The Bodley Head
Bernard Shaw

SHAW'S MUSIC

VOLUME I

The Bodley Head
Bernard Shaw

SHAW'S MUSIC

The complete musical criticism
in three volumes

Second Revised Edition

Edited by

Dan H. Laurence

VOLUME I
1876–1890

THE BODLEY HEAD

LONDON

A CIP catalogue record for this book is
available from the British Library

ISBN: 0-370-30247-8
      0-370-30333-4 Set of 3 vols
      0-370-31270-8 Pbk

Printed and bound in Great Britain for
The Bodley Head Ltd,
31 Bedford Square, London WC1B 3SG
by Mackays of Chatham PLC
Set in Clowes Plantin Light by CCC.
This edition first published 1981
Second revised edition 1989

CONTENTS

Shaw's Music

is published in three volumes
Volume I: 1876–1890
Volume II: 1890–1893
Volume III: 1893–1950 with appendix and
biographical and general indexes
to the entire edition

For
HALLIGAN AND IBBS

Star Billing

INTRODUCTION*
by Dan H. Laurence

"I could make deaf stockbrokers read my two pages on music," Shaw once wrote in reference to his criticism in The World, "the alleged joke being that I knew nothing about it. The real joke was that I knew all about it."

Shaw's extraordinary musical knowledge resulted from an exposure to music almost from infancy. The Shaws were naturally a musical family: "All the women could 'pick out tunes' on the piano," Shaw reminisced in the preface to Immaturity, "and support them with the chords of the tonic, subdominant, dominant, and tonic again. Even a Neapolitan sixth was not beyond them. My father played the trombone ... My eldest uncle [William] ... played the ophicleide, a giant keyed brass bugle, now superseded by the tuba ... My Aunt Emily played the violoncello. Aunt Shah ... used the harp and tambourine." Shaw's mother had a mezzo-soprano voice "of remarkable purity of tone," which she developed under the mesmeric influence of a singing-teacher friend, George John (Vandeleur) Lee. This "method" she eventually passed on to her son, who, as a boy, aspired to be an operatic baritone. It was Lee who first took young George to the opera, and it was his Amateur Musical Society concerts in Dublin's Antient Concert Rooms, in which Mrs Shaw was a frequent participant, which gave the boy much of his earliest knowledge of the Italian opera repertoire. At fifteen Shaw could "sing and whistle from end to end leading works by Handel,

*A revised version of an introduction published originally in How to Become a Musical Critic, 1961.

Haydn, Mozart, Beethoven, Rossini, Bellini, Donizetti and Verdi," and all this he owed, as he acknowledged in the preface to London Music in 1888–89, to "the meteoric impact of Lee, with his music, his method, his impetuous enterprise and his magnetism, upon the little Shaw household." The extent to which this early and profound influence left its mark upon Shaw ("music," he told a friend, "has been an indispensable part of my life") is reflected in the emphasis on music prevalent throughout his writing. Music is a dominant element in the five novels written between 1879 and 1883. Immaturity, Shaw's first novel (written at 23) abounds in musical personages, ranging from the young composer at a party "flapping his hands" as he performs the final bars of "what he presently informed his audience was a Scandinavian Rhapsody in the form of a study for the loose wrist" to a series of devastating portraits of music critics and connoisseurs, including the gentleman who describes a Turkish rondo as "Mozart in one of his playful moods. Mozart with his German depth temporarily held in abeyance by his Gothic humor and his Latin melodiousness—his infantile vivacity getting the mastery of his profound learning and of that stupendous fatalism which, in the G minor symphony, seems to foreshadow the giant Beethoven."

The Irrational Knot opens with a satire on Music for the People workingmen's concerts sponsored by well-intentioned but benighted Christian Socialist parsons and social-conscious "society" folk (a subject Shaw was to expound upon with more seriousness in Francis Hueffer's Musical Review in 1883): "Tickets will be distributed to the families of working men by the Rev. George Lind . . . Symphony in F: Haydn. Arranged for four English concertinas by Julius Baker. Mr Julius Baker; Master Julius Abt Baker; Miss Lisette Baker (aged 8); and Miss Totty Baker (aged 6½) . . . Song: Rose softly blooming: Spohr. Miss Marian Lind ... Nigger melody. Uncle Ned. Mr Marmaduke Lind, accompanied by himself on the banjo."

In Cashel Byron's Profession the prizefighter hero of the novel translates into pugilistic terms his understanding of the battle between Wagner and his critics: "I made out from the gentleman's remarks that there is a man in the musical line named Wagner, who is what you might call a game sort of composer; and that the musical fancy, though they can't deny that his tunes are first-rate, and that, so to speak, he wins his fights, yet they try to make out that he wins them in an outlandish way, and that he has no real science."

But it is in Love among the Artists that Shaw most fully reveals the extent of his knowledge of music and the powerful influence it has exerted upon him. His protagonist, Owen Jack, is a modern composer-genius of Beethovenesque intensity and ferocity, intractable and violent in his contempt for the second-rate, and demoniacally possessed as he composes:

Jack was alone, seated at the pianoforte, his brows knitted, his eyes glistening under them, his wrists bounding and rebounding upon the keys, his rugged countenance transfigured by an expression of extreme energy and exaltation. He was playing from a manuscript score, and was making up for the absence of an orchestra by imitations of the instruments. He was grunting and buzzing the bassoon parts, humming when the violoncello had the melody, whistling for the flutes, singing hoarsely for the horns, barking for the trumpets, squealing for the oboes, making indescribable sounds in imitation of clarinets and drums, and marking each *sforzando* by a toss of his head and a gnash of his teeth. At last, abandoning this eccentric orchestration, he chanted with the full strength of his formidable voice until he came to the final chord, which he struck violently, and repeated in every possible inversion from one end of the keyboard to the other.

When Jack's Fantasia for pianoforte and orchestra is accepted for performance by Manlius, the conductor of the Antient Orpheus Orchestra, and the Polish lady pianist who is performing with the orchestra misjudges the speed of a movement under the direction of Manlius, Jack impetuously springs to the conductor's desk and, in an explosion of sound, conducts the rehearsal himself:

"Louder," roared Jack. "Louder. Less noise and more tone. Out with it like fifty million devils." And he led the movement at a merciless speed. . . . It was an insensate orgy of sound. Gay melodies, daintily given out by the pianoforte, or by the string instruments, were derisively brayed out immediately afterwards by cornets, harmonized in thirds with the most ingenious vulgarity. *Cadenzas*, agilely executed by the Polish lady, were uncouthly imitated by the double basses. Themes constructed like ballads with choruses were introduced instead of orthodox "subjects." . . . The Polish lady, incommoded by the capricious and often excessive speed required of her, held on gallantly, Jack all the time grinding his teeth, dancing, gesticulating, and by turns shshsh-shing at the orchestra or shouting to them for more tone and less noise.

Music is equally important as an element in Shaw's dramatic works. Mozart's Don Giovanni, which motivates the entire play, sets the mood and the scene specifically for the Don Juan in Hell sequence of Man and Superman, with the stage directions calling for "a ghostly violoncello palpitating on the same note endlessly" and "wailings from uncanny wind instruments." The Act III, mystical rite in The Tragedy of an Elderly Gentleman (the fourth play in the Back to Methuselah cycle) opens with "Invisible trumpets utter[ing] three solemn blasts in the manner of Die Zauberflöte," after which "organ music of the kind called sacred in the XIX century begins." In Passion, Poison, and Petrifaction, by way of contrast, a choir of invisible angels ends the burlesque with an unexpected rendition of Wont You Come Home, Bill Bailey. Higgins, in Pygmalion, returns with Eliza from the success of the Embassy Ball "half singing half yawning an air from La Fanciulla del Golden West," and a pianoforte duet of a wedding march (Lohengrin, surely) climaxes the tomfoolery The Music Cure.

A considerable number of Shaw's dramatic characters are, to one degree or another, musicians. Clementina Buoyant is addicted to the saxophone, with which she charms alligators. Randall Utterword trills a flute solo of Keep the Home Fires Burning as the curtain descends on bomb-torn England at the end of Heartbreak House (the play itself is labeled a fantasia). Andrew Undershaft parades with Major Barbara's Salvation Army band, blaring away on a trombone, as Adolphus Cusins bangs the time with his drum for *Immenso giubilo*. Charteris in The Philanderer, describing Julia's heartbreak, makes his point by sounding a discordant chord on Grace's piano, doing so, incidentally, by sitting on the bass end of the keyboard. Iddy Hammingtap in The Simpleton sermonizes on harp music. Count O'Dowda, Fanny's patrician parent, finds "Beethoven's music coarse and restless, and Wagner's senseless and detestable. I do not listen to them: I listen to Cimarosa, to Pergolesi, to Gluck and Mozart." Lady Corinthia Fanshawe, the "Richmond Park nightingale" of Press Cuttings, is "devoted to music and can reach F in alt with the greatest facility—Patti never got above E flat." Alastair Fitzfassenden, who marries the millionairess Epifania, has "a startlingly loud singing voice of almost supernatural range"; he can "sing Caruso's head off," but "Nature unfortunately forgot to endow him with a musical ear."

The plays themselves, as Shaw revealed, were conceived on musical principles, being opera without music. The Inquisitor's speech, he told O. B. Clarence, who performed in the rôle, "is an operatic solo as much as *Il Balen* in Verdi's Trovatore. There is nothing I like better than composing arias, cavatinas, and *grand finales* for good actors." His dialogues were frequently envisaged as duets, trios, and quartets. In the casting of the plays Shaw insisted on variety in pitch as "indispensable to an intelligible and agreeable performance." Candida, accordingly, should be a contralto, Marchbanks a tenor, Morell a baritone, Prossy a soprano, and Burgess a bass. A conversation in which people all speak at the same speed and pitch, Shaw contended, is not only extremely disagreeable but disastrous. His instructions to performers invariably were given in musical terms. "Begin the big speech at the end *pianissimo* and *adagio*," he advised Esmé Percy. "You can't build up from a *forte con brio*. To get your whole compass you must start from zero." Granville Barker "was not far out," said Shaw, "when, at a rehearsal of one of my plays, he cried out, 'Ladies and gentlemen: will you please remember that this is Italian opera."

It might be propounded that, even had Shaw never written any formal musical criticism, we should still have been able to detect, from his novels and plays, that he was, as Eric Blom wrote in a recent edition of Grove, "one of the most brilliant critics ... of music who have ever worked in London, or indeed anywhere." Fortunately, conjecture is unnecessary, for the criticism does exist and, with publication of the present edition, the full range of Shaw's accomplishment may now be examined in perspective.

Shaw's very first journalistic experience upon his arrival in London in 1876 was that of a musical critic. It is, however, hardly to have been expected that the editor of any London publication would knowingly engage the journalistic services of a stripling of twenty, fresh from provincial Dublin, for so specialized an assignment. The employment, as Shaw explained in an autobiographical essay How to Become a Musical Critic (1894), came as the result of a deception played upon the non-related Captain Donald Shaw, editor of The Hornet, a satirical weekly. Vandeleur Lee cagily palmed himself off on editor Shaw as a musical critic and privately arranged for his *protégé* to pen the notices. It was a mutually advantageous arrangement, for both attended the concerts and operatic performances on complimentary tickets, and the Shaw household benefited from the urgently needed additional income. Donald Shaw eventually sensed he had been hoodwinked, but the editor and the ghost never met. The one major drawback, as Shaw subsequently noted, was that he had no opportunity to correct proofs of his criticisms.

The deception was sustained for nearly a full year, from 29 November 1876 to 26 September 1877. In later years Shaw was to claim that the paper expired shortly thereafter, due principally to the negative effect of his criticisms, but in actuality *The Hornet* survived until February 1880. Shaw also alleged, hyperbolically, that the editor "had mutilated and interpolated my notices horribly," but of all the Hornet contributions (preserved by Shaw in a large cutting-book), only one Wagner article reveals any serious "anti-Wagnerism," and this is now known from extant correspondence to have been drafted by another hand, revised by "Lee" at the editor's request, and then re-revised by the editor. As for the "puffs," which Shaw alleged the editor had frequently inserted, it is difficult to find in the entire body of the criticism more than a handful of real compliments, and this praise, when it appears, has the ring of sincerity; the artists thus extolled were to continue to receive Shaw's approbation in subsequent criticism and reminiscence. Only in the praise bestowed upon Sterndale Bennett's overture to Parisina (28 March 1877) does there appear to be ground for suspicion.

The criticism in The Hornet does reveal, however, that Shaw at twenty had already developed a remarkable capacity for detecting the weaknesses of musical performances. He expatiated on the importance of *ensemble* versus the "star system" in opera, on "scratch" performances, on inadequate rehearsal time, on clumsy staging and ugly *décor*. He excoriated the vibratos, tremolos, wobbles, and goatbleats of the questionably celebrated French and Italian *artistes* who performed with London opera companies. He attacked (as he was later to do as a dramatic critic of Shakespearean productions) the vulgarization and mutilation of classic works. He harped on the audience's bad manners and on the national insensibility to good music. He scored "the absurdity of being the only music-patronizing nation in the world which systematically tolerates opera delivered in a foreign tongue," and which insisted on translating every French, German, and Russian work, not into English, but into Italian!

In his early criticism Shaw was frequently ruthless, his crusading zeal leading him to an emulation of David's slaying of his tens of thousands. The legendary Tamberlik in his celebrated duet in Rossini's Otello, we are told, for the C sharp "substituted a strange description of shriek at about that pitch. The audience, ever appreciative of vocal curiosities, eagerly redemanded it." A Liszt composition is described as having "a brief *andante* of advanced commonplace." The sharpness of the flute-playing of Oluf Svensden, it is suggested,

[14]

constituted "an unhappy craving to be conspicuous at any cost." The ghost apprentice had not yet learned how to substitute the rapier for the bludgeon, though his critical perception was intuitively correct.

More than seven years elapsed before Shaw had an opportunity to return to musical criticism, but this long hiatus, during which he had devoted himself largely to literary exercise (but also to studies of harmony, counterpoint, and temperament), resulted in development of style and improvement in articulation which are dramatically apparent when one compares Shaw's criticism of the analytical program of Liszt's Mazeppa in 1877 with that of the Inferno in 1885, or his contemporary description of Wagner's performance as conductor in London with the retrospective portrait in Herr Richter and His Blue Ribbon. The maturing critic focused his attention upon many of the same faults which had been targets of his earlier attack, but his approach had become more subtle, his assault more controlled, his brash self-assurance tempered by time and experience into a colorful and charming egotism. And at last his innate sense of humor came into play in that now-famed effervescent personality known to us as Corno di Bassetto.

It must not, however, be supposed that Corno was conceived as spontaneously or facilely as Shaw and T. P. O'Connor would have had us believe. It is true that Shaw joined the editorial staff of The Star at its inception in January 1888, under the editorship of O'Connor and his two brilliant young assistants, H. W. Massingham and Ernest Parke. And it is equally true that after a week or two of thwarted attempts, via the Star's leaders, to turn the Liberal paper into a Socialist one, Shaw was obliged to withdraw from the staff. "Dear Chief," he wrote to O'Connor, "This is my resignation. I am not worth my salt to the Star; and you will be more at your ease without having constantly to suppress my articles. ... So I must give myself the sack; though what is to become of you and Massingham when you have no one to guide you through the mists of sentimental Utopianism is more than I can foresee. The special Providence that protects children be your safeguard!"

The romantic tale woven by Shaw, and later embroidered by O'Connor in his Memoirs of an Old Parliamentarian, is that Massingham, being unwilling to lose his young Socialist friend, reminded T. P. that the paper had no musical critic, and that Shaw, having an extraordinary knowledge of music, would be the ideal man for the position. To this O'Connor claimed he instantly agreed, for he knew that Shaw "had just emerged from that desolating interval in life in which employment either does not exist or is sparse and fitful; and I had gone through so much agony in the same interval of my life that I could not think of putting a man back into the abyss from which he had only just emerged."

There is not, however, a grain of truth in the story. Shaw resigned on 9 February 1888, noting in his diary on the 10th that he went to the Star office in Stonecutter-street for the last time, during which visit he wrote a sub-leader and arranged with O'Connor to write occasional signed articles and to send notes. For several months, as a free-lance journalist, he made odd contributions to The Star, but he was contributing with greater frequency to the Pall Mall Gazette and, at the same time, providing art criticism for The World. There was no question of his becoming musical critic of The Star; the position was already filled. Anyone examining the pages of The Star for the bulk of the year 1888 will find its musical criticism signed "Musigena," a pseudonym which masked the identity of a fellow-Socialist, E. Belfort Bax, the uncle of Arnold Bax. In June 1888

Shaw gravitated towards the job that was eventually to be his by accepting Massingham's offer that he cover those occasional musical events which conflicted with performances being reviewed by Bax. In July, when Bax was preparing to leave for a holiday in Zürich, he arranged with Shaw to serve as his substitute. Thereafter, until early in 1889, Shaw continued as second-string critic. It was not until February 1889 that Shaw replaced Bax completely and, in need of a pseudonym, created his *alter ego.* Corno di Bassetto, after months of anonymity, made his presence known to readers of The Star on 15 February—"a veritable Siegfried," as Stephen Williams eulogized in 1951, "leaping with whoops of joy to the holy task of denouncing the decadence of Wotan and smashing through the brilliant quackery of Loge."

London suddenly found itself being entertained by a weekly column of "Musical Mems" that was an olla-podrida of wit and wisdom on music, drama, ballet, socialism, vegetarianism, pugilism, and anything else its author cared to throw in for good measure. Shaw had found his ideal *métier*, and at a cost to The Star of only three guineas a week. "There never was such musical criticism on land or flood," O'Connor later boasted, but when Shaw wrote to him in March 1890 to ask for an increase in salary, O'Connor demurred. The Star, he replied, could do very well without Shaw. A second letter of resignation followed immediately: "The giving up of the Musical Mems will be a gigantic—a Himalayan mistake. However, a wilful man must have his way." As O'Connor did not call his bluff, Shaw wrote *finis* to Corno di Bassetto in May 1890; a week later he contracted with Edmund Yates to do a column on music for The World, where for more than four years the initials "G.B.S." were to appear weekly. These articles represented Shaw's most mature journalism, the judgments of a man who, in his own words, had "something to say and a reasonably human way of saying it." They also constituted his valediction as a professional musical critic.

Any assessment of Shaw's XIX century musical criticism must include several incontrovertible facts. No critic of his time—no performer for that matter—possessed so thorough a knowledge as Shaw did of the Italian repertory which dominated the London musical scene. This did not, however, blind him to other musical values, as it seemed to do to many of his colleagues. Few were more perceptive than Shaw in recognizing the genius of Wagner, not only as a great musician, but as a profound thinker and moralist. Those who challenge Shaw's later statement that he was a pioneer crusader for Wagner's works in London do so without any real knowledge of the London musical scene, in which as late as 1890 only Wagner's earlier works "were known or tolerated." Orchestral passages from the operas and a handful of arias had gained popularity in the concert halls, the overture to Tannhäuser becoming a veritable *cliché*; but the half dozen master works of Wagner—the Ring operas, Parsifal, and Meistersinger—were conspicuous by their absence from the opera stages, and one was obliged to journey all the way to Bayreuth to hear them. The Ring cycle had, in fact, been performed in London only once, in 1882; ten years later it would be heard again, not in the repertory of an English company, but in a production imported from Germany for the occasion. For more than a decade Shaw fought what was virtually a one-man critical crusade to obtain for Wagner in London more than an occasional incompetent English representation of his operas.

Shaw also perceived the profound significance of the music of Bach at a time when few in England were ready and able to appreciate it; Bach belongs, he predicted, "not to the past, but to the future—perhaps the near future." And he championed the cause of Mozart, whose "German music with Italian words" had not yet received the recognition that Shaw insisted be accorded it. "Most conductors," he mourned, "can make nothing of Mozart—many of them honestly believe there is nothing in him . . ." Mozart, whose Zauberflöte Shaw considered to be "the first oratorio of the religion of humanity," was, to him, the greatest of all the musicians. "He taught me how to say profound things," Shaw once told Ferruccio Busoni, "and at the same time remain flippant and lively."

Perhaps most important of all, Shaw perceived clearly the ineptitude of British music as produced by the pedantic "university school" of composers—Sterndale Bennett, Parry, Stanford, Cowen, Macfarren, and Sullivan "the organist of Chester Square"—the traditionalists who dictated British musical taste under the pernicious influence of a shallow "European culture." As Ernest Newman noted in his Sunday Times review of Music in London in 1932, "Shaw turned upon the spectacle of the English musical world of the day an eye unclouded by tradition, a judgment unaffected by social or official considerations. He declined to take people like the Parrys and the Stanfords and the rest of them seriously as composers, or the colleges as the providentially appointed trainers of the musical youth of the nation." To Shaw XIX century British music was "a little Mozart and water." If the English language was to be treated musically, he argued, "it must be done in the style of Purcell, and not in that of Verdi."

When the non-academic Elgar appeared on the horizon at the turn of the century, Shaw was certain that British music had taken a decisive step forward. "I consider," he wrote to the editor of the Morning Post in 1911, "that the history of original music, broken off by the death of Purcell, begins again with Sir Edward

Elgar." Elgar, he expostulated in an interview at Glastonbury in 1916, "is the first musician who, after a century of imitation of Handel, Mendelssohn and Spohr, began to write music like an Englishman." The older British composers were killed by the academic system, he insisted; the younger ones were *making* style and were full of experiments. "I hold the view," he concluded, "that after two hundred years during which our abler men would not touch music, we are now coming into our own again as a great musical nation." The emergence of Vaughan Williams, Delius, Bax, Britten, Walton, and Tippett as contributors to XX century musical development more than fulfilled the prophecy. But it is not unusual that Shaw should have been right in this instance; as Ernest Newman pointed out, "time has proved the rightness of nine contemporary estimates of his out of ten."

That Shaw occasionally blundered in his evaluations cannot be questioned; he never claimed to be infallible, though he once exclaimed jocularly, in The World, that the first precept in a contemplated book, Advice to Old Musicians, would run, "Dont be in a hurry to contradict G.B.S., as he never commits himself on a musical subject until he knows at least six times as much about it as you do." If Shaw had a weak spot it was in the area of the Romantics. Brahms he saw as "a musical sensualist with intellectual affectations," whose absolute music was "abundant, fresh, hopeful, joyous, powerful," but who, "when he touched a literary subject of any dimensions," became "a positive blockhead." Though he could praise Gounod he had to admit that "at bottom, his music is tedious." Liszt and Berlioz came off little better, though Newman suggested one reason for the undervaluing of Berlioz might have been that his works were not too intelligently performed in London at the end of the century.

At the heart of Shaw's antipathy to the successors of Beethoven there seems to have been an intense distaste for their conservatism, their refined, earnest, "Sunday-school profundities," especially in the area of sacred music, of which Mendelssohn, with his pop religious oratorios, was to Shaw the worst offender. The virtual worship of Mendelssohn by the Victorians was sufficient to unleash an emotional barrage from a man whose criticism ever was personal and passionate. And one might argue with considerable conviction that Shaw's early estimate of Brahms *was* the correct one, for which his subsequent apology was unnecessary.

Shaw's errors of judgment were, on the whole, remarkably few, and his insights sound. "In a few years," he commented in 1894, "the musical taste of this century will strike us exactly as we are now struck by the literary taste of the century which thought Pope a greater poet than Chaucer." Shaw's pantheon of musical greats in 1889, including Bach, Handel, Haydn, Mozart, Beethoven, and Wagner, would receive respect more readily from music lovers today than most of these composers did a century ago in London, when a programmist could describe Mendelssohn as "a master yielding to none in the highest qualifications that warrant the name."

For the most part Shaw instinctively recognized the true artist and rejected the false one. And though he wrote less frequently of music in the XX century than he had in the XIX, his acumen was little blunted. He strove to keep abreast of the times, at least as much as the BBC's programming would permit, and he was now as self-assured about Richard Strauss as he had been about Wagner, as confirmed in his opinion of Beecham and Boult as he had been in that of Manns and Richter. In 1914 he commented, in a letter to Cedric Glover, "I always applaud Schönberg and Scriabin vigorously because they are enlarging our musical material so usefully ... I was quite proud of myself for guessing which was to be the final chord of the fifth Orchestral Piece, which was more than I had been able to do in the four previous ones."

Wagner, as Shaw was endlessly fond of repeating, said music "is kept alive on the cottage piano of the amateur," and every evening at Ayot, for thirty years, Shaw sat down to the Bechstein just before bedtime and played and sang for his wife Charlotte. After her death in 1943 the keys were silent—until the day early in 1950 when an exuberant Greer Garson burst in for a visit and wheedled Shaw into accompanying her in a bevy of music hall ditties. Once again, in his 94th year, he drew from the shelf his orchestral scores, bound in vegetarian vellum, from which he would play and, quaveringly, sing the scores of Mussorgsky's Boris Godunov, Verdi's I Masnadieri, Strauss's Ariadne auf Naxos, and Elgar's Dream of Gerontius. Iconoclastic to the end, he refused to indulge in the practice of old men by reminiscing nostalgically about the past to prove that things were better then than now. Almost with his dying breath he insisted that we sing better today than our grandparents did.

For three-quarters of a century Bernard Shaw appraised the English musical scene. He wrote with logic, wit, directness, conscience, courage, and a liveliness of intellect which was unique in his time and remains so in ours. The musical journalism he produced is probably as brilliant as any that literate man can ever hope to see. Just try to name another critical journalist in the English language who remains as readable after nearly a century.

DAN H. LAURENCE

London, *August 1960*
San Antonio, *March 1980*

EDITOR'S NOTE

The three volumes which comprise this edition contain in chronological order all of Bernard Shaw's known published musical journalism and occasional pieces on musical subjects, including the complete texts of Music in London 1890–94 (3 vols., 1932), London Music in 1888–89 (1937), and How to Become a Musical Critic (1961), as well as The Perfect Wagnerite (1898; finally revised 1930) and more than 125,000 words of hitherto uncollected writings, identified as such by insertion of the letter "U" in square brackets at start and finish of each uncollected text.

The materials throughout have been edited to conform with Shaw's own established style in the Standard Edition, including all of its now well-known peculiarities. It should be recognized, however, that this style was evolved over a period of years, with inconsistencies between the earliest-set Standard Edition volumes and the ones set in the 1940's. Further, many of the volumes, including Music in London, in the Collected Edition (1930–32) and the Standard Edition (1931–32), were prepared for the printer and proofread, not by Shaw, who was busily working at his play Too True to be Good and the Ellen Terry–Bernard Shaw correspondence, when not traveling in the U.S.S.R. and South Africa, but by Charlotte Shaw, by an extraordinarily careless proof-reader at R. & R. Clark, Ltd., which printed the editions, and by a professional researcher employed by Shaw to copy out texts from old newspapers and journals.

As a consequence, the present editor has had to make

a considerable number of arbitrary decisions in matters of style, sometimes sacrificing uniformity to cater to Shaw's whims, as in his communication of 8 April 1944 to the printer William Maxwell: "I rather like various spellings; so dont bother about them. I always bung in a Z when I can, except in enterprise, which Blanche [Shaw's secretary Blanche Patch] always types enter-prize, which is phonetically right, but too suggestive of an intermediate prize." The spellings of names in The Perfect Wagnerite are anglicized variants employed designedly by Shaw, and are therefore retained though at odds with the spelling in the journalism.

Paragraphs which Shaw deleted from London Music either for reasons of space or because he questioned their interest for latter-day readers have been restored; there has been no substitution, however, of original newspaper texts for the texts revised by Shaw for the later publication. A number of silent deletions have been made, of brief announcements of forthcoming perform-ances, non-committal reports of meetings of musical societies, and any similar matter which does not fall into the category of criticism or commentary. Only one substantial deletion occurs: Shaw's report of Andrew Lang's lecture on literature which was included, inex-plicably, in London Music.

Footnotes are the editor's except where Shaw's author-ship is indicated by insertion of the initials "GBS" in square brackets at the end of the annotation. Headings for untitled criticisms consist, as far as possible, of phrases extracted from the text.

The unsigned writings were identified from a large number of sources: unpublished diaries, notebooks, account books, correspondence, extant manuscripts, and cuttings books preserved by Shaw, as well as from marked files of journals in which they were originally published.

I am grateful as ever to Barney Blackley, my editor at The Bodley Head, for much sound advice and for his infinite patience. I also owe a debt, not for the first time, for the valuable assistance of Sir Rupert Hart-Davis, Dr Felix F. Strauss, Raymond Mander and Joe Mitchenson, George Goossens, Lois Garcia, Paul Myers and the staffs of the drama, music, and dance collections of the Library for the Performing Arts, New York.

Equally helpful in various ways have been Janet Adam Smith, Olga Buth, Dr Norbert Greiner, Colin Mabberley, Cyril Russell, Leslie Staples, Dr John Strauss, Harley J. Refsal of Luther College, who re-translated Shaw's report of Grieg's London reception written for the Dagbladet (Oslo), the Royal University Library of Oslo, Lars Langåker, Director of the Norwegian Information Service, New York, and the Österreichische Bundesbahnen Zentraldirektion-Bibliothek. Finally, a special acknowledgment to Ralph Bateman for the enormous burden of preparing a comprehensive index to the edition, and for doing it so well.

At the front of the first volume of Music in London in 1932 Shaw inserted a brief note: "There are people who will read about music and nothing else. To them dead *prima donnas* are more interesting than saints, and extinct tenors than mighty conquerors. They are presumably the only people who will dream of reading these three volumes. If my wisdom is to be of any use to them it must come to them in this form. And so I let it go to them for what it is worth." The disclaimer is reprinted here to complete the record. It is probably, however, the one time in his life that G.B.S. underrated himself.

D.H.L.

EDITOR'S NOTE TO SECOND EDITION

Four pieces of writing by Shaw on musical subjects have come to my attention since the first publication of Shaw's Music in 1981. These have now been added to the text in an Appendix to Volume 3, along with two annotations I was unable to provide earlier. A number of corrections in the text and in the index have also been made. This new edition happily provides the opportunity for me to make grateful acknowledgment of the assistance, not hitherto credited, of D. L. Cheke, Warren F. Michon (Senior Librarian of the New York Public Library Music Division), the Harry Ransom Humanities Research Center of the University of Texas at Austin, and James Tyler (Curator of the Bernard F. Burgunder Shaw Collection, Cornell University Library).

D.H.L.

Niagara-on-the-Lake, Ont.
July 1988

SHAW'S MUSIC

PREFACE

*Written in 1935 as a preface to London Music in 1888–89
as Heard by Corno di Bassetto . . ., published in 1937*

When my maiden novel, called Immaturity, was printed
fifty years after it was written,* I prefaced it with some
account of the unhappy-go-lucky way in which I was
brought up, ending with the nine years of shabby genteel
destitution during which my attempts to gain a footing
in literature were a complete and apparently hopeless
failure.

I was rescued from this condition by William Archer,
who transferred some of his book reviewing work to me,
and pushed me into a post as picture critic which had
been pushed on him, and for which he considered
himself unqualified, as in fact he was. So, as reviewer for
the old Pall Mall Gazette and picture critic for Edmund
Yates's then fashionable weekly, The World, I carried
on until I found an opening which I can explain only by
describing the musical side of my childhood, to which
I made only a passing allusion in my Immaturity
preface, but which was of cardinal importance in my
education.

In 1888, I being then 32 and already a noted critic and
political agitator, the Star newspaper was founded under
the editorship of the late T. P. O'Connor (nicknamed
Tay Pay by Yates), who had for his very much more
competent assistant the late H. W. Massingham. Tay
Pay survived until 1936; but his mind never advanced
beyond the year 1865, though his Fenian sympathies
and his hearty detestation of the English nation disguised
that defect from him. Massingham induced him to

* Written in 1879; first published in 1930.

[29]

invite me to join the political staff of his paper; but as I had already, fourteen years before Lenin, read Karl Marx, and was preaching Socialism at every street corner or other available forum in London and the provinces, the effect of my articles on Tay Pay may be imagined. He refused to print them, and told me that, man alive, it would be five hundred years before such stuff would become practical political journalism. He was too goodnatured to sack me; and I did not want to throw away my job; so I got him out of his difficulty by asking him to let me have two columns a week for a feuilleton on music. He was glad to get rid of my politics on these terms; but he stipulated that—musical criticism being known to him only as unreadable and unintelligible jargon—I should, for God's sake, not write about Bach in B Minor. I was quite alive to that danger: in fact I had made my proposal because I believed I could make musical criticism readable even by the deaf. Besides, my terms were moderate: two guineas a week.

I was strong on the need for signed criticism written in the first person instead of the journalistic "we"; but as I then had no name worth signing, and G. B. S. meant nothing to the public, I had to invent a fantastic personality with something like a foreign title. I thought of Count di Luna (a character in Verdi's Trovatore), but finally changed it for Corno di Bassetto, as it sounded like a foreign title, and nobody knew what a corno di bassetto was.

As a matter of fact the corno di bassetto is not a foreigner with a title but a musical instrument called in English the basset horn. It is a wretched instrument, now completely snuffed out for general use by the bass clarinet. It would be forgotten and unplayed if it were not that Mozart has scored for it in his Requiem, evidently because its peculiar watery melancholy, and the total absence of any richness or passion in its tone, is just the thing for a funeral. Mendelssohn wrote some chamber music for it, presumably to oblige somebody who played it; and it is kept alive by these works and by our Mr Whall. If I had ever heard a note of it in 1888 I should not have selected it for a character which I intended to be sparkling. The devil himself could not make a basset horn sparkle.

For two years I sparkled every week in The Star under this ridiculous name, and in a manner so absolutely unlike the conventional musical criticism of the time that all the journalists believed that the affair was a huge joke, the point of which was that I knew nothing whatever about music. How it had come about that I was one of the few critics of that time who really knew their business I can explain only by picking up the thread of autobiography which I dropped in my scrappy prefix to Immaturity. For the sake of those who have not read the Immaturity preface, or have forgotten it, I shall have to repeat here some of my father's history, but only so far as is necessary to explain the situation of my mother.

Technically speaking I should say she was the worst mother conceivable, always, however, within the limits of the fact that she was incapable of unkindness to any child, animal, or flower, or indeed to any person or thing whatsoever. But if such a thing as a maternity welfare centre had been established or even imagined in Ireland in her time, and she had been induced to visit it, every precept of it would have been laughably strange to her. Though she had been severely educated up to the highest standard for Irish "carriage ladies" of her time, she was much more like a Trobriand islander as described by Mr Malinowski than like a modern Cambridge lady graduate in respect of accepting all the habits, good or bad, of the Irish society in which she was brought up as part of an uncontrollable order of nature.

She went her own way with so complete a disregard and even unconsciousness of convention and scandal and prejudice that it was impossible to doubt her good faith and innocence; but it never occurred to her that other people, especially children, needed guidance or training, or that it mattered in the least what they ate and drank or what they did as long as they were not actively mischievous. She accepted me as a natural and customary phenomenon, and took it for granted that I should go on occurring in that way. In short, living to her was not an art: it was something that happened. But there were unkind parts of it that could be avoided; and among these were the constraints and tyrannies, the scoldings and browbeatings and punishments she had suffered in her childhood as the method of her education. In her righteous reaction against it she reached a negative attitude in which, having no substitute to propose, she carried domestic anarchy as far as in the nature of things it can be carried.

She had been tyrannously taught French enough to recite one or two of Lafontaine's fables; to play the piano the wrong way; to harmonize by rule from Logier's Thoroughbass; to sit up straight and speak and dress and behave like a lady, and an Irish lady at that. She knew nothing of the value of money nor of housekeeping nor of hygiene nor of anything that could be left to servants or governesses or parents or solicitors or apothecaries or any other member of the retinue, indoor and outdoor, of a country house. She had great expectations from a humpbacked little aunt, a fairylike creature with a will of iron, who had brought up her motherless niece with a firm determination to make her a paragon of good breeding, to achieve a distinguished marriage for her, and to leave her all her money as a dowry.

Manufacturing destinies for other people is a dangerous game. Its results are usually as unexpected as those of a first-rate European war. When my mother came to marriageable age her long-widowed father married again. The brother of his late wife, to whom he was considerably in debt, disapproved so strongly that on learning the date of the approaching ceremony from my mother he had the bridegroom arrested on his way to church. My grandfather naturally resented this maneuver, and in his wrath could not be persuaded that his daughter was not my granduncle's accomplice in it. Visits to relatives in Dublin provided a temporary refuge for her; and the affair would have blown over but for the intervention of my father.

My father was a very ineligible suitor for a paragon with great expectations. His family pretensions were enormous; but they were founded on many generations of younger sons, and were purely psychological. He had managed to acquire a gentlemanly post in the law courts. This post had been abolished and its holder pensioned. By selling the pension he was enabled to start in business as a wholesaler in the corn trade (retail trade was beneath his family dignity) of which he knew nothing. He accentuated this deficiency by becoming the partner of a Mr Clibborn, who had served an apprenticeship to the cloth trade. Their combined ignorances kept the business going, mainly by its own inertia, until they and it died. Many years after this event I paid a visit of curiosity to Jervis-st., Dublin; and there, on one of the pillars of a small portico, I found the ancient inscription "Clibborn & Shaw" still decipherable, as it were on the tombs of the Pharaohs. I cannot believe that this business yielded my father at any time more than three or four hundred a year; and it got less as time went on, as that particular kind of business was dying a slow death throughout the latter half of the XIX century.

My father was in principle an ardent teetotaler.

[33]

Nobody ever felt the disgrace and misery and endless mischief of drunkenness as he did: he impressed it so deeply on me in my earliest years that I have been a teetotaler ever since. Unfortunately his conviction in this matter was founded on personal experience. He was the victim of a drink neurosis which cropped up in his family from time to time: a miserable affliction, quite unconvivial, and accompanied by torments of remorse and shame.

My father was past forty, and no doubt had sanguine illusions as to the future of his newly acquired business when he fell in love with my mother and was emboldened by her expectations and his business hopes to propose to her just at the moment when marriage seemed her only way of escape from an angry father and a stepmother. Immediately all her relatives, who had tolerated this middle-aged gentleman as a perfectly safe acquaintance with an agreeable vein of humor, denounced him as a notorious drunkard. My mother, suspicious of this sudden change of front, put the question directly to my father. His eloquence and sincerity convinced her that he was, as he claimed to be, and as he was in principle, a bigoted teetotaler. She married him; and her disappointed and infuriated aunt disinherited her, not foreseeing that the consequences of the marriage would include so remarkable a phenomenon as myself.

When my mother was disillusioned, and found out what living on a few hundreds a year with three children meant, even in a country where a general servant could be obtained for eight pounds a year, her condition must have been about as unhappy and her prospects as apparently hopeless as her aunt could have desired even in her most vindictive moments.

But there was one trump in her hand. She was fond of music, and had a mezzo-soprano voice of remarkable purity of tone. In the next street to ours, Harrington-street, where the houses were bigger and more fashionable than in our little by-street, there was a teacher of singing, lamed by an accident in childhood which had left one of his legs shorter than the other, but a man of mesmeric vitality and force. He was a bachelor living with his brother, whom he supported and adored, and a terrible old woman who was his servant of all work. His name was George John Vandeleur Lee, known in Dublin as Mr G. J. Lee. Singing lessons were cheap in Dublin; and my mother went to Lee to learn how to sing properly. He trained her voice to such purpose that she became indispensable to him as an amateur *prima donna*. For he was a most magnetic conductor and an indefatigable organizer of concerts, and later on of operas, with such amateur talent, vocal and orchestral, as he could discover and train in Dublin, which, as far as public professional music was concerned, was, outside the churches, practically a vacuum.

Lee soon found his way into our house, first by giving my mother lessons there, and then by using our drawing room for rehearsals. I can only guess that the inadequacies of old Ellen in the Harrington-street house, and perhaps the incompatibilities of the brother, outweighed the comparative smallness of our house in Synge-street. My mother soon became not only *prima donna* and chorus leader but general musical factotum in the whirlpool of Lee's activity. Her grounding in Logier's Thoroughbass enabled her to take boundless liberties with composers. When authentic band parts were missing she thought nothing of making up an orchestral accompaniment of her own from the pianoforte score. Lee, as far as I know, had never seen a full orchestral score in his life: he conducted from a first violin part or from the vocal score, and had not, I think, any decided notion of orchestration as an idiosyncratic and characteristic part of a composer's work. He had no

[35]

scholarship according to modern ideas; but he could do what Wagner said is the whole duty of a conductor: he could give the right time to the band; and he could pull it out of its amateur difficulties in emergencies by sheer mesmerism. Though he could not, or at any rate within my hearing never did, sing a note, his taste in singing was classically perfect. In his search for the secret of *bel canto* he had gone to all the teachers within his reach. They told him that there was a voice in the head, a voice in the throat, and a voice in the chest. He dissected birds, and, with the connivance of medical friends, human subjects, in his search for these three organs. He then told the teachers authoritatively that the three voices were fabulous, and that the voice was produced by a single instrument called the larynx. They replied that musical art had nothing to do with anatomy, and that for a musician to practise dissection was unheard-of and disgusting. But as, tested by results, their efforts to teach their pupils to screech like locomotive whistles not only outraged his ear but wrecked the voices and often the health of their victims, their practice was as unacceptable to him as their theory.

Thus Lee became the enemy of every teacher of singing in Dublin; and they reciprocated heartily. In this negative attitude he was left until, at the opera, he heard an Italian baritone named Badiali*, who at the age of 80, when he first discovered these islands, had a perfectly preserved voice, and, to Lee's taste, a perfectly produced one. Lee, thanks to his dissections, listened with a clear knowledge of what a larynx is really like. The other vocal organs and their action were obvious

* Cesare Badiali, highly reputed Italian basso, first sang in London in 1859. Vandeleur Lee's claim to have heard him sing "when he was nearly eighty" was an exaggeration, as Badiali died in 1865 at the age of 55.

and conscious. Guided by this knowledge, and by his fine ear, his fastidious taste, and his instinct, he found out what Badiali was doing when he was singing. The other teachers were interested in Badiali only because one of his accomplishments was to drink a glass of wine and sing a sustained note at the same time. Finally Lee equipped himself with a teaching method which became a religion for him: the only religion, I may add, he ever professed. And my mother, as his pupil, learnt and embraced this musical faith, and rejected all other creeds as uninteresting superstitions. And it did not fail her; for she lived to be Badiali's age and kept her voice without a scrape on it until the end.

I have to dwell on The Method, as we called it in the family, because my mother's association with Lee, and the *ménage à trois* in which it resulted, would be unpleasantly misunderstood without this clue to it. For after the death of Lee's brother, which affected him to the verge of suicide, we left our respective houses and went to live in the same house, number one Hatch-street, which was half in Lower Leeson-street. The arrangement was economical; for we could not afford to live in a fashionable house, and Lee could not afford to give lessons in an unfashionable one, though, being a bachelor, he needed only a music room and a bedroom. We also shared a cottage in Dalkey, high up on Torca Hill, with all Dublin Bay from Dalkey Island to Howth visible from the garden, and all Killiney Bay with the Wicklow mountains in the background from the hall door. Lee bought this cottage and presented it to my mother, though she never had any legal claim to it and did not benefit by its sale later on. It was not conveniently situated for rehearsals or lessons; but there were musical neighbors who allowed me to some extent to run in and out of their houses when there was music going on.

The *ménage à trois*, alternating between Hatch-st.

and Dalkey, worked in its ramshackle way quite smoothly until I was fifteen or thereabouts, when Lee went to London and our family broke up into fragments that never got pieced together again.

In telling the story so far, I have had to reconstruct the part of it which occurred before I came into it and began, as my nurse put it, to take notice. I can remember the ante-Lee period in Synge-st. when my father, as sole chief of the household, read family prayers and formally admitted that we had done those things which we ought not to have done and left undone those things which we ought to have done, which was certainly true as far as I was personally concerned. He added that there was no health in us; and this also was true enough about myself; for Dr Newland, our apothecary, was in almost continual attendance to administer cathartics; and when I had a sore throat I used to hold out for sixpence before submitting to a mustard plaster round my neck. We children (I had two sisters older than myself and no brothers) were abandoned entirely to the servants, who, with the exception of Nurse Williams, who was a good and honest woman, were utterly unfit to be trusted with the charge of three cats, much less three children. I had my meals in the kitchen, mostly of stewed beef, which I loathed, badly cooked potatoes, sound or diseased as the case might be, and much too much tea out of brown delft teapots left to "draw" on the hob until it was pure tannin. Sugar I stole. I was never hungry, because my father, often insufficiently fed in his childhood, had such a horror of child hunger that he insisted on unlimited bread and butter being always within our reach. When I was troublesome a servant thumped me on the head until one day, greatly daring, I rebelled, and, on finding her collapse abjectly, became thenceforth uncontrolable. I hated the servants and liked my mother because, on the one or two rare and delightful occasions when she

[38]

buttered my bread for me, she buttered it thickly instead of merely wiping a knife on it. Her almost complete neglect of me had the advantage that I could idolize her to the utmost pitch of my imagination and had no sordid or disillusioning contacts with her. It was a privilege to be taken for a walk or a visit with her, or on an excursion.

My ordinary exercise whilst I was still too young to be allowed out by myself was to be taken out by a servant, who was supposed to air me on the banks of the canal or round the fashionable squares where the atmosphere was esteemed salubrious and the surroundings gentlemanly. Actually she took me into the slums to visit her private friends, who dwelt in squalid tenements. When she met a generous male acquaintance who insisted on treating her she took me into the public house bars, where I was regaled with lemonade and gingerbeer; but I did not enjoy these treats, because my father's eloquence on the evil of drink had given me an impression that a public house was a wicked place into which I should not have been taken. Thus were laid the foundations of my lifelong hatred of poverty, and the devotion of all my public life to the task of exterminating the poor and rendering their resurrection for ever impossible.

Note, by the way, that I should have been much more decently brought up if my parents had been too poor to afford servants.

As to early education I can remember our daily governess, Miss Hill, a needy lady who seemed to me much older than she can really have been. She puzzled me with her attempts to teach me to read; for I can remember no time at which a page of print was not intelligible to me, and can only suppose that I was born literate. She tried to give me and my two sisters a taste for poetry by reciting "Stop; for thy tread is on an empire's dust"* at us, and only succeeded, poor lady, in awakening our sense of derisive humor. She punished me by little strokes with her fingers that would not have discomposed a fly, and even persuaded me that I ought to cry and feel disgraced on such occasions. She gave us judgment books and taught us to feel jubilant when after her departure we could rush to the kitchen crying "No marks today" and to hang back ashamed when this claim could not be substantiated. She taught me to add, subtract, and multiply, but could not teach me division, because she kept saying two into four, three into six, and so forth without ever explaining what the word "into" meant in this connexion. This was explained to me on my first day at school; and I solemnly declare that it was the only thing I ever learnt at school. However, I must not complain; for my immurement in that damnable boy prison effected its real purpose of preventing my being a nuisance to my mother at home for at least half the day.

The only other teaching I had was from my clerical Uncle William George (surnamed Carroll) who, being married to one of my many maternal aunts (my father had no end of brothers and sisters), had two boys of his own to educate, and took me on with them for awhile in the early mornings to such purpose that when his lessons were ended by my being sent to school, I knew more Latin grammar than any other boy in the First Latin Junior, to which I was relegated. After a few years in that establishment I had forgotten most of it, and, as aforesaid, learnt nothing; for there was only the thinnest pretence of teaching anything but Latin and Greek, if asking a boy once a day in an overcrowded class the Latin for a man or a horse or what not can be called

* Lord Byron, Childe Harold's Pilgrimage, Canto III (1816), xvii.

teaching him Latin. I was far too busy educating myself out of school by reading every book I could lay hands on, and clambering all over Killiney hill looking at the endless pictures nature painted for me, meanwhile keeping my mind busy by telling myself all sorts of stories, to puzzle about my vocabulary lesson, as the punishments were as futile as the teaching. At the end of my schooling I knew nothing of what the school professed to teach; but I was a highly educated boy all the same. I could sing and whistle from end to end leading works by Handel, Haydn, Mozart, Beethoven, Rossini, Bellini, Donizetti and Verdi. I was saturated with English literature, from Shakespear and Bunyan to Byron and Dickens. And I was so susceptible to natural beauty that, having had some glimpse of the Dalkey scenery on an excursion, I still remember the moment when my mother told me that we were going to live there as the happiest of my life.

And all this I owed to the meteoric impact of Lee, with his music, his method, his impetuous enterprise and his magnetism, upon the little Shaw household where a thoroughly disgusted and disillusioned woman was suffering from a hopelessly disappointing husband and three uninteresting children grown too old to be petted like the animals and birds she was so fond of, to say nothing of the humiliating inadequacy of my father's income. We never felt any affection for Lee; for he was too excessively unlike us, too completely a phenomenon, to rouse any primitive human feeling in us. When my mother introduced him to me, he played with me for the first and last time; but as his notion of play was to decorate my face with moustaches and whiskers in burnt cork in spite of the most furious resistance I could put up, our encounter was not a success; and the defensive attitude in which it left me lasted, though without the least bitterness, until the decay of his energies and the growth of mine put us on more than equal terms. He never read anything except Tyndall on Sound,* which he kept in his bedroom for years. He complained that an edition of Shakespear which I lent him was incomplete because it did not contain The School for Scandal, which for some reason he wanted to read; and when I talked of Carlyle he understood me to mean the Viceroy of that name who had graciously attended his concerts in the Antient Concert Rooms. Although he supplanted my father as the dominant factor in the household, and appropriated all the activity and interest of my mother, he was so completely absorbed in his musical affairs that there was no friction and hardly any intimate personal contacts between the two men: certainly no unpleasantness. At first his ideas astonished us. He said that people should sleep with their windows open. The daring of this appealed to me; and I have done so ever since. He ate brown bread instead of white: a startling eccentricity. He had no faith in doctors, and when my mother had a serious illness took her case in hand unhesitatingly and at the end of a week or so gave my trembling father leave to call in a leading Dublin doctor, who simply said "My work is done" and took his hat. As to the apothecary and his squills, he could not exist in Lee's atmosphere; and I was never attended by a doctor again until I caught the smallpox in the epidemic of 1881. He took no interest in pictures or in any art but his own; and even in music his interest was limited to vocal music: I did not know that such things as string quartets or symphonies existed until I began, at sixteen, to investigate music for myself. Beethoven's sonatas and the classical operatic overtures were all I knew of what Wagner called absolute music.

* John Tyndall, Irish physicist and natural philosopher, who did much to popularize science, was the author of On Sound (1867).

I should be tempted to say that none of us knew of the existence of Bach were it not that my mother sang My Heart Ever Faithful,* the banjo-like *obbligato* of which amused me very irreverently.

Lee was like all artists whose knowledge is solely a working knowledge: there were holes in his culture which I had to fill up for myself. Fortunately his richer pupils sometimes presented him with expensive illustrated books. He never opened them; but I did. He was so destitute of any literary bent that when he published a book entitled The Voice, it was written for him by a scamp of a derelict doctor whom he entertained for that purpose, just as in later years his prospectuses and press articles were written by me. He never visited the Dublin National Gallery, one of the finest collections of its size in Europe, with the usual full set of casts from what was called the antique, meaning ancient Greek sculpture. It was by prowling in this gallery that I learnt to recognize the work of the old masters at sight. I learnt French history from the novels of Dumas *père*, and English history from Shakespear and Walter Scott. Good boys were meanwhile learning lessons out of schoolbooks and receiving marks at examinations: a process which left them pious barbarians whilst I was acquiring an equipment which enabled me not only to pose as Corno di Bassetto when the chance arrived, but to add the criticism of pictures to the various strings I had to my bow as a feuilletonist.

Meanwhile nobody ever dreamt of teaching me anything. At fifteen, when the family broke up, I could neither play nor read a note of music. Whether you choose to put it that I was condemned to be a critic or saved from being an executant, the fact remains that

* Mein glaübiges Herze frohlocke sing' Scherze, from Bach's cantata No. 68.

when the house became musicless, I was forced to teach myself how to play written music on the piano from a book with a diagram of the keyboard in it or else be starved of music.

Not that I wanted to be a professional musician. My ambition was to be a great painter like Michael Angelo (one of my heros); but my attempts to obtain instruction in his art at the School of Design presided over by the South Kensington Department of Science and Art only prevented me from learning anything except how to earn five shilling grants for the masters (payment by results) by filling up ridiculous examination papers in practical geometry and what they called freehand drawing.

With competent instruction I daresay I could have become a painter and draughtsman of sorts; but the School of Design convinced me that I was a hopeless failure in that direction on no better ground than that I found I could not draw like Michael Angelo or paint like Titian at the first attempt without knowing how. But teaching, of art and everything else, was and still is so little understood by our professional instructors (mostly themselves failures) that only the readymade geniuses make good; and even they are as often as not the worse for their academic contacts.

As an alternative to being a Michael Angelo I had dreams of being a Badiali. (Note, by the way, that of literature I had no dreams at all, any more than a duck has of swimming.) What that led to was not fully explained until Matthias Alexander, in search, like Lee, of a sound vocal method, invented his technique of self-control.

I had sung like a bird all through my childhood; but when my voice broke I at once fell into the error unmasked by Alexander of trying to gain my end before I had studied the means. In my attempts to reproduce the frenzies of the Count di Luna, the sardonic accents of Gounod's Mephistopheles, the noble charm of Don Giovanni, and the supernatural menace of the Commendatore, not to mention all the women's parts and the tenor parts as well (for all parts, high or low, male or female, had to be sung or shrieked or whistled or growled somehow) I thought of nothing but the dramatic characters; and in attacking them I set my jaws and my glottis as if I had to crack walnuts with them. I might have ruined my voice if I had not imitated good singers instead of bad ones; but even so the results were wretched. When I rejoined my mother in London and she found that I had taught myself to play accompaniments and to amuse myself with operas and oratorios as other youths read novels and smoke cigarets, she warned me that my voice would be spoiled if I went on like that. Thereupon I insisted on being shewn the proper way to sing. The instructive result was that when, following my mother's directions, I left my jaw completely loose, and my tongue flat instead of convulsively rolling it up; when I operated my diaphragm so as to breathe instead of "blowing"; when I tried to round up my pharynx and soft palate and found it like trying to wag my ears, I found that for the first time in my life I could not produce an audible note. It seemed that I had no voice. But I believed in Lee's plan and knew that my own was wrong. I insisted on being taught how to use my voice as if I had one; and in the end the unused and involuntary pharyngeal muscles became active and voluntary, and I developed an uninteresting baritone voice of no exceptional range which I have ever since used for my private satisfaction and exercise without damaging either it or myself in the process.

Here I must digress for a moment to point a moral. Years after I learnt how to sing without spoiling my voice and wrecking my general health, a musician-reciter (Matthias Alexander aforesaid) found himself disabled by the complaint known as clergyman's sore throat. Having the true scientific spirit and industry, he set himself to discover what it was that he was really doing to disable himself in this fashion by his efforts to produce the opposite result. In the end he found this out, and a great deal more as well. He established not only the beginnings of a far reaching science of the apparently involuntary movements we call reflexes, but a technique of correction and selfcontrol which forms a substantial addition to our very slender resources in personal education.

Meanwhile a Russian doctor named Pavlov devoted himself to the investigation of the same subject by practising the horrible voodoo into which professional medical research had lapsed in the XIX century. For quarter of a century he tormented and mutilated dogs most abominably, and finally wrote a ponderous treatise on reflexes in which he claimed to have established on a scientific basis the fact that a dog's mouth will water at the sound of a dinner bell when it is trained to associate that sound with a meal, and that dogs, if tormented, thwarted, baffled, and incommoded continuously, will suffer nervous breakdown and be miserably ruined for the rest of their lives. He was also able to describe what happens to a dog when half its brains are cut out.

What his book and its shamefully respectful reception by professional biologists does demonstrate is that the opening of the scientific professions to persons qualified for them neither by general capacity nor philosophic moral training plunges professional Science, as it has so often plunged professional Religion and Jurisprudence, into an abyss of stupidity and cruelty from which nothing but the outraged humanity of the laity can rescue it.

In the department of biology especially, the professors, mostly brought up as Fundamentalists, are informed that the book of Genesis is not a scientific document, and that the tribal idol whom Noah conciliated by the smell of roast meat is not God and never had any objective existence. They absurdly infer that the pursuit of scientific knowledge: that is, of all knowledge, is exempt from moral obligations, and consequently that they are privileged as scientists to commit the most revolting cruelties when they are engaged in research.

Their next step in this crazy logic is that no research is scientific unless it involves such cruelties. With all the infinite possibilities of legitimate and kindly research open to anyone with enough industry and ingenuity to discover innocent methods of exploration, they set up a boycott of brains and a ritual of sacrifice of dogs and guineas pigs which impresses the superstitious public as all such rituals do. Thereby they learn many things that no decent person ought to know; for it must not be forgotten that human advancement consists not only of adding to the store of human knowledge and experience but eliminating much that is burdensome and brutish. Our forefathers had the knowledge and experience gained by seeing heretics burnt at the stake and harlots whipped through the streets at the cart's tail. Mankind is better without such knowledge and experience.

If Pavlov had been a poacher he would have been imprisoned for his cruelty and despised for his moral imbecility. But as Director of the Physiological Department of the Institute of Experimental Medicine at St Petersburg, and Professor of the Medical Academy, he was virtually forced to mutilate and torment dogs instead of discovering the methods by which humane unofficial investigators were meanwhile finding out all that he was looking for.

The reaction against this voodoo is gathering momentum; but still our rich philanthropic industrialists lavish millions on the endowment of research without taking the most obvious precautions against malversation of their gifts for the benefit of dog stealers, guinea pig breeders, laboratory builders and plumbers, and a routine of cruel folly and scoundrelism that perverts and wastes all the scientific enthusiasm that might otherwise have by this time reduced our death and disease rates to their natural minimum. I am sorry to have to describe so many highly respected gentlemen quite deliberately as fools and scoundrels; but the only definition of scoundrelism known to me is anarchism in morals; and I cannot admit that the hackneyed pleas of the dynamiter and the assassin in politics become valid in the laboratory and the hospital, or that the man who thinks they do is made any less a fool by calling him a professor of physiology.

And all this because in 1860 the men who thought they wanted to substitute scientific knowledge for superstition really wanted only to abolish God and marry their deceased wives' sisters!

I should add that there is no reason to suppose that Pavlov was by nature a bad man. He bore a strong external resemblance to myself, and was wellmeaning, intelligent, and devoted to science. It was his academic environment that corrupted, stultified, and sterilized him. If only he had been taught to sing by my mother no dog need ever have collapsed in terror at his approach; and he might have shared the laurels of Alexander.

And now I must return to my story. Lee's end was more tragic than Pavlov's. I do not know at what moment he began to deteriorate. He was a sober and moderate liver in all respects; and he was never ill until he treated himself to a tour in Italy and caught malaria there. He fought through it without a doctor on cold water, and returned apparently well; but whenever he worked too hard it came back and prostrated him for a day or two. Finally his ambition undid him. Dublin in those days seemed a hopeless place for an artist; for no success counted except a London success. The summit of a provincial conductor's destiny was to preside at a local musical festival modeled on the Three Choirs or Handel Festivals. Lee declared that he would organize and conduct a Dublin Festival with his own chorus and with all the famous leading singers from the Italian opera in London. This he did in connexion with an Exhibition in Dublin. My mother, of course, led the chorus. At a rehearsal the contralto, Madame Demeric Lablache, took exception to something and refused to sing. Lee shrugged his shoulders and asked my mother to carry on, which she did to such purpose that Madame Lablache took care not to give her another such chance.

At the Festivals Lee reached the Dublin limit of eminence. Nothing remained but London. He was assured that London meant a very modest beginning all over again, and perhaps something of an established position after fifteen years or so. Lee said that he would take a house in Park Lane, then the most exclusive and expensive thoroughfare in the West End, sacred to peers and millionaires, and—stupendous on the scale of Irish finance—make his pupils pay him a guinea a lesson. And this he actually did with a success that held out quite brilliantly for several seasons and then destroyed him. For wheras he had succeeded in Dublin by the sheer superiority of his method and talent and character, training his pupils honestly for a couple of years to sing beautifully and classically, he found that the London ladies who took him up so gushingly would have none of his beauty and classicism, and would listen to nothing less than a promise to make them sing "like Patti" in twelve lessons. It was that or starve.

He submitted perforce; but he was no longer the same man, the man to whom all circumstances seemed to give way, and who made his own musical world and reigned in it. He had even to change his name and his aspect. G. J. Lee, with the black whiskers and the clean shaven resolute lip and chin, became Vandeleur Lee, whiskerless, but with a waxed and pointed moustache and an obsequious attitude. It suddenly became evident that he was an elderly man, and, to those who had known him in Dublin, a humbug. Performances of Marchetti's Ruy Blas with my sister as the Queen of Spain, and later on of Sullivan's Patience and scraps of Faust and Il Trovatore were achieved*; but musical society in London at last got tired of the damaged Svengali who could manufacture Pattis for twelve guineas; and the guineas ceased to come in. Still, as there were no night clubs in those days, it was possible to let a house in Park Lane for the night to groups of merrymakers; and Lee was holding out there without pupils when he asked me to draft a circular for him announcing that he could cure clergyman's sore throat. He was still at Park Lane when he dropped dead in the act of undressing himself, dying as he had lived, without a doctor. The postmortem and inquest revealed the fact that his brain was diseased and had been so for a long time. I was glad to learn that his decay was pathological as well as ecological, and that the old efficient and honest Lee had been real after all. But I took to heart the lesson in the value of London fashionable successes. To this day I look to the provincial and the amateur for honesty and genuine fecundity in art.

* Shaw's memory failed him here. Patience was rehearsed in June 1883, but the scheduled performance was cancelled.

Meanwhile, what had happened to the *ménage à trois?* and how did I turn up in Park Lane playing accompaniments and getting glimpses of that artstruck side of fashionable society which takes refuge in music from the routine of politics and sport which occupies the main Philistine body?

Well, when Lee got his foot in at a country house in Shropshire whither he had been invited to conduct some private performances, he sold the Dalkey cottage and concluded his tenancy of Hatch-street. This left us in a house which we could afford less than ever; for my father's moribund business was by now considerably deader than it had been at the date of my birth. My younger sister was dying of consumption caught from reckless contacts at a time when neither consumption nor pneumonia was regarded as catching. All that could be done was to recommend a change of climate. My elder sister had a beautiful voice. In the last of Lee's Dublin adventures in amateur opera she had appeared as Amina in Bellini's La Sonnambula, on which occasion the tenor lost his place and his head, and Lucy obligingly sang most of his part as well as her own. Unfortunately her musical endowment was so complete that it cost her no effort to sing or play anything she had once heard, or to read any music at sight. She simply could not associate the idea of real work with music; and as in any case she had never received any sort of training, her very facility prevented her from becoming a serious artist, though, as she could sing difficult music without breaking her voice, she got through a considerable share of public singing in her time.

Now neither my mother nor any of us knew how much more is needed for an opera singer than a voice and natural musicianship. It seemed to us that as, after a rehearsal or two, she could walk on to the stage, wave her arms about in the absurd manner then in vogue in

[51]

opera, and sing not only her own part but everybody else's as well, she was quite qualified to take the place of Christine Nilsson or Adelina Patti if only she could get a proper introduction. And clearly Lee, now in the first flush of his success in Park Lane, would easily be able to secure this for her.

There was another resource. My now elderly mother believed that she could renounce her amateur status and make a living in London by teaching singing. Had she not the infallible Method to impart? So she realized a little of the scrap of settled property of which her long deceased aunt had not been able to deprive her; sold the Hatch-street furniture; settled my father and myself in comfortable lodgings at 61 Harcourt-st; and took my sisters to the Isle of Wight, where the younger one died. She then took a semi-detached villa in a *cul-de-sac* off the Fulham Road, and waited there for Lucy's plans and her own to materialize.

The result was almost a worse disillusion than her marriage. That had been cured by Lee's music: besides, my father had at last realized his dream of being a practising teetotaler, and was now as inoffensive an old gentleman as any elderly wife could desire. It was characteristic of the Shavian drink neurosis to vanish suddenly in this way. But that Lee should be unfaithful! unfaithful to The Method! that he, the one genuine teacher among so many quacks, should now stoop to outquack them all and become a moustachioed charlatan with all the virtue gone out of him: this was the end of all things; and she never forgave it. She was not unkind: she tolerated Lee the charlatan as she had tolerated Shaw the dipsomaniac because, as I guess, her early motherless privation of affection and her many disappointments in other people had thrown her back on her own considerable internal resources and developed her self-sufficiency and power of solitude to an extent which kept her

[52]

up under circumstances that would have crushed or embittered any woman who was the least bit of a clinger. She dropped Lee very gently: at first he came and went at Victoria Grove, Fulham Road; and she went and came at 13 Park Lane, helping with the music there at his At Homes, and even singing the part of Donna Anna for him (elderly *prima donnas* were then tolerated as matters of course) at an amateur performance of Don Giovanni. But my sister, who had quarreled with him as a child when he tried to give her piano lessons, and had never liked him, could not bear him at all in his new phase, and, when she found that he could not really advance her prospects of becoming a *prima donna*, broke with him completely and made it difficult for him to continue his visits. When he died we had not seen him for some years; and my mother did not display the slightest emotion at the news. He had been dead for her ever since he had ceased to be an honest teacher of singing and a mesmeric conductor.

Her plans for herself came almost to nothing for several years. She found that Englishwomen do not wish to be made to sing beautifully and classically: they want to sing erotically; and this my mother thought not only horrible but unladylike. Her love songs were those of Virginia Gabriel and Arthur Sullivan, all about bereaved lovers and ending with a hope for reunion in the next world. She could sing with perfect purity of tone and touching expression

> Oh, Ruby, my darling, the small white hand
> Which gathered the harebell was never my own.

But if you had been able to anticipate the grand march of human progress and poetic feeling by fifty years, and asked her to sing

> You made me love you.
> I didnt want to do it.
> I didnt want to do it,

she would have asked a policeman to remove you to a third-class carriage.

Besides, though my mother was not consciously a snob, the divinity which hedged an Irish lady of her period was not acceptable to the British suburban parents, all snobs, who were within her reach. They liked to be treated with deference; and it never occurred to my mother that such people could entertain a pretension so monstrous in her case. Her practice with private pupils was negligible until she was asked to become musical instructress at the North London College. Her success was immediate; for not only did her classes leave the other schools nowhere musically, but the divinity aforesaid exactly suited her new *rôle* as schoolmistress. Other schools soon sought her services; and she remained in request until she insisted on retiring on the ground that her age made her public appearances ridiculous. By that time all the old money troubles were over and forgotten, as my financial position enabled me to make her perfectly comfortable in that respect.

And now, what about myself, the incipient Corno di Bassetto?

Well, when my mother sold the Hatch-street furniture, it never occurred to her to sell our piano, though I could not play it, nor could my father. We did not realize, nor did she, that she was never coming back, and that, except for a few days when my father, taking a little holiday for the first time in his life within my experience, came to see us in London, she would never meet him again. Family revolutions would seldom be faced if they did not present themselves at first as temporary makeshifts. Accordingly, having lived since my childhood in a house full of music, I suddenly found myself in a house where there was no music, and could be none unless I made it myself. I have recorded elsewhere* how, having purchased one of Weale's Handbooks which contained a diagram of the keyboard and an explanation of musical notation, I began my self-tuition, not with Czerny's five-finger exercises, but with the overture to Don Giovanni, thinking rightly that I had better start with something I knew well enough to hear whether my fingers were on the right notes or not. There were plenty of vocal scores of operas and oratorios in our lodging; and although I never acquired any technical skill as a pianist, and cannot to this day play a scale with any certainty of not foozling it, I acquired what I wanted: the power to take a vocal score and learn its contents as if I had heard it rehearsed by my mother and her colleagues. I could manage arrangements of orchestral music much better than piano music proper. At last I could play the old rum-tum accompaniments of those days well enough (knowing how they *should* be played) to be more agreeable to singers than many really competent pianists. I bought more scores, among them one of Lohengrin, through which I made the revolutionary discovery of Wagner. I bought arrangements of Beethoven's symphonies, and discovered the musical regions that lie outside opera and oratorio. Later on, I was forced to learn to play the classical symphonies and overtures in strict time by hammering the bass in piano duets with my sister in London. I played Bach's Inventions and his Art of Fugue. I studied academic textbooks, and actually worked out exercises in harmony and counterpoint under supervision by an organist

* The Religion of the Pianoforte, in the Fortnightly Review, February 1894. See Vol. III, p. 105.

friend named Crament,* avoiding consecutive fifths and octaves, and having not the faintest notion of what the result would sound like. I read pseudo-scientific treatises about the roots of chords which candidates for the degree of Mus.Doc. at the universities had to swallow, and learnt that Stainer's commonsense views would get you plucked at Oxford, and Ouseley's pedantries at Cambridge. I read Mozart's Succinct Thoroughbass (a scrap of paper with some helpful tips on it which he scrawled for his pupil Sussmaier); and this, many years later, Edward Elgar told me was the only document in existence of the smallest use to a student composer. It was, I grieve to say, of no use to me; but then I was not a young composer. It ended in my knowing much more about music than any of the great composers, an easy achievement for any critic, however barren. For awhile I must have become a little pedantic; for I remember being shocked, on looking up Lee's old vocal score of Don Giovanni, to find that he had cut out all the repetitions which Mozart had perpetrated as a matter of sonata form. I now see that Lee was a century before his time in this reform, and hope some day to hear a performance of Mozart's Idomeneo in which nothing is sung twice over.

When I look back on all the banging, whistling, roaring, and growling inflicted on nervous neighbors during this process of education, I am consumed with useless remorse. But what else could I have done? Today there is the wireless, which enables me to hear from all over Europe more good music in a week than I could then hear in ten years, if at all. When, after my five years office slavery, I joined my mother in London and lived with her for twenty years until my marriage, I used to drive her nearly crazy by my favorite selections from

* See Vol. II, page 931.

Wagner's Ring, which to her was "all *recitative*," and horribly discordant at that. She never complained at the time, but confessed it after we separated, and said that she had sometimes gone away to cry. If I had committed a murder I do not think it would trouble my conscience very much; but this I cannot bear to think of. If I had to live my life over again I should devote it to the establishment of some arrangement of headphones and microphones or the like whereby the noises made by musical maniacs should be audible to themselves only. In Germany it is against the law to play the piano with the window open. But of what use is that to the people in the house? It should be made [a] felony to play a musical instrument in any other than a completely soundproof room. The same should apply to loud-speakers on pain of confiscation.

Readers with a taste for autobiography must now take my Immaturity preface and dovetail it into this sketch to complete the picture. My business here is to account for my proposal to Tay Pay and my creation of Bassetto. From my earliest recorded sign of an interest in music when as a small child I encored my mother's singing of the page's song from the first act of Les Huguenots (note that I shared Herbert Spencer's liking for Meyerbeer) music has been an indispensable part of my life. Harley Granville-Barker was not far out when, at a rehearsal of one of my plays, he cried out "Ladies and gentlemen: will you please remember that this is Italian opera."

I reprint Bassetto's stuff shamefacedly after long hesitation with a reluctance which has been overcome only by my wife, who has found some amusement in reading it through, a drudgery which I could not bring myself to undertake. I know it was great fun when it was fresh, and that many people have a curious antiquarian taste (I have it myself) for old chronicles of dead musicians and actors. I must warn them, however, not to expect to find here the work of the finished critic who wrote my volumes entitled Music in London, 1890–94, and Our Theatres in the Nineties.* I knew all that was necessary about music; but in criticism I was only a beginner. It is easy enough from the first to distinguish between what is pleasant or unpleasant, accurate or inaccurate in a performance; but when great artists have to be dealt with, only keenly analytical observation and comparison of them with artists who, however agreeable, are not great, can enable a critic to distinguish between what everybody can do and what only a very few can do, and to get his valuations right accordingly. All artsmen know what it is to be enthusiastically praised for something so easy that they are half ashamed of it, and to receive not a word of encouragement for their finest strokes.

I cannot deny that Bassetto was occasionally vulgar; but that does not matter if he makes you laugh. Vulgarity is a necessary part of a complete author's equipment; and the clown is sometimes the best part of the circus. The Star, then a hapenny newspaper, was not catering for a fastidious audience: it was addressed to the bicycle clubs and the polytechnics, not to the Royal Society of Literature or the Musical Association. I purposely vulgarized musical criticism, which was then refined and academic to the point of being unreadable and often nonsensical. Editors, being mostly ignorant of music, would submit to anything from their musical critics, not pretending to understand it. If I occasionally carried to the verge of ribaldry my reaction against the pretentious twaddle and sometimes spiteful cliquishness they tolerated in their ignorance, think of me as heading one of the pioneer columns of what was then called The New Journalism; and you will wonder at my politeness.

* The "Bassetto" criticism was written in 1888–90 (though Shaw occasionally used the pseudonym subsequently). The theatre criticism was written in 1895–8.

You may be puzzled, too, to find that the very music I was brought up on: the pre-Wagner school of formal melody in separate numbers which seemed laid out to catch the *encores* that were then fashionable, was treated by me with contemptuous levity as something to be swept into the dustbin as soon as possible. The explanation is that these works were standing in the way of Wagner, who was then the furiously abused coming man in London. Only his early works were known or tolerated. Half a dozen bars of Tristan or The Mastersingers made professional musicians put their fingers in their ears. The Ride of the Valkyries was played at the Promenade Concerts, and always encored, but only as an insanely rampagious curiosity. The Daily Telegraph steadily preached Wagner down as a discordant notoriety-hunting charlatan in six silk dressing-gowns, who could not write a bar of melody, and made an abominable noise with the orchestra. In pantomime harlequinades the clown produced a trombone, played a bit of the pilgrims' march from Tannhäuser *fortissimo* as well as he could, and said "The music of the future!" The wars of religion were not more bloodthirsty than the discussions of the Wagnerites and the Anti-Wagnerites. I was, of course, a violent Wagnerite; and I had the advantage of knowing the music to which Wagner grew up, wheras many of the most fanatical Wagnerites (Ashton Ellis, who translated the Master's prose works, was a conspicuous example) knew no other music than Wagner's, and believed that the music of Donizetti and Meyerbeer had no dramatic quality whatever. "A few *arpeggios*" was the description Ellis gave me of his notion of Les Huguenots.

Nowadays the reaction is all the other way. Our young lions have no use for Wagner the Liberator. His harmonies, which once seemed monstrous cacophonies, are the commonplaces of the variety theatres. Audacious young critics disparage his grandeurs as tawdry. When the wireless strikes up the Tannhäuser overture I hasten to switch it off, though I can always listen with pleasure to Rossini's overture to William Tell, hackneyed to death in Bassetto's time. The funeral march from Die Götterdämmerung hardly keeps my attention, though Handel's march from Saul is greater than ever. Though I used to scarify the fools who said that Wagner's music was formless, I should not now think the worse of Wagner if, like Bach and Mozart, he had combined the most poignant dramatic expression with the most elaborate decorative design. It was necessary for him to smash the superstition that this was obligatory; to free dramatic melody from the tyranny of arabesques; and to give the orchestra symphonic work instead of *rosalias* and rum-tum; but now that this and all the other musical superstitions are in the dustbin, and the post-Wagnerian harmonic and contrapuntal anarchy is so complete that it is easier technically to compose another Parsifal than another Bach's Mass in B Minor or Don Giovanni I am no longer a combatant anarchist in music, not to mention that I have learnt that a successful revolution's first task is to shoot all revolutionists. This means that I am no longer Corno di Bassetto. He was pre- and pro-Wagner; unfamiliar with Brahms; and unaware that a young musician named Elgar was chuckling over his irreverent *boutades*. As to Cyril Scott, Bax, Ireland, Goossens, Bliss, Walton, Schönberg, Hindemith, or even Richard Strauss and Sibelius, their idioms would have been quite outside Bassetto's conception of music, though today they seem natural enough. Therefore I very greatly doubt whether poor old Bassetto is worth reading now. Still, you are not compelled to read him. Having read the preface you can shut the book and give it to your worst enemy as a birthday present.

MID-ATLANTIC,
Sunday, 2 June 1935.

MUSICAL BUZZINGS OF
A GHOST APPRENTICE
(*The Hornet*, 1876–77; unsigned)

PAULINE
29 November 1876

[U] Mr Cowen's Pauline was produced for the first time on Wednesday last, the 22nd November, by Mr Carl Rosa, in the presence of a large and favorably disposed audience. The book, by Mr Henry Hersee, is an adaptation of the late Lord Lytton's wellknown play* to operatic purposes, in compliance with the exigencies of which our old friend, Colonel Damas, has disappeared altogether, and the remaining characters ever and anon desert the smooth language of the original for verses for which the adapter in his preface has modestly disclaimed any poetic merit. In the musical illustration of the drama thus supplied, Mr Cowen has had all the advantages which can be conferred by the indulgent attitude towards a young composer in whom they felt a national interest, a story of established popularity, the best artistic talent available in English opera, an orchestra and chorus of unusual excellence, and a conductor who spares no pains in the presentation of any work he undertakes.

Under these circumstances, it cannot be contended that Mr Cowen had not a fair field for his experiment as an operatic composer. We would be loth to bear hardly on so painstaking a musician as Mr Cowen is known to be, still more so to discourage a young musician who has

---

* Edward Bulwer-Lytton's The Lady of Lyons, first performed at Covent Garden in 1838, proved to be one of the most successful and enduring plays of the century, achieving 20 London productions before Cowen made it into an opera.

come to the front amidst a dearth of native talent; but the fact remains that the music of Pauline possesses little originality, and displays an utter absence of dramatic faculty. The moment the composer quits the *aria cantabile* form, in which he has already achieved some renown, he betrays weakness, which sometimes verges on absurdity. The musical merit of the opera, therefore, depends principally on the songs with which it is liberally interspersed, and of these not one has any, save the slenderest, connexion with the drama, the words being of the ordinary type manufactured for ballads, and mostly without any bearing on the action.

The opera begins with an introduction consisting of a short *andante maestoso*, afterwards made use of in the *ensemble* of Act III., and a melody which also recurs in Claude Melnotte's famous description of his visionary palace at Como. On the rising of the curtain we find the widow Melnotte awaiting Claude's return from a *fête* outside her cottage. A chorus of villagers ensues, in which they hail the hero as their prince. When they retire, he expresses his passion in a song, One Kind Glance, sung by Mr Santley in his usual finished style. It narrowly escaped an *encore*. We may add that the position adopted by the accomplished baritone, who sang the second verse with one foot placed on a chair, was by no means graceful, and interfered decidedly with his respiratory powers. In the awkward recitative, So do I scatter her image to the winds, in which Claude vents his indignation at the insult to his messenger, we have the first exemplification of the composer's means of delineating the more violent emotions, and we hail with relief the advent of a melody which for a few notes seems to be the familiar Auld Robin Gray, but which develops into a pretty duet of mutual consolation between mother and son. On the entrance of Glavis and Beauseant, the act concludes unhappily with a *trio* for the three men,

[62]

which is the worst feature in the act. Apart from its barrenness as a musical composition, it is scored in a grandiose style, that, applied to the paltry situation of a plot against a scornful girl, is simply absurd.

Act II., which takes place in the garden of M. Deschapelles, opens with a ballet and chorus, commonplace and thinly instrumental, the harp being conspicuous by its abuse. Although the incident of Claude's cool disposal of the snuffbox and ring lent by his tempters seems hardly susceptible of musical treatment, Mr Cowen has embodied it in a sestet, which fairly preserves the humor of the original. In the scene which follows, Damas's challenge of the pretended prince's Italian is ingeniously replaced by a sneering request from Beauseant that Claude will try a guitar for him, on which artless pretext Claude accordingly favors us with Inez was beautiful, an effective song with a pretty *pizzicato* accompaniment. The description of the palace at Como is preserved *verbatim* from the original play, and the composer has successfully translated it into melody. The scene would be charming but for the unpleasant recitative, Oh false one, which follows. The concluding duet is spoiled by a monotonous accompaniment for the harp, of which instrument we have had already more than enough. A lively song for Glavis in nine-eight time, Love has Wings, was redemanded; and the act closed with a wedding march and chorus, which present no special features for criticism.

The third act, at Melnotte's cottage, begins with a song, From its mother's nest, which will probably be heard again on the concert platform. It was excellently sung by Miss Yorke, who received a hearty *encore*. It is a pity that Mr Cowen has seen fit to injure this pretty song by the tasteless flute passages at the end of each verse. The scene between Claude and Pauline, on her discovery of his real station, contains an air, From my first years, and a charming duet, Yet, ere I go, which is the gem of the opera, and stands in agreeable contrast to the crude *agitato* passages with which it is surrounded. The intrusion of Beauseant is unhappily treated. It is difficult to judge the effect of his duet with Pauline, inasmuch as Miss Gaylord and Mr Celli sang flat throughout. The entrance of Claude to the rescue is illustrated by mock-heroic drum passages, which are but a sorry compensation for the fine stroke of character achieved by Lord Lytton in furnishing the "mountebank" with an empty chair. After a very unattractive air—I was tempted to crime,—sung by Claude, the act ends with a tolerably effective *ensemble* constructed on the opening bars of the introduction. In the *entr'acte* which precedes Act IV., we again hear the melody of the duet, Yet, ere I go, this time as a violin solo. We were scarcely prepared for the treatment it received at the hands of so able an artist as Mr Carl Rosa's leader, who played it flat from beginning to end. The most noteworthy numbers of the last act are a song, conventional in type, delivered by Miss Gaylord with much feeling, and a very pretty chorus of bridesmaids, Blooming and bright.

The orchestral portion of the opera displays little judgment. The effect is frequently impoverished, owing partly to excursions into the higher octaves, where the volume of tone is necessarily thin. We have already alluded to the injudicious use of the harp—a fault which has prevailed amongst our composers since the production of M. Gounod's Faust, where the instrument is employed with such exquisite effect. But exactly as in Faust the harp is introduced with a sparing hand, and always well-supported, so in Pauline, and other works of the same calibre, it is lavishly used throughout the score, and frequently left to bear the entire burden of the accompaniment. As with the voice, so with the orchestra, Mr Cowen is most successful when his theme is some simple air, which is usually allotted to the oboe or violin. When he attempts passionate recitative or dramatic effect, the intention is not realized, or [results in] an indulgence in passages so cacophonous that they can only be accounted for as mistaken efforts at originality, colored, perhaps, by a little Wagnerian affectation.

Miss Julia Gaylord impersonated the scornful Lady of Lyons with the greatest success, displaying unexpected pathos in the last two acts. Her singing was marked by real feeling, and though sometimes uncertain in intonation, owing to defective method, was, on the whole, most creditable to her. Miss York's Widow Melnotte was all that could be desired, and was received with enthusiastic applause throughout. Mrs Aynsley Cook as Madame Deschappeles, was, as she always is, thoroughly efficient. Mr Santley's performance of the part of Claude was even and finished, the success of many of the songs being mainly due to his artistic rendering of them. Mr Turner, as Glavis, the better to convey the foppishness of the character, adopted the unaccountable expedient of moving about as though his ankles were tied together. The effect was sufficiently ridiculous. The ungrateful part of Beauseant fell to the lot of Mr Celli, who appeared in various costumes, now revengeful in a "Hardress Cregan"* walking suit, and anon Satanic in pink satin. We are the more sorry to observe Mr Celli's melodramatic propensities, as we believe that with some study in the right direction, and his constant reference to his favorite part of Mephistopheles, he is capable of becoming a good actor. After each act, composer and artists were called before the curtain, and the librettist also appeared to receive the congratu-

* Hardress Cregan is a character in Dion Boucicault's melodrama The Colleen Bawn (1859).

lations of the audience. Finally, a brief *ballet d'action* was performed by the conductor and composer, in which Mr Carl Rosa felicitated Mr Cowen in dumb show on the success of his work, and Mr Cowen mutely testified his conviction of how much that success was due to the exertions of Mr Carl Rosa.[U]

ENGLISH OPERA
6 December 1876

The English opera season is at length over. For a time, at least, theatre-going lovers of music must be content with the brassy delights of pantomime and the affecting symphonies which accompany the development of transformation scenes. Mr Carl Rosa has started on a provincial tour, which will, we hope, prove as successful as his London season has been. During that season he has not hesitated to depart from managerial precedent so far as to keep his promises, and he has fairly carried out his program of discarding the star system and aiming at excellence of *ensemble*. For this he deserves our gratitude, rather than the reproaches with which he has been assailed for enlisting Mr Santley as "a star," and for excluding Mozart's operas from his repertory. Cavillers would do well to bear in mind that avoiding the star system does not mean engaging none but second-rate artists. When an *impresario* offers us an impoverished orchestra, incompetent subordinates, and defective *mise en scène* in order to meet the sensational terms of popular *prime donne*: then we have just cause for complaint. But Mr Carl Rosa has not done this. On the contrary, his company is in all respects improved since the accession of Mr Santley.

As to the clamorers for Mozart, their importunity practically amounts to asking for a display of weakness in the production of works which demand all the highest qualifications which the most gifted artists can bring to their work. We have had an opera of Wagner's [The Flying Dutchman] very creditably produced; we have had Fidelio, which some—notably those who speak of Mozart's works as trifles—declare the greatest of operas; we have had Pauline, specially written by one of our own composers; and if we are not satisfied, Mr Carl Rosa is not to blame in the matter.

The only special event of the closing week was a morning performance of Faust, for the benefit of the society for the relief of distressed Americans, the part of Marguerite being undertaken for this occasion by Madame Van Zandt, who, like the other artists, volunteered her services. Under these circumstances, a minute criticism of the lady's performance would be uncalled for. It will suffice to say that, with the exception of a trifling hitch in the church scene, she sang the music correctly, and achieved a floral success. We would suggest, however, that in future the persons who kindly undertake to throw bouquets should study the score beforehand, and offer their tributes at the proper opportunities. On Wednesday last, bouquets dropped promiscuously throughout the performance, and one, bearing a message of peace and charity, fell most inappropriately into the hands of Mephistopheles. The military band in the fourth act played strepitously— most offensively so, indeed. Mr Ludwig, who appeared as Valentin, effectually spoiled his song by delivering the words with a strong foreign inflexion: an affectation which cannot be too strongly reprehended.* In other

* Ludwig was the professional name adopted by Irish tenor William Ledwidge. Throughout Shaw's early critical years— until, in fact, the custom waned—he disparaged this practice by British musical artists of masking their national origin with foreign names and mannerisms.

respects, the cast was the same as usual, Miss Yorke being conspicuous by her meritorious impersonation of Siebel.

On Tuesday, the 28th ult., Cagnoni's opera The Porter of Havre was performed before a rather limited audience. This pretty opera holds a position somewhat analogous to that of Marta. It is not great, but it is never disagreeable. It contains some beautiful numbers, the orchestration (in the style of Meyerbeer) is solid, and the plot, though absurdly constructed, is entertaining. Above all, in some of its scenes are familiar pictures of home life—impossible on the Italian stage—the power of presenting which is one of the most charming attractions afforded by English opera.

The last two nights were devoted to Fidelio and The Water Carrier. The association of these is the more appropriate as it gives us an opportunity of tracing the extent to which Beethoven followed Cherubini—his acknowledged model—in the structure of his only opera. As performed by the Carl Rosa company, the dialogue is retained according to the intention of the composers, and we escape the recitative impertinences with which Balfe and others have vulgarized these works for representation on the Italian stage.

MOZART AND HAYDN WITH STRINGS

6 December 1876

[U] At the Popular Concert on the 25th ult., Mozart's string quartet, No. 2 in D minor, was performed. This work, with its *andante* which seems to forecast the sweetness and depth of the Zauberflöte, its *finale* with variations, and its gay minuet and trio, is generally heard at least once during each season, and is always welcome. On this occasion, the minuet was encored. On the following Monday, the same master was represented by his quartet in D major, No. 7, and the Strinasacchi sonata for pianoforte and violin. The quartet, composed about a year later than the wellknown Jupiter symphony, displays in common with it that clear form and contrasted variety of effect, in the command of which Mozart has never been equaled. It was executed by Madame Norman-Neruda, MM. Kies, Zerbini, and Piatti, with vigor and sonority of tone, but with some want of refinement in the delicate *forte pianos* of the minuet. The Strinasacchi sonata, written hurriedly at the request of a friend, is one of the composer's less important works, and, with those who were fortunate enough to hear Madame Neruda's performance of Beethoven's Kreutzer sonata, with Mr Hallé at the previous concert, it must have suffered by the inevitable comparison. The pianoforte part was in the able hands of Miss Zimmermann, who also played Mendelssohn's fantasia, Op. 28, with her accustomed skill, the *presto finale* being taken at a dazzling speed.

Judging by the high standard taught us by the artists themselves, they scarcely did justice to Haydn's quartet, No. 6, of Op. 17. The gigue-like *presto* was satisfactorily rendered; but in the following movements the concert of the instruments was less perfect, and the F in *alt*, sustained by the first violin in the *largo*, was hardly up to the pitch. Miss Butterworth was the vocalist on Saturday; and on Monday Signor Gustave Garcia sang Handel's Tyrannic Love and Schubert's Appeal in an exaggerated style, which obtained for the latter an ill-deserved *encore*.[U]

MUSICAL INTERVALS

13 December 1876

[U] Last week, on Thursday and the following days, Mr A. S. Ellis gave a series of demonstrations of musical intervals, at the Exhibition of Scientific Apparatus at South Kensington. As such matters are interesting only to the intelligent section of the musical public, the attendance on each occasion was rather limited, but, we are glad to say, not wholly confined to persons scientifically or technically concerned. A few ladies were present, and the demonstrations were followed with the closest attention, many questions being addressed to the lecturer at the conclusion. Mr Ellis, in the course of his remarks, dwelt principally on the effects of equal temperament, the imperfection of which he illustrated in the most intelligible manner by producing on Herr Appun's instruments the perfect harmonic intervals and the false or tempered ones of the pianoforte, &c., in succession: the difference being appreciable by any listener—however ignorant of the principles involved—accustomed to discriminate between harmony and discord.

As the great majority of us receive our musical education almost entirely through the pianoforte, it will be seen that such demonstrations are of general importance. Most amateur and many professional players have a vague knowledge, derived from hearsay, that there is some mysterious difficulty which has to be reconciled in the tuning of their pianofortes; but as to the definite meaning of temperament, the existence of partial tones, the source of beats, and so on, they are wholly ignorant. They avoid such questions, and sneer

[70]

at them as troublesome matters of theory, which possess no practical value. Yet all these "bitter words" represent very simple matters, quite within the comprehension of the most ordinary intellect; and so far from their being useless in actual music, it may be stated that, without a knowledge of the harmonics of a string or the phenomena of sympathetic vibrations, no person can employ the pedal of a pianoforte, except empirically. It is much to be desired that acoustics should form a regular branch of musical instruction, and we strongly recommend those who desire to hear those intervals which they have hitherto known only in the abstract to pay a visit to "Room 2" at South Kensington.

Perhaps the most generally interesting object there is the enharmonic harmonium of Mr Bosanquet, which is not merely a piece of acoustical apparatus but a musical instrument, giving us nearly seven notes for each one we can obtain on the pianoforte, and affording even greater facilities than Herr Appun's instrument for the contrast of the true with the tempered intonation. It is to be regretted that the announcement of Mr Ellis's demonstrations was not more widely circulated and couched in more popular language, and we hope that the subject will not be allowed to drop. Small though the number of scientific musicians may be, yet the success of the work of Helmholtz*, Professor Tyndall, and others on the subject would seem to indicate that general interest in it is steadily increasing, and that there is at least a hope that the musicians of the future may be something more than the jealous dogmatists of the past—and, we fear, to some extent of the present generation also.[U]

The only novelty at the Saturday Popular Concert on

* Hermann von Helmholtz, German physicist, investigated the mechanisms of hearing and offered an explanation of the perception of the quality of tone.

the 2nd instant was a Sonata for pianoforte and violin by Rheinberger, introduced by Madame Norman-Neruda and Mr Hallé. It was unfortunately placed at the end of the program, and neither the romantic beauty of the work, nor the ordinary politeness due to the artists, availed to secure it a hearing until the last overcoat in the hall was comfortably buttoned and everybody prepared to rush forth at the first notes of the *coda*. It is not calculated to advance our national reputation that these concerts should be so largely frequented by foreigners, who naturally conclude that our pursuit of music is mere fashionable affectation, and that we are incapable of behaving ourselves properly.

LISZT THE CHARLATAN
20 December 1876

Mazeppa, a symphonic poem for orchestra, by F. Liszt, was performed for the first time in England, at the Crystal Palace on the 9th inst. The program introduces the work as "a gigantic musical picture of the terrible three days' ride related in Victor Hugo's soul-stirring poem, and of the poet's allegorical representation of the unbridled flight of genius, and its final triumph through suffering and adversity." Then follows a brief dissertation on the comparative merits of Lord Byron and Victor Hugo as emotional poets; the usual thematic analysis of the music; and, finally, a reprint of the entire poem. It will be seen that no trouble was spared to enable the audience to realize the composer's intention, or to arouse their interest in his work.

The first portion is an *allegro agitato*, of which we are told "This remarkable movement illustrates the three days' flight of the wild steed, and the almost indescribable anguish and despair of its human victim, as related in the first fourteen verses of the poem." It opens with a sudden clash of cymbals, at which the section of the audience which is not familiar with the eccentricities of higher development bursts out laughing. The sequel consists of rapid triplets, with a good deal of piccolo, drum, and cymbal, relieved by an effective melody for the brass: the whole producing an effect sufficiently entertaining, and at times very amusing, but not even remotely approaching the sublime. It may be revived at intervals with an alteration of program, as, for instance, "A Sudden Shower," "A Storm in a Teacup," or "Macbeth, The Witches' Cauldron," any of which it would illustrate more appropriately than the rushing of a wild horse, which is perhaps the only phenomenon of an exciting description that it does *not* suggest. After a brief *andante* of advanced commonplace, the "symphonic poem" concludes with an *allegro marziale*, in the constant modulations and stirring marches of which we see, not "glory and greatness achieved through suffering and adversity," but the favorite effects of the clever pianoforte transcriber achieved on a large scale through the resources of orchestra. Opinions respecting the work as a whole must depend altogether on the standard from which it is judged. If we consider it as a fantastic caprice designed to illustrate the more grotesque external incidents of the story, it deserves some admiration for its piquancy and skilful scoring. But if we apply the broad gauge, which the composer himself challenges, and look for a picture of complicated emotion, and a display of the powers of music much as we find in the symphonies of the great masters, we unhesitatingly condemn it as false art, due to the conception, not of a true musician, but of a charlatan.

[U] At the same concert Bennett's beautiful and original

symphony in G minor was performed with the sympathetic expression which Mr Manns' orchestra sometimes attains. The overture was Schumann's Genoveva, and here the execution lacked crispness, a defect readily felt in a work which is in itself somewhat turgid. Miss Anna Mehlig played a concerto of Hiller's carelessly on a toneless piano, and a few songs were contributed by Miss Ida Corani and Mr Celli, amongst them the air from Tannhäuser, *Oh tu bell' astro incantator*; also an aria from Giralda, which might well have been spared, as it possesses no interest, and was not invested with any artistic graces by the singer. The remainder of the program was devoted to the interests of the royalty system.[U]

Schubert's string quintet in C, Op. 163, beautiful though its themes are, is decidedly too long. The composer fell into the error—an habitual one with him—of developing the principal movements at a length quite disproportionate to his resources in variety of form, and hence the effect of the quintet as a whole is wearisome. Apart from this, the work is full of the melancholy tenderness characteristic of Schubert's style, and the compact central movements, with the quaint *scherzo* and funereal trio are sources of unalloyed pleasure. It was moderately well played at the Monday Popular Concert on the 11th inst. by MM. Piatti, Ries, Zerbini, and Pezze, led by Herr Straus. Miss Anna Mehlig displayed her technical ability in a performance of Schumann's Toccata in C, Op. 7, and, being deservedly encored, played one of those mysterious *morceaux* which we are accustomed to hear on such occasions. She was also heard in Brahms's pianoforte quartet in G minor, and with Signor Piatti in a polonaise by Chopin. The arrangement of Brahms's quartet is unusual. It opens with the customary *allegro*, followed by an *intermezzo* with trio, the former melancholy in character, and

[74]

played with muted violins. This is succeeded by an *andante*, which is perhaps the most important movement in the work. The *finale* is in the *rondo saltarello* form, so favored in modern instrumental music, and its performance elicited a burst of genuine applause. The entire work, though less striking than the quartet in C minor, recently introduced at the Popular Concerts, is a sufficient example of the genius of a master of whom we in this country know far too little.

MESSIAH IN THE ALBERT HALL
27 December 1876

[U] On Monday, December 18th, a performance of the Messiah by the Albert Hall Choral Society took place, conducted by Mr Barnby. Dr Stainer presided at the organ, and the solo parts were sustained by Mlle Titiens, Madame Trebelli-Bettini, Herr Behrens, and Mr W.H. Cummings. The assembly of a large audience bore testimony to the unfailing popularity of the greatest of oratorios.

The performance, on the whole, was unsatisfactory in the extreme. The conductor throughout seemed to be actuated by one motive: that of getting through his work as quickly as possible. We believe Mr Barnby will find few musicians to agree with him as to the *tempo* of Oh, thou that tellest, which was played more in the trivial measure of a dance tune than with the solemn emphasis of a sacred air. Many other movements suffered in the same way, and the dignity of style demanded by oratorio was not once attained. In order to conduct such a work as the Messiah successfully, a faculty for controling large masses is required; and this Mr Barnby apparently does not possess. The chorus seemed to regard him as a useful index in starting, and the orchestra played with very little reference to him at all. Under such circumstances, it is not to be wondered at that the performance was an unprofitable one, destitute of grandeur, and irritating by the inadequacy of the effect to the resources at hand.

The choruses were, in most instances, correctly sung, the chief exception being Let us break their bonds asunder, which became disorganized. But no mechanical accuracy (such as it was—it did not extend to an attempt at phrasing) could compensate for the utter absence of spirit displayed by the Albert Hall Choir. The stirring For He shall purify, and the sublime Hallelujah, might have been mere singing exercises, for any sense of their significance that appeared on Monday night.

The orchestra, from whom we should have expected more, achieved, if possible, less than the chorus with regard to artistic execution. A dry, rasping style of bowing was adopted in the overture, as being, we presume, the best adapted to the requirements of fugue. The exquisite accompaniment to the recitative And lo! the Angel of the Lord was robbed of all its beauty; and in that to And suddenly, the phrases were exaggerated into a series of *forte pianos*. In accompanying He shall feed His flock, the *legato* was carried out by slipping from note to note in a most inartistic manner. Whenever the full power of the orchestra was employed, the coarseness of the brass became painfully obtrusive. In the Pastoral Symphony the flute was a shade sharp. This is a defect against which an artist who values his reputation cannot guard too jealously, as the unmusicianlike device of tuning slightly above the pitch, in order to secure an undue prominence, is becoming common in our orchestras, and threatens to prove a serious evil.

Mr Cummings, who undertook the tenor music, at once displayed his inefficiency by his feeble rendering of Comfort ye, and his uncertain execution in the air Every Valley. The florid passages in Thou shalt break them can scarcely be said to have been executed at all; and in Behold and see, the expression was overstrained, and the style undignified. Mr Cummings's least successful effort was But thou didst not leave, which was transposed half a tone. Herr Behrens, who sang a few of the bass numbers, betrayed an equally limited acquaintance with his part and the English language. He frequently selected the middle of a phrase as a suitable opportunity for taking breath; and in Why do the nations he substituted semiquaver passages for the triplets, and stumbled through rather than sang the air. He yielded But who may abide to the contralto—an arrangement by which the audience were gainers. The air The trumpet shall sound, which had figured conspicuously in the announcements, was omitted. Mlle Titiens, who might have helped to make amends for the general inferiority of the performance, was unable to do so, being, unfortunately, in bad voice.

Of Madame Trebelli-Bettini, we have purposely deferred mention, as we feel that she is entitled to a place apart from the rest. During the numbers allotted to her, which seemed all too few, her beautiful vocalization, perfect phrasing, and pathetic tones obliterated for the moment all consciousness of the surrounding shortcomings. Her singing of He shall feed His flock could not have been surpassed. For a great operatic artist to deliver the touching airs of the Messiah without once having recourse to dramatic coloring, whilst conveying throughout the truest lyrical expression is, indeed, one of the highest achievements of executive musical art.

The Crystal Palace concert of the 16th inst., the last of the winter series, was devoted to the celebration of Beethoven's birthday, the works performed having been selected entirely from his compositions. The concert room was crowded to inconvenience. The chief item in the program was the choral symphony, of which the instrumental portions and principal vocal parts were admirably performed. The choruses were mechanically executed, and hence the Ode to Joy was the least effective movement in the symphony. An occasional lack of power in the weightier passages was probably due to the extremely unfavorable acoustical conditions of the concert room. The fifth pianoforte concerto was played by Madame Arabella Goddard with vigor and accuracy. But something more than these is required for an interpretation of Beethoven's music, and, consequently, much of the beauty of the work was lost. It should be mentioned that the pianoforte used was a feeble instrument, such tone as Madame Goddard could produce from it being of the most commonplace quality. The popular overture to the ballet of Prometheus was excellently played. Madame Blanche Cole sang the cavatina, Praise of Music, very fairly, though falling short of the inspired style which it calls for. Mr Lloyd proved unequal to Adelaide, rendering it conventionally, and falling into the common error of taking the impetuous *allegro* too slowly. Madame Antoinette Sterling, in singing *Wonne der Wehmut* and *Neue Liebe*, treated them with her peculiar mannerism and characteristic disregard of metric accent, charming in a ballad, but quite the reverse in a song by Beethoven.[U]

NEARLY A BLANK

3 January 1877

The past fortnight has been, musically speaking, nearly a blank. At Christmas the divine art is wont to retreat into private life! There are plenty of carols, but no concerts; and even the church bells, in hopelessly false intervals, ring out a special appeal to the public to be taken down from their cold eminence and consigned to the crucible. And as, in spite of our protests, they daily assert beyond dispute our national insensibility to music, it would be as well to comply with their demand and allow the hours to pass away undisturbed.

[U] At the concert in the Westminster Aquarium, on the afternoon of the 22nd December, Miss Woolf's overture The Fall of Pompeii and a symphony by M. Halberstadt were performed, the latter for the first time. In the composition of his symphony, which consists of the usual four movements, M. Halberstadt has displayed his command of orchestral effect, principally of the operatic type, and much ingenuity in the use of wellworn passages and commonplace themes. The symphony is, in fact, one of those pieces of patchwork which are periodically compiled by distinguished professors possessing no faculty for original composition, who once a year or so produce a work to be applauded for a moment by their pupils and friends and then forgotten. It has nothing of the advanced German stamp about it; on the contrary, it rather surprises us with reminiscences of the once universal, but now rapidly vanishing, school of Rossini. It was conducted by the composer and received with loud applause, in which the orchestra disinterestedly joined. Miss Woolf's overture was performed at so early an hour that we were unable to hear it. We hope, however, to have another opportunity of doing so, as the composer, in venturing from the ordinary practice of songwriting into the department of orchestral music of which the best examples are constantly before the public, has taken a bold step. An interesting item on the program, from a phenomenal, if not artistic, point of view, was a movement from Mozart's ninth concerto, correctly and intelligently played by Mlle Douste, who is, we are informed, but six years of age. The *cadenza*, usually improvized by the player, was supplied by M. de Fontaine, who might have saved his reputation for good taste by suppressing his responsibility for this—as it proved—very vulgar ornament. In response to an *encore*, the young artist executed a fugue with perfect clearness, a feat of much greater difficulty than the concerto presented. Mr Thurley Beale sang two songs: Gounod's Nazareth and Schubert's Wanderer. Mr Beale's strength does not lie in the walk of art to which these songs belong, and he failed to do them justice. The concert concluded with Herold's too-often-heard overture to Zampa.[U]

A PERNICIOUS SYSTEM

17 January 1877

In the present century of universal progress, no art, perhaps, has attained to such subtly-varied developments as that of advertizing. We used to hear that an outlay of some thousands in advertisements would ensure a return of cent. per cent. This, however, is now a vulgar and old-fashioned principle; and of late years the far more ingenious method of bringing one's wares into notoriety at the expense of the public has been brought nearly to perfection, especially by the music trade, abetted by the less independent singers of the day. Thus, a few of the leading firms have started musical journals in order to secure an impartial review for each work published by them, and a just exposure of the demerits of such trash as rival establishments may attempt to impose on the public. A more immediately remunerative plan is the institution of dreary entertainments known as "ballad concerts." It is well known that the best way to sell a song is to have it sung. Consequently, when Messrs Blank and Co. announce a concert for which they have engaged the most eminent vocalists of the day, more is implied thereby than is evident to the unsophisticated concert-goer, who conceives the undertaking to be a legitimate speculation. He finds the concert stupid, but he does not attach any significance to the fact that all the uninteresting and worthless items which spin out the long program (excepting only those which constitute the attraction and are sung by artists who have achieved an independent position) are published by Messrs Blank and Co. Probably, if he did awake to the true nature of the transaction, he would decline to contribute in future to the advertizing expenses of the enterprising firm; and as such uninitiated frequenters of concert rooms are, as a rule, the only persons who pay for admission, the whole pernicious system of publishers' concerts would fall unsupported to the ground, bringing with it the concomitant nuisances of royalties and similar varieties of blackmail, alike degrading to art and oppressive to composers of real merit.

[U] The Monday Popular Concerts were resumed on the 8th inst., when Mlle Marie Krebs appeared for the first time this season, and achieved the somewhat heroic feat of executing the Sonata Appassionata from memory. Nevertheless, this fashion of dispensing with the book, which has come into vogue of late years, we hold to be not only unnecessary, but undesirable, except in the case of compositions intended to display technical proficiency only. In the interpretation of Beethoven's greater sonatas, the strain on the executive powers is sufficiently engrossing without further distracting the attention from the feeling of the tone-poem by adding the difficulty of remembering it by rote. Mlle Krebs played the Appassionata with her usual steadiness and brilliancy; but the majesty and pathos of it were not fully brought forth, and in the *allegro* there was some sacrifice of clearness to speed. She also played with perfect success in the sonata in F major for pianoforte and violoncello, one of Beethoven's earlier works, Signor Piatti contributing to make this—what it undoubtedly was—the most satisfactory performance of the evening. Mozart's Divertimento No. 3 (for strings and two horns), and Haydn's quartet, No. 2 of Op. 50, formed the remainder of the instrumental portion of the program, but did not prove very agreeable, the imperfect tune being occasionally quite painful. The quartet was heard for the first time, and we look forward to hearing it again with a more sympathetic leader than Herr Straus. Mme Thekla Friedlander sang three songs, and was encored in Sebastian Bach's *Willst du dein Herz mir schenken.*

The 26th March, 1877, being the fiftieth anniversary of the death of Beethoven, it is suggested that the occasion should be duly celebrated in England. About a month since, on the great master's birthday, Mr Manns' commemorative concert at the Crystal Palace proved a success, and we hope the experiment will be repeated. Perhaps some of our numerous choral societies might find courage to attack the little known Missa Solemnis, one of the most remarkable of the extraordinary works produced by Beethoven in his latter days. [U]

BIORN:
From a Musical Point of View
24 January 1877

[U] Of the many difficulties which beset criticism, the most hopeless is the effort to review work which, without rising to originality or stooping to bad craftsmanship or absurdity, preserves a dead level of respectable mediocrity, and opposes to the most acute censor a purely negative completeness, in which there is nothing to be admired, nothing that can reasonably be condemned, and, in short, nothing but the constant demand for something with a semblance of novelty to justify its existence at all. Such is the music of Biorn, a grand romantic opera by Lauro Rossi, which was produced at the Queen's Theatre on the 17th inst., for the first time.

Signor Rossi's music is neither better nor worse than the generality of operas which are poured forth profusely in Italy, where they fill a program for a few nights and then are heard no more. It is as free from inspiration as from crudity, and the composer never fails in his vein of melody, occasionally repeating himself, never directly plagiarizing, but alway suggesting some wellknown composer—Verdi, perhaps, most frequently. A detailed criticism of the opera would be monotonous. The best number is a chorus of waiting women, in the fourth act; the worst, the portions of declamatory recitative allotted to Lady Elfrida. Of Mrs Fitzinman Marshall's performance as Elfrida we forbear to speak, as an apology was made for her on the score of illness. Miss Cora Stuart was fortunate in having the only part in the opera with which it was possible to feel any sympathy, and she achieved the main success of the evening. Mlle Corandi as Hela apparently suffered from a slight nervousness at first, which interfered with the certainty of her delivery. The part of Biorn was taken by Signor Mottino, who has a heavy baritone voice, but lacks ease of style, and sings with a perceptible *vibrato*. The subordinate parts were satisfactorily filled.

A contingent from the band of the Scots Fusilier Guards, under the direction of Mr J.P. Clarke, assisted on the stage. The scenic effects, with which the opera is loaded, were excellently presented, and with a trifling exception were produced without any of the shortcomings usual on first nights. Indeed, but for the liberal and sometimes unaccountable supplies of lightning and thunder, the opera would have proved rather dull. On the whole, we are unable to attach the slightest musical importance to the production of Biorn, and we are of opinion that the exertions expended in its production might have been much more worthily employed.[U]

WALTZES BY BRAHMS

24 January 1877

[U] On Saturday afternoon, the 13th inst., the concert room at St James's Hall was crowded to an unusual extent. Mr Sims Reeves sang Adelaide and a very charming song, Awake, by Signor Piatti, to the composer's *obbligato*. It was encored with enthusiasm. Mlle Marie Krebs played the Sonata Pathétique, her rendering of the rondo being most spirited and original. She was also heard in Mozart's pianoforte quartet in G minor, which was executed with a good deal of dash, but not without a few slips on the part of the first violin. Schubert's octet was repeated, the second *andante* and minuet being omitted.

At the concert on the following Monday the most interesting feature was the introduction for the first time of a set of waltzes for the pianoforte by our expected guest, Herr Brahms, arranged for four hands (on this occasion the skilful ones of Mlle Krebs and Miss Zimmermann), with a romantic commentary for voices, which was sung by Mlles Löwe and Redeker, MM. Shakespeare and Pyatt. The performance was quite satisfactory, and must have been delightful to all whose temperaments were sufficiently poetic to grasp the spirit of the composition. Another novelty was a rondo by Chopin for two pianofortes, which would have been perfectly executed had the players been more accurately together. As it was, some of the chords formed startling echoes rather than simultaneous sounds. A Spanish quartet (so-called) by Schumann followed, and the concert concluded with Beethoven's second pianoforte trio. Mr Henry Holmes was the leader at both concerts.[U]

MUSIC FOR CONNOISSEURS
31 January 1877

[U] Welcome, indeed, to connoisseurs were two parts of the program of the Popular Concert of the 20th, the sonata Les Adieux, and a strange relic of the XVII century, introduced for the first time by Signor Piatti and Sir Julius Benedict, in the shape of a sonata for violoncello and pianoforte by the now forgotten Antoniotto. It consists of two *adagios*, in which much genuine poetry is displayed, and two quick movements, which are merely quaint. Signor Piatti, who executed the sonata with his usual finish, had considerably the advantage of his accompanist in the matter of acquaintance with the work. Mlle Marie Krebs played the Les Adieux better than she has played anything else this season at the Popular Concerts, and was recalled twice by the audience. Mendelssohn's quintet for strings, Op. 87, was rendered rather coarsely as to the *allegros*, but the slow movements were excellently given. Herr Straus displayed unusual delicacy in the *andante*, which was encored.

On Monday Mlle Krebs played the celebrated

thirtytwo variations on an air in C minor*—a work which presents some technical difficulties, particularly in its broken time, but which is by no means a worthy example of the master's resources in the variation form. The arrangement of the program was injudicious, as it comprised no less than three different items containing variations—in fact, the only instrumental piece which did not either consist of or include an air so treated was Beethoven's great quartet in F major, Op. 59, of which the executive honors are due chiefly to Signor Piatti. The instruments were very rarely in tune throughout, and though the artists were cordially applauded at the conclusion, the performance was not firstrate. Mlles Redeker and Friedlander, who are established favorites at these concerts, sang duets by Rubinstein and Schumann. Mlle Redeker especially has been deservedly successful in her sympathetic rendering of the songs of Schubert. The concert concluded with Beethoven's sonata for pianoforte and violin, No. 1 of Op. 12, one of the composer's most Mozartean productions. It was executed by Mlle Krebs and Herr Straus.

Mr Richard Blagrove, who has espoused the neglected cause of the concertina, gave the first concert of his second season on Thursday evening, the 25th inst. He announces his intention of devoting the profits of these concerts to a fund for providing original compositions written for several concertinas. Although we cannot help a passing reflection that it may be possible to have too much of a good thing, we wish Mr Blagrove every success. [U]

* Beethoven, G.191.

ROSSINI'S STABAT MATER

7 February 1877

[U] Miss Agnes Zimmermann was the pianist at the Popular Concert, on Monday, the 29th ultimo, when she played Beethoven's sonata in C major, No. 3 of Op. 2. It is a relief to hear some of the earliest works of the master in these days, when players so seldom condescend to go behind Op. 10 or 13. Miss Zimmermann's playing is always thoroughly satisfactory: being accurate, free from affectation, and only lacking that natural gift of the highest expression, which is so rare, and so impossible of acquisition, that we have no right to complain of its absence. Schumann's extraordinary quartet in A major, Op. 41, was played with spirit and, it is gratifying to note, received with marked approbation. The leader, Mr Henry Holmes, subsequently introduced an *adagio* from a Salon Stücke by Spohr. In response to a warm *encore*, he played a difficult, but somewhat dry, study. Mr Holmes is always welcome at chamber music concerts. He plays with feeling, and generally in tune: qualities which are frequently conspicuous by their absence from the quartets at St James's Hall. Schubert's pianoforte trio, Op. 99, was the last item in the program, which should have been closed by a more concise work. At the end of a concert the audience are rarely in a mood to follow the lengthy developments in which Schubert indulged; and on Monday the final *allegro* was played to empty benches. Mlles Friedlander and Redeker contributed duets by Schumann and Rubinstein, with their customary success.

A new vein, which may be described as the familiarly-mysterious, has been struck in the almost exhausted

[87]

mine of song names. We are apprised that at the next ballad concert Mme Sherrington will sing Somebody, and Mr Lloyd will sing Sometimes. We hope this is not an effort of our popular tenor to imitate Mr Sims Reeves.[U]

On the 1st instant, at the Albert Hall, Mendelssohn's Lobgesang and Rossini's Stabat Mater were repeated. With the exception of Mr Sims Reeves, the cast was entirely different from that of last December. We are glad to note a decided improvement in the orchestra and chorus. The symphony preceding the vocal portions of the Hymn of Praise was very fairly played, especially the *allegretto*, in which the brass is little employed, and which is in itself perhaps the best part of the instrumental work. In following out the idea suggested by Beethoven's ninth symphony, the comparative weakness and paucity of invention displayed by Mendelssohn are emphasized by contrast; and whether from this reason or not, the symphonic prelude to the Lobgesang has always appeared to us an elaborate and lengthy working up of somewhat feeble materials. Mr Sims Reeves's delivery of the tenor music was full of devotional feeling, and the intensity of expression conveyed in the cry, Watchman, will the night soon pass? made a deep impression. Miss Anna Williams and Miss Braham sang out of tune, and the duet I waited for the Lord suffered for it.

In the Stabat Mater the principal parts were in the hands of Mesdames Lemmens-Sherrington and Antoinette Sterling, Messrs W. H. Cummings and R. Hilton. The last-named gentleman rendered the baritone music inartistically, and entirely failed to realize the sharp markings of the Pro peccatis. Miss Sterling was remarkable as usual for her earnest feeling and originality of style. If she would but deign to pay a little attention to phrasing and carefully avoid stooping to mannerism, she might take rank amongst the greatest of our oratorio singers. Madame Sherrington marred an otherwise satisfactory interpretation of the soprano music by the introduction of a shake very much out of keeping with the character of the Inflammatus.

In the duet Quis est homo, the trombones, which have become a nuisance to frequenters of the Albert Hall, exerted themselves with their usual offensiveness. It is true that Rossini marked the semiquaver emphasized by the trombones *fortissimo*, but the *maestro* had studied the instruments in the hands of artists, and not in the circus. The strangest thing is that Mr Barnby, who should know better, apparently approves of the hideous bark—there is really no other equivalent in the language—from which the audience visibly shrink. Excepting further a sharp drum, the orchestra was otherwise efficient.

PLACIDA, THE CHRISTIAN MARTYR

14 February 1877

[U] An attractive feature in the program of the Popular Concert of Saturday, the 3rd inst., was M. Blumenthal's Message sung by Mr Sims Reeves, and accompanied by the composer. The result must have been far from gratifying to M. Blumenthal, for the audience received with marked coldness one of the worst renderings of his favorite song we have ever had the misfortune to hear. Later on, the popular tenor made amends by his singing of Signor Piatti's Awake, awake, although even in this he suffered by comparison with his performance on a previous occasion. Spohr's sextet for strings, Op. 140, was played in an unfinished style as to the quick movements, a defect which seems inevitable under the leadership of Herr Straus. On the following Monday, when Herr Joachim made his *rentrée*, was heard the first really wellplayed *allegro* since the departure of Madame Norman-Neruda: that of Beethoven's quartet, Op. 59, with the fugued *finale*. The great violinist also played in a Haydn quartet; and for a solo Sebastian Bach's Chaconne in D minor. Being encored, he played a familiar gavotte by the same master, whose music he treats in a peculiar style, which is the more welcome because it differs from the traditional insistence on hard outline to which we are accustomed. Mlle Marie Krebs, at this and the previous concert, played sonatas by Dussek and Clementi, so well as to suggest a regret that her rare executive powers were not employed on compositions of greater interest. Mr Edward Lloyd attempted Beethoven's beautiful song The Quail, and completely failed to grasp the conception, his rendering being simply in the style which he has found so successful in the treatment of ordinary ballads. Signor Zerbini's accompaniment was merely mechanical. Mr Lloyd's singing of Gounod's When thou art nigh, was satisfactory.

On Monday afternoon, the 5th inst., the Musical Association held their first monthly meeting of this year at Harley-street. Mr Higgs read a remarkably clear, though necessarily compressed analysis of Bach's Art of Fugue, which was followed with the closest attention, and led to a discussion in which Mr H.C. Banister and other gentlemen took part; it is needless to add, without arriving at any conclusion, as to the vexed dogmas of contrapuntal art.

Mr William Carter's Placida, the Christian Martyr was performed on Thursday last at the Albert Hall. Mr Carter's cantata, if not a very interesting, is at any rate an eminently inoffensive, work. It constantly refreshes the listener with reminiscences of familiar masters. Tediousness is prevented by the remarkable rapidity of the action, which dispenses with dramatic details as far as possible. The processional march, the moving bass and triplets for brass in which were evidently suggested by Mendelssohn, was encored on Thursday night; why, we do not at all understand, for if the truth must be told, it is a very vulgar composition, and decidedly the worst number in the work. The vocal portions were satisfactorily executed, except those assigned to Fabian and Nero. Signor Foli sang out of tune, and Mr Llewellyn Winter did not do justice to the musical reputation which was the sole virtue of the Roman tyrant. An inadequate performance of Mozart's Requiem followed. This great work did not seem to inspire any feeling of interest in either chorus or orchestra, and the final fugue—which was taken at about half the proper speed—was delivered to a desert of vacant chairs, with here and there a lonely listener. We are strongly of opinion that if a competent presentation of the Requiem be not attainable, it should not be attempted at all. The soloists were Mesdames Sherrington and Patey, Messrs Lloyd and Foli, the portions entrusted to them being the most praiseworthy in the performance.[U]

DIABOLICALLY CONVENTIONAL
21 February 1877

[U] At the Saturday Popular Concert on the 10th, Herr Joachim played Tartini's celebrated Trillo del Diavolo, a composition which dates from a period when the grotesque had not as yet become a necessary association with the diabolical in music. The preliminary *largo* contains all the poetic merit of the work, and he who suggested the subsequent movements must have been unusually conventional as a devil. Miss Zimmermann played Schubert's first sonata very well indeed. The final movement, however, would have gained in effect had the speed been more moderate. The vocalist was Miss Gowa, who has a mezzo-soprano voice of good quality, and displays some histrionic power in the delivery of her songs. Her method is defective, especially as to breath, the correct management of which she must master if she wishes to rank as a competent public singer. On the 12th, Mr Barton McGuckin, who has achieved some celebrity as a tenor vocalist in Ireland, made his first appearance at the Popular Concerts, and was favorably received. His voice is good, and if he exerts himself to impart a little more interest and variety to his singing, he will, doubtless, take a creditable position. The concert was opened by Cherubini's quartet in E flat, which effectually distracted the attention of the audience for the remainder of the evening. Herr Joachim played a good deal out of tune in the learned *allegro agitato*. Beethoven having unfortunately accredited Cherubini as a great composer, it has become the fashion to speak reverently of the abilities of the Italian contrapuntist, and to listen to his music occasionally, but not often. The quartet in E flat contains one fine episode in the *larghetto*; the rest is about as interesting as a fugue by Albrechtsberger or an enigmatical canon of the XV century. Mlle Marie Krebs played a series of sketches by Sterndale Bennett, entitled The Lake, The Millstream, and The Fountain, the last of which was encored. The Millstream is a charming piece of descriptive music. The Lake is a Mendelssohnian *andante tranquillo*—a style which displays Mlle Krebs at her weakest. Further on, she took the pianoforte part of Schumann's violin sonata in D minor, and acquitted herself gallantly, considering her evidently limited foreknowledge of the work. Madame Schumann's *rentrée* took place on the 24th, too late for notice.

On Thursday last a recital was held at the concert room of Messrs Hodge and Essex, at Argyle-street, having for its object the introduction to the English public of American chamber organs, by J. Estey and Co. The capabilities of the instrument were illustrated by Mr Augustus Tamplin, who played a Bach fugue, Schubert's Ave Maria, and what was truly described as a fantasia on Don Juan. As these recitals take place weekly, and are open to the public, it is unnecessary for us to offer an opinion on the merits of the organs, further than to say that the recitals, if they cost nothing, are still worth going to. Mlle Zimeri contributed a few songs, which proved of only secondary interest.[U]

MUSIC AT SYDENHAM

28 February 1877

The second Crystal Palace concert of this year took place on Saturday afternoon, the 17th. The program included Cherubini's earnest and refined overture to Medea, Haydn's Oxford symphony, and an overture to Alfieri's tragedy of Saul, the latter being heard for the first—and possibly the last—time in England. It is a fair specimen of a modern concert overture, being provided with a program which instructs us as to the intention of the various passages. Thus, the trombone solos, which, we should mention, were played without any of the noisy vulgarity which our experience elsewhere has led us to associate with that instrument, are illustrative of the wrath of Saul; the harp indicates the soothing minstrelsy of David; and when a trumpet and side drum leave the orchestra and perform vigorously in the lobby, we know that the Philistines are approaching, and that the end of the overture is at hand. Excepting such brief suggestions

[93]

as Beethoven prefixed to the movements of a very few of his works, or the fanciful titles which Schumann gave to his pianoforte pieces, detailed programs seem to be a complete mistake. They may impart a certain interest to a composition for those who are incapable of appreciating abstract music, but they do so at the expense of the dignity of an art whose true province is foreign to the illustration of commonplace and material detail. In the present case, however, the program is emotional rather than incidental, and Signor Bazzini's overture, if not strikingly original, is sufficiently entertaining to justify its introduction by Mr Manns.

Mlle Marie Krebs played Beethoven's fourth concerto in her characteristic style, crisply and steadily. Throughout the concert the orchestra acquitted themselves most satisfactorily. The performances to which we are accustomed in London seem to move in a narrow circle from weak incompetence or coarse violence to the perfection of lifeless finish, according to the incapacity, the misdirected energy, or the cold autocracy which distinguished the conductors. At Sydenham, thanks to Mr Manns, we can hear an orchestra capable of interpreting with refinement and expression the greatest instrumental compositions, more especially those of Beethoven.

[U] In the selection of the vocal portion of the program, an improvement was apparent, for which the experience of the past year left ample room. Mlle Sophie Löwe sang two songs from Egmont, very well indeed. Madame Antoinette Sterling was heard in Mr Sullivan's setting of the wellknown lines by Adelaide Procter, entitled The Lost Chord, and also in the Slumber Song from Bach's Christmas Oratorio. This lady's singing of Bach's music baffles criticism. If we were to analyze her rendering technically, phrase by phrase, we might be enabled to display our acumen by pointing out a good many faults, but we would still be constrained to admit that the effect of the song was realized. As we have no wish to make such an exhibition of pedantic absurdity, but are only too glad to hail any manifestation of that true artistic instinct which the artificial training of public singers so seldom fails to weaken or destroy, we do not hesitate to rank Madame Sterling as a worthy exponent of the music of the unsurpassed John Sebastian Bach, whose works we so seldom hear. If her own individuality were a little less obtrusively asserted, Madame Sterling would leave nothing to be desired that a little study would not easily accomplish.

Beethoven's Pastoral symphony has been pressed into the service of the Royal Aquarium, and is advertized as a Vision of Music. It is illustrated by appropriate scenery and interspersed by appropriate songs. This is popularizing Beethoven with a vengeance. But if not a very legitimate way of inducing us to listen to a great work, it will probably be an effectual one, and both pecuniarily and esthetically the end may justify the means.

The sixth triennial Handel Festival at the Crystal Palace is announced for the 25th June. Let us hope that the composer may be saved from his friends, and the function of writing or selecting "additional orchestral accompaniments" exercised with due discretion.[U]

THE QUICKSANDS OF HONEST CRITICISM
7 March 1877

The Hornet regrets to have to inform its readers that it has been getting some grievous knocks lately, owing to its unreasonable tendency to be honest in the matter of musical criticism. Some weeks since it ventured to express itself strongly on the subject of advertizing songs, &c., at the expense of the public, by means of reviewing in journals conducted by publishing firms, royalties, ballad concerts, and similar disinterested undertakings of a culture-fostering description. The remarks were directed generally at a system which The Hornet believes detrimental to the advancement of music, because it reduces the concert room to the level of the market, and degrades the artist into what is vulgarly termed a "tout." No individuals were assailed and, sagacious and deeply versed in human nature as The Hornet is, it never occurred to it that anyone would claim the honor of being personally alluded to in the article. Closely though the cap might fit, it was not to be expected that many claimants for its honors would be forthcoming.

But The Hornet was deceived. Messrs Boosey and Co., the music publishers, of Regent-street, with unexpected candor, have confessed themselves hit by the random dart. They courteously add that the article was malicious and unfair, as to which The Hornet is perfectly content to allow the public to judge betwixt itself and Messrs Boosey. To complete the blow, they refuse to advertize any further in these columns—an announcement which has caused unspeakable dismay in the nest, and will, no doubt, speedily accomplish its financial ruin.

The Hornet publishes these facts because it is well that the public should be apprised of the difficulties which beset a critic who is resolved to do justice to himself and his duty to his readers. Not very long ago a certain colossal temple of art, erected to the memory of the late Prince Consort, goaded by the irreverent comments of a Hornet (who refused to accept a thousand performers as a substitute for a decent performance), endeavored to exclude the sensitive insect, evidently preferring to reserve their favors for more complaisant critics. The attempt meets with the success it deserves, and The Hornet will criticize such performances as impartially as ever.

Finally, as it is not fond of airing itself in its own columns, it will withdraw its injuries from the notice of its readers until again stimulated by some aspirant to the honors of counter-concerts and stall-purchased criticism.

MADAME SCHUMANN'S ART

7 March 1877

[U] One of the best Popular Concerts of the season was that of Monday evening, the 26th ult., when Spohr's pretty Nonetto was performed by Messrs Joachim, Zerbini, Svensden, Lazarus, Dubrucq, Wotton, Wendtland, Reynolds, and Piatti, in a thoroughly satisfactory manner, the executants being recalled with hearty applause at the conclusion. The quartet was Haydn's in C major, Op. 33, which was rendered with exceptional excellence. Herr Joachim played a sonata of Handel's as we have not heard him play before, this season, and was encored. In fact, this concert seemed to be one of the rare occasions on which the artists can enter thoroughly into the spirit of their work, a frame of mind which will not be commanded, and but seldom coaxed. The vocalist was Herr Henschel, who possesses a fine baritone voice, but whose style is not unmixedly agreeable and not at all refined. Madame Schumann played Beethoven's Les Adieux sonata. If any words could do justice to the poetic expression and *beauty* of touch which distinguishes Madame Schumann's art, they are such as would appear overstrained and out of place in these columns. But we may at least recommend the many pianists who set such store by the vulgar quality of brilliancy never to omit an opportunity for studying the greater attributes of pianoforte playing as exemplified by one whose like we shall not easily hear again.

An overture entitled The Enchanted Forest, the latest composition of Sir Julius Benedict, was produced for the first time, at the Crystal Palace Saturday concert, on the 24th February. It is a pretty and varied composition, containing weird horn passages descriptive of the magic wood, and brisk hunting airs: the whole forming an agreeable if not a very weighty or original work. The symphony was Mozart's in G minor, the execution of which left nothing to be desired, save perhaps a trifle more crispness in the first *allegro*. It is to be doubted whether the effect aimed at by the composer is not to some extent frustrated by the employment of the large body of strings contained by the modern orchestra. It is certain that Mozart did not contemplate any such overweight in his small but masterly score, and it is scarcely fair to play his symphony with the same number of violins as [in] the Tannhäuser overture.

Spohr's violin concerto in D, No. 9, was one of the prominent attractions of the program, Herr Joachim's rendering of the *adagio* being perfect. He also played, with Mr Oscar Beringer, a Saraband by Leclair, and three Hungarian dances by Brahms, which were unhappily placed towards the end of an unusually lengthy program. The vocal items were contributed by Mrs Osgood, who sang Hauptmann's weak *Gia la notte*, and the air from Der Freischütz's Though clouds by tempests, the beautiful accompaniment to which was excellently given by the orchestra. Miss Mary Cummings made her first appearance in public at this concert, selecting an air from Eli, and Meyerbeer's *Nobil donna*. She suffered somewhat from nervousness, which, though it did not affect her voice (a heavy mezzo-soprano), caused her to hurry through the cavatina from Les Huguenots at a startling pace. She made a favorable impression, more especially by her singing of the first air. The concert concluded at a late hour with Wagner's overture to Tannhäuser, which held the audience seated despite the loss of the express at 5.15 entailed by waiting. The exciting violin accompaniment to the Pilgrims' Chorus produced its wonted effect, and the overture was received with enthusiastic applause.[U]

A PAMPHLET ON THE VOICE

Review of Arthur Barraclough's Observations on the
Physical Education of the Vocal Organs. 7 March 1877

This is one of a large number of pamphlets which have been called forth by the success of certain works on the voice, which have recently come into general notice. Mr Barraclough, being, as we presume, a teacher of singing, has made some observations in the exercise of his profession which possess the merit of being quite incontrovertible, and strictly in accordance with the results of scientific research. Such, for instance, is the statement that voice production results from the action of muscles controlled by the will, that every period of activity must be followed by a period of repose, and that Nature's laws cannot be violated with impunity. If the public consider these facts sufficiently startling to call for an outlay of a shilling on a pamphlet embodying them, Mr Barraclough's book will probably have a large circulation. If, on the contrary, it should occur to them that the said facts are abundantly promulgated else-where, and are, indeed, the property of most intelligent

[99]

schoolboys, they will lay down the Observations with a passing wonder why they should have been printed at all.

Mr Barraclough's special knowledge of voice production may be estimated by his references to singers as "vocal athletes," to "force of blast" as a condition of vocalization, and to physical exhaustion as a necessary consequence of singing which must be provided for, on the principle of training a prizefighter. He mentions that "the vocal ligaments are brought together," a fact which we would recommend him to test by the laryngoscope before issuing a second edition of his work. And to clergymen who suffer from loss of voice, he recommends daily practice at reading lessons, which would infallibly leave them without any voice at all, their affection not being [from] want of practice, as Mr Barraclough erroneously supposes, but an improper method of production, usually brought about by the endeavor to read with a sombre inflexion not natural to them.

Matter of this kind, eked out to twentytwo pages by some commonplace remarks, and a misquotation of Shakespear, constitutes the Observations on the Physical Education of the Vocal Organs, without throwing the smallest light, even suggestively, on one of the most important musical questions of the age, and, unfortunately, one of the most obscure.

AN EVENING OF BALLADS
14 March 1877

[U] Song manufacturers will hail with sorrow the approaching close of the concert season. The "last but two" of the London Ballad Concerts took place last

Wednesday evening. The program consisted of no less than twentyeight items (including *encores*), good, bad, and indifferent; some being worthy old songs; some, feeble new ones; but all published by the enterprising concert givers. The audience was not fastidious, and although they declined to consider Roeckel's songs a treat, and obviously preferred the old favorites, still they applauded genially throughout. Madame Lemmens-Sherrington, accommodating herself without scruple to the tastes of her hearers, exhausted the resources of claptrap in Home, sweet Home, Comin' thro' the Rye, and a couple of modern songs, on the sale of which she probably has the customary royalty, as it is not otherwise conceivable that she or anyone else would sing them.

Mr Sims Reeves, having done a little stroke of business with I cannot say Goodbye, achieved a considerable stroke of art by his rendering of Tom Bowling, in reply to an enthusiastic *encore* for which he gave Come into the garden, Maud. Both songs were delivered with a pathos which fully justified the great reputation of the singer. Madame Goddard played a few pieces in a splashy style suited to the occasion, and which she assumes with ease, thanks to the extraordinary technical attainments and lack of esthetic feeling. Mr Edward Lloyd, whose high position as a ballad singer is now completely established, sang Sullivan's Sweethearts charmingly in response to an *encore* of Phillis is my only Joy. Mr Maybrick paid his tribute to the abilities of the mysterious composer Adams* by selecting Nancy Lee, which was well received. He also sang that very stupid old song The Leather Bottle, in concluding which he made an effect quite the reverse of refined by dwelling

* A teasing reference to the fact that the wellknown concert singer Michael Maybrick sang songs of his own composition published under the pseudonym Stephen Adams.

on a long note. Miss Helen d'Alton was heard in the quaint and welcome Barbara Allen, which would have been more appropriately placed in the first part of the program than close to the end of the second.

Excepting, perhaps Tom Bowling, the most genuine success of the evening was Sullivan's setting of The Lost Chord, with which Madame Antoinette Sterling, by her sympathetic voice and wealth of expression, evoked a vehement burst of applause culminating in a redemand of the entire song. Equally emotional was her rendering of Sweet and Low by Wallace. Some glees were contributed by the London Vocal Union. These gentlemen, despite an occasional tendency to get out of tune and glare reproachfully at one another, acquitted themselves very fairly, and seem to enjoy a creditable measure of popularity.

On March 8, Mr William Carter's choir performed Mendelssohn's Elijah at the Albert Hall. Signor Foli was announced for the part of the Prophet, but his place was taken by Signor Campobello, who is scarcely equal to so dignified a *rôle*. Madame Patey, Madame Lemmens-Sherrington, and Mr Lloyd filled the principal remaining parts satisfactorily, Madame Patey especially distinguishing herself by her rendering of O rest in the Lord. The choruses were executed with accuracy, but without spirit. The orchestra was somewhat above its usual standard, although the trumpets were disagreeably harsh in one or two places. This defect, by the bye, used to be more noticeable from the opposite side of the orchestra. Altogether, the performance was not sustainedly interesting throughout, a result due partly to a want of weight in the representative of Elijah, and partly to the apathy with which the choir delivered even their most dramatic numbers—the frantic invocations of Baal, for instance.[U]

A SEMI-PASSION

At the Albert Hall, on Thursday last, a portion of Bach's St Matthew Passion was performed by Mr Barnby's choir. We say a portion because the omissions were extensive, though, doubtless, justified by the necessity for accommodating a work of singular religious intensity to the tastes of an audience only half content to simulate an interest in what the majority of them are incapable of appreciating. The full force of Bach's treatment of the scriptural narrative is of a kind which can be felt only by unsophisticated or highly cultivated communities. A modern metropolitan audience consists chiefly of persons who retain nothing of the simplicity which must have characterized a Leipzig congregation a hundred and fifty years ago, and who have not yet reached that stage of development at which the popularly dramatic element in music ceases to be indispensable; consequently, the works of the great cantor are listened to with cold respect, whilst enthusiasm is reserved for those compositions of a later date in which the passion is all on the surface, and in the rarest beauties of which is indicated a disquietude in sympathy with the unsettled march of modern ideas.

The accuracy with which the difficult choral parts were executed on Thursday evening testified to the care with which the work had been rehearsed. In the chorales, the effect of the voices, freed from the constraint of false temperament involved by accompaniment, was particularly agreeable. Unfortunately, Mr Barnby seems to lack that magnetic hold of the forces under his command which constitutes the gift of conducting, and a painful tendency to drag is always apparent in his choir. Mr Cummings undertook the arduous part of the Evangelist. He repeated the text as fast as possible, and with little regard to the dignity of the narrative. His attempts at expression were few and unfelicitous, and his intonation was occasionally defective. Mr Thurley Beale delivered the august words allotted to him mechanically. He made no effort in Twas in the cool of eventide, the only aria which he essayed. Miss Anna Williams sang the soprano music correctly, but without expression. In the aria For love of us, the tune was imperfect, and the reeds in the orchestra somewhat behind the flute *obbligato*, which was played by Mr Svensden. The result was rather startling than agreeable, and the audience were clearly somewhat bewildered.

Madame Antoinette Sterling alone displayed sufficient poetic power for the interpretation of the Passion music, her rendering of See the Savior's outstretched arm being especially excellent. She also sang Have mercy with great intensity, and her performance generally left nothing to be desired, except, perhaps, a little more purity of style. The violin *obbligato* to the last-named song was very satisfactorily executed by Mr Pollitzer, and the orchestra throughout was fairly efficient, the score affording no opportunity for those strepitous displays which often distinguish performances under Mr Barnby's direction. Dr Stainer presided at the organ, and discharged his important functions with his usual ability.

[U] The ninth London Ballad Concert, which took place on the 14th, was of unusual interest, the program consisting of old English and Scotch songs, which have outlived the applause of many generations. Miss Edith Wynne, one of our few true ballad singers, sang Tell me my heart, by Bishop, and for an *encore* the same composer's Love has eyes. Her best effort was On the banks of Allan water, which she delivered with much pathos. She also sang the familiar Robin Adair. Madame Cave Ashton contributed The Bailiff's Daughter of Islington, and The Blue Bells of Scotland, engaging the interest of the audience by the simplicity of her style. Madame Antoinette Sterling sang Caller Herrin' as only she can sing it; also The Three Rovers, for which, on being encored, she substituted Dont be sorrowful, darling. Mr Sims Reeves very properly refused to repeat The Bay of Biscay, O!, his rendering of which was highly popular, without being vulgar. His contribution to the Scotch portion of the program was The Macgregors' Gathering. It must certainly be admitted that when Mr Sims Reeves chooses to sing he distances all competitors with ease.

Mr Lloyd being indisposed, Mr Shakespeare sang his songs, but cannot be said to have taken his place. Nor can Mr Maybrick be congratulated on his share of the program, which included Hearts of Oak, A Friar of Orders Grey, &c. Madame Goddard played fantasias on English and Scotch airs, and fascinated her hearers with a strikingly unpleasant imitation of a bagpipes, which must have astonished those who had studied her program for a recital on the 23rd inst., where she figures as the exponent of Bach, Handel, and Schumann. The London Vocal Union gave a part-song entitled Old Towler, devoted to the celebration of the chase, with so much spirit that it was repeated.[U]

SCHUMANN'S FAUST

28 March 1877

An extra Popular Concert was given on the afternoon of the 21st, for the performance of the first and fifth of Beethoven's posthumous quartets. The selection was an admirable one, for the two works in question illustrate some phases of feeling which belong peculiarly to the great master's individuality, and have been expressed in music by no other composer. The quartet in F major, Op. 135, contains one of those majestic slow movements which occur in Beethoven's earliest and latest works, and in which he has conveyed intense melancholy without any sacrifice of dignity or suggestion of morbid sentimentality. In the *scherzo* and *finale* of the E flat quartet is expressed the riotous humor which seems to have increased in recklessness with the years and troubles of the writer. In both works are to be found other beauties, of which it would be impossible to treat with the pen; but the characteristics above-mentioned contrast so strongly that they produce a striking effect when heard in succession, as was the case on Wednesday last. The executants were MM. Joachim, Ries, Straus, and Piatti. Herr Henschel was the vocalist, and was— thanks to his fine voice—received with marked favor. Madame Schumann played the Waldstein Sonata in a manner which would have sustained a comparison with the performance of any other artist save one—Madame Schumann herself. The sonata was certainly not rendered with her usual exquisite delicacy and feeling, a misfortune for which a very cold concert room and a very bad piano are probably responsible.

At the third concert of the Philharmonic Society, on the 22nd inst., Schumann's music to the last scenes of Goethe's Faust was performed for the first time in London. It probably astonished many hearers, in whose minds music to Faust was associated in idea with limelight and earthly passion. It may safely be asserted that there are fifty English readers familiar with the story of Gretchen for one who is acquainted with that strange flight into purely ideal regions, wherein the poet depicts the opening of the uneasy philosopher's immortal career. Speculations on the "eternal feminine" are more congenial to the German than to the English temperament. It is, consequently, improbable that many of the audience on Thursday last knew very clearly what they were to look for. When the object and scope of Schumann's music become more familiar to us, we will be better able to appreciate its thoroughness; for sustainedly earnest and beautiful as it undoubtedly is, it never once rises to a sublimity independent of the poem.

Another novelty introduced at this concert was a scene from Tristan and Isolde, a music drama which, in order of development, is the latest of Wagner's works. It is not exactly a song in the ordinary acceptation of that term, for the sharpest amateur could never hope to whistle it. It is worked out with elaborate richness of orchestration, yet its brief lines have all the charm of simplicity. Despite its unfavorable place in the program, it was vehemently encored, and with this unreasonable demand Mrs Osgood complied, singing on both occasions with admirable taste and feeling.

Beethoven was represented by a *terzetto* in his Fidelio style and by the Choral Fantasia, the pianoforte part of which was excellently rendered by Miss Agnes Zimmermann. Indeed, we have never heard her play better—a fact which implies no trifling measure of merit. The orchestra, saving a few slight drawbacks, was satisfactory throughout the concert, and did justice to the late Sir Sterndale Bennett's Parisina, an overture which will compare without derogation with any of Mendelssohn's. They also distinguished themselves by the fire with which they executed the overture to Der Freischütz. A word of commendation is due to the unusual steadiness of the horns in the *adagio*.

[U] The last ballad concert of the season took place on the 21st, at the St James's Hall. Mr Sims Reeves had succumbed to the severe weather, and his songs were sung by Mr Shakespeare. Mr Lloyd sang, as usual, excellently, was encored twice, and responded to the first re-demand with Sweethearts, which he sings extremely well, and which is—at his hands—a great favorite with the audience. Mr Maybrick sang The Vicar of Bray and a song by the composer of Nancy Lee. There is only one obstacle to Mr Maybrick's claim to be considered an inoffensive singer—the habit he has contracted of emphasizing the penultimate note of each song he sings. Even when the note is properly attacked and adequately sustained (which in Mr Maybrick's case it is not), the effect is vulgar. Miss Frances Brooke, in the Lady of the Lea, displayed some power of reading a ballad intelligently; but her intonation is uncertain. Madame Edith Wynne sang (in Welsh) The Bells of Aberdovey charmingly, and was encored—a tribute which was also paid to her rendering of Let me dream again. Of the effect which Madame Antoinette Sterling produces with The Lost Chord we have spoken already. Her delivery of The Three Fishers was characterized by unexaggerated pathos and entire freedom from conventionality. It is a remarkable testimony to the value of simple truth in art that Madame Sterling, who never condescends to claptrap, evidently holds the foremost place in the estimation of the ballad concert-goers. Madame Arabella Goddard—unrivaled in manual dexterity—expounded the pianoforte school of Thalberg with vigor and success, to the great delight of her hearers. [U]

OPERA PROSPECTUSES

4 April 1877

[U] After raising public expectation to a high pitch by maintaining an impenetrable silence in the midst of rival prospectuses and portentous advertisements that Drury Lane Theatre was to be let for the season, Mr Mapleson at length unfolds the plan of the coming season from his old quarters in the Haymarket. His manifesto is brief and businesslike, and contains nothing startling. The newcomers reach us before their reputation; the old supporters of Her Majesty's Opera are still at their posts. We will again hear Mlle Titiens as Lucrezia and Semiramide; Madame Nilsson returns, flushed with her late triumphs on the Continent, to repeat her old successes as Gretchen and Valentine, and to achieve a fresh one as Senta; and Madame Trebelli-Bettini, with consummate art, will sweep the entire range of the lyric drama, from Azucena to Cherubino. Monsieur Faure will essay the character of Vanderdecken in Wagner's Der Fliegende Holländer, with what success it matters not at all; for have we not all long since made up our minds that M. Faure is the most accomplished actor, the most finished vocalist, the finest gentleman, and, in general, the most absolute paragon of operatic excellence that can be conceived? And is it likely that we are going to admit, under any circumstances, that our enthusiasm may be a trifle overstrained? Perish the thought. We doubt not that in the great French baritone's presentation of the accursed mariner will be discovered a subtle profundity calculated to throw into despair all past and future artists who may attempt the part.

The chief "revival" of the season will be Signor

Tamberlik, who will reappear after an absence of many years. The name of Signor Gayarré is also in the list. He seems to be much in request, for Mr Gye announced him, the other day, amongst the Covent Garden artists. Perhaps, however, there are two Signori Gayarré; otherwise, indeed, the double announcement is inexplicable. Sir Michael Costa will resume his position as conductor. Mlle Katti Lanner is re-engaged as *première danseuse*. These arrangements call for little comment. Mr Mapleson is necessarily looking too anxiously towards the unfinished building on the Embankment to devote himself to a season of brilliant novelty. The strength of his company remains unimpaired, and it is of approved quality. In recognition of the renewal of interest in Cherubini's music, caused by the success of Les Deux Journées, with Mr Carl Rosa, Medea will be produced, with Mlle Titiens in the title *rôle*, as in 1864. A further advance, after the example of English opera, might with advantage be made by discarding Signor Arditi's recitatives, and so performing the opera according to the composer's intention. Rossini's Otello may also be expected, with Madame Nilsson and M. Faure in their old parts of Desdemona and Iago. Gluck's Armida is promised, and will prove interesting as the work of a composer who broached theories which, through the instrumentality of Wagner, have in our time revolutionized music. The season will be a brief one, the subscription including only thirty nights. April the 28th will be the opening night.[U]

CATHEDRAL REFORMS
11 April 1877

[U] At the meeting of the Musical Association, on the 2nd inst., a paper on music in cathedrals was read by Mr Barrett. It was couched in the forcible strain of commonsense, protesting against ecclesiastical conservatism. The chairman expressed an opinion that its publication would induce some reforms in the management of our cathedrals—an opinion which we see no reason for sharing, inasmuch as it is the fashion of such reverend councils to resent suggestions which imply that there is any room for improvement within their jurisdiction, and to adhere ultimately to their own traditions until public opinion ceases to suggest, and threatens to enforce. The abuses reprehended by Mr Barrett were the neglected education of the choristers, the inferior social status of lay-clerks, and the sensational tendency of modern church music. A discussion on these subjects elicited some warm references to the asserted right of the choirboys in the Abbey to admission at Westminster School. It seems strange that this right, if it really exists, cannot be established by taking action in a particular case, the expenses to be contributed by those interested in the result.[U]

The forthcoming Wagner Festival at the Albert Hall, announced by Messrs Hodge and Essex,* ought to prove the genuineness of our appreciation of the greatest of modern composers, by presenting to us his music

* Performances of the Wagner Festival were given in the Royal Albert Hall on May 7, 9, 12, 14, 16, and 19. Two additional "Farewell Concerts" were held on May 28 and 29.

divested of the attractions of the stage. Our Wagnerian education has, by the force of circumstances, hitherto been retrogressive. Lohengrin was the first work of the advanced school with which we became familiar; and this was not in itself inappropriate, for Lohengrin is the first opera in which Wagner is all himself. Its form is complete and symmetrical, and its construction exhibits no trace of the disturbing influence of the old style of Weber and Meyerbeer, which may be regarded as Wagner's starting point. This disturbing influence is so palpable in the incongruous mixture of old forms and new effects throughout the Tannhäuser that those who represented Wagner's music as inconsistent and chaotic were, for once, enabled to gratify their prejudice against the master with some degree of truth.

Yet this opera formed the next step in our experience of what has been absurdly called "the music of the future." It was inefficiently presented to us; and its vague outline, the natural product of the period of transition during which it was composed, was unsatisfactory to an audience whose hopes had been inspired by the perfect form of Lohengrin. But the retrograde from Lohengrin to Tannhäuser found a sort of homeopathic remedy in a further step back to Der Fliegende Holländer, in which the conflicting elements are as yet accommodated to oneanother, and which possesses what the other operas of Wagner grievously lack—human interest.

Such is the curious course which constitutes our preparation for the most advanced works of the composer who will shortly revisit us. How far it will be successful remains to be seen.

BACH AND DON PASQUALE

18 April 1877

On Wednesday, the 11th inst., the Bach choir—following their precedent of last year—gave a performance of the Mass in B minor, at the St James's Hall. In order that the Kyrie might be heard without interruption, the audience were invited to be seated at ten minutes before eight, an arrangement which the majority signified their appreciation of by arriving punctually at ten minutes past. The work was, however, listened to with attention; and the number who availed themselves of the pause before the Agnus Dei to leave the hall was, despite the great length of the Mass, unusually small. Considering the difficulties presented to an amateur chorus by the complicated polyphonic construction of Bach's music, the performance was a fairly satisfactory one. A few of the numbers dragged a little, and in all an extreme caution was evident, which interfered with that spontaneity which is essential to the full effect of massive choral works.

On the other hand, the choir displayed a praiseworthy accuracy and sense of the importance of their task. Many of the numbers of the Credo, which forms the grandest portion of the service, were followed by loud applause. Madame Lemmens-Sherrington and Madame Patey sang with their customary efficiency, the masterly duet Detur unum Dominum, &c. being rendered with particular success. Signor Foli was, as usual, in difficulties with his articulation, a peculiarity which the Latin language seems to render additionally prominent. Mr Cummings sang the tenor music as he sings always, which was, doubtless, gratifying to admirers of his voice and style.

The numerous *obbligati* were well played as a rule, the difficult one to the Quoniam, for the horn, and that for the violin to the Benedictus, executed by MM. Wendtland and Straus, deserving particular notice. The exception was the flute-playing of Mr Svensden, which was sharp throughout. As we have noticed the same want before with this artist, we are forced to conclude that it arises not from accidental circumstances, such as variation of temperature, but either from defective ear or an unhappy craving to be conspicuous at any cost. Herr Otto Goldschmidt conducted, and was warmly received by his choir.

[U] At the Royal Italian Opera, on Thursday last, Mlle Marimon (who was announced for the part of Norina in Don Pasquale) was unable to appear. Mlle Smeroschi, who took her place, acted with considerable spirit; but her favorite expedient of accomplishing executive difficulties by dashing at them was only occasionally successful, and proved an indifferent substitute for the finished *roulade* of perhaps the best vocalist on the stage. Her intonation is sometimes incorrect; but generally speaking she filled the part with tolerable success. Unfortunately, in an opera like Don Pasquale—in which everything depends on the excellence of four principal singers—something more than this is required to sustain the interest to the end of the three acts.

The honors of the performance fell to the lot of M. Capoul, whose grace and fervor secure the approval of his audience in spite of his vicious French method of producing his voice. His rendering of the familiar *Com' è gentil* was the only *encore* of the evening. Signor Ciampi was the Don, and he conducted his impersonation according to the approved traditions of the Italian *buffo* style. That is to say, he sang as little as possible, and talked as much as possible, in a flat and brawling tone, sufficiently disagreeable in itself, but quite irritating when uttered interjectionally during the airs of the other characters. We do not know what effect an Italian *buffo* produces on most cultivated Englishmen—we can only speak for ourselves; but we imagine it might find a parallel if Mr Harry Paulton or Mr J.L. Toole* could be induced to perform in their characteristic style to a polite Roman or Florentine audience. Signor Cotogni, as Malatesta, was operatic in the same sense in which we speak of an actor as "stagey." He sang correctly, but with a powerful *tremolo*, and discharged the necessary stage business efficiently. The choruses were given with vigor and precision, but, as the wont of choruses is, without refinement.

Signor Bevignani conducted. There are two conductors at Covent Garden, and probably neither considers himself responsible to the public for the shortcomings of the orchestra. The fact remains that the band is intolerably coarse, continually drowning the singers' most strenuous efforts in the *tuttis*, and destitute of delicacy in the lighter passages. For the credit of the house, the artists, and the conductors we trust that one of the largest and most fully appointed of our orchestras will not be permitted to rank also as the worst. We have witnessed more interesting performances than that of Don Pasquale on Thursday; but it was, on the whole, a respectable one. The attendance was so numerous as to give ample promise of a busy season.

Signor Gayarré appeared as Raoul in Les Huguenots on Saturday to a tremendous house. He sang tamely at

* Harry Paulton was a wellknown "low" comedian, who had appeared since 1872 in comic operas at the Alhambra. J. L. Toole, who had been making a reputation for himself as a comic, subsequently took over the Charing Cross Theatre in 1879, renaming it Toole's, where he made a great success with farce until his retirement in 1895.

first, but in the duel septet and the grand *duo* with
Valentine, he roused his audience to enthusiasm. His
acting, however, was by no means up to the mark. Mlle
Bianchi did fairly as the Queen, but her scale-singing is
defective. Mlle d'Angeri was as usual.[U]

SIGNOR GAYARRÉ'S
SELF-COMPLACENCY
25 April 1877

The announcement that the latest successor of Mario
was to appear as Raoul, in Meyerbeer's Les Huguenots,
attracted to Covent Garden Opera House a large
audience desirous to judge of Signor Gayarré's powers
from a part which affords every possible opportunity to
an artist, both vocally and histrionically. Signor Mario's
mantle has, by this time, been assumed by so many
aspirants that it has become somewhat threadbare, and
the public are slow to believe in its virtue. Some of the
wearers have striking personal advantages, without
either voices or dramatic ability. Some are singers who
cannot act, others are actors who cannot sing. A great
many can neither sing nor act nor look well—nor, in
fact, offer any reasonable excuse for their appearance in
opera at all, except that the public, not knowing any
better, is content to endure them for a season.

Of this class Signor Gayarré is an illustrious example.
We believe he once had a voice—and a robust voice,
too—though not of remarkably fine quality, and to
abuse its wreck without taste or artistic skill constitutes
his present employment. His movements are awkward,
and his few attitudes are suggestive of nothing but a
self-complacency the grounds for which are wholly
indiscernible. Why he should have been cast for a

character such as Scribe's ingenuous and rash hero, when M. Capoul—who, though by no means immaculate, has, at any rate, some pretensions as an artist—was available, we are unable to guess. Signor Gayarré's Raoul was simply below criticism. After the most exciting situation in lyric drama—the duet in the fourth act of Les Huguenots—he was honored with a single call. His C sharp in the duel septet evoked some applause. Except at these points, his performance seemed to produce no favorable impression. We hope it will be long before another such tenor appears, to be heralded with a flourish of puffery, and criticized with as much gravity as if he were really a singer.

[U] Mlle d'Angeri as Valentine acted with great energy in the conventional lines of the part. Her singing, until she overcomes her constant *vibrato*, can only be allowed to pass muster by a stretch of courtesy. But for this defect she would rank as a capable and most useful artist. Mlle Bianchi, who has lately been making notable advances in her profession, essayed the florid music of Marguerite de Valois with tolerable success. She seems, however, to be under a delusion as to the nature of a shake—a delusion which is shared by some greater artists. She delivers it in a series of spasmodic expirations, and the tone becomes flatter and flatter to the end, which usually conducts her unexpectedly into another key. Mlle Scalchi as the page Urbain gained the only *encore* of the evening for *Nobil donna*, and was generally most efficient. The Nevers of Signor Cotogni lacked refinement, and the part did not stand out with sufficient prominence. The remarkable "character" part of the old Huguenot retainer Marcel became quite colorless in the hands of Signor Bagagiolo, whose singing was, however, fairly satisfactory. Signor Capponi sang the music of the fanatical Governor of the Louvre coarsely, and did not act at all.

Signor Vianesi conducted, and under his direction the orchestra quite surpassed themselves in rough and inartistic execution. The choruses were quite worthy of the accompaniment, and the Rataplan in particular was received with a contempt which was richly merited. The simple detail of the bells, which produce so striking an effect by their interruption of the impassioned duet in the fourth act, was neglected. The benediction scene gave the impression of a disorderly mob; and the *finale* of the last act, from the entrance of the assassins, mutilated as it is, was not sung at all, Mlle d'Angeri alone proving equal to the occasion by sustaining a few random notes. Considering the performance as a whole, and with special reference to the tenor, the orchestra, and the chorus, we consider it to be the worst in our unhappy experience, even of the operas of Meyerbeer.

For an enjoyable musical evening we are indebted to Mr Richard Blagrove, whose fourth concert took place last Thursday at the Royal Academy of Music. The concert room in Tenterden-street is so comfortable, and the surroundings so quiet, that it forms an agreeable refuge for those who are curious to hear something novel in music, and are tired of the blaze and crush of the opera. The idea of a quintet by Mozart played on concertinas varying in size from a small oyster keg to a large hatbox may seem alarming; but the result is thoroughly agreeable, and proves that Mr Blagrove is an enthusiast and not a speculator. A pretty and rather brisk movement, specially composed for these concerts by M. Silas, and unaccountably termed an *adagio*, was performed last week for the first time. Mrs Blagrove lent valuable assistance in an arrangement of a portion of Hummel's septuor in D minor, and subsequently accompanied Mr Blagrove in some Welsh airs and a selection from La Sonnambula. The English concertina closely resembles the clarinet in tone—and, indeed, at

a pinch, a worse substitute for Mr Lazarus than Mr
Blagrove might easily be found. The substitution of
reeds for strings produces a marked change in the effect
of such works as Mozart's quintet in G minor, but does
not detract from their charm. The vocalists were Miss
Bessie Stroud, who was unwise enough to attempt
Schubert's Ave Maria, and Mr Shakespeare, who sang
a song of his own composition. He falls somewhat short
of his celebrated namesake in point of originality, but
his song was warmly received.[U]

THE GREAT VIRTUOSO
2 May 1877

On Saturday, the 21st, the afternoon concert at the
Crystal Palace was conducted by Herr Rubinstein, and
the program consisted entirely of his works. For a reason
which we will presently state, we shrink from the task
of presenting a criticism of this remarkable performance.
Greater pens than we can hope to wield have already
told the world of the great pianist seizing his hearers by
the ears with wings of golden fire. Highly popular
essayists have circulated columns of exalted and original
imagery, wherein we find Beethoven turning in his
grave and gazing at the score of the Ocean symphony
with admiring despair. Rubinstein is the Jupiter, the
Cyclops, and the what other potent personality you will,
of the pianoforte. One enthusiast, having apparently
rushed straight from the exciting pages of Les Trois
Mousquetaires into musical criticism, calls his idol "the
d'Artagnan" of the instrument.

In short, after the approved fashion of modern
Germany, our public prints have been pouring forth
columns of such nauseous eulogy, not to say ignorant

nonsense, on the works and performances of Herr Anton Rubinstein that, if Beethoven were not, fortunately for himself, beyond the reach of all journalism, whether penny daily or sixpenny weekly, it is not impossible that he would, indeed, turn in his grave with a characteristic grunt of disgust. For ourselves, we would out-Herod Herod in wild applause of the genius displayed by the great *virtuoso* at his concert, only—we wernt at it.

AMATEUR OPERA

2 May 1877

[U] On Wednesday, the 25th ult., was given the first *matinée* of the "Troubadours," a new club of musical amateurs, who propose, in addition to a similar meeting every Wednesday during the season, to undertake no less an achievement than an Italian opera every year. The operas (when they come off) are to be in aid of some institution, and, probably, the amateurs will give more charity than they are likely to receive from the critics. However, the club has evidently been well organized, for the attendance on Wednesday at Park Lane was both numerous and select, and the program was satisfactorily executed. The works performed were by Gounod, Bellini, Verdi, Blumenthal, &c. Miss Bessie Waugh was the accompanist, and Mr Vandeleur Lee conducted. It is said that two operas are in active preparation by the club; and the production of one, at least, may be expected before the end of the season.

The retirement of Mr Santley from the boards is announced for the conclusion of Mr Carl Rosa's opera tour. Who is to take his place we cannot at present imagine, but Mr Santley undoubtedly shews to greater advantage in the concert room than on the stage. He is no actor, although his earnestness and genial manner, and the fact that he is by no means singular in his deficiency, to a certain extent neutralize this objection. But nothing could compensate for the injury done to his voice by singing parts which make frequent excursions below his range, such as The Flying Dutchman, which he repeated so often last year at the Lyceum. Therefore, we think that the loss to English opera notwithstanding, Mr Santley is to be congratulated on the step he has taken.[U]

MEN AND WOMEN OF THE DAY:
Richard Wagner*

9 May 1877

[U] Wagner's present visit to this country is made under circumstances very dissimilar to those that brought him here before. In fact, he makes just such a triumphal return as did Louis Napoleon to the shores of France, from which he had fled a penniless exile. Hitherto, Wagner's arrival has not altogether been heralded by a flourish of trumpets wheras now the enumeration of the instruments that he brings with him, seriously stated in the following matter-of-fact manner like a laundress's list, would augur that, literally no less than figuratively, he is likely to make a considerable noise. For he is accompanied by twentyfour first and twentyfour second violins, twenty violas, twenty violoncellos, twentytwo double basses—one hundred and ten strings in all; six flutes, six oboes, two *corni inglesi*, six clarinets, one bass clarinet, six bassoons, one *contrafagotto*, eight horns, six

* This essay was drafted by an unidentified writer, revised by Shaw, and further revised by the editor of The Hornet. It is reprinted here for its curiosity value and because Shaw preserved it among the cuttings of his contributions to the journal.

trumpets, four trombones, four tubas, one contra-bass tuba, two pairs of kettle-drums, one triangle, one pair of cymbals, one side drum, one glockenspiel, and six harps. Surely, since King Nebuchadnezzar set up the golden image, no such an assemblage of musical instruments was ever collected together.

The apostle of the music of the future first landed here in 1840, an unknown man. In 1855 he came here at the invitation of his firm supporter, Ferdinand Praeger, and conducted eight of the Philharmonic Society's concerts. He was not highly thought of, either by the public or the press; but the late Prince Consort was one of his warmest admirers. Certainly no man ever had more artistic supporters and antagonists than Wagner. Born at Leipzig, May 22, 1813, he was educated in the Universities of that town and of Dresden. Early in his career [he] distinguished himself as a poet and a librettist. His first work was a blood-and-thunder tragedy, with fiftytwo murders or deaths by natural causes, a crowd of ghosts and spectres, and half a dozen survivors of some sixty *dramatis personæ*. As a *pianiste* he was considered a failure, for he would persist in playing by ear. Under Weinlig he studied harmony, and became a finished contrapuntist, and at the age of twenty he brought out a serious opera Die Feen, which was followed by The Novice of Palermo, given successfully in 1836, or thereabouts. His next work, played during his directorship of the Magdeburg Opera, failed completely. It was a setting of Shakespear's Measure for Measure. Rienzi, his first work of importance, was written just thirty years ago, and despite the influence of Meyerbeer, who cordially admired the young composer, then in his 24th year, it was refused in Paris. Only a year or two ago some of the numbers were cordially hissed at one of M. Pasdeloup's concerts in the Cirque d'Hiver. This was followed by Die Fliegende Holländer

(The Flying Dutchman), but while the music was pronounced vile, the book was given to another composer to reset. This he did with complete lack of success. Better luck, however, attended the prophet in his own country. In 1842, Rienzi was produced at the old Opera House in Dresden. It created a furore, and the King of Saxony at once made the composer his own *kapellmeister*. In rapid succession came Der Fliegende Holländer, Tannhäuser, and Lohengrin, while his only comic opera, Die Meistersinger von Nürnberg, was given with great effect at Weimar.

To enter into any exposition of the merits of Richard Wagner as a composer would require a space considerably exceeding, not only this column, but an entire number of our paper. The old notion that he was a mere noisy charlatan has vanished before his music, which proves at each hearing more beautiful and intelligible. Its method is clear to everyone who can appreciate poetry, whilst the rules which it violates are known only to the few, and by them little respected. That his absolute rank must be amongst the greatest composers is evident, but only a future which will have forgotten his voluminous writings on opera, his factious partisans, his egoism, his contemptuous notice of Mendelssohn as a gentleman amateur, his fierce hatred of Meyerbeer, whose genius and originality paved the way for the "music of the future," and his personal eccentricities, can decide how his fame will stand in relation to that of Beethoven, of Mozart, and of John Sebastian Bach. As a dramatic poet, Liszt and others have not hesitated to compare him with Shakespear. Posterity will only smile at their arrogant presumption, and regret that the hand that produced Tristan und Isolde should have wasted so much of its cunning on the absurd myths and shadowy personages with whom it is impossible to feel a ray of sympathy.[U]

VERDI'S CLOYING SUCCESSION
OF ARIAS

9 May 1877

[U] On Thursday last Mlle Carolina Salla made her *début* at Her Majesty's Opera, in the character of Adelia in Verdi's Un Ballo in Maschera. A well-filled house testified rather to the interest of the occasion, and the attraction of novelty which still attaches to the house, than to the popularity of the opera, which consists mainly of a cloying succession of arias inadequately relieved by a very small proportion of concerted pieces. Mlle Salla's talents are not of the extraordinary order; she has a rather unsympathetic voice, which she forces, and her histrionic achievements are limited to the usual "business" of the operatic stage, executed, however, with some fervor. The main success of the evening was Madame Lablache's striking impersonation of Ulrica, which was a principal feature of the first act, and indeed of the entire opera. The *scena, E lui*, concluded on C in *alt*, and [was] declaimed with the fine dramatic power which especially distinguishes this artist.

Mlle Mila Rodani was effective as Oscar, and displayed much skill in the management of a not very powerful voice. Signor Fancelli, whose organ of tune seems to have improved since last season, discharged the part of Riccardo satisfactorily. His vocalization in the famous quintet *E scherzo od e follia* was clumsy, and lacked the graceful finish essential to the effect of this delicate *morceau*. We are sorry we cannot congratulate Signor Rota on his Renato. His articulation is defective, and his method of tone production open and inartistic. He distinguished himself by starting the *Eri tu* a beat late—

to the evident discomfiture of Sir Michael Costa—and singing it out of tune. The minor parts were filled as minor parts usually are. With a few trifling exceptions—notably the flat intonation of the flutes in the transition to the key of D in the introduction—the orchestra was excellent.[U]

NOISE FOR CHARITY
30 May 1877

[U] On Saturday last a concert was given at the Albert Hall for the benefit of the Royal Cambridge Asylum for Soldiers' Widows and that section of the entertainment-seeking public who are not afraid to face the combined power of nine military bands. It is worth remarking that the people who like this sort of thing are usually foremost in denouncing Herr Wagner and his school as mere noise manufacturers. The list of patrons was extensively advertized, and fully guaranteed the quality of the concert in a vulgar, if not an artistic, sense. The absence of Mlle Titiens through severe indisposition cast some shadow over the occasion, but as her place was taken by Madame Trebelli the audience had no reason to complain on musical grounds. Amongst the items in the program was Mr W. Cusins's Princess of Wales march, which was conducted by the composer.

Nothing very novel has been doing at the opera houses for the past week. Meyerbeer's Robert le Diable has been produced at the Haymarket, with Mlle Salla in the part of Alice, a performance to which we allude elsewhere.* At Covent Garden the usual *répertoire* is being drawn on. Les Huguenots is announced for June 6th, with M. Capoul as Raoul. We think the management

* The review of the opera apparently was not written by Shaw.

is acting wisely in withdrawing Signor Gayarré's representation of the part. As yet there is no intimation from either house of the production of Der Fliegende Höllander, which figured so conspicuously in the prospectuses of both establishments. The orchestral beauties of the work will ensure its renewed success in the hands of Sir Michael Costa; and for the same reason it may be confidently predicted that jewelers' cotton will be at a premium at Mr Gye's house before Signor Vianesi has led his brassy forces through the first thirty bars of the overture.[U]

THE WAGNER FESTIVAL

6 June 1877

On the 29th of last month the last concert of the Wagner Festival took place at the Albert Hall. It is not, however, our intention to criticize any of the concerts in particular, but simply to make a few remarks about the festival generally. Herr Wagner, as a conductor, must be very unsatisfactory to an orchestra unused to his peculiarities. He does not, as has been stated, lack vigor, but his beat is nervous and abrupt; the player's intuition is of no avail to warn him when it will come; and the *tempo* is capriciously hurried or retarded without any apparent reason. Herr Richter, whose assumption of the *bâton* was hailed by the band on each occasion with a relief rather unbecomingly expressed, is an excellent conductor, his beat being most intelligible in its method, and withal sufficiently spirited. The orchestra acquitted themselves imperfectly as a rule, the inner parts dragging sometimes so much as to destroy the effect, more especially in such brisk contrapuntal movements as occur in Die Meistersinger.

The vocalists were of exceptional excellence. Frau Materna justified her great reputation, not only as to the brilliancy of her tone and her great powers of endurance, but in the equally important matter of expressive delivery and distinct articulation. Frau von Sadler Grün's voice is of that rare quality which has some indefinable sympathy with melancholy. Her rendering of Brangäne's ominous warning in the Tristan und Isolde conveyed the spirit of the verse to perfection, and her performance of Senta's music in Der Fliegende Holländer has fixed for us a high standard for future reference. No less remarkable was her singing as the woodbird in Siegfried. Owing to a severe cold, the mellow and powerful voice of Herr Unger was heard at a disadvantage. Herr Karl Hill made good his claim as a singer of the first rank by his expressive and refined singing of the parts of Vanderdecken and King Marke.

At each concert Herr Wagner was received with tempestuous applause. On the 19th May he was presented with an address, and a laurel wreath was placed on his brow, which latter distinction was probably more gratifying to his feelings than favorable to the dignity of his appearance. After the last concert he made a brief speech to the orchestra, expressing a satisfaction at their performance which we hope was sincere. Addresses were also presented to Herren Richter and Wilhelmj.*

* August Wilhelmj, noted violinist, was the entrepreneur who sponsored the Festival on behalf of his friend Wagner.

MEN AND WOMEN OF THE DAY:
Madame Christine Nilsson and M. Faure

6 June 1877

[U] In one of our portraits this week our readers will recognize the features of Madame Christine Nilsson. We do not propose to give here a sketch of her personal history. Such details may be sought with justifiable interest in the case of statesmen, or those who enjoy what is called "the confidence of the nation," but with the private life of artists the public has no concern; and the landmarks in the professional career of a *prima donna* possess too wearisome a sameness to leave any impression on the memory. Therefore, we will confine ourselves to artistic considerations only, no less from the necessity of making our columns entertaining than in obedience to the rules of good taste.

Madame Nilsson is beyond question the most gifted of our leading *soprani*. This position she has made good, notwithstanding the most serious technical deficiencies, by the force of her inborn dramatic instinct and the charm of a voice whose beauty asserts itself in spite of a most destructive method of production, the effects of which are but too obvious towards the conclusion of her performance in those operas which demand constant and severe exertion from the representative of the heroine. Nor are her vocal circumstances without a parallel in her employment of her rare histrionic talents. Madame Nilsson possesses genius; but it is undisciplined genius. Her greatest impersonations, abounding as they do in passages of great power, are never quite consistently sustained throughout. Take, for instance, that in which she has won her brightest laurels: the operatic version of

Goethe's Gretchen. In the second act we expectantly await the appearance of the innocent and timid girl returning from prayer. Instead of this we see a self-possessed woman come forth with assured step, listen composedly to the overtures of a tenor whose nervousness is not always feigned, give him what is popularly called "his answer," and pursue her homeward way with a manner sufficiently suggestive of her ability to take the best possible care of herself to daunt even the cynical perseverance of Mephistopheles.

In the garden scene all this vanishes. Nothing could be more truthfully conveyed than the confusion in which she endeavors to hide the jewels she has put on from the eyes of Faust. Thenceforth, the charm of the impersonation increases. We are carried away in defiance of bad phrasing, breathing in awkward places, wilful trifling with the *tempo* to the destruction of all rhythm, and any other liberty which the impulsive audacity of the singer may suggest. Her acting at the death of Valentin, once witnessed, cannot easily be forgotten; and in the church scene she attains the highest tragic expression of which the part admits. The curtain falls and rises again on the prison scene, when we are astonished to find the capricious charm again absent, and as in the second act the ideal Gretchen replaced by the real Madame Nilsson.

Similar dramatic suspensions are noticeable in all her greatest parts. As Elsa in Lohengrin, after sustaining the character admirably through three acts, she unaccountably loses ground in the fourth, and conveys an impression rather of obstinate sulkiness than distracting grief. As Valentine in Les Huguenots she absolutely excites antagonism by her bearing at first, and inspires little interest subsequently until the great duet of the fourth act, in which she rises to the occasion and fairly electrifies her audience. For the full evocation of her great powers, some task which exercises them to the utmost seems requisite. In those scenes, in attacking which the greatest artists must feel at a disadvantage, she achieves a brilliant victory. On lighter occasions she is merely *la prima donna assoluta*, a little spoiled perhaps by success. In such a temper she disdains conventionality, and occasionally evinces a patronizing appreciation of the performances of her colleagues that must be humiliating rather than flattering to them. However, if Madame Nilsson be fairly judged, it will be found that her faults are such as a little study and self-discipline may easily overcome, whilst her merits are of that rare type of which it is commonly said that they are born and not acquired, and which constitutes the arbitrary attribute which we call genius.

We couple a portrait of M. Faure with that of Madame Nilsson, not because we conceive that any analogy exists between their artistic talent, but because accident has associated them in some of their most celebrated impersonations. M. Faure's principles of stage conduct may be summed up thus: "Keep well to the front, and take your time." So successful has this line of action proved, that he has come gradually to be accepted by a sort of critical conventionalism as the greatest living operatic baritone. Nevertheless, the quality of his voice is not remarkable: he is a vocalist of the French school, and a bad one; and he is an essentially commonplace actor. His two most admired parts are Don Giovanni and Mephistopheles. The first affords the highest test, both vocal and histrionic, to which an artist can be subjected, and in it M. Faure fails. Of the second, a character about which more has been written than read, good taste and a dramatic instinct, which need be no more than superficial, are quite sufficient to ensure a respectable performance, and M. Faure's performance is eminently respectable, not to say occasionally a trifle dull. In less central parts, where brilliancy as an actor and attractive vocalization are not absolutely necessary—Nevers, in Les Huguenots, for instance—M. Faure is most satisfactory; and, indeed, there would not be two opinions respecting his great utility on the operatic stage were it not for the exaggerated encomiums which have been lavished on him, with no other effect than that of placing him in a false position and raising expectations which his gifts do not enable him to realize.[U]

HER MAJESTY'S OPERA: LUCIA

6 June 1877

[U] On the 29th ult., Mlle Chiomi made her first essay on the lyric stage in the character of Lucia, in Donizetti's opera of that name. She looked charming, and sang like a *débutante*. It is so unfair to judge of an artist's capabilities by a performance at the disadvantages which a first appearance necessarily entails that we prefer to pass over the present instance as lightly as possible, simply recording that Mlle Chiomi received much applause, and our conviction that she will need some further study before taking high rank as an artist. Signor Fancelli took the place of Signor Gillandi, who was unwell, and achieved a pronounced success. At the present time, when we are afflicted not only with a dearth of good tenors but a decided prevalence of bad ones, Signor Fancelli may justly claim a place amongst the first of our operatic singers. The other parts were cast as on previous occasions, and the orchestra was, as usual, satisfactory. As the opera, with the same cast, is advertized for reproduction tomorrow, we shall defer our detailed criticism til next week.[U]

THE PHILHARMONIC CONCERTS
6 June 1877

[U] The program of the seventh concert of the Philharmonic Society on the 28th May included no novelty. Nevertheless, all the items were established favorites, and the concert proved highly enjoyable. Indeed, the Philharmonic concerts are so seldom dull that it is surprising that they are not more fully attended. The symphony was Spohr's Consecration of Sound; the overtures, Egmont and Tannhäuser. Herr Straus played Macfarren's violin concerto in G minor in his characteristic trenchant style, introducing a very long and ungraceful *cadenza*. He was greeted with loud applause at the conclusion of the concerto, which was excellently performed. Signor Campobello sang *Vedrò mentr'io sospiro* from Le Nozze di Figaro, coarsely. Madame Sinico sang *Deh vieni, non tardar* from the same opera, and *Connais-tu le pays?* from Mignon with her usual efficiency. The orchestra was throughout extremely good. Great praise is due to Mr Cusins, whose conducting and personal influence on his band shew his musicianly interest in and appreciation of his work.[U]

OPERA AND EMPTY BRAVADO
13 June 1877

[U] The operatic events of the past week have not been specially interesting. On the 5th Rigoletto was produced at Her Majesty's, with Signor Galassi in the title *rôle*.

His impersonation was highly satisfactory. His earnestness and remarkable voice secure his success in parts which do not require great delicacy of treatment. Signor Talbo, who appeared as the Duke, rather overacted his part, and spoiled *La donna è mobile* by concluding on a weak B natural. His preference for his higher register is, however, excusable, as it is the best part of his voice. He bids fair to be a useful singer. Mlle Valleria was the Gilda, and Madame Trebelli a perfect Maddalena.

On Thursday Mlle Chiomi again appeared as Lucia. She would do well to bear in mind that excessive energy can never convert stage business into acting. Her voice is somewhat hard, and the upper notes are usually flat, which is caused by defective method rather than incorrect ear. She marred the first *scena* by a profusion of antiquated ornament. Mlle Chiomi's attractive appearance is, however, a strong point in her favor. Signor Fancelli was again successful as Edgardo; and Signor Rota, as Enrico, proved himself a master of the art of shouting. He also displayed his perseverance as a gesticulator by incessantly moving his right arm to and fro after the unsightly fashion of an amateur violinist.

On the 5th inst. Mr Henry Ketten gave a pianoforte recital at the St James's Hall. The system of modern *virtuosi* is remarkable. Let any man obtain some favor from the public as a player or singer, and straightway he concludes himself competent to entertain an audience for three hours by his unaided exertions. He generally finds himself mistaken. Even Herr Rubinstein's hearers are sometimes fain to cry "Hold, enough!" and he can play in several styles. Mr Ketten can only play in one, and that not a very agreeable one. He is unable to render a simple melody in the *cantabile* style, being simply an instrument of percussion. He plays rapidly, but inaccurately; and his use of the pedal is abhorrent to an educated ear. Under these circumstances his choice of

Beethoven's prodigious sonata, Op. 106* (with incidental preludes by Henry Ketten) was an empty bravado, which, we trust, he will not repeat. A chaconne of Handel's and Bach's Italian concerto were steadily executed, and a few of the player's own compositions were favorably received. Mr Ketten's muse is, at any rate, prolific, his Serenade Espagnole being marked Op. 60. [U]

VOCALISTS OF THE SEASON:
Madame Trebelli

13 June 1877

[U] Madame Trebelli has, as most of us know, been for many years the leading contralto of Mr Mapleson's opera company. To her exertions it is mainly due that at Drury Lane and the Haymarket the performances have generally an artistic value far above those at Mr Gye's house. It may sound rash to ascribe the superiority of a whole company to the merits of one member of it, but it must be considered that many of the fine impersonations to which we are accustomed at Her Majesty's are matched by the efforts of rival artists at Covent Garden. The talents of Mesdames Nilsson and Patti, of MM. Faure and Graziani preserve an equal balance in the estimation of the public; but with Madame Trebelli the scale turns. Possessing a voice of exceptional richness, and a finished style which only a classicist can fully appreciate, she is without a rival amongst contraltos or a superior amongst singers.

We have artists who rely on inspiration only, and we

* No 29, in B flat (the "Hammerklavier").

have to condone their impure style and lack of technical skill in consideration of their rare natural gifts. Madame Trebelli alone combines the truest lyrical expression with a style and phrasing so perfect that the greatest virtuoso of the pianoforte or violin might profit by hearing her sing the works of Handel and Mozart. Her mastery of every detail displays a conscientious devotion to music and a subtlety of taste rarely met with. Her delivery of the English text in oratorio might put to shame the majority of our clerics. (How few foreign artists have paid us the compliment of conquering our language, even superficially!) She never trifles with her work: never betrays indisposition or indifference, and never unduly obtrudes her own personality, which nevertheless lends a charm to all her performances.

In opera she is unsurpassed; and in the works of Mozart, particularly as Zerlina, Cherubino, &c., she leaves all competitors (in the first-named part she has at least one distinguished one) far behind. Of her dramatic ability it suffices to say that she has given us the Cherubino of Mozart instead of that of Beaumarchais, and that in her Zerlina we have the coy tenderness which the music teaches, without a trace of the pert vulgarity which we too often see associated with this most beautiful part. An actress who can achieve such things will not be found wanting in the coarser melodramas illustrated by Verdi and his school. Madame Trebelli is peculiarly entitled to the respect and gratitude of musicians because, although gifted by nature with a voice and person in themselves sufficient to ensure a wide popularity, she has by assiduous attention added to them a technical perfection but rarely aimed at, and still more rarely achieved, by her colleagues. Such refinements, acquired in the face of the obtuseness of the multitude to their value, are the strongest proof of her love of art. It will always be a grateful task to pay a public tribute to the fame of an artist whose greatest excellencies are unfortunately "caviare to the general."[U]

ROSSINI'S FLORID OTELLO

20 June 1877

The chief event of last week at Her Majesty's was the revival of Rossini's Otello, with Signor Tamberlik in the title *rôle*. Madame Nilsson's Desdemona was so fine a performance as to give intense interest to an occasion which would have been somewhat dull without it. In the last act especially, the effect on the audience was evidenced by the manner in which some untimely applause was suppressed. Equally moving was her acting in the *finale* of the second act. Henceforth her Desdemona may rank amongst the most remarkable of her impersonations.

In order to represent the operatic Othello respectably, a voice and some faculty for acting are indispensable. Signor Tamberlik possesses neither of these qualifications. He sings in a doubtful falsetto and his movements are unmeaning, and frequently absurd. For the C sharp in the celebrated duet *L' ira d' avverso fato*, he substituted a strange description of shriek at about that pitch. The audience, ever appreciative of vocal curiosities, eagerly redemanded it. Signor Carrion, as Roderigo, seemed laudably anxious to make as much of his part as possible, and succeeded—more, probably, to his own satisfaction than to that of the audience. He sang his music correctly, but the quality of his voice is not pleasant. M. Faure's Iago was generally understood to be a deeply-studied conception. Possibly it was, for there was no indication of it on the surface. His vocalization lacked the crispness necessary for Rossini's florid music, and his acting consisted merely of shaking hands warmly with his colleagues for no apparent reason. Signor Foli was an efficient Elmiro. His rendering of *Nel cor* was, however, rather slovenly. The orchestra was excellent; and Sir Michael Costa displayed unwonted animation. The various instrumental solos were [satis]factorily executed, particularly that for the horn, which precedes the second scene of the first act. The opera was well mounted, and the scenery appropriately handsome. Nevertheless, we doubt whether Othello's garden was happily placed in the bed of a river; and we are sure that the gondola of the Doge would glide all the more smoothly for a little lubrication.

[U] Herr Wachtel's appearance as Manrico, [in Il Trovatore] on the 12th, was deservedly successful. His acting and singing were alike excellent. His high C, which he gave three times in the *Di quella pira*, is a genuine note and not, as we commonly hear, a scream. His use of the *mezza voce* is artistic, and is not a device to conceal weakness or total absence of real voice. He shared with Madame Trebelli the honors of the occasion. Mlle Nandori was an efficient but colorless Leonora.

On Friday last, Il Barbiere was produced at Covent Garden, with Madame Patti as Rosina. Her performance in that part is too familiar to call for notice. In response to the usual *encore* in the lesson scene she sang Home, sweet Home,* to the unbounded delight of her hearers. Indeed, the opera proved so intolerably wearisome that some of the audience had already displayed their

* Home Sweet Home was originally written for the opera Clari; or, The Maid of Milan (1823), with its music by Sir Henry R. Bishop and its lyrics by the American poet John Howard Payne. Adelina Patti sang it so often, even incorporating it in the music lesson scene in The Barber of Seville, that it became her musical signature.

appreciation of the sentiment of the ballad in the most practical way. Signor Cotogni was the Figaro, but he cannot be said to have sung the part. His acting was exaggerated and farcical. Words could scarcely paint the dreariness of Signor Ciampi as Bartolo. Signor Ordinas was the conventionally grotesque Basilio, and Signor Nicolini's Almaviva was not calculated to raise the clouded spirits of the house. Mlle Corsi was excellent as Bertha. The orchestra performed in a style that, to say the least, was not first-class. Signor Vianesi conducted.[U]

VOCALISTS OF THE SEASON:
Signor Nicolini

20 June 1877

[U] Signor Nicolini is one of the most popular of our operatic tenors. This description would have been but doubtfully appropriate some weeks ago, when it seemed as if we were about to indulge in one of our periodical bursts of indignation at his expense. At present, whether it is that we have learned from our great essayist that such displays of feeling are ridiculous and misplaced*; or that Signor Nicolini, like Orpheus, has charmed us from our moral pedestal by the sweetness of his numbers: the fact remains that his popularity has emerged

* Shaw may be thinking here of Sir Francis Bacon's essay Of Discourse, in which he says: "Discretion of speech is more than eloquence; and to speak agreeably to him with whom we deal is more than to speak in good words or in good order." Sir Rupert Hart-Davis suggests alternatively that the essayist was Macaulay, who in his review of Moore's life of Byron (1831) wrote: "We know no spectacle so ridiculous as the British public in one of its periodical fits of morality."

unabated from the trial, and his hold of the many-headed derived fresh security from its temporary relaxation. Therefore, an expression of opinion as to his demerits as an artist cannot now be considered as taking him at a disadvantage. If it is retorted on us that generous and enlightened criticism should rather dwell on his merits, we reply that we have not yet discovered what his merits are.

Signor Nicolini is interesting as an exponent of a school of singing (if we may use the term) which has lately become popular, and which may be considered as a monument of the extraordinary gullibility of the world in matters musical. The education of a singer, according to the approved Italian method, has been facetiously described as consisting of two distinct processes: the destruction of the natural and the creation of the artificial voice. This is at least half true, for the first operation is generally accomplished to a nicety. Unfortunately, here the system breaks down; and the student (should he possess a robust constitution, and survive) finds himself thrown on the world without any voice, but with the consolation of being no worse off than most of his profession. So he cultivates his head voice, in which register he can sing florid music with tolerable fluency; pulls together any ruins of chest notes which he happens to retain; and so manufactures a compound sound which is neither the voice of man, woman, nor boy, and which inflicts exquisite pain on all listeners who can pretend to any purity of taste. Its common characteristics are an impure and unsteady tone, an uncertain pitch, an undignified expression, and a constant *tremolo*.

Nevertheless, the public listens, imputes its unpleasant sensations to ignorance, applauds and *encores* as only the very ignorant can do, and eventually has its judgment so corrupted by habit that legitimate vocalization becomes actually repugnant to its ear. Therefore, though we began by stating that Signor Nicolini is one of our most popular tenors, we had no intention of implying any artistic excellence on his part. Flattery itself could scarcely deem his voice an agreeable one, or his style and presence impressive. The list of his qualifications is soon exhausted. He has a competent knowledge of stage business, and fills up a blank in a cast when no one better is to be had. No more remains to be said. To expatiate further on his peculiarities would be neither a graceful nor an interesting task.[U]

WAGNER AT COVENT GARDEN THEATRE
27 June 1877

On the 16th inst. the popularity which Wagner's Flying Dutchman [earned] in the hands of Mr Carl Rosa last year was followed up by its production at Covent Garden, with Mlle Albani and M. Maurel in the principal parts. Some weeks ago we departed from the usual cautious reserve of critics as far as to predict a failure for the orchestral portion of the opera. Signor Vianesi's band has obligingly borne out our statement, but not without a faint effort to redeem its reputation. The strings and reeds were a little better than usual, whilst the brass exercised an unwonted self-denial in the matter of noise, and so added indecision and feebleness to their customary defects of coarse tone and absence of phrasing. The rendering of the picturesque and forcible overture was quite colorless; and throughout the opera the bold phrases which constantly recur were so meanly interpreted that those who had formed their expectations of the work from the spirited representation at the

Lyceum must have been sadly disappointed by its new aspect under the *bâton* of Signor Vianesi. The scenic arrangements were elaborate, but not always appropriate. The phantom ship was represented by a substantial structure which moved with the deliberation of a canal barge, and in the last act came to pieces, or rather folded itself up with a gravity that tacitly rebuked all inclination to excitement. The violence of the waves sometimes lifted them entirely from their bed, and revealed strange submarine monsters disporting themselves in perpendicular jumps below. The billows in the opening storm were represented by an ingenious application of the principle of the corkscrew to a sheet of green canvas. The atmospheric effects were the most successful.

From Mlle Albani, as the acknowledged exponent of Wagner in this country, an interesting impersonation of Senta was expected. She was, as she always is, extremely conscientious, and the music displayed the clear beauty of her upper notes to great advantage. But Mlle Albani has not attained to that highest art which lies in the concealment of art, and consequently her acting lacked spontaneity, and had a melodramatic tinge wholly repugnant to the pure simplicity of the ideal Senta. Nevertheless, her performance may still claim a high degree of merit for its earnestness and the care with which it had evidently been studied. M. Maurel, as the Dutchman, looked very well, and sang very well. It is the more to be regretted that he should mistake fervid affectation for true acting, and so neutralize his great natural gifts. His demeanor suggested an inartistic self-consciousness, and in one or two situations he verged dangerously on the ridiculous. Signor Bagagiolo's fine voice carried him through the least intelligent impersonation of Daland we have ever witnessed. Signor Carpi was a tolerable Erik. Signor Rosario was an unsatisfactory pilot, and made nothing of the charming song in the first act. The small part of Mary was undertaken by Mlle Ghiotti. The choruses were executed without any regard to light and shade, and suffered accordingly, more especially the spinning song. The performance generally shews that Mr Gye has good material at his command if it could only be put to any good account. Its misuse is more to be deplored in the present case because it is not so much the reputation of Covent Garden which is at stake as the popularity already too long withheld from the works of Wagner.

ETELKA GERSTER

27 June 1877

One of the most important musical events of the season took place at Her Majesty's Theatre on Saturday night, when Mlle Etelka Gerster, a lady who has already achieved a considerable reputation in Germany, made her *début* before an English audience, in the character of Amina in Bellini's La Sonnambula. Her success was a gratifying proof that our national habit of believing blindly (or, rather, deafly) in any worthless artistic material that *impresarios* think fit to impose on us, has not quite blunted our appreciation of genuine merit. Mlle Gerster is evidently a born musician. The quality of her voice, though not equally agreeable throughout its range, is generally clear and sympathetic. She sings up to F in *altissimo* with facility and fine tone. She phrases correctly, and her articulation is distinct, without being affected. She executes *roulade* with fluent rapidity, and does all her work with an intelligent certainty which only those who possess the true musical temperament ever display. Her histrionic powers are so considerable as to ensure for her a celebrity in the future as an actress as well as a vocalist. When she acquires the perfect finish that comes from long experience, she will be qualified to take a place in the first rank of lyric artists. Her performance evoked the most enthusiastic recognition from the audience. We are so accustomed to the heartless applause of *claqueurs* at first appearances that it was quite a relief to hear the true ring of the outburst that followed the first few notes of the artist. *Ah! non credea* was rapturously encored; and Mlle Gerster received four calls at the conclusion of the opera, in addition to three between each act. She is to be congratulated on having made a remarkable and well-deserved success.

[U] Signor Fancelli played Elvino. His acting in the second act was weak, and he sang *Prendi l'anel* flat. His performance was otherwise satisfactory. Signor del Puente was a commonplace Count. Nervousness prevented Mlle Robiati from making anything of the small part of Lisa. Both orchestra and chorus were excellent. [U]

On Thursday last, Flotow's charming, but unpopular, Marta was produced before a limited audience. The difficulty of inducing the public to patronize this opera is the more curious as those who do venture on it invariably evince the greatest appreciation of its freshness and graceful flow of melody by constant *encores* and warm plaudits. However, there are reasons for its want of attraction. It is too long; it contains rather much of the Last Rose; it requires a faculty for light comedy, which is almost unknown on the lyric stage; and it is so comprehensible that the public are wont to consider it a waste of money to pay for it what would secure an opera by Beethoven, or some other master, equally intelligible to them.

If we may judge from the performance on Thursday, Marta is not a favorite with Sir Michael Costa. The overture was taken too rapidly at the *larghetto*, and too slowly at the *allegro*. The prelude to the second act was hurried, and the effect in both numbers was lost. We hear no such defects when Rossini is interpreted at the Haymarket. Of Mlle Chiomi's Marta there is nothing to be said, except that it was extremely unfinished, and that her intonation (from nervousness, possibly) was false throughout the first scene. Much more study will be necessary before Mlle Chiomi can be heard with pleasure in principal parts beside an artist so accomplished as Madame Trebelli, whose Nancy left nothing to be desired, either vocally or histrionically.

The part of Lionello is not suited to Signor Fancelli, but he acquitted himself very creditably under the circumstances. Signor del Puente was a moderately respectable Plunketto, and received for the *Chi mi dirà* an *encore* which the conductor refused to recognize. Signor Zoboli was the Tristane. Some humor was displayed by the stage manager in the selection of costumes. Not content with the time-honored custom, which clothes the foster brothers in a garb such as no peasant ever wore at any period of the world's history, he introduced a company of soldiers in the attire of the Wars of the Roses. The attendants of Queen Anne were habited as Italians of the XV century; and the monarch herself led the fashion, in a style obsolete about 150 years before her birth. These matters do not trouble the public much; but it is well to point them out occasionally, lest they should be carried too far.

VOCALISTS OF THE SEASON:
Signor Fancelli

27 June 1877

Signor Fancelli is a fortunate man. He is a tenor with a voice. The time has been, and will be again, we hope, when no man could hold a leading position on the stage without varied artistic qualifications. At present a great deal of audacity, a little affectation, some judicious puffing, and sufficient lung power to make a noise at brief intervals for three hours or so complete the list of acquirements necessary for a *primo tenore*. If he be able to shout, he will do well to sing a bar or two occasionally in a light falsetto. The critics will fall into raptures over his exquisite management of the *mezza voce*, and the public will follow the critics. If he cannot do this, he has only to be careful not to lapse into inoffensiveness. Critics are only human, and they will attribute their anguish whilst listening to the tenor to anything sooner than to his defects. If they can see no excellences, they will invent some.

For instance, it is easy to say that a singer "phrases" well, because so few know what phrasing means. A certain tenor of this season, who is the very worst singer we ever heard, had this accomplishment specially manufactured for him by critics who felt it to be their duty to admire him, and who were at a loss to see what they should admire him for. Yet his case was by no means an exceptional one. For men who desire a reputation in art for which they have nothing to shew, Italian opera in England opens the only suitable field. In a state of affairs such as we have hinted at, it is obvious that (since the public always retain their natural predilection for what is good, beneath their affected raptures at what is mere imposture) an artist who has any real qualifications has a much fairer opportunity than if he were surrounded by really gifted rivals.

Such a qualification, and such an opportunity, Signor Fancelli possesses. He is not an actor, but what he does is done in earnest, and he sustains comparisons only with men who cannot act and who are not in earnest. There are exceptions, perhaps, but they are too few to affect him. He has a real voice, and a fine one, and in this respect he is about alone amongst our operatic tenors. Opera-goers hail him with delight as a relief from the hideous varieties of throaty vibration with which they have been surfeited. His tasks this season have been arduous, and he has discharged them ably, as far as his gifts permitted him. That he is above the vanity which disdains a small contribution to the completeness of a performance, he proved by undertaking the few bars in Otello sung by the gondolier passing without. The inevitable comparison with the two other tenors who figured in the cast proved immeasurably to his advantage. If Signor Fancelli's taste and histrionic power were only equal to his voice and sincerity of intention, we should have on our stage an accomplished singer and actor. As it is, we have a most useful artist, and one that we always hear with pleasure.

A DUCAL OPERA
4 July 1877

[U] Art workmanship is popularly held to be a privilege of the base untitled. Consequently, on the occasion of the production on Saturday of the Duke of Saxe-Coburg-Gotha's opera Santa Chiara, Covent Garden presented a scene of desolate splendor, enlivened in the higher places of the auditorium by a few spectators, most of whom, having a large amount of space at their disposal, assumed a recumbent attitude and so heard out the three weary acts at their ease.

Santa Chiara is a very respectable composition for an amateur. One has not even the consolation of laughing at it. There is nothing crude, nothing ludicrously weak in it. Only there is nothing original. A tolerable duet, a fair funeral dirge, a passable song, a middling Neapolitan dance and chorus—but beyond this, nothing! His Highness of Saxe-Coburg-Gotha never once appears. Instead, we have commonplace Donizetti in the opening phrases of the airs (further on they lose all form), an occasional succession of harsh chords from Der Flie-gende Holländer, a faint reminiscence of Gounod and Verdi here and there, and an intolerable quantity of second-hand Meyerbeer—that is to say, the external forms of Meyerbeer, divested of his striking individu-ality, his inexhaustible variety, and the piquant contrasts which prevent his longest operas, when justly per-formed, from flagging. The instrumentation of Santa Chiara is Meyerbeer, enriched from the revelations of Wagner. The noble composer has borrowed everything, and assimilated nothing. Instead of impressing his own stamp on his levies, he has simply obliterated that which they originally bore. In every number the same want of form and invention is evident. The successive portions, even of the songs, have no relationship, and when they are half finished, the hearer neither recollects the beginning nor desires to hear the conclusion.

Of the three acts the first is the dullest. The second is, perhaps, the best. It contains some good church music, and the best *ensemble*, *Qual rimorso*, in the work. The *finale*, consisting of a funeral chant, interrupted at the close of each strain by the strokes of midnight, is forcible and dramatic. The last act has a respectable duet for

[147]

tenor and soprano, and is much better than the first. Of the plot we can give our readers no idea, although we have studied the book diligently. There is a lady, in whom "pride of rank transcendeth," who is poisoned by her husband. She dies temporarily, after the manner of Juliet, is canonized, and appears subsequently as a saint, after which her husband stabs himself in order to permit the tenor to marry her.

The performance was in nowise remarkable. Signor Capponi was coarse, M. Capoul affected, and Signor Cotogni pretty good. Mlle Smeroschi sang sufficiently well for the occasion; and Mlle d'Angeri's *tremolo* was in such force that she cannot be said to have sung at all. The orchestra, we are glad to say, was better than usual. The scenery was about the best portion of the entertainment. We may remark that the libretto is crowded with impertinent and ungrammatical detail: the instructions to the performers reading like a burlesque of those employed by Wagner. The opera has been repeated once.

Mr Mapleson will hardly sustain the reputation of his house by such performances as that of La Figlia del Reggimento on Friday last. Mlle Rodani and Signor Carrion attracted but a small audience, and entertained them very indifferently indeed. If Sir Michael Costa could only realize the manner in which his orchestra takes advantage of his absence, he would probably never entrust M. Sainton with the *bâton* again.

On the 27th ult. a concert was given by Mr Leslie's choir for the benefit of the Directors. The program was so long that a significant reference to it averted one *encore*. The performance was generally excellent. Messrs Lloyd and Santley, Miss Robertson, and Madame Patey were amongst the vocalists, and sang with their usual success, save the last, for whom an apology was made on the score of indisposition. [U]

VOCALISTS OF THE SEASON:
Mlle Albani

4 July 1877

Mlle Albani has for some years past sustained the enterprise of Mr Gye in a range of those leading parts which stop short on the one hand of the florid brilliancy of Rosina and Caterina, and on the other of the weighty grandeur which we look for in Semiramide and Lucrezia. Since her first appearance here she has steadily improved her position, and at present her hold of the musical public is assured. Mlle Albani's artistic abilities, though not of the rarest, are still of a very estimable order. She has to thank nature for a faculty for hard work, and a voice of the most beautifully clear quality in its highest register. Everything else she owes to her own unspared exertions. It is to be regretted that these exertions seem to be always directed to the attainment of new and often visionary excellences, and never to the remedying of defects which are painfully obvious, and which mar, more or less, her most admired performances. Her intonation is frequently false; and the fatal *tremolo* is already perceptible even in her clearest notes. No amount of talent could neutralize these two faults, which seem to gain ground every season.

Yet Mlle Albani is apparently unconscious of their existence, and wastes the attention that might correct them on evolving forced dramatic effects which only rob her achievements of the simplicity essential to really fine art. That the production of her voice is often forced, and always accompanied by ungraceful facial contortion, should, perhaps, be imputed to her illustrious master, Signor—or, as he delights to be styled, Commendatore—

Lamperti. But it is nonetheless a serious drawback to the enjoyment of the spectator. She is said to be qualified by special training for the impersonation of Wagner's heroines, and consequently her Elsa, Elizabeth, and Senta have always been regarded with peculiar interest. There is no necessity for alluding in detail to her reading of the various parts in her extensive *repertoire*. All exhibit the same characteristics. Earnest study, anxious striving after effect, and the sensuous charm of her voice are to be set off against art which is not concealed, defective management of the breath, artificial gesture, and an absence of genius which can never be compensated [for] by talent, however sedulously cultivated. That she has no claims to [be] what is arbitrarily called a classical singer she proved by her indifferent performance at the Handel Festival last week. Nevertheless, it is but just to add that Mlle Albani's capabilities have proved sufficient to gain for her an enthusiastic following, and deservedly so; for conscientiousness, which we consider her greatest merit, can hardly be too highly esteemed. During her last visit to Paris her success, which we had not the pleasure of witnessing, was reported as extraordinary; and the appreciation evinced of her powers at her late appearance as Senta at Covent Garden was one of which any artist might justly be proud.

THE HANDEL FESTIVAL
4 July 1877

Another Handel Festival has passed away, bearing testimony in its progress to the undiminished popularity of our most imposing musical institution. The occasion, considering its magnitude, affords but little matter for comment. The stale wonderment which the great chorus never fails to elicit has already been exhausted; and Sir Michael Costa has probably enjoyed the triennial laugh in his sleeve over the journalistic exaggerations of the difficulties he has had to contend with. As a matter of fact, the time for regarding an *ensemble* of 4000 performers as a prodigy has gone by; and the sooner we begin to consider the feasibility of adding another thousand or so to the number, and varying the *repertoire* a little, the longer our national interest in the Festival is likely to last. We do not mean to imply that the highest interests of music would be served by increasing a choir already so large as to entail conditions of performance incompatible with strict justice to the master. But a justification of such a course might be found in the increase of sensational attraction; for the aims of the Festival givers necessarily are, firstly, commercial; secondly, phenomenal; and, lastly, artistic.

The performance of the Messiah on the first day was excellent in the choral numbers, and generally respectable in the arias. It would be invidious to select any particular chorus for mention. All were executed with perfect precision; and the text was enunciated with surprising distinctness. It is unfortunate that spirited renderings are considered incompatible with the safe conduct of large masses. However, all that could be done to relieve the somewhat mechanical rigidity of the great choruses by careful observance of *forte* and *piano* was done to the utmost, and the effect was, on the whole, stirring and impressive. The orchestra, though at times rather brassy, was satisfactory, the phrasing being conscientiously followed with the result of a fairly artistic reading. The solos were the weak points of the performance, except in a very few instances. Mlle Albani sang her first recitatives out of tune, and in the subsequent arias made no effect, Rejoice greatly being conspicuously weak. Madame Patey acquitted herself most meritoriously in the numbers allotted to her, which produced an impression due to her care and earnestness. Madame Edith Wynne, in I know that my Redeemer liveth, struck the first really sympathetic chord in her listeners, and suggested regrets that her share in the performance was not greater. Mr Cummings sang the tenor music in the first part feebly as [is] his wont, but with more finish than usual. Owing to the high pitch of the organ, Mr Sims Reeves was not available for the Passion music; but Mr Vernon Rigby reproduced his mannerisms with more success than usually falls to the lot of imitators. Mr Santley did not seem in as happy a mood as usual. Nevertheless, he sang Why do the nations and The trumpet shall sound as perfectly as could have been desired. Herr Henschel took the rest of the baritone music; and it is sufficient to say of him that his bad pronunciation was his misfortune, and his bad phrasing his fault.

The program for the second day was too varied to admit of detailed notice within our limits. In addition to the vocalists (Mlle Albani and Herr Henschel excepted) before mentioned, Mesdames Patti, Sherrington, and Suter, MM. Foli and Edward Lloyd sang—the last-named artist making a decided addition to his already high reputation. Mr Best played an organ concerto. The Israel in Egypt was given on the concluding day, according to custom. We cannot omit this opportunity of warning conductors against the common error of endeavoring to make all performances of the Messiah as like the Festival one as possible. The transept of the Crystal Palace is larger even than the Albert Hall; and the crashing brass and retarded rhythms which are appropriate enough to the vast Handel orchestra become misplaced and intolerably offensive in any smaller space.

HER MAJESTY'S OPERA:
ANOTHER LUCIA
11 July 1877

[U] Mlle Etelka Gerster, the one really valuable addition which our stock of *artistes* received this year, has followed up her success as Amina by appearing as Lucia in Donizetti's opera of that name. She again exemplified her resources as a vocalist by her fluent execution, her admirable phrasing, and the captivating purity of tone in her higher notes. Her acting, though occasionally too obviously studied and embodied in gesture not always free and graceful, fully justified the high expectations created by her performance in La Sonnambula. We believe that when Mlle Gerster has attained the ease and perfect finish that experience will surely bring to her, we shall have an *artiste* who may hold her own even when contrasted with our recollections of the incomparable Ilma di Murska. It is to be regretted that she has not favored us with a better selection from her repertory than Bellini's charming but somewhat trivial La Sonnambula and an opera of Donizetti's, which, despite a few pleasant numbers, every true musician must cordially detest. Her exceptional range would enable her to conquer the part of Astrifiammante* in the Zauberflöte with ease; and her refined taste and careful phrasing would have a worthier field in the music of Mozart than in the meretricious strains of Donizetti.

The dress in the first act is not what it might be, nor is the one in the second act in strict accordance with

---

* The name given to the Queen of Night in the Italian translation (Il Flauto Magico) of Mozart's opera.

English tastes—in the matter of sleeves. With these slight errors corrected, and a little less extravagance on the part of her dresser in the matter of powder, we feel assured that Mlle Gerster will establish herself as one of the favorites at Her Majesty's Theatre.

The other parts in Lucia were cast as before. Signor Fancelli was satisfactory as Edgardo, although histrionically weak. Signor Brocolini does not always sing in tune, and consequently his Raimondo is not always acceptable. Signor Rota's impersonation of Enrico was a very poor one. The orchestra was at times rather noisy. The military drum and cymbals, never very welcome, are particularly objectionable at Her Majesty's, the instruments used being utterly destitute of tone. It would be cheaper, and equally effectual, for Sir Michael to employ a stage carpenter to bang the orchestra door at a pre-arranged signal.

By the bye, why is it that the Master of Ravenswood, whenever he appears on the stage in the opera, proceeds to fling his cloak and hat on the ground with a melodramatic air? It is ridiculous in the first act, impolite in the second, and only justified by the prospect of suicide in the third. Yet tenors cling fondly to this absurdity. But we have alluded to the want of originality on the operatic stage elsewhere.[U]

MR FLORENTINE'S CONCERT
11 July 1877

[U] In obedience to the courteous invitation of Mr Carlos Florentine, we repaired on the 2nd inst. to his concert at the St James's Hall, taking care to arrive "punctually at eight." We felt somewhat aggrieved by the fact that the entertainment did not commence until fully twenty minutes after, when a trio was performed under considerable difficulties, there being no copy for the vocalists save the one on the pianoforte. Most of the items in the program were familiar, but they were nonetheless welcome. Madame Antoinette Sterling sang Balfe's Rowan Tree with a characteristic charm which baffles description. Also The Lost Chord, which was redemanded. We have noticed her rendering of this song before, and so exhausted on paper the subject which we find inexhaustible in the concert room. Madame Lemmens-Sherrington favored us with a vocal pastoral symphony by Zaubert, containing much imitation of an impossible bird. Being encored, she substituted, by way of novelty, Come Back to Erin. She subsequently made the most of a capital piece of claptrap by Molloy, entitled Jamie.

Mr Edward Lloyd sang The Message, one of his most enjoyable efforts, and his favorite Sweethearts, which he sings extremely well. Signor Foli sounded his low F-sharp, under pretence of *Qui sdegno*, a song which he simply cannot sing. He was better suited in I fear no foe, which he delivered with spirit, and only escaped an *encore* through the lateness of the hour. The *artistes* above mentioned (substituting Miss Belval for Madame Sterling) sang *Un di se ben*, which went correctly enough, but was obviously a "scratch" quartet. Mlle Enequist sang *Ah, fors' è lui* and other songs; but we prefer not to dwell on her share of the performance. Her method of singing effectually precludes her from succeeding as a vocalist. The remaining songs were undertaken by executants not ranking above respectable amateurs. Amongst them Mr Trelawney Cobham's rendering of a ballad by Leslie deserves special mention.

Herr Wilhelmj's contribution to the program proved most welcome. He played his paraphrase of the air from the Meistersinger with his usual freedom of style and intensity of expression. Dr Ganz accompanied very indifferently, and inflicted on the audience a Reverie and galop of his own composition. Such productions may be tolerated occasionally from young ladies in drawing rooms, but their intrusion on the concert platform amounts almost to an impertinence. Mr Carlos Florentine's share of the entertainment was becomingly modest, and he received much applause for Honor and Arms.*[U]

VOCALISTS OF THE SEASON:
M. Capoul
11 July 1877

[U] We have selected M. Capoul for the subject of our column this week because we are of opinion that his reputation presents a problem worthy of consideration by those who are alive to the extremely low degree of excellence exhibited in operatic performances in England. He is the leading, perhaps the best, tenor at one of our great opera houses. Yet he is far from having any claim to a first place in the ranks of lyric art. About his voice audiences differ. Some uphold him as the personified ideal of a finished singer; others, who never admit more than one sort of excellence in the same person, declare that he is an exquisite actor, but has no voice. Both views are fair specimens of the critical incapacity of the great body of music-hunters. As a matter of fact, M. Capoul has a very fair voice, an indifferent method of producing it, and worse than indifferent taste in using it. In style he is more refined than most of his colleagues. But, unfortunately, there are so many offensive mannerisms to set off against this advantage that we often

* An aria from Handel's oratorio, Samson (1743).

feel that we could tolerate a little coarseness if we could gain therewith some variety and self-respectful modesty. For in these things M. Capoul is lamentably deficient. With the air of a man perfectly satisfied with himself he treats us repeatedly to the cheap trick of alternating an effected *mezza voce* with bursts of chest voice, and apparently believes that this is art. He stands on tiptoe, waves his arms abroad, and with impassioned gesture expresses as intelligibly as he could in words, "Behold me in my elaborate frame! Here is excellent music written by men of talent to display my voice. Here are several worthy people behind me, whom you could see if I had not taken care to spread myself well across the footlights, engaged expressly to sustain my melody with judicious harmonies! But do not let them distract your attention from Victor Capoul!"

Now, the public do not relish appeals of this kind. They are not acute critics, but they have the common-sense not to take palpable affectation for solid merit. They can discern, after a few repetitions, between a mere claptrap effect and a legitimate exercise of art. They feel what tires them; and M. Capoul, always singing with the same artifices and making the same gestures, is at times very tiresome indeed. We have heard a lady observe that she always enjoyed M. Capoul's singing except when she looked at him; and her sentiments seem to be so far shared by the public that, for those songs which are sung behind the scenes— *Com'è gentil*, for instance—the French tenor usually receives a special meed of applause. The reputation as an actor which he has achieved in spite of all this constitutes the problem we have referred to. Why is it that the male artists who are most extolled for their histrionic powers on the operatic stage are decidedly inferior to the third- and fourth-rate performers at our ordinary playhouses? Why, for example, do we, who are used to witness acting of very high merit in most of our metropolitan theatres, persuade ourselves that M. Faure is a great actor, and M. Capoul a good one? Unless it results from an idea that the buskin is the natural heritage of the French nation, it must be that the absurd conventionalities and traditions which cumber the lyric boards have so blunted our perception that we have become incapable of distinguishing exaggerated fervor and egotistical demeanor from true artistic impersonation.

To break with such traditions rests with the *artistes*, and not with the public. How agreeable a performer might M. Capoul be if he would but realize that he has something to learn; and that he is but a means, and not the end, of those performances in which he participates? We may be mistaken in our judgment of him; and he may approach his art in a humbler spirit than he betrays by his behavior. If so, his efforts are strangely misdirected. In any case, he is one example amongst many that, rare as originality is in any art, in none is its absence so general and so slavishly manifested as under the complex conditions of opera representation.[U]

THE OPERA SEASON IN RETROSPECT: I

18 July 1877

[U] In ending his season at Covent Garden Mr Gye will close on Saturday with a performance of Verdi's Aïda. In the meantime Madame Patti will take her benefit in *Faust* on Thursday; and Mlle Albani will appear on

Friday as Lucia, Hamlet being played this (Wednesday) evening for her benefit.*

In his preliminary manifesto Mr Gye mentioned five strange operas, of which at least three were to be performed. The promise stands fulfilled, the choice having fallen on Wagner's Flying Dutchman, Nicolai's Merry Wives of Windsor, and Santa Chiara, a work which ought never to have been produced. Wagner's opera fared hardly. On the first night the stage carpenters abetted the endeavors of the orchestra to make the picturesque music-opera fail. On the second the band lost their allies, but still contrived to do some damage. At its last chance, when both disadvantages were modified, Mlle Albani was prevented by a severe cold from doing justice to her important part. Nicolai's pretty opera was pushed aside until the close of the season, and consequently had no chance of succeeding. Santa Chiara failed.

The season proved barren of new vocalists. Signor Tamagno was promised, on condition that his affairs would permit of his coming. Apparently they did not; for he is still a stranger to us. Signor Gayarré was announced by both Mr Mapleson and Mr Gye. Eventually Mr Gye bore off the prize, a fact on which his rival is much to be congratulated. Of the lady artists named in the prospectus some half dozen were unknown to English audiences. Of these many appeared not at all; and those who did made no mark. Mlle Albani has improved her position. She has adopted a safe method

* It was a custom in theatre and opera in England, until early in this century, for each principal performer in a company to be entitled to receive from the management the proceeds from a "benefit" performance at the end of the season. This performance was generally attended by the enthusiastic admirers of the particular actor or singer, who would wisely choose to appear in a successful and popular *rôle*.

[159]

of voice production; and if she vanquishes the *tremolo*, her future is assured. Mlle Bianchi has made a notable advance since last year. Mlle Smeroschi has settled into what is called a useful artist. Madame Marimon, unquestionably the best vocalist on the stage, remains far too much in the background. Mlle d'Angeri, in spite of her evident ability, has succumbed completely to the *tremolo*, and steadily declines in the esteem of the public. The other *artistes* have held their places without any noteworthy improvement. M. Maurel's voice is somewhat weightier than it was, but his deportment has become unpleasantly affected. Signor Bagagiolo's volume of tone has fallen off, we hope temporarily, as his claims as an artist are not great. Signor Tagliafico seems to have succeeded fairly at the stage management.

The orchestra, during the greater part of the season, played in a style more suited to a circus or a dancing-saloon than to an opera house. Signor Vianesi's superabundant energy bore little fruit until a few weeks since, when a marked improvement was manifest. We suspect that the conductor has a good deal of work on his hands at Covent Garden, and is often forced to produce works very inadequately rehearsed. Nevertheless, it is hard that the public, which pays monstrous prices for indifferent performances, should suffer from the defective arrangements of Mr Gye or his managers. Signor Bevignani is a nonentity, and for the much-to-be-desired improvement which we hope to find next season in the band, Signor Vianesi alone must be looked to. It is to be regretted that Herr Rubinstein's opera Nero, about which there is much curiosity, was not produced instead of the worthless manufacture of the Duke of Saxe-Coburg-Gotha.

At Her Majesty's, Mlle Etelka Gerster has been repeating her impersonation of Amina in La Sonnambula, and Lucia. Signor Tamberlik appeared on the 9th as

Manrico, and on the 11th as Ottavio, a part much better suited to his slender resources in the matter of voice. He announces his benefit on the 23rd inst., when he will resume the *rôle* of Otello, and give his admirers one more chance of hearing the C sharp which they fondly imagine is a chest note.

Madame Nilsson's benefit and last appearance but one this season will take place on the 25th. She has again selected Les Huguenots for the occasion; and, as we think, wisely. Her acting in the fourth act is one of the most remarkable of her dramatic successes.[U]

VOCALISTS OF THE SEASON:
Mr Edward Lloyd
18 July 1877

[U] Hitherto we have confined ourselves to critical sketches of operatic artists. But in a few weeks or less opera will have vanished from our minds, and the singers whose tremulous high C's we so blindly admire will give place to singers of more sterling merit, who are not ashamed of their nationality. And of these who so popular as Mr Lloyd, whose amiable bluffness has become familiar to us on many concert platforms? His appearance amongst us is comparatively recent, but his agreeable voice, pleasant personality, and good taste have already placed him second to Mr Sims Reeves, and to him only. This position might, in our opinion, be considerably improved by Mr Lloyd at the expense of some earnest study. At present his qualifications are limited. He is a ballad singer—a charming one, it is true, but still nothing more. When he essays oratorios he loses ground at once: he sinks to the level of a merely useful singer. In essaying songs of the highest type he suffers still more, for he betrays weakness. When we think of his merits as an artist it is not to Adelaide or The Quail that our memory turns, but to Sweethearts. Now, this is not as it should be. It argues a total want of depth and a knack of giving a ballad prettily rather than the power of interpreting music with refined sympathy. We are loth to believe that Mr Lloyd can go no further than this; but we are not sure that he has gone much further.

In the natural course of events Mr Sims Reeves's place in the artistic ranks will one day be vacant, and Mr Lloyd will be looked to to step into it. It rests with himself in a great measure to qualify himself, not only to step into it, but to fill it. He will, in any case, be able to make more noise than his predecessor; but will he be content with this? We hope not. We do not think that he will ever make an audience feel Tom Bowling as Mr Sims Reeves can; but he can delight one thoroughly by his rendering of ballads of a more artificial sort. It is in the works of Handel and Mendelssohn that he will find himself at a disadvantage so formidable that only the most earnest and constant effort will enable him to sustain the comparison. We have heard such works interpreted with more than the utmost pathos Mr Lloyd has ever shewn, combined with irreproachable technical skill; and we shall feel the want of both in the future. If he is not then competent to supply that want, he must be prepared, in spite of the lavish applause with which our music mobs lull *artistes* into false security, to fall second to the first newcomer who can make good his claim to the possession of the "Divine fire." [U]

THE OPERA SEASON IN
RETROSPECT: II
25 July 1877

[U] The short season at Her Majesty's is at length drawing to a close. The illness of Mlle Titiens has altered the usual course of events at the Haymarket this season. Semiramide and Lucrezia, for the first time for many years, have lain unheard. To the same lamentable cause must be ascribed the failure of that part of Mr Mapleson's scheme which concerned the revival of Cherubini's Medea and the production of Gluck's Armida. Less intelligible is the non-appearance of The Flying Dutchman. Most admirers of Wagner had set their hearts on seeing Madame Nilsson as Senta; and though we have little faith in M. Faure's ability to do justice to the heavy part of Vanderdecken, we think the management would have found its account in redeeming its promise.

Rossini's Otello was duly performed; but the once universal popularity of the Italian master has long been waning. Its attractions were, however, reinforced by the curiosity of the public with regard to Signor Tamberlik; and so it fared sufficiently well. But the spectacle of an artist who has survived his voice and who possesses no compensatory gifts is a painful one. The opera must have failed but for the powerful acting of Madame Nilsson. Herr Wachtel, despite the general admiration excited by his performances, appeared too seldom to affect the character of the season. Signor Gayarré, on the contrary, contributed considerably to its success by transferring his services to Covent Garden. Signor Talbo did not fail. Signori Carrion and Cabero did not succeed.

Signor Fancelli discharged a heavy share of the season's labor with deserved success.

Of the lady artists who were newcomers, Mlle Gerster alone made any mark. Her *début* must be considered a notable event in the annals of opera. Mlles Salla and Nandori were thrown into the shade, and Mlle Chiomi fairly extinguished by it. The last-named vocalist can only achieve distinction at the expense of severe study, if, indeed, she has not wholly mistaken her vocation. Mlle Naresi, a very estimable artist, was announced, but did not appear.

The orchestra was, as a rule, good; but its members seized the opportunities afforded by the absence of Sir Michael Costa to shew how badly they could play when they chose. A word must be said of Mlle Katti Lanner. She has established her position at Her Majesty's as an artistic dancer; and her pupils, headed by the precocious Mlle Muller, testify to the soundness of her administrative powers.

On Tuesday the 17th Mlle Gerster performed the part of Elvira in Bellini's I Puritani for the first time in this country, repeating the impersonation on the following Saturday. The comparative smallness of the audience testified to the unpopularity of an opera which, despite a few charming melodies and the traditions of the celebrated Rubini quartet,* has so little variety in its cloying rhythms that it vies for dulness with any Italian opera on the stage. The public, already familiar with her Lucia and Amina, naturally cared little to hear the new

* Giovanni Rubini is one of the greatest of the legendary tenors, said to have introduced the vibrato and the sob, for whom Bellini wrote numerous operas, including I Puritani. The "quartet" was first sung, both in Paris and in London, in 1835 by Rubini, Giulia Grisi, Antonio Tamburini, and Luigi Lablache.

singer in a part so similar as Elvira. Nevertheless, the opinion of those who did go was unmistakable; and, whatever the management may have done, Mlle Gerster achieved another brilliant success. The numbers in which she bore a prominent part were received with loud plaudits. The Polacca, which was encored, served to display Mlle Gerster's exceptional range, which is only the least of her qualifications. Her rendering of the entire part exemplified her admirable phrasing and execution, and her power of impressing with great tenderness of expression a voice not naturally sympathetic. There were also indications of the probability of her voice attaining considerable volume of tone when it has been developed by a few years' further use.

Her acting was energetic and often passionate, but overstudied in appearance; and her gestures were crude and lacked the spontaneous grace indispensable to finished effect. Fortunately, her faults are on the right side. Experience will tone down exaggeration and rectify the common mistake of overloading every scene with sustained action. Vocally she has much less to learn. If her accentuation of the phrasing were slightly modified the better to conceal her art, little further could be desired.

The other *rôles* were satisfactorily filled. Signor Fancelli's part was curtailed; but what he sang he sang very respectably. Herr Rokitansky's rough style was appropriate in the part of Giorgio. Signor Rota, as Riccardo, was tolerable. The *Suoni la tromba* was taken too fast; but it was the sooner over. What a boon this duet must be to the clamorers for "melody" and Wagner extirpation. Everybody can whistle it. To hear it is to learn it. To learn it is to detest it.[U]

VOCALISTS OF THE SEASON:
Madame Lemmens-Sherrington
25 July 1877

[U] An invasion having been made on to the concert platform by discussing Mr Edward Lloyd, it seems natural to turn to the consideration of an artist constantly associated with him thereon. Madame Sherrington is the principal soprano of that small band of vocalists who are familiar to London audiences in the genial relaxation of the ballad concert. She is a clever lady, familiar with the weaknesses of the public and unscrupulous in taking advantage of them. Hence she rarely escapes that outcome of popular ignorance, the *encore*. She is an accomplished mistress of claptrap, and an extensive patroness of the royalty system. When some worthy old song of long-extinct copyright is redemanded at her hands, she dexterously substitutes Come Back to Erin. Her favorite vehicles for display are those ballads which contain effective contrasts, or can be directed with a certain amount of personal application at the audience. She also cultivates the warbling-bird species of composition, and not infrequently displays her imitative powers so liberally as to provoke the crustier sort of critics to hint that the St James's Hall is not the London Pavilion.

Nevertheless, Madame Sherrington, although she systematically makes the unskilful laugh, does not always make the judicious grieve. When serious work is to be done no one can be more grave than she. She is useful in every department of her art, has achieved distinction as an oratorio singer, and has never been connected in the public mind with even a suspicion of inefficiency. Her method of singing is admirable, and her voice remains unimpaired in spite of the continuous labor of years. Her talents, though not of the highest order, enable her to sustain with dignity the heaviest and most dramatic parts in oratorio. But it is as a ballad singer that her reputation stands highest, and it is of this species of art that she has the most complete command. Unfortunately, it is also that which affords the largest scope for those violations of good taste to which we have alluded, and which she is not likely to discontinue as long as the public evince so keen a relish for them. It is a commercial age, and artistic propriety must be content to have the worst of it.[U]

THE MERITS OF MEYERBEER
1 August 1877

Few operas have suffered more from the pruning-knife of the stage manager than Meyerbeer's historical romance [Les Huguenots]. The fifth act, performed as it usually is with the opening scene excised and the *finale* recklessly mutilated, rarely induces an audience to sit after midnight for its sake. This season it vanished entirely from the boards, its omission being justifiable on the principle that what cannot be done properly is best left undone. The remaining acts are so extensively and tastelessly curtailed that many critics, unacquainted with the score, have denounced the opera as a fragmentary arrangement of musical odds and ends. In its original form the work is undoubtedly too long for the most patient audience. But the method which has been adopted of extracting central portions from the concerted pieces, as in the *finale* to the second and third acts, is so barbarous that a reconstruction of the version for performance would be extremely desirable, until the public are prepared to devote two nights to one opera. The score contains nothing unworthy of a hearing. We are acquainted with no work of similar length which is more highly finished in all its parts; which contains such a profusion of original and varied melody without being eked out by conventional manufacture; which displays greater fertility in orchestral device; and which at the same time bears so exclusive a stamp of one individuality. The merits of Meyerbeer are now rarely disputed. The conservative critics, having glorified Mayer* and Paisiello in order to disparage Rossini, at length praised Rossini at the expense of Meyerbeer; and now, nothing discouraged, invent rhapsodies about Meyerbeer for the purpose of depreciating Wagner.

[U] Madame Nilsson, in her impersonation of Valentine, did not display any marked advance on her effort of last year, except by her more modest and womanly bearing in the second act. In the fourth she treated the conventional rendering of the part with great power and pathos. But her performance, brilliant in many isolated points, was not thoroughly sustained. And, apart from the intense expressiveness of her tone in a few passages, her vocalization was unsatisfactory, notably in the duet with the basso in the scene on the Pré-aux-Clercs. Madame Trebelli, as Urbain, seemed quite happy and gave the audience every reason to share her feelings. With the exception of Signor Foli's Marcel the remaining parts were filled in a most commonplace manner. Signor Fancelli did his best as Raoul. Signor del Puente, as Nevers, attempted to embellish the recitative which precedes the *finale* of the third act, and illustrated thereby the remark of Michael Angelo that to alter is not

* Johann Simon Mayr, German-born dramatic composer in Italy, whose successful opera Saffo (1794) was followed by some seventy additional operatic works.

to improve. The choruses, with a few exceptions, were satisfactorily executed, and the orchestra acquitted itself most creditably. It is a pity that the pitch of the bells on the stage is not adhered to by the band. The Bohemian ballet was carefully arranged and deservedly successful.[U]

VOCALISTS OF THE SEASON:
Sir Michael Costa

1 August 1877

To those profane persons who have been moved to laughter by the appearance of the celebrated conductor amongst our "Vocalists," we address the assurance that no one has a more influential voice in regulating our operatic repasts than Sir Michael Costa. Nay, he is the most successful of our vocalists, for his voice never fails—and of whom else can as much be said?

The struggle for existence in modern London has been aptly described as a constant march against time. By dint of constantly beating time, Sir Michael has secured the foremost place in the very thin ranks of our conductors. His place is undisputed. With the exception of Mr August Manns, whose labors are confined to the nobler field of abstract music, he is the only chief under whose *bâton* orchestras display good training. The merits which he successfully cultivates are precision and refinement, and both go so far in music that their attainment alone would entitle him to his high position. Nevertheless, they are not everything. In rendering the heavily loaded scores of the composers of the new German school, and the well-filled compositions of Beethoven and even Meyerbeer, the music, if played correctly and steadily, will answer for itself. The combination of noise and commonplace which constitutes the usual accompaniment of an Italian opera requires little of artistic treatment, save the avoidance of coarseness. And in all such works the band swayed by Sir Michael Costa at Her Majesty's Theatre invariably gives complete satisfaction. It is only when they essay the light but exquisitely constructed scores of Mozart that we are compelled to admit that the rare delicacy and dash necessary to their effect is wholly wanting. The master who receives the fullest justice from Sir Michael is Rossini, to whose music he is wedded by taste and nationality. The works of the great Germans he attacks conscientiously, but without the keen relish which he exhibits when his own school is the subject of exposition. His ideas of speed are not uniformly satisfactory. Generally speaking, he errs on the side of slowness.

That highest faculty of a conductor, which consists in the establishment of a magnetic influence under which an orchestra becomes as amenable to the *bâton* as a pianoforte to the fingers, we do not give Sir Michael Costa credit for. Instead, he has the common power of making himself obeyed, and is rather the autocrat than the artist. To one who is only called on to direct competent players, this is amply sufficient. The performers are all able artists, who know that they will not be permitted to play carelessly, and this knowledge naturally ensures satisfactory results. When, as sometimes happens, an emergency arises and confusion reigns momentarily amongst his forces, Sir Michael quietly puts down his wand and allows the matter to remedy itself as best it can.

He has acquired much fame from his conducting of the Handel Festival; but we have, on a former occasion, expressed our opinion that the difficulties of this achievement are fancifully exaggerated by the public. In conclusion, we are sorry to say that he has been guilty of some grave breaches of musical taste. It may be justifiable to rescore the oratorios of Handel, but no true musician can sympathize with Sir Michael Costa when he tampers with Beethoven, as he has done in more than one instance, by presumptuously reinforcing the brass parts with trombones.

ON OPERA IN TRANSLATION
8 August 1877

A not very brilliant season has been succeeded by a week of absolute stagnation, musically speaking. *Impresarios*, artists, and audiences have vanished from amongst us in quest of new singers, new triumphs, and such health as can be gained from the mountain winds of Switzerland, or the more economical atmosphere of the rearward apartments of apparently deserted premises. The critics are divided between operatic retrospects and the prospects of English opera during the autumn and winter with Mr Carl Rosa. We have so low an opinion of the merits of Italian opera in this country, and so steady a conviction that its downfall is only a question of time and musical culture, that we turn willingly to the rival enterprise which has relieved us from the absurdity of being the only music-patronizing nation in the world which systematically tolerates opera delivered in a foreign tongue. And, be it remembered, not in the language for which the music was written, but in a vile Italian substitute for the original French or German libretto.

Those persons who object to English versions on the score of their literary demerits are presumably unacquainted with the Italian language, or they would scarcely assert the superiority of the translations which we hear so maltreated by German, Spanish, Swedish, French, Irish, and American artists at our opera houses.

[171]

The few Italian singers, mostly of minor importance, do even less justice to their native tongue than the foreigners, pronouncing their recitatives in a species of gabble which we can scarcely identify with the musical language which we have heard declaimed by Signor Salvini.* In other countries the artists pay their audiences the compliment of mastering their speech, and presenting them with an intelligible and most enjoyable entertainment. The pre-eminence of Italian as the language of song has been urged to the serious detriment of opera in this country. English is the only tongue capable of enlisting the sympathy of the Englishman. It is far nearer to the German, in which the greatest operas have been written, than Italian; and it is also capable of greater variety of inflexion and expression. It is more amenable to musical requirements than French. Once cultivated on the lyric stage, an example would be constantly before the public which might perhaps modify the corruption which the unfortunate vowel experiences in London. But these are secondary matters.

The great point is that English is our national tongue, and, therefore, the only one which should be tolerated in our national opera houses. When we are at last roused to draw comparisons between the dreary emptiness of the evening spent in Covent Garden or the Haymarket, listening to performances which are foreign in heart and form, and the familiar and sympathetically rendered versions which excite the enthusiasm of shilling galleries for even Wagner, it is certain that we should as soon think of going to hear Mr Irving in a German translation

* Tommaso Salvini, Italian tragedian, first performed in London in 1875. Shaw, who apparently saw his Othello in May 1876 and his Hamlet in 1884, referred to Salvini in an 1889 lecture on acting as "the greatest actor of the day."

of Hamlet as to an Italian opera. After this hint of our views, we need scarcely add that Mr Carl Rosa has our warmest wishes for the success of the enterprise which he has inaugurated with so much energy.

[U] It is said that Herr Chandon has been engaged by Mr Mapleson for the season of 1878. He will be remembered by visitors to the Wagner Festival of last May as a steady singer with a strong baritone voice of more resonance than quality, and withal somewhat coarse in his style. But he will appear to greater advantage when no longer contrasted with Herr Karl Hill, whose taste and expressive delivery might render the least severe critic fastidious.

A series of ten operas in English is in course of production at the Crystal Palace, by the Rose Hersee Opera Company. The list of vocalists is not particularly attractive, but there are materials for some pleasant performances, nevertheless.[U]

OPERA AT SYDENHAM
15 August 1877

[U] The musical barrenness of last week was momentarily relieved on Bank Holiday by entertainments at the Royal Aquarium, the Alexandra Palace, and more especially at the Crystal Palace, where Beethoven's Battle of Vittoria was performed under the direction of Mr Manns, the orchestra being reinforced by military bands. There was also a ballad concert, supported by Mesdames Sterling and Campobello, Messrs Shakespeare, Foli, and Barton McGuckin. The last-named gentleman is an Irish tenor of some reputation in his own country, where audiences are neither easily pleased nor particularly ceremonious in demonstrating their displeasure.

[173]

The series of opera in English now in course of performance at Sydenham is not likely to prove very attractive. Madame Rose Hersee is only acceptable in very light parts, whilst Signor Campobello, not a very intelligent or interesting singer, is entirely deficient in histrionic power. Yet they are the principal artists in a troupe which essays Don Giovanni and Le Nozze di Figaro, operas which demand a greater variety of artistic accomplishments from their exponents, and bear ill treatment worse, than any others on the stage. It might be well for Mr Carl Rosa to engage the entire troupe and so obtain the control of an enterprise which, as at present directed, is not likely to advance the cause of English opera.

But even Mr Carl Rosa himself can hardly be adding much to his provincial renown. We learn from the Dublin journals that Mr Santley's place has been taken by Mr Aynsley Cook. Mr Cook is a useful artist in his way, but the announcement of his appearance as Vanderdecken in The Flying Dutchman is rather a strong inducement to playgoers to stay at home. Surely the acceptance of Wagner in the Green Isle was sufficiently imperilled by the manner in which Mr Gye produced Lohengrin there some years ago,* without Mr Rosa dealing it a further stroke at the expense of his own interest in the opera which proved such a mine to him last year at the Lyceum. On the other hand,

* On 29 August Shaw amended his statement in a brief paragraph, noting that it was William Ludwig who had assumed the part of Vanderdecken in Dublin, with Aynsley Cook playing Daland. "With regard to a further exception to a remark of ours concerning Lohengrin in Dublin" he added "we beg to say that we did not style the cast 'indifferent,' and that we are perfectly aware that the name of Mr Gye was not used in connexion with the undertaking."

Madame Blanche Cole, always an agreeable singer, will perhaps find more sympathy amongst audiences than the estimable but somewhat uninteresting Madame Torriani.

The Paris Figaro announces the formation of a third Italian opera company for Drury Lane next year. As London, so far from clamoring for three opera houses, displays every year an increasing reluctance to support two, we presume the new scheme is intended to oust one or other of the existing ones. If so, let us hope that the competition will have the usual effect of lowering prices and improving quality. There is room for both operations at present. But why not start English opera on an imposing scale instead of adhering to that hollowest of fashions: the Italian opera? Surely the time is as ripe for the inauguration of a new system which will enlist our sympathies as for an attempt to reinvigorate an old and sapless one, which only retains our attention by expensive sensationalism.

One of the best known song writers of the present generation met with a sudden and violent death on the 5th instant, when Mrs Marsh, better known as Virginia Gabriel, was thrown from her carriage in Grosvenor Place. Mrs Marsh's talents were admirably suited to the taste of her time, and a great many of her ballads (who does not recollect Ruby?) enjoyed a popularity rarely accorded to the ephemeral productions which our music publishers scatter forth weekly. [U]

VOCALISTS OF THE SEASON:
Madame Antoinette Sterling
15 August 1877

[U] Madame Sterling shares, with Mr Sims Reeves, the chief place amongst our ballad singers. She is a perfectly unconventional artist, marked out for ignominious failure by the verdict of all critics of the safe old croaking school; and destined to succeed always, and irresistibly, before audiences who only recognize music as an excellent thing when it reaches to those painfully pleasant emotions which, in the Londoner, are not particularly near the surface. She seizes, with unerring instinct, the true coloring of ballads of all forms, subjects, and nationalities. It matters nothing at all whether the occasion be an English, an Irish, or a Scotch night, whether the song is The Lost Chord, The Rowan Tree, or Caller Herrin'. Madame Sterling sings; and everybody, from the unmusical pest, who claps for the mere sake of making a noise, to the skilled musician, who entertains a rooted aversion to applause in any form, straightway either vociferously demands, or gladly acquiesces in, an immediate repetition. This result is attained without claptrap.

Like that of all artists of strong individuality Madame Sterling's style is colored by a remarkable mannerism. Such peculiarities, however, are invariably attractive. It is only affectation that repels. Ballad singing is usually accompanied by coquettish smirks, a smile at the end of each stave, and an absurd prolongation of the pathetic phrases, by way of apology for the absence of legitimate effect. The mob applaud, and the judicious hearer recoils disgusted. However, the judicious hearer is in most concert rooms an uninfluential member of a minority of some half a dozen persons, whose disapproval matters very little to the vocalist. These petty practices Madame Sterling has never condescended to employ. Those who do not care for artistic merit of too abstract a sort are caught by her peculiar accent and characteristic short delivery. She never misses the full effect and weight of a word, yet she never dwells on one, but relies simply on the rapid sympathy inspired by her voice's strange tone quality.

It must not be supposed, however, that the domain occupied in music by the ballad is the only one in which Madame Sterling shines. In a far-removed classical region she reappears as almost the only one of our concert singers who is capable of doing justice to the poetic genius of Sebastian Bach. His sacred songs, replete with meaning, afford a suitable field for the display of her special talent, and if in interpreting them she betrays that she is something less than a finished technical artist, she also proves that the great composer was a great deal more than an ingenious contrapuntist. In the wide intermediate space occupied by operatic music and pieces designed for the display of vocal accomplishments Madame Sterling is less successful. Her disdain of scholastic dogma and [her] determination to appear only as the self-taught exponent of music as a moving art rather than an entertaining accomplishment have been amply rewarded. But it has prevented her from mastering the delicate artificial refinements of correct phrasing and fluent execution which are essential, not only to opera, but in the greater part of the oratorios of Handel.[U]

THE PROMS

22 August 1877

The Promenade Concerts at Covent Garden, which have become an institution during our unmusical autumns, are now in active operation. On last Wednesday, the first "classical" program of the season was performed, and its reception afforded another proof of the fallacy of the commonplace theory that the public dislike good music, which is so frequently advanced as an excuse for giving audiences the worst possible value for their money. The concert opened with the Anacreon overture, a work in which Cherubini, in addition to his constructive skill, displays a vivacity and fire which are not always to be found in his polished and scholarly compositions. A movement from the beautiful fragment of a symphony in B minor by Schubert produced its usual effect, and the scherzo from Mendelssohn's Midsummer Night's Dream, although somewhat roughly performed, was encored.

The principal attraction, however, centred in the performance of the first of Mozart's three most popular symphonies, that in E flat. The manner in which it was executed by "the most eminent musicians of the day" suggested an unpleasant idea of the spirit in which they approached their work. Instead of an orchestra conscientiously endeavoring to do justice to a great work, the audience were entertained by the spectacle of a number of individuals bent on displaying the consummate ease with which they could rattle through so simple an affair as a score of Mozart's. There was much vigorous bowing, which was not necessary; there was no delicacy, which was the chief requisite; little attention was paid to the conductor, who is never in his element when dealing

[178]

with high-class German music; and the result was, of course, the comparative failure of the symphony.

It was followed by a transcription for orchestra and military band of Handel's See the Conquering Hero comes, in which the delighted listeners had the pleasure of hearing the simultaneous explosions of six cornets, six horns, four euphoniums, one ophicleide, and seven trombones, in addition to the full orchestra of reeds and strings. The trumpets alone remained silent, probably in order to avoid undue noise. A selection from M. Gounod's new opera Cinq Mars revealed the unwelcome fact that the composer of Faust, in his last production, has fallen back on manufacture as a substitute for inspiration. As it comes from a first-rate establishment, it is manufacture of a good sort, but as music it is valueless. Signor Arditi's selection was satisfactorily performed, as his band contains many accomplished soloists, of whom we may particularize MM. Hughes and Lazarus as the best. Mr Howard Reynolds has a remarkable physical aptitude for the cornet, and plays with some taste; but his style is not at all legitimate. The remainder of the instrumental portion of the program was made up of popular dance music, one item being a polka by Signor Arditi, accompanied by the vigorous rataplans of a youthful contingent from the Coldstream Guards.

[U] Mlle Debillemont played Handel's variations on the air known as The Harmonious Blacksmith and a gavotte by Bach. She is a well-taught player and, her style being sufficiently vigorous, she easily finds favor with the promenaders, who do not greatly value depth or strict taste. Mlle Pommereul was heard in Beethoven's romance in F for the violin, which was encored. Her tone was thin and flat throughout, but she seems to possess abilities considerable in so young a performer. [U]

[179]

The vocalists are not above the promenade concert average, and Mlle Dérivis, who displayed her weakness in *Batti, batti,* and the shadow song from Dinorah, is decidedly below it. Signor Giannini, the tenor, does his best. Signor Medica, the baritone, does his worst. It is impossible to witness the performance of this very young singer without a sensation compounded of mirth and pity. As he sings he repeatedly makes a stereotyped gesture with his disengaged hand, and glares about him with the eagle eye of affectation. He has no artistic style, but his voice is a noisy one, and he seems to delight in the sound of it. We expect modesty of demeanor even from singers who have just reason to be proud of their gifts, and Signor Medica, having neither the one nor the other, seems to have adopted the dignified principle that the best palliative of groundless arrogance is boundless absurdity.

VOCALISTS OF THE SEASON:
Mr Santley

22 August 1877

Mr Santley is the best baritone singer with whom the London public is familiar. He has a voice; he knows how to produce it; he has acquired the art of managing his breath properly; and he conscientiously interprets the works which he sings without adding or subtracting a note. The taste of the present age has, it is true, voted all these accomplishments and gifts to be superfluous and old-fashioned. Your modern audience plausibly argues that it is no great feat for a man to sing if he has a voice, and clamors for the sensational performances of artists (foreigners preferred) who have mastered a few unpleasant tricks during the final shattering of the vocal

[180]

organs, which usually precedes their appearance in public. It is the birthright of an Englishman to do as he likes; and if he chooses to pay through the nose for the privilege of hearing a French baritone sing through the nose, he can adduce in his defence the natural fitness of the transaction, and the fact that the national taste rarely gives itself the slightest trouble about artistic excellence.

There is always, however, a mass of persons in existence who possess more or less musical and, consequently, unfashionable taste; who profess to like what they know; and who have the far more valuable faculty of knowing what they like. They like Mr Santley because he is both a competent and an honest singer. He cannot boast of genius, and yet, at the present moment, he stands quite unrivaled in his position. At the opera houses his successors only disparage themselves by suggesting comparisons with him. In the concert room we have no choice between him and some estimable nonentity who merely fills a gap in the harmony. Since the lamented death, some years since, of Signor Agnesi, we have had no baritone of any serious pretensions established amongst us, and the result is that Charles Santley, who, though a very good singer, is neither a great nor a poetic artist, is, beyond dispute, the chief of his own department of the musical profession in England.

He has been much before the public in opera, and the introduction of Wagner's Flying Dutchman to London is probably due to his influence. If it be so, he rendered an important service to art progress at some expense to himself, for his exertions in the part of Vanderdecken were seriously, though, we hope, temporarily, detrimental to his voice, the music lying in great part much below his natural range. His greatest success was in the high and light *rôle* of Mikeli, in the Les Deux Journées of Cherubini. Although not unsuccessful in portraying simple pathos, acting is evidently no part of his vocation. His bearing on the stage is congenial and familiar, but quite unsuited for characters requiring dignity or refinement. His secession from the boards is, therefore, not to be regretted. He is seen to greater advantage on the concert platform and [with] the Handel orchestra, and he is removed from the temptation to cultivate an artificially weighty style which opera holds out.

We desire to emphasize our recognition of one of his merits as a man, if not a musician. It is that he is an Englishman who is not ashamed of his nationality. Despite the managerial pressure which must have borne on him at the outset of his career in favor of Sant, Santelli, Santalini, Saint Lis, and other seductive disguises, he had the courage to be "Mr Santley." We wish other native artists had the good sense to follow his example. Or if they must deceive themselves (they can scarcely imagine that they deceive the public) can they not do it with some show of plausibility? Why insult ordinary perception by putting an *o* after each syllable of a good Scotch name, as Burns often did with a line of poetry? Does not "Signor Talbo" sound, to say the least of it, a little disingenuous? If Mr Slater thinks his name more befitting a critic than a composer, can he not adopt the worthy name of Barry without misspelling it?*
There is no custom for which we have a more hearty contempt than that prevalent amongst our artists of adopting foreign names. It is a species of fraud on our national reputation as a musical people (such as it is), and is practised only through affectation or a slavish regard for false conventionality.

* Dublin-born Edward Slater, a prolific composer of popular songs, had adopted Odoardo Barri as his professional name.

THE ONCE DREADED BEETHOVEN

29 August 1877

[U]The once dreaded name of Beethoven attracted an unusually large audience to Covent Garden on the 22nd. The program might, perhaps, have been more judiciously arranged, and the movement from the violin concerto should have been omitted. Its performance displayed only the weakness of clever Mlle Pommereul, and its *encore* from the *cadenza* was an absurdity which was only accomplished by the perseverance of a small clique, in opposition to the general feeling. The overture, Coriolan, suffered from want of sharpness and dash. The "metronome" movement from the eighth symphony was encored, as it always is. The symphony was that in B flat, No. 4, and its execution was in nowise remarkable. In deference to popular impatience symphonies are played at Covent Garden without the repeats; and, considering the conditions of performance, we think this a wise arrangement.

An interesting item in the program was the beautiful largo from the Pianoforte Sonata, No. 3 of Op. 10, arranged for orchestra by W. Hepworth. The arrangement is for the most part successful, but although their melancholy tones are in keeping with the sentiment of the work, we think the four horns are too constantly employed. No other brass instruments appear in the score. The weakest point is unfortunately at the climax of the movement in the *crescendo* near the end, where the *arpeggios,* so effective in the original version, are completely overpowered by the wood and heavier stringed instruments, which in their turn fail to give the effect produced by the bass on the pianoforte. Mlle

Dérivis would have sung an air from Fidelio well if the tremulousness of her voice had permitted her. A miscellaneous selection completed the program. [U]

VOCALISTS OF THE SEASON:
Mr Vernon Rigby

5 September 1877

In the musical as in all callings, originality, or the power of creating an independent mode of exposition, is a gift possessed only by a few. Mr Vernon Rigby is not one of the few. Nor is he one of the musical mob—the vast army of singers who commence with an awkwardly-assumed style derived from their teachers and, in course of time, drift into respectable nothingness with no style at all. He has apparently recognized the fact that his own resources contain no germ of artistic individuality, and so has adopted at second hand a pre-existing individuality which had done good service during many years of trial. Such a process has a delusive semblance of easiness about it. A public singer is successful. He makes his success in full view of everybody who chooses to study him. He is conspicuous on a platform. The lights are turned up. There is no deception. He who has eyes and ears can perceive how it is done.

After this manner, it appears to us, did Mr Vernon Rigby set to work to discover the potent spell of Mr Sims Reeves. He has succeeded in producing a counterfeit coin not altogether unacceptable to those who are unfamiliar with the original. The voice metal is genuine in both, though of a somewhat baser quality in the copy; but the distinctive stamp of the latter is an imitation, and, of course, an imitation correct only in trick and external flourish. Somehow the essence of the mysterious thing always escapes the imitator, who gains nothing for his pains but a set of sorry antics, and a rueful conviction that, after all, every true man's apparel does *not* fit your thief.

The apparel of Mr Sims Reeves, both artistic and material, is of more than usual eccentricity, and has so much of the grotesquely manneristic about it that it sits even on him oddly enough at times. But his is forgiven because it covers a spark of true feeling. When Mr Vernon Rigby puts it on, it covers nothing, but aspires to be attractive on its own account. That it fails needs not be said. But it does worse. It becomes irritating. The borrowed articles of the singer offend that sensitive appreciation of fitness in art which the really musical listener possesses, and, although we question very much whether there can be said to be a truth in impersonative art without a twisting of terms, still, for a singer to assume the mannerisms of a brother artist, instead of assuming an ideal character of his own conception, seems to us as false as anything may well be.

Yet Mr Vernon Rigby, though thus unwilling to rely on his own invention for a good style, is in other respects decidedly egotistical in his musical attitude. When he takes a leading part in an oratorio, which he frequently does, he gives his audience to understand that any interest in Handel or Haydn they may feel disposed to evince must be strictly subsidiary to their attention to the celebrated tenor who deigns to lend the lustre of his voice to the works of these composers. The critic who demurs to this, and who looks for breadth of style and regard to the due relation of the various parts to the entire composition, is likely to be considerably disappointed. Mr Rigby has a nice voice. We are sorry we cannot give him credit for his other accomplishments, seeing that they are not fairly his own, or exonerate him from artistic failings which, in our opinion, go far to nullify them.

MUSICAL REVIEWS
12 September 1877

[U] From Mr Joseph Williams, 24 Berners-street, W.:
The Fairy Dell; So sings the Lark; The Patrol; Tis I, my love. By Franz Abt. These compositions are all melodious and agreeably constructed, except The Patrol, the words of which are absurd even for Mr Edward Oxenford. They contain in almost every phrase reminiscences of other composers, from Mozart to Arthur Sullivan.
From Messrs Weeke's and Co., 16 Hanover-street:
The Fairy Glen Waltzes, by A.F. Delmar, will not distract the attention of the dancers by their originality.[U]

MUSICAL REVIEWS
19 September 1877

[U] From Messrs J.B. Cramer and Co., 201 Regent-street:
Deutsche Mädchen Lieder Waltz. In this Herr Hartmann, Mus. Doc. of Trinity College, Dublin, has conceived the unhappy idea of making use of airs by Mozart, Weber, &c., as themes for a waltz. We can recommend the work to those who are unacquainted with the original airs.
Oh, chide me not for loving; Sweet Rosabelle; Jack's Bequest. By C.H.R. Marriott. Mr Marriott is a facile manufacturer of little tunes. The first-named song is the best of the three. With reference to the last we beg to

warn composers, publishers, and all whom it may concern that we have had enough of Jack. We have borne his wedding, his vow,* and his bequest, calmly. But the limit of our endurance is reached, and if we hear any more of him, our critical pen shall be dipped in gall for his reception.

Roses on the Stream; Fare thee well, and if for ever. By A.D. Duvivier. These songs are somewhat above the average of such publications. The music of the latter is not worthy of Byron's poetry, being incoherent in design. Both are a little labored, but it cannot be said of M. Duvivier that he "hath no feeling of his business."† [U]

A TYPICAL "POPULAR" VOCALIST
26 September 1877

Amongst artists the struggle for existence resolves itself into a struggle for popularity. Popularity is attained by different persons in different ways. Twice or thrice in a century some gifted being appears, and, by an occult power, gains the idolatry of the public in a night or two, retaining it often for years after the last traces of the original fascination have succumbed to age, misuse, or the intoxication of success. Others enter the arena in humble guise, and toil laboriously in the pursuit of artistic excellence, their love of music sustaining them against the coldness of unscrupulous rivals who resent conscientiousness, and the indifference of the mob to exalted considerations of all kinds. They often have to wait; but, as a rule, the solid weight of genuine art

* Jack's Wedding by Arthur Carnall and F. E. Weatherly and Jack's Vow by William Charles Levey and Edward Oxenford were also published in 1877.

† Hamlet, V,i,71.

material establishes itself at last, and that unassailably. Nevertheless, the process is a slow one for this age of quick returns and impatient aspirations; and a quicker method of succeeding is usually adopted.

The outward and visible signs of this royal road to popularity are of infinite variety, according to the ingenuity of the traveler. If a female vocalist (and such are the most brilliant professors of the science of claptrap) desire to shine in this way, she must bear in mind that her work begins from the moment her audience first catches sight of her. Let her then smile and trip forth as captivatingly as possible. If she have to make her way through an orchestra, a little judicious embarrassment as she threads the row of fiddlers (who will tap their desks vigorously and so ensure a reception) will often lay the foundation of an enthusiastic *encore* before she utters a note. A prettily whispered conference with the conductor or accompanist will dispose of the suffrages of every youth present of average susceptibility. The fashion in which the sheet of music is held is of much importance, but no positive rule can be laid down respecting it. To dispense with the copy altogether is sometimes advisable as being impressive, but, perhaps, the most irresistible plan is to have a small card or scrap of paper on which the words are scribbled. A timely lapse of memory is useful when the singer has the gift of displaying confusion agreeably.

The purely musical portion of the task is of minor importance. If the song be English, the words must be pointedly delivered at the audience in a confidentially colloquial style. The pathetic parts should be drawled, and those notes made the most of which best display the power of the voice. In justice to all present, each line must be delivered to the right and left of the platform alternately; and the vocalist must bear in mind that it is impossible to smile too often. In Italian music, shakes must be introduced at every suitable or unsuitable opportunity. They must by no means be steadily delivered, as such a mode savors of old-fashioned classicalism, but shot forth in a series of jerks. During the process the pitch may be allowed to fall half a tone, but not more, as it might be difficult to regain the key with sufficient rapidity. Considerations of this kind are, however, immaterial, as very few persons will have the least idea as to whether the singer is in or out of tune. Applause should be promptly improved by reappearance and many obeisances. If an *encore* be doubtful, it should be accepted as a matter of generosity to the public.

From these few and unskilful hints may be gathered the manner in which popularity can be obtained without taste, culture, or voice. Those who adopt it are not necessarily devoid of these attributes, but they pervert rather than improve them. Of their school more than one that we could name is a prominent professor of this theory; and in drawing attention to this *spurious imitation of real art,* we now remind them that, though speaking now in general terms, we may be led on some future occasion to particularize offenders.*

OPERA IN ITALIAN

*The Saturday Musical Review, 22 February 1879;
unsigned*

[U] If any man, having nothing else to do, will take the trouble to scan the charges for admission to the Court, the Prince of Wales's, or any of our first-rate theatres, and compare them with the tariff of either of our opera

---

* Fortunately for the threatened "offenders," this was the last critical buzz of the ghost apprentice in The Hornet.

houses, he will find a difference sufficiently startling to raise the question whether the prices exacted by the managers are justified by their expenses or by the superior gratification derivable from their entertainments. The commercial aspect of opera is necessarily dependent on the esthetic, which involves, not only the propriety of lyric drama as a musical form, a consideration which the public have long since settled for themselves; but the common sense question whether to visit Her Majesty's or Covent Garden Theatre in the season be really a profitable way of spending an evening.

As we believe that for many years past no speculator in opera in England has been pecuniarily successful during any extended period, we feel justified in concluding that the present system is as little satisfactory to the managers as to their patrons. There are several reasons for this on the surface. The large salaries paid to the artists, the necessity for a complete orchestra, the chorus, and the employment of a conductor, and other functionaries who have no place in the economy of ordinary theatres, contribute to swell the expenses of an operatic company beyond those of any other scheme for the entertainment of the public. Yet if we consider the high prices charged, and the great capacity of the houses used; if we allow for the exaggerations which the gossips of the press delight to indulge in, of the salaries of the leading singers, and compare the number of such singers with the host of *débutantes,* and others whose appearance is only explicable on the ground that they pay heavily for the privilege of performing; if we bear in mind that the works produced have either survived their copyright, or been stolen from the composers by advantage of law, and are produced with little rehearsal save what they obtain at the public expense on subscription nights; and if we refer to the perfection of detail achieved elsewhere in return for much lower prices, the conviction will be forced on us that our Italian opera is pecuniarily unremunerative, simply because it is esthetically monstrous. We shall not attempt within our space to exhaust the prolific subject of its defects, but something we are bound to say in justification of our opinion that things are not as they should be on our lyric stage.

The function of dramatic music is to express the emotion which accompanies the action of a play, which play as a primary and indispensable requisite should be completely intelligible to the audience, down even to the minutest details of the dialogue. The degree in which any opera dispenses with this condition marks the degree in which it descends beneath the highest models; and the extent to which the listener can be content with a broad outline of the argument is the extent to which he may be looked on as one with a sensual relish for sweet sounds, instead of an intelligent perception of music. To the fact that out of a hundred persons who attend an opera from other than social reasons, not more than ten propose to themselves anything further than the gratification of this lower harmonic appetite, is due the existence in England of so ludicrous an anomaly as opera in Italian; for, be it observed, out of the many works which our Swedish, German, French, and American artists sing in bad Italian, only a few were originally written in that language; and these few are the least meritorious, and at the present time, happily, the least popular. The first requisite for the true appreciation of opera being thus denied to us, and that for no satisfactory reason, we are naturally indifferent to the acting of scenes which we cannot easily follow. The laws of supply and demand are as potent in the theatre as elsewhere; and, consequently, we have at our opera houses a system of gesticulation so unmeaning, so impotent to excite even derisive mirth, that the ghastliest and most ludicrous traditions of the old melodramatic stage would, if revived, be more tolerable to us. Even the few artists who are capable of better things only escape momentarily from the false atmosphere generated by their own thoughtlessness and the ignorance of the public, when the power of the composer dominates artist and audience, and conquers in spite of every disadvantage. Nor do the public seem to be offended by this false conventionalism. Praise which would sound exaggerated if applied to our greatest actors, is lavished in chamber, clique, and column, on the shallowest French charlatanry and the dreariest Italian buffoonery. Aspirants whose demerits are such as should debar them from participation in a piece performed by amateurs, are permitted to appear in the most responsible parts, and often meet with considerable encouragement. And hereby we have arrived at this: that with musical enthusiasts amongst us sufficiently numerous to crowd concert rooms where the loftiest abstract music prevails, our opera houses are abandoned to followers of fashion who feel no higher interest than a personal favoritism which is never based on artistic appreciation. For this evil the critical press is in part responsible. A comparison of the musical criticism in vogue with that concerning literature or the graphic arts will suffice to mark its degradation, the inevitable result of the timidity of critics who can only judge one performance by reference to another, and are unable to handle their subject with the certainty conferred by knowledge, or the independence which springs from resolute truthfulness.

The truth is that Italianized opera in England is aristocratic in the worst sense. It has become effete because it has never appealed to the people. Its audience has worn evening dress and kept late hours so long that its vitality has escaped; its power of discerning between sensational sham and true power has become confused; and it applauds with palsied hands spiritless desecrations of Mozart, or dodders feebly over the music of the future, so much louder and more stimulating than the music of the past. Whatever we may think of Wagner, we owe him thanks, inasmuch as he has taken fashionable opera by the throat, and shaken the old paralytic shrewdly. He has given us works that must be performed, with words that must be understood. One of these works, welcomed with enthusiasm in English, was treated with indifference when it was reproduced in Italian guise— a good sign, pregnant with the hope that we may yet see a popular performance of—let us say Don Giovanni— good enough to edify the people, to educate the critics, and to justify our national culture. [U]

AMATEUR OPERA
AT LONDONDERRY HOUSE

The Court Journal, 8 July 1882; unsigned. Review of a performance of Gilbert and Sullivan's Trial by Jury and scenes from Gounod's Faust and Verdi's Il Trovatore, for which Shaw had served as rehearsal pianist and stage manager. Written at the request of Vandeleur Lee, who planted it in the Journal.

[U] The fine banqueting hall of Londonderry House, Park Lane, was crowded on Saturday evening by a fashionable audience assembled to witness an amateur operatic performance in aid of the fund for the relief of distressed Irish ladies. The room was brilliantly lighted, and the historical portraits of illustrious members of the Stewart-Vane-Tempest families were seen to advantage. Conspicuous were the portraits of the eminent statesman Viscount Castlereagh, who represented this country at the Congress at Vienna, which followed the Revolutionary and Napoleonic wars; and of Baron Stewart (third

Marquis), the gallant Peninsular general. The room also contains some fine statuary presented to Charles William (third Marquis), by the Emperor Nicholas of Russia in 1837, and busts of Pitt and Castlereagh.

The performance, which was efficiently conducted by Mr Vandeleur Lee, began at nine o'clock, and terminated just before midnight. We append the program.

The amateurs, in selecting such familiar operas as Faust and Il Trovatore, set themselves a difficult task, which, upon the whole, they satisfactorily fulfilled. All present must have heard the familiar strains from the most popular works of Gounod and Verdi repeatedly; and it was hardly judicious, therefore, to invite a comparison with the most consummate vocalists of the present and the past. However, we can speak well of Mrs Herbert Chatteris's performance, which, vocally and dramatically, was of the highest order. Mrs Inez Bell also filled her part in an adequate manner. Miss Gordon Archibald obtained a recall after singing Siebel's air *Le parlate d'amor*. Mr Barnes Newton, as Manrico, gained credit by his delivery of *Ah! che la morte*, and earned a share of the applause which greeted Mrs Inez Bell's rendering of the popular duet *Si la stanchezza*. The remaining characters were assumed by Captain Holled Smith (the Count di Luna) and Messrs Hirchfield and Maitland.

The amateurs were quite at home in comic opera, and a most enjoyable representation of Gilbert and Sullivan's Trial by Jury took place. The piece, it will be remembered, is founded upon an alleged breach of promise of marriage, and Captain Barrington Foote, R.A., was the representative of the gay deceiver.

> "It was wrong of him to do so,
> For the girl had bought her trousseau."

With yellow hair parted in the middle, an eyeglass, light garments, and vacant look, he sang and played admirably. Captain Liddell, R.A., was a most facetious judge. The offer of his breast for the bride to recline upon, and the brilliant inspiration to marry the fascinating plaintiff himself, the jury acquiescing with the words, "For he's a judge, and a good judge too," caused, as usual, much hilarity. Captain Barrington Foote's song, Lovesick boy, and Captain Liddell's ditty, How I became a judge, were humorously rendered, and the concerted music especially was very good, reflecting great credit on the pretty bevy of bridesmaids and the jury. Captain FitzGeorge, R.N., was the plaintiff's counsel, and Viscount Feilding was a droll usher of the court. Mrs Godfrey Pearse looked very pretty in bridal attire, and she played and sang with charming effect.

The difficult task of conducting this enterprising body of amateurs was discharged by Mr Vandeleur Lee, who, with the sympathetic cooperation of an orchestra of remarkable excellence, skilfully led the vocalists through the dangers of Italian opera, and dexterously rescued them from the consequences of their errors, which, it should be added, were surprisingly few.

The performers were subsequently entertained at supper by the Marchioness of Londonderry, to whose interest and hospitality the Amateur Opera Committee are largely indebted for a financial success which will, we are informed, enable Mr Herbert Chatteris, the honorary treasurer, to place at the disposal of the fund for the relief of distressed Irish ladies a substantial sum.

The costumes, fittings, stage scenery, and decorations for the operas were supplied by Messrs L. and H. Nathan, 17, Coventry-street.[U]

MUSIC FOR THE PEOPLE

The Musical Review, 10 and 17 March 1883 ; unsigned

The employment of a generic term, such as "the people,"
to denote one section of the community is not wholly
defensible, but the sanction of custom must be an excuse
for its use in the present instance; and, after all, it is a
more complimentary expression than the "proletariat,"
or the "lower orders," and not more open to question
than the "working classes"—which last is frequently
adopted by toilers with the hand in a somewhat invidious
sense. By the people we mean the vast number of
struggling breadwinners whose life is passed outside the
regions of art, and beyond the reach of its ennobling
influence. That the art of music, with which we are
especially concerned, has no place, and can have no
place, in the existence of an immense majority of the
population unless external action places it at their
command, will not be contended. The prices of
admission to concerts and opera in the metropolis are
practically prohibitive except to persons in easy circumstances, and to a less extent the same rule applies to the
great provincial centres. On the continent imperial and
municipal authority assumes a more parental aspect
than with us, and the principle of subsidies is universally
recognized as the one means whereby the community
generally may be enabled to enjoy first-rate performances in the theatre and the concert room. It would be
idle to lament the absence of such machinery at home.
Great Britain is committed to a policy of *laissez-faire* in
art matters, or, more strictly speaking, in musical
matters, and until a revolution occurs in our national
method of treating the subject it is only to the

philanthropic efforts of individuals that we can look, in the first instance, for an alteration of the musical famine under which so many suffer.

For a long period the matter was treated with profound indifference generally, but quite recently a feeling seems to have arisen in the minds of certain well-meaning persons that something might be done, and the result is the formation of two or three societies having for their direct and sole purpose the giving of cheap musical entertainments to those who can only afford a few pence for an evening's amusement. We say advisedly the result is the formation of these societies, for the practical outcome of the movement can scarcely be said to have commenced, owing either to the feebleness or misdirection of the efforts in the cause. The proceedings of an association styling itself the People's Concert Society have come under our observation once or twice, and it may be allowed that in this instance the executive seem to have some lucid idea of the nature of the work to be accomplished. A series of concerts was first tried about four years ago, at the hall of the Eleusis Club, a radical institution, in the King's Road, Chelsea, the programs of which consisted chiefly of instrumental chamber music, the movements of a trio or a sonata being frequently interspersed with vocal pieces. The latter were always of a superior class and were interpreted generally by efficient amateurs, the instrumental executants being professionals whose names are familiar in the musical world. The charges for admission were a penny and threepence. The society is still in existence, for we have heard of concerts being given of a similar nature at the East End during the present season. Persons of Sabbatarian tendencies may be scandalized to hear that Sunday evening concerts have been tried at which a collection for expenses has taken the place of a charge for admission. Whether the society's operations have met with an encouraging amount of support we have no means of knowing, but it cannot be said that the measures taken to enforce the fact of its existence on the lethargic public mind have been as vigorous as could be wished. Perhaps a lack of capital has necessitated the adoption of a modest policy up to the present time.

In another instance, however, there has been an amount of trumpet-blowing worthy of the inauguration of a great work. If the promoters of the temperance music hall movement are not triumphant in the task they have undertaken, it will certainly not be for want of sufficient advertizing. But it is questionable whether the attempt to work in two directions at once is not inimical to progress in either. Sobriety is a good thing and healthy amusement is another, but the working man's tastes will not be elevated by the association of music with total abstinence; for he will resent the attempt to dictate what he shall drink or avoid, and severely stay away from the coffee music hall. Of course temperance people may come, but persons of moderate opinions, being denied the privileges which they can obtain in the theatres and ordinary music halls, are not likely to avail themselves of entertainments so dearly purchased. Thus the Victoria Hall, which might be made a centre for the diffusion of art among the humbler ranks of society, only appeals to one section, and that a comparatively small one. The executive may reply that the spread of temperance principles is their primary object, music being merely employed as a helping influence in the cause. That may be, but it would be grossly unfair to gauge the tastes of the entire artisan class by the measure of success obtained in this instance. We have yet to learn what would be the result of an enterprise in which musical culture was made the first consideration, the liberty of the subject being fully maintained in matters of bodily refreshment.

A few remarks on the nature of the work actually carried on in the Victoria Hall may be desirable. The ballad concerts, given once or twice weekly, were at first sustained by professional aid, often given gratuitously— a system, it is needless to say, which could not be maintained for any length of time. Grave objections were made by ordinary concert givers, but they were scarcely necessary, as the supply of competent performers was certain to fail after a while, and we believe the professionals are now receiving remuneration in the regular way. It would be unwise to judge hastily, but from the experience of two or three visits to the hall, we should imagine that the management underestimates, rather than overestimates, the critical capacity of its audiences. For example, at a so-called Scandinavian concert, given on the 13th ult., a number of weak songs, weakly interpreted, were received with polite indifference, *encores* being reserved for Beethoven's violin Romance in G, Op. 40, some Hungarian airs nicely rendered by Mlle Brousil, and a couple of Swedish melodies capitally sung by Mlle Enequist. A newly-formed choir gave a selection of part-songs very creditably, and these were also warmly received, while the dance tunes, played by an indifferent band, went almost without a hand. At a rough guess, there may have been 1500 people in the hall, and if the whole of them had been skilled musicians the verdict on each item could not have been more discriminating. The demeanor of all present was equally remarkable, perfect silence being preserved while the music was being performed; and the observer could not, therefore, fail to gain a favorable impression of the musical receptivity of the dwellers in and around the New Cut.

Perhaps the most successful and most generally

satisfactory of all the associations in the metropolis whose operations come within scope of the present inquiry is the Bow and Bromley Institute. Music is not the sole end and aim of this institution, but the art has a large place in its working, and its interests are furthered in a straightforward and practical manner. Here, every Saturday evening during the winter months, organ recitals are given, at which the most accomplished English and foreign performers appear, the charges for admission being sixpence and threepence. A means is hereby provided for enabling the humblest classes to become acquainted with at least one variety of the best music, performed in the best manner, at a nominal cost; and it is cheering to know that the movement has been attended by unequivocal success. Although the hall will accommodate 1200 persons, the number of those who desire admission is generally in excess of these figures. Further, the programs are neither exclusively nor mainly composed of overtures and operatic selections; on the contrary, the works of Bach and Mendelssohn are largely drawn upon, and we have the best authority for saying that they are as highly appreciated as the lighter excerpts of the French school. The printed programs contain brief and pithy descriptions of the various pieces, enabling the audiences to follow the music with some intelligent interest. The Bow and Bromley Institute has also an excellent Choral Society, under the direction of Mr W. G. McNaught, and frequent performances are given of the most elaborate oratorios and cantatas. The work here, it should be noted, is carried out on strictly businesslike principles, without any pretence at philanthropy or any intrusion of the goody-goody element. Herein, we believe, lies the secret of its success. There may be other institutions than those already named in which the diffusion of musical taste among the masses is made a feature, but, if so, their doings have not attained sufficient prominence to warrant attention in this place.

It has frequently been observed that true musical feeling is to be found in greater abundance in some of our large provincial centres than in the metropolis. This is unquestionably true in the sense that towns like Birmingham, Manchester, or Leeds are not of such unwieldy magnitude as to hinder general sympathy for and interest in any movement emanating from a central point in their corporate existence. We shall see later on how the vast size of London is directly inimical to the establishment of such an institution as the Birmingham Musical Association, on which some remarks may be fittingly offered in connexion with our present subject. Three or four years ago it seems to have occurred to some influential residents in the hardware capital and its vicinity that the musical prestige which the town has long possessed might be extended by a more direct cooperation of the artisan class in the art and its cultivation. The result of this feeling was the formation of the above-named association, with Mr Jesse Collings, M.P., as its president. Birmingham possesses a magnificent Town Hall and various musical societies. The Mayor grants the use of the former, free of rent, and the assistance of the latter is secured for the concerts of the Association, which are given on Saturday evenings from October to April. The third annual report lies before us, and it is at once an interesting and [an] encouraging document. It appears that during the season 1881–82 twentyseven concerts were given, at which the average attendance was 2629 persons. As the receipts average £45:11:7, it follows that the charge for admission equaled fourpence a head.

What kind of music was it, then, which drew these crowded assemblages of working people? The report furnishes an extremely satisfactory answer. Among the choral works which were performed in their entirety were Bennett's May Queen, Gounod's Gallia, Bridge's Boadicea, Gade's Crusaders, and Macfarren's May Day, together with selections from various oratorios and cantatas. Many of these were given with full orchestral accompaniment, and the following instrumental works were presented entire: Beethoven's Symphony in C, Mozart's Pianoforte Concerto No. 4, the Rosamunde ballet music, and a number of overtures. Upwards of 2700 choralists and fifty instrumentalists took part in the concerts, the majority twice and many three times. As most of the societies to which these performers belong were remunerated by donations to their funds, it may fairly be said that the Birmingham Musical Association is a self-supporting concern, or, at any rate, no more dependent upon voluntary help than are the majority of our leading musical societies throughout the country. Thus firmly established, this enterprising body has of late busied itself with the formation of a special amateur band and chorus, to belong exclusively to the association. The invitations issued met with so warm a response that the limits of 250 originally assigned to the chorus and of seventy to the band were at once reached and even exceeded.

In face of such facts as these, it would be idle to deny the existence of an immense latent capacity for musical culture in the ranks of the people, and it only remains to inquire why the example of Birmingham is not generally followed, and especially in London. The primary difficulty in this overgrown Babylon is the absence of any central machinery which could be utilized for the purpose. Hammersmith and Stepney, Kentish Town and Rotherhithe lie practically as far away from oneanother as Liverpool and Manchester. It needs but little observation to prove that the outlying theatres and music halls depend exclusively upon local audiences for patronage. High class concerts given in any one of the four districts named would, therefore, have no concern for the dwellers in the other three. What we require is not one society, such as that of Birmingham, but a dozen; and unfortunately the resources of each district are not equal to the task of initiating any movement of the kind.

Help from without being practically out of the question, matters remain as they have always been, save for a few spasmodic attempts to cope with the difficulty. But another adverse influence is that anti-musical feeling which refuses to recognize the value of the art, save as a means to gain some other end. Our principal musical festivals have only been sustained by connecting them with philanthropic work, and in two directions at the present time in the metropolis music is relegated to the position of a handmaid in the cause of religion and sobriety. We have already seen how the promoters of the temperance movement utilize their opportunities at the Victoria Hall; but a far more lamentable misuse of means remains to be noticed. The purchase of Exeter Hall by the Young Men's Christian Association has afforded scope for the exercise of religious prejudices, which might, but for this circumstance, have been deemed incredible at the present day. Here is one of the finest halls in London, centrally situated, in possession of an excellent organ, and for well-nigh fifty years associated with musical celebrations on the grandest scale, doomed to re-echo nothing better than the celebrations of the Salvation Army. It would be as idle to attempt a serious argument with those who deem Handel, Bach, and Mendelssohn sinful as to enter upon a contest of logic with the inmates of Hanwell Asylum; but it is little less than exasperating to observe golden chances thrown away by those who are presumed to have a direct interest in the promotion of refining and civilizing influences among the masses. It is pleasant to note that in one or two instances—notably at Bristol and Leeds—a feeling is beginning to manifest itself in favor of the severance of the galling chains which have so long bound music and charity together, and it is therefore not too much to hope that some idea of the dignity and value of art will eventually find its way among those who undertake important schemes of a philanthropical nature in London. But at present the silver lining to the cloud is barely discernible.

One of Shaw's favorite leisure pastimes in the 1880's was the creation of musical settings for poems and lyrics, designed for his own entertainment and that of his friends, never with commercial publication in mind. Of the three Shaw compositions which are known to have survived, one is a setting of Shelley's verses commencing When the lamp is shattered, dated 23 June 1883. It is reproduced here from the original in the Manuscript Department and Southern Historical Collection of the University of North Carolina Library at Chapel Hill, the gift of Archibald Henderson. The remaining two compositions, settings of Caroline Radford's lyrics How she Comes (March 1884) and Ah, Love, I Lack thy Kisses (September 1884), will be found in the Henry W. and Albert A. Berg Collection, New York Public Library.

I

When the lamp is shattered
The light in the dust lies dead ;
   When the cloud is scattered,
The rainbow's glory is shed ;
   When the lute is broken,
Sweet notes are remembered not ;
   When the lips have spoken,
Loved accents are soon forgot.

II

   As music and splendour
Survive not the lamp and the lute,
   The heart's echoes render
No song when the spirit is mute :—
   No song but sad dirges,
Like the wind in a ruined cell,
   Or the mournful surges
That ring the dead seaman's knell.

III

When hearts have once mingled,
Love first leaves the well-built nest;
The weak one is singled
To endure what it once possessed.
O Love, who bewailest
The frailty of all things here,
Why chose you the frailest
For your cradle, your home, and your bier?

IV

Its passions will rock thee,
As the storms rock the ravens on high:
Bright reason will mock thee,
Like the sun from a wintry sky.
From thy nest every rafter
Will rot, and thine eagle home
Leave thee naked to laughter,
When leaves fall and cold winds come.

HERR RICHTER AND HIS BLUE RIBBON

The Dramatic Review, 8 February 1885

Herr Richter's popularity as an orchestral conductor began, not in the auditorium, but in the orchestra. It dates from his first visit here in 1877 to conduct the Wagner festivals at the Albert Hall. At these concerts there was a large and somewhat clumsy band of about 170 players, not well accustomed to the music, and not at all accustomed to the composer, who had contracted to heighten the sensation by conducting a portion of each concert. It is not easy to make an English orchestra nervous, but Wagner's tense neuralgic glare at the players as they waited for the beat with their bows poised above the strings was hard upon the sympathetic men, whilst the intolerable length of the pause exasperated the tougher spirits. When all were effectually disconcerted, the composer's *bâton* was suddenly jerked upwards, as if by a sharp twinge of gout in his elbow; and, after a moment of confusion, a scrambling start was made. During the performance Wagner's glare never relaxed: he never looked pleased. When he wanted more emphasis he stamped; when the division into bars was merely conventional he disdained counting, and looked daggers—spoke them too, sometimes—at innocent instrumentalists who were enjoying the last few bars of their rest without any suspicion that the impatient composer had just discounted half a stave or so and was angrily waiting for them. When he laid down the *bâton* it was with the air of a man who hoped he might never be condemned to listen to such a performance again. Then Herr Richter stepped into the conductor's desk; and the orchestra, tapping their desks noisily with their bows, revenged themselves by an ebullition of delight and deep relief, which scandalized Wagner's personal admirers, but which set the fashion of applauding the new conductor, whose broad, calm style was doubly reassuring after that of Wagner. He, meanwhile, sat humbly among the harps until he could no longer bear to listen quietly to his own music, when he would rise, get into the way of the players, seek flight by no thoroughfares and return discomfited, to escape at last into the stalls and prowl from chair to chair like a man lost and friendless. As it is difficult to remain in the room with the greatest living composer without watching his movements, even at the risk of missing some of his music—which, after all, you will have other chances of hearing—you perhaps paid less attention to Herr Richter than he deserved.

After the Wagner festival nothing remarkable in the way of conducting occurred in London until the following year (1878), when, at a series of concerts given by Madame Viard-Louis, Mr Weist Hill achieved some extraordinary successes, which the London public would probably have recognized in the course of, say, ten years or so, had Madame Viard-Louis been able to prosecute her undertaking at a loss for so long. But this was impossible; and next year Herr Richter came again to conduct "Festival Concerts," so called because the managers knew that his reputation as conductor of the Bayreuth Festival was likely to attract the public far more than his artistic ability. In 1880, however, his position was secure; and since then we have had "Richter Concerts" annually. These concerts had many pleasant peculiarities, which their good example soon rendered less peculiar. The conductor seemed to be familiar with the music, and did not conduct at sight from a score from which he hardly ventured to raise his eyes lest he should lose his place. He did not pose and gesticulate like a savage at a war dance, nor did he, like an overbred man of St James's, scorn to appear more impressionable than a regimental bandmaster. He seemed to think about his business rather than about himself, and, in rare snatches, when the band had fallen into perfect swing, about the music rather than about his business. In these ecstatic moments his extended arms would pulsate almost imperceptibly; and poetic admirers would compare him to a benignant bird balancing itself in a cloud of blond sunshine (the blond sunshine being diffused from his fair Saxon locks). A point missed would bring him quickly to earth, alert, yet still gracious; but a point overdone—nothing short of monumental stolidity could endure his eye then. For the rest, he could indicate the subdivisions of a bar when it was helpful to do so; and he declined to follow the fashion, set by acrobats of the pianoforte, of playing all *allegros* against time, on the principle that fastest is cleverest.

The public felt the gain in dignity, and respected Herr Richter for it, probably without knowing why. Then he let slip the secret that the scores of Wagner were not to be taken too literally. "How" exclaimed the average violinist in anger and despair "is a man to be expected to play this reiterated motive, or this complicated figuration, in demisemiquavers at the rate of sixteen in a second? What can he do but go a-swishing up and down as best he can?" "What, indeed?" replied Herr Richter encouragingly. "That is precisely what is intended by the composer." So the relieved violinists went swishing up and down, and the public heard the hissing of Loki's fires in it and were delighted; whilst those who had scores and were able to read them said "Oh! thats how it's done, is it?" and perhaps winked. And Herr Richter flourished, as he deserved; so that even when his band is positively bad, as it was once or twice at the German Opera last year, or weary and demoralized, as it cannot but become towards the end of a long concert in the stuffiness of St James's Hall, his credit shields them from the censure of the few who know, and from the suspicion of the many who dont. He has now been engaged to conduct the Birmingham Festival, and Sir Arthur Sullivan, who appreciates him better than the general public, whose admiration of a musical celebrity is always half superstitious, thinks that a post of such honor should have been given to a native conductor. He has suggested Mr Cowen, Mr Villiers Stanford, and Mr Barnby as competent substitutes. But Mr Villiers Stanford is an Irishman; Mr Cowen is a Jew; and Mr Barnby, though an industrious and enterprising musician, accustomed to deal with large choirs, has been more successful with new works like Verdi's requiem or Parsifal than with our stock oratorios, which somehow have a stale sound under his direction which Herr Richter has not yet succeeded in imparting to any performance entrusted to his care. Besides, Mr Barnby's reputation is local. If he were selected, dozens of other local celebrities, who doubtless consider themselves equally efficient, would raise the cry of favoritism, if not of downright jobbery. To select the only popular conductor who enjoys a European reputation was the least invidious course open to the Festival Committee; and it is difficult to imagine any alternative which would not have caused more general dissatisfaction both to the profession and to the public.

It is certainly true that Herr Richter, years before he had even chosen the profession in which he is so eminent, succumbed to those "temptations to belong to other nations" which the hero of Pinafore withstood. He is not an Englishman, and he does not even intend to become one: a course quite open to him, as Sir Arthur pointed out when reminded of the supremacy of the late

Sir Michael Costa. Costa was an Englishman by domicile; and Sir Arthur himself, who was born a little westward of these shores, and who is of a darker and southerlier strain than the Saxon Richter, can claim no more. Since, however, we use a musical scale which is not specially English, but European and American also, we must go east of the Ural mountains or south of the Mediterranean to find a real "musical foreigner." Still, there is something in the remark of Sir Arthur Sullivan that "a German who cannot speak English appears oddly selected to conduct English choruses." It is less to the point that Herr Richter is not, as Costa was, conductor of the Sacred Harmonic Society and of the Italian opera, that being clearly so much the worse for the Italian opera, whilst the Sacred Harmonic, by appointing Mr Charles Hallé as successor to Costa, set the Birmingham committee the example of appointing a foreigner. And if the conductorship of a series of concerts of established reputation justified the position allowed to Costa, the Viennese conductor is qualified in that respect by the Richter concerts, which are not second in popularity or musical importance to any in London. Indeed, the increased alertness of our older institutions dates from the year in which Herr Richter gave them something tolerable to compete with. I have a particularly deadly-lively recollection of the seasons which immediately preceded his invasion; and I do not think he came a day too soon, nor have I ever met a musician who did. The objection that he is not a master of the English tongue, though invalid against a conductor of orchestral concerts or of German opera, deserves to be weighed when an English oratorio is to be performed. Orchestras only need to be sworn at; and a German is consequently at an advantage with them, as English profanity, except in America, has not gone beyond a limited technology of perdition, extremely monotonous in the recurrent

irritation set up by an unsatisfactory rehearsal. But
choristers must have their pronunciation corrected by
somebody if we are ever to escape from that hearty
British "Thah wooaht Ee-li-jar," with which our choirs
are accustomed to denounce Mr Santley for troubling
Israel's peace. Herr Richter clearly cannot do this with
authority. If anyone else will undertake to polish the
elocution of the Birmingham choir in the course of a few
rehearsals, he has a fair claim—other things being
equal—as against the foreigner. Pending the production
of his testimonials, we seem to bear with the foreigner
very cheerfully.

THE INFERNO AT ST JAMES'S HALL

The Dramatic Review, 15 February 1885

Mr Walter Bache has now given us a dozen opportunities
of hearing the serious products of Franz Liszt. His
twelfth orchestral concert of the works of that eminent
pianist, biographer, essayist, patron of genius, Hungarian rhapsodist, and musical enthusiast took place on the
3rd instant. The chief composition in the program was
"a symphony to Dante's Inferno, Purgatorio, and
Paradiso," particularly the Inferno. When, in order that
allowance may be made for my personal bias, I declare
at once that I do not like this symphony, I consider that
I am expressing myself very moderately indeed; and
were I to act strictly upon critical precedents, I should
proceed to prove to my own satisfaction that the form
of the symphony is wrong, the progressions forbidden,
the decay of modern music largely attributable to its
influence, and the total result lamentably different to
what might have been expected had it occurred to
Mozart to set the Divine Comedy to music. But as all

these remarks would be equally appropriate to much modern music of which I am very fond, I will forgo them, and content myself with thanking Mr Bache for the opportunity of making up my mind that the Dante symphony, though doubtless a treat to the composer's disciples, is not suited to my constitution. I shall justify as best I can my opinion that the work is shallowly conceived and detestably expressed; and the reader, if curious on the subject, can study the very different view advanced by Richard Pohl in his book about Franz Liszt, and judge between us. The shortest way would undoubtedly be to go and hear the symphony played; but this, with my experience of Mr Bache's concert fresh in my recollection, I distinctly decline to advise any sober person to attempt.

It is hard to say what the characteristics of Dante's Hell are. Turmoil, hurry, incessant movement, fire, roaring wind, and utter discomfort are there; but so they are also in a London house when the kitchen chimney is on fire. Convey these by music, and the music will be just as appropriate to the one situation as to the other. To convey nothing else is to miss the characteristic which differentiates the Inferno from any other noisy and unpleasant place; and this is what, as I think, Liszt has done: therefore I call his conception a shallow one. I am seriously of opinion that if the symphony were dubbed anew The Conflagration, and a careful analytical program compiled, assigning the various episodes of the *allegro* to The Alarm, The Fire Gaining Ground, Awakening of the Inmates and their Flight, Gathering of the Crowd, Arrival of the Engines, Exertions of Firemen and Struggle of Police with the Mob, with the Falling in of the Roof as a climax, not one of the audience would perceive the slightest incongruity between the music and the subject. The plan could be carried out to the end of the symphony.

The Francesca episode might be labeled Complaint of the Lady of the House to Captain Shaw.* To that gallant officer might be attributed the soothing recitative-like passage for the bass clarinet, at present supposed to represent the poet's sympathetic address to the unfortunate lovers. The *andante* would be appropriate to the mingled feelings of relief and regret following the extinction of the flames; the incidental fugue might portray the firemen searching the blackened ruins by lantern light; whilst the vocal conclusion would be in its place as the Thanksgiving of the Householder. The music is far more adequate to this program than to that of the composer, whose logic is like that of Shakespear's Welshman. "I warrant you shall find" says Fluellen "in the comparisons between Macedon and Monmouth, that the situations, look you, is both alike. There is a river in Macedon; and there is also moreover a river in Monmouth; and there is salmons in both."† There is haste, confusion, and discord in Dante's Hell; and there is haste, confusion, and discord in Liszt's symphony. So far, "the situations, look you, is both alike." But not a whit more alike than dozens of situations even more remote from the Divine Comedy than the one I have suggested. Dante's poem is unique because of those features of it that are not to be found elsewhere. Liszt's symphony is commonplace because disturbance and noise are commonplace. But to do justice to it on its own level, I admit that the degree of noise is not altogether commonplace. The symphony is exceptionally loud.

The proceedings begin at the gate of Hell with a phrase founded on that useful old favorite formerly known as the chord of the diminished seventh. This is

* Eyre Massey Shaw was for thirty years (1861–91) Chief of London's Metropolitan Fire Brigade.
† Shakespear's King Henry V., Act IV., Scene 7.

delivered *fortissimo* by the three trombones and the tuba in unison, and repeated twice with modifications of increasing harshness. The effect is purely a question of the power of the trombones. Such as it is, it is just half what six trombones and two tubas would produce. As additional instruments could easily be procured from the band of the Grenadier Guards, who are accustomed to enhance similar effects at Promenade Concerts, Mr Bache, if he really likes this description of music, might find the reinforcement worth its cost. As it is, the result of the opening is to deafen and irritate the listener, and to leave him more than ever convinced that the art of using the trombone to express the terrors of the supernatural was born and died with Mozart, who would certainly have regarded a *fortissimo* passage for three trombones in unison in a serious work as an outrage on public decency. It is impossible, from lack of space, to follow the symphony point by point. The trombones go from bad to worse. Their parts, at first marked *ff*, soon appear with the three f's, in his enthusiasm for which Liszt outdoes the Farmers' Alliance. Volleys of strident barks from the brass alternate with shuddering triplets from the strings, and mingle with clarinets buzzing in their lowest register on the hackneyed Der Freischütz model; drum rolls that soon cease to convey anything to the worried ear except a monotonous thumping and stamping, like applause at a public meeting in a hotel breaking out on the floor above your bedroom in the middle of your first sleep; and all the howling and hurrying commonplaces of orchestral *diablerie* piled upon oneanother to exasperation point. When it was over on Friday evening, a majority of the audience, in spite of their disposition (which I shared) to make much of Mr Bache in return for his enterprise and devotion, shewed by their silence that the composer had gone too far in offering them this obscene instrumental orgy as a serious comment on a great poem.

The remainder of the work was so far Dantesque that it produced an impression which ordinary readers of the Divine Comedy often confess having experienced. They find the Purgatorio duller than the Inferno, and the Paradiso duller than either. For my own part I was in no humor to be consoled by elaborate prettiness from harp and English horn, viola and flute, and so forth, for what I had just suffered. The choir of ladies, among whom were Mr Malcolm Lawson's votaresses of St Cecilia, furnished a pretty background to the orchestra; but they did not seem well accustomed to sing together; and the final Magnificat, monotonously exalting itself by modulations from one key to another a tone above, and accompanied by muted violins hissing like a badly-adjusted limelight, was not so soothing as it was intended to be. At last a senseless episode, like the duel in Don Giovanni gone mad, turned out to be the *coda*; and, with a final Hallelujah, the welcome end came.

Putting Dante and the pretensions of the composer to illustrate him out of the question, and regarding the work merely as an example of the resources of the orchestra, the symphony seems to me useless even from a student's point of view. Qualities of tone which have never been made effective except when used very sparingly are resorted to almost continuously. Combinations which have been used with delightful results elsewhere occur only to fall flat upon ears tortured beyond the desire of any orchestral combination except a few bars rest. Though in many places ethereal sweetness and smoothness have been so elaborately planned that a glance at the score raises pleasant expectations, the effect proves to be only a paper one; or perhaps the players are too far demoralized by the violence and strain of the context to do justice to the pretty platitudes which the composer has sought to worry, by mere stress of orchestration, into melody and beauty. If there be any of those charmingly piquant effects which decorate the Hungarian rhapsodies, they are so discounted as to be unnoticeable. Comparisons with Berlioz are suggested by the fact that his aims and method are imitated by Liszt, as they have been by Raff. But Liszt's range is very narrow as compared with that of Berlioz. He produces certain vigorous and strident effects which are acceptable until he gives you too much of them, which he invariably does: a notable example being his setting of the Rákóczy March, which was also in the program the other evening. But though he aims strenuously at Berlioz's formidable maximum of tone, he has not the secret of it, and degenerates into intolerable noise in the attempt to reach it. He never surprises you, as Berlioz does, by producing several different effects from combinations of the same instruments. He outdoes Berlioz in bidding for the diabolical by noise and fury; but he quite misses the strange nightmare sensation, the smell of brimstone, as Schumann called it, which characterized Berlioz's exploits in the infernal field. Pre-eminence in the infernal is, perhaps, hardly worth disputing; but one must compare Liszt with a composer against whom he is perceptibly measurable. To compare his works with those of Bach, Handel, and Mozart, or even with the occasional savage aberrations of Wagner and Beethoven, would dwarf him too absurdly.

A few other works were performed at the concert. There was the March of the Three Holy Kings, with its pretty *trio* in D flat, which I had sufficiently recovered from the Inferno to enjoy. A "dramatic scene" entitled Joan of Arc at the Stake, with happily very little stake and a great deal of Joan, was sung by Mademoiselle Alice Barbi, who will probably sing it, not with more pleasure to others, but with perhaps a little more comfort to herself, when she attains some additional skill in managing her breath. I offer the suggestion with due reserve, conscious that the lady is likely to know more of her art than I do. Mr Bache played the pianoforte concerto in E flat, and received a laurel crown of the dimensions of a life-buoy in acknowledgment. I am sorry for the sake of my credit with him that I came away unconverted.

THE BACH BICENTENARY
The Dramatic Review, 28 March 1885

The Bach choir is a body of ladies and gentlemen associated under the direction of Mr Otto Goldschmidt "for the practice and performance of choral works of excellence of various schools." It made itself famous on the 26th April 1876, by achieving the first complete performance in England of John Sebastian Bach's setting of the High Mass in B minor. The work disappointed some people, precisely as the Atlantic Ocean disappointed Mr Wilde. Others, fond of a good tune, missed in it those compact little airs that can be learnt by ear and accompanied by tonic, sub-dominant, tonic, dominant, and tonic harmonies in the order stated; or, pedantry apart, by the three useful chords with which professors of the banjo teach their pupils, in one lesson, to accompany songs (usually in the key of G), without any previous knowledge of thoroughbass. As there was nothing for those unfortunate persons who did not like the Mass but to listen to it again and again until their state became more gracious, the Bach choir repeated it in 1877, in 1879, and again on Saturday last. As that day is supposed to be the 200th anniversary of Bach's birthday, a special effort was made; the performance was given in the Albert Hall; the society was reinforced by picked choristers from Henry Leslie's and other noted choirs, to the total number of over five hundred singers; and orchestral instruments that have fallen into disuse since Bach's time were specially manufactured and studied by eminent players for the occasion.

Those faults in the performance for which the conductor and the choir can fairly be held responsible were not due to any want of care or earnestness in preparation. One chorus, Credo in Unum Deum, fell into confusion, the singers being apparently bewildered by the burst of applause with which the audience had just received the Cum Sancto Spiritu. This, however, was an accident: the number was sung accurately at the last rehearsal; and had the conductor been in a position to stop and start afresh, or to repeat the chorus, the mistake would have been remedied. Here, for once, was an opportunity for the British public to set matters right by an *encore*. It is needless to add that the British public did not rise to the very simple occasion. Among the inevitable shortcomings may be classed the loss of effect in some of the brighter numbers—notably the Pleni sunt cœli—by the jog trot which seems to be Mr Goldschmidt's *prestissimo*. It is ungracious to complain of a conductor who has achieved a result so admirable and difficult as a good performance of the great Mass; and it is quite possible that Mr Goldschmidt may have experimentally determined that a single extra beat per second would endanger the precision upon which so much depends in Bach's polyphony; but there were moments on Saturday when the audience must have longed that Mr Goldschmidt would go ahead a little—when some may have profanely felt that one glass of champagne administered to the conductor would have made an acceptable difference in the effect. Mr Gold-schmidt has, however, well earned his right to have his own opinion on the question; and he shewed when, in the Gloria and the Cum Sancto Spiritu, he got from B minor into D major, that he is capable, on occasion, of a flash of that spirit which earned for Bach himself the compliment that "in conducting he was very accurate; and in time, *which he generally took at a very lively pace,* he was always sure."

The renovation of the obsolete *oboe d'amore* (love-hautboy), and the execution of the trumpet parts upon the instrument for which they were written, instead of, as usual, upon the clarinet, proved very successful, and furnished a fresh illustration of the fact that our modern "orchestration" falls as far short of Bach's orchestral music as the medley of dance tunes and stage thunder which constitutes a Parisian grand opera falls short of one of his cantatas. The *oboe d' amore* is pitched a third lower than the ordinary oboe. It fell into disuse in the last century. After some time its loss was felt; but unfortunately its place was then filled, in the scores of Rossini, Meyerbeer, and Wagner, by the English horn: an instrument which produces something of the plaintive effect of the *oboe d' amore,* but the tone of which can be described only as a mongrel compound of the snarling of a bad clarinet and the whining of a bad oboe. The *oboe d' amore* has the true oboe tone, and is far superior in dignity and sweetness to the English horn. Whether it is equally manageable is best known to Messrs Horton and Lebon, who have been at the pains to master it; but if it be, I should not be sorry to see it finally banish the English horn from the orchestra. A performance of the overtures to William Tell and The Flying Dutchman with the English horn parts taken by this new-old love-hautboy would furnish an interesting test of the comparative merits of the instruments. Perhaps the forthcoming South Kensington Exhibition* will be so good as to arrange such a performance.

The rehabilitation of the old-fashioned trumpet was still more interesting. Owing to the weakness of conductors, the indolence or incompetence of players, and the ignorance of the public, trumpet parts are habitually played upon the cornopean (I prefer to give the thing its hideous English name): an instrument that, accompanied by the harp, can, in skilful hands, draw tears from a crowd at the door of a gin-palace by The Pilgrim of Love, or Then youll remember me, but the substitution of which for the trumpet in the concert room is an imposture and an outrage. It is easier to play, however; and whenever trumpet players find a conductor whom they dare trifle with, they play the cornopean. On precisely the same ground, and with less injury to the general effect, clarinetists might play their parts on the English concertina, which is far more like a clarinet in tone than a cornopean is like a trumpet. The result of tolerating the easier instrument has been that no composer now ventures to write for the easy cornet passages that Handel never hesitated to write for the difficult trumpet. Herr Julius Kosleck, of Berlin, shewed us on Saturday that the old trumpet parts are as feasible as ever. He brings out the high D with ease, executes shakes, rivals our finest flautists in the purity of the tone he produces in the upper register, and seems able to do,

* The International Inventions Exhibition opened at South Kensington in May 1885. Division II, according to the official program, consisted "of Musical Instruments of a date not earlier than the commencement of the present century; and of Historic Collections of Musical Instruments and Appliances ..." Shaw purchased a season ticket on 25th May and reviewed most of the variegated musical programs at "the Inventions" from May to October in The Dramatic Review, Our Corner, and The Magazine of Music.

with his prodigiously long, straight instrument, all the feats that the first-cornet heros of our military bands accomplish in their "*staccato* polkas," and the like double-tongueing atrocities. It is to be hoped that our native players will not suffer themselves to be beaten by the Berliner. The modesty which leads them to declare the trumpet too difficult for them has often been overcome by the simple argument of "No song, no supper," paraphrased for the occasion as "No trumpet, no engagement." Conductors can now reinforce their authority by threatening to send for Herr Kosleck.

The principal vocal parts were entrusted to Miss Anna Williams, Madame Patey, Mr Edward Lloyd, and Mr Kempton, who replaced Signor Foli, absent through illness. The audience, somewhat stunned by the stupendous choruses, hardly appreciated the delicacy and subdued fervor of the airs and duets, as to the execution of which it must suffice to say that the airs might have been worse, the duets might have been better, and both might have been more frequently rehearsed. This is a safe and widely-applicable critical formula, not disagreeably precise, and yet not inexpressive as critical formulæ go.

It is the custom of the Bach choir to give two concerts every year, concentrating themselves on the great composer at one and avoiding him at the other. Thus the festival now in question was preceded by a concert at St James's Hall on the 19th of last month, when Mr C. H. H. Parry's setting of certain scenes from Shelley's Prometheus, composed for the Three Choirs Festival of 1880, was performed for the first time in London, as was also Friedrich Kiel's Star of Bethlehem. The latter work was quite new: Kiel, famous in Berlin as a learned teacher and contrapuntist, being little known in this country. The Star of Bethlehem is a short oratorio of excellent workmanship; and the composer, if his talent

[223]

is not sufficiently many-sided to rank as genius, is yet so thoroughly qualified in other respects that our choral societies might well spend on his works some of the energy which they occasionally waste on composers that are not qualified at all. The English version has been adapted from the English Bible by Mr J. Maude Crament, himself a contrapuntist of some note, as an energetic helper of the Bach choir ought to be. It is, like his version of the Christus of the same composer, successful both from a musical and literary point of view.

One word on the economic side of these concerts. My program cost me more than it was worth, even as programs go. My seat also cost me more than it was worth, as seats at concerts go; but I was advised of that beforehand, and was at liberty to stay away if I did not like the price. But a program, once you are entrapped in St James's Hall, is an absolute necessity, because the last thing you can gather from an English vocalist is the lyric verse he is supposed to be singing; and you must, therefore, either refer to a book for the subject of the music, or trust to the singer's facial expression, which usually varies with the difficulty of the note rather than with the intensity of the dramatic situation. As the Bach choir is very rich, and allots the best seats privately to its members or their friends before the public are accommodated, it can surely afford to make its charges at least as low as those of heavily-handicapped individual concert givers.

ENGLISH OPERA AT DRURY LANE

*The Dramatic Review, 11 April 1885; signed "Ignotus."
Although this was the pseudonym of editor Edward Paget
Palmer, Shaw identified himself as the author in his diary
entry for 8 April 1885*

On Monday last, the Carl Rosa company opened their
campaign at Drury Lane. They are as happy, healthy,
and respectable as ever. They knock their voices about
with their old confident robustness; their elocution
fluctuates as of yore between artless colloquialism and
toastmasterly magniloquence; and their acting is still
the acting of Richardson's show. They are not yet tired
of tacking tawdry strips of obsolete *cadenza* to the end
of their songs, nor have they ceased to remind the
judicious spectator, by their inveterate aping of the
follies of the Italian lyric stage, of Artemus Ward's
unlucky assumption of "an operatic voice" when serenading his sleeping wife.* Nevertheless they are welcome. With a corrupt foreign school to lead them astray,
no native school to reclaim them, and an ignorantly
good-natured public to encourage them, they make the
most of their opportunities, and treat their patrons far
better on the whole than their Italian rivals treat theirs.

The opera performed on the opening night was
Maritana. Poor Maritana! Its infinite blarney may keep
its hotch-potch of bluster and sentiment alive longer
than many more thoughtful works. There is not an
original idea in it—not even an original turn given to a

* Artemus Ward Among the Fenians, in Charles Farrar
Browne, Complete Works (1871). Browne, an American
humorist who wrote under the pseudonym of Artemus Ward,
was very popular in England. He died there in 1867.

borrowed idea. The authorship of the inimitable Bunn is conspicuous in the singableness, the sentiment, and the outrageous absurdity of the lyrics. He never wrote words quite so pleasant to sing, so melting to hear, so irresistibly funny to read as those of When other lips and other hearts, but Let me like a soldier fall is by no means unworthy of him. A literary man who is not musical may always be detected by his inability to perceive the least merit in Bunn. Musicians know better, and envy Balfe and Wallace their librettist.

Don Cæsar de Bazan (variously called Sezzar and Scissor by the Carl Rosa artists) was impersonated by Mr Maas, who, not quite at ease with his breast "expanding to the ball," declined an enthusiastic *encore* for the song in which that heroic phenomenon is prefigured, but repeated There is a flower that bloometh, very willingly. Mr Maas's style is no longer heavily ecclesiastical, as it was some years ago, when he played Rienzi at Her Majesty's, and when Miss Georgina Burns made her first striking success in London as the Messenger of Peace. His voice is soft, rich, and unforced; and the delight of the public in it seems to be boundless. On the other hand, his gifts are not various. In passages where promptitude, force, and incisive declamation are required, Mr Maas is a trifle sleepy. Don Cæsar's warning to the captain of the guard, Know sir, who I am: Count of Garofa, &c. &c., is not very terrible as Mr Maas delivers it. In point of voice, the tenor was the best of the combatants; but there were traces of staleness and sluggishness about the fighting condition of the noble scamp that were all in favor of the captain of the guard.

Madame Georgina Burns as Maritana and Mr Ludwig as Don Jose obtained the usual *encores* for Scenes that are Brightest, and In Happy Moments. They were less successful in the duets of the first act, the soprano being hard and hurried, and the baritone hollow and toneless. In the concerted music they were far surpassed by Mr Maas and Miss Marian Burton, who listened to the voices with which they had to blend their own. Madame Georgina Burns and Mr Ludwig sang throughout as if they were stone-deaf to every part except those of Maritana and Don Jose.

Miss Marian Burton, though her voice is not yet quite solid, and although she appended a dreadful "ornament" to Hark, those Chimes, made a very favorable impression as Lazarillo by her appearance, her intelligent acting, and her sympathetic singing. Her phrasing is sometimes that of a not over-conscientious ballad singer, and, if not remedied, will prove a serious disqualification for parts of a higher order than Lazarillo; but Miss Marian Burton does not seem the sort of person to persist in bad habits when she is once made aware of them.

Lazarillo, by the bye, is an armorer's apprentice, a grimy, coaly, rusty person, with stains of the stithy on his shirt and skin, and with a scorched leathern apron on. Miss Marian Burton, however, turned out like the pastrycook in Geneviève de Brabant, in spotless lawn, impossibly dainty and clean. Now, as she has an opportunity of appearing in the last act at her very prettiest, in blue satin and lace, might she not sacrifice a little to realism by putting on the leathern apron and a touch or so of rust and soot during her apprenticeship to the brutal armorer? Surely the opera is unreal enough without such utterly incredible details as those of the costume and complexion she adopted on Monday night.

The chorus, regardless of the tanning sun of Spain, presented faces and arms of the whitest and pinkest, spoiling the scenery, and offending the eye. They also offended the ear. They are not, as many choruses are, voiceless; but the tone they produce—if tone it may be called—is coarse and unmusical at best, and execrable at worst. This is inexcusable, as any body of choristers can be made fairly efficient if trouble enough be taken with them. They make some attempt at acting too, as most choruses have done since the Meiningen company played Julius Cæsar here. Anyone desirous of a hearty laugh should hasten to witness the gesticulations of the Carl Rosa chorus as they listen to The Harp in the Air.

Maritana does not tax the ingenuity of the stage manager very heavily. Nevertheless, Mr Maas in the concerted piece, See the culprit, got into difficulties that could easily have been avoided. And the gymnastic feats of Miss Marian Burton with the muskets from which she has to withdraw the bullets should not be performed under the immediate supervision of the firing party.

Did Vincent Wallace regard the scene in which the Marquis and Marchioness appear as a harlequinade, with the clown and policeman omitted, and the pantaloon and the old woman retained? The effect is amusing, but not conducive to the dignity of English opera.

GORING THOMAS'S NEW OPERA

Unsigned notes in The Dramatic Review, 18 April 1885

[U] It is pleasant to have to record an unqualified success for the production of Mr A. Goring Thomas's *Nadeshda* by the Carl Rosa Opera Company, on Thursday evening last, at Drury Lane. There was an *encore*, even before the curtain rose, for the prelude; and the performers and the composer were repeatedly called before the curtain at the end of each act. Tremendous applause followed Madame Alwina Valleria's delivery of a song with chorus, placed opportunely at the climax of the second act, which is the brightest part of the opera. Miss Josephine Yorke, Mr Barton McGuckin, and Mr

Leslie Crotty each made a distinct success in their parts of Princess Natalia, Voldemar, and Ivan. Mr Burgon, with a little more ease and experience, will prove a valuable acquisition to the company.

Mr Barton McGuckin's stage deportment is impressive—almost too impressive sometimes. Incongruous reminiscences of Mr Barry Sullivan,* and even of Mr Bradlaugh†, float across the mind when Mr McGuckin's princeliness becomes solemn or his affection paternal. But he has advanced remarkably as an actor.

Mr Randegger does not make the most of the Carl Rosa orchestra. He accepts as a *pianissimo* what Herr Richter would probably describe as a tolerably vigorous *mezza forte*. On Thursday he disregarded nearly all the more delicate gradations indicated by the composer. In response to an enthusiastic call for Mr Goring Thomas at the conclusion of the performance, Mr Augustus Harris appeared and bowed gratefully.[U]

NADESHDA

The Dramatic Review, 25 April 1885

[U] Nadeshda, a romantic opera in four acts, the libretto by Julian Sturgis, the music by A. Goring Thomas, was performed for the first time by the Carl Rosa Company at Drury Lane Theatre on Thursday, the 16th April. The action takes place in Russia in the middle of the last century. Not this time, however, in the Russia of sledges, eternal snow, and Astrakan

---

* Romantic Shakespearean actor, whose Dublin performances had thrilled Shaw in his youth.

† Charles Bradlaugh, a platform spellbinder, was England's leading secularist as well as a social and political reformer.

trimmings. In glowing summer, the serfs of the Princess Natalia, sufficiently warmed by the northern sun and the frequent knoutings administered by order of their mistress, are celebrating in their gayest attire the accession of Voldemar, the Princess's elder son, to the lordship of the estate. They, confident after the manner of serfs that a change of masters must put an end to all their troubles, revile the knouting Princess who is abdicating, and praise the Prince who is succeeding her. Ostap, a sentimental socialist of the period, with a scowl and a prodigious knife, endeavors to awaken them to the probability of, as he puts it, the cub wolf growing fiercer than its dam, the eaglet than the worn-out eagle. In vain: his views are too advanced for them. They chaff him about a girl named Nadeshda, and he retires, clutching his knife and scowling. From the tenor of the general conversation it appears that this Nadeshda is regarded by her neighbors as somewhat fanciful, but gifted with an excellent disposition and considerable personal attractiveness. She presently appears, laden with flowers. Ostap intimates that he has something particular to say to her if she will allow him. She holds out no hope to him of a satisfactory reply to his communication, and begs him to think no more of her. He expresses his determination to knife the whole universe first, and withdraws. Then Nadeshda, left alone, anticipates Wordsworth in an impassioned address to the beauties of nature, more particularly to a river which has been for a long time the sole confidant of her vague aspirations. The distant voices of her companions recall her to commonsense, and she disappears; but not before she has conveyed quite definitely, if a little periphrastically, that she is in want of a lover.

Voldemar and his brother Ivan now come out for a walk. Voldemar's virtue and heroism are apparent from his fair complexion, powdered wig, and tenor voice. But

Ivan, being dark and a baritone, is at once recognized as a villain. Voldemar speaks jubilantly of their boyhood and the games they used to have together. Ivan remembers that period very well, but hints that the games included schoolboy lickings of which he received the lamb's share. Voldemar soothes him by promising to give him whatever he asks for "tomorrow," and, seeing that Ivan does not believe him in the least, confirms his promise by a solemn pledge. Nadeshda, still looking for a lover, returns just then, and thinks that Voldemar will suit her very nicely. Both brothers fall in love with her on the spot; and the matter drops for the present.

Now comes the festival in the hall of the castle, where the serfs present an address in Russian fashion to their new master. There are songs; processions; pantomimes full of edification for unruly wives, who, it is inculcated, should be soundly thrashed by husbands desirous of domestic bliss; hunt-the-slipper, with a gold ring instead of a slipper; and, finally, the presentation of an offering of bread and salt by Nadeshda. Everybody is delighted except Ostap, who still clutches his immense knife and scowls. Voldemar cannot turn his eyes from Nadeshda. Ivan now steps forward and begs to remind his brother of his promise. He will not abuse such princely generosity by an exorbitant demand. All he requires is the serf Nadeshda. Voldemar is confounded. Nadeshda, terrified, implores him to refuse. But Voldemar is a man of honor, and will keep his word at all costs. Still, as he reminds Ivan, his promise is not due until "tomorrow," when Nadeshda will not be his to give away. "How so?" says Ivan. "Because I set her free now" says Voldemar. Shylock's discomfiture is nothing to that of Ivan. He draws his sword on his brother, who promptly puts him out of the house. Ostap meanwhile scowls jealously, and asks "Have I a knife?" That he can for a moment overlook so obvious a part of his equipment sufficiently shews the extent to which his mind is disturbed. Strange to say, the Princess Natalia, though on the premises and not indisposed, takes no part in these proceedings. For this Mr Julian Sturgis is much indebted to her, as she would have been very much in his way throughout the entire scene.

Now that the festivities are over, Ostap's socialism, though sentimental, proves to have been economically sound; for the serfs are toiling as before, and the knout is apparently as active as ever. To Nadeshda's cottage comes, after sunset, Voldemar. Nadeshda, having anticipated Wordsworth by half a century, now, with the help of Voldemar, anticipates the garden scene from Gounod's *Faust* by twice that period. The lovers part at last; but Voldemar, foreseeing that Mr Sturgis will want him later on, announces that he will spend the night strolling near at hand. The Princess Natalia, with a retinue of knouters, now appears, guided by Ostap, and attended by Ivan, who has roused her family pride by telling her that Voldemar intends to marry a serf. Nadeshda is dragged from her dwelling, and Ostap is ordered to knout her. Horrified, he takes to his heels; and the Princess's favorite corrective is about to be applied by a stalwart retainer when Voldemar rushes in, loses his temper, and declares his intention of marrying Nadeshda forthwith. A family quarrel ensues; and Voldemar goes off in search of a priest, whilst the Princess retires in dudgeon. Ivan then proposes to Nadeshda that she shall fly with him. This being wholly unreasonable, she declines; and Ivan resorts to violence. Her cries bring Ostap to the rescue. He knifes Ivan, and, to save further trouble (the librettist having no further occasion for him) commits suicide.

Matters being smoothed so far, the marriage ceremony is about to proceed when the Princess interposes with a request for a private interview with Nadeshda, to which the bridegroom most emphatically objects. It takes place, nevertheless; and the Princess shows Nadeshda an imperial order for the banishment of——. She threatens to fill up the blank with the name of Voldemar if he persists in marrying the daughter of a serf. Thereupon the nice point arises as to which of the two women will in that case be guilty of Voldemar's ruin. The Princess admits that the responsibility will be doubtful, but is quite clear as to the facts. Nadeshda then offers to suffer banishment herself for Voldemar's sake. The Princess compliments her on her pluck, but accepts her offer; and Nadeshda is going straight away into exile in her bridal dress, when Voldemar returns and declares his intention of going with her. The Princess disinherits him then and there, and sends for Ivan. Ivan, mortally knifed, is not in a position to profit by his succession to the estate. He is brought in only to profess his regret for past deviations from the path of virtue, and to make a comparatively pious end. The Princess, broken down by her bereavement, relents; and the serfs, delighted at the death of Ivan and the defeat of the Princess, say solemnly "Yet, whilst we wail, still may the good prevail," and on that optimistic pretext finish the opera merrily with an epithalamium.

Forty years have elapsed since Bunn and Fitzball wrote the *Bohemian Girl* and *Maritana*: yet the old-fashioned English opera libretto shows no sign of decay. Arline, the artless child of nature, lives again in Nadeshda, no longer dreaming that she dwelt in marble halls, but still dreaming hard. The indomitable soul of the gypsy queen has passed into the haughty Princess Natalia. The chirping flute and the rippling violin embroider the airs of the impossible heroine: the terror-striking trombone lends impressiveness to the declamation of the unwomanly tragedy queen. We miss, it is true, the humor of Florestan, and the high comedy of

Don César; but Ostap and Devilshoof, Don José and Ivan, Thaddeus and Voldemar, are as closely akin as Box and Cox.* Their oaths are inviolable, their ancestors ever in their thoughts, their hands often on their swords. Mr Sturgis has with daring originality forborne to mention that Nadeshda is the long lost changeling child of some eminent Russian noble; but that she actually is so, no experienced playgoer can for a moment doubt.

Mr Goring Thomas, who does not aim beyond a purely descriptive treatment of the simpler emotions, and is content to be grandiose or sentimental as occasion demands, has spared himself no pains in setting to music a work that, if produced at a West End theatre as a drama, would be ridiculed by the very people who seem to think it (or anything) quite good enough for an opera. What Mozart would have thought of it when he was adding to the greatness of one of Molière's greatest works, and shewing Beaumarchais that there were more sides than one to his philosophy, is not fairly in question here, as all that happened a hundred years ago. Besides, Mr Goring Thomas has no more of the Mozartian power of representing men and women musically than— to select the most flattering comparison—Beethoven had. He describes emotions only, and these none of the profoundest. Gloomy discordant rumblings in the orchestra indicate villainy on the part of the vocalist: swaggering martial strains denote dauntless courage or pride of race: the course of true love runs smoothly for

* Florestan is the imprisoned husband in Beethoven's Fidelio. Don César and Don José are rival noblemen in Wallace's Maritana. Devilshoof is a gypsy who gives asylum to the Polish rebel Thaddeus in Balfe's The Bohemian Girl. Box and Cox (1847) is a one-act farce by J. M. Morton, adapted into a comic opera Cox and Box (1867) by F. C. Burnand, with music by Arthur Sullivan.

once in nine-eight or twelve-eight time, clinging, cloying, and yearning. But before he can be ranked, not with Mozart, but even with M. Gounod, Mr Goring Thomas must make many more and subtler distinctions between human moods than he has made in Nadeshda. The mere labor value of his score, measured by the technical work he has put into it, is, perhaps, more than double that of an ordinary Balfe, Wallace, Donizetti, or Bellini opera. But the writer of an opera needs to be more than a musician: he should be an observer of men and manners—a descriptive sociologist of a high order. No composer so qualified would waste serious work on the Princess Natalia's invocation of her ancestress in the third act of Nadeshda. The toleration of such blatant nonsense has brought ridicule upon the stage; and Mr Goring Thomas cannot do more to bring ridicule upon music than by seriously and skilfully setting blatant nonsense to music. A modern composer, standing on the shoulders of Wagner and Berlioz (not to go further back to the men whose trick we have lost), hardly deserves to be patted on the back as Mr Goring Thomas has been for using the materials they have shewn him, and his own scholarship and industry, only to elaborate the childishness of Balfe and Wallace.[U]

DVOŘÁK AT THE PHILHARMONIC

Unsigned notes in The Dramatic Review, 25 April 1885

[U] At the Philharmonic last Wednesday a new symphony by Antonin Dvořák was conducted by the composer. The work has neither title nor program, and is described simply as No. 3 in D minor, Op. 70.* It

* The symphony has since been renumbered No. 7.

consists of the usual four movements in the customary order (if any musical arrangement can be considered customary nowadays), all full of varied and charming episodes in addition to their regular subjects, and all worked out with an imaginative ingenuity very welcome at present, when we suffer from so much ingenuity that is purely mechanical. The symphony seems to be the expression of the composer's happy and romantic vein; but the happiness and romance are of a serious Northern sort: there is nothing of the forced carnivalesque gaiety and tarantella torture that high-spirited modern composers occasionally goad us with. People who imagine scenery for the music they hear need not dread being dragged by Dvořák into a blinding sunlight in an Italian street with a drunken crowd of gaudily attired bacchanalians reveling at high pressure. His music suggests nothing more blinding than the lights of a fishing village on a Northern rock-bound coast on a starlit night. The Northern taste for stimulants only peeps out in the elaborate *codas* on which Dvořák bestows so much pains.

It was Beethoven who, probably fascinated by the grandeur and impetuosity of some of Mozart's operatic *finales*, began this practice of deliberately forcing the grace and piling up the weight in order to make an exciting finish to the fast movements of symphonies. Sometimes, for fun, he overdid it. The conclusion of the C minor symphony, and that of No. 8, are jocose extravagances. But the public unfortunately acquired a taste for it, and began to consider the moderation and dignity of the old-fashioned perorations insipid. Since then, nearly every overture or quick movement has been expected to end with a tremendous rally. It is to be hoped that amateurs are awakening to the fact that one rally is very like another, and that they should not publicly abuse the effects of music as they would be ashamed to abuse the effects of brandy. The *codas* in

Dvořák's new work are very elaborate; but instead of being mere headlong attempts to wind up brilliantly they are interesting sections of the movements in which they occur. One of them concludes, like Beethoven's Coriolan, with a *diminuendo ;* and another with a brief but dignified *maestoso*.

Of the already familiar works in the Philharmonic program the most successful was Weber's Konzertstück, played to perfection by Mlle Clotilde Kleeberg and the orchestra. It was a most dainty performance throughout—one that actually left nothing to be desired. What is more, the audience appreciated it. Mlle Kleeberg was called to the platform three times at the conclusion.

There were three overtures in the program: Spohr's to Faust, Beethoven's to Fidelio (the seldom played one in C, known as No. 1 Leonore) and an obsolete work formerly admired as the overture to Don Giovanni. It appears to have been written by a man named Mozart. It was placed at the end of the concert, in order that advanced musicians should have an opportunity of leaving before it was played. The position was not ill chosen, as it sounded better after the other overtures than the best of them might have sounded after it. M. Dannreuther would hardly have believed it.

Sir Arthur Sullivan conducted. Under his *bâton* orchestras are never deficient in refinement. Coarseness, exaggeration, and carelessness are unacquainted with him. So, unfortunately, are vigor and earnestness. The No. 1 Leonore overture, one of Beethoven's most impetuous compositions, would not have hurt a fly on Wednesday evening. It is well for Sir Arthur to be fastidious; but one cannot help thinking that he would get a firmer grip sometimes if he took his gloves off.

One of the indiscretions of Sir Arthur's youth was revived at this concert. Mr Edward Lloyd and Miss Etherington sang a duet from his Kenilworth, written for the Birmingham Musical Festival of 1864. It is interesting as containing the germ of the tenor song from the masterpiece of the composer's maturity—H.M.S. Pinafore.[U]

THE RICHTER CONCERTS

Unsigned notes in The Dramatic Review, 2 May 1885

[U] The Richter concerts began on Monday last at St James's Hall, where they will for some weeks to come supply the want of Monday popular orchestral concerts. The hall was crowded and the reception of the conductor enthusiastic. The band acquitted itself admirably in Schubert's unfinished symphony in B Minor. In the first section of the *allegro,* which was played so exquisitely that the players fell short of their own performance in repeating it, the woodwind was subdued to such sighing, whispering, and rustling as are seldom heard in an English concert room. On the other hand the Tannhäuser overture was spoiled by the trombones. The three gentlemen in charge of these instruments confidently delivered the pilgrims' chorus with all possible coarseness, flat throughout. As this has happened before at the Richter concerts, it may be inferred either that the conductor enjoys it, which is hardly credible of a musician of his taste, or that he has been so unfortunate in his experience of trombone players that he despairs of reconciling the full power of the instrument with purity of tone and accuracy of pitch. But a visit to the Crystal Palace will convince him that English players can be persuaded by Mr August Manns to do what his triad of German sackbuttists will not—and therefore presumably cannot—even attempt.

It so happened that when Herr Richter first formed

an orchestra in London some of our best players were engaged at the opera and elsewhere. He has done well to retain the men with whom he made his reputation here; but they should requite him by taking care that their performances shall be as excellent in each detail as in the aggregate. This they do not always do. The brass band—horns excepted—is inferior to the wood band; and the latter is not always so faultless as it was on Monday in the Schubert symphony.

Liszt's pretty and amusing Hungarian rhapsody in D minor and G major was nearly, but happily not quite, encored. This is *the* Rhapsodie Hongroise which our sisters and cousins struggle with in C sharp minor and F sharp major, the keys in which the work is most playable, if not most readable, for the pianoforte, but which would involve an orchestra in useless difficulties.

Wagner's Parsifal prelude, which was performed this day fortnight at the Crystal Palace, was again heard at the Richter concert. It is very beautiful and very solemn—desperately solemn, in fact. Would it be irreverent to remark, now that its beauty and solemnity have been admitted, that it contains some startling commonplaces, and that one of its most august themes recalls the air crooned by Mime, the dwarf blacksmith, in Siegfried?

The symphony was Beethoven's No. 7. It may seem an utterly Philistine thing to leave a concert without waiting to hear this most exuberant of musical revels conducted by Hans Richter; but that is what the critic of the DRAMATIC REVIEW reprehensibly did. When efficient ventilation and electric lighting shall enable a band to attack an exacting symphony with unrelaxed energy and unblunted sensibility after more than an hour's hard work, the symphony in A will be worth waiting an extra hour for even by those who have often heard it before. But these conditions are not as yet realized in St James's Hall; and there is consequently always a marked falling off in the performances towards the end of the concerts.

"Words of the concert: one shilling." This is what they call an analytic program at the Richter concerts, and what they charge for it. The programs are in no way superior to the eloquent and learned commentaries of Sir George Grove and Mr Barry at the Crystal Palace, or those of Sir G. A. Macfarren and Mr Joseph Bennett at the Philharmonic. But—apparently in a spirit of pure extortion—they are sold (or offered for sale) at double the price.

At the Browning and Shakespear performance at St George's Hall on Thursday, the serenade in the second act of A Blot in the 'Scutcheon was sung by Mr Edwin Bryant to music composed for the occasion by Mr A. C. Mackenzie. The air is a reminiscence of the serenade in the first act of Goetz's Taming of the Shrew, Mr Browning's poetry having apparently produced the same effect on Mr Mackenzie as Shakespear's on Goetz. The Browning Society will probably regard this as a compliment to Shakespear, whilst the New Shakspere Society will congratulate Mr Browning on it.

Mr Mackenzie has also composed an introduction to the third act of the Blot. A small string band, eked out by a pianoforte, and conducted by Mr Berthold Tours, occupied the orchestra, and discoursed this and other more or less appropriate music in the course of the evening. Their performance of Cherubini's overture to Medea was not an unmixed success; and the relevance of Ambroise Thomas's Caïd to The Comedy of Errors is not patent; but on the whole the little band did very well.[U]

ROMANTIC MUSIC

Unsigned notes in The Dramatic Review, 9 May 1885

[U] The program of the Fifth Philharmonic Concert on Wednesday last, though fairly attractive, somehow failed to fill St James's Hall. The condition of the cheaper seats at the back of the room is a reliable gauge of the popularity of any concert of high-class music. On Wednesday they were empty. At the Richter concerts they are usually crowded. This is to some extent the penalty the Philharmonic Society is suffering for past shortcomings. It is marching fairly with the times now, and producing some new work at nearly every concert. Unfortunately, it did not adopt this policy until the successes of its competitors, and the decay of its own reputation, forced it to recognize that senile inertia, hackneying the classics to save itself the trouble of selecting new work and helping new composers, was not true conservatism. The Philharmonic is now awake at last; and its credit, though evidently not yet re-established, is certainly convalescent. There were two items in the last program that have been heard less than a hundred times in London before. One was Dvořák's pianoforte concerto in G minor, the other, a couple of movements from Berlioz's Romeo and Juliet.

The solo part in Dvořák's concerto was played by Herr Franz Rummel, and the work was conducted by the composer. It has all the characteristics which are making Bohemian music popular in this country. All ordinary men love romantic music; and the healthy Englishman is no exception. But his insular brutality revolts against the lachrymose obstreperousness of the romantic Italian and the theatrical sentimentality of the

[241]

romantic Frenchman. As a tonic for both he prescribes a cricket match, or a football scrimmage with as much kicking in it as possible. Hence his appreciation of Bohemian music, which is intensely romantic and yet not unmanly. It has the gypsy charm about it. It is the music of men who live in the open air; who do not know how to read novels; who breed clever wrestlers and cudgel players, and whose failings are of a material hen-stealing sort that finds no expression in their songs. Herr Dvořák's music is such as we might expect from a very highly evolved gypsy genius, always fascinating, but neither demoralizing the hearer nor compromising the dignity of the composer.

A significant feature of the concert was the use of a pianoforte manufactured by a famous American firm. This, at a Philharmonic concert, looks like a collapse of the monopoly of supplying pianofortes for our leading concerts that has been maintained so long by an old established English firm. In richness of tone the superiority of the American pianofortes, and even of European imitations of them, was and is so great that their exclusion hitherto from our concert platforms has been due solely to the great obligations under which the kind and considerate assistance of the English firm on various occasions had placed almost every pianist of reputation, and many who remain comparatively obscure. Probably no excess of deliberate bribery could have effected this result, which was creditable to the feelings of the firm and of the artists, but not wholly advantageous to the public.

The second promise of Mr Carl Rosa was redeemed on Thursday night by the performance at Drury Lane of Jules Massenet's Manon for the first time in London. The parts were allotted as at the production of the opera in January last at the Royal Court Theatre, Liverpool; except that the Chevalier des Grieux, then played by

Mr Barton McGuckin, was impersonated on Thursday by Mr Joseph Maas. Madame Marie Roze's acting as Manon Lescaut is no less remarkable than that by which she has surprised the public in Carmen. No manifestation of delight on the part of the audience was lacking to the success of the performance. Applause, bouquets, repeated calls before the curtain, and general enthusiasm, confirmed the soundness of Mr Carl Rosa's judgment as emphatically on this occasion as on that of Nadeshda. Important parts were filled by Messrs Ludwig, Burgon, Clifford and Lyall.

Apropos of Carmen, which now divides with Gounod's Faust the position of the most popular of modern operas, it would be interesting to learn how many of the artists who appear in it at Drury Lane have read the admirably told story by Prosper Merimée on which the opera is founded. It seems safe to guess that Mr Ben Davies has not. As Don José Lizarrabengoa, he is the sturdiest, most good-humored, and least jealous of British brigadiers. His aspect does *not* recall the Satan of Milton. It is true that he is *"un jeune gaillard, de taille moyenne, mais d'apparence robuste"*; but he signally lacks the *"regard sombre et fier"* that completes the description. A man less likely to stab any woman than Don José ben Davies never trod the stage. This, cheerful as it is, mars the interest of the drama, in which José is the only character who greatly moves our sympathy. The entanglement of the unlucky soldier by the evil fascination of Carmen loses much of its pathos in the hands of a jolly and rather stolid Britisher of the frankest Tommy Atkins type.[U]

MANON

The Dramatic Review, 16 May 1885

In fitting the story of Manon Lescaut to the stage for M. Massenet, MM. Meilhac and Gille took for granted that their audience had read the novel upon which their libretto is founded. In France this assumption may have been justified, but the average Englishman is about as likely to have read the famous seventh volume of the Mémoires et aventures d'un homme de qualité produced by Prévost d'Exiles in 1731, as the average Frenchman is to have read Clarissa Harlowe. Those who find the libretto bewildering will do well to read the novel, which is prodigiously superior to the opera. The now scarce 1838 edition, with the vignettes of Tony Johannot, or the scarcer 1797 edition, exquisitely printed by Didot and illustrated by Lefebvre, may be recommended to dainty readers. The much vaunted *édition de luxe* of 1875, with the preface by Alexandre Dumas *fils,* and the etchings by Leopold Flameng, will repay careful avoidance. Those who do not hold with M. Dumas that *"il n'y a de livres malsains que les livres mal faits"* had better read the novel before presenting a copy to the young lady of fifteen of whom much has been said of late in these pages.

When M. Jules Massenet descended on our shores for the first time in 1878 with an instrumental suite descriptive of scenes from Macbeth, he established his reputation as one of the loudest of modern composers. Something of that *esprit de corps* which led a celebrated artillery regiment to sing with ungrammatical enthusiasm We are the boys that fears no noise* seems to have determined him not to allow even a simple chord to a recitative to pass without a pluck at the strings and a slam on the drum capable of awakening the deaf. When the curtain descends on a thrilling "situation" he pours forth all his energy in a screeching, grinding, rasping *fortissimo* of extraordinary exuberance and vigor. He is perhaps better at a stage tumult than any living composer. Ever and anon there comes in Manon a number that stuns the hearer into drowsy good humor, and leaves him disposed to tolerate anything that gently tickles his exhausted ears and does not tax his attention too heavily. The quartet with chorus in the fourth act must be almost as audible on Waterloo Bridge as in the first row of stalls in Drury Lane Theatre.

About the music generally there is little to be said, but that little is in its favor. It is pretty, spirited, easy to follow, varied with considerable fancy and ingenuity, never dull, and only occasionally trivial or vulgar. As Manon is technically an *opéra comique,* the dialogue is spoken, and the speaking is accompanied by the old-fashioned *mélodrame,* or descriptive orchestral accompaniment, the effect of which is in every case happy. The instrumentation is so excessively strident at times that it would conceivably satiate even Liszt, whilst the immoderate fury to which the composer abandons himself at each climax of the drama, reminds one of the Verdi of Ernani and Il Trovatore; but on the whole the orchestral work has a distinct style, and is by no means a mere hotch-potch of borrowed effects. Of Wagnerism there is not the faintest suggestion. A phrase which occurs in the first love duet breaks out once or twice in subsequent amorous episodes, and has been seized on by

* A nautical ditty, arranged by C. M. Cady (Cleveland, Ohio, 1871).

a few unwary critics as a Wagnerian *leit motif*. But if Wagner had never existed, Manon would have been composed much as it stands now, wheras if Meyerbeer and Gounod had not made a path for M. Massenet, it is impossible to say whither he might have wandered, or how far he could have pushed his way.

The performance at Drury Lane on the 7th was favored by the rare suitability of the parts to the artists who undertook them. "*J'ai l'humeur naturellement douce et tranquille,*" said poor des Grieux to the Abbé Prévost; and Mr Maas, whatever his disposition may be, certainly has a voice and stage manner exceptionally *douce et tranquille.* He wins all the sympathy that readers of the novel feel, in spite of their moral sense, for the amiable hero whose honor rooted in dishonor stood, and whose faith unfaithful kept him falsely true. Manon, or Mannong, as they call her in their hearty English way at Drury Lane, was irresistible in the first two acts. Madame Marie Roze is not a first-rate singer, and time was when to have described her merely as a bad singer would have conveyed but a feeble impression of her shortcomings. When Tietjens's central place became vacant, Madame Marie Roze was put into it as a stopgap by a management at its wits' end to find a passable substitute. There is no room here to chronicle a tenth of the labors she undauntedly attacked in that extremity. When Lohengrin had to be played she took her voice in her hand (so to speak) and rushed through the part of Ortrud. When there was no Pamina left in England, she fell fearlessly on Mozart and was defeated with heavy loss to the hearers. The scars of that campaign are on her voice to this day. Yet through it all she disarmed the critics. Something pleaded for her in their manly breasts (it was certainly not any pre-eminent artistic excellence on her part), and she was allowed to clothe herself, unchallenged, with the prestige of *prima donna* at Her

Majesty's Opera, London. It was supposed to be on the strength of this that America subsequently accepted her, and that she was hailed in the provinces as a great artist when she at last placed her services at the disposal of Mr Carl Rosa.

But it now appears to be delightfully and surprisingly true that there were better reasons for her success. She has returned to us with not only much more of her voice left than any reasonable person could have expected, but with new claims as an actress of remarkable ability. Her Carmen is as undeniably the best we have seen here as Madame Trebelli's is the best we have heard. She might be said to realize Mérimée's heroine down to her boots, were it not that the novelist expressly mentions Carmen's "white silk stockings with more than one hole in them," wheras on the stage Carmen's stockings appear intact. Manon is a fresh triumph for Madame Marie Roze. The intelligence and determination that have enabled her to achieve it are still masked by the infantine simplicity, the plaintive eyes, and the innocent beauty that used to blunt the critical pen and sweeten the critical ink. But the artlessness that was once only too genuine now conceals carefully premeditated acting, based on an exhaustive study of the original description of the character. Manon in the inn yard at Amiens, and in the little set of apartments in Paris, is more charming than any novelty the lyric stage has shewn us for some years past. No art can quite redeem the subsequent scenes from the repulsiveness of their moral infamy; but as the gilding is very thick, and the bustle incessant, the spectator finds it easier to laugh, to stare, and—if soft-hearted—to cry, than to think into the ethics of the case. As a singer Madame Marie Roze is far more judicious than she used to be. By giving up her old fashion of desperately assaulting vocal difficulties in the hope of vanquishing them by force or by good luck, she has saved her voice from serious deterioration; and it is now fairly clear and strong. In using it she makes the most of what she can do; and what she cannot do she gracefully dodges. She is to be congratulated on having made an extraordinary advance in her profession, and that, too, in a department of it which rarely receives a pretence of adequate attention.

Mr Ludwig, who plays the rascally soldier, Lescaut, once had some tone in his voice, and perhaps was capable of becoming an actor. But he has shaken all the tone away (most unfortunately managing to retain the voice), and, busy as he is posing, rolling the eye, and sawing the air, has no leisure even to think of acting. Yet his deportment as Lescaut is far more rational than that of Mr Burgon as des Grieux, senior, whose proceedings are so absolutely unaccountable as to exempt him from criticism. Yet the audience were pleased with Mr Burgon on the first night, and the strange signals he made with his hat, and his singing of Go wed some Maiden fair and tender must be recorded as popular successes. Mr Maas, by the bye, in altering I pray you, sir, do not mock me, into I pray *thee*, was disrespectful enough to *tutoyer* his father. Mr Lyall is as funny as usual in the part of Guillot, introduced by the authors of the libretto to evade the disagreeably close relationship that exists in the story between the two lovers of Manon who procure her arrest. There are many pretty concerted pieces for the subordinate characters, and much lively choral work. In the riotous scene at the Amiens inn, where a crowd of passengers bawl and struggle for their luggage, the choristers for the most part adopt the tactics which have been allowed to pass in the riot scene in the Meistersinger, where the singers disregard their parts, shout whatever comes into their heads, and make as much noise as possible.

Mr Joseph Bennett has done his best to translate the

French libretto into English that will fit the notes and yet comply with ordinary literary conditions. Nevertheless, quotations would be out of place here, as it is no part of the function of grave musical criticism to create uproarious mirth.

CHORAL WORKS

Unsigned notes in The Dramatic Review, 16 May 1885

[U] Two choral works, Beethoven's Calm Sea and Prosperous Voyage, and a rhapsody for contralto solo and chorus of men by Brahms, were performed at the Richter concert last Monday. The Richter choristers have improved. Not only can they sing quite softly on occasion, but they frequently sing in tune, though they have yet to learn to sustain a note without a continuous alteration of the pitch. There was a long selection from the Niblung Ring, which must have seemed a strange jumble to those who did not know what it was all about. There are signs of wear on Wagner's music already: much of it will be voted old-fashioned by half the world before the other half gets over its novelty. Those who love, like Mr Gilbert's cut-throat, "to listen to the merry village chime"* should hear Glinka's charming Kamarinskaja played by the Richter orchestra. The concert wound up with Beethoven's not abstruse but aboundingly strong and spirited second symphony. Both the conductor's reading of it and its execution by the band were, to our taste, absolutely unexceptionable.

Mr Geaussent's choir, at a concert in St James's Hall

* In the Police Sergeant's song, When a felon's not engaged in his employment, in The Pirates of Penzance.

[249]

on Wednesday evening, performed Mr A. C. Macken-zie's dramatic cantata, Jason. When a modern composer wishes to catch the spirit of Greek art, he generally betrays his secret opinion that Phidias was tame, and Praxiteles cold-blooded, by proceeding to dance in the fetters of extreme decorousness, and to pipe as much under his breath as possible. The music which Mr Mackenzie offers as descriptive of Jason's struggles with the bulls and the dragon, and of the conflict of the armed men, is scholarly and elegant, but not much more exciting than a spelling bee. Perhaps the effect was partly discounted by the very small orchestra, which occasionally set the teeth of the audience on edge by accidentally playing chords of a more advanced descrip-tion than any to be found in Tristan und Isolde. The players may therefore be presumed to have had little or no opportunity of rehearsing their work, for, a few mistakes apart, they acquitted themselves like artists. But a band a thousand strong could not reinforce Mr Mackenzie's music enough to make it a match for Jason. The setting of the calmer passages of the poem, however, may be commended without reserve for its grace and tenderness. The whole cantata proves the advantage of refined workmanship, and also, perhaps, how important it is that composers should discriminate between their invention and their memory. It is a little too evident that Die Meistersinger is a favorite with Mr Mackenzie; and one of the movements in Medea's *scena*, A Royal Maiden, is so obviously a refraction in Mr Mackenzie's memory of Tannhäuser's chant in praise of Venus, that the author of the analytical program, though he stretches critical indulgence to the utmost in the composer's favor, has thought it best to forestall this inevitable comment by suggesting it himself. Madame Albani and Messrs Edward Lloyd and Santley were the vocalists. The engagement of these eminent artists was more fortunate for Mr Mackenzie than for the concert giver; for the announcements failed to attract a large audience, and in spite of the economy practised in the orchestral department, the concert can hardly have proved as remunerative as it deserved to. Mr Geaussent's choir has been admirably trained: the only notable shortcoming was in the chorus of armed men, in which the voices were almost inaudible. The contraltos especially distinguished themselves by the fulness and beauty of their tone.

Herr Antonin Dvořák has "dedicated with feelings of deep gratitude to the English people" a setting of Vítěslav Hálek's patriotic hymn entitled The Heirs of the White Mountain, composed by him in 1871, but only just published. As an attempt to express the aspirations of a nation in bondage, it would perhaps be better appreciated on the other side of St George's Channel. "There is a certain pathos" says Mr Joseph Bennett "in the dedication of this work to a people who long ago conquered all the liberties that a nation can desire." Leaving this distinguished art critic to settle with Mr William Morris whether the majority of Englishmen enjoy all the liberties they can desire, we may congratulate Mr Geaussent's choir on having been the first to introduce the hymn, which is a striking expression of Bohemian national sentiment. The thrilling whisper in which the possibility of freedom is first hinted at produces an effect not easily to be forgotten. Herr Dvořák conducted the work in person.

The New Shakspere Society gave its annual concert on the 8th inst., at University College. These entertainments are in some respects extremely funny. They invariably begin by a XVI or XVII century madrigal, sung without accompaniment by three vocalists seated at a table. Those who know the long practice in singing together, the perfect intonation, and the familiarity with the particular work in hand that is needed in this most difficult and half-forgotten art of madrigal singing, can imagine the effect of letting loose a scratch trio of second- or third-rate ballad concert professionals once a year upon contemporary settings of Shakespear for the edification of a purely literary and antiquarian society. At the occasion in question, a madrigal by Weelkes, an unusually beautiful and interesting specimen of the music for which England was once famous, was murdered in an indescribable manner. However, it mattered but little. Shakespear, fortunately for himself, was dead; and the new Shakspereans revelled in the frightful cacophony which they innocently supposed to be XVI century quaintness. Their eyes sparkled with delight at mis-tuned dissonances that wrung groans from the writhing Dramatic Reviewer. The more modern music that followed was, with a few exceptions, fairly sung. A setting of the dirge from Cymbeline by Alice Borton shewed considerable talent on the part of the composer.[U]

MOSZKOWSKI'S JOHANNA D'ARC

Unsigned notes in The Dramatic Review, *23 May 1885*

[U] The 1885 series of Philharmonic concerts closed on Wednesday evening, when Herr Moritz Moszkowski conducted his "great Symphonic Poem" (such is the strong language used by the Philharmonic directors) entitled Johanna d'Arc. Herr Moszkowski is a Berlin pianist and composer, known in this country by two sets of so-called Spanish dances arranged as duets for the pianoforte, the first set pretty and not too commonplace; the second more elaborate, but not otherwise more meritorious. Johanna d'Arc is a symphony with a program after the fashion of the late Joachim Raff, founded on Schiller's tragedy of The Maid of Orleans. The first movement describes "Joan's pastoral life. Her exalted mission is revealed to her in a vision." This vision appears as an intensely orchestrated solo for the violin, between the first section of the movement and the fantasia. Its effect was not wholly celestial at the Philharmonic. Mr Carrodus, like other famous violinists, is subject to playing flat, and he was suffering from a particularly severe attack of this distressing complaint on Wednesday. The rest of the movement is as orthodox in form as symphonic movements are made nowadays. The first subject is pretty and pastoral; the second is a spirited little march in B major, scored with drum and piccolo, and incongruously recalling *L'amour, ce dieu profane!* from Ambroise Thomas's Caïd. The themes are too trivial to bear their lengthy working out and circumstantial repetition in the second and third sections of the movement, by which they are worn threadbare and made tedious.

The *andante* is superscribed "Inner Consciousness—Former Memories." In only one instance is it possible to discriminate between the consciousness and the memories. Herr Moszkowski has introduced and rather insisted on a striking phrase from the intermezzo which precedes the 4th act of Gounod's Faust. This cannot be one of Johanna's "former memories," as she died some centuries before M. Gounod was born. It must therefore be taken as an expression of the prophetic side of her inner consciousness. By way of *scherzo*, there is a "Procession of the Conquerors to the Coronation at Rheims." This is of course a march. Herr Moszkowski may rest assured that we already have as many marches of this kind as we want: in fact we can easily spare him one or two to repay him for taking his own away, if he will be so forbearing as to do so. The final *allegro* is said to represent "Johanna in Prison: her Release, Triumph, Death, and Apotheosis." All these occur, not according to history, but according to Schiller, whose Maid of Orleans, it will be remembered (provided you read Schiller), escaped from prison and died on the field of battle. In this movement, lugubrious strains for the bass strings a prison make, and bassoons and horns a cage. Then piccolo music, again of the Caïd type, tells of approaching rescue. The Maid breaks her chains (*pizzicato*); and battle, murder, and not particularly sudden death ensue.

There is not a single theme or progression in the whole work that excuses Mr Charles E. Stephens for calling it "great"; but it is quite interesting enough to justify its performance at a Philharmonic concert. Much, if not all of the second and third sections of the first movement, could well be spared, consisting as they do of repetition and elaboration that would not have been undertaken had not the supposed requirements of the sonata form furnished a pretext for them. Herr Moszkowski is imaginative and tuneful. He is never absolutely dull, and would not be tedious if he would only let his tunes alone when he has done with them. It is not reasonable to assume that an air of the sort that M. Planquette composes for his comic operas becomes infinitely interesting when ushered into a symphony and submitted to symphonic treatment, such treatment frequently amounting to nothing more than dismembering it and playing it half a dozen times over in half a dozen different keys on half a dozen different combinations of instruments to an accompaniment of its own fragments. Herr Moszkowski's themes are all the less fit for repetition because most of them are nothing but repetitions of the same phrase on different degrees of the scale. They resemble Mozart's *Non più andrai, Finch' han del vino*, &c. &c., in this respect, but not in any other.

Poor Johanna d'Arc, heavily discounted by Wagner's overture to The Flying Dutchman, which preceded her, was swept into oblivion by Beethoven's pianoforte concerto in E flat, which followed. The German ocean, with surges racing past into the wake of the phantom ship, blasts tearing through the rigging, cold black storm clouds, and snatches of melody borne on the wind, came between the critic and the garish reality of St James's Hall until his imagination was suddenly dried up by the observation that Sir Arthur Sullivan was taking the last page much too slowly. The famous phrase of the Dutchman's doom, simple as it is, was not perfectly played by the brass instruments; the final interval of a fifth being taken with a slovenly skip that vulgarized it disagreeably. This and the deficient velocity of the *coda* excepted, the overture was admirably executed. The great concerto went almost faultlessly. Herr Franz Rummel played the first movement with great spirit and delicacy. He fell off a little in the final allegro as all players do except those who have attained the calm, grace and power of perfect mastery. Herr Rummel has not yet acquired the classic taste for repose of style. He is alternately exciting and fascinating where the greatest players are alternately grand and poetic. His reputation had been greatly strengthened by his performance of Dvořák's concerto at a previous concert; and his playing on Wednesday has confirmed his popularity at St James's Hall. It may be added, for the information of students in general, and young ladies who have learned in Leipzig and elsewhere to talk about *technique*, that Herr Rummel holds his hand so low that his fingers often slope downward to the wrist as he plays.

The remainder of the program consisted of Gounod's charming bucolic overture to Mireille; a fine song,

Sorge Infausta, from Handel's Orlando; and Anacreon's ode, I wish to crown my quiv'ring lyre, set by Sir Arthur Sullivan in 1868 for the Gloucester Festival. The composer used part of the music a second time when he tuned his quiv'ring lyre to When Frederic was a little boy, in H.M.S. Pinafore.* Mr Santley sang the ode seventeen years ago, and he sang it again the other night. If Mr Santley's pronunciation were as pure as his vocal style he might still, at his best, challenge any living baritone known to London audiences. His singing of the aria by Handel was excellent.

The appointment of Sir Arthur Sullivan as conductor of the Philharmonic, though it has not filled the room at every concert as the appointment of Herr Richter would certainly have done, has proved on the whole satisfactory. The standard of refinement in orchestral performances which it is desirable that a society with the honorable traditions of the Philharmonic should maintain, has been raised by Sir Arthur, who only wants a little more fire to make him eminent as a conductor. It is true that he was received with energetic hisses on Wednesday night; but that was because he was twelve minutes late—apparently because someone else, who ought to have known better, was ten minutes late. But the hatchet was buried at the end of the concert, when he received a hearty ovation from audience and orchestra.[U]

* Ruth's song, When Frederic was a little lad, is in The Pirates of Penzance.

MADAME NILSSON

Unsigned notes in the Dramatic Review, 30 May 1885

[U] The Daily News interviewed Madame Christine
Nilsson the other day, and received many valuable
wrinkles in *l'art d'être prima donna*. Old as the Daily
News is, for ladies love unfit: the power of beauty it
remembers yet. It found Madame Nilsson's geniality
agreeably tempered by "the profound gaze of her great
thoughtful blue eyes, just as the music of her vibrant
and sympathetic voice is in contrast with the firm grasp
of her hand revealing force and will beneath its dainty
envelope." Madame Nilsson would appear to be a hard
hitter with both hands; for beside the above comparatively cool reference, we find the D. N. ardently
describing "the beautiful white hands held forth in
greeting." And again, "She receives her visitor with a
hearty shake of the hand, or rather hands; for with that
charming vivacity which is one of her chief characteristics she extends both in sign of greeting." Happy Daily
News! Those hands, it protests, receive no adequate
expression in Cabanel's portrait of Madame Christine as
Ophelia. "Probably the painter thought, and with some
justice, that the intense vitality typified by the singer's
hands would ill accord with the lilies and languors"—
and so on. The fascinating members are, it appears,
"neither childishly small, boneless, and nerveless, nor
large and coarse, but well proportioned, handsome,
capable-looking hands—evidently the hands of a person
who can do something valid." They can, for instance,
perceptibly affect the heart from which proceeds "the
largest circulation of any liberal paper in the world."

After such a theme as these magnetic hands, quotations as to "the fair head covered with short curls of the hue known as *blonde cendré*," or "the great serious blue eyes which look calmly out with an 'equal-to-either-fortune' expression" (how admirably our great daily describes when its full powers are roused by a genuine emotional crisis!) would only tantalize the readers of the DRAMATIC REVIEW; whilst the information that Madame Nilsson has for several years past been "practising her voice" in the Belgrave Road would be an anti-climax.

Madame Nilsson's notions of training herself for her feats on the stage are the usual odd mixture of science and superstition. She repudiates stimulants and late hours, and when the infatuated Daily News remarked that it "thought champagne was good for soprani, and stout for contralti," she contemptuously declared that "conviviality meant strong drink, followed by bad singing." "The best and only thing to sing on" said Madame Nilsson, very truly "is the effect of a sound wholesome meal eaten some hours before. To drink a pint of liquid of any kind before singing is madness." (The D. N. had feebly intimated that if it were about to sing in an opera, it would imbibe a pint of stout, because it had heard that Malibran used to do so.) On the whole Madame Nilsson's habits go far to explain why she retains her enviable strength and grace unimpaired, whilst so many of her colleagues fall off, not to the shadow, but, quite on the contrary, to three times the bulk of their former selves.

Madame Nilsson's superstitions are few and harmless. Though she likes to play the violin, she denies herself that beneficial exercise because someone (who must be little short of another Daily News in his ideas of hygiene) told her that "the cramped attitude and powerful vibration might affect her singing in the evening." The reply to this is that you should not play the violin in a cramped attitude; and that the "powerful vibration" of the instrument is far less objectionable than that of the carriage in which Madame Nilsson takes the fresh air because—and here is another of her superstitions—she is afraid that exercise on horseback, in which she delights, would also interfere with her efficiency as a vocalist. If Madame Nilsson will only adhere to her early hours and sensible diet, she may fearlessly ride and play the fiddle to her heart's content. Neither practice is likely to do her anything but good.

The Royal Academy of Music are convening a public meeting on the subject of musical pitch. The particulars have not yet been announced; but the secretary, Mr John Gill, undertakes to send tickets of admission to musicians, physicists, and persons interested in music, provided they apply to him before two o'clock today.

Most good singers, who can use their middle and lower registers effectively, and who do not enjoy a high pitch for its own sake, would probably advocate a return to the old pitch of Mozart's time, at which the A on the second space of the treble staff gave 422 vibrations per second. The instrumentalists have incurred, and probably deserve, the odium of steadily forcing the pitch up since then. However that may be, the pitch did rise until a stand was made by the solemn proclamation at Paris in 1859 of A with 435 vibrations as the *diapason normal*. Even this was quarter of a tone higher than Mozart's. (The irresponsible amateur, in order to shew how much higher he can sing than the first singers of Don Giovanni, will tell you offhand that the pitch is two or three tones higher than it was a hundred years ago—but never mind him.) The French pitch did not mend matters in this country, where the Philharmonic pitch, adopted by Messrs Broadwood in tuning their concert grands, was as high as 455, four-fifths of a semitone higher than the *diapason normal,* and nearly a semitone and a third higher than Mozart's. The Steinways, in America, tune their pianofortes to a pitch even higher than this. The organs at the Albert Hall, the Crystal Palace, the Royal Academy of Music, St James's Hall, and the Alexandra Palace are all up to Philharmonic pitch, or within a few vibrations of it. As altering the pitch of an organ is a costly process, there is not much likelihood of the forthcoming meeting doing anything more practical than vainly protesting against the misdeeds of the men who built these organs, and so deprived the Handel Festival of the services of Mr Sims Reeves, who resolutely refuses to produce his high A with more than 435 vibrations per second. [U]

THE MARRIAGE OF FIGARO
The Dramatic Review, 6 June 1885

On this day last week Mr Carl Rosa concluded his triumphant season at Drury Lane by conducting a performance of Mozart's opera, Le Nozze di Figaro, now a hundred years old. A century after Shakespear's death it was the fashion for men, otherwise sane, to ridicule the pretensions of the author of Hamlet to intellectual seriousness, and to publish editions of his works prefaced by apologies for his childishness and barbarism, with entreaties to the reader to judge him indulgently as a man who "worked by a mere light of nature."* At present, a century after Mozart's death, we have among us men, only partially idiotic, who hold similar language of the composer of Figaro, Don

* Nicholas Rowe, in his edition of Shakespear's plays (6 vols., 1709).

Giovanni, and Die Zauberflöte. Now the truth about Shakespear was never forgotten—never even questioned by the silent masses who read poetry, but skip notes, comments, and criticisms. And that the many heads of the mob are perfectly "level" on the subject of Mozart, is shewn by the fact that Figaro or The Don will still draw a house when nothing else will, though not a single perfectly satisfactory representation of either opera is on record. It is true that the infallibility of the mob is as yet only a dogma of Mr Sydney Grundy's*; but this matter does not rest on mob authority alone: Wagner, when not directly expressing his unmitigated contempt for his own disciples, delighted to taunt them by extoling Mozart; and Gounod, standing undazzled before Wagner and Beethoven, has confessed that before Mozart his ambition turns to despair. Berlioz formed his taste in ignorance of Handel and Mozart, much as a sculptor might form his taste in ignorance of Phidias and Praxiteles; and when he subsequently became acquainted with Mozart in his works, he could not quite forgive him for possessing all the great qualities of his idol Gluck, and many others of which Gluck was destitute, besides surpassing him in technical skill. Yet Berlioz admitted the greatness of Mozart; and if he did not fully appreciate him as the most subtle and profound of all musical dramatists, much less as his own superior in the handling of his favorite instrument, the orchestra, he never was guilty of the stupid fashion that has since sprung up of treating him as a sort of Papageno among composers.

This exordium is intended to help a few readers, who may have been perverted by the Papageno propagandists, to realize the magnitude of the task which Mr Carl

* This may allude to Grundy's play The Silver Shield, which had opened at the Strand Theatre on 19 May.

Rosa successfully attempted last Saturday. For his own part, he came forward as a conductor to carry out his own reading of the work, and not as Mr Randegger does—and does very well—merely to keep the band together and accompany the singers. There is an old tradition that the Figaro overture should be played against time so as to finish within three and a half minutes. There are two hundred and ninetyfour bars in the overture; and there are only two hundred and ten seconds in three and a half minutes. Consequently seven bars have to be played every five seconds. This gives the most effective speed. But the conductor must keep it uniform throughout: he must not indulge in *rallentandos*. Unfortunately this is just what Mr Carl Rosa did. He lingered affectionately over the delightful little theme in A just before the repeat, and then spurted to make up for lost time. The orchestra responded gamely; and the final chord was passed well within the two hundred and tenth second; but the finish was a scramble, which was the greater pity as the *rallentando* which necessitated it was in bad taste. Mr Carl Rosa's conducting is marred by two bad habits of his: he hurries at every *crescendo;* and he prolongs his pet passages as much as possible. Physically, he gives himself much unnecessary trouble. Throughout the overture he actually made two down beats in each bar, as if the music were written in two-four instead of common time. In a less familiar work the effect might have been to confuse the players, and Mr Carl Rosa can hardly have steadied his own nerves by slashing the unoffending air nearly six hundred times in less than four minutes. However, if he did those things which he ought not to have done, he at least did not leave undone those things which he ought to have done. He conducted the performance instead of allowing the performance to conduct him; and the largest share of the effect produced would not have been produced had he not been there. His treatment of the *allegro maestoso* movement in the baritone aria, *Vedrò mentr' io sospiro*, revealed all its dignity, which must have surprised many Italian opera-goers present. In this case he reduced the speed to which we have become accustomed; and he did the same, but with questionable judiciousness, in the first section of the great *finale* to the second act, where the *allegro*, interrupted by the discovery of Susanna, is resumed in B flat at the words *Susanna, son morta*. On the other hand, he took Figaro's aria, *Aprite un po'*, at the beginning of the last act, at a rattling *allegro molto*, a quite unjustifiable proceeding, as it bothered Mr Barrington Foote and violated Mozart's direction "*moderato.*" Later in the same act the movement marked *andante* in six-eight time, *Pace, pace, mio dolce tesoro*, was also taken far too quickly. There were three important omissions, besides those which have become customary. These were the duet *Via resti servita, madama brillante* for Susanna and Marcellina in the first act; the sestet *Riconosci in questo amplesso* in the third act, which was perceptibly weakened by the hiatus; and that extraordinary pæan of a base soul, *In quegl' anni*, for Don Basilio in the fourth act.

Before dealing more particularly with the singers, acknowledgment must be made of their general superiority in point of taste and conscientiousness to their Italian rivals as we last heard them at Covent Garden. They sang, with so few exceptions that they may all be stated here, faithfully what Mozart wrote. Madame Marie Roze, finding a few notes in *Deh vieni, non tardar* too low for her, sang them in the higher octave. Mr Barrington Foote in *Non più andrai* and Mr Burgon in *La Vendetta* embellished their parts by two very innocent (and easy) little scales, as merely human bassos always do and always will. Finally, in that song in which Mozart makes merry with the horns, Mr Barrington Foote

[263]

altered the penultimate note with such disastrous effect that he will probably trust Mozart's judgment in future rather than his own. This was all. Lovers of music who have had, at Covent Garden, to submit to the vulgar liberties taken without public rebuke by Madame Pauline Lucca with such songs as *Voi, che sapete,* or who have stared at the cool reliance upon popular ignorance with which Signor de Reszke used to omit the difficult passage of triplets and the F sharp in *Vedrò mentr' io sospiro,* against which Mr Ludwig so heroically bruises himself, will appreciate the fidelity of Mr Carl Rosa's artists, and will be glad to hear that they were applauded as heartily and encored as freely as if they had treated the audience to all the stale *fioriture* of their singing masters.

Madame Marie Roze was Susanna. She began very well, and remained so up to the middle of the second act, when her intonation became a little uncertain. Thenceforth she fell off vocally; and by the time the last act was reached she was singing much as the Marie Roze of ten years ago was wont to sing. Her acting was better, but she appeared too conscious of her own sprightliness, marred her dialogue by mirthless laughs, and was too tender-hearted to box Mr Barrington Foote's ears soundly in the garden scene. It would, perhaps, be inhuman to suggest that Mr Foote should try next time the effect of a vigorous pinch on the realism of Madame Marie Roze's acting. She would suffer; and probably he would too, subsequently; but the public would compensate both by the laughter and applause which make reputations behind the footlights. Miss Julia Gaylord, as Cherubino, delighted the audience by her vivacity, which indeed put her out of breath once or twice at critical moments. She made no attempt at the serious side—the Mozartian as distinct from the Beaumarchais side—of the page's calf-love for the countess, and was

[264]

quite as impudent in her presence as elsewhere; but she did justice to as much as she could see of her part, sang *Voi, che sapete* very prettily, and was encored heartily. Miss Georgina Burns played the countess. Her voice does not improve with use, but it is still brilliant. It may be said of nearly the whole cast that their voices are the worse for wear, instead of, as should be the case, the better. The exceptions are Mr Burgon, who did very well as Bartolo, and Mr Lyall, whose voice, if not very fresh or powerful, remains precisely as it was when the oldest inhabitant first heard it. As Basilio he had a grotesque hat and a red umbrella, and more Mr Lyall needs not to make him happy. Mr Barrington Foote's voice is not heavy enough for the music of Figaro, but his enunciation is very clear; and though he is not exactly a comedian, he is funny enough to pass for one on the lyric stage.

The orchestra, when playing the last section of the march in the third act, managed to get hideously out of tune, probably in consequence of the effect of the heat of the house on the woodwind instruments. With this exception they played admirably, as indeed any body of competent players could not help doing with such exquisite work in hand. The *fandango* was evidently designed by an artist capable of understanding the value of the opportunity offered by the only number in this wonderful opera that falls to the share of the dancer.

Though English performers in English opera are not quite so scarce as Italian performers in Italian opera, there was a mixture of nationalities at the Marriage of Figaro. The Countess was English and so was Figaro. The Count was Irish, Susanna French, Cherubino American, and the conductor German. The good humor of the audience was boundless. Besides the pre-arranged floral compliments to the *prime donne,* there was much cheering after the national anthem, and repeated calls for Mr Carl Rosa, who was at last led out by Mr Augustus Harris. As Mr Carl Rosa bowed himself off, a wreath was thrown, and Mr Augustus Harris snatched at it and made an unsuccessful attempt to lasso the retreating conductor with it. Failing, he disappeared in pursuit, and presently returned dragging Mr Carl Rosa forcibly with him, laurel crowned. Even after this Mr Carl Rosa had to come out again bowing. At the second bow he incautiously approached the footlights. Instantly there was a dead silence, broken only by a cry of "Speech! Speech!" Mr Carl Rosa blenched and precipitately dived behind the curtain; and the audience dispersed, highly pleased with him, with Mozart, and, for less obvious reasons, with themselves.

AÏDA GALLICIZED

Unsigned notes in The Dramatic Review, 13 June 1885

[U] At the Gaiety Theatre, French opera is in possession every second night. The only novelty, so far, is Lakmé, a three act opera by M. Léo Delibes. The book, by MM. Gondinet and Gille, treats of the adventures of Gerald, an English officer in India, who, with Rose, Ellen, Mistress Bentson, Frederic, and other perfidious islanders, excites the hatred of Nilakantha, a priest of Brahma. Lakmé is Nilakantha's beauteous daughter; and Gerald falls in love with her. Nilakantha kills him; but Lakmé bears his body to a retreat in the forest; brings him to life again; and proposes that he shall pledge her his eternal fidelity in a draught of sacred water. He agrees; and she goes to fetch the water. Just then Rose, Ellen, and Frederic enter; the fife and drum band of the regiment strikes up; and when poor Lakmé returns, Gerald is unable to conceal his preference for England, home, and duty. So she poisons herself, and the curtain descends. Mistress Bentson and the English ladies do not appear in the Gaiety version. The music, like the English officer, is very French; and there is too much chanting that is supposed to be Hindoo, but is actually the sham Egyptian music from Aïda Gallicized. There is "sparkling" dance music, and sentimental love music, modulating in Gounod fashion; but nothing that calls for serious criticism.

Lakmé has been produced here in recognition, not of its merit, but of its convenience for the display of Mlle Marie Van Zandt's talent. She is clever, confident, has considerable natural facility in executing *roulade,* and can touch E natural in *alt.* On the other hand, her voice, for so young an artist, is surprisingly deficient in freshness of tone; and only those notes which she takes very lightly are held steadily. When she ventures to sing with any energy, she is hardly better than her colleagues, who for the most part sing with a shattering *tremolo* and a nasal tone to which French audiences are better accustomed than English ones. Mlle Van Zandt is the only member of the original cast who appears at the Gaiety. Gerald and Nilakantha are now impersonated by MM. Dupuy and Carroul. These parts were filled by MM. Talazac and Cobalet when Lakmé was produced for the first time at the Opéra Comique in April 1883. M. Soulacroix, who has been heard at Covent Garden, plays the secondary *rôle* of Frederic as satisfactorily as a very vivacious French gentleman can be expected to play in the part of a British officer.

The mounting of the opera is quite as good as it need be. In the second act there is a capital crowd of Hindoos, Chinamen, Persians, British tars, with a solitary representative of Tommy Atkins; and the scene, though shorn of the humors of Mistress Bentson, is lively and amusing. The Bayadère ballet is better danced from a ballet master's point of view than most of the opera is sung from a musician's. Signor Bevignani conducts an orchestra of about forty players, selected from his old forces at Covent Garden. Their share of the performance might be worse. It also might be better.

Mr Eugen d'Albert, who became famous here as one of the prodigies brought to light by the Royal College of Music at South Kensington, and who subsequently went abroad and devoted himself to serious composition, must regard Herr Richter with somewhat mingled feelings. Mr d'Albert has composed an overture; and Herr Richter has had it played at his last concert, and played irreproachably. So far, Mr d'Albert is deeply indebted to the great conductor. But, unless a work have a whole concert to itself, much of the effect depends on how it is placed in the program. Mr d'Albert's overture, for instance, had the second place, the desirability of which depends a good deal on the sort of work that occupies the first place: somewhat also on that which comes third. Herr Richter made the following inhuman arrangement:—1. Mozart's great symphony in E flat. 2. Mr d'Albert's overture. 3. The Tannhäuser overture and ballet, as arranged for Paris in the days of the celebrated anti-Wagner riot. It is not to be wondered at that the new overture fell flat between this cross fire from the heaviest artillery of the XVIII and XIX centuries. Most conductors can make nothing of Mozart—many of them honestly believe there is nothing in him; but Herr Richter did not miss a single point in the symphony; and Mr d'Albert's work was nowhere after it. His overture is very long, and very slow. In form it resembles the preludes to Wagner's latest music dramas, and is made up of phrases which are all in rhythm, harmony, and instrumental treatment, direct reminiscences of motives from the Bayreuth master's works. Mr d'Albert is at no loss for technical resources to re-embody the ideas he has borrowed, no doubt in earnest enthusiasm, and without a thought of plagiarism; but the cool reception of his overture on Monday ought to convince him that second-hand Wagner will prove as intolerable tomorrow as mock Shakespear or Mozart-and-water have proved in the past. We have endured, in Joachim Raff, one cuckoo composer of XIX century music. Mr d'Albert will, we hope, spare us another.

At the same concert, a performance on a small scale of Berlioz's Symphonie Funèbre et Triomphale was tried and found wanting. A similar experiment this year at the Crystal Palace with the Te Deum, another of the composer's "monumental" works, went to shew that where Berlioz's intentions cannot be fully carried out, his works are best left alone; and this result was fully confirmed at Monday's concert. Performances of this symphony, of the Te Deum, and of the Requiem, ought to be feasible under the auspices of the Inventions Exhibition at the Albert Hall, where an orchestra of 200 performers could be engaged without heavy pecuniary loss. Nothing less than this will suffice. Such performances as those at the Crystal Palace and St James's Hall will only destroy the popularity which Mr Charles Hallé's production of the Faust a few years ago gained for Berlioz. The very first bar of the Symphonie Funèbre, written for eight side drums, and played at the Richter Concert upon one! shewed the futility of the attempt to dispense with the extraordinary forces for which the work was designed. The only satisfactory feature of the performance was Herr Müller's playing of the Oraison funèbre on the trombone. At a previous concert, Herr Richter's trombonists, by their delivery of the pilgrims' chant in the Tannhäuser overture, goaded the DRAMATIC REVIEW into describing them irreverently as "a triad of German sackbuttists," and comparing them very unfavorably with the English players at the Crystal Palace. Had they played on that occasion as Herr Müller played on Monday, the reproach would never have been incurred.[U]

RICHTER'S GEMS

Unsigned notes in The Dramatic Review, 20 June 1885

[U] A symphony by Robert Fuchs, a Styrian composer, one of the Professors of the Vienna Conservatoire, was performed at the Richter concert on Monday. A concise, vigorous work, put together with skill and firmness, it gives a more favorable impression of the composer's strength than his pretty but not very interesting string serenade, which was played at St James's Hall some years ago. The symphony is in C major, and the two middle movements are a short and catching intermezzo in the relative minor, *presto*, which was nearly encored (we are rapidly acquiring sufficient familiarity with serious music to qualify us for the barbarism of encoring a movement from a symphony); and an *adagio* in E major. The whole work is as free from the modern sickly pianoforte flavor and want of sound craftsmanship as a symphony of Haydn's, though Herr Fuchs cannot boast of anything comparable to the inexhaustible invention and unwithering freshness of that evergreen genius.

The Fuchs symphony was supplemented by a strong program selected from the gems of previous concerts. There was the Komarinskaja of Glinka, an ingenious web of tunes and chimes that supplies the Richter amateurs, many of whom are persons of commendably lofty views and serious aims, with a scrap of music that, though light, is not beneath their notice. Herr Henschel sang his two favorite pieces: the song of Pogner from the Meistersinger, and the Farewell and Fire Charm from the Walküre. Herr Henschel's tone is as fine and his enunciation as clear as ever. The two selections epitomize everything that is irrestible in Wagner. The melody, overflowing from all the parts, vocal and instrumental, of the Meistersinger song, is as refreshing as the farewell of Wotan is terrible and pathetic, like the voice of a god in trouble. Even the militant anti-Wagnerists have admitted the fascination of Brynhild's slumber, surrounded by Loki's surging, flashing, rippling flood of fire; perhaps the most successful direct presentation of a scene by music that has been made in this century, which has witnessed no small number of desperate attempts at such music-pictures. The No. 3 Leonore overture followed, and perhaps suffered a little by being placed at the end of the concert, when the fine edge had been taken off the orchestra by the symphony and the Wagner music; but is was played with great spirit, the players charging the coda with tremendous gallantry and carrying it by storm.

Next Monday's Richter concert will be the last of the season. As usual, Beethoven's choral symphony will be performed with the assistance of the choir. Miss Amy Sherwin, Miss Goldstein, Mr Edward Lloyd, and Mr Frederic King will sing the solo parts. Mr Villiers Stanford's setting of a portion of Walt Whitman's Burial Hymn of President Lincoln is also in the program. The overture will be that to Wagner's Flying Dutchman, which was last played in London at the final concert of the Philharmonic series. The comparison between its effect when conducted by Sir Arthur Sullivan and by Richter will be interesting.

At the Inventions on Tuesday afternoon, the concert of the Strauss orchestra in the Albert Hall crowded the amphitheatre and arena to such an extent that the police had some difficulty in keeping the doors closed against the unfortunate visitors who came too late to find room.

Herr Strauss, resolved to shew that he can be classical on occasion, conducted an arrangement by his late brother, Josef Strauss, of the first movement of the Moonlight Sonata. The triplet accompaniment, scored for the harp, was played by Madame Pistor-Moser, and the melody by Herr Wagnes, on the horn. The dance music was as bright as usual. The more serious items were of a mild character, and were very prettily executed.

On Wednesday, Friday, and Saturday next, concerts of English glees and madrigals composed between 1590 and 1830 will be given at the Inventions Exhibition by members of the Round, Catch, and Canon Club. Shakespear enthusiasts should attend and listen to the music that inspired the last act of The Merchant of Venice.[U]

A SUBSTITUTE FOR STRAUSS

The Dramatic Review, 27 June 1885

When Herr Richter disbanded his orchestra on Monday last, London was left to face three months without concerts of high-class music. Only the well-to-do amateurs will be any the worse, for there is practically no regular provision made at any time throughout the year for the mass of people who like good orchestral music, but who cannot afford to spend more than a couple of shillings a week on gratifying their taste. Of weekly concerts of recognized excellence, we have two sets: the Saturday afternoons at the Crystal Palace in the winter and early spring, and the Richter concerts from spring to midsummer, with a few extra performances very late in the autumn or early winter. These concerts are not cheap enough for the people. A Crystal Palace Saturday Popular, taking place on a half-crown day, with an extra charge for admission to the concert room, a sixpenny program, and a railway journey, makes a larger hole in half-a-sovereign than many amateurs care to make in five shillings. The lowest charge for admission to a Richter concert is two-and-sixpence; and the analytic program, though fattened by six pages of advertisements, costs an additional shilling, for which it is perhaps the worst value in London. The consequent dependence of both series of concerts on the patronage of comparatively rich people is shewn by the fact that they cease when the moneyed classes leave London, and recommence when they return.

Yet music is never really out of season. Fashionable singers may go and come with the Mayfair birds of passage; but so do fashionable preachers: yet no one seriously proposes to close St Paul's or Westminster Abbey during the autumn. The moment our concerts reach the people, they will become independent of fashion and season; and until they are thus independent, it is useless to pretend that they are popular. One of the standard out-of-season entertainments is the promenade concert, decorated with huge blocks of ice that do not cool anyone but only shew how independent music is of the weather. In spite of the fact that these concerts cater for two classes of people, each of which frightens the other away from them, they have proved beyond all question that classical music, a complete orchestra, and admission at one shilling, will attract a crowd in London. That is to say, one of our public needs is a weekly concert of good orchestral music for one shilling.

There is now such an opportunity of supplying this need as has never before arisen. The immense popularity of the yearly exhibitions at South Kensington is due, not to the interest of the people in fishery, in hygiene, or in inventions, but to their love of a crowd, a band, and "a gardens." The crowd satisfies the mere instinct of gregariousness; and the units of the crowd enjoy the garden much as the coster, as Mr Gilbert has quite accurately observed, "loves to lie a-basking in the sun."* But the music ministers to an active taste. It turns the scale in favor of South Kensington against the parks, or the embankment, or any other accessible place where there is a crowd and some greenery. It attracts even those who dislike crowds and public gardens, just as the promenade concerts at Covent Garden Theatre attracted people who loathed every feature of a promenade concert except the orchestra. Hence a great deal of money has been and is daily being spent at the Kensington exhibitions on military bands.

But a military band is not an orchestra. The feats of the British bandsman with the clarinet are amazing: he achieves with ease fiddle passages which no student of the orthodox treatises on orchestration would dare to write for his instrument; yet he cannot be to the musician all that the violinist is. The most insinuating tenor saxhorn cannot make us forget the viola; nor can the contrabass helicon, as it wraps the stalwart soldier in its brazen coils, compel to its slow utterance the seismatic tremors of the doublebass. Transcriptions of the overtures to William Tell and Masaniello, ballet music, selections from operas, Turkish patrols, and arrangements of The Lost Chord for cornet solo, afford small satisfaction to the masses who crave for symphonies, and are curious concerning the three manners of Beethoven.

Why, then, does not the Council of the Inventions Exhibition establish a first-rate orchestra at South Kensington? They cannot allege that it would cost too much: the mere imagination of the orchestra they might

* Gilbert and Sullivan, The Pirates of Penzance (When a Felon's Not Engaged in His Employment).

have had for the money which they have so ignorantly squandered on a small Austrian quadrille band, with an established reputation for being the very thing that we do not want here, makes the mouth of the musician in the London wilderness to water, and his teeth to gnash with disappointment. Here are a multitude of competent native or domiciled English players stranded at the closed doors of our opera houses and concert rooms, face to face with a music-loving multitude of Londoners thirsting for a good orchestra with a speciality for Beethoven's symphonies. Here, too, are the Inventions commissioners, with a unique market for bringing this supply and demand to equilibrium, and an opportunity of redeeming, by the same stroke, their exhibition from the reproach of being only a pretentious Cremorne or Rosherville. What, in this enviable position, have they done? They have engaged a foreign band, the speciality of which is not Beethoven's symphonies, but Strauss's sons' waltzes, which, even if people went to the Inventions to dance, would still be objectionable, not only because they are intolerably hackneyed, and have been so any time these fifteen years, in spite of the rest given to them by the popularity of Waldteufel and his slow waltz, but also because they remind us of the sheol of sensual vulgarity into which we suffered the French empire to lead us in the days when the beautiful Blue Danube first became rife among us.

The method of puffing this band adopted by the management was of a piece with the engagement. They advertized the sum they had agreed to pay Herr Eduard Strauss, and left the public to infer that the excellence of his band was in proportion to the largeness of the amount, which, it is as well to repeat, would have sufficed to engage an English orchestra equal to any in Europe. And they will probably justify their investment by pointing to the fact that audiences sufficient to overflow the Albert Hall crowd to see the dancing conductor, and to tap their feet and wag their heads to the seductive swing of his numbers, accentuated by those neat flicks of the side drum and chirps from the piccolo in which much of the Strauss magic consists. But the duties of the Council are not fulfilled when a crowd is assembled. The promise of a mammoth Christy Minstrel show, a variety entertainment, or a prizefight, would mass the visitors to the Inventions in the Albert Hall at a stated hour: there would be a difference in the character and class of the audience, and possibly also in the subsequent history of England, but not in the number of heads. The Executive is practically availing itself of state aid to crush out private enterprises for the entertainment of the people. The theatres have suffered in all directions; and no fresh undertaking is likely to start handicapped by state competition. If under these circumstances the South Kensington authorities do not keep their exhibitions up to the highest practicable artistic standard, they will debase the moral and musical currency, and prevent private enterprise from restoring it. The safest, easiest, most profitable, and most creditable course open to them is to set at once about establishing a first-rate English orchestra on the foundations laid by Mr August Manns at the Crystal Palace, and by Mr Weist Hill at the Alexandra Palace. When the people have been educated by some years of popular concerts at which orchestral music of the highest class can be heard for a shilling, they will be better able to understand such entertainments as the "Historic Concerts," which will next month illustrate the steps by which Music progressed from the Missa brevis of Palestrina to the Wein, Weib, und Gesang waltzes which the Inventions Council offer us as the flower of modern European music.

A word of apology is due to Herr Eduard Strauss for

grumbling so discourteously over his engagement. He has done all that he professed to do, and all that well-informed musicians expected. To quarrel with him because he has not astonished us as his father astonished our fathers nearly fifty years ago, or because he plays the sort of music that he is celebrated for playing, and was expressly engaged to play, would be unreasonable. The fault rests entirely with those Trustees of our metropolitan culture who blundered in art by neglecting a great opportunity of advancing music in England, and in economy by purchasing an inferior commodity abroad when a better was to be had for less money at home.

THE CONFERENCE ON MUSICAL PITCH

Unsigned notes in The Dramatic Review, 27 June 1885

[U] The Conference on Musical Pitch at St James's Hall on Saturday last was more amusing than might have been expected, even by those who know the diversity of the interests involved, and the way in which some of our eminent musicians, under cover of addressing a few general remarks to a public meeting, will nag at adversely opinionated fellow musicians for fifteen minutes at a stretch, in a manner highly diverting to those who are in the secret, though occasionally a little wearisome to the uninitiated. Sir George Macfarren was in the chair. After some interesting speeches from Mr Santley and Dr Stainer, and a little enlightenment from Mr A. J. Ellis and Mr Bosanquet, Mr Duvivier threw out skirmishers with a view to controversy. He began pertinently enough by pointing out that certain instrumental effects devized by composers in the past were quite altered by the elevation of the notes from the very characteristic low register of the clarinet to the higher register. But Mr Duvivier soon succumbed to the temptation to act as a musical *agent provocateur* by introducing irrelevant disparagements of modern orchestration that were evidently intended as a challenge to the disciples of Wagner. Fortunately the first resolution was put to the meeting immediately after Mr Duvivier's speech; and the challenge was forgotten.

Later on, Mr Rockstro, the flautist, had a lively passage of arms with Dr W. H. Stone. Mr Rockstro said that if the pitch were lowered, all the flautists would have to buy new flutes (the prices of modern flutes run into three figures occasionally). Dr Stone ridiculed this statement, and insisted that any flautist, by turning the *embouchure* of his instrument, could lower the pitch half a tone. Dr Stone, in fact, would not admit the necessity of replacing any instrument except the clarinet; and he pointed out that if the pitch were lowered half a tone, the A clarinets could be used as B flat clarinets, so that the clarinettists would not have to replace their whole set of instruments. On the subject of the cost of such replacements, opinion differed widely. Mr Cousens said £40,000 for the army alone. Mr Blakely guessed £200,000, though whether he included volunteer and militia bands in his estimate did not appear.

On the whole, there was an unlooked-for conflict of opinion as to the absolute facts concerned. Many of the speakers assumed French pitch to be a semitone lower than concert pitch, although Mr Bosanquet was careful to point out at an early stage of the discussion that French pitch is only two-thirds of a semitone below concert pitch. Mr Duvivier stated the vibration number of C at French pitch differently from Mr A. J. Ellis; and Mr Rockstro and Mr Charles Stephens were at odds on the subject of English concert pitch. Again, Mr Bosanquet stated that the pitch of most country organs

[278]

is French; but it subsequently appeared that the Society of Arts pitch, which is somewhat sharper, prevails. No speaker explained why the pitch had risen. Singers protested against the elevation; players of wind instruments complained of it; eminent authorities on the violin asserted that the best instruments of Stradivarius and Amati are either strained and spoiled by the screwing up of the strings, or deprived of their tone by the devices employed to make them strong enough to bear the strain; and violoncellists, compelled to employ thin strings instead of the thick ones of Lindley's day, lamented the consequent loss of power. Why the old Handel pitch, which lasted for a couple of centuries, should have risen in spite of everybody concerned having an interest in keeping it down, was not elucidated. Mr Ellis could only say that at the Congress of Vienna a set of instruments presented by the Emperor of Russia to one of the household regiments was manufactured to the high pitch; and that as these instruments were occasionally used at the opera, the orchestra had to tune up to them. But why they were so manufactured Mr Ellis could not say—or, at any rate, did not say.

Resolutions were eventually passed approving of a uniform pitch; of the French normal diapason as the most convenient standard; of taking immediate steps to induce our principal orchestras and our military bands to conform to that standard; and of a committee consisting of five musical men of science, thirteen executive artists, and three manufacturers of musical instruments, to give effect to the views of the meeting. One of these resolutions was informally passed. An amendment was moved and rejected; and Sir George Macfarren took the Noes to the amendment as Ayes to the substantive motion, which he omitted to put. Some of the dissentients objected to French pitch without approving of the present concert pitch; and a few resisted any alteration whatever. The latter class were composed of players who feared that an alteration would put them to the heavy expense of purchasing new instruments; and of Madame Patey, who wrote strongly recommending the high pitch for its superior brilliancy. But Madame Patey is a contralto; and contraltos gain renown by singing low notes just as sopranos do by singing high ones. Hence the contraltos have exactly the same reason for keeping the pitch up that sopranos have for keeping it down. The Shakespearean gentleman who could sing "both high and low"* was not trained by a modern singing master. If he had been, he would have had no middle to his voice, and must have depended on an effective compass of a fifth or thereabouts for vocal fame.

If French pitch be impossible without new instruments, how was it that the pitch came down at Covent Garden when Madame Patti insisted on it, and at Her Majesty's Opera when Madame Nilsson did likewise? At both houses, by the bye, the pitch, on very warm evenings, has been known to rise half a tone in the course of the performance. No wonder Madame Patti rebelled. French pitch is always declared by orchestral players to be impracticable; but it has never proved so when the conductor was determined to have it, except when, as at the Albert Hall, an organ stands in the way. For the pitch of that organ Mr Ellis says we have to thank the late Sir Michael Costa, who was, it appears, a stickler for the high pitch. On the whole, Sir Michael ought to have known better. Mr Carl Rosa, unfortunately, seems much of his opinion.

The Round, Catch, and Canon Club made a great

* O mistress mine, where are you roaming?
O, stay and hear; your true love's coming,
That can sing both high and low
Twelfth Night II iii

success last Wednesday at the Inventions with a selection of English glees and madrigals. The extraordinary charm of these glees is due to the smooth harmonic progressions of the old-fashioned counterpoint, and to the absence of accompaniment, which permits the singers to sing perfectly in tune, if they are capable of it by nature. Nearly all modern music is forced out of tune by accompaniments played upon keyed instruments, in which, by an objectionable but very convenient compromise known as "equal temperament," every note is made to do duodecuple duty in the twelve different keys, more or less imperfectly. The imperfection is only perceived by ordinary ears as a roughness in the chords. If anyone would compare these rough equal temperament chords at their worst with the smooth chords of human voices perfectly in tune, let him go to the Albert Hall, and hear an organ recital followed by a madrigal sung by the Round, Catch, and Canon Club. The Albert Hall organ in full blast, with the two or three echoes for which the building is famous in full play, and the beats of the equal temperament chords of the larger pipes rattling like a train of artillery wagons charging along a newly macadamized road, produces probably the most infernal din—the epithet is too moderate, but it is the only one that presents itself—ever offered as a substitute for music. After it, Horsley's By Celia's Arbor, sounds heavenly. On Wednesday, the audience encored it rapturously.

When, after all these exquisite part songs, the Strauss band entered and attacked Rossini's gaudy overture to La Gazza Ladra, the contrast was unbearable; and the writer of these lines precipitately fled from the building, and did not return until they played the North Sea waltz of the younger Johann Strauss—not the great original Strauss. Herr Eduard Strauss should give us more of his father's music, and less of his own and his brothers'.

No musician in search of a new sensation should miss the Siamese band at the Inventions. They now give concerts in the Albert Hall; and the audience crowds about the orchestra to look at these grave foreigners squatting cross-legged before their strange instruments, clad in the court dress of Siam, which, in delicate compliment to western habits in general, and our great railway companies in particular, is closely copied from the uniform of the English ticket collector. Most of us laugh at the music, and can find no whistleable tunes in it; but it is by no means impossible for a western European to enjoy it and even partly appreciate it; and the players are unmistakably skilful and artistic. The instrumental effects are of considerable variety. The scoring (if one may call it so) of the Sensano, or "Sweet Melody," would have delighted Berlioz, who might have imitated it by a combination of muted violins, trills on the low notes of two flutes playing in thirds, an inverted pedal sustained by an English horn, a worn-out Collard pianoforte, and a kitchen clock out of order and striking continually in consequence. Much more brilliant and sonorous effects are produced in airs of bolder design, such as The Malays of Lobhabury (which is enormously superior to our comic songs with similar titles), The Sorrow Parting, and the Siamese national anthem, during which it is the fashion at South Kensington to stand. The Pegu Affliction has afflicted countries further west than Pegu (if Pegu *is* a country); for it is nothing but Auld Lang Syne powerfully treated as a declamatory recitative. The Brother is a *moto perpetuo* for a wooden dulcimer, with florid accompaniments.

Several solos are introduced, notably one on the Siamese Stradivarius, and on the Takhay, which resembles in tone the reeds one cuts from a stalk of standing corn. The strokes of the kitchen clock instru-ment—the Siamese triangle—are phrased into groups of

[282]

two notes by letting the metal vibrate freely only for the first note of the group, and damping it for the second. The band has evidently been informed that when the foreign devils clap their hands after a piece, they desire to hear it again. To this barbaric custom the Siamese gravely conform; and the foreign devils consequently have to submit to *encores* which they did not quite intend to insist on. The Siamese scale appears to contain an approximation to every note in our scale, with the conspicuous exception of the leading note, the absence of which not only gives an oddly inconclusive air to the tonic at the end of a piece when it is approached by an ascending passage, but renders God Save the Queen impossible. Nevertheless the Siamese play it without the leading note, substituting the minor seventh. The excruciating effect of this in the second bar may be imagined. It reminds one of the penultimate note of John Anderson, my jo. It is to be hoped that Mr A. J. Ellis will find out what the Siamese think of our equally tempered scale. Some of their chords are smoother than ours; and as their thirds sound very flat to our corrupted ears, they are probably justly tuned, as the thirds in our system are very sharp.[U]

ART CORNER

Extracts from a monthly series of notes on music, drama, and art, in Our Corner, July 1885

[U] The musical season this year has been a fairly busy one. Italian operas, at the rate of two every week, with Madame Patti singing at each representation, have been keeping the fashionable tradition alive at Covent Garden since the 16th of last month. But the real opera season was that of Mr Carl Rosa's company at Drury Lane

[283]

Theatre, which opened on the 6th of April with Wallace's Maritana, and closed on the 30th May with a surprisingly good performance of a work of a very different stamp, Mozart's music-comedy Le Nozze di Figaro, still as fresh and wonderful as it was when it was composed nearly a century ago. Two new operas were produced in the interim. These were Mr Goring Thomas's Nadeshda, and M. Jules Massenet's Manon. Both have been fortunate enough to please the public. They are full of pretty and stirring music, noisy at times, but, on the whole, very superior in workmanship to operas of the same class composed a generation ago. Mr Goring Thomas is careful and ambitious in his composition: M. Massenet is no less so; but he is more inventive and spontaneous, and so seems to work less laboriously. He is passionate where the Englishman is sentimental, and impetuous where Mr Thomas seeks only to be massive and imposing. He had, however, a much more inspiring subject in the story of Manon Lescaut than the childish drama, half idyll, half Richardson's-show-tragedy, which Mr Julian Sturgis is said to have adapted from a Finnish romance for Mr Thomas.

Manon Lescaut dates from the first half of the XVIII century, when society appears to have been so corrupt that a gentleman could preserve some self-respect under circumstances in which an Englishman would be expected nowadays to loathe himself. M. Massenet's librettists, MM. Meilhac and Gille, in dramatizing Prévost d'Exiles's novel, have therefore kept the Sunday side of their hero, des Grieux, well before the public, and have suppressed the episodes in which his failings led him into actual disgrace. To whitewash Manon would have been not only impossible, but bad policy in catering for a Parisian—perhaps no less so for a London—audience, even were the British doctrine of justification by whitewash a rational one. Manon is certainly more human, if less respectable, than Nadeshda, who is one of those Galatea figures manufactured by the male poet solely for his own delight; and this is perhaps why M. Massenet's opera is so much more lively than Mr Goring Thomas's. Neither work contains anything profound or original; but M. Massenet has his own style in handling the orchestra (it is occasionally a very obstreperous style, by the way), wheras Mr Goring Thomas has everybody's knowledge of instrumentation and no orchestral style at all. As a musical colorist he is far surpassed by the French composer.[U]

We have had French opera at the Gaiety Theatre; but it has only served to shew the remarkable natural talent of Mlle Van Zandt, whose sole extraordinary qualification is an agile soprano voice with a range that includes E natural in *alt*. She is supported by a company of striking examples of the defects of the French school of singing, from which she is herself by no means free.

The Richter concerts, taking place on Monday evenings at St James's Hall, came to a close on June 22nd. Herr Richter's reception when he went to his desk at the first concert was so enthusiastic that he must feel assured that the musical amateurs of London have entire faith in him, and are ready to praise whatever he conducts without regard to the quality of the performance. Much of this faith is only fashionable superstition; but he won it honestly and takes no unfair advantage of it. The orchestra began the season admirably, and improved as it progressed, some of the performances being quite irreproachable, though there is a weak place or two in the wind band. The choir assisted in Beethoven's Calm Sea and Prosperous Voyage,*

* This choral work, Op. 112, is not to be confused with Mendelssohn's better-known overture, Op. 27, bearing the same name. Both are based on the pair of poems by Goethe.

Brahms's Harz Mountains Rhapsody, and Berlioz's massive Symphonie Funèbre et Triomphale. The impression produced by these choral performances is that not one of the choristers individually possesses a voice, but that at this grave disadvantage they do wonders collectively. They certainly no longer spoil the concerts, as they did once or twice in former seasons. The performance of the Berlioz symphony was interesting, as it is in the list of works which the composer called "architectural" or "monumental," and in which he expressly sought to produce prodigious effects by the employment of prodigious resources. Thus the Symphonie Funèbre et Triomphale was planned for performance by a band upwards of two hundred strong, including over one hundred and twenty wind instruments, drums, &c. Of course no such force was available at St James's Hall, and Berlioz would undoubtedly have repudiated such a paltry substitute as Herr Richter was able to offer. The effect was unsatisfactory; and the composer's reputation has been unfairly damaged by it: a result which those who were present at the production, on a similarly reduced scale, of the gigantic Te Deum at the Crystal Palace in April were quite prepared for. To play either of these works without at the very least doubling the ordinary numbers of a concert orchestra is as unjust to the composer as a performance of a Haydn quartet on the jew's harp would be.

Another novelty, at the same concert, was an overture by M. Eugen d'Albert, a young musician of whom great hopes were entertained during his connexion with the South Kensington School of Music, now the Royal College. To musicians familiar with the later works of Wagner there is nothing novel or interesting in the overture, Mr d'Albert having sacrificed his individuality, doubtless with sincere devotion, at the Bayreuth shrine. His work was admirably played, but the significant coldness of the audience at the end was all the more conclusive. An orchestral piece from Liszt's Christus, representing the song of the Bethlehem shepherds, would have pleased better but for its tedious length, and the absolutely unreasonable character of much of the matter that spins it out. The first hundred bars contain some passages which shew that pastoral effects of instrumentation, hackneyed as they are, are not yet exhausted. If Liszt had spared us the inevitable sample of his would-be passionate and sublime manner which disturbs the movement later on, the shepherds' song might become popular. Most of the programs have included a Beethoven symphony, but perhaps the highest proof of Richter's ability as a conductor was his success with Mozart's symphony in E flat. Many of our conductors, who gain considerable credit by their achievements in our grandiose and sensational XIX century music, are so completely beaten by Mozart that their performances have undermined the composer's immense reputation instead of confirming it. Herr Richter, however, held his own masterfully; and the only reputations damaged were those of the composers whose works were close enough to the E flat symphony in the program to suffer from the inevitable comparison. It was curious to observe in the two last movements of this work that the power of music to produce hysterical excitement when used—or abused—solely as a nerve stimulant, which is the only power that the XIX century seems to value it for, is used by Mozart with exquisite taste and irresistible good humor to relieve the audience from the earnest attention compelled by the more serious part of his work. Could he have foreseen that this half jocular side of his art would be that most seriously elaborated by his successors, and that his great compositions would appear as tame to some musicians of a later generation as a recitation from Shakespear presumably is to a howling dervish, his too early death might not have lacked consolation.

The Philharmonic concerts, which were not so well attended as they deserved, were conducted this year by Sir Arthur Sullivan, whose care and refinement have greatly improved the performances of the Philharmonic orchestra, but who certainly kills the music he conducts when vigor and impetuosity of treatment are required. The most important new works produced were a "symphonic poem" entitled Joan of Arc, by Moszkowski, the composer of the well-known Spanish dances for piano and four hands, and a symphony by Dvořák. Joan of Arc, a long and elaborate piece of program music, contains nothing very fresh, and a good deal that is decidedly stale. Herr Antonín Dvořák's symphony, which was conducted by the composer in person (as was Joan of Arc also), is in the key of D minor, and is numbered Opus 70. It suggests that a suite of gypsy songs and dance tunes must have evolved, like an organism, into the higher form of a symphony. The quick transitions from liveliness to mourning, the variety of rhythm and figure, the spirited movement, the occasional abrupt and melancholy pauses, and the characteristic harmonic progressions of Bohemian music, are all co-ordinated in the sonata form by Herr Dvořák with rare success. To English ears his music seems to be particularly grateful, for Dvořák has become so popular that he has dedicated an early work of his to the English nation "with feelings of deep gratitude." It is so long since the English nation produced any particularly English music (having since Purcell's death compassed nothing but secondhand Handel, secondhand Mendelssohn, and lately a little secondhand Wagner of the Meistersinger sort) that they ought to appreciate this compliment from a composer so intensely national in his work as Dvořák. The subject of the dedication is a patriotic hymn entitled The Heirs of the White Mountain, by Vítězslav Hálek, translated by Dr Troutbeck. It was performed at St James's Hall, on the 13th May, by Mr Geaussent's choir. On the same occasion Mr A. C. Mackenzie's Jason was produced. The choir, though not very numerous, sang very well indeed, and the solo parts were undertaken by Madame Albani and Messrs Lloyd and Santley. Had the title of the work been Love in a Village, the adequacy and charm of the music would not have been questioned. Jason and Medea, unfortunately for Mr Mackenzie, have graver associations.

September 1885

New works of art do not come to light in London during the month of August. Picture shows are closed, and Music condescends to promenade concerts at which the orchestra serves as a blind to a drinking bar, the patrons of which pay most of the expenses, and hear least of the music. Thus Music exploits Vice; and Vice is probably none the worse for making the acquaintance of Music, though Music is undeniably a little the worse occasionally for her contact with Vice. But a large body of Londoners who, to our great disgrace, have no other opportunity than the promenade concerts of hearing an orchestra for a shilling, and who can afford no more, are enabled to hear an overture or two when they please, and occasionally a symphony or concerto. The Inventions Exhibition could and should have given these people what they want long ago; but the only orchestral concerts at South Kensington have been those of Herr Eduard Strauss, whose handful of players proved themselves a capital *quadrille* band, but did nothing to satisfy lovers of serious music, and were certainly not worth the large sum expended upon them by the

[289]

Council of the Exhibition. They played dance music with a somewhat forced gaiety and dash, and ventured on a few good overtures, of which the conductor made but poor work. The rest of their programs contained arrangements of pretty drawing-room pieces, which were agreeable enough to those who knew of nothing better. Eduard Strauss is the youngest of three sons of Johann Strauss, who, with his celebrated band, made a sensation in London in the year of the Queen's coronation. That band, like its creator and conductor, now belongs to musical history only, though many persons undoubtedly believed last season that the Strauss at the Inventions was the celebrated Strauss, just as reasonably as the French peasants who voted for the imperatorship of Louis Napoleon believed that they were giving their suffrages to the hero of Austerlitz.

Johann Strauss had three sons, Johann, Josef, and Eduard; and he was determined that none of them should be musicians. But they all three baffled him. The waltzes of Johann the younger, the composer of the Blue Danube, caused his father's dance music to be almost forgotten. He had a Strauss orchestra; but he eventually devoted himself more and more to his present occupation of composing for the theatre. Die Fledermaus and other comic operas of his have been performed in London, at the Alhambra. Josef Strauss died some years ago after a visit to Russia. He too formed a Strauss orchestra, as did our recent visitor Eduard, who is said to have been trained, according to his father's wish, as an architect. He has the musical temperament of his family, but a musically endowed man may be either a Richter or a Christy Minstrel, according to his extra-musical qualifications. Eduard Strauss holds an intermediate position between the two extremes.

His only rivals at the Inventions Exhibition were military bands, notably those of the Grenadier and

Coldstream Guards. The Grenadier band is popularly supposed to be the better of the two; and it is in fact by far the larger and more completely equipped. The compass of its intensity of sound is immense, the gradation from *pp* to *ff* (now frequently displayed at full length in claptrap marches of the Turkish Patrol pattern) lasting an extraordinarily long time. The conductor, Mr Dan Godfrey, is a popular hero on Saturday nights: the belief of the audience in him is boundless. But the Coldstream band, mechanically inferior as it is, is artistically the better of the two, Mr Thomas having the advantage of Mr Godfrey in point of refinement, although, like most English bandmasters, he is shy of doing more with his band than he is likely to be generally and vociferously thanked for. The position of a capable military bandmaster is not any easy one. He is largely dependent on the officers of the regiment, many of whom are pretty sure to consider coarse playing and trivial music the best value for their subscriptions. He has to insist ceaselessly on a delicacy in the playing of wind instruments which his men do not appreciate, until he has come victorious out of a long struggle with them. His power to enforce thorough practice and rehearsal, though despotic in comparison with that enjoyed by ordinary conductors, is discounted by the compulsion he himself is under to accept and train such players as chance sends him, instead of to select and engage the best talent in the town. And, worst of all, he is expected to be ready at a moment's notice with a string of trumpery marches and dances which deprave his own taste and those of his men; whilst anything more serious than the overture to William Tell brings him little, if any, immediate encouragement or credit. But in the long run good music would certainly repay him for the labor of getting it up. If Mr Thomas has the courage and perseverance to include an overture by

Mozart or Beethoven, and at least one movement from a Beethoven symphony, in each of his Inventions programs; to stick to that policy; to induce the Council to advertize it; and to make it known as a speciality of his band, Mr Godfrey will soon be relegated to the second place in popular esteem, and the Coldstream Guards will have admittedly the first band in the service. The trouble of obtaining or making the necessary rearrangements of the orchestral scores ought not, at this time of day, to be considerable.

[U] Some very good work has been done at the Inventions in what are called "historic concerts." A series of performances of the unaccompanied vocal music of the contrapuntists of the XV and later centuries was of extraordinary excellence, and may be accepted as more than a set-off against the mistake of the Strauss engagement and a few minor blunders. The Round, Catch, and Canon Club, a double quartet of singers; and the Bristol Madrigal Society, numbering 120, and especially strong in boy's voices, gave concerts of Old English music which it would not be easy to overpraise. In London, benighted as we are to the treasures of English art, and the beauty of unaccompanied concerted singing, these performances were especially timely and valuable. Shortly after they took place, a London choir attempted Palestrina's Missa Brevis and Allegri's famous Miserere. The result was a failure so disgraceful that the announcement of a second performance of the same kind was withdrawn, and has not since been heard of. But this mishap was redeemed in the same week by three concerts of old Dutch music by eight singers from Amsterdam under the direction of M. Daniel de Lange. Although the music they sang was from two to five centuries old, the impression they made will not be forgotten easily. At the first of the three concerts, their singing was excellent beyond description. Some ignorant and meddlesome person probably told them that their refinement was too subtle to be effective in the Albert Hall; for they were a shade less careful and louder on the two following occasions; but they still exceeded all ordinary performances far more than they fell short of their own previous achievement. Their names were Mesdames Gips and Van Rennes, Esjer and Veltman (sopranos and contraltos); MM. Rogmans and Jebak (tenors); M. Spoel (baritone); and M. Messchaert (bass.) M. S. de Lange, a masterly organist, played compositions by Handel, Bach, and a XVI and XVII century Dutch composer named Jan Pieter Sweelinck, a musician of remarkable genius, hitherto practically unknown to us. Since this triumph the musical council of the Inventions has been enjoying its laurels almost inactively. A ridiculous "ocarina" concert, and a number of recitals on exhibited instruments for purposes of advertisement, have been relieved only by a trombone concert at which Messieurs Case, Geard, Antoine Matt, and J. Matt obtained a fair hearing at last for their grand, but unpopular, instrument. They performed, among other pieces, the two short movements for trombone quartet written by Beethoven in 1812, and first played at his own funeral.[U]

The Court band of the King of Siam, which plays certain compositions that have been handed down by aural tradition and have never, it is said, been committed to writing, plays occasionally at the Albert Hall. Their performance, though most of the visitors evidently find it merely outlandish, is not wholly beyond the range of Western sympathy. Some of the airs and instrumental effects are not unpleasant. The Siamese scale contains no leading note, and the attempts of the band to play God Save the Queen and other European airs are rather trying in consequence; but they succeed better with Scotch airs such as Auld Lang Syne, which is very like

[293]

their own Pegu Affliction. But a little of the Siamese music goes, it must be confessed, a very long way.

November 1885

Another attempt to establish a standard musical pitch has been made and abandoned in despair. The King of the Belgians attacked the problem royally by decreeing that all military bands, musical schools, theatres, and other institutions subsidized by the Government throughout Belgium should tune to French pitch. Our minister at Brussels wrote to the Foreign Office quoting the decree. The Foreign Office, at a loss how to dispose of this communication, sent it on to the Royal Academy of Music as being presumably something in the line of that institution. The directors of the Academy thereupon convened a public meeting, which took place at St James's Hall on the 20th June last; and a very lively meeting it was. The upshot was the appointment of a committee to carry out certain resolutions which had been passed. This committee began by trying to get the pitch of our military bands authoritatively fixed by the War Office. But the Commander-in-Chief pleaded "financial and other difficulties too great to be overcome" and declined to trouble himself in the matter. The Committee, feeling that it would be presumptuous to persist in the face of difficulties which had daunted so brave and able a tactician as the Duke of Cambridge, abruptly dissolved itself, declaring that "the impossibility of controling the musical arrangements of her Majesty's forces renders such an establishment" (of a uniform pitch in accordance with that which prevails in Europe) "totally impracticable." And so the matter drops for the present.

The difficulty is, as usual, an economic one. For example, a flute such as is used by a professional player in a concert orchestra costs about thirty guineas. If the pitch for which that flute was constructed be altered so much that a new instrument will have to be substituted, then every professional flute player in the country will have to disburse thirty guineas for a new flute, and wait for a chance of partly recouping himself by selling the old one to some amateur who does not play in concert with other performers. The same heavy tax would, under the same conditions, fall on oboe, clarinet, and bassoon players. The outcry which a proposal to alter the pitch provokes from the orchestra may be imagined. But against it must be placed the outcry of the singers against the strain put upon their voices by the excessively high English pitch, and the protests of musicians against the performance of the music of Mozart and Handel in what are practically higher keys than those in which it was intended to be heard.

Our pitch is rather more than a semitone sharp to Handel's tuning fork, so that his compositions in the key of D are heard nowadays in what he would have called the key of E flat. The change is a disadvantage to tenor and soprano singers as far as their highest notes are concerned, though to contraltos and basses, whose lowest notes are of course facilitated by the rise in pitch, it is an advantage. Hence soprano and tenor singers protest against the high pitch, whilst contraltos advocate it. Mr Sims Reeves has sacrificed engagement after engagement at musical festivals sooner than sing to the high pitch set by the organs at such performances. Madame Nilsson and Madame Patti have insisted on French pitch at the opera. But Madame Patey declares that the high pitch is an improvement. She is a contralto. And so the battle rages between the vocalists and the instrumentalists, whilst the instrument makers take one side or the other according to their pecuniary interest or the difficulties created by the exigencies of construction. But a combination among our conductors, if they could

[295]

be induced to agree as to the most desirable pitch, and to be inexorable in making the attainment of that pitch a condition of a player's engagement, would soon settle the question.

Expert players of wind instruments can modify the pitch of the notes they produce very considerably by their blowing, by turning the embouchure, drawing out mouthpieces, crooks, and tuning-slides, inserting washers, and other devices. They have to do this constantly even when playing at the pitch for which their instruments were designed, because mechanically perfect instruments are physical impossibilities. The upper octave of the flute, as far as it depends on the holes and keys of the instrument, is so sharp that it would be useless if the player could not flatten the notes by his method of blowing. Some players have such power of correcting mechanical defects by their embouchure that for the sake of certain advantages in power of tone they cause their flutes to be constructed in such a way that no ordinary player can use them. Players on reed instruments have less latitude of this kind; but except in the case of the clarinet they can by the aid of mechanical alterations vary the pitch within half a tone, which is quite sufficient for the purpose in question. The clarinet alone is said to be intractable, but as every clarinet player is expected to possess at least three instruments, in A, in B flat, and in C respectively, something can be done to meet the difficulty—if it really exists—by considering the A clarinet as a clarinet in B flat, which instrument many players improperly use almost exclusively. Brass instruments have resources in shanks and tuning-slides for flattening, and string instruments present no difficulty. Old Italian violins would be much improved by a return to thicker strings and removal of the fortifications which have been added in modern times to protect them against the strain of the high pitch. Nearly all the admitted difficulties can be got over without new instruments. Those that are supposed to be most formidable have been known to disappear with such alacrity before a determined conductor two minutes after they had been declared utterly insuperable by the player, that it may be doubted whether they are anything more than conservative excuses.

Perhaps the greatest obstacle to a reform is the expense of retuning great organs such as those in the Albert Hall and the Handel orchestra at the Crystal Palace, an operation which would cost a large sum per instrument, particularly if the alteration were not exactly a semitone, and so should necessitate the modification of every separate pipe and reed. If the proprietors of the organs could be induced to suffer this outlay, and if the War Office and the officers of the various regiments could be persuaded to make a tremendous investment in new clarinets, there would still have to be faced a certain amount of grumbling from the public and artistic agony on the part of conductors at the temporary falling off in the effect of orchestral performances which would inevitably follow a change of pitch. This would disappear when the players became accustomed to the new pitch; but in the meantime there would be much murmuring, and much crowing from the advocates of the high pitch. It will be seen that the matter is by no means a simple one, and that alteration involves unforeseen trouble in many quarters. The avoidance of such trouble in future is, however, one of the most tempting results of the establishment of a uniform pitch, not only throughout England, but throughout Europe.

[U] A determined attempt is being made at Her Majesty's Theatre to accustom the British public to the Italian three-act *ballet d'action*. Excelsior has now been played nearly a hundred and thirty times, and it certainly does not disappoint those who are curious enough to go to see it. The music is, of its kind, excellent; and the dancing, in which a considerable body of men and children are employed, is graceful and spirited. The action, which illustrates the progress of steam, electricity, and engineering enterprise, is interesting and amusing; and there is not a single dance, group, or scene, in which the personal attractions of the female performers are relied on to please the audience. A bishop might, in pursuance of Mr Stewart Headlam's advice, witness Excelsior without a misgiving as to the perfect good faith both of the performers and the spectators in the purely artistic character of the entertainment. The ample stage room at Her Majesty's, and the combinations of bright positive colors, thoroughly Italian in taste, produced an effect which is very cheerful and almost classic in its refinement and simplicity. Under Mr Hawtrey's management the ballet has been supplemented by Planché's Secret Service, in which Mr Hermann Vezin is supported by Mr Frank Archer and Mr Arthur Dacre. Miss Kate Vaughan now appears in the second act of Excelsior, and gains what her Italian colleagues must think rather cheap applause by her dancing of a feeble waltz by Signor Tosti.[U]

December 1885

Mors et Vita, the sacred trilogy composed by M. Gounod for the last Birmingham Festival, and received there with something short of enthusiasm, was performed for the first time in London at the Albert Hall by Mr Barnby's choir on the 4th of November. M. Gounod is no Voltairean: he is the romantically pious Frenchman whose adoration of the Virgin Mother is chivalrous, whose obedience to the Pope is filial, and whose homage to his God is that of a devoted royalist to his king. It follows that he is not a deep thinker. But his exquisite taste, his fastidious workmanship, and an earnestness that never fails him even in his most childish enterprises, make him the most enchanting of modern musicians within the limits of his domain of emotion and picturesque superstition. Religious music is not now the serious work it used to be. One hundred and fifty years ago it was still possible for a first-rate intellect to believe that in writing for the Church its highest powers were enjoying their worthiest use. A Mass and a series of religious Cantatas embody the greatest achievements of John Sebastian Bach, the greatest composer of his age (which implies much more than that he was merely the greatest musician). Mozart, the immediate inheritor of Bach's supremacy, was so orthodox a man in his nonage that he exulted when, as he phrased it, Voltaire "died like a dog." Yet religion got no grip of his mature power. His reputation as a moralist and philosopher rests, not on his Masses, but on his two great operas, and on his allegorical music-play Die Zauberflöte, which might have been composed by a modern Positivist or Agnostic Socialist.

Beethoven's masterpiece, the Choral symphony, culminates in a setting of Schiller's Ode to Joy, a poem that might almost have been written by Shelley. After Beethoven, composers who, like Schumann, were thinkers as well as musicians, unconsciously dropped the Bible and the liturgy, and devoted themselves to secular poetry and to such works as the second part of Goethe's Faust. Berlioz was no exception: the Requiem Mass was to him only a peg to hang his tremendous music on; to a genuinely religious man the introduction of elaborate sensational instrumental effects into acts of worship would have seemed blasphemous. Mendelssohn was, like M. Gounod, no very profound thinker. The decay of what is called orthodoxy appeared quite as strikingly in its failure to call into action the highest faculties of philosophic composers who were not consciously heterodox, as in its overt repudiation by many commonplace persons at and about the revolutionary epoch. And so nowadays religious music means either a legend from scripture, melodramatically treated exactly as a legend from Hoffmann or an opera libretto would be, or else a Mass in which the sensuous ecstasies of devotion and adoration, the hypnotic trances and triumphs which make religion a luxury, are excited in a refined fashion by all the resources of the accomplished musician, just as they are in a cruder way by the tambourines and cornets of the Salvation Army. Mors et Vita, like Rossini's Stabat Mater and Verdi's Requiem, belongs to this class; but in it there is also some of the descriptive melodrama of the modern oratorio.

Just as the introduction to the last act of M. Gounod's Roméo et Juliette is descriptive of the sleep of Juliet, so the introduction to the second part of his new sacred trilogy is entitled Somnus Mortuorum. The resurrection at the sound of the trumpets is then musically set precisely as if it were a scene in a ballet. A curious effect is produced by sharpening the fifth of the chord figured by the fanfares of the trumpets, which thus play the intervals of the augmented triad as if it were a common chord. As may be supposed, the resolution of the discord is somewhat urgently demanded by normal ears long before the dead are fairly awake. This central episode in the work is preceded by a requiem, and followed by scenes descriptive of the judgment and the new Jerusalem. Long before it is all over—it lasts three hours—one feels that a more vigorous composer would have made shorter work of it. At bottom, M. Gounod's piety is inane, and so, at bottom, his music is tedious. The charms of beauty and natural refinement without brains may be undeniable; but they pall. M. Gounod's religious music is beautiful; it is refined; it is negatively virtuous in the highest degree yet attained; the instrumentation is continuously delightful; the whole would realize a poetic child's conception of the music of angels. But men grapple with the problems of life and death in the XIX century in another fashion. Feeling that the consummate musician is a puerile thinker, we are compelled to deny that he is a great composer whilst admitting the loveliness of his music.

Of the performance it need only be said that Madame Albani, Miss Hilda Wilson, Mr Lloyd, and Mr Santley were fully efficient in the solo parts. The orchestra was admirable. The huge chorus sang accurately, and proved that they had been diligently drilled. The Albert Hall Choral Society is progressing, though there is still room for a considerable improvement both in tone and intelligent delivery. They might do better, considering their numbers and opportunities; but it can no longer be said of them as aforetime that they could not possibly do worse.

HISTORIC CONCERTS

Unsigned notes in The Dramatic Review, 4 July 1885

[U] The original members of the Band of Lansquenets, of the XVI century, are happily dead; but they have left their flutes and their drum behind them. The drum is of the sort used by the *virtuosi* that accompany Punch and Judy shows; and the flutes are brown keyless flageolets, not very accurately pierced, and not absolutely identical in pitch. They are of various sizes, the largest resembling a leg of an old-fashioned bed, and the smallest—a most dreadful instrument—a leg of the small stool belonging to the same suite of furniture. They are eight in family, and when they discoursed the March of the Lansquenets at the Historic Concerts in the Inventions Exhibition, the effect was voted "quaint." The incessant beating of the loosely stretched drumhead; the weak whistling of the soprano flutes; and the mournful woodiness of the tenors and basses moving in thirds, sixths, and fifths with them—all being more or less out of tune from defects of construction that no skill on the part of the players could neutralize—made a whole which was certainly quaint enough: almost as quaint as the waits at Christmastide. But a little of it was calculated to go a long way.

These Lansquenets' flutes are called *flauti dolci*, or sweet flutes. On the same inscrutable principle, in our own day, we have execrable machines made with concertina reeds, fed with bands of perforated paper, and played by turning a handle, advertized as the Dulciana, the Melodina, the Harmonista, and The Cottager's Joy. The "sweet flute" has an inimitable plaintive silliness that is all its own; but it is not sweet. The common cross flute, now fast becoming obsolete, was an improvement on it. M. J. Dumon played three pieces by Bach and Handel on an old ivory one-keyed specimen that Frederick the Great may (or may not) have performed upon. The want of power and unevenness of quality that provoked Mozart and other composers to speak so unkindly of the flute were very perceptible. The modern flute, as constructed by Boehm, is one of the most powerful instruments we have, as M. Dumon's pupils demonstrated in response to an *encore* for the Lansquenets' march . Yet the faults of the old flute were partly the faults of its qualities. The pieces played upon it by M. Dumon to the harpsichord accompaniment (executed by M. Wouters) had a flavor unattainable nowadays with Boehm flutes and Steinway grands.

The harpsichord was particularly interesting to

musicians as an important part of the working "plant" of Bach, Handel, and Mozart, the greatest composers known to us. Great as they were, they were nevertheless as subject to the conditions imposed on them by their tools and materials as Phidias and Praxiteles. The conceptions of artists are limited by their practicability. No composer, however boundless his imagination, ever conceives chromatic scales in *altissimo* for the bass trombone. For the same reason, no contemporary of the harpsichord ever conceived Chopin polonaises or Rhapsodies Hongroises, as the result of an attempt to play them would have been an unmeaning jangle, culminating in the knocking of the instrument to pieces. The foreign gentlemen in fur-collared overcoats and long moustaches who are in such force at the pianoforte exhibits at the Inventions may be congratulated on being contemporaries of Steinway instead of Hass. They hammer the modern iron-framed pianoforte recklessly, reveling in fistfuls of chords, and quite content, if they can get their thumbs and little fingers on the right notes, to let the rest of their digits strike what they may chance upon, any combination of sounds making a satisfactory chord to them provided it be loud enough. Place one of these gentlemen before a harpsichord, and ask him to play six bars of a suite by Handel or a sonata by Mozart, and you will presently know whether he can really play or not. The thin tone of the harpsichord and the staccato effect of runs and scales upon it have certain advantages. The harmony does not become muddled as it so often does on modern pianofortes; and many old-fashioned passages acquire character and piquancy when played upon it. There are two harpsichords in use at the Historic Concerts. One, with a double keyboard, by Hass, is a fine representative of the concert grand of 1734. It has been raised to French pitch, and consequently is probably harder and more metallic in tone than its maker intended; but the difference, at most, can be but trifling. The other, a smaller instrument, is very inferior, and does not hold in tune. At the second concert it had got so far out that Mlle Ulmann's performance on it of a few celebrated pieces by Couperin and Rameau was rather trying to one's ears.

As to the *viola da gamba*, it is not too much to say that M. Jacobs might safely challenge any violoncellist to surpass his performance upon it. The instrument he uses dates from the XVII century; no violence has been done to it to get it up to modern concert pitch; and the tone is full and pure, and very even over the whole compass of the instrument, there being none of the differences of character from string to string which are so remarkable in the violoncello. The *viola da gamba* has six strings. M. Jacobs played a sonata by Tartini admirably.

Mlle Elly Warnots sings some XVI century songs, some of which were probably familiar to Mary Stuart and to Henri Quatre. For "historic" concerts it is necessary to find singers who are artists of culture and intelligence, and not mere vocalists. Mlle Warnots fulfils these conditions satisfactorily. A somewhat unexpected feature of these concerts is their great attraction for visitors to the exhibition and the genuine enjoyment of the music by the comparatively few persons for whom there is room in the concert hall, from the doors of which numbers of people were turned away on Wednesday and Thursday. The excellence of the performance is highly creditable to MM. Victor Mahillon, J. Dumon, and other members of the Brussels Conservatoire. The program will be repeated for the last time at five o'clock this afternoon.

Next week there will be a concert of Italian and English madrigals on Wednesday, and on Thursday a lecture by Dr Bruce on North English vocal melodies.

Meanwhile, Herr Strauss gives two concerts daily in the Albert Hall. On Thursday last he introduced an orchestral arrangement by his own hand of Chopin's polonaise in A. Some added decorations, scored for the piccolo, are striking; and it is perhaps just as well that Chopin, who was a short-tempered man, was not there to hear them. On the same occasion a performance of Mendelssohn's Ruy Blas overture, a work in which the great string power of our English orchestras usually comes out strongly, gives a fresh illustration of Herr Strauss's inability to beat us at serious work. At the same time it must be admitted that his band has acquitted itself in many respects very well indeed. Not to be behindhand, Mr Godfrey occasionally selects a Strauss waltz for performance by the bandsmen of the Grenadier Guards, who play it with a spirit and precision upon which Herr Eduard Strauss could hardly improve. All the bands at South Kensington are the better for the publicity they enjoy, and the much discussed competition of the Strauss orchestra. The engagement of the band of the Pomeranian Hussars is now almost at an end. For a cavalry band, it is not bad; but is necessarily inferior to such first-rate infantry bands as those of the Grenadier and Coldstream Guards, with their varied resources in wood, wind, and even—in the case of Mr Godfrey's band—in a couple of bass strings. The Pomeranian pitch, by the bye, is monstrously high; and the tone is arid and piercing, instead of being brilliant.[U]

BRASSES AND PIPES

Unsigned notes in The Dramatic Review, 11 July 1885

[U] A lecture at the Inventions is sometimes amusing, sometimes very much the reverse. Mr Blaikley, for instance, gave one recently on brass instruments. Primarily, of course, the object of the lecture was to advertize Messrs Boosey's wares; but Mr Blaikley's claims to be heard on the subject are independent of the interests of the firm with which he is connected. But he should keep elementary acoustics out of his lectures at the Inventions. People who have studied the subject know everything he deals with already, except his point about conical tubes and Helmholtz's mistake respecting them. The rest of the audience are simply bewildered by his remarks about vibrating columns and the position of their nodes. The most useful lecture would be illustrated by a complete set of instruments, and might run as follows: "You see, ladies and gentlemen, this monstrous trumpet—as you would call it—nearly half as long as this room is wide. It is what the soldiers play on in Mr Godfrey's band. You look incredulous; but allow me to roll it up into a convenient shape, and you will recognize it at once. (Exhibit euphonium, and wait for applause.) Now, when your little boy (laughter) asks you what is that big thing that the soldier is playing, you reply, seeing that it is very large and made of brass, 'That is a bassoon, my son.' (Applause.) But you are wrong, as usual. (Sensation.) It is a euphonium. *This* is a bassoon. (Exhibit bassoon—do not wait for applause.) This, which you call a flageolet, is really an oboe (murmurs of dissatisfaction); and this, which you suppose to be a cornopean, is a slide trumpet. You will probably never learn to distinguish accurately between a clarinet and an oboe, a trumpet and a cornet. (Disturbance.) But this at least you all know to be an ophicleide. (Hear, hear, and applause.) You err, my friends: it is in fact a tuba or bombardon. (Loud hisses.) There is all the difference in the world between them. Now, as to the quality of tone. That, you are doubtless aware, depends on the material of which the instrument is made—in this instance, brass. (Signs of assent.) I will now give you a practical illustration of how much the material has to do with it. (Play See the conquering hero on the tuba.) You hear the effect of the brass? (Great applause.) I will now play the same tune on a brown paper model of that tuba. (Do so.) You perceive that the effect is exactly the same (groans) and that you will do well in future to confine the expression of your musical opinions to circles into which no reliable information has as yet penetrated." (Platform stormed, and lecturer rescued by the police in a damaged condition.)

A lecture of another sort was given on Thursday afternoon by the Rev. J. Collingwood Bruce, on the Northumberland small pipes and the ballad music of the north of England. Dr Bruce, scholar, divine, antiquary, enthusiast, and, in his way, a bit of a wag, gave a quaint lecture illustrated by songs and pipe tunes. The latter were played by the Duke of Northumberland's piper, William T. Green, and by a very skilful unattached artist named Thomas Todd. Todd's pipe was the sweeter instrument of the two, and there was something bardic about his appearance; he looked more the harper than the piper. Green, on the other hand, is a typical piper, and was evidently impatient of his new metropolitan boots, which creaked when he marched up and down the platform playing, and pinched him when he sat still. A small choir sang the songs very fairly, winning an encore for Bobby Shaftoe. As Dr Bruce observed, the north country music "amuses the fancy and pleases the ear without exhausting the intellect." He did not gain quite so ready an assent when he remarked that the pipes are to be valued chiefly as a domestic instrument. It may be, as he said, that "domestic joys are better than those of the public assembly"; but to a Middlesex householder a public assembly, even of the Clerkenwell Vestry, would be a welcome refuge from a home haunted by more than a very little and very occasional performance on the Northumbrian bagpipes.

Next week there will be three concerts of ancient Netherlandish music at the Inventions. On Tuesday Palestrina's Missa Brevis, with the traditional embellishments as performed by the Papal Choir, will be in the program. Visitors should not be afraid of these concerts because they are called "historical." They have hitherto proved highly enjoyable, apart from all chronological considerations.

On Wednesday last a concert was given at the Albert Hall by the Bristol Madrigal Society, which is nearly forty years old. Pearsall was one of its first members. It has a roll of one hundred and twenty singers, admirably trained, and in good practice, their most difficult selections being sung with precision and without the least apparent anxiety or effort. The boys' voices are especially beautiful and even. There were twenty items in the program, some of them only quaint museum specimens of the art, but others masterpieces of English music. Chief among these was Wilbye's Sweet honey-sucking bees, now nearly three centuries old and not worn out yet, nor likely to be. As samples of what has been done in our own age by Pearsall, Sir Patrick Spens, which is practically a ballad in ten real parts, and the famous carol In dulci jubilo, let us our homage shew, &c., were sung. Both were encored.

Whilst the Bristol Madrigal Society was in full song,

a substantial British Matron walked proudly into the amphitheatre with her daughter. On hearing the strains for which England was once famous throughout Europe, she hesitated, and said in a distinct and audible voice "This isnt Strauss, is it?" Her daughter looked suspiciously at melodious Bristol, and replied doubtfully "I dont think it can be." "Then come out of this" said the matron, and retired somewhat indignantly. No doubt she referred the question to a policeman in the corridor. If the policemen at the Inventions were the Encyclopædia Britannica in blue binding, they would break down under the cross-examination to which they are daily subjected. It is pitiable to see an innocent young constable, who only knows that he is to keep the door of the music room shut during the pieces, assailed by "Is the Appassionata Sonata over yet?" "Is this the way to Queen Elizabeth's lute?" "Where's Beethoven's piano? You dont know! Well: the program boy said you did." "I want to see Handel's tuning-fork" (as if the policeman had it concealed about his person). "Will they play anything from the Mikado today?" "Which entrance ought we go out by to get to the Commercial Road?" &c. &c. &c. &c. &c.

Many of the spinets and harpsichords in the historical collection at the Albert Hall conform to Mr Weller's specification of the pianoforte inside which Mr Pickwick was to have been conveyed from the Fleet prison to America. "The works" have been taken out of them; and the visitors who, being specially requested not to touch, always do touch furtively whenever the attendant is not looking, elicit no sound from the instrument.[U]

AN ENGLISH FAILURE
AND A DUTCH TRIUMPH

Unsigned notes in The Dramatic Review, 18 July 1885

[U] Not since the days of Charles II. has England sustained a humiliation from the Dutch like that which has just befallen her at the Inventions Exhibition. Compared with such utter shame as we have now been put to, the bombardment of Sheerness by de Ruyter is something to congratulate ourselves upon. Here are the facts. On Tuesday last, an English choir, conducted by Mr W. S. Rockstro, gave at South Kensington a concert of sacred music of the XVI and XVII centuries. On Wednesday and Thursday, eight Dutch singers from Amsterdam, conducted by Monsieur Daniel de Lange, did the same. On the one hand was a strong body of British singers, with their countrymen's reputation as the greatest part singers in the world to uphold in an International Exhibition. On the other, a mere double quartet of Dutchmen and Dutchwomen, with faces that we have often seen in picture galleries on the canvases of Rembrandt, Hals, Terburg, Jan Steen, but never in a concert room. What Briton could ever have believed these people to have either voices, musical traditions, or great composers? It is true that the existence of clever persons of Dutch extraction, such as Beethoven and Sarah Bernhardt, has been vouched for; but that a Dutchman could do anything before being extracted except paint "old masters," is in flat contradiction to every British prejudice.

To such prejudices the record of this week will strike cold. Mr Rockstro's choir sang Palestrina's *Missa Brevis* for four voices. Nothing like that performance will ever be heard from the Dutch company. They also sang Allegri's famous Miserere, which is sung once a year (in Easter week) at the Sistine Chapel in Rome. If they sing it as Mr Rockstro's choir sang it, once a year is too often. Once a century would be too often. Such displays should not be cheapened by frequent repetition. Most English ladies and gentlemen can sing reasonably out of tune without perceptible effort; but the extraordinary aptitude of Mr Rockstro's vocalists for this species of entertainment is far beyond anything usually available even in private circles. They avoid the correct pitch as if by instinct, and flatten and sharpen the most temptingly easy intervals so as to inflict the maximum of anguish on the expectant listener. Yet on Tuesday they did not seem to do this on purpose. Many of the men made wry faces, and regarded oneanother with a "Why cant you sing in tune?" expression that sometimes, when an unbearably excruciating progression maddened them, intensified to a glare of Cain-like hatred. The ladies did not mind so much: they apparently did not care how the others sang, so long as they themselves were a good comma sharp. At the beginning of each movement they took the pitch from the harpsichord. The pitch at the finish depended altogether on the length of the movement, during which they shewed no particular preference for one key more than for another. Even when they had made a choice they seldom stuck to it for half a dozen bars at a time. The audience said "Palestrina's music is very quaint." What Palestrina would have said had he been there to hear is past imagining; nor indeed does it matter, as it would probably have been totally unfit for publication. But it is to be hoped that the audience, on reflection, will absolve the composer from the intentions imputed to him by Mr Rockstro's choristers.

Nor ought they to shift the blame too hastily from

Palestrina to Mr Rockstro. The undertaking was an extremely difficult one, and it was evident that the conductor had done his utmost to secure a satisfying result. The fact that there was no absolute breakdown proves how much trouble must have been taken. But the materials for a good performance were not present, and though Mr Rockstro is to blame either for having selected them injudiciously—if he had any choice—or for not declining the task if he had none, he no doubt did his best with the forlorn hope that he volunteered to lead. A few of them would have done better in a good choir, but that is the very utmost praise that can be accorded. Besides the Mass and the Miserere, a few anthems by Redford, Tallis, Farrant, and Orlando Gibbons were sung (if one may use the expression), and a gentleman played a Preludium and Arrangement of *Een Kindeken is uns Geboren*, by Dr John Bull. This was the most enjoyable item in the program, but there was no reason for playing it on a Kirkman harpsichord. As far as historic accuracy was concerned, it might as well have been played on a Steinway grand.

The day after the English failure came the Dutch triumph. At three o'clock on Wednesday, a few handfuls of people, languidly curious about a Concert of Ancient Netherlandish Music, strolled into the Albert Hall, and found an organist at work there. There was nothing strange in that, as the Albert Hall in these days is rarely free from an organist. But this was a masterly organist, and from such the Albert Hall enjoys an almost complete immunity. Further, a lady was managing the stops for him as if she knew this organ—which was nevertheless a foreign one to her—by heart. He was playing a remarkable piece of music consisting of a figure with a strongly marked rhythm repeated over and over again with a grip and culminating power worthy of Wagner, a freedom and breadth almost worthy of Handel, and a harmonic treatment that would not have discredited Bach. Except for the purity of the harmony, and the preparation and resolution of the discords, Wagner would have been guessed as the most likely composer of the three. On purchasing a program, the visitor discovered that this powerful music was by one Jan Pieter Sweelinck, a Dutch contemporary of Shakespear's. Here was a revelation. When the fantasia was over, about two persons applauded: conclusive evidence that the audience did not know a good organist from a bad one, and saw nothing startling in the discovery of an Elizabethan Wagner. Enter then to the platform four Dutch ladies, four Dutch gentlemen, and a man with a face as striking as that of Liszt. He was the conductor, M. Daniel de Lange, presumably brother to the organist, M. S. de Lange. The audience stared, and the strangers seemed a little chilled and anxious. They stood up and sang the 122nd psalm as set for four voices by Wagner Sweelinck. It would be futile to attempt to describe their singing. The audience was cool and apparently a little bewildered at first. The more foolish Philistines soon took themselves elsewhere to try their weight, ride in the air car, or smoke in the gardens. It was not until the concert was over that the Netherlanders, coming forward in a body to acknowledge a second round of almost emotional applause, perceived that the Britishers, stupid and slow as they had appeared at first, were accessible after all to something better than Strauss. For that one concert all the sins against music of the Inventions Council may be forgiven them. The sufferings inflicted by Mr Rockstro's choir were forgotten before six bars of Sweelinck's psalm were over.

At the second concert on Thursday, the singing was less perfect than on the previous day, one or two of the choir being apparently a little indisposed; but even at that disadvantage the performance was of extraordinary

[313]

excellence. The impression previously made by Swee-linck's music was confirmed; but the greatest effect was produced on this second occasion by the oldest work: a number from the mass Fortuna Desperata, composed in the XV century by Jacob Obrecht. The singers were Mesdames Gips and van Rennes (sopranos), Esser and Veltman (contraltos), Messieurs Rogmans and Jebak (tenors), Spoel (baritone), and Messchaert (bass). Madame Esser and MM. Rogmans and Messchaert appear to be musicians of exceptionally sympathetic temperament; but it would be invidious to claim pre-eminence for them over their colleagues when the merits of all are so remarkable. They sing with perfect ease and purity of intonation, not a note being forced. They will perform for the last time this afternoon at three o'clock. If their fame has spread since Wednesday as it deserves to, the Albert Hall will be full.

On Wednesday evening, at Prince's Hall, Mr Edersheim's music to Byron's Hebrew melodies was sung by Madame Antoinette Sterling, Miss Fonblanque, Miss Hilda Coward, Signor Foli, Mr Herbert Reeves, Mr King, and other artists. Mr Edersheim's undertaking so considerable a work as the setting of these poems shews him to be a musician with serious intentions; and he writes, as might be expected, with earnestness and refinement. But only two or three of the settings can be called true compositions. The rest are scales, major, minor, and chromatic, and figurations of chords, harmonized with some taste, and made as tuneful as possible, but still rather suggestive of those singing exercises which profess to combine musical interest and beauty with gymnastic utility. Mr Edersheim was fortunate enough to procure the assistance of distinguished singers, who took his songs with all possible seriousness, as indeed they have often, for the sake of a royalty, taken much worse music. A Miss Hettis-Lünd made her first appearance in public, not without some promise. There is a certain simple concert drill as to moving, standing, acknowledging the accompanist's share of the song by waiting for him to finish, and the like, into which Miss Lünd has yet to be initiated. The same remark applies to Miss Nita Capella, who also made her first appearance. Miss Dinelli, Miss Snowdon, and Mr Coward also assisted.[U]

PIANOFORTE AND ORGAN

Unsigned notes in The Dramatic Review, 25 July 1885

[U] The 19th volume of the Encyclopædia Britannica, just issued, includes Plain Song, by Mr W. S. Rockstro, and Pianoforte, by Mr A. J. Hipkins. Mr Hipkins, conscious that his connexion with Broadwood exposes him to suspicion of partiality, has been scrupulous in allotting to their authors the credit of the numerous inventions by which the modern pianoforte has evolved since Cristofori's contrivance of the escapement action nearly two hundred years ago. His article, which occupies fourteen pages, and is fully and clearly illustrated, is of especial interest to Londoners just now, as many of the instruments referred to are to be seen at the Inventions Exhibition. Of the American pianofortes with overstrung iron frames, the invention of which is claimed by both Steinway and Chickering, Mr Hipkins remarks that "overstringing as at present effected is attended with grave disadvantages, in disturbing the balance of tone by introducing thick, heavy basses, which, like the modern pedal organs, bear no just relation to that part of the keyboard where the part-writing lies." He also questions the durability of pianofortes with a tension of twentytwo tons on the frames, as is the case with American and German concert grands. Both these criticisms must be admitted to be just when the ideal pianoforte of the future is taken as the standard of excellence; but the old-fashioned English piano is not therefore likely to maintain itself on the concert platform against the much richer and more powerful instruments made on the American system. It must be understood, of course, that the American system has been adopted largely both in England and on the continent, and that the opinion here stated does not imply a recommendation of the pianofortes of any particular maker either in America or elsewhere.

Almost the only class of musicians who seem to be having a thoroughly good time of it in London at present are the organists. There are an immense number of organs at the Inventions. Besides the two in the music room, and the one in the Albert Hall, there are so many in the Central Gallery that, even after making due allowance for getting lost in the building and counting the same organ over and over again in one's wanderings, the total number can hardly be computed at less than twentyseven. On these instruments recitals are given at all hours; so that the program is half filled with the lists of pieces to be performed on them. Mr Smith of St Matthews, Hampstead; Mr Jones of St Marks, Southwark; Mr Brown of St Lukes, Stepney; and Mr Robinson, of St Johns, Hammersmith, find themselves famous. Crowds press on them so closely as they play, that—their elbows being at the level of the noses of the persons immediately behind them—they cannot draw a stop without peril of also drawing the cork (pugilistically speaking) of some too eager admirer of their manipulative skill. Unfortunately they do not consult oneanother before selecting their pieces; and a certain want of variety in the programs is often the result. For instance, a visitor enters the exhibition from Kensington

Gore. A deafening jangle in the Albert Hall causes him to refer to his program, where he finds that he is listening to War March of the Priests—Athalie—Mendelssohn. When he has had enough of it, he passes through the conservatory, where he hears majestic strains from the Guards' band. A contrivance resembling a date rack informs him that item No. 6 in the list is being performed. Consulting his program, he ascertains that No. 6 is Mendelssohn's War March from Athalie. Proceeding to the Central Gallery, and threading an avenue of pianos, which he is either requested by placard not to touch, or verbally importuned to try by salesmen who seem to regard him as a Rubinstein, he is overpowered by a flood of harmony from Messrs Willis and Sons' organ. Greatly struck by the grandeur and dignity of the music, he turns again to his program and reads "March of the Priests, Athalie, Mendelssohn-Bartholdy." Having heard this composition before, he does not wait, but investigates the results of inventive genius until he is recalled by a trumpet-like fanfare from Messrs Brindley and Foster's organ. Something in the melody stirs vague associations with the past. The program seems to swim before his eyes, and his hand is not steady; but he succeeds in deciphering "March, Athalie, Mendelssohn." He hears it to the end; has a turn in the aquarium; and wanders to where Mr H. Wedlake's organ is discoursing a vigorous and lofty theme. He recognizes it as something he has heard before; but he cannot think of its name, unless it be the Hallelujah Chorus. He determines to put a cross in the margin of his program, so that he will remember to speak to his wife of the majesty of Handel when he gets home. On attempting to do so, he finds, not Handel, but Mendelssohn. It is not the Hallelujah Chorus, but the march from Athalie.

Uttering a slight imprecation, he retires, and watches

the fountains playing until a ravishing air, wafted into the grounds from Messrs Bryceson Brothers' electric organ, brings him back full of delight and curiosity. Again referring to the program, he learns that the organist is busy with the march from Athalie. He is a little surprised, but finds the march growing on him. When it is over he endeavors to *encore* it; but the crowd does not applaud sufficiently, and he is disappointed until another look at the program informs him that the march will be played again later in the evening on Messrs J. W. Walker and Sons' organ. Whilst in search of this instrument he stumbles upon a gentleman who is trying the vocalion in the Siamese court. Charmed by the rhythmic character of the *morceau*, he waits, and asks the gentleman what he has been playing. "Oh, a march" says the gentleman "Mendelssohn's, you know, from Athalie, you must have heard it often." He admits that he has and withdraws. On his way to Messrs Walkers' exhibit, he is arrested by the now almost familiar fanfare from Messrs Henry Jones and Sons' organ, upon which Mr Trego is just striking up the War March of the Priests. Finally, when the organs are shut up for the night, he thinks of home, and goes out to take a last look at the illuminated gardens. The band breaks forth into a wellknown tune. This time he needs no program to tell him that he is listening to Mendelssohn's splendid war march. "But why" he asks "are the people taking off their hats?" "Because" replies the policeman "the band is playing God Save the Queen!"

The vocalion, by the bye, is a standing puzzle to the Inventions visitors, many of whom are goaded to ask the bystanders what it means. As the average sightseer is always ready to explain what he does not understand, statements that the vocation is "a specious of horgan and 'armonium combined" are freely forthcoming. As a matter of fact the sounds of the vocalion are produced by harmonium reeds in combination with strings which reinforce certain harmonics of the reeds so as practically to extinguish the fundamental tones. Thus the note C is produced by a reed tuned to sound the F a twelfth below, but with its second harmonic (C) so strongly reinforced by a string that it alone is heard when the reed is put into vibration. The resultant quality of tone is as smooth and nearly as sweet as the flue pipes of an organ, for which the vocalion seems to be the next best substitute. To say that it is better than the harmonium would be faint praise, as it could hardly be worse than that detestable instrument, to which the world has never been reconciled by even the cleverest playing and the most carefully calculated dispersion of the harmony or other device for mitigating its harshness. The vocalion was invented some years ago by Mr Baillie-Hamilton. [U]

MUSICAL INSTRUMENTS AT THE INVENTIONS EXHIBITION

The Magazine of Music, August 1885

No less satisfactory exhibition can be conceived than a collection of musical instruments surmounted by notices that visitors are requested not to touch. Even a Stradivarius violin is not pleasant to look at when it is standing on end in a glass case. You may not hold it to the light to make the lucid depths of the varnish visible; you must not foreshorten its curves by placing it in the position in which it should be played—the only position in which a fiddle does not remind you of a plucked fowl hanging by the neck in a poulterer's shop; you cannot hear the sound, apart from which it is the most senseless object extant; and your personal independence is irritated by the feeling that what prevents you from satisfying your curiosity by force of arms is not your conscience, but the proximity of a suspicious policeman, who is so tired of seeing apparently sane men wasting their time over secondhand fiddles and pianofortes, that he would probably rather arrest you than not, if only you would give him a pretext for the capture. A harpsichord with a glass lid on the keyboard is disappointing; but a clavichord similarly secured is downrightly exasperating; for if there is one instrument that every musician would like to try, it is the *wohltemperirte klavier* of Sebastian Bach.

To relieve such feelings, which must afflict all visitors to the gallery of the Albert Hall more or less, the Council of the Inventions Exhibition has arranged a series of historic concerts, at some of which a few of these instruments have already been heard. The six-stringed *viola da gamba* has actually raised the question whether it is not at least equal to the violoncello, instead of being the "nasal and ungrateful" instrument we have been taught to imagine it. But the few pieces played upon it by M. Jacobs were chosen to shew it to the greatest advantage, and certainly did not furnish an exhaustive test of its capacity. The old Italian violins were not played, as they are supposed to be already familiar to us. This, however, is a mistake. The Strads now in use by certain great violinists have all been tampered with to enable them to bear the tension of modern concert pitch. Take a Stradivarius or Amati fiddle, exactly as it left the maker's hand; fit it with the thick strings used in the XVII century; and an attempt to tune it at the pitch of the Albert Hall organ will probably spoil it or smash it. At the old pitch of Handel's tuning fork, which is a little flat to French pitch, the instrument would give us the true Stradivarius tone, which is just as strange to us as that of the *viola di gamba*. The excellence of the modernized Strad, with its added fortifications and its threadlike strings, is only obvious to the large class of amateurs whose imaginations, when prompted by an analytic program, discern divine harmonies in any plausible noise made in their presence. The Council at South Kensington could not devize a more practically important experiment than a performance, at the old pitch, by some competent artist upon an authentic and untampered-with violin by Amati, Stradivarius, or Guarnerius, followed by a repetition of the piece at concert pitch on a modernized instrument by the same maker.

An old regal, a chamber organ, with flue pipes and one reed stop, was used at the historic concerts. It was a whole tone flat to the other instruments; but the discrepancy was easily overcome by transposition. The effect of Luther's Ein' feste Burg, accompanied by the regal, was as fine as it would have been detestable had a modern harmonium been used. Small old-fashioned organs, in mean-tone temperament, are still to be found in some country churches; and the sweetness of their tone, and the smoothness of the chords and progressions played in the practicable keys upon them, will make many a church-goer grieve when they are replaced by modern equally-tempered instruments, with all the jangling abominations that represent power, and all the theatrical prettinesses that represent pathos to the XIX century organ builder. The merits and limits of these old organs are those of the regal also.

The simple cross flute, with its six holes and one key, though still played by Christy Minstrels, itinerant musicians, and innumerable amateurs, is now known in the orchestra chiefly by traditions of the dislike which its imperfections provoked in Mozart and other great masters of instrumentation. Except in the quality of one or two of its upper notes, it proved greatly inferior to the modern Boehm instrument when directly contrasted with it at the historic concerts. There are a few pure and silvery notes at the top of its compass, and an occasional abjectly plaintive, but distinctly audible one, sprinkled here and there lower down. But the rest of its sounds are so weak that, at a little distance, they were lost in the tinkling of the harpsichord. Mozart's practice of doubling the flute part by a bassoon in the octave below was probably suggested more by the necessity of reinforcing the weak places in the flute's compass than by any fancy for the effect of the two timbres in combination. The still older *flute-à-bec, flauto dolce*, or lansquenet flute, of which four sorts, treble, alto, tenor, and bass, were played in the simplest diatonic harmony, with a flaccid side drum of the kind used by showmen marking time, is a wooden flageolet, the most agreeable tones of which may be compared to the cooing of an old and very melancholy piping crow. The specimens used at the historic concerts were only approximately identical in pitch; and the piercing was of the roughest ante-Boehm order. The effect of the *flauti dolci* music was, on the whole, quaintly execrable.

So many abuses have come in with the modern pianoforte that its superiority to the harpsichord is not a subject for unmixed rejoicing. But its superiority is none the less undeniably vast. All that can now be said for the harpsichord is that it checkmated slovenly and violent playing; that it forced composers to cultivate clearness of construction and intelligent part writing; and that it preserves for us the intended effect of certain ornate passages, favored by Handel and Bach, which seem merely *rococo* when played on a pianoforte.

So far, these concerts of instrumental music, though excellently carried out, have been planned as exhibitions of old-fashioned chamber music only. It is greatly to be desired that some orchestral concerts be attempted with a view to reproducing the effects heard by Bach, Handel, Haydn, and Mozart, during what may be called the pre-clarinet period of orchestration. The Haydn orchestra might be revived by altering the ordinary proportions of string to wind players, multiplying the bassoons, and, of course, lowering the pitch, which should be done by thickening the strings used. The effect of this on the tone from the basses would be remarkable. There are various methods by which the pitch of wind instruments can be lowered, when the players are disposed to lower it, which they seldom are. The clarinet is an exception; but music in which the clarinet is used is practically modern music, and need not be included in the programs. The Bach orchestra, with its three trumpets, the first of them playing florid passages up to the high D, and its two *oboi d' amore*, was reproduced with splendid success at the Bach bicentenary performance of the Mass in B minor last spring. The *oboe d' amore* has been resuscitated by the Mahillons at Brussels; and it amply justifies Bach's preference for it. In quality of tone it is purer, sweeter, and more dignified than the English horn; and it is certainly not less powerful. As to the trumpet, no instrument needs rehabilitation more urgently. In the show cases of modern instruments at the exhibition, dozens of cornets, many of them elaborately decorated and even bejeweled, are conspicuous; but only in one or two instances is a solitary trumpet, labeled "slide trumpet, for classical music," to be seen in a modest corner. These slide trumpets are not the instruments Bach wrote for. They are hard to play, and their tone is so vile that Herr Richter and other first-rate conductors connive at the substitution of the more manageable cornet. Though this is a musical fraud, and a deplorable one, it is certainly better to have a good cornet well played than a bad trumpet ill played. It has been repeatedly said that

[323]

Bach's trumpet parts are impracticable; and they are commonly executed nowadays by the clarinet; but Julius Kosleck of Berlin has exploded that superstition by playing the first trumpet part of the great Mass at the highest English concert pitch on an old-fashioned straight trumpet, without missing a note. It is said that Mr Morrow, the wellknown English trumpet player, has ordered a similar instrument. If this be true, there is some hope that what was once called "the heroick art" of playing the trumpet may be revived among us. We have had quite enough of the attempts of cornet players to produce genuine trumpet effects.

Besides the music of the past, the music of the future might have a place in the Inventions scheme. There are important classes of new instruments which are kept out of use because musicians have no opportunity of hearing them. Many of the pretended musical novelties in the Exhibition are, it is true, quite sufficiently illustrated by portraits of some distinguished person wiling away the tedium of high life by performing upon them. But on the other hand there are whole families of genuine additions to the resources of the orchestra that have not yet got further than a place in a few of our military bands. Probably not one student in the Royal Academy or Royal College of Music could "spot" a saxophone blindfold; and it is doubtful whether the name of the sarrusophone would convey any meaning to them. Yet a knowledge of the effect of applying the single and double reed to metal instruments should surely form part of the education of the rising generation of composers. As yet the "recitals" on new instruments have been of the nature of advertisements rather than of experiments. In an exhibition of inventions, all the practical publicity should not be appropriated to relics of the past. Practical publicity for a musical instrument implies, not that the public can see it, but that they can hear it.

SINGING, PAST AND PRESENT

The Dramatic Review, 1 August 1885

The most famous singing-master that ever lived was Porpora, who was in his prime in the first half of the XVIII century. George Sand's novel Consuelo has made him known to the general reader. That his pupils were extraordinary singers is not a figment of the novelist's imagination. Specimens of the outrageous vocal feats which they habitually executed, and which they compelled composers to devize for them, may be seen in the works of Hasse, Porpora himself, Handel, and Mozart. The only artists we have who can compare with these singers are our circus acrobats, who make their living by performing athletic impossibilities with grace, ease, and perfect tranquillity. These acrobats are not exceptional men any more than soldiers and sailors are exceptional men. Any boy of the proper age, and free from deformity or marked physical disability, will do as well as another for the purposes of the acrobat trainer in want of an apprentice. Ordinary gentlemen who cannot rub the backs of their heads against their heels without breaking their backs, or sit down on the floor in the posture of a T square without splitting themselves, may rest assured that had they devoted themselves to the study of gymnastics at a sufficiently early age under competent direction, they should by this time have been able to converse with their friends in far more complicated attitudes without inconvenience. And there is no doubt that our apparently degenerate XIX century singers, whom the contents of a dozen ammoniaphones could not bring safely through the songs written by Mozart in his boyhood for de Amicis and Rauzzini, could, in the hands of Porpora, have done everything that Porpora's average pupils did. Exceptionally gifted people existed in Porpora's time, and exist now.

An artist's powers are partly native, partly acquired. Some people can do easily at the first challenge what costs others long training and teaching. But it is probable that, though the degree of skill that men and women are born with varies a good deal, the utmost additional skill that they can acquire by study is a constant quantity. For instance, if Porpora taught all he knew to each pupil, and we represent that quantity of imparted skill by the number 5, then a finished pupil of Porpora's would possess his or her natural gifts as a singer plus 5. Let us assume that nature does as much for the singer as art, and rate an average pupil's inherited capacity as 5 also. His total skill when trained by Porpora would then be represented by 10, consisting of natural skill 5, plus taught feats and trained skill 5. An exceptionally gifted person, a Caffarelli or Farinelli, would have natural skill equal to more than 5. Let us say, for Caffarelli, 7. Porpora added his 5 to the 7, leaving Caffarelli pre-eminent with a total of 12 as against the 10 of the average pupil of his master.

But let us now suppose that Caffarelli, instead of practically being given or sold when a child as an apprentice to Porpora, and sacrificing himself so completely to his profession as to have his soprano voice preserved artificially at the cost of his virility, had lived in our day; been educated in an ordinary English school; and had his attention turned to music by being assured, after attempting to sing Hybrias the Cretan, or Goodbye, to his sister's accompaniment, that he ought to study for the profession, because Lloyd and Santley get sums of guineas (variously stated at from five to a hundred and fifty by his friends) in one night for singing these very songs no better—to the friends' taste—than he. Caffarelli, if he cannot afford the terms of a private professor, accordingly takes his 7 of natural skill either to a conservatory, or academy, or college, or institute. At some of these, so far from adding to his 7, he may chance to have it reduced to 0 by the extinction of his voice. At any of them he is likely to gain 2 in elocution, style, &c., and to lose 3 in freshness of tone and soundness of voice. $7 + 2 - 3 = 6$. He comes out of his conservatory or academy with a loss of 1. All his average competitors have still, as in the XVIII century, natural ability equal to 5; but they too lose 1 by their academic training; and so the average for trained singers is 4 as against 10 under Porpora's method and system. Thus the modern Caffarelli, scoring 6 to his competitors' 4, is still two above the average, and is therefore just as pre-eminent as the old Caffarelli, who scored 12 to his competitors' 10. Hence we have great singers now as our great-great-grand-fathers had, although the acrobatic operas of Handel and the juvenile Mozart are inexecutable.

Of the results of private teaching it is better to say nothing. Every private teacher with whom I am or have ever been acquainted, has rediscovered Porpora's method, can explain it at considerable length, teaches exclusively on it, and is the only person in the world who can do so, all others being notorious quacks and voice destroyers. There are a great many unique persons in London, and most of them are teachers of singing. But even they will admit and lament that they cannot score Porpora's 5, because their pupils begin at too late an age, and obstinately refuse to spend six years over one page of exercises in the hope of being subsequently told "Go forth, young man: you are now the greatest singer in the world." The difficulty, in fact, is not to implant that conviction in an ordinary English tenor, but to eradicate it. He feels it, without being told, in less than six months. So, even granting that our rediscoverers of Porpora's method really do add 3 out of his 5, and only miss the other 2 because no apprenticeship takes place, we are still left with an average of 8 (5 natural + 3 imparted) against Porpora's average of 10 (5 natural + 5 imparted).

Before we drop too many tears over this decadence of the art of singing, it is as well to consider whether all that we have lost is worth regretting. The old vocal acrobats were, like other acrobats, more anxious to dazzle the public and to make money as fast as possible than to make the highest use of their exceptional skill; and they used all the power that skill gave them to thwart composers who tried to save the opera house from sinking into a mere arena for the feats of vain singers. When Mozart was a boy, he dared not have written such easy music as Don Giovanni for the stage. Nowadays, a composer hardly dare write anything so difficult as some of it has become. Mozart's lifelong fight was against supermusical virtuosity in singing; and when he became famous enough to have his own way, he wrote no more of his old Italian florid passages with skips of nearly two octaves between almost impossible intervals. The constantly cited music of the Queen of Night in the Zauberflöte, and the much more extravagant passages in Die Entführung aus dem Serail, are comparatively plain sailing: they require exceptional compass, but nothing comparable to acrobatic powers. Handel, who, when Cuzzoni refused to sing *Falsa imagine*, at once set about throwing her out of the window, bullied his singers into a wholesome fear of him; but he finally made up his mind that music could get on better without them; and, indeed, any reader of THE DRAMATIC REVIEW who will take the trouble to make himself acquainted with such of the music written for Porpora's pupils as can no longer be sung effectively by our best singers, will find that its impracticability is a distinct gain.

The history of stage speaking is much the same as that of stage singing. English actors were as famous throughout Europe in the XVI century as Italian singers were in the XVIII. The plays of the pre-Shakespear period prove that the old dramatists, or rather stage poets, depended on their actors for effects of elocution which no modern actor can produce, or would dream of trying to produce. Chapman and Marlowe, with their passion for the grandiose, seem to have tempted these elocutionists to ruin their art by bombast and violence, exactly as Rossini and Verdi, in our century, have brought Italian opera singing to a condition in which the operatic tenor hardly takes precedence in popular estimation of the organ grinder and the penny ice man. The actors who abused their schooling and took to shouting found fate waiting for them in the plays of Shakespear. An actor who should habitually attempt to shout his way through Othello, Macbeth, or Lear would, by the ruin of his voice and the wreck of his moral and physical health, remove himself expeditiously from the stage. That the decadence of the old school, through the very excellence of which elocution had become the end and drama the means, was accelerated in this way, must appear very probable to anyone who has noted the quick work that Wagner's music makes with the shouting tenors and screaming sopranos who render Verdi so terrible to us. You cannot play Shakespear and live, unless you know how to speak rationally; and you cannot sing Wagner on the "tension of cords and force of blast" principle, with any prospect of lagging superfluous on the stage after a few years' work. All ambitious actors play Shakespear, and so, in self-preservation, must acquire a non-destructive method. Singers of Bayreuth music-dramas must do likewise. In this way Wagner's music is

[329]

at present bringing about a busy revival of the art of singing, and is discrediting and destroying many ignorant and demoralized pretenders who have long infested the lyric stage, and who very naturally declare that Wagner's music means ruin to what they take to be the human voice. The same process is constantly in action. The Elizabethan and Victorian ages are striking examples of it; but the struggle between the poet and the player, the composer and the singer, both manifestations of the inward struggle in each man between the aspiring human side of him and the vain and greedy monkey side, are as busy in the centuries when art is happy and has no history as when it is disturbed by the advent of a Shakespear or a Mozart.

THE GRAVE TROMBONE

Unsigned notes in The Dramatic Review, 8 August 1885

[U] On Wednesday last, at the Inventions Exhibition, Mr George Case, the wellknown trombone player, delivered a lecture partly on his instrument and partly in spoken words concerning its history and utility. The trombone has been much misunderstood in general society. The gravity of its tones, and the habitual solemnity of feature which its embouchure produces in the player, contrasted with the laughable action of the slide, have a serio-comic effect which has made it the butt of much unenlightened ridicule. As a domestic instrument it is not popular, because it takes up a great deal of room when in action, and is apt to split the ears of both groundlings and second-floorlings when experimented upon by amateurs. Hence, it is not ordinarily believed that the trombone has been called the king of instruments; that Berlioz applied the adjective "Olympian" to it; or that the trombone player may claim a position of the first dignity in the orchestra. He certainly enjoys—and frequently abuses—a greater power of spoiling an otherwise excellent performance than any other player can pretend to. For the trombone is like the little girl in the nursery rhyme. When it is good it is very, *very* good, but when it is bad it is horrid. Mr Case protested earnestly on Wednesday that trombone players are often blamed by critics for disagreeable effects due to the composers' ignorance of the instrument's peculiarities. Such cases probably occur sometimes, though far oftener the injustice is done to the composer, who is blamed for the coarseness due to the deficiencies of taste or skill in the player. But there is no doubt that Sterndale Bennett's recommendation to composers to treat trombone players as gentlemen, pathetically insisted on by Mr Case, has been disregarded by the majority of composers. To turn from such scoring as that of *Possenti numi* in Die Zauberflöte, or from the last act of Don Juan to the innumerable compositions in which the trombone has either to play senselessly and continuously with the basses or else be heard only when noise, pretence, and vulgarity are required by the composer, is a common experience of the trombone player. When he has any artistic feeling (which is not invariably the case) it must be a very bitter experience.

Mr Case's lecture was not a very satisfactory one. He evidently started with the conviction that the secret of delivering a popular lecture on the trombone is to say as little as possible about the instrument. This is a compound mistake. The public, far from caring little about musical instruments, are usually very curious about them, as Mr Case might have inferred from the number of people who stare at the displays in our instrument-makers' shop windows. Further, the audience in the music room at the Inventions Exhibition is presumably always specially interested, as there is plenty of entertainment at hand elsewhere for those who are otherwise disposed. Now, when a number of people assemble to pick up some information about a brass instrument, it is quite safe to assume that they want to know its name, how it is played, and what it sounds like. Mr Case avoided these points on the plea that they were only interesting to the professional player, and confined himself to some necessarily sketchy historical matter, and to a minute account of what the Germans used to call the instrument, what the Moors used to call it, what the French used to call it, and so on. This was all very well; but it was not what the audience wanted. They wanted to be shewn the different sorts of trombones now in use so that they might learn to distinguish between them. Then they wanted to hear the difference in the sounds produced by them, illustrated by a few passages devized to contrast the characteristic tones of the alto, tenor and bass. Then they wanted to see the various shifts used—how a scale is played, for instance. Finally, an example of what a skilful performer can do in the way of *bravura* playing would have satisfied and probably amused them.

Mr Case told them hardly anything that they might not have learned from books of reference without his intervention. It was evident, in fact, that he privately did not believe that the public really cared about him or his instrument, and that his duty, as a goodnatured man, was to let them down as easily as possible, and give them plenty of musical interludes. Should he repeat his lecture, he will do well to overcome this mistaken modesty, to be as communicative as possible, and to talk shop without stint. He may depend on meeting much more indulgence than he needs, and much more interest than he expects. The illustrations selected by him were performed by himself on the alto trombone, Messrs

Geard and Antoine Matt on tenors, and Mr J. Matt on the bass trombone. Mr Geard, as first tenor, had the post of honor, and the quality of his performance justified his title to the position. Mr Henry Dart made shift with the unfinished organ of Messrs Michell and Thynne as best he could in Luther's Ein' feste Burg, and in a remarkable setting by Heinrich Schütz (1629) of David's lamentation, *Fili mi Absalon*, for organ, four trombones, and bass voice. This was sung by Mr Stanley Smith. The Equalen, composed by Beethoven in 1812, and first performed at his funeral, followed. Mr Case subsequently decided that Beethoven's harmony was superior to the old-fashioned counterpoint of Schütz and Luther; but this decision, though a pretty safe one, will hardly be unanimously voted sound. On the whole, the little trombone concert was an artistic success. Mr Phasey, who, in his capacity of tuba player, has often sat at the left hand of the trombone triad, came out in a new light as an orchestral conductor by wielding the *bâton* during the *Fili mi Absalon*.

Mr Case, by the bye, stated that the trombone effects in the supper scene of Don Giovanni were borrowed by Mozart from Gluck. This is not quite accurate. The few bars sung by the statue which interrupt the recitative in the graveyard scene of Don Giovanni are almost note for note the same as the utterance of the oracle in Gluck's Alceste. But the supper scene, the only other place in Don Giovanni in which the trombones are used, is original: its instrumentation practically turned over a new leaf in the art. Nothing written before or since is like it. The critic, *blasé* beyond the reach of the Freischütz, Robert le Diable, Berlioz's Faust, or Wagner's fiery mountain, is still not safe from a shudder at that awful stir in the orchestra which makes us feel that the stone man is going to speak. The trombones, which are never for a moment used to imitate or represent the voice of the statue, yet anticipate and accompany it so as to prompt an impression of suspense and supernatural awe which the unaided human voice could not suggest. The effect has been repeatedly imitated, but never with success. A German commentator has observed that the trombone parts were probably added after Mozart's death by someone else. Perhaps they were. It is also possible that the title of Hamlet refers to the ghost and his murder, and that the part of the Prince of Denmark was added, after Shakespear's death, by an inferior hand. The world knows nothing of its greatest men.

The mention of Alceste reminds a Londoner that he is distinguished from the Berliner and Parisian by his ignorance of the operas of Gluck, whom he knows solely as the composer of *Che farò senza Euridice?* Yet Gluck's average work was second only to Mozart's best; we have put up with season after season of operas that are no more to be compared to Gluck's than Bernini's sculpture is to Phidias's, or Gustave Doré's drawing to Holbein's. There was a Gluck society in London once: the present writer recollects hearing a very creditable recital of this very Alceste in the concert room of the Royal Academy of Music in Tenterden-street some years ago, and being much struck by an admirable performance of the part of Hercules by a Mr Theo. Marzials, presumably the gentleman since famous as the composer of some good songs, and of a few others not so good, except for keeping the pot boiling in intervals of inspiration. What has become of the Gluck Society?

The Siamese band has succumbed to a mad ambition to perform the music of western Europe. On Wednesday last they announced a composition entitled Krob Chakewarn, or The Glory of the Universe. The krob chakewarn part was genuine Siamese, as far as a barbarian critic could judge, but the glory of the universe was recognized, after a pause of incredulous astonishment, as the soldiers' chorus from Gounod's Faust. The main theme, in B flat, was grappled with successfully; but the episode in F had to be abandoned after a painful struggle, by which the audience apparently suffered more than the musicians, who maintained an air of imperturbable self-satisfaction, evidently considering that the turn they had given to Gounod (and to his admirers) was as charming as it was novel and unexpected. It is to be hoped that some friend of England will hint to them that the only western melody that we can stand when played with a scale containing no leading note is John Anderson, my jo. Western music, however, is not strange to the Siamese. Their military bands are like ours: the instruments being imported from France. The Court band at the Inventions officially plays traditional music in a traditional fashion. But, as the inhabitants of Courtfield Road are painfully aware, the bandsmen have an ungovernable fancy for attempting to execute popular music hall and other London melodies on their instruments. Fancy Wait til the clouds roll by practised on a powerful stone dulcimer without the leading note, in a quiet road every evening after dinner! [U]

A VIENNESE LADY ORCHESTRA

Unsigned notes in The Dramatic Review, 15 August 1885

[U] The musical amateur who is tired of the military bands and endless organ recitals at the Inventions, and who likes his music under breezier conditions than prevail at promenade concerts, will do well to turn where the spacious decks and palatial saloons of the Thames steamers tempt at each pier the *flâneur* of the Embankment to commit himself to the mercy of the waves of Lambeth Reach and the winds that are wafted from the wilds of Battersea Park. In this outlandish suburb, the Albert Palace lifts its crystal dome to the autumn sun, the influence of which upon the pen of the journalist is becoming very perceptible just now. The Albert Palace began life years ago as the Dublin Exhibition, in which capacity it sheltered many vast audiences and famous singers, from the late Madame Titiens down to Mr Ira D. Sankey.* The musical promenades that took place in it were made memorable by the performances of the band of the 1st (or King's) Dragoon Guards, which, under the direction of a gifted but eccentric Austrian, named Schramm, at one time attained to a perfection that Mr Dan Godfrey and his Grenadier Guards have never come within measurable distance of. But these transitory glories passed away. Schramm died at Ballincollig, in Cork, and was forgotten; and the Exhibition, as became an Irish institution, got into difficulties. It had passed some time before into the hands of Lord Ardilaun, then Sir Arthur Guinness, whose celebrity is coextensive with the popular taste for stout; and he had entrusted its management to a Mr Edward Lee.

This happened during the first viceregency of Earl Spencer, who had even then incurred much of the unpopularity which he has ever since suffered in Ireland. He made great sacrifices of his personal convenience to gain the goodwill of the people, going to concerts, theatres, sports, flower shows, regattas and ceremonies of all sorts with the constancy of a martyr. But as fast as he dug away the mountain of odium by his complaisance, the Castle bureaucracy, the police, or the Government were sure to pile it on again with an extra boulder or so

* A popular American evangelist, whom Shaw had seen in Dublin in 1875.

to boot. It was in a more than usually spasmodic attempt to propitiate Dublin that he visited the Exhibition and desperately knighted the manager, who thenceforth was Sir Edward Lee. The town was startled; a little scandalized; somewhat amused, though not enough so to take the matter with perfect good humor; and, on the whole, disposed to emphasize the fact that the latest recipient of the spurs was an Englishman. So it hissed more than ever: and the title, as far as the Lord Lieutenant was concerned, was thrown away. The Exhibition failed in due course, and Sir Edward Lee returned to his fatherland; but he pined for the edifice in which he had been ennobled, and began to dream of re-establishing it amid a more sympathetic population. The dream of the projector nowadays soon becomes the scheme of the managing director. A company was formed; and the vast glasshouse was detached from its stone nucleus in Earlcourt Terrace, Dublin, and transported piecemeal to the south boundary of Battersea Park, where it arose again as the Albert Palace, and was opened to the public this very year.

Something of its former splendor is lacking. The murky red paint which, to conceal the London smoke, covers the once white framework, is indescribably ugly and depressing. The orange-colored panes with which the roof has been glazed somehow remind the disheartened visitor of ginger-ale and general cheapness. The internal decoration is Philistine to the utmost degree; and some of the incidents of the place are paltry and suggestive of the Edgware Road on Saturday night. But, on the whole, the Albert Palace is roomy and cheerful; and if Brixton and Battersea learn the way to it, and find a reasonably good band there, and plenty of dresses and wearers of dresses to look at, the Palace may succeed as a suburban promenade. At present, it offers an attraction which eclipses the late Strauss concerts at South

Kensington, and which is the occasion of this brief historical retrospect.

At the south end of the Dublin Exhibition was a large transept, which was of no particular use when the exhibits were removed, and the place was an exhibition in name only. The transept has been rearranged at Battersea at the opposite end of the building as a concert room, and dubbed "Connaught Hall." The galleries have been adapted to the new requirements by various devices, which do not seem particularly ingenious, as the space wasted is enormous, and the seats and positions far from comfortable. There is a small orchestra, and a large and revoltingly ugly organ. But as the orchestra is in a fair north light, the floor vastly spacious, and the walls and roof of glass, no pleasanter place for an afternoon concert in fine warm weather exists in London. And here, every afternoon and evening, are to be heard and seen the "Viennese Lady Orchestra."

Excepting only a procession of policemen at a funeral, nothing less brilliant can be conceived than the common spectacle of an "English Gentleman Orchestra" as they tumble up through the hatchways to the platform when the stroke of three or eight pipes all hands. Fancy, instead of this, the apparition in full sunlight of a charming person of the other sex in a crimson silk military tunic and white skirt. Fancy at her heels a string of nearly sixty instrumentalists, all more or less charming, and all in crimson tunics and white skirts. Fancy a conductor distinguished by a black silk skirt, and sleeves made somewhat shorter and wider than the others, so as to give free play to a plump wrist and arm. This is no vision of an autumnal journalist at a loss for copy; it is to be seen daily at the Albert Palace, as the following wide-awake details are intended to prove. The tunics are made with stand up collars, and are crossed with three "frogs" of white silk cord, of which there are

[338]

further decorations at wrist and throat. Their wearers spread themselves like a vast bouquet over the orchestra, those who have not flutes or violins in their hands taking possession of the big drum, the cymbals and the double basses. Then a few male creatures sneak apologetically in with trombones, horns and clarinets. They feel their position acutely, and hurry to some very low chairs at the back, where they are hidden behind a rampart of red tunics and white skirts. The drummer alone is unabashed. He is a well-favored young gentleman, with dark eyes and moustache; and he is conscious that though anybody can bang the *grosse caisse*, no woman ever born can handle the kettle drums, which are his especial charge. During the opening march he marks time *ad libitum* on a side drum with extraordinary spirit and with a high-stepping action that adds greatly to the effect; but his subsequent more orthodox performances on the *timpani* are executed with a wooden drumstick, with a vigor that would startle such light-handed artists as Mr Chaine or Mr Smith.

The effect of the "lady orchestra" as a whole is novel and very pleasant. They are inferior to the Strauss band in precision and perfection of detail; but the Strauss impetuosity was forced, false, and often misplaced and vulgar: these Viennese ladies seem inspired by a feminine delight in dancing that makes them play dance music in a far more captivating fashion than their male rivals. They have grace, tenderness and moderation: qualities which are very refreshing after two months of the alternate sentimentality and self-assertion of Eduard Strauss, than whom, by the bye, Madame Marie Schipek, the conductor, is a much more dashing violinist. Like him, she conducts with her bow, and acts as leader alternately. Her conducting is not conducting in the Richterian sense: there is no reason to suppose that she could use a *bâton*, so as to produce an original

[339]

interpretation of a classical work; but she marks time in the boldest and gayest Austrian spirit, and makes the dances and marches spin along irresistibly. Fräulein Anna Kohlert contributes solos on the zither; but her performance is not extraordinary; there are humble players in our minor music halls who do as much with the instrument as she can. Her touch is rather rough. The programs are usually made up of a march, a waltz, an overture, a polka, or other dance, a solo on the zither, cello, &c., a selection, and a galop. There are two concerts daily: one in the Connaught Hall at half-past three, and one in the nave at half-past seven. Anyone who goes once is extremely liable to go again.[U]

PROMENADES AND FACKELTANZ

Unsigned notes in the Dramatic Review, 22 August 1885

[U] At Covent Garden Mr Freeman Thomas keeps alive the only form of entertainment that as yet enables the Londoner to hear a full orchestra for a shilling. The promenade concert, as established among us, is an anomalous institution consisting of a first-rate orchestra playing first-rate operatic and classical music, and a drinking bar with a lounge and rendezvous for disreputable seekers and purveyors of pleasure. Attempts to bring the audience up to the level of the music by discouraging the pleasure seekers have not proved remunerative. Deliberate debasement of the music to the level of the drinking-bar has been tried with consequences still more disastrous. The more thoroughly a casino policy is carried out behind the orchestra, and a St James's Hall (musical) policy before it, the better the promenade concerts succeed. Among the results are symphonies accompanied by the popping of soda water corks, students and musicians wandering among grace-less rakes, ladies looking down from the boxes into an arena which they dare not be seen crossing, women of the town weeping over sentimentally virtuous ballads in the intervals of conversation with the brothers and sons of the contemptuous ladies upstairs, and Music declining to make any social distinctions, and behaving itself generally towards the evil and good, the just and the unjust, as impartially as the sun or the rain.

Mr Gwyllym Crowe occupies the position of conduc-tor at Covent Garden this year. This must be taken as implying, not that Mr Gwyllym Crowe conducts, but rather, as Samuel Weller* forcibly said, so far from it, on the contrary, quite the reverse. The orchestra conducts him; and he, like an amiable and easy-going musician, lets them have their own way. And his example might be followed with advantage by others. On Tuesday night, for instance, Madame Enriquez made an experiment with Spohr's Rose softly blooming, which is a reminiscence of Mozart's *Voi, che sapete*, and a very difficult song for any but a first-rate singer, though in appearance it is innocence itself. Madame Enriquez began too fast; and the orchestra, in the gentlest way imaginable, tried to draw her back into the proper *tempo* until, finding her intractable, they aban-doned her to her fate. It overtook her at the ornamental chromatic passage at the end of the second verse. Owing to an unusual proportion of idiots at large in the promenade, the song was encored; but Madame Enri-quez wisely substituted Ye banks and braes, and perhaps resolved privately to leave Spohr to oblivion in future. Mr Joseph Maas was more successful with Tosti's Only a year ago, Come into the garden, Maud, and When other lips, a sentimental selection that shewed the

* Character in Dickens's Pickwick Papers.

popular tenor at his best. Mr Maas has an earnest way of closing his eyes and addressing the audience as if breaking some particularly painful intelligence to them. He does this with a tenderness that only a very strong-hearted critic could resist. It is doubtful, however, whether the effect would not be just as touching if the eye closing were omitted; and it is certain that ribald promenaders, with no ear for Mr Maas's rich voice, would be deprived of an excuse for laughing at him. Mr Stedman's choir of fourteen girls (whose united ages may be roughly guessed at 250 or thereabouts) and an assortment of boys, are retained to sing Mr Gwyllym Crowe's popular—almost too popular—vocal waltz *Fairy Voices*, which is less vulgar if not less commonplace than the *See-Saw* which now makes exile sweet to the Londoner. It is very good of Mr Gwyllym Crowe to compile pretty waltzes for us; but it is to be hoped that he will take a holiday some of these autumns and leave us to make up our programs as best we can with Weber's *Invitation*, Berlioz's *Scène au bal*, and other makeshifts.

The instrumental music was chosen from the better class of romantic operas. The inevitable *William Tell* overture was played tolerably well. Mr Howell, who played the opening phrases for the violoncello, is faithful to the old school in his observance of the traditional rule to play a little sharp in a solo for the sake of prominence. Mr Dubrucq played the oboe when he ought to have played the English horn. Most of the audience were none the wiser; but the obligation on orchestral players to abstain from these petty frauds, and on conductors to refuse to connive at them, is a question of conscience, and is just as binding at a promenade concert as at the Crystal Palace or St James's Hall. The pretty *entr'acte* from Gounod's *La Colombe* presents no difficulty to an orchestra, except the final chain of shakes for the violins, which did not come off as well as usual on this occasion.

The details of Auber's dainty Zanetta overture were thrown away in the large space of Covent Garden under Mr Crowe's somewhat lax discipline. Meyerbeer fared better in the execution of his Indian ballet from L'Africaine, and in his third Marche aux Flambeaux, composed in 1854 for the marriage of Prince Frederick of Hesse and the Princess Anne of Prussia. This characteristic work is not easy enough to be played carelessly. The brass is very effectively used in it, and certain florid passages and feats of double-tongueing afford a welcome opportunity for display to cornet players. Mr Ellis made the most of them on Tuesday evening. On the whole, the Marche aux Flambeaux was better played than the other instrumental pieces— possibly because, as it headed the program, the artists were fresh when they attacked it.

A Marche aux Flambeaux, or Fackeltanz, is a German court ceremony which takes place at royal marriages. It is not exactly a march, and not exactly a dance; it is a procession which is supposed to be a dance, but which lasts so long that if it were actually danced the august persons concerned would forget their rank and lie down on the floor to rest before it was half finished. At Berlin the order of the Fackeltanz is as follows:—the Kaiser and his consort, with the newly-married couple, are seated on a dais before the throne, surrounded by the innumerable majesty of Germany. The cabinet ministers, headed by the Grand Marshal of the Court, approach with prodigious lighted tapers in their hands. At the foot of the dais they bow, and, turning to the right, march round the hall, followed by the bride and bridegroom, the band meanwhile playing the Marche aux Flambeaux, which is always in the rhythm of a polonaise. When the circuit is completed the Emperor takes the bride round again, still headed by the unfortunate ministers. Then the Empress takes the bridegroom. And so on until every royal lady present has been taken round by the bridegroom, and every Prince has taken round the bride. This walk round is accepted by convention as equivalent to a dance. When it is over, the cabinet ministers give their torches to pages, who conduct the married pair to their apartments. The bride's garters—silk ribbons embroidered with her initials—are then distributed among the aching processionists as they disperse to their armchairs and slippers at home.

Prince Bismarck knows better than to take part in the Fackeltanz; and it is probable that if it were introduced in this country in compliment to the young German gentlemen who woo and win our Princesses, ministers would become remarkably Radical on the subject of the dowries and pensions that grease the path of true love at our English court. If they could not avert the Fackeltanz in that way, they might even go the length of tempting their supporters, by an only three-lined whip, to stay away from a division and land them in the shelter of Opposition. Thus the promotion of a Royal match, might, by means of the Fackeltanz, become a reliable party move for dislodging a gouty or corpulent cabinet.

The Birmingham festival will not make such a large hole as usual in the Covent Garden orchestra this year. Herr Richter is very properly standing by his own men rather than by the late Sir Michael Costa's, some of whom have become in the course of time rather pressingly eligible for superannuation. No injustice seems to have been done to the public by the alterations. Mr Lazarus, for instance, though decidedly a veteran, and not a member of the Richter concert orchestra, retains his place, not because he occupied it on former occasions, but because he is still the greatest available clarinet player. Herr Richter has not only brought the orchestra up to date; but he is about to adopt Handel's views with reference to the Messiah. The contralto is no longer to be permitted to usurp the bass aria, But who may abide; and the beautiful minor section of The Trumpet shall sound, to the words For this corruptible shall put on incorruption, will not henceforth be "usually omitted." The old system of announcing a performance of a masterpiece, and then giving as little of it as the ignorance of the public may be depended on to put up with, seems to be fading from the concert room as well as from the stage.[U]

THE SEARCH
FOR ANOTHER MESSIAH

Unsigned notes in The Dramatic Review, 29 August 1885

[U] All the musical news this week is Birmingham news. The daily papers have published columns of particulars of Gounod's Mors et Vita, Mr Cowen's Sleeping Beauty, and Dvořák's Spectre Bride, Mr Mackenzie's *scena*, entitled Invocation, and Mr Anderton's cantata Yule-Tide, have been heard and let down with the usual polite phrases. Mors et Vita will, it is stated, be performed in London on the evening of November 4 (Wednesday), in the afternoon, on November 14 (Saturday), and at St James's Hall, on the 1st December.

M. Gounod's oratorio is dedicated to Pope Leo XIII. The descriptions at hand do not represent it as a cheerful work. It begins with a Requiem. Judgment follows Death; but the upshot is happy, as Judgment leads to Life. This is a large order for M. Gounod. Exquisite as he always was in his sentiment, and graceful as he is in his piety, he is hardly the man to take the field with Bach and Handel, who were as much more modest in choosing their subjects as they were more powerful in handling them. When we read of great use of represent-ative themes, and "faint *tremolando* passages" represent-ing the beginning of the resurrection of the dead, we are left but little hope of having anything in Mors et Vita, except a more or less impressive ballet in three acts, descriptive of a funeral, a graveyard and paradise. About the religious music of the XIX century there is a desperate triviality which shews how far human seri-ousness has been divorced from the legendary externals of our creeds. Our really serious music is no longer recognized as religious, whilst our professedly religious music, though laboriously composed in the "impressive" style, is no more serious than is the third act of Robert le Diable. We have already had from M. Gounod the Redemption musically illustrated by a March to Calvary, with "orchestral effects" (effects without causes, Wagner called them). And now we have the resurrection depicted by *tremolando* passages and more "effects" for six trumpets. Religious music of this sort is only remarkable as *naïve* blasphemy, wonderfully elaborated, and con-vinced of its own piety. Doubtless, many of the public are pleased, much as they would be if, on going to church, they found sensational novels bound up in their Bible covers, and were surprised to find Scripture so amusing. The critics are much of the same opinion: Mendelssohn is still their idol; and it was Mendelssohn who popularized the pious romancing which is now called sacred music; in other words, the Bible with the thought left out. M. Gounod proved his capacity in this direction by giving us Faust with all Goethe's thought left out, and, the result having been so successful (and, it must be confessed, so irresistibly charming), it is natural that he should turn his attention to the Bible, which is worshipped in England so devoutly by people who never open it, that a composer has but to pick a subject, or even a name, from it, to ensure a half-gagged criticism and the gravest attention for his work, however trivial.

The truth is that when Bach and Handel passed away, there was no more serious music composed until Mozart wrote Die Zauberflöte, which is still generally regarded as an unusually insane extravaganza. Then Beethoven gave us the choral fantasia and the ninth symphony, and that is about all we yet know, except some cantatas by Schumann and Brahms, and that part of Wagner's work which, so far, seems to be quite worth the trouble he took with it. Schumann's Faust has a third part worthy of Mendelssohn or Gounod, and it alone has been performed here: the earlier scenes of Faust's experience of care, blindness, and death having been neglected expressly on account of their alleged inferiority. As might be expected, their inferiority meant simply the vulgarity and stupidity of those who discovered it. Meanwhile, intentionally sacred music, so-called, has grown more and more profane. Even Beethoven, at the very time when he wrote the choral fantasia and the ninth symphony, failed when he deliberately attempted to write a stupendous Mass, which, compared to the choral symphony, has nothing stupendous about it, except the ugliness of its over-strained counterpoint. Mozart's Requiem, the only religious work of his philosophic period, gained some inspiration from the shadow of his tragic death; but it also is a *tour de force* in counterpoint, with the important difference from the Mass in D that Mozart achieved a triumphant and apparently easy success as a contra-puntist, wheras Beethoven suffered a laborious and somewhat ungraceful failure. But neither Mozart nor Beethoven would be a jot less famous if their Masses had never been written, wheras the reputation of Handel without the Messiah, or that of Bach without the Mass in B minor, the Passion music, and the Cantatas, would half vanish. It is, in fact, nearly a century and a half since any religious work of the first class has been produced by a musician. So that, in spite of the extreme seriousness with which the critics are just now taking Mors et Vita, it is on the whole just as improbable that M. Gounod has written a really profound oratorio as that Sir Frederick Leighton has painted a worthy companion piece to Michael Angelo's Last Judgment.

The moral of all this is that our Festival committees are mistaken in their policy of looking for sacred oratorios. They seem to believe—on the unsound principle that what has been done once may be done again—that another Handel may turn up some day with another Messiah. But he will not. If Handel were alive today, his Messiah would wear another guise, which would probably not be recognizable by the Birmingham committee as a sacred one, and which would certainly not be explicitly religious. It is not the hood that makes the friar nowadays anymore than it was before Marches to Calvary, *tremolando* resurrections, and edification by orchestral effects became rife in the land. These things should be commissioned by General Booth,* who exploits religious emotion in a coarse and unskilful, though effectual way, exactly as M. Gounod exploits it with refinement and mastery. No really great work will ever be patched up from them; and the sooner our festival makers intimate to composers that they are prepared to rate secular poetry, provided there be good thinking in it, above ballet music to sensational scenes from the New Testament, the sooner they are likely to get that new Messiah for which they are presumably waiting.

It is to be hoped that no reader of the above will

* "General" William Booth was a religious leader, founder of the Salvation Army.

suppose that the DRAMATIC REVIEW is either insensible to the loveliness of M. Gounod's operas and the Schubertian number and variety of his exquisite songs, or disposed to deny his right to treat scriptural narrative in a purely legendary and romantic way if he pleases. But it is necessary to insist just now on the fact that legendary and romantic music must not be allowed to claim the elevation connoted by the words "sacred" and "religious." In doing so it is hardly possible to avoid reminding the British public that Mendelssohn and Gounod, great as is the pleasure we derive from their music, are not in the very first rank as composers, not the peers of Mozart, Bach, Handel, Wagner, or even Beethoven. The reminder seems additionally ungracious as neither of them has ever claimed any such distinction, except perhaps as far as the Wagner part of the comparison goes. [U]

MOTETS AND MADRIGALS

Unsigned notes in The Dramatic Review, 5 September 1885

[U] People who like to pick up motets and madrigals by ear have had exceptional opportunities at the Inventions Exhibition this week. On Tuesday, in the Albert Hall, between two o'clock and half-past six, Mendelssohn's Why rage fiercely the heathen, and Morley's Fire! Fire! were sung nine times over in the various styles prevalent at Dover, Birmingham, Leicester, Nottingham, Sheffield, Liverpool, Burslem, Manchester, and Chelsea. From each of these places came a choir one hundred strong to compete for prizes of £100, £60, and £30. The test appointed was the singing of the two compositions named, and any one other piece, to the highest satisfaction of Messrs W. A. Barrett, H. Leslie, and W. G. McNaught, the judges. On Wednesday and Thursday a second competition between choirs upwards of fifty strong, for prizes of £60, £35, and £15, took place before a tribunal composed of Messrs A. O'Leary, Ebenezer Prout, and Eaton Faning. There were no less than fourteen entries for this. Yesterday a prize was offered for the best choir of upwards of thirty female voices; and for this a drawing-room class from Redhill "walked over." The prize, however, was withdrawn, as there was no competition. This was a mistake on the part of the Council. A choir attaining a high standard of excellence should be rewarded, competitors or no competitors, though the judges should of course be empowered to withhold the prize from an undeserving performance. Prizes of £60 and £40 for choirs of men's voices upwards of sixty strong, and £30 and £20 for choirs upwards of thirty, obtained three entries in each class. The results of the competitions will probably be announced today.

It is no very high praise to say that the worst of the large mixed choirs at this competition did better than the scratch assemblies of metropolitan ladies and gentlemen who bawl their way through the works of the great composers at the Crystal Palace and St James's Hall under Mr August Manns and Herr Richter. There will not be much difficulty in awarding the first prizes; but the attempt to determine any order of merit in the inferior grades will probably end in the three judges tossing "odd man out" for a decision. The nature of the occasion, and the hours at which it took place, precluded many critics from hearing the entire competition; but each of them records at least one "treat," and the general public attended in great numbers. The performance on the second day by the Hanley Glee and Madrigal Society may be mentioned here as exceptionally fine. On

Tuesday the Nottingham Philharmonic Society made a great effect; but their brilliancy is a little forced, and suggests that the society must recruit constantly to make up for wear and tear of voices. In some cases it was evident that great trouble had been taken to perfect very unpleasant effects. The conductor of the Chesterfield Harmonic Society, for instance, has laboriously trained a good choir to produce disagreeably sudden *diminuendos* and explosive *crescendos* with great precision. To a nervous man the echoing Albert Hall during this performance was about as cheerful as a draughty house with the doors slamming every fifty seconds. The Chesterfield Society sang, in addition to the test pieces, Macfarren's Break, break, break, which ended half a tone lower than it began. The Popular Ballad Concerts Choir sang very pleasantly and naturally, leaving the light and shade to take care of itself—which it did, to some extent. The Peckham Tonic Sol-faists produced capital tone, but had the opposite fault to the Ballad Concerts people; they seemed mechanical and over-drilled. The Burslem Tonic Sol-fa choir are said to have achieved a tremendous success on Tuesday. The chief prize will therefore probably go either to them or to the Nottingham Philharmonic Society.

In the important point of pronunciation, most of the performances were deplorable. The Hanley Glee and Madrigal Society were as excellent in this as in other respects; but their case was exceptional. Considering how unintelligibly many of our best singers deliver their words, the deficiencies of choristers in elocution are not to be wondered at, though they are certainly not to be passed over without strenuous remonstrance. Once upon a time a singer was not supposed to know the rudiments of his profession until he could pronounce the syllables *Do, Re, Mi*, &c., with the vowels perfectly pure, and the consonants perfectly sharp and unmistakable. Nowadays

[351]

choir trainers may be seen beaming with satisfaction whilst their pupils sing a sight-reading exercise to such sounds Dahoo, Rahee, Mihyee, Fawr, and other mongrel diphthongs. Ears that can complacently endure this sort of thing are not likely to be too exacting in other respects.

Might one venture to suggest the establishment of a prize for conducting, to be awarded by a committee of deaf men? We in London do not lack variety and picturesqueness in the action of our favorite conductors. As practised by Mr August Manns, conducting is a vigorous broadsword exercise. Herr Richter fingers his *bâton* as delicately as a fine fencer fingers his foil, or a fine violinist his bow, moving his arm gently and evenly from the elbow joint. Mr Carl Rosa slashes from his wrist. Sir Michael Costa also struck from the wrist; but he did not slash: he was cool, precise, and steady— almost uncomfortably so. Signor Arditi flourishes his *bâton*, and keeps time by flexure of his knee joints. The restrained war dance of Herr Eduard Strauss was not conducting; but as it was intended as such, it may be mentioned here as an unfavorable specimen. A week ago it seemed safe to say that all possible varieties of *bâton*-handling were familiar to London. But the conductors who appeared at the Albert Hall this week introduced several new styles to us, one or two of which might be appropriately called the Whirling Dervish style, or, even to borrow an idea from Mr Mantalini,* the Private Madhouse style. There were conductors with vertical action who prodded at the firmament, horizontal action conductors who seemed to be frantically waving their singers further back from them, elongating and collapsing conductors, expanding and contracting conductors, ambidexterous conductors, like drowning swimmers

* Character in Dickens's Nicholas Nickleby.

catching at straws right and left, and stiff one-handed conductors, like semaphores. Their emotions were as varied as their actions. Some conducted imploringly, others threateningly, others pompously or pedantically, a few persuasively, a great many in a sudden manner extremely disconcerting to strangers. The non-conductor was there, as he is everywhere; but the prevalent fault was fussiness. One gentleman who brought up a suburban Tonic Sol-fa choir was demonstrative to a degree that would have brought his sanity in question had he not been a musician, and therefore a privileged gesticulator. His choir did him credit, and did not deserve to be treated as if they were a flock of errant sheep in a bewildering network of streets, and he their drover.[U]

SACRED MUSIC:
A REPLY TO MR COMPTON READE

Unsigned notes in The Dramatic Review, 12 September 1885

[U] There is a severe music famine in the metropolis now, and this column would be very much emaciated but for Mr Compton Reade,* who has kindly provided food for it in the shape of a letter to the editor, challenging certain profound observations on sacred music made here on the 29th of August.

When Mr Compton Reade first took up the subject of music in the pages of the DRAMATIC REVIEW, he made

* The Rev. Compton Reade was a critic and novelist, whose recent novel Who Was Then the Gentleman? had been reviewed anonymously by Shaw in the Pall Mall Gazette on 15 July 1885.

his mark at once by saying of Handel that "as a harmonist it is superfluous to add he is nowhere, his chords having been subsequently supplied by Mozart." This startling superfluity seems to be due to the discovery by Mr Compton Reade that Mozart, when writing additional accompaniments to the air The people that walked in darkness in the Messiah, harmonized a passage which Handel wrote in plain unison. Mozart had no business to do this, but as a great musician paying a tribute to the beauty of a theme written by a master whom he greatly admired, he may be excused the liberty he took, especially as he could not possibly have foreseen that a century later such a very superfluous generalization as Mr Reade's would be based on the few chords that he read into And they that dwell in the Shadow of Death. It is true that another passage in the same stirring criticism implied that Handel used "common chords and interminable twiddles"; but the occurrence of an occasional common chord in the original score of the Messiah and other works would not by itself upset the assertion that Handel as a harmonist was "nowhere." The statement is only cited here as an illustration of the firmness and fearlessness with which Mr Compton Reade utters his convictions in the face of adverse facts. For if the score of a music-drama by the most advanced modern harmonist—Wagner's Tristan und Isolde for instance—were placed before Sir Walter Macfarren or any equally competent musician with a challenge to him to point out one chord in it that was unknown to Handel, he would probably be unable to select one without a misgiving that when the musical curiosity— for it would be a curiosity—was published, letters would pour in containing instances of the use of that particular chord in half a dozen of Handel's scores. People who talk about new chords, like those who at this time of day still believe that Monteverde discovered the chord of the dominant seventh (as the Pall Mall Gazette recently assured its readers), are either repeating the follies of critics who wrote before the historic method prevailed in criticism, or are, like Mr Reade, generalizing with heroic rashness on instances of the tampering to which many great compositions have been subjected, ostensibly to make them acceptable to modern taste, but really to save the trouble of carrying out the composer's intentions. If Handel could revisit the glimpses of the moon, modern harmonists would astonish and perhaps scandalize him, not by new chords, but by neglecting to prepare their discords by breaking burglariously from one tonality into another without the ceremony of modulation, and by writing in keys that were impracticable on keyed instruments in his time. Many of our composers would be "nowhere" with a vengeance if they were handicapped by the rules to which Handel, for good reasons, submitted.

It is useless to point out here that the results achieved by Handel under restraint were as great as the greatest that have since been achieved in comparative freedom. Mr Reade is within his right when he declares that Handel's music consists of "icy melodies and effusive rhodomontade," and speaks of "the mere mechanism of Bach." *De gustibus non est disputandum.* But there are questions of fact as well as of task involved in his letter of last week, in which he declares that he has read our critique of Gounod's Mors et Vita with wonder. It is characteristic of his impetuous style that he should have read what he attacked with wonder instead of with attention. For example, he has read the remark that "neither Mozart nor Beethoven would be a jot less famous if their Masses had never been written" with so much wonder that he has come away from it under the impression that it "put Mozart first on the list of religious composers." The logic of this is obscure; but the shortest way to set the matter right is to restate the contention which Mr Reade has misunderstood.

Here is the contention. Handel and Bach, in their most serious moods, were moved by religious subjects to exercise their greatest powers. But the later generation to which Mozart belonged was not susceptible to this influence. He was pious in his childhood; and he could always represent the devotional mood with great tenderness in music, as he could represent any other mood; but religion could not inspire him to put forth all his powers, as it had inspired Handel and Bach. In its old form it was not real enough nor serious enough to him. But when the ideal of a regenerated human society reached him in his masonic lodge, it did what the church had failed to do—moved him to his grandest utterances. The Zauberflöte was the first oratorio of the religion of humanity. Beethoven's setting of Schiller's Ode to Joy was the second. The inextinguishable vital spark which in Handel's day still dwelt in Lutheranism has passed into Positivism and Socialism; and a Mass or a Lutheran oratorio is now either a barren *tour de force* by a great man (Mozart's Requiem and Beethoven's Mass in D are instances) or a ballet by a comparatively small man descriptive of incidents from the scriptural narrative, with airs theatrically expressive of sentimental piety.

Mr Reade will see (if his wonder has subsided sufficiently) that his own view as to Mozart's inferiority to Wesley as a composer of religious music is not contradicted, but confirmed by the view which he has attacked. It may be a libel to say that Mendelssohn was neither religious nor serious; hence nothing of the kind was said here. But it does not follow that Mendelssohn's works are as serious as Bach's because Mendelssohn was as serious as Bach in writing them. A child may be as earnest in building a castle of sand as an architect in building a Parliament house: indeed, the faith of the child in its work may be greater than that of the architect. But that does not remove the frivolity of the sand-castle.

As to Spohr and Haydn being omitted from a list of composers of the very first rank, Spohr was omitted as a matter of course, he not having done more to entitle him to such a position than Gounod or Mendelssohn. Haydn was passed over after more deliberation, much as Sir Walter Scott might be passed over by a literary critic in compiling a list of great poets beginning with the names of Dante, Shakespear and Goethe.[U]

HISTORICAL INSTRUMENTS
Unsigned notes in The Dramatic Review,
19 September 1885

[U] The historical collection of musical instruments at the Inventions Exhibition is now much better worth a visit than it was some months ago. There are no rows of cases furnished with elaborate labels and no instruments, or with curious instruments and no labels. The labeling is complete and fairly accurate as far as the descriptive part is concerned, though in one or two instances single-reed instruments have received names proper to double-reed ones and *vice versa*. The catalog, too, has been compiled and issued. The collection is an extraordinary one, and, if the historical particulars furnished—especially the dates—be correct, a valuable one to students of the orchestra. The variety of woodwind instruments is amazing. In some of them the instruments of the present day are anticipated exactly: others must have seemed as eccentric when they were made as they do now. The construction of instruments, in spite of the improvements of Theodore Boehm and others, is still empirical and tentative; and manufacturers are continually making experiments which occasionally result in monstrosities. These are often the favorites of their makers, who display all the blindness of parental affection in trying to establish them as new instruments or as improvements on old ones. The cases at South Kensington do not lack specimens of such abortions, which are in much better preservation than the normal instruments. This is natural enough, since they were not worn out by constant use, and were kept as curiosities on account of the singularity of their appearance.

Another advantage to the collection, from a popular point of view, is the wet weather, which drives the bands into the Albert Hall in the evening. The instruments can then be examined—or rather stared at—by gaslight, to military music. For the information of country readers, it should be explained that the collection is placed in the highest gallery of the Albert Hall, which forms an uninterrupted circular promenade round the building. Behind the organ the way is through a suite of drawing rooms, furnished in the fashions of the XVI, XVII, and XVIII centuries respectively, with, of course, lutes, virginals, and harpsichords, according to date. Thus the visitor can fancy himself in the very room in which Shakespear read his sonnets to "the dark lady," and watched her fingers walk with gentle gait over the blessed wood of the virginals, whilst the saucy jacks leapt to kiss the tender inward of her hand. The illusion is greatly heightened by the band of the Coldstream Guards playing a selection from the Mikado outside.

There are two pianofortes in the gallery which stimulate the interest of the sightseers far more than the St Helier's Stradivarius or Queen Elizabeth's lute. One of them has been painted by Mr Burne-Jones.* The other, the property of Mr Alma-Tadema,† who designed it, is a stable, massive structure of polished oak, brass, and ivory, with well proportioned but mechanical lines and curves. The white inner surface of the lid is inscribed with the autographs of more or less distinguished persons who have used the instrument. The bench is a far more humane piece of furniture than the piano, which suggests an expensive American "casket" (coffin). It is difficult to contemplate it for five minutes without looking about for a heavy woodchopper. On the other hand, a musician could live with the instrument painted by Mr Burne Jones, and like it better every day. Visitors who have not their thinking apparatus ready are disagreeably affected by it at first; but those who know enough to consider that a pianoforte should be taken seriously will come back to have another and another look at it. It is the instrument best worth looking at in the Exhibition, the Stradivarius fiddles and the Rucker's harpsichords not excepted.

There is a negative attraction, too, at the Inventories. The British Army quadrilles—the autumn manœuvres of music—are no longer to be heard there nightly. But they are not homeless. Mr Gwyllym Crowe took them in at the Covent Garden promenade concerts yesterday, with "extra military bands." No matter. Even the British Army quadrilles cannot last forever. We shall grow out of such elaborate tomfoolery some day.

On Monday last, a hardshelled lover of classical music, who occasionally elevates the tone of this column by

* Edward Burne-Jones was an English painter and designer influenced by William Morris, Rossetti, and the pre-Raphaelites.

† Lawrence Alma-Tadema was a Dutch-born painter who specialized in classic subjects.

[359]

some scientific comments on high class compositions, was discovered in the act of witnessing a burlesque at the Gaiety Theatre.* As the music of the Vicar of Wide-awake-field is not by John Sebastian Bach, but by "Florian Pascal," the gentleman's conduct seemed to call for explanation. This he arbitrarily refused to supply; but he expressed himself strongly on certain points in the performance. He says it is hard that a man cannot drop his program, or sneeze, without the noise being taken as an *encore* by the conductor, Mr Hamilton Clarke. Having further in view that conductor's fair reputation as a musician, he cannot understand why all the concerted music is either suppressed or merely shammed. There should surely be a scrap of hunting chorus to the song sung by Miss Agnes Consuelo in the first scene. Again, there is in the second act a tuneful part song to some balderdash (if the authors will excuse that perfectly justifiable expression) about Morn, hateful morn, and Night, lovely night. Why are the parts not sung? On Monday the septet was a soprano solo with a comic accompaniment of wrong notes from Mr Arthur Roberts. Miss Consuelo, being a singer of some preten-sions, did not omit the extravagantly inappropriate royalty song which "Florian Pascal," with the customary eye to the music shops, has thrust into the score of the burlesque; and the audience did not seem to object, as they paid Miss Consuelo the compliment of an *encore*. But why the conductor should have started a sentimental ballad at a speed of 120 crotchets a minute, which increased to nearly 170 before the song was over, was

* Shaw had gone to witness the performance of the leading lady, Agnes Consuelo, to whom he had been giving vocal lessons. The authors of this burlesque of Goldsmith's The Vicar of Wakefield were H. P. Stephens and William Yardley. The composer hiding behind the pseudonym "Florian Pascal" was Joseph Williams.

not apparent to anyone unfamiliar with the traditions of Gaiety conducting. In our classicist's opinion, the Gaiety's traditional formula for ease and spirit must be slovenliness and slapdash, and its traditional rule: "If anything proves troublesome, leave it out; no one will be any the wiser." If Mr Hamilton Clarke would only extend to the stage the influence which he exercises in the orchestra, in which there is an evident attempt to do vulgar work with as much refinement as possible, the sacred lamp would burn all the brighter. At present it is flickering.

The essay by Sir George Macfarren which first appeared as the article "Music," in volume 17 of the ninth edition of the Encyclopædia Britannica, is now published separately. It is a most interesting and valuable summary of the historical information collected and the conclusions arrived at during a long life devoted wholly to music. Half a century has elapsed since Sir George wrote his first symphony. He can remember the great Rossini boom, the great Meyerbeer boom, the great Verdi boom, and the great Wagner boom. The extraordinary rise and growth of Beethoven's popularity in England has occurred during his lifetime. He now delivers his judgment very cautiously. Although to him every step gained by Wagner has been a loss to art, he loves the fate of the Bayreuth master to be decided by Time. Of Liszt and Gounod he says that "a future generation must judge" the "compositions styled oratorios" which they have produced. He still maintains that the completion of the chromatic scale by valves in brass instruments is "a serious evil, and has an incalculably pernicious effect upon the orchestration of the day." Alfred Day's treatise on harmony remains where it has always stood in his estimation, "comprehending whatever is practically available, and reconciling the previously apparent discrepancies between principle and use." "Opera" he declares "reached perfection under the masterly, magical, nay, superhuman touch of Mozart, whose two *finales* in Figaro and the two in Don Giovanni are models which should be the wonder of all time and yet can never be approached." Bravo, Sir George! The paragraph devoted to Offenbach has a sting in its tail. "He (Offenbach) has several imitators in the country of his adoption, *and is represented in England by Sir Arthur Sullivan!*" [U]

WHAT DID MR READE EXPECT?

*Unsigned notes in The Dramatic Review,
26 September 1885*

[U] Mr Compton Reade wrote to the DRAMATIC REVIEW last week pursuing the subject of religious music, and rather plaintively alluding to a "desire to be severe" with him in this column. What did Mr Compton Reade expect? Some remarks were made here on the subject of religious music. He attacked them without apparently having taken the trouble to read them carefully, and laid himself open to abundant ridicule by his misapprehension of the position to which he had gratuitously taken exception. Nevertheless, a well-meant attempt was made to disentangle his ideas by restating the case; and no stress was laid on any of the weak points in his criticism except such as were likely to mislead the general reader. Surely this was not an unduly severe reception. Mr Compton Reade evidently thinks that it might have been more indulgent. Undoubtedly it might; but, on the other hand, it certainly might have been much more severe without creating a reaction in Mr Reade's favor. How far it overshot or fell short of the golden mean may be left to the readers who are interested in the controversy. A point or two in Mr Reade's last letter may be noted here.

In the first place, he has explained himself satisfactorily as to Handel. He began by bringing against that composer the same accusation as was brought against the late M. Jullien by his less successful rivals, and against the royal composer of the Galatea Waltz by the Fenians. He stated, in short, that as Handel was nowhere as a harmonist, his "icy melodies" and "effusive rhodomontade" had to be harmonized by another hand. He now says that he "did not mean to infer that the great George Frederick was ignorant of counterpoint, or that he had no notion of harmony." The only reasonable reply to this is that if Mr Reade uses language for the purpose of concealing his thoughts, he is himself a little severe in bringing an accusation of unfairness against those who assume that he means what he writes. Again, he says that unless his memory is "the most treacherous of sieves," Mozart stood first and Beethoven last in a catalog of composers in which precedence went by eminence in religious composition. Whilst congratulating Mr Reade on his masterpiece of mixed metaphor, it must be added that his memory *has* failed him. The list referred to had no reference whatever to the religious works of the composers included in it. Consequently the only inconsistency which Mr Reade has pointed out is one between statements which were made here and statements which were not made here.

When Mr Reade declared that "Mozart's Masses may be religious—according to your ideas of religion—but surely do not deserve the epithet *serious*," his view was cordially assented to. Whereupon he immediately awoke to the importance of the other side of the question, and accused the assenter of "sneering" at Mozart's religious works. From which it would appear that Mr Reade's

[363]

opinion of Mozart is whatever the Dramatic Reviewer's opinion is not.

The citation of Mr Charles Reade's selection of one of Gounod's Christmas songs for "the harp music in Drink" as the final award of supreme excellence in religious composition; and the description of the typical Bach product as "a chorale in 12 or 24 real parts" with "a theme," need no comment. It has been evident from the beginning of the controversy that Mr Compton Reade's sense of religious fitness (to use his own phrase) is satisfied by the dulcet chromatic chords, the tender progressions, and the caressing modulations by which Spohr and Gounod provide him with "sweet and beautiful aids to devotion." When these musical delicacies were here ignored, a sense of injustice seems to have rankled in him, as it probably did in many others to whom the war songs of the Salvation Army and the hymns of Mr Ira D. Sankey are musically all in all; and he hit out at the omission with characteristic impetuosity. He is, he says, "a Christian, sincere enough." It is plain that even as a critic he is sincere enough; but he is neither considerate enough nor accurate enough to conduct a discussion with any prospects of raising a definite issue, much less arriving at a conclusion. So far he has taken no discoverable trouble to ascertain his own meaning or to state it exactly. But perhaps the difference may be generally stated thus. The Dramatic Reviewer distinctly considers that the Kyrie alone of Bach's Mass in B minor outweighs the whole of Beethoven's Mass in C and Gounod's Messe Solennelle together. Therefore to him the path from Bach to Gounod has been downhill. Mr Reade finds nothing but "mere mechanism" in Bach; but he cannot listen unmoved to the beautiful Benedictus of Beethoven's earlier Mass, as indeed neither can the Dramatic Reviewer. To Mr Reade, therefore, the path from Bach is a path uphill, or rather a flight from the earth to the curtains of heaven. The difference must remain until he replaces his vague impression of imaginary chorales in 12 or 24 real parts with a vivid memory of the magnificent march of Bach's harmony, and his melody that anticipates and yields to every thought and emotion of the sensitive singer.

The great John Sebastian—to imitate Mr Reade's friendly unceremoniousness—has been alive now for two hundred years, and is more vigorous than ever, whilst poor Dalayrac, who moved Berlioz as Spohr and Gounod move Mr Reade, is as dead as Albrechtsberger, who "thought in double counterpoint." "Mere mechanism" does not last two centuries; and each age forgets the "sweet and beautiful aids to devotion" of its forerunner, because it can always produce its own. Pretty songs are like pretty bonnets. Lovely as they are, we can afford to throw them away when they go out of fashion, because they can be replaced at little cost with new ones just as good. But we cannot afford to throw down our cathedrals at every change of fashion in architecture. We keep Bach and Handel in constant repair for the same reason.[U]

PRIZES AND PIRACY

Unsigned notes in The Dramatic Review, 3 October 1885

[U] The fashion of offering prizes for original musical compositions, introduced by the Philharmonic Society last season, is spreading. Mr Freeman Thomas has made a bid in this way for an overture to be produced at the Covent Garden promenades; and Messrs Brinsmead and Sons announce that they have thirty guineas ready for any British-born subject who can compose a pianoforte concerto to the superlative satisfaction of

Mr W. G. Cusins. Messrs Brinsmead define what they want as "a concerto for pianoforte and full orchestra." One would like to know what "full orchestra" means just now. Not that any practical difficulty is likely to arise on this point; but a musician, if he had to lay down strict conditions for a competition, would be rather puzzled when he came to consider what the standard full orchestra really is. Mozart's symphony in G minor, one of the greatest extant works of its kind, is written for a mere handful of instruments: Berlioz's Funereal and Triumphant Symphony employs a whole battalion of players. On the whole, it is to be hoped that Mr Cusins will give most marks to the thinnest score instead of to the fullest, other things, of course, being equal. Economy in scoring helps the circulation of music in the provinces and among the people, and is favorable to the development of individual excellence in orchestral players. The "effects" obtained by the employment of extra instruments in compositions designed on the standard model are hardly ever worth the additional money they cost.

Another point insisted upon by Messrs Brinsmead—that the competitors must be "British-born subjects"—may be recommended to the attention of the Irish National League, and will probably lead to the boycotting of Brinsmead pianofortes and the moonlighting of all those who play upon them. Irishmen are subjects of the British crown; but they are not "British-born." Mr Villiers Stanford, for example, would be disqualified if he condescended to submit a concerto to Mr Cusins for the sake of a possible thirty guineas. Now, the average Irishman is familiar with the name of Balfe, and able to whistle I dreamt that I dwelt, and When other lips. He may by chance have heard of Sterndale Bennett, but he knows nothing of his music. Of the works of Purcell, or of Wilbye and his contemporaries, the Milesian amateur has not the faintest suspicion. Hence his favorite assertion that all the English composers have been Irishmen. He will certainly attribute Messrs. Brinsmead's proscription of his countrymen to international jealousy. If, as is possible, the proscription was unintentional, perhaps Messrs Brinsmead will be so good as expressly to say so. Their offer would be handsomer without the addition of "No Irish need apply," particularly as there are many students in our musical academies and training colleges who are not "British-born," but whose future work will certainly go to the credit of English music.

Particulars of Messrs Brinsmead's offer may be quoted for the benefit of the British-born who have not seen it. "The score only must be forwarded, not later than October 31, to Mr George Mount, 5, Belsize Park Gardens, N.W. The name of the composer must nowhere appear on the work, which must bear a motto or device, and be accompanied by a sealed letter endorsed outside the envelope with the same motto or device, and containing within the composer's name and address. It is intended to produce the successful work during the season 1885. The composer will be required to provide legible and well-written parts in sufficient number for the orchestra; and the directors reserve the right to perform the work at any future time from these copies; but all other rights will rest with the composer or his assignee."

In the American Mikado case,* Judge Wallace has

* Rupert D'Oyly Carte and John Stetson, his American representative, had taken legal steps to enjoin theatrical pirates from giving unauthorized performances of the Gilbert and Sullivan comic opera, The Mikado. An injunction was refused, however, by Judge William J. Wallace of the U.S. Circuit Court. At least three pirated productions were staged in America prior to the first authorized performance on 19 August.

decided that the preparation of orchestral parts from a published pianoforte arrangement is not only not an invasion of the common law rights in the unpublished original score, but not even an infringement of the copyright in the pianoforte arrangement. This decision will be binding in New York, Connecticut, and Vermont, unless it be reversed in the United States Supreme Court. From a musician's point of view the only possible explanation of such a decision is either incapacity for logic, or a deplorable want of knowledge of the subject on the part of the court. From the point of view of an American lawyer it may, however, be sound public policy to defeat the attempts of English artists to obtain copyright in their works in the United States, though such a policy exposes American artists to a much more crushing competition than any to which Free Trade would expose the protected American manufacturer. Still, there is no other ground on which a sane man (provided he knew what he was talking about), could declare a score made from a pianoforte arrangement an original work. If an American painter procured a photograph of Mr Holman Hunt's "Flight into Egypt," copied the design and the light and shade on canvas, and exercised his invention in the coloring only, his claim to have produced an original work would be scoffed at by the most superficial amateur. To score a pianoforte arrangement is a precisely analogous operation, although it is easier beyond all comparison to fill in a score than to color a design with oil paint. The decision of Judge Wallace will seriously affect music publishers, as a practice has arisen of late of having pianoforte arrangements of important works made by American citizens, and copyrighted by them in the United States. If these arrangements do not protect the score, our transatlantic cousins will soon have the pleasure of hearing Gounod's Mors et Vita, with spurious orchestration by the local bandmaster. That trick has been done many a time in England to save the hire of the authentic parts, as many a musician who enjoyed a glimpse behind the scenes in the bad old times can tell; but to enforce such a practice by law just when the public are becoming sufficiently instructed to know that it ought to be punished seems unworthy of the chosen land of Theodore Thomas.*[U]

BERLIOZ ASCENDING

Unsigned notes in The Dramatic Review, 10 October 1885

[U] The Bristol Musical Festival Committee announces three performances. The reader will anticipate the particulars. The Messiah, the Elijah, and a miscellaneous concert beginning with a new cantata by a local organist, of course? Not at all. Positively no Elijah, no local cantata, no selections, but instead, Belshazzar, Berlioz's Damnation of Faust, and the Messiah. This honorable prominence allotted to Berlioz at an English musical festival, and the remarkable discovery that the complete works of Handel are not comprised in the three volumes containing the Messiah, Israel in Egypt, and Judas Maccabeus, deserve a word of acknowledgment. We do not yet know half enough of Handel. As Britons we are convinced that we know more of his music than any other nation does, because we are more persistent in repeating the Messiah. And, as there is no sign of the Messiah wearing out, it cannot be said that we sing it too often; but we certainly sing the other oratorios of

* German-born director of the Chicago Conservatory of Music and stimulator of American musical taste.

Handel too seldom—so seldom that there are hardly any great composers with whose work in the gross we are not more familiar than we are with his.

A better acquaintance with the works of Berlioz will do much to hurry our music through and out of a perilous phase. In our musical childhood we like descriptive music: in our musical adolescence we crave for sensational orchestration: subsequently we take what we can get, and are more or less thankful. But whilst we are still intoxicating ourselves at orchestral orgies, it is important that we should have them as good as they can be made; and for that we must go to Berlioz. Whether the festive provincial, when he has become accustomed to enjoy Faust's terrible gallop to hell, will contentedly return to the much milder dissipation of Elijah's ride in a whirlwind to heaven, remains to be seen. If he is capable of drawing comparisons, he will, at least, be in no danger of mistaking the orchestration of Liszt and Raff for first-rate work.

The above suggests a program which might suit Mr Gwyllym Crowe at the Promenade Concerts. Why not add to the hackneyed classical nights, humorous nights, and British Army nights, a novelty under the title of a Newmarket night? Program: The Spectre Hunt, from Weber's Freischütz; Liszt's symphonic poem Mazzeppa; the elopement of Lenore with her lover's ghost on horseback, from Joachim Raff's Lenore symphony; Elijah's ride to heaven in a fiery chariot, by Mendelssohn; Race of Faust and Mephistopheles, on two black thoroughbreds, to Sheol, by Hector Berlioz. Should the relief of a ballad be called for, Signor Foli can be at hand with Prince Poniatowski's Yeoman's Wedding Song, Ding dong, ding dong, we gallop along. Schumann's little piece, The Rocking Horse, might employ the pianist of the evening. Turf authorities could then decide whether Berlioz's alternative quaver and couple of semiquavers represents a canter or a gallop, and whether the swishing triplets of Liszt are not at least as suggestive of a frying-pan in full action as of the flight of the fiery untamed steed. There is really no reason why sporting men should be kept out of our concert rooms by Bach, Gluck, Mozart, and others who took their art seriously (Gluck, by the bye, was once guilty of making the bass strings in the orchestra imitate the barking of Cerberus at Orpheus). There is plenty of horsy music, easily graduated from the simple passage by which Haydn conjured up the noble steed, who, with flying mane and fiery look, impatient neighed, to the elaborate Ride of the Valkyries, by Richard Wagner.

Concerts with special programs, such as the one just sketched, may prove the beginning of a rational classification of musical compositions. At present the program of an orchestral concert often reminds one of an old Drury Lane playbill of the days—or rather nights—when the entertainment was opened by a melodrama, continued by one of Shakespear's tragedies, relieved by a grand Christmas pantomime, and concluded by a screaming farce. To the uninitiated British public all plays were mysterious products of a higher intelligence and an occult technique, whether Shakespear or Fitzball were the author. It is to be feared that a good many of us are in the same condition today with regard to music. One symphony is as grave an undertaking to us as another. If Mr Irving were to announce that at his next revival of Hamlet, the tragedy would be preceded by The Wreck Ashore, everybody would perceive the incongruity. But the Philharmonic Society is just as likely as not to regale its subscribers next season with Mozart's symphony in G minor preceded by Moszkowski's Joan of Arc symphony, although it is certain that the admirers of Mozart will regard M. Moszkowski's symphonic ballet music much as frequen-

ters of the Lyceum regard Mr Buckstone's melodrama.*
Against the mixture of high-class and low-class music
at our opera houses, where the talent of the artists, with
all the accessory resources of the theatre are squandered
one night on a common blood-and-thunder Italian
piece, and (consequently) found wanting the next when
an opera of the highest class is put forward, it seems
useless to protest in the face of the economic difficulties
which stand in the way of any sudden alteration of the
system. But we have surely progressed far enough to
make feasible the successful establishment of a second
class of orchestral concert for the performance of
romantic and descriptive music, selections from operas,
and the like, so as to take the second-rate novelties which
the public desire to hear off the hands of Herr Richter
and the Philharmonic Society, leaving them free to
restore to life the many half-forgotten classics which are
now crowded out by new compositions which certainly
must be performed somewhere, but which the most
cultivated concert-goers do not want to hear and which
the most cultivated artists do not want to play. There is
no more sense in setting Herr Richter to take a turn at
the work of Mr Gwyllym Crowe than there would be in
setting Mr Irving to do the work of Mr Augustus Harris.

Plenty of opportunities for the cultivation of specialities at different series of concerts will be available during
the forthcoming season. There will be a Brinsmead
series, and a set of concerts conducted by Mr A. C.
Mackenzie. Here we have a couple of openings for a
new departure. Two established societies have changed
their conductors—a most momentous step. Mr W. H.
Cummings has accepted the *bâton* at the Sacred

* John Buckstone (1802–79), actor-manager at the Haymarket Theatre for quarter of a century, was a prolific author
of tragic dramas and farces.

Harmonic. There is a certain novelty in the reappearance of a retired tenor as a conductor. Tenor singers are traditionally supposed to be capricious, vain, selfish, and deficient in intelligence. The French describe a childish and conceited person as *bête comme un tenor*. Mr Cummings is happily not this sort of tenor. He is an accomplished musician, and an authority on the subject of English music and its history. He has never lost an opportunity of reminding the British public that one of the greatest composers that ever lived was an Englishman named Purcell. Perhaps, since the Yorkshire Feast Song and Dido and Eneas do not come within the Sacred Harmonic field, Mr Cummings will persuade the Society to produce some of Purcell's religious music. If it were only to gratify connoisseurs in counterpoint, in which Purcell practised a variety of remarkable feats, the experiment would be worth trying.

The other instance of a new conductor in an old society is Mr Villiers Stanford, who has succeeded Herr Otto Goldschmidt at the Bach Choir. The change is a promising one. Mr Stanford is that very exceptional combination—a young Irishman who is also a scholarly musician. He will supply the Celtic fire so sadly missed in the performances conducted by Herr Goldschmidt, whose many invaluable qualities, however, will make him regretted unless Mr Stanford maintains the high standard of industry and artistic conscientiousness which made the Bach bicentenary festival this year such a success. Herr Goldschmidt presumably regards it as the crowning achievement of his conductorship, and takes the opportunity to retire whilst its honors are fresh upon him.[U]

A ROYAL REBUFF

Unsigned notes in The Dramatic Review, 17 October 1885

[U] The stir lately made by the Royal Academy of Music at the instigation of the King of the Belgians leaves us as far as we were before from a settlement of the standard pitch question. The committee appointed by the meeting held in St James's Hall last June, an account of which appeared in this column, has dissolved itself in despair. All that it did was to memorialize the Field Marshal Commander-in-Chief, begging him, in effect, to do as the King of the Belgians had done, *i.e.* command all the military bands in the service to play henceforth at French pitch. This daunted even the Duke of Cambridge. He excused himself on the ground of "financial and other difficulties"; and the committee, discouraged by the royal rebuff, fell to pieces forthwith. It is to be regretted that they did not take some steps to ascertain and report on the difficulties, "financial and other," alleged to stand in the way of tuning down less than a semitone. Some more precise information is needed as to the outcry that new instruments will have to be purchased by orchestral players if the English pitch be discarded. Is this true; and if so, how true? It is said that the clarinet presents a difficulty. But is there a single clarinetist in the country who cannot, by drawing the mouthpiece of his instrument out of the socket, inserting washers, or modifying his reed and his blowing, get down at least half a tone when he is once thoroughly persuaded that no excuse will be accepted, and that the only alternatives are the sacrifice of his engagements, or the expenditure of a hundred guineas for a new set of clarinets? The confident allegations of impossibility made by the partisans of the high pitch against the French normal diapason would lead one to suppose that a performance at French pitch had never taken place within the last half century in England. The thing has been done without the purchase of a single new instrument, and can presumably be done again as often as our conductors choose to insist upon it. It is true that the results of playing at a strange pitch would not be delectable at first; but the new conditions would soon cease to be strange, and the players would learn how to coax their instruments into tune. This is what they have to do at any pitch; for all the keyed wind instruments used in the orchestra have imperfections which must be corrected by the player.

The fact is that conductors and players do not object to the high pitch; and, except at the opera house, they have proved too strong for the singers. At the festivals, the pitch of the organ overrules all. It is the organ builders who have baffled Mr Sims Reeves throughout his long struggle against the ruinous Philharmonic pitch.

Mr Ebenezer Prout is to decide which is the best of the seventy-odd overtures evoked by the Promenade Concerts competition. Without disparagement to Mr Prout, or to Mr W.G. Cusins, who has accepted a similar position from Messrs Brinsmead, one judge is not enough. Down east, in Blue Anchor Yard, they allow three judges to a glove fight. Surely less counsel should not be taken in judging between composers of overtures and concertos. Mr Prout, as an authority on instrumentation, might be associated with Dr Stainer to criticize the harmony, and Mr Gwyllym Crowe to give due weight to the poetic originality (if any) displayed by the competitors.

At Her Majesty's Theatre they still persevere in the

attempt to accustom us to ballets three acts long. And they certainly deserve to succeed. Excelsior is one of the pleasantest entertainments at present accessible in London. It is not like the ordinary *ballet d'action*—a pantomime with a romantic plot; nor is it that least diverting of inanities: a *ballet divertissement*. The action is not that of individuals, but of civilization; and its victories are those of man over nature, and not—as in most Terpsichorean festivals—of nature over man. The ladies of our ordinary ballets are always beautiful; but their costumes are monotonous, their gymnastics limited and not always graceful or natural, and their complexions all apparently from the same makeup box. A dance of huntsmen—not young ladies in scarlet satin coats and jockey caps, but actual men in huge boots and spurs—is received nightly at Her Majesty's with an enthusiasm which all the glories of the Alhambra, even in the days of that very charming ballet Yolande, failed to evoke. The relief given by the employment of men and children; the purely artistic character of the spectacle, the designers of which have absolutely ignored that section of the public which degrades the ballet by regarding it as a mere exhibition of female beauty; and the novelty and success of the attempt to set people thinking by a form of entertainment to which we had all but lost the habit of bringing our brains, are doing much to raise the character of the art of dancing to something of its ancient dignity. The bright Italian coloring, and the amazing spins of Signor Cecchetti, with the lively but not unrefined music, are only minor points of excellence in a very hopeful performance.[U]

ENCORES

Unsigned notes in The Dramatic Review, 24 October
1885

[U] It is worth noting that musical enterprise is unusually hopeful and active in preparing for the winter season, although in the summer fashionable Italian opera was unable to achieve even a respectable death struggle. Next month the Albert Hall Choral Society, Novello's Oratorio Concerts, Brinsmead's Symphony Concerts, and the Richter Concerts will leave little leisure to the amateurs who make a point of missing nothing. The comparatively frivolous autumn musical entertainments are preparing for dissolution. At the Covent Garden promenades great efforts are being made to crown the season with concerts of exceptional splendor. Such artists as Madame Norman-Neruda, Madame Trebelli, Mr Sims Reeves, and Mr Santley have appeared on the same night, the prices being doubled for the occasion. Of this doubling of prices the public have no right to complain. The inveterate mendicity with which they have abused the *encore* system night after night, so as to obtain exactly twice what they have paid for, would justify any extremity on the part of the managers and artists.[U]

A hearty *encore* is not in its nature an appropriate subject for economic scrutiny, but not one in ten of such *encores* as have become habitual at Covent Garden is an expression of musical enthusiasm or gratitude to the artist who receives the pretended compliment. In every average audience there is a certain proportion of persons who make a point of getting as much as possible for their money—who will *encore*, if possible, until they have had a ballad for every penny in their shilling, with the orchestral music thrown in as a makeweight. There is also a proportion—a large one—of silly and unaccustomed persons who, excited by the novelty of being at a concert, and dazzled by the glitter and glory of the Bow-street temple of Art, madly applaud whenever anyone sets the example. Then there are goodnatured people who lend a hand to encourage the singer. The honest and sensible members of the audience, even when they are a majority, are powerless against this combination of thoughtless goodnature, folly, and greed. And so the system becomes rooted, and can only be neutralized in an unsatisfactory way by favorite artists declining to be set down in the program for more than half the songs they intend to sing.

There are doubtless many concert-goers who *encore* from a genuine desire to hear over again a performance which has just given them great pleasure. One cannot help wondering whether their consciences ever ask them why they permit themselves to do at a concert what they would be ashamed to attempt elsewhere. Imagine the sincere encorist consuming a bath bun and asking the confectioner to give him another for nothing because the first was so nice. Yet that would be no more unreasonable than is the common practice of acknowledging the charm of Mr Sims Reeves's singing of Tom Bowling by a demand (without additional payment) for Come into the garden, Maud.

It is, however, of little help to dwell on an abuse without suggesting a remedy. The simplest one would be to send round the hat, with an announcement that as soon as the singer's terms for one song had been collected, the *encore* would be complied with. It would be amusing to witness the effect of such a measure on the enthusiastic crowd who surge about the orchestra at Covent Garden cheering Mr Lloyd and Mr Santley, and who next day recount the number of ballads they enjoyed over and above what they paid for. It might do much to convince them at last that *encores* are not nitrogenous food—singers cannot live on them. Also that beggars in broadcloth inside a theatre are not a whit more respectable morally than the beggars in rags outside.

LISZT-LESS

Unsigned notes in The Dramatic Review, 24 October 1885

[U] This evening Herr Richter will launch the winter season with an orchestral concert. On Monday afternoon Mr Walter Bache will follow with a pianoforte recital which will *not* be devoted wholly to the compositions of Liszt. Compositions by Bach, Beethoven and Chopin will be admitted. This is far better than the plan of "Liszt, and nothing but Liszt," which Mr Bache has adopted on some past occasions. At all pianoforte recitals there is the drawback of too much piano. To superadd too much Liszt was not the way to obtain for that composer the esteem which Mr Bache claims for him.

The announcement of Liszt's St Elizabeth for the 6th of April next year at Novello's oratorio concerts has elicited the usual rumor that the Abbé is about to visit this country, and that he will be present at the performance. No musical season is complete in England without this rumor. If it be not fulfilled soon now it will never be fulfilled at all. Liszt completed his seventyfourth year on Thursday last.

Mr A. J. Hipkins, the foremost English authority on the history and construction of the pianoforte, gave his long-promised lecture on the spinet, harpsichord, and clarichord, at the Inventions Exhibition on Wednesday, and again yesterday evening. This may be regarded as the last effort of the Council to be serious and historical in their musical aims. In a fortnight the exhibition will be closed.

A recent interesting feature at the Inventions is the band of the Mounted Artillery. It is announced as a string band; but it is, in fact, a complete orchestra. Its efficiency proves how much a refined conductor, by dint of working with care and perseverance in a thoroughly artistic spirit, can do with the material at the disposal of a military bandmaster. The Cavaliere L. Zavertal deserves the gratitude of South Kensington for having trained a band which, unlike even the best of the crack bands in the service, is absolutely free from vulgarity. At a late concert in the Albert Hall, Weber's second symphony—opportunities of hearing which do not often occur—was in the program. It was preceded by the Schiller march, which made the curious impression that Meyerbeer's music, empty as it is, never fails to produce when carefully and sympathetically executed. [U]

RICHTER WAXES STOUT

Unsigned notes in The Dramatic Review, 31 October 1885

[U] The only novelty at the Richter concert this night week was the substitution of a euphonium for the second trombone, in consequence of the absence of Mr J. Matt. The mooings and bellowings of this strange orchestral animal, hidden between the first and third trombones, did no very great harm to the general effect, though in one or two passages the tone of the trombone triad was perceptibly weakened and fuddled by it. The band was in excellent condition, and was one hundred strong, owing to the inclusion in the program of such heavily-scored works as Wagner's Emperor March, and one of Liszt's Hungarian Rhapsodies. The string quartet, the only part of the orchestra in which the numbers can be varied according to the taste or means of the concert giver, contains sixtysix players: sixteen first violins, sixteen seconds, twelve violas, twelve violoncellos, and ten double basses. For the wind and drum parts of an ordinary Beethoven symphony, fifteen players are required, so that at a Richter concert the symphony would be performed by eightyone artists. Now, Beethoven himself was considered extravagant for suggesting that there should be at least seventy players in a full orchestra. So it will be seen that Herr Richter does not treat us stingily in this matter.

The *Kaisermarsch*, which opened the concert, was performed in a sufficiently stupendous manner. Compared to it, all our stock grand marches of Meyerbeer and Mendelssohn are mere quicksteps. Its epic magnificence was inspired by that infernal carnival of blood and iron, the Franco-German war of 1870-71; and it may be classed with the downfall of the French empire as one of the two good things that sprang from that convulsion of evil. The march will be liked none the worse when its origin is forgotten. Posterity is likely to be more surprised than pleased if its analytical-program writers insist on assuring it that this thundering outburst of fervent and jubilant song was "composed in honor of King Wilhelm of Prussia on his becoming Emperor of Germany." Such is Mr C. A. Barry's version of the matter. But we may hope that the march was written as much in honor of the accomplishment of German unity as of King William's new title. It would be humiliating to have to class, even in a subject index, so powerful a composition with God bless the Prince of Wales.

The most popular item in the program was the introduction to Tristan, with the death song of Isolde as arranged for use at orchestral concerts. This is the music that delights men who are unfamiliar with the forms through which the earlier composers expressed themselves. It has brought into the concert room a thoughtful class which formerly declined to regard music as a serious art. These people, never having wasted their time on dance tunes mechanically constructed upon alternate chords of the tonic and dominant, experience none of that ludicrous discomfiture on hearing a tonic discord which led to so many protests that Wagner's music was melodyless cacophony. In poetry, Mr Browning has achieved the same feat and incurred the same abuse. He is read by men who regard the reading of most other poetry as a waste of time; and his verse has been declared no verse at all by persons with a turn for "The rose is red: the violet, blue" manner of lyric. The applause which followed the Tristan prelude at St James's Hall on Saturday would have sufficed in an opera house to bring Madame Patti before the curtain at least ten times. Even Herr Richter, who is somewhat less ready with his acknowledgments, had to add an unwonted number of bows to the performance. Popularity, by the bye, seems to agree with Herr Richter. If musical criticism were concerned with the breadth of a conductor's waistcoat as it is with the breadth of his style, this would be the place to remark that Hans Richter has grown perceptibly stouter since his first visit to this island.

Liszt's Hungarian Rhapsody in F requires, as usual, a good deal of special pleading in the analytic program in order to justify its pretension to be a grave work of art. At the very outset the subdued drum roll, and the two horns in F dreadfully sounding their very deepest note, seem pregnant with doom. This is only Liszt's way: it is as harmless as the scowl of Mr Vincent Crummles.* True, the slow movement is *quasi marcia funèbre*; the quick one, *allegro eroico*; but the solemnity does not last: before five minutes have elapsed the reverend composer is dancing among the oyster shells amid the most inspiriting whistling and jingling imaginable. A Hungarian rhapsody is the gayest of diversions at a classical concert.

The symphony was Schumann's in D minor, in which the four movements are continuous. It dates from 1841, and, as might be expected, the plan is Beethoven's, though the tunes are Schumann's. Some of the themes reappear in more than one of the movements, and Mr Barry does not fail to assure us that these recurring themes "impart a sense of unity to the work as an organic whole." This remark has been made before: it will be made again. The customary reference to the C minor and choral symphonies (which are not, in the least, cases in point) will be added. The attention of great minds will be thus attracted to the subject of unity, and the value of that particular form of it which consists in using the same idea twice over will be settled. Pending that settlement, the DRAMATIC REVIEW will preserve a sceptical attitude. A leading motive it understands: a referring-back with obvious intention (as in the ninth symphony) it can follow; but its sense of artistic unity has not yet been reduced to a perception of absolute identity.

The members of the Richter orchestra must be at present in a state of stony numbness produced by constant railway traveling in northern latitudes during the cold of this week. They played at Newcastle-on-Tyne on Monday, at Glasgow on Tuesday, at Edinburgh on Wednesday, at Dundee on Thursday, and at Glasgow

* Character in Dickens's Nicholas Nickleby.

again yesterday. They will complete their labors by a second performance this morning at Edinburgh.

Dr Francis Hueffer, having undertaken to deliver a series of lectures for Mr Hermann Franke, has been publicly described by that enterprising gentleman as "the eminent Music-Historian." Dr Hueffer is, in fact, critic of music to the Times newspaper; author of Richard Wagner and the Music of the Future, and of The Troubadours; and a poet into the bargain. In the latter capacity he wrote the libretto to Colomba,* prefacing it with some remarks on Bunn which excited discussion. He hardly did justice to Bunn's curious power of writing verses which, when sung, are lyric and pathetic, but, when read, present a combination of bathos and raging nonsense that any country might be proud of. Dr Hueffer has also composed several songs. His lectures are to be on Wagner, Berlioz, and Liszt, and will be delivered at Glasgow, Edinburgh, Manchester, Liverpool, Birmingham, Nottingham, Oxford and Cambridge. But why must London wait?

Herr von Serres, manager of the Austrian State railways, has borne off Madame Montigny-Rémaury in wedlock from the profession to which, as a pianoforte player, she was a valuable acquisition. She visited us several times of late years, and produced, especially in concerto-playing, a striking impression. Her nervous energy, which was always excited to an intense degree by playing in public, enabled her to produce an impression of great brilliancy and impetuosity without sacrificing the clearness of her execution and the emphasis of her phrasing to excessive speed.

A new symphony by Brahms has been played for the first time at Saxe Meiningen by the grand Ducal

* A lyrical drama with music by A. C. Mackenzie (1883), from a tale by Prosper Merimée.

Orchestra. It is stated that "as the score and parts at present exist only in manuscript, it is unlikely that the new symphony will be heard in England during the present year." Doubtless it will not; but as to the alleged reason, it may be said that there is time to copy and rehearse half a dozen symphonies between this and 1886. [U]

FUGUE OUT OF FASHION

The Magazine of Music, November 1885

To the average Briton the fugue is still an acute phase of a disease of dulness which occasionally breaks out in drawing rooms, and is known there as classical music. It has no pleasant tune in four strains to add to such stores of memory as Grandfather's Clock and Wait till the clouds roll by. Its style vaguely suggests organ music or church music. Its polyphonous development defies the amateur who picks up things by ear: not that Dutchman himself, who astonished the Philharmonic Society by playing chords on the flute when Sterndale Bennett was conductor, could have whistled a fugue. Those who are, comparatively speaking, connoisseurs, guess the piece to be "something by Handel." Outsiders, who have often wondered what a fugue may be, cease talking and listen curiously, generally with growing disappointment culminating in a relapse into whispered conversation. This is a relief to the player, who, conscious of having taken a desperate step in venturing on a fugue in a drawing room, becomes more and more diffident as the hush indicates that the company have adopted the unusual course of listening to the pianoforte. Many a player, under stress of too much attention, has lost heart; paused on the first dominant seventh that presented itself; and glided off into a waltz, which never fails to set all tongues going again except perhaps those of a few sentimental young people who have overpowering recollections of the last partner with whom they danced that very waltz. The classicists who rail at dance music should never forget the cluster of associations, rich with the bloom of youth and the taste of love, which the lounger, without the slightest previous knowledge of music, can gather from a waltz by Waldteufel.

Professional pianists, and those hardy amateurs who are not to be put out by any concentration or diffusion of the attention of their audience, usually confine themselves to their own compositions in the drawing room. They do not play fugues because they cannot write them. The standard precept runs:—"Learn thoroughly how to compose a fugue, and then *dont*"; and on the second clause of this they act perforce, since they have neglected the first for lack of the economic pressure which is needed to make the average man take serious pains with any subject. It does not pay an ordinary professor of music to learn double counterpoint any more than it pays a journalist to write Latin verses. Fugues are unsaleable: of the considerable number written every year by students, candidates for degrees, and organists, hardly one comes into the market, and for that one there is seldom a purchaser. As to the value of the practice in double counterpoint gained by fugal composition, all that can be said from a commercial point of view is that a musician can make as much money without it as with it. And even from an artistic point of view there are some plausible nothings to be said against the weary climb up Fux's Gradus ad Parnassum. If Beethoven had not worried himself as he did over counterpoint, we might have been spared such aberrations of his genius as the Mass in D. Cherubini's music might have been more interesting if he had not been stopped short by satisfaction with the scientific smoothness and finish which his technical resources enabled him to attain. Besides, one can pick up the art of fugue at any time if occasion should arise. Spohr never wrote a fugue until he had to furnish an oratorio with an overture. Then he procured a copy of Marpurg, looked at the rules, and wrote a respectable fugue without further preparation. Mozart tried his hand successfully at all sorts of contrapuntal curiosities the moment he came across examples of them. It may be true that the best contrapuntists were also the most skilful composers; but their good counterpoint was the result of their skill, and not their skill the result of their counterpoint. To study fugue, not for immediate use in composition, but for its own sake, eventually leads to writing it for its own sake, which means writing dry and detestable music. Such are the excuses at hand for the student who has privately made up his mind that life is not long enough for a thorough course of counterpoint.

Since even the most urgent advocates of such a course falter when the question is no longer one of learning how to write fugues, but of actually writing and publishing them, even the student whose aims are purely artistic finds himself at last debating whether fugue is not obsolete. Many have answered the question in the affirmative. The old-fashioned deliberate form no longer seems to express anything that modern composers are moved to utter. It is not the power to write fugues that is lost, it is the will. The St Paul proves that Mendelssohn could write elaborate fugues and embroider them with florid orchestral accompaniments; but the Elijah suggests that in his mature judgment these features of his earlier oratorio were but scholarly vanities. Meyerbeer and Donizetti were academic adepts; and Meyerbeer at least was never lazy, perfunctory, or hurried; yet neither of them made any considerable direct use of their knowledge: many comparatively unschooled composers, who only got up Marpurg as Spohr did, to write an Amen chorus or an oratorio prelude (just as a barrister gets up a scientific point when it happens to be the pivot of a case in which he holds a brief), have left more fugal counterpoint on record than either of them. Wagner wove musical tissues of extraordinary complication; but the device of imitation had no place in his method. The history of fugue as employed by the great composers during the last hundred and thirtyfive years, is one of corruption, decline, and extinction. Sebastian Bach could express in fugue or canon all the emotions that have ever been worthily expressed in music. Some of his fugues will be prized for their tenderness and pathos when many a melting sonata and poignant symphonic poem will be shelved for ever. Lamentation, jubilee, coquetry, pomposity, mirth, hope, fear, suspense, satisfaction, devotion, adoration— fugue came amiss to none of these in his hands. The old vocal counterpoint reached its zenith then, as the five-act tragedy in blank verse did in the hands of Shakespear. The decadence was equally rapid in both instances. Within half a century after Bach's death, Mozart was not only expressing emotions by means of music, but expressing them in the manner of a first-rate dramatist, as they are modified by the characters of the individuals affected by them. Like Bach, he was not merely an extraordinary man—Offenbach, strictly speaking, was that—but an extraordinary genius. And yet he made no use in his greatest work of the form which was as natural to Bach as the German language. The customary omission of the brisk little *fugato* at the end of Don Giovanni does not obscure the superlative excellence of that opera. In the Figaro there is not even a *fugato*. In the Zauberflöte the chorale sung by the two armed men is accompanied by some fugal writing of impressive beauty, which, with the Recordare of the Requiem, shews what Mozart could have done with the imitative forms had he preferred them. But this only gives significance to the fact that he did without them. In the last movement of the Jupiter symphony, and in the Zauberflöte overture, the fugue and sonata forms are combined. But the overture is distinctly a *tour de force*, a voluntary reversion to an old form, undertaken by Mozart partly from his rare sympathy with what was noble and beautiful in the old school; partly because, in the overture to Don Giovanni, he had already produced a model for the modern opera overture which he could not himself surpass, and which remains unique to this day. The Jupiter *finale* is historically more important. It is the first notable instance of the XIX century tendency to regard fugue, not as a vehicle of expression, but as a direct expression in itself of energy, excitement, and bustle. This view seized Beethoven, who took a great deal of trouble to acquire skill in double counterpoint and canon, in order to use it for certain *tours de force* which were much less successful than Mozart's. But in his natural characteristic works he used it only to produce a sort of spurious fugue or *fugato*, consisting of a vigorous subject treated with a fast and furious *stretto*, and then thrown aside. He had no command of the form: on the contrary, it commanded him. A particular effect to which it lent itself had caught his fancy, that was all. His *fugato* was invariably an ebullition of animal spirits. In it the parts had no vocal fitness: the accents of human emotion which occur in every bar of Bach's subjects and countersubjects are absent in Beethoven's fugal compositions. He brutalized the fugue as completely as he humanized the sonata. After his spurious fugue came Meyerbeer's spurious *fugato*, in which the subject, instead of being continued as countersubject to the answer, drops its individuality by merging in the harmony. In the prelude to Les Huguenots all the fugal effects which Meyerbeer cared for were produced in a striking way without the trouble of writing a bar of double counterpoint. Handel's fugal setting of the words He trusted in God that He would deliver Him. Let Him deliver Him, if He delight in Him! is a masterly expression of the hatred, mockery, and turbulence of an angry and fanatic mob. Meyerbeer, in the third act of his famous opera, obtained an effect of the same kind, sufficient for his purpose, by means of a sham fugue. This was his deliberate choice: he was perfectly competent to write a genuine fugue, and would undoubtedly have done so had not the counterfeit suited the conditions of his work better.

Little mock fugal explosions are not uncommon now in opera. There is a ludicrous example in the overture to Vincent Wallace's Maritana. Verdi has occasionally threatened the theatre-goer with a display of fugal science, but the pretence has never been carried very far. Similar symptoms, also speedily suppressed, appear in the third act of Boïto's Mefistofele. Gounod often gives us a few pretty bars in canon, or a theme, with a bold skip or two at the beginning, introduced and answered in the rococo "dux and comes" style. There is a charming *fughetta* in the first act of Bizet's Carmen. But all these examples are either whims, pursued for a few measures and then abandoned, or exciting panto-mime music to what is called by stage managers and prizefighters a rally. Wagner and Goetz, the only men of our time who have been, like Handel and Bach, great both as harmonists or chord writers and as contrapuntists or part writers, have not dealt in fugue. They have associated themes with definite ideas, and practised all the combinations which their logic led them to in consequence. It has not led them to the device of imitation, which has been therefore left to men who, like the late Frederick Kiel of Berlin, have possessed great talent and industry without originality or genius. Imitation is often very pretty, and it always, by giving the part writing a definite and obvious aim, produces an air of intelligibility in the composition which is very welcome to the many people who are apt to get befogged when they endeavor to follow music of any complexity. But nowadays the life has gone out of it: we practice it principally for its own sake now and then, but never for the purpose of expressing subjective ideas.

MORS ET VITA

Unsigned notes in The Dramatic Review,
7 November 1885

[U] On Wednesday night, at the Albert Hall, an immense audience confirmed the verdict of Birmingham by voting Gounod's Mors et Vita, on the whole, a bore. No cultivated musician will endorse this opinion without considerable qualification; but it may be doubted whether there exist half a dozen enthusiasts who are in a hurry to devote three hours more to another hearing of the work. For it lasts three full hours, without allowing for an interval between the first and second parts. A performance that begins at half-past seven and is not over until twenty minutes to eleven would make most audiences restive, even if the composer were at liberty to range from grave to gay, from lively to severe, as at the opera. In an oratorio this is of course out of the question; and in Mors et Vita there are hardly any of those exciting mundane incidents which help the British public through the popular works of Handel and Mendelssohn. Mors et Vita will be described by many honest Philistines as being as long as an oratorio and as dull as a Mass. It is, in fact, a Requiem Mass with a Paradiso appended to the Inferno. The ideas dealt with are nearly all subjective: there is no stoning of saints, leaping upon altars, fiery chariots, or suggested spectacular melodrama of any sort; nor is there anything parallel to the raging mob in the St Matthew Passion, or the chorus of scoffers in the Messiah.

Yet there is a great deal of what is called program music. At the beginning of the second part there is an orchestral "sleep of the dead," which is a little more impressive, and also a little duller, than the exquisite Sommeil de Juliette, from the composer's Roméo. The sleep is interrupted by trumpets calling the dead to judgment. Imagine half a dozen cornets playing the augmented triad in chords and fanfares; and connect that with your ideas of the last trumpet if you can. We are apt to pity the ignorant Asiatic who is overborne by the awful majesty of the hundred-armed idol in his temple; but the people who listen reverently to half a dozen cornets in the Albert Hall, and feel their conception of the apocalyptic vision realized by it, must surely be hardly in a position to give away much brainweight to the simple Oriental. After this there is a rustle, a murmur, a confused treading of countless feet, a multitudinous tramping, a hurried march, more augmented triad from the brass, and a vocal announcement of the order of procedure from Mr Santley. All this is as naïvely inadequate to the subject as a medieval miracle play or mystery.

In fact, much of Mors et Vita may be described as a mystery with modern ballet music. Audiences are growing accustomed to this. Since the Almighty was brought upon the stage in Boïto's Mefistofele, speaking, or rather singing, through the mouths of the chorus, we seem to have become hardened to incongruity and indifferent to piously-intended blasphemy. The Supreme Judge has a good deal to say in the third part of Mors et Vita, and he says it with dignity and refinement, quite *en grand seigneur*, being apparently conceived by M. Gounod on the lines of that noble gentleman, Athos, in Les Trois Mousquetaires. Here, again, M. Gounod is undoubtedly innocent of any intentional irreverence; and the grace of his enchanting music, by making us forget its subject matter, banishes our sense of its absurdity. But he has treated the Christian religion with the same utter frivolity as he formerly treated Goethe's Faust; and criticism must now allow itself to be bribed to ignore that fact by the sensuous beauty of his music.

Admitting, then, that M. Gounod's deficiency in insight and range of thought renders it impossible to apply a Bach or Mozart standard in estimating him, what are the merits of his latest work? Well, nearly all his old merits. In variety and invention he has fallen off a little; but the loss is more than made good by his perfected mastery. The orchestration and the part-writing are impeccably beautiful from beginning to end. There is not one miscalculated effect; no thickness, roughness, or confusion; no clumsily placed chords, or forced or unvocal progressions; all is clear, smooth, articulate, harmonious, and in exquisite taste. Many of the strains are quite angelic. St John's vision of the heavenly Jerusalem is a trance in melody; and the orchestral epilogue to the requiem is magnificent, the effect of its strange cadence, aided by the consummately skilful disposition of the brass instruments, being extraordinary. The instrumentation never lacks the intensely poetic character to which so much of the charm of the composer's Faust is due.

On the other hand, the sequences and repetitions are almost beyond all patience. Mr Compton Reade complains of Handel on this score; but the mind recoils from the contemplation of Mr Reade's probable condition

[393]

when he hears Mors et Vita. Handel is a mine of invention in comparison to Gounod (or indeed to most modern composers) in the matter of repetition. Long as the work is, there are only four leading motives in it: and of these the third, expressing the happiness of the blessed, is reiterated *ad nauseam*, its very sweetness eventually being a disadvantage to it. The second, with its alternate major and minor forms, is the happiest. The choruses consist in too great part of some phrase repeated over and over on different degrees of the scale, or in different keys. But a double chorus in the true old vocal counterpoint, without accompaniment, is one of the gems of the work. It is a setting of the words "*A custodia matutina usque ad noctem.*"

The performance was, on the whole, an admirable one. Madame Albani's clear upper register was an unfailing source of pleasure in the suave, singable strains of which Gounod knows the secret. Miss Hilda Wilson and Messrs Lloyd and Santley did their duty as it should be done. The orchestra played as though Herr Richter had been still there to conduct them; and Mr Barnby marshalled them as expressly as usual. The choir quite surpassed themselves in their speciality of producing less tone in proportion to their numbers than any other known body of vocalists. In the third part of the trilogy there is a beautiful chorus *Ecce tabernaculum* to be sung *piano* in unison. It is so written that the middle and lower registers of the voice, where screaming and bawling are impossible, alone come into use. On Wednesday night the effort to sing *piano* extinguished the little tone that each singer had to spare, and a more diverting spectacle than this huge army of choristers making a feeble buzzing which the four skilled singers on the platform could have drowned without an effort, need not have been desired by the most heavily bored spectator. The orchestra cut through it trenchantly, though they, too, were playing as quietly as possible. Except in this respect, however, the chorus were thoroughly up to their work. The traces of Mr Barnby's diligence were almost too obvious. His care to prevent them from prolonging the final quaver of a phrase, repeatedly led to its curtailment to a demi-semiquaver, the effect being suggestive of what is called "saying Bo! to a goose." As the performance is to be repeated this afternoon, Mr Barnby might with advantage urge them not to be zealous overmuch, and, above all, to work their vocal apparatus with less noisy friction and more vocal tone.

The second Richter concert, originally announced for Wednesday, was shifted to Tuesday so as not to clash with Mors et Vita at the Albert Hall. The evening was wet, and the concert room was not quite so full, nor the band quite so fine (though both very nearly) as at the first concert. The No. 2 Leonore overture excited, as usual, a desire to hear the *coda*, at least, of the No. 3. The fine tone and delicate execution from the violoncellos was remarkably brought out by Beethoven's score. Mozart's *andante*, with variations in D minor for strings and two horns, shewed, by contrast, how heavily the great composer's strength is usually discounted by the gingerly way in which conductors commonly handle his work. They seem either to be afraid of his music or to have but little faith as to there being anything in it. Richter grapples with it like a man, and the result amply justifies him. The symphony was Brahms, in D minor: an elaborate work, with every bar as good as the composer could make it. Such thorough and skilful workmanship goes far, and the romantic melodies and charming devices with which the symphony abounds go further; but its beauties are kaleidoscopic: there is no real coherence in it; and the middle sections of the movements, especially the first, are tedious and barren.

[395]

Madame Valleria and Mr Edward Lloyd sang the great love duet from the first act of Die Walküre. They sang it in English, but it might as well have been sung in the original for anything the audience could distinguish. The episode of the sword, the opening of the door revealing the moonlit night in spring, and the reminiscences of Odin, accompanied by the haunting Walhall motive (which now seldom fails to send a perceptible thrill through the audience) reconciled Mrs Grundy to the extreme indecorum of Sieglinde's behavior, and to the disagreeable violence of her passion. The share of the orchestra was a trifle less successful than usual, owing to the brass being a little rough and out of sorts—probably an effect of the unpleasant weather.[U]

THE BRINSMEAD *VERSUS* RICHTER

Unsigned notes in The Dramatic Review,
14 November 1885

[U] The first of the Brinsmead Symphony Concerts took place last Saturday at St James's Hall. Messrs Brinsmead have behaved handsomely in their undertaking. They have fixed the price of admission to the cheapest seats at a shilling; and they supply programs free of charge. The orchestra, consisting of seventy of the Philharmonic band, is potentially, if not actually, first-rate. The string quartet numbers fortyeight players: twelve first violins, twelve seconds, eight tenors, eight cellos, and eight double basses. The appointment of Mr George Mount as conductor, if not an absolutely luxurious arrangement, is one of which there is no reason to complain. The performers emerge from a grove of exotics into public view. And some structural alterations have been effected in St James's Hall by which the audience in the concert room can enjoy occasional snatches from the program of the Christy Minstrels on the lower floor.

The gratuitously distributed programs, be it understood, are no mere lists of the pieces to be performed. They are analytic pamphlets such as are unblushingly sold for a shilling at the Richter concerts. The persuasive pen of Mr Joseph Bennett, sceptical Bayreuth pilgrim and copious critic of the Daily Telegraph, has been enlisted by Messrs Brinsmead to give literary value to their gift; and he in turn has gracefully found a place in the first program for an analysis of Mr Ebenezer Prout's symphony in F, by Mr W. A. Barrett, who points out, with the artless eloquence of a born programmic rhapsode, that Mr Prout's scoring, "though presenting nothing strained in its design, is nevertheless of a nature calculated to be effective." It will be seen that the programs, albeit free, shew no falling off from the remarkable literary standard attained by their sixpenny and shilling exemplars.

In comparing the Brinsmead orchestra with the Richter orchestra one is struck at once with the majority of English players in the one and of German in the other. The consequence, according to our favorite national boast, ought to be a considerable superiority in the effect of the strings from the English orchestra. The actual result is just the reverse. The English inferiority in power is of course accounted for by the inferiority in numbers, the Richter quartet being eighteen stronger than the Brinsmead; but there is a still greater inferiority in quality of tone, delicacy of execution, and, above all, of discipline. On Saturday night, our "best body of strings in Europe" began by rattling through Mendelssohn's Melusine overture off hand, with a disagreeable air of depending on their reputation and caring little about either the conductor or the audience. The playing

[397]

from the wind and drums, on the other hand, was refined and conscientious, and fairly substantiated the boast of English excellence. It should be added that Mr Mount did not give his band a fair chance. He hurried along as if preoccupied with the novelty of the occasion and the burden of his duties. Of those variously significant pauses which constitute the better half of the art of the conductor as well as the orator, there were none. No one doubts Mr Mount's ability to read music and to beat time; but his higher qualifications were brought in question rather than proved by his opportunity on Saturday. Happily that opportunity is not exhausted, and Mr Mount, when he grows accustomed to his new band, has yet time to achieve a distinguished success even in competition with Herr Richter.*

Mr Prout, who conducted his own symphony, gained the chief success of the evening. The orchestra smartened up considerably to do him honor; and the result was a capital performance of his skilful and enjoyable work. Mr Prout, as the author of a treatise on instrumentation, is supposed to be an English Berlioz or Gevaert. His effects certainly never miss fire, nor does he ever ridiculously overset the balance of tone between the various bands in the orchestra, as many symphonic poets do. Mr Prout refuses to write symphonic poems—perhaps because he is too cheerful; perhaps because he knows how to write a symphony. Whenever the distinction involves a real difference, it is generally for the worse on the part of the symphonic poet, who ought to know better than to make it. All symphonies are poems, or ought to be.

The procession music from Moritz Moszkowski's

* Shaw's brief, duplicative note in the "Art Corner," Our Corner, December 1885, concluded: "Herr Richter's conducting is still to that of his competitors as the declamation of a first-rate actor is to the lesson reading of an average curate."

symphonic poem, Joan of Arc, was commented on in these columns last spring, when the composer conducted the entire work at a Philharmonic concert. It does not seem to have grown since then.

The Chevalier Emil Bach's performance of Beethoven's pianoforte concerto in E flat would have been quite satisfactory but for a slight deficiency in power, perhaps due to intentional moderation, always a rare quality, and one of which it is dangerous to complain, lest the immoderate legion be unduly encouraged. The pianoforte used, though its tone, which was remarkably even throughout its compass, told well throughout the hall, and its touch seemed swift and clear, was yet a shade too bricky (the term is meant to convey the character of sound produced by the stroke of a trowel on a brick) to be quite grateful to the ear. Messrs Brinsmead would do well to replace it at the next concert with an instrument of richer tone.

If the above suggestion be taken in good part, perhaps another would not be repudiated. It is, that the printer of the program should not persist in describing the *timpani* as *tympani*. Indeed, whilst we are in England, may we not as well put a bold face on it and call them drums, without further ado?

Admission at a shilling is supposed to involve the presence of a certain proportion of mob which must be diverted to intervals with a song. Messrs Brinsmead accordingly engaged Mr Maas, who sang Adoniram's fine invocation from the first of Gounod's Reine de Saba with great effect. He also attempted *Dalla sua pace*, from Don Giovanni; but here our popular tenor was floored, not so much by Mozart as by Mr Mount, who could make nothing of this exquisite song. Mr Mount's failing is undue haste. The effect on the perfect calm of *Dalla sua pace* can be imagined by those who know the work.

On the whole, Messrs Brinsmead have treated the

[399]

public much better than most concert givers do. None of the few shortcomings alluded to above were in any way their fault. Yet one result of their enterprise has been to demonstrate that the day for "orchestras of seventy performers" in St James's Hall is gone by. There should be, at least, sixty string players, and there had better be sixtysix. If anyone still imagines that the difference can be compensated by the substitution of English for German players, he has but to go to a Brinsmead concert and then to a Richter, and he will be cured of his delusion.

An opportunity for making the comparison suggested above occurred this week. The first Brinsmead concert was on last Saturday; the last Richter on Wednesday. At the latter was performed Weber's Euryanthe overture; Sachs's monologue from Die Meistersinger; the rainbow scene from the Das Rheingold; and the ninth symphony. In the Wagner extracts the vocal parts were not all that they might have been. One of the Rhine daughters sang out of tune; and Loge accentuated the eccentricity of his music perilously. But the great effect of Donner's voice echoing from the clouds was achieved to perfection by the orchestra. In spite of the apparent complication caused by the great number of parts written for the violins—all of which, however, are playing different figurations of the same chord—this scene is one of the simplest as well as the most effective ever written for the orchestra. Its execution on Wednesday was very successful, the only faults being the vocal shortcomings, and the overpowering of the rainbow theme in the last few bars by the wind instruments, the repeated chords from which must have seemed quite unreasonable to hearers whose memory did not supply the hidden thread of melody on which they were strung.

The performance of the ninth symphony was a very fine one. Even into the chorus Herr Richter has knocked some intelligence and some sort of feeling for the quality of the scrap of tone they produce. His management of the first movement could hardly have been surpassed, and shewed how much vigor is usually sacrificed by the excessive speed and clockwork monotony of the ordinary English treatment of the work. He started at Beethoven's marked time of 88 crotchets per minute, but reduced the speed for the second subject to 70, working thence up to the 88 again, and again slackening to 78. The *scherzo*, marked 116 bars a minute, he took at 113 bars, which was remarkably accurate, but which again illustrated his care to sacrifice nothing to mere speed. It is to be hoped that his example may eventually discredit the railway system which has hitherto too much prevailed in our concert rooms.[U]

THEATRE ORCHESTRAS

Unsigned notes in The Dramatic Review,
21 November 1885

[U] The now celebrated Heckmann quartet gave their first concert of the season at Prince's Hall this day week (last Saturday). Chamber music in west London has hitherto been left mainly to Messrs Chappell and their Monday Popular Concerts. It has been left in very good hands; but there is hardly any mortal enterprise, and certainly no musical one, that will not get rusty as the years pass, unless it be kept up to the mark by emulation. The St James's Hall players have been allowed to fix their own standard of excellence for a long time past; and they have certainly not abused their monopoly: their standard is fairly high. But considering their position in London, London's position in England, and England's position in Europe, a fairly high standard is not high enough. The best string quartet in London ought to be one of the wonders of the world. The Monday Popular quartet is not quite that yet. Its average tone is too thin and its average style too tame. It may be said that chamber music must necessarily sound so in a large concert room; but those who believe this do not know the capacity of the violin in the hands of a great player. Madame Norman-Neruda, in her happier moments, can make her instrument peal grandly throughout St James's Hall; and if we could find four players whose average would be as good as Madame Neruda's best, we should have a string quartet worth boasting of. We shall probably get it as soon as we are worthy of it; which seems a little way off as yet. Meanwhile, the Heckmann quartet is doing useful work in putting the older establishment on its metal.

Foremost among the musicians who never seem to have profited by the technical lessons which chamber music teaches, are the composers of our comic operas. The consistency with which these talented gentlemen compel managers to dispose to the worst possible advantage of the money set aside for paying the orchestra, proves that they care but little for the economics of orchestration. They apparently start with the conviction that a grand orchestra is absolutely necessary, no matter how small the theatre may be. This necessitates a large number of players; and as the amount which the management can afford to spend on the orchestra depends on the size of the theatre, the larger the band the less its individual members receive. When, in consequence of this, the salaries are third-rate, third-rate players have to be engaged; and the string quartet is impoverished to make room for trombones, a big drum and cymbals, and a harp. The resultant orchestra is so bad that any section of it left to play by itself for a moment becomes ridiculous: there is nothing for it but to keep them all working away constantly, making as much noise as possible to cover up deficiencies. Experienced leaders of bad theatre bands therefore ridicule all attempts at artistic scoring and rearrange in their own dreadful fashion all the music their Falstaff's armies have to execute. So that the very effects for which the quality of the orchestra is sacrificed become impossible in consequence of that sacrifice.

The remedy is a simple one. Any manager can convince himself by sitting out a few concerts of good chamber music that four or five stringed instruments, in capable hands and skilfully written for, can produce a greater variety of effects and a greater volume of tone than the two dozen or thirty miscreants (Pickwickianly speaking) who make a hole in his treasury every week for keeping all people with sensitive ears away from his theatre. Let him then resolve to devote the money he is squandering on twentyfour bad players to the remuneration of twelve good ones, or of fifteen bad players to four good ones. Mr Armbruster did something of this sort at the Court Theatre; and the step was generally recognized as being in the right direction.

Let us suppose that a manager wishes to commission a new comic opera, and that he cannot afford to pay more than about a dozen really good players. His best plan would be to engage three first violins, three seconds, two violas, three violoncellos, and two double basses. He should then warn the composer to do the best he could with that force; and if the composer knew his business, he could do very well indeed with it. It is true that if a manager cannot afford a wind band, he has no business to produce operas at all; but he should always insist on a good string quartet as the nucleus of his orchestra, and add wind instruments to the extent of his resources. A glance at the scores of such masterpieces of instrumental accompaniment as Mozart's operas, and even of portions of Wagner's Meistersinger, will shew how much can be done without using more than three pairs of wind instruments in addition to the strings.

These remarks have some bearing on the exploit of Mr Edward Jones at the Opera Comique, where Miss Consuelo and Mr Harris are maintaining an orchestra which is only an unappreciated extravagance.* Mr Jones apparently believes that every different effect requires a different instrument. He therefore aims, for the sake of the utmost variety of effect, at the utmost variety of instruments. Hence, cymbals, triangle, big drum, side drum, glockenspiel, two trombones and cornets, in addition to the reasonable horns, bassoons, clarinets, oboes, and flutes. Perhaps the score contains parts for a third trombone, a second pair of horns, an English horn, a bass clarinet, a double bassoon, a pair of harps and a third drum, all suppressed by the niggardliness of the management. However that may be, Mr Jones may be reconciled to the necessity of cutting his coat according to his cloth by the assurance that all the desirable effects which he has distributed among so many instruments might be produced by a modest orchestra of strings, two horns, two bassoons, two clarinets (or oboes, or flutes; but not all three) and the drums. Twenty good men and true could thus get him a reputation as a workmanlike composer, wheras his inordinate forces at the Opera Comique have, so far, only gained him certain friendly but very disagreeable recommendations to have his score touched up by a skilled hand. He would discover, too, that each instrument can speak several languages instead of one. The score of Berlioz's Faust must be after Mr Jones's own heart; but nothing in it is more remarkable

* Agnes Consuelo and F. J. Harris were presenting a comic opera, The Fay o' Fire, with a libretto by Henry Herman and music by Edward Jones.

than the amazing variety of effects produced by the same instruments and by the same combinations of instruments. It is time enough to insist upon a grand orchestra when you have exhausted the resources of a small one.

All this applies to the orchestras at the theatres where music is only a pastime between the acts as well as to the comic opera houses. But where the band is only employed to clear the theatre at the end of the performance, the worse the music is, the better for its purpose. At the Criterion Theatre, for example, Mr Wyndham, when the curtain falls, immediately un-chains a fiddle, a cornet, and a piano. It would be more humane to turn on a hose, and more polite to adopt Artemus Ward's plan of a printed notice that "Persons who do not leave the hall when the performance is over will be removed by the police."* Perhaps Mr Wyndham has no ear for music.

Musicians who find themselves next Monday in the neighborhood of St Alfege's Church, Greenwich, might do worse than enter and help to celebrate the three hundredth anniversary of the death of Thomas Tallis, the reputed father of English cathedral music. A selection from his works will be sung.[U]

---

* The passage in Artemus Ward Among the Mormons (Charles Farrar Browne, Complete Works, 1871) that Shaw had in mind reads: "Ladies and gentlemen, my lecture is done—if you refuse to leave the hall, you'll be forcibly ejected."

THE NEED FOR A NEW CONCERT ROOM

Unsigned notes in The Dramatic Review,
28 November 1885

[U] A notable feature of the present season is the quantity of musical entertainment that is to be had under cost price. Messrs Novello's oratorio concerts, it is understood, cannot possibly pay: St James's Hall is not large enough to hold the multitude whose money would be required to cover the expenses. Messrs Brinsmead repudiate profit from their orchestral concerts. They give many programs, and announce that if, in spite of their liberality, their enterprise leaves a balance in hand, it will be handed over to charitable institutions. A suggestion has already been implied in these columns that twenty more string players are urgently needed in the Brinsmead orchestra. If there is any reason to expect a balance in hand, here is a means—charitable to the public—of anticipating it.

As to Messrs Novello's difficulty, it has been evident for a long time past that London is waiting for a concert room larger than St James's and smaller than the Albert Hall. St James's Hall is now old enough to be in high favor with Conservatives. We have become used to its inconveniences, and many musical associations have, in a measure, endeared it to us. The system of admitting the public to the orchestra, when its hemicyclical knifeboards are not occupied by a choir, is a boon to amateurs who love to get inside the orchestra, as it were. The exceptional height of the platform, though it might tax the nerves of singers unaccustomed to perform on the edge of a sheer precipice, and though

[406]

it certainly strains the cervical vertebræ of the occupants of the front stalls, is highly acceptable to the people in the balcony and to the gods in the loft at the back of the room, just under the roof. The hall has been successfully used for grotesquely different purposes. Madame Schumann has played there many times to those who are fortunate enough to delight in her poetic and refined execution. Mr Bradlaugh sometimes thunders from the platform against his enemies, whilst hundreds of volunteers from the Radical clubs keep order by methods not akin to the spell of Madame Schumann's art. In the budding spring the ropes and stakes arise in the place of Richter's desk; and the amateur pugilist, gory but game, pounds his panting antagonist in the final bout for the championship of the year. On these occasions, also, the admirers of Madame Schumann are few and far between, and the bowl flows more copiously at the adjacent places of refreshment than it does on concert nights. Next evening, perhaps, the hall will echo to the strains of divine service. On the whole, the permanent attendants enjoy a varied education. But at music, oratory, pugilism, and prayer alike, the spectator finds one end of his spine tired by the height of the platform, the other end incommoded by the lowness of the seats, and the pervading smell of dinner which nauseates him in his moments of repletion, and tantalizes him in the pangs of hunger. Taking one consideration with another, there is certainly room for a new hall, which may deviate extensively from the old model without risk of an explosion of popular indignation.

Here another suggestion may be hazarded. At an orchestral concert there is no reason for placing the band at the end of the room. At a Richter concert, if the orchestra were leveled and made circular, at least four halls, each as large as the St James's auditorium, might radiate from the musical centre without any of the persons therein losing a note of the music. Now, Millbank prison, a panopticon building of this sort, designed by Bentham, is condemned, and is practically in the market. Let Mr Hermann Franke form a company to purchase the building; furnish the cells luxuriously as private boxes; and let them out by the season for a series of first-rate orchestral concerts. The band would, of course, be stationed in the centre, from which the long avenues of cells radiate. The pris—the subscribers, that is—could entertain their friends as if in their own drawing rooms, whilst enjoying the music echoing down the corridors that now resound only to the challenge of the warder. Upon the abolition of the present compulsory character of the attendance, the present difficulty of egress would be replaced by a pleasanter competition for ingress. No time must be lost if this unique chance is to be secured. Already the speculative builder, in quest of town lots, has his eye on Millbank, and it will soon be too late to consecrate this monument of our civilization to the service of music.

But to return from Millbank to the gratuitous concerts of Messrs Brinsmead and Novello. Are these gentlemen actuated by purely artistic or philanthropic motives? Probably not. Every advance in the popularity of oratorio in this country means an increase of business for Messrs Novello, who print and publish popular editions of all the oratorios. They print them very well indeed; and their editions are genuine editions, and not mere reprints with old typographic errors reproduced to prove that the distinguished musician, whose name is on the title page as editor, has not examined a single bar of the work. Consequently, though Messrs Novello have an axe to grind at their concerts, it is an axe which does public service. Messrs Brinsmead have their pianofortes to advertize. They are eclectic makers, not famous as inventors, but wide-awake producers of instruments embodying all the successful improvements of every inventor from Hawkins to Chickering and Steinway. Now, up to very recent times, all pianofortes, except those of one or two English makers, have been practically boycotted at London concerts. The extreme friendliness of the mammon of unrighteousness laid pianists under irresistible obligations; and they often would not touch in London one of the various instruments which, on the other side of the water, they had declared to be the very best pianofortes in the world. Consequently, manufacturers who could afford it found it expedient not only to make pianofortes, but to give concerts at which they could secure a hearing for them. Hence, probably, the Brinsmead concerts. But one cannot help surmising that the exigencies of competitive advertisement may yet compel the traders in music and instruments to provide not only the performances but the audiences. Then tickets will be given away in the streets by sandwich men; and rival touts will struggle in Piccadilly to decide whether the possibly unmusical wayfarer shall be dragged into St James's Hall to hear Smith and Co.'s concert, conducted by Richter, or into Prince's Hall, to hear Brown Brothers' piano played by Rubinstein.

Another variety of axe-grinding, and yet popular and useful, concert is the ballad concert, now in full swing at St James's Hall, under the auspices of Messrs Boosey. The ballad concert is the hothouse of the royalty song, and there is nothing in all art so conducive to the conclusion that England is an asylum for idiots as the average royalty song. But the public is so far of that opinion that the programs at the ballad concerts are well stiffened with songs of admitted merit and established popularity. M. Pachmann and Madame Norman-Neruda play there too. This is an advance on the bygone, but not very remote period, when the instrumental music consisted of a schoolgirl's pianoforte piece, contemptuously dashed off against time by Madame Arabella Goddard.[U]

PROGRAMS
The Magazine of Music, December 1885

When the unsophisticated visitor from the country to the metropolis goes to a Richter concert, not because he knows or cares enough about music to make the faintest class distinction between the overture to La Gazza Ladra and the prelude to Tristan und Isolde, but because a Richter concert is one of the sounds of London, and therefore not to be missed by the complete tourist, his first experience is the payment of half-a-crown for admission. (Here let millionaire readers, who habitually pay half-guineas for stalls, forbear and read no more. The economic considerations which dictate this article have no weight with such.) His next is an encounter with a gentleman who carries a bundle of white pamphlets, and cries incessantly "Book of the words! Program! Book of the words!" A book will evidently not only be a guide through the unknown ways of a Richter concert, as to the nature of which the tourist's notions are of the vaguest, but will serve as a memento of the occasion in after years in the quiet country home. "One shilling, please" says the vendor. That is forty per cent. on the price already paid for admission. The visitor is staggered; but he is too much of a sportsman to grudge a shilling during a holiday trip, and he pays with assumed cheerfulness, privately adding the incident to his stock of instances of London roguery. Whilst waiting for the concert to begin, he opens his purchase and reads. It contains some historical information which is not of the slightest interest to him, and much technical detail which he does not understand. He can just gather that it becomes him to prepare with awe for the treat in store for him. Having always believed that the musicians in a band played by ear the tune agreed upon, whilst the basses improvized the harmony as they went along, he can make nothing of the references to the score. Vague notions of plan, pre-arrangement, and rehearsal oppress him with a sense of his own ignorance. He looks furtively at his neighbors; but they do not seem puzzled. They may, it is true, be only pretending to understand their "book of the words"; but no sign of imposture is perceptible. What can he do but imitate their serenity as best he can? When the band begins at last, he cannot make head or tail of the noise they are making. Occasionally they break into something like a tune, and then he smiles and beats time with his foot; but his neighbors frown and "shsh" angrily at him, and the tune is presently "developed" as the book calls it; that is, it becomes no tune at all. At the end of the concert he plucks up a little, and goes off to supper, after which he feels that now that it is all over he is glad he went. If asked subsequently whether he liked it, he will not reply directly, but will observe seriously that it was very fine—very fine indeed. But he has one solid grievance, if he chooses to ventilate it. He has been compelled to pay a shilling for a book of which only one page—the bare list of pieces, worth some fraction of a farthing—was of any use to him.

Take another case at the opposite extreme of musical culture. An experienced concert-goer and accomplished musician goes also to the Richter concert. He also requires only a list of the compositions to be performed. He has read over and over again, at the Crystal Palace and elsewhere, what Sir George Grove and Mr C. A. Barry have to say about the No. 3 Leonore overture.

When "the movement comes to an impressive close on the tonic of the original key," he knows it without referring to a printed statement. He has read what Schumann said about Brahms and about everybody else, and he does not believe the little anecdotes as to what Beethoven said of "the young Franz Schubert." He objects to have his attention called to "remarkable modulations" that are only remarkable on paper. The old works he knows; and he would fain follow the new ones without being pestered and prejudiced at every step by somebody else's opinion, particularly when that opinion is only a forced remark made because the writer, being paid to say something, did not consider it honest to be silent even when he had nothing to say. Yet all this can the amateur not avoid unless, as many prudent matrons do, he cuts the advertisement from the newspaper and keeps it in his pocket for reference. Even then there may not be light enough to read small print by in a half-crown seat beneath the gallery. The chances are that he has to succumb to "One shilling, please," and to swallow the impertinences of the analyst with as few wry faces as possible. Occasionally, when the work is quite new, he derives an ill-natured satisfaction from the false estimates into which the analyst has been led by the necessity of judging the score by eye instead of by ear. For, though it is by no means safe to infer the intention of the composer from the achievement of any particular orchestra, still rasher is it to infer his achievement from his intention as expressed on paper. This, however, is neither here nor there; for the pleasure of finding out that an analyst is fallible is decidedly not worth a shilling. And when the work analyzed is a familiar one, as nine-tenths of the works performed at classical concerts are, not only is this gloomy triumph denied to the musician, but the analysis, instead of being a brand new essay on the work, is a stereotyped reprint that has done duty many times before, and will as many times again. It is quite maddening to calculate how this reduces the cost to the concert giver, whilst the concert-goer cannot escape "One shilling, please."

And here we come to the interests of the general musical public, who approve of analytic programs as on the whole helpful and interesting. Professional concert-goers may both find and make useful memoranda in them, and they are particularly convenient when the critic goes to sleep during the performance of a new work, as, when the next thunderclap from the drum wakes him, he can, by referring to the analysis, guess how much he has lost during slumber. But were programs fifty times as convenient, a shilling is a shilling, and in this instance a shilling is too much. It is a monopoly price, and represents, not the cost of production of the book, but the utmost sum that a sufficient number of persons will reluctantly yield sooner than go without. Now this most pestilential principle assures the least happiness of the smallest number. Suppose the audience to consist of a thousand persons. Suppose that each of them will pay sixpence for a program, but that only five hundred will pay a shilling. A thousand programs will be printed in any case, the first time the experiment is tried. A return of £25 will, let us further suppose, satisfy the greed of the management. ("Greed" may not be polite, but, as has been already said, a shilling is a shilling.)

Now, in the interest of the greatest number, this return should be secured by the sale of the thousand programs at sixpence. But in the interest of the concert giver, five hundred will be sold at a shilling, and only five hundred provided at the next concert. Five hundred of the audience will thus go programless, and the rest will suffer the exasperation of having had to submit to double extortion. And in the future the price will go up and the supply diminish, until a point is reached at which the profits decline instead of increase. For instance, it would not pay to raise the price to ten shillings, as nobody would buy at that price, and the expenditure for printing programs, which are valueless except as waste paper after a concert, would be a dead loss. The public, in short, will be "exploited" until it strikes. At present the demand for a shilling causes a partial strike; but there are sufficient "knobsticks"—*i.e.* compliers with the demand—to cover the loss occasioned by the strikers.

But a strike of purchasers on a rising market is foredoomed to failure. The only remedy lies in competition. Inside the concert room there can be no competition: the concert givers have a monopoly there. But the monopoly ceases at the street door. If any private speculator, upon ascertaining the program of a concert from the advertisement in the daily papers, chooses to compile an analytic program, print it, sell it at the doors for ninepence, and gain for it a reputation for trustworthiness, the public will buy outside at ninepence instead of inside at a shilling. The concert giver, after a few vain placards to the effect that authorized programs are to be had within only, will have to reduce his price to sixpence, only to be again underbid by the man outside. If the latter have the requisite qualities and capital, he will finally compel all concert givers to contract with him for the supply of analytic programs, and he will conduct that branch of music publishing as a separate industry. The fear of competition from rival speculators would thenceforth prevent him from taking advantage of the transferred monopoly to re-establish the old extortionate prices. Nay, it is quite possible that by developing the practice of inserting advertisements in the programs, he might eventually find it to his interest to give them away gratuitously, embellished with handsome portraits of celebrated singers who have been soaped, or ammoniaphoned, or miraculously cured of a cough.

If no speculator is hardy enough to adopt this suggestion, the abuse will continue, and be aggravated as time goes on. One-and-sixpenny programs will soon appear, and we may yet pay half-a-crown for a pamphlet of stereotyped matter costing less than a penny to produce. Let the reader who has just paid a shilling for his program at one of the three recent Richter concerts take that expensive volume and compare it with this Magazine (the circulation of which, by the bye, is not compulsory, as that of a concert program practically is), and consider whether something cheaper ought not to be forthcoming in this age of competitive license. Tenderhearted people who very properly mistrust modern cheapness, may note that a reduction in the price of programs would trench on profits and not on wages. Even profits would probably be increased in the long run by a concession to the impecuniosity of the art-loving middle classes; but it would be a waste of time to work this probability out in the hope of influencing such very bird-in-the-hand politicians as the monopolists who charge a shilling for an analytic program.

BERLIOZ'S EPISODE

Unsigned notes in The Dramatic Review, 5 December 1885

[U] Handel's concerto in B flat, for harp with orchestra of strings and two flutes, appeared fresher and more novel at the Crystal Palace last Saturday than it is likely to have done a century and a half ago, before its style had gone out of fashion. As compared to the great

[415]

achievements of Handel, it is a trifle; but as we in the XIX century are unable, from one cause or another, to trifle so masterfully, Mr Manns was right in supposing that the public would be willing to devote a few minutes of its Saturday half-holiday to sampling the small beer of the illustrious Saxon. The public, indeed, was graciously pleased to evince unmistakable symptoms of gratification; and Mr Lockwood, who played the solo part with perfect precision, was warmly applauded. Mr Manns interpreted the direction *andante allegro* in the first movement as equivalent to the modern *allegretto*, and the effect proved that he was exactly right in doing so. The elegiac sadness of the *larghetto*, with its grand cadence, is in Handel's most sensitive vein of melody, which still goes straight home in spite of lapse of time and change of taste.

After Handel came—Felicien David! Miss Amy Sherwin was ill-advised to bring his flimsy couplets into such damning contrast with Mendelssohn's Athalie overture and the Handel concerto. In vain did she endeavor to interest the audience in *le Mysoli* by assuring them that it was a *charmant oiseau*. In vain did Mr Alfred Wells tootle with his flute as skilfully as she warbled with her voice. David's graceful puerilities were hopelessly put out of countenance. An occasional fault in intonation suggested that Miss Sherwin felt that she was put at a disadvantage by her selection, and was ill at ease in consequence. However, she was reassured at the end of the song by a hearty recall.

Two overtures were played: that of Mendelssohn to his setting of Racine's Athalie, and Wagner's to Tannhäuser. It is significant that though Mendelssohn is England's musical idol, and Wagner still abhorred of many of her sons, yet the Tannhäuser overture is played at the Palace every year, wheras the Athalie overture had not been heard there for seven years before this day week. Yet it is one of the most striking of Mendelssohn's compositions for the orchestra. It is an unequal work, the beginning and end being greatly superior to the middle, the weakness of which, especially the fantasia on the chorale-like theme with which the brass and oboes and bassoons so augustly open the overture, is only redeemed by its unflagging fire. But in the concluding *maestoso* movement the march of the harmony is magnificent, and bolder than anything in the Tannhäuser overture. The effect of the culminating dissonance, in which for four bars the violins and woodwind instruments maintain a shake on C sharp against the tonic pedal D ground out by the basses, the drums, and the third trombone, with brilliant *arpeggios* from the strings and harp on the chord of the minor ninth, all pulsating faster and faster with repeated *sforzandos*, is most exciting and original.

The Tannhäuser overture is getting just a little hackneyed. It suffers from frequent repetition, inasmuch as the pilgrims' chant, which is all but worthy to be ranked with the great air in the same rhythm from Mozart's Die Zauberflöte (*Possenti Numi*), grows upon the hearer, wheras the Bacchanalian racket of the Venusberg gains nothing by reiteration except the proverbial offspring of familiarity. Stimulating as this delirious mænad music whirl is, it is apt to become stale; and those who delight in it soon require a stronger dram with a new flavor, and so turn to the newest musical illicit distiller, who is prepared to out-Herod Wagner.

The main feature of the concert, however, was Hector Berlioz's Episode in the Life of an Artist: a Fantastic Symphony in Five Parts. Berlioz wrote a program for this work, and requested that it should be distributed among the audience at each performance. Instead of doing this, the Crystal Palace managers reprint, "by kind permission," an analysis by Mr W. A. Barrett, who gives an account of his own, prefacing it with the remark "Here is the gist of the matter Berlioz would have his audience charge their minds with." The reader naturally infers that Berlioz gave a longwinded account of his own symphony, and that Mr Barrett has kindly condensed and improved it. Yet Berlioz is brief enough in all conscience. He says "A young musician of morbid sensibility and ardent imagination poisons himself with opium in a fit of despair caused by love. The dose, not sufficient to kill him, plunges him into a heavy sleep, accompanied by the strangest visions, during which his sentiments, his sensations, his reminiscences, are translated by his diseased brain into musical ideas and images. The woman he loves becomes for him a melody—a fixed idea—which returns upon him and sounds in his ears everywhere." This is a literal translation. Now hear Mr Barrett, and compare.

"The composer conceives the idea of realizing for a while a young musician, whose soul is consumed by that indefinite yearning, that soul sickness, which has been called the 'vague passion,' and which forms the subject of so much modern rhythm, miscalled poetry. For the first time he meets, unexpectedly, a woman who seems to realize all the perfection which he had longed for in his mind. Being a musician, it is natural almost that his ideal should become real only to his soul in the form of a phrase of melody, which appears in each movement. In this he supposes himself to be possessed of the power to trace the character of the loved one—timid, yet noble; passionate, yet sweetly tender."

If Berlioz were alive to read this, he would probably be passionate, but not sweetly tender, though he might be unable to refrain from a laugh at "vague passion" as a translation of his *"vagues de passion."* Mr Barrett postpones the opium trance, which is the key to the nightmarish character of the whole work, until he comes to the fourth part, the march to the scaffold, which he calls March to the Gallows, in spite of the tremendous crash with which the guillotine axe cuts short the *idée fixe* at the end of it. He touches off the character of the loved one on the authority of his own imagination, which is undeniably a fervid one, but which should be exercised on his own fantastic symphonies, and not on those of Berlioz. Even as a mere translator he is too expansive. He Englishes the fifteen words in which the composer describes the second part, into a paragraph containing sixtyfour. The feat deserves to be recorded at length. Here is Berlioz.

"*Il retrouve l'aimée dans un bal au milieu du tumulte d'une fête brillante.*"

Which, in the analytic hands of Mr Barrett, reappears thus: "Alone amid the giddy whirl of a festival, where all is centred that can charm the senses and delight the eye, the artist gazes on the fair and comely forms that float by in the whirling and exciting dance. But his fancies wander hither and thither, and the beloved one follows his every thought, and ripples and troubles the fountain of his moody dreamings." Bravo, Mr Barrett!

The performance of the symphony was only partially successful. Mr August Manns took the first movement too slowly. This may seem like dogmatizing on a matter of taste; but it is in fact a matter of authority—of the authority of Berlioz—who expressly states that the first *allegro* should be played at the rate of 132 minims per minute. The writer, feeling that the movement was missing fire, took out his watch and "clocked" Mr Manns as if he were competing in a Sheffield handicap. Mr Manns was beating only 112 minims—two thirds of the proper speed. The difference was too great: the music lost the character, *agitato e appassionato*, that Berlioz insisted on; and the *idée fixe* made its zigzag way leisurely through the web of sound instead of darting through it like a flash of lightning. The rest of the work was satisfactorily performed, though the almost morbid delicacy of execution and extreme contrasts of crash and whisper indicated in the score were set aside in some instances as impracticable or outrageous. It will always remain an open question whether the symphony is worth the time and trouble its performance costs. In actual life, young men under the influence of the emotions it represents are unmitigated nuisances to themselves and to their acquaintances; and the public is apt to be impatient of their "reveries and passions" even when they are translated into music. Still, there is an infernal fascination about Berlioz's work that never fails to impress imaginative hearers when the performers get adequate steam up. The sounds in the orchestra lose their technical character, and become cries, mutterings, footsteps, and plagues of darkness. It is by no means certain that the public understands the blasphemous mockery of the Dies Iræ hooted slowly by the bassoons and two ophicleides, derisively repeated twice as fast by the horns and trombones, and finished as a mad dance by the fiddles; but all can appreciate the strange effect of the strings struck with the wooden part of the bows, and the peals of thunder in the pastoral scene. Like certain superior kinds of stage thunder, these last are expensive, as they require the services of four drummers.

Mr Manns' disagreement with Berlioz in the first movement, and in that only, of the symphony, is made the more remarkable by his conscientiousness in other details. His concerts are superior to those even of Herr Richter in some respects. For example, in the overture to Athalie the trumpet parts were played on trumpets, and not on cornets, as they certainly would have been at St James's Hall, where Herr Richter tolerates these detestable orchestral impostures with apparent complacency. In the Tannhäuser overture, the long shake for the tambourine in the *diminuendo* which precedes the re-entry of the pilgrims' chorus, was not played as a roll on the big drum (an exceedingly effective way, nevertheless, of obtaining the result aimed at by Wagner). In every respect Mr Manns conducted, as he has always done, in the spirit of a genuine artist; and it is greatly to be regretted that his work has not been more accessible to the many Londoners for whom the Saturday concerts are too distant and too expensive to be frequently enjoyed.

On Tuesday last Gounod's Mors et Vita was performed at Messrs Novello's Oratorio Concert at St James's Hall, where the platform is unfortunately not large enough to accommodate the requisite orchestral and choral force. The choir acquitted itself well on the whole, though the tenors were weak. Mr Mackenzie conducted. The soloists were Mesdames Albani and Trebelli, Messrs Lloyd and Santley. Like all M. Gounod's works, Mors et Vita gains greatly by repetition.
[U]

SAINT-SAËNS AND RAFF

Unsigned notes in The Dramatic Review,
12 December 1885

[U] M. Camille Saint-Saëns has been playing at St James's Hall. It may seem superfluous to add that the instrument he played was the pianoforte; but the time has been in St James's Hall when M. Saint-Saëns has gone up to the neglected organ and played a Bach fugue; and it is to be hoped that he will do so again. Unfortunately, an organ solo generally gives an English audience an illusory sensation of being in church: a sensation which, strange to say, they do not seem to enjoy. On Saturday last, however, M. Saint-Saëns refrained from the organ, and played his C minor concerto, and a septuor for strings, pianoforte, and trumpet—a very effective combination.

The septuor is something to receive thankfully, if it were only for the pat on the back which it gives to the trumpet player. In the days of Bach and Handel, the trumpeter was an important man, and Mozart found him rather apt to give himself airs. Nowadays he has so little love for his instrument, and so little artistic feeling for his parts, that he invariably substitutes the cornet, which is easier to play, though much more difficult to listen to. When used cautiously for *cantabile* themes of a sentimental character, it is not absolutely objection-able; but it imparts an atrocious vulgarity to trumpet music. It has been denounced in these pages before, and will be again, as something may be done to extirpate a flagrant nuisance by complaining of it with sufficient persistence.

The symphony at the Brinsmead concert, which was conducted by M. Ganz, was Raff's in E major, called Lenore. Lenore, the heroine of Bürger's ballad, was so disappointed when the troops returned from the war without her lover, that she flew in the face of Providence, and used language that went beyond the licence even of a broken heart. That night she heard a tap at the door, ran down and found her Wilhelm there in his war panoply, with his horse. He will not come in; he will not take anything, she cannot guess why, because she does not see the little fountain of blood that spurts from a hole in his left breast, as portrayed in Retsch's outlines. Insisting on an immediate elopement, he places her behind him on the horse, whose hoofs rattle on the bridge as they dash off on a demoniac ride back to the cemetery, in which poor Wilhelm is now permanently established. It is a most awful business, and Lenore dies of it, but she is forgiven her sin at last.

Nothing suits your modern orchestral composer so well as the weird—the diabolical—the infernal. It is very exciting, very easy, and justifies any extravagance. The best part of Raff's symphony is, however, the natural part. The supernatural ride is far inferior to that in Berlioz's Damnation of Faust. The first movement, which depicts the happiness of Lenore and Wilhelm before he goes to the war, is bright, impetuous, and carried along with breadth and freedom. The slow movement consists of several pretty, though vulgar melodies, and contains some harmonic beauties of an audaciously Raffish description. The third movement is the long march past of the returning troops, interrupted for a few moments by the agitation of the stricken Lenore, but presently resumed and continued in its unvarying tramping rhythm until it dies away in the distance. The last movement is the phantom ride. It is poor and second-hand, and contains a passage which was composed by Wagner for The Flying Dutchman, just as the second subject of the first movement was composed by Auber for The Crown Diamonds. Raff's compositions are extraordinarily numerous, and in some points extraordinarily ingenious; but he seems to have used the first ideas that came to him, without any scruple as to their quality. Sometimes he was fortunate in his ideas; sometimes he was not. He was never deep, and he was often too shallow and careless to be even superficially refined. If his powers of conception had been as remarkable as his powers of execution he would have been a great composer. As it was, his best is no better than Schubert's "middling."

At the next Brinsmead concert ... the symphony will be Berlioz's Episode in the Life of an Artist, for which it is to be hoped that Mr Joseph Bennett will write a new analysis, instead of borrowing that of Mr Barrett. The proper course would be to follow Berlioz's directions by printing an exact translation of his program. That done, the analytic spirit can have as much vent as it requires. Mr Ganz will conduct. As he has played at a performance of the work conducted by Berlioz himself, he should possess the authentic tradition as to its performance.

The second concert of the Heckmann quartet took place last Tuesday at Prince's Hall. Their remarkable powers were effectively displayed by certain passages in the work by Dittersdorff, with which they began; but now that the virtues of the Heckmann combination are well established, the replacement of Dittersdorff on the shelf would be generally regarded as a well-advised measure. It was followed by Mozart's great quartet in C—the one that begins with a poignant series of false relations. In the days when that quartet first saw the light, people used to complain that there was no melody in Mozart's music; that it might be profound, but that it was all discord. When Beethoven came, they passed their complaint on to him, and asked him why he could not be tuneful, as Mozart was. Only yesterday they were throwing Beethoven in Wagner's teeth in the same manner; and they will ask the next man why he cannot satisfy the intellect and ravish the ear at the same time, as Wagner did.

The quartet in C was followed by Beethoven's in F— that with the Russian air in the *finale*. It consists of three beautiful but apparently interminable fantasias; and it gives some color to the remark that Beethoven did not always know when to stop. When the audience, quite ready to go home, are disappointed for the third or fourth time by the interrupted cadence of the last movement, they privately intimate to the shade of Beethoven that it is possible to have too much of a good thing. The higher judgment of Mozart was made conspicuous by the juxtaposition of the two famous quartets.[U]

A PRIDE OF FAUSTS

Unsigned notes in The Dramatic Review,
19 December 1885

[U] Many Londoners will go to the Lyceum tonight*
with an impression that they are going to witness
something in the nature of an operatic performance.
The state of mind of the Frenchman, much quoted just
at present, who, when the German mentioned Goethe's
Faust, said, "In France we pronounce the name
Gounod," is the state of mind of a considerable
proportion of metropolitan theatre-goers. This is so
much the worse for themselves; for Mr Wills (if he has
treated his theme seriously), and, above all, for the
gentleman—Mr Hamilton Clarke, is it not?—who has
to provide the incidental music. His work will be
compared by hundreds of the audience with Gounod's;
a few will compare it with Wagner's, Mendelssohn's,
Schumann's, Berlioz's, Boïto's, and Liszt's. One or two
may even compare it with Lindpaintner's and Prince
Radziwill's.

The last-named and least known Faust composer
produced a prodigious score, and sold copies to half the
crowned heads in Europe. They got value for their
money, too, for the pair of folio volumes are well worth
looking at. The instrumentation is fanciful. Faust's first
thirty lines, for example, are accompanied by the chord
of C sharp, sustained on the harmonica, an instrument
in which the sounds are produced by friction from glass

---

* W. G. Wills's adaptation of Goethe's Faust was presented
that evening by Henry Irving, who appeared as Mephistopheles, with Ellen Terry as Margaret.

bowls, and which has the property of throwing nervous people into convulsions. The work is throughout serious and elaborate; but it is really an opera with a spoken *libretto*. The actors are directed in many places to recite to the rhythm of the music, and are otherwise all but made to sing. On the whole, the Prince's music, in spite of the trouble he evidently took with it, must have been a terrible nuisance to the performers and to the public. Lindpaintner's overture, but for its thinly veiled conventionality, might suggest an asylum with a number of lunatics rushing up and down stairs and slamming the doors, but occasionally stopping to listen to a melancholic patient learning the flute in the drawing room.

Schumann's Faust is the only setting of Goethe's work that evinces much appreciation of the philosophical side of it. Of the story of Gretchen it contains only a brief garden scene, her prayer to the Mater Dolorosa, and the church scene. The second part, in which Faust (blind) mistakes for the noise of his philanthropic engineering enterprise the rattling of the spades of the lemures as they dig his grave, and dies, is the most interesting. Mr Santley might do worse than induce some of our concert givers to produce it. The part of Faust would repay his attention.

Berlioz's vividly imaginative treatment of the picturesque element in the popular section of the great poem can be compared not to anything else in music, but only to the indescribable lithographs of Eugène Delacroix. Spohr wrote an opera called Faust, which was first produced in London in 1840, and was revived in 1852 with considerable success; but it has nothing to do with Goethe's Faust. Wagner wrote a Faust overture; and Mendelssohn's Walpurgisnacht deals with just such a scene as that for which Mr Irving has called in Italian aid from Her Majesty's Theatre.

Gounod's Faust is now nearly thirty years old; but its

popularity does not yet wane. In it Faust is a refined but weak sentimentalist, who assigns the reversion of his soul to Mephistopheles on condition of being made young again. Mephistopheles is a mountebank who grimaces in the glow of a red limelight; cowers when a cross-handled sword is shaken at him; laughs sardonically at his own humor; and is, perhaps, the most childish and ridiculous travesty of a serious conception that the public has ever disgraced itself by taking in earnest. Nevertheless, his cynicism contrasts racily with Faust's sentimentality; and his music is very fascinating. In dealing with poor Margaret, M. Gounod was in his depth and at his best, and there is no need to describe the result. The Valentine of the opera is by no means so natural, though doubtless more agreeable than Goethe's ruffianly soldier, who dies remarking that he commits himself to God, and would be happy in doing so if he could first get his hands on the wretched old duenna who has connived at his sister's ruin. The question of today is: Will Mr Irving proceed on Gounod's lines or on Goethe's? Will he distort his eyebrows and smile in a red halo? Will he shrug his shoulders and point with his toes and utter strident ha-has? It is much to be hoped that he will not, and much to be feared that the public will not recognize him as Mephistopheles if he does not. If he has decided to comport himself rationally, may his example react upon the operatic stage, where the counsels of commonsense are sadly in need of practical instances in their favor.

A scrap about Mozart occurs in a book called Wieland and Reinhold, which has been published in Germany. The great poet in 1793 wrote to Reinhold as follows: "I should be pleased if you could time your visit so as to hear the operetta Der Baum der Diana. The music is said to be extraordinarily charming, wheras Mozart's Figaro, from which we all expected so much, is the most disagreeable thing I ever heard in my life." Nevertheless, Mozart's music still makes its way. The latest description of the overture to Don Giovanni is "a mingling of animal vivacity and fateful trumpet tones." [U]

THE FOURTH BRINSMEAD CONCERT

Unsigned notes in The Dramatic Review,
26 December 1885

[U] Last Saturday, in St James's Hall, Messrs Brinsmead produced at their fourth concert the famous thirty-guinea prize concerto. Mr Oliver King, the composer, is the author of some elegant trifles for the pianoforte, and of a symphony in F, entitled Night. He is also pianist to H.R.H. the Princess Louise, Marchioness of Lorne, so that Mr W. G. Cusins, in awarding him the prize, has made a courtly choice, as becomes a musician who has himself had the advantage of royal patronage. No doubt all the rejected candidates will infer that the thirty guineas has gone by favor and not by merit. This, however, is a disadvantage of the one-judge system. Nothing is more natural than that the taste in music which recommends two musicians to the same circle should also recommend them to oneanother.

There is no reason to suspect that the competition drew anything better than Mr King's concerto. It consists of the usual three movements—an *allegro moderato* in G sharp minor; an *andante* in E; and a *finale* in A flat. Its form presents nothing unusual, unless comparative orthodoxy be considered so. The character of the concerto, though excessively sentimental, is on the whole refined and quiet without being timid or conventional; and the workmanship is elaborate and carefully finished throughout. The use of muted violins

[428]

is perhaps overdone in the slow movement. The composer has evidently a special fancy for the strings, which best express his favorite vein of sentiment. He frequently subdivides them, giving solo parts to the leaders. His feeling for the wind instruments is less lively, and his apparent lack of taste for the peculiarities of the pianoforte will probably hinder his work from attracting pianists. Though by no means deficient in individuality, the concerto was not sufficiently powerful or original to rouse the audience to enthusiasm after Berlioz's Fantastic Symphony and Beethoven's Egmont overture; but Mr King had no reason to complain of the cordial applause which greeted him when he bowed his acknowledgments side by side with Madame Frickenhaus, whose performance of the pianoforte part was unexceptionable.

The Brinsmead orchestra has improved greatly since its half-hearted performance at the first concert under Mr Mount. The playing on Saturday last left nothing to be desired in clearness of detail, delicacy of execution, or refinement of tone. In point of weight, the strings fell short, owing to their numerical deficiency. The symphony, Berlioz's Episode in the Life of an Artist, cannot be adequately rendered in St James's Hall by an orchestra with only two dozen violins. Berlioz expressly demands "at least" 15 firsts and 15 seconds. There were only 8 violas, 8 violoncellos, and 8 double basses, instead of the desiderated 10, 11, and 9; and some of the earthshaking effects for the bass strings in the first movement were lost in consequence. Since Messrs Brinsmead are prepared to give up all the direct profits of these concerts to philanthropic uses, no ingratitude to them for their enterprise is implied by the suggestion that the cause of art and the claims of philanthropy would be served alike by providing a dozen more players with an engagement.

The performance of the Fantastic Symphony was more successful than the recent one at Sydenham. Somehow, a wintry afternoon at the Crystal Palace is not favorable to sympathy with the intense ardor of the opium-poisoned artist of whose dreams the symphony is a distorted musical reflection. The Brinsmead orchestra played the work very finely indeed; but Mr Ganz, like Mr Manns, took the *allegro agitato* too slowly: the sudden change from mere melancholy to "volcanic love" which should accompany the entry of the *idée fixe*, with the "delirious anguishes" and "jealous furies" that follow, can by no means be represented by an orchestra jogging along under easy sail at the rate of sixteen minims less than Berlioz's explicit *tempo*. The scene in the fields, the least popular movement in the work, was unusually effective on this occasion, though here again, as in the waltz, Mr Ganz was not quite up to speed. On the other hand, he hurried the sinister "*marche au supplice*"; but here the enhanced effect justified him. The final diabolical orgy came off with great spirit. The substitution of bass tubas for ophicleides, now nearly always made, produces a more dignified tone in the Dies Iræ than Berlioz intended. There is something peculiarly outlandish in the hoot of an ophicleide. No tuba can bellow in quite the same way, nor, indeed, do manufacturers of brass instruments at all regret the disability. The ophicleide will probably not survive Mr Hughes in London orchestras.

The program of the symphony was, as usual, not that of Berlioz, who is evidently regarded as a doubtful authority on the subject by our concert givers, as they always fall back on Mr Barrett's analysis, written by him for Mr Ganz's concert in 1882. It is high time for Mr Barrett to revise his work, which consists of a program and analysis. The former he should burn for several reasons, but chiefly because Berlioz wrote a sufficiently full and exact program, which should be used as a matter of justice to the composer even if Mr Barrett's were better written, instead of being, as it is, very much the reverse. Also, because it repeats Schumann's blunder of supposing that only the two last scenes take place during the opium trance, and not the whole work, as Berlioz clearly states. The analysis is less objectionable; but it begins with an absurd quotation of the two bars of pure prelude with which the work opens, wheras the very remarkable theme in C minor, which begins in the third bar, and which is the proper subject to quote, is not given. One might just as well quote the first two bars only of Beethoven's Eroica, Mendelssohn's Italian, or Raff's Lenore symphony.

One word more about this apparently inevitable program of Mr Barrett's. When Berlioz, in his description of the first movement, speaks of "*ce vague des passions*," he is quoting Chateaubriand, who somewhere wrote that the further nations advance in civilization, the more intense becomes "*cet état du vague des passions*." Gautier has given in the earlier chapters of Mademoiselle de Maupin a capital description of the unaccountable disquietude referred to. But neither Berlioz, nor Chateaubriand, nor Gautier ever called it "the vague passion." Why, then, should Mr Barrett do so?

Before the Fantastic Symphony, Miss Gertrude Griswold sang *Il est doux: il est bon,* from Massenet's Hérodiade. The gentleman who is *doux et bon* is no other than St John the Baptist; and the idea of singing such things about so august a person would shock an Englishwoman, even if the music were Handel's. Being, as it is, intensely passionate and sentimental French operatic music, the situation is still more impossible in London. Miss Griswold nevertheless outfaced the incongruity—perhaps, indeed, she was unconscious of it—and did M. Massenet justice. She subsequently sang

[431]

several other songs; but the claims of the Heckmann quartet at the other side of Piccadilly had to be attended to immediately after the conclusion of the prize concerto.

Herren R. Heckmann, O. Forberg, T. Allekotte, and R. Bellmann made their parting bows at the conclusion of their fourth and last concert after playing Beethoven's famous quartet in C sharp minor, Op. 131. They have already earned for themselves a considerable reputation among lovers of chamber music; and although no very large section of these have yet formed a habit of going to Prince's Hall, there is a fair prospect for Herr Franke of establishing the Heckmann Concerts as firmly as Mr Chappell has established the Popular Concerts, if he can hold out through a few seasons more. The strong points of the Heckmann quartet are volume of tone, energy, and remarkable consentaneousness. Their weak points are dignity of style and delicacy, though of the latter they occasionally prove themselves capable in an extraordinary degree. But Herr Heckmann often leads with more spirit than discretion, playing wildly and with somewhat too large a proportion of notes out of tune in the quick movements. In the *adagios* his intonation is generally faultless. Herr Bellmann is the most nearly immaculate of the four.[U]

PALMY DAYS AT THE OPERA
The Magazine of Music, January 1886; unsigned

When old-fashioned people deplore the decadence of the modern theatre, and regret the palmy days of the drama, superstitious ones are apt to take the desirability of palminess for granted, without troubling themselves to ascertain the exact conditions which constituted it.

On inquiry, we are led to infer that long runs, elaborate scenery and dresses, efficient performance of minor parts, and prose dialogues, are degenerate; but that prompters, changes of program every night, poster playbills printed in blue color that adheres to everything except the flimsy paper, and "historical" costumes—*i.e.* costumes belonging to no known historic epoch—are palmy. Between the merits of these things, the young London play-goer can hardly judge; for he has no experience of palminess. There are many persons of culture still under thirty who are familiar with the palmy flat, vanishing from the scene with the scene-shifters' heels twinkling at its tail; who have touched the orchestra palisade from the front row of a palmily stall-less pit; who have seen the creations of Shakespear enter and quit the scene to the strains of Handel; and whose fingers have been a sorry sight after smudging the playbill for three hours. But these experienced critics are from the country, and began their play-going careers whilst palminess and stock companies still lingered there, as they do, perhaps, to this day. But the West Londoner, who only visits first-class theatres, has only one way of studying palminess. He must go to the opera, where he will soon get quite enough of it to convince him that the theatre in John Kemble's time, when it was carried on much as Italian opera is now, had quite enough drawbacks to reconcile a reasonable man to the changes which have since taken place.

There are no long runs at the opera. Faust is played one night, and Lucia the next; Lohengrin follows, and so on. Here is a splendidly palmy training for the singers. No stagnation in one play for three hundred nights, until the characteristics of his part fasten themselves upon the actor as mannerisms, never afterwards to be got rid of. No rusting of one's powers of study by disuse, nor dawdling in drawing rooms when one should be

[433]

busy with the divine art at rehearsal. No season passing away without a single performance of one of Mozart's operas, as seasons so often pass without a representation of Shakespear's plays. Development of powers in their fullest variety, by constant alternation of tragedy and comedy, classicism and romanticism, Italianism and Germanism; leading, of course, to enormous superiority of the lyric to the ordinary actor.

At this point it becomes somewhat obvious that the palmy theory lacks experimental verification. On the ordinary stage, crippled as it is supposed to be by long runs, everyone is expected to act; and the more important characters are expected to act very well. At the opera the tenor is not expected to act at all; and the baritone, though admittedly an eminently dramatic figure, would not, if he condescended to spoken dialogue, stand the smallest chance of being allowed to play Rosencrantz at a revival of Hamlet at the Lyceum or Princess. And if, by bringing strong private influence to bear, he succeeded in getting cast for Bernardo, and attempted, at rehearsal, to apply to that part the treatment which gained general admiration for his Conte di Luna, he would undoubtedly be at once conveyed, under restraint, from the stage to bedlam. Fancy a Don Felix or a Benedick at any West End theatre exhibiting the manners of an average Don Juan or Count Almaviva! Conceive any respectable dramatic company daring to act that great and neglected work of Molière's, Le Festin de Pierre,* as our opera singers usually act the masterpiece which Mozart founded on it. Yet musical critics frequently speak of the dramatic power and tragic intensity of the latest and absurdest Lucia or Traviata in terms which no sober critic of the

* Don Juan; ou, Le Festin de Pierre (1665), which provided the inspiration for Don Giovanni.

kindred profession ever applies to the most skilful achievements of Mrs Kendal.

But, then, the variety of resource, the freedom from mannerism—from Middlewickism! Unhappily that has not come off yet. Operatic actors, so far from being free from mannerisms, wholly substitute mannerisms of the feeblest sort for acting; and as for variety of resource, there is not a penny to choose between an average *prima donna's* treatment of any two of her parts, however dissimilar in conception. Her Lady Henrietta is exactly the same as her Marguerite; her Marguerite is not distinguishable by a deaf man from her Juliet, except by her dress and wig; and her Semiramis is only a swaggering Juliet. Even the few singers, male or female, who are specially celebrated for their acting, would be celebrated for their deficiency if they were placed in an equally prominent position in drama, and judged by the standard set by Ristori and Salvini.

As to the development of "study," or the power of learning new parts by constant change of program, it is to be noted that wheras the power of prompting and of taking a prompt during actual performance is becoming a lost art at our theatres, opera singers never venture before an audience without a prompter in the middle of the stage to pilot them through their business. As there is no possibility of sufficient rehearsal, it is part of their qualification, as it still is of the actor in the remote places where the palmy system is still rampant, to get through a part in which they are not even letter-perfect, much less note and letter-perfect. Who has ever heard an opera go absolutely without a hitch, except it was a very new opera which had been recently the subject of special effort in preparation, or a very old one played by a company of veterans? How many singers, when they have once picked up enough of their part to get through it without disgrace by dint of watching the prompter, ever give any further study to its details? At the ordinary theatres a hitch is as exceptional an occurrence as the forgetting of the Lord's Prayer, or the benediction by a Dean. Our actors gain both study and practice from long runs. It is true that they are condemned too often to play for months shallow and characterless parts which they get to the bottom of in a week; but that is the fault of the abject condition of the drama in England, and not of the system of long runs, which gives artists time to get thoroughly inside their parts, and frees them during considerable periods from daily rehearsals, to dawdle in the drawing room if they like, but also to study in the library, the picture gallery, the museum, the gymnasium, or the concert room, as their bodily or mental wants may suggest. The old system of a changed program every night and a hurried rehearsal every day meant insufficient time to prepare one's part, and no time at all to prepare oneself for playing it. To the actor as to other men, leisure means light. He may not always make a good use of his leisure; but in that case he will eventually succumb to competition of the men who do.

As to the advantage of having performances of the greatest operas each season, it may be admitted that a few great works are included in the narrow and hackneyed repertory of our opera houses; but it must at the same time be asked whether such performance as they get is in any sense worthy of them. Don Giovanni is certainly kept before the public; but in what plight? With fine movements omitted in the second act; with the *recitatives* gabbled through in a manner which could not be adequately described without the employment of abusive epithets; and with most of the parts played so as to inspire a faint wonder as to whether ten or twenty more earnest rehearsals, followed by a run of a hundred nights, would suffice to reveal them to the players. When this is all we can do for Don Giovanni we had better keep it on the shelf, as we now keep Shakespear when we have not time to take due trouble with him. The actor who knows one part, and consequently one play thoroughly, is superior to the actor who can scramble with assistance through a dozen. The one gets into the skin of one character: the other only puts on the clothes of twelve. One impersonation is worth more than many impostures. Long runs mean impersonations: palminess means imposture. Let us rejoice over the departure of the palmy days of the theatre.

STREET MUSIC

Unsigned notes in The Dramatic Review, 2 January 1886

[U] The music of the week has been chiefly performed *al fresco* during the small hours. It has raised no special question, except perhaps as to the exact degree of nocturnal disturbance that would legally justify a resort to firearms. But in common with all concerted street music, it presses upon us the need for establishing a uniform standard pitch. Regularly every Friday there comes, within earshot of a member of the musical staff of this Review, a band, the members of which are supposed to be fellow-countrymen of Beethoven. Their instruments, fitted with cylinders instead of valves, look German and cheap. There are cornets, flugelhorns, saxhorns, a couple of yellow ochre clarinets, and a bombardon. No two of these instruments have the same pitch; but they are not so far apart as to produce any discord used in music; between the sharpest instrument and the flattest the difference is about nine-tenths of a semitone, always excepting the bombardon, which is about three-quarters of a tone sharp to the average pitch of the rest. They play the overture to Tancredi; the

Lord Chord; two selections of folk songs—one English and the other German; an Iolanthe fantasia; and several waltzes which baffle recognition, as the inner and bass parts are improvized by the performers, and the treble played from memory. A householder in the street, evidently a man of no small hardihood, likes this program, and has it performed in its entirety before his premises every Friday at noon. The Dramatic Reviewer lives opposite. Not wishing to be unneighborly, he goes out at twelve o'clock, and takes care not to return until the street is quiet again, save for the traffic, the negro melodists at the two corner public-houses, and a few stray barrel pianofortes.

Now, the Dramatic Reviewer has no desire to interfere with street bands which gratify other people, provided they are genuine bands, and not a fortuitous aggregation of rascals who, having by ill-luck become possessed of instruments, and learnt how to make a noise with them, agree to combine their several nuisances into one intolerable plague of discord. The Legislature should interfere. If Mr Auberon Herbert*, or Mr Herbert Spencer protest, in the name of individual liberty, and cry *laissez-faire*, they must be ignored on the ground that one half of the public is too ignorant to protect itself, and the other half restrained from doing so by existing laws, which are already a violation of these very principles of individual liberty and the doctrine of *laissez-faire*. If the liberty of the members of the Friday band includes the right to interrupt the professional labors of the Dramatic Reviewer with sackbut and shawm, then *his* individual liberty should include the right to interrupt *their* professional labors with a fire

* Auberon Herbert was a crusading journalist, editor of Free Life. Like Herbert Spencer, the great rationalist philosopher, Herbert was a strong advocate of individualism.

engine charged with boiling oil and molten lead. If Mr Auberon Herbert would avoid this *reductio ad absurdum*, he must admit that the subject is a proper one for State interference.

The following measures are quite as practical as some that are now being rigorously carried out. Every person found singly in the streets with a wind instrument should be compelled to wear a muzzle of a pattern to be approved of by the council of the Royal Academy of Music. In the case of bagpipers, the instrument should be confiscated and destroyed. Two or more musicians in company should be dealt with as a band in the following way: they should be compelled to elect a responsible leader, recognizable by some badge or decoration. On the challenge of any householder or other person of substance, this leader should produce a tuning-fork, free reed, or pitchpipe giving the normal diapason of his band. If on trial at a given temperature any of the instruments were found to be incurably out of tune, both the player of that instrument and the leader should suffer a month's hard labor, and be thereafter musically outlawed for the rest of their natural lives. Pawnbrokers' shops should be searched for second-hand brass instruments and German concertinas; and the law as to their possession should be assimilated to that concerning dynamite. Amateurs wishing to practice should, until they can obtain a diploma from an examining board, be confined to a four-mile radius measured from the centre of Salisbury Plain. And so on. Bad music is a worse evil than hydrophobia. A nation which taxes and muzzles dogs, and yet allows German bands to blackmail it without restraint, had better at once utilize some empty space and conceal a couple of useless excrescences by wearing its ears inside its head.

This is supposed to be an appropriate time for a review of the music of the past year. Holders of that opinion cannot do better than turn over the back numbers of this Review, the establishment of which eleven months ago was the first event upon which the musical world of 1885 is to be congratulated. In the spring followed the bicentenary festival of the great John Sebastian Bach, with a performance of his Mass in B minor according to the original score—trumpets, *oboi d'amore*, and all the impossibilities triumphantly included. Then there was a successful season of English opera, with a new English opera—Mr Goring Thomas's Nadeshda—disputing first place with a new French one—M. Massenet's Manon. Even more satisfactory was the absence of all popular interest in Italian Opera during a brief airing of that decrepit imposture at Covent Garden. The exploits of the musical section of the council of the Inventions Exhibition resulted in what will, it is to be hoped, prove a revival of interest in pure vocal counterpoint, and in the art of harmonious and human singing, as opposed to the abominable shouting and screaming with which the opera has infected us. The three concerts of ancient Netherlandish music given at the Albert Hall by a double quartet of Dutch ladies and gentlemen (or Hollanders, as they would prefer to be called) more than atoned for the blunder of throwing away on Herr Strauss's quadrille band a sum which would have secured the services of a first-rate English orchestra. In the winter, besides the usual musical events, a new series of oratorio concerts were started by Messrs Novello, and a new series of orchestral concerts by Messrs Brinsmead. At the Birmingham Festival Herr Richter succeeded Sir Michael Costa almost without opposition. Both there and at the Philharmonic Concerts, Herr Antonin Dvořák's fame as a composer increased among us. M. Gounod favored us with a new oratorio. On the whole, Music has fared far worse than in 1885.[U]

GROVE'S: VERSE TO WATER-MUSIC

*Unsigned review of a "part" of Sir George Grove's A
Dictionary of Music and Musicians. The Pall Mall
Gazette, 15 January 1886*

[U] This work, the greatest of Sir George Grove's many
services to music in England, is at last coming within
measurable distance of the letter Z. The last part issued
begins with "Verse" and ends with "Water-music." It
therefore includes "Violin," "Vogler," and "Wagner"—
that is to say, one technical subject of great importance,
and two exceptionally interesting biographies. These
last are as complete and as unstinted as might be
expected from the editor's evident delight in the
biographical department, in which he himself set an
excellent example by his exhaustive monograph on
Beethoven. The growth of Abt Vogler's reputation in
this country since 1865 is not due to his music, which is
never performed, but to the poem with his name which
Mr Browning published in that year. His history has
hitherto been obscure, the best remembered fact about
him being the sovereign contempt which he inspired in
Mozart. Those who are interested in him can now, by
turning to the Rev. J. H. Mee's article in the Dictionary,
learn much more about the Abbé than Mr Browning
knew when he wrote Dramatis Personæ.

The account of the Bayreuth master is from the pen
of Mr Edward Dannreuther, and extends over fiftyseven
and a half columns. The author's intimacy with Wagner
seems to have imposed a certain reserve on him: the
personality of the great composer eludes us throughout
the elaborate itinerary and list of compositions, writings,
and performances. In this itinerary there is an omission

on p. 353, where no mention is made of Wagner's departure from Paris in the spring of 1842. The reader is consequently puzzled by finding the composer making an excursion to the Bohemian hills, apparently from the French capital. The section devoted to Wagner's artistic theories is brief, and suggests that Mr Dannreuther is either tired of explaining the subject, or sensible of the uselessness of second-hand expositions of it. The general effect of the biography is to leave the reader extremely curious to know more about its extraordinary hero, and Mr Dannreuther is careful to give very full information as to the means of gratifying this curiosity as far as that can be done by the perusal of existing publications. Some very interesting passages from the composer's conversation are given. Little is said of the ignorant and foolish clamor which arose against his music here and elsewhere until the public shamed the hostile critics into observing at least the common decencies of discussion. One famous remark of Wagner's on the subject is, however, quoted. The poets, he said, thought highly of his music, and the musicians had some respect for him as a poet; but the professional critics would never countenance him in any capacity. [U]

MUSIC STUDY IN GERMANY

Unsigned review of Music Study in Germany: From the Home Correspondence of Amy Fay. The Pall Mall Gazette, 19 January 1886

[U] It is not surprising that this book, which appeared in Chicago in 1881, should have attracted the attention of Sir George Grove, to whose musicianly interest in it we are probably indebted for its republication on this side of the Atlantic by Messrs Macmillan. It is a record of five and a half years spent in Berlin by an American girl studying pianoforte playing under the ill-starred Karl Tausig, under Kullak, Liszt, and Deppe. Berlin between 1869 and 1875 was a lively place for a young musician. Miss Amy Fay dashed into her studies with great pluck and enthusiasm. Whether it was her nationality, her talent, her personal appearance, her character, or all four combined, that brought her so easily on good terms with her neighbors and her musical heros, cannot, of course, be ascertained from her own letters. She was, at any rate, handy with her pen, and was no sooner settled in Europe than she began the correspondence with her relatives at home from which the volume under consideration was afterwards compiled. In America she had admired no one except Gottschalk; but in Berlin she began by shutting her ears and opening her mouth, thinking every goose a swan. She humbled herself like a saint by unceasing contemplation of her own imperfections. "My constant thought is" she writes "when *will* my passages *pearl*? When will my touch be perfectly equal? When will my octaves be played from a lightly hung wrist? When will my thumb turn under and my fourth finger over without the slightest perceptible break?"

These agonies of aspiration and despair, and the drudgery of finger exercises, were compensated by the ecstasy of finding in every concert room a Walhall, and in every virtuoso a divine hero—"a two-edged sword" as she says in one of her many outbursts about Liszt. Fellow students with wonderful eyes, destined to command Europe by their genius, were as plentiful as blackberries in 1869. It is interesting to turn the leaves and see these exciting and delicious raptures going the way of all the illusions of youth as the young American devotee grows in years and wisdom. The two-edged swords become longhaired men playing Beethoven's Sonata in F minor

[443]

more or less badly. Girls who, in the refulgent sunset of youth, seemed destined to be queens of musical Europe, reappear in the dawning of wisdom and womanhood as dowdy incipient governesses.

She began her studies under Tausig. When she first played to him "he kept calling out all through it in German, 'Terrible! Shocking! O Gott! O Gott!'" which naturally made poor Miss Fay cry, although she was resolved not to be beaten, and finished her piece with heroic cussedness before giving way. He was not a reassuring teacher. His pupils were "as thin as rails" with excessive study; and when he played a passage and bade them imitate him, it was as if he had required them "to copy a streak of forked lightning with the end of a wetted match." Presently, however, he tired of teaching, and abruptly abandoned his conservatory (conservatory here meaning a forcing-house for young pianists). Shortly afterwards all hope of his changing his mind was put out of the question by his death. So Miss Fay went to Kullak, who was much more amiable than Tausig, but who put her even more out of countenance by liberal displays of his own superiority as a pianist. With him, nevertheless, she remained until 1873, when she made a pilgrimage to Weimar, the shrine of Liszt, whose acquaintance she soon made. "He is just like a monarch" she wrote; "and no one dares speak to him until he addresses one first, which I think no fun." Liszt took a fancy to her, drew her out, encouraged her, let her play as she pleased, and made the best of it. The result was that when she returned to Berlin, Kullak, who before the Weimar trip had been "a great master, thoroughly capable of developing artistic talent to the utmost," appeared "so pedantic" that she found him intolerable after three or four lessons. Just then she met by chance Ludwig Deppe, who speedily convinced her that the four years she had spent paying gifted pianists to quarrel with her for not playing as well as they, were so much time wasted, and that she had better get taught to use her fingers forthwith. So she gave up Kullak and the concert at which she was about to appear as his pupil, and went to Deppe, who, to her great humiliation, set her to work on Czerny's "School of Velocity," which she had left behind her, as she thought, at school for ever.

She retained her faith in Deppe until her return to America in September 1875. The publication of her letters a few years later was quite justified by the lively sketches they contain of many famous musicians, besides the account of public feeling in Berlin during the war. Her judgments and criticisms, though surpassingly rash and unmeasured, are amusing, and often very happily expressed. The little sketches of Natalie Janotha, Herr Moszkowski, and others whose fame has spread to London since Miss Fay was at Berlin, will be read here with special interest. Readers who are not musical will find some entertainment in the impression made by German etiquette on the free American girl, and will most likely agree with her that "the best plan is the old-fashioned American one—namely, give your children 'a stern sense of duty,' and then throw them on their own resources."[U]

PRINCIPLES OF SINGING

Unsigned review of Albert B. Bach's The Principles of Singing. The Pall Mall Gazette, 13 February 1886

[U] Treatises on singing are eagerly purchased nowadays by great numbers of half-educated young people who are fond of the theatre and of music and who are averse to the sordid ways of commerce, and to the severe intellectual efforts which alone can open the doors of the

learned professions. Lazy and good-for-nothing individuals they are for the most part, with a sufficient turn
for art to make them quite willing to become famous
and well paid as great artists provided a royal road to
that eminence be found for them; and they invariably
feel that they have made a considerable advance when
they have purchased a book on the subject of the art they
happen to prefer. The demand thus created enables
publishers to take up textbooks which would otherwise
be unremunerative and so incidentally to place the
counsels of experienced singers and teachers within
reach of the few earnest students and inquirers who
really profit by them. Mr Albert Bach's book will of
course not teach any one to sing, but it will convey
much useful information, and some salutary warnings
to any young vocalist who may consult it.

Should another edition be called for, however, Mr
Bach will find some revision necessary. On page 92 we
read of "the foundation of the opera under Peri Caccini
Monteverdi," as if these three men were one; while, on
the opposite leaf, Faustina, the wife of Hasse, is
mentioned as if she were two persons. On page 119, in
the diagram representing the strokes of the conductor's
baton in triple time, the second beat is drawn to the left
instead of to the right. On page 155 it is stated that "the
tension of the lips reaches the highest degree" in forming
the vowel *ee*, a sound with which the lips have nothing
to do. On page 32 is a short paragraph to the effect that
the timbre of wind instruments depends greatly on the
materials of which they are made. Here Mr Bach is in
direct conflict with Mr Blaikley, who, as a practical
instrument maker, may be inferred to be better qualified
to pronounce on the subject than a professor of singing.
The assertion on page 166 that "in all voices the middle
register is best," may be true in Edinburgh, where Mr
Bach practises, but it certainly does not hold good in

England or in the countries whence our public singers come. Possibly Mr Bach intended to convey that the middle register is best worth cultivating. Grave exception will be taken to the recommendation to persons conducting the studies of children "to endeavor to extend the natural limits of one register so as to make one or two of its notes reach into the adjoining register," a practice which should be strictly limited to the extension of a higher register downward.

No fresh controversy is likely to arise over Mr Bach's pages on the physiology of the vocal organs. He is evidently not fond of the laryngoscope, and has been content to take at second-hand from the best available sources his information on points extraneous to art. Appended to his book are about a hundred and twenty pages of exercises, of which those on the various intervals are likely to prove specially useful.[U]

MUSIC AS A DEGREE EXERCISE

Unsigned note in The Pall Mall Gazette,
22 February 1886

[U] The first performance of works composed as exercises for the degree of Doctor of Music in the London University took place on Saturday afternoon, in the presence of the Vice-Chancellor, Sir James Paget, and other dignitaries, who listened with great gravity to Mr W. H. Hunt's Stabat Mater and to a portion of a requiem by Mr Augustus Hayter Walker. A very creditable performance was achieved by a small choir of ladies and gentlemen, a Mustel organ, and a pianoforte, with two players serving as orchestra. Mr Hunt seems to have paid more attention to the sacred works of Rossini and Gounod than to those of Mendelssohn,

whose influence, once paramount in all religious compositions by English students, seems just now on the
wane. Mr Walker's harmony is much more studied and
expressive than that of Mr Hunt, whose intentions are
merely tuneful, and whose genius is reproductive rather
than original. Originality, however, is a power which it
is as well to conceal in a degree exercise. Although the
performance was, of course, unsuspected by the general
public, there was a fair sprinkling of friends of the
novices and members of the university present.[U]

MR ROCKSTRO'S HISTORY OF MUSIC

*Unsigned review of W. S. Rockstro's A General History
of Music. The Pall Mall Gazette, 24 February 1886*

[U] This very compendious work begins with Hermes
Trismegistus making a tortoise shell into a lyre on the
banks of the Nile, and ends with M. Gounod's Mors et
Vita and M. Massenet's Manon. A history of all
intervening music is condensed into five hundred pages
of large and liberally leaded type. Within such limits the
mere technical descriptions, with the necessary statement of dates, names, places, and compositions, crowd
out the criticism. Not that Mr Rockstro, whose
imagination always kindles when music is his theme,
has confined himself to a dry record of births, deaths,
and opus numbers. On one page he writes from the
fulness of his heart, as Berlioz wrote of Dalayrac. Over
the leaf he recovers himself, and reassumes the historian
and critic. But in this way discrepancies arise which
might lead a reader previously ignorant of music to
suppose that Méhul was a greater composer than
Mozart, because Mr Rockstro utters, in his gratitude to
the composer of Joseph, a eulogy that he feels would be

superfluous and at best inadequate in the case of Don Giovanni. There is no common measure in his criticisms: Raff gets as much praise as Beethoven. It would be unfair to say that all Mr Rockstro's geese are swans; but some such inference might be drawn if his past services to the art had not established his right to a more favorable construction.

In a record which includes a work first heard at the Birmingham Festival in 1885, it is surprising to find no mention of the great Netherlander Pieter van Sweelinck, whose compositions were resuscitated for us with such striking effect at the very remarkable concerts of ancient Netherlandish music given at the Albert Hall last June, in connection with the Inventions Exhibition. Surely the statement that Orlandus Lassus was "the last great genius of the Netherlands" is a little hard on Sweelinck. A much more astonishing omission is that of Signor Verdi, whom Mr Rockstro excuses himself from dealing with on the ground that "the tentative character of his later works is so self-evident, that all attempts to classify them, until the school shall have more fully developed its guiding principles, would be both misleading and invidious." However this may be, a list of "the most important works given to the world since the middle of the XIX century" which contains Madame Sainton-Dolby's cantata St Dorothea, but not Il Trovatore, is rather a curiosity of musical literature than a piece of history. And, though the English operas of Balfe, Wallace, Loder, Smart, and Hugo Pierson are duly recorded, there is not a word about the revival of comic opera in our own generation by Sir Arthur Sullivan and Mr W. S. Gilbert.

The best illustrations in the volume are those borrowed from Sir George Grove's Dictionary of Music and Musicians. The other portraits of the great composers are apparently taken from the photographs exhibited in

[449]

most music shops. Any one who compares the brilliant *jeune premier* offered on page 277 as a representation of Mozart with a good engraving after the portrait by Tischbein,* will see at once that the former is a libel that expresses nothing but the vulgar misconception of one of the most thoughtful of modern artists.

An appreciative notice of Wagner proves that Mr Rockstro, though a veteran critic, is not behind his time. It is, however, as a book of reference that his history will chiefly be valued.[U]

HULLAH AND MUSIC

Unsigned review of The Life of John Hullah, LL.D., by his Wife. The Pall Mall Gazette, 3 March 1886

[U] John Pyke Hullah was born in 1812; and it is but just two years since he died. The threescore years and ten which he fulfilled were as eventful musically as politically. In their first decade, Haydn and Mozart were the gods of modern music, and Beethoven an ignorant pretender, seeking to conceal the poverty of his ideas by presenting them in strange, uncouth forms, and making up for his lack of melody by overcharged instrumentation and abundance of discord. Soon Spohr was critically elected to the vacant post of greatest living composer of sacred and instrumental music. Mendelssohn succeeded him, with added glory, as the greatest of all composers, ancient or modern, and held that dignity until it could no longer be denied to Beethoven, who was posthumously installed as the Titan of music, his old distinction as the dunce being passed on to Schumann to keep warm

* Johann Tischbein, court painter to William VIII. of Hesse-Cassel.

for Wagner, who only recently shuffled it and his mortal coil off together at Venice.

In the theatre, too, great reputations waxed and waned; much conservative criticism was set at nought; and much progressive enthusiasm dashed. The once universal Rossini, whose Semiramide appeared to our greener grandfathers a Ninevesque wonder, came at last to be no longer looked upon as a serious musician. Meyerbeer, the impressive, the original, the historical, the much imitated inimitable, is now only "the Jew that Wagner drew." Donizetti came and went, with Bellini and others of less note. Yet there were new sensations in store. With the turn of the half-century came Verdi, vulgar and yet Victor Hugoesque, with his irresistible torrents of melody, a little muddy and mixed, but copious and impetuous enough to sweep away the critics who stooped for a spoonful to analyze. With him came Gounod, the French Mendelssohn of the stage. Their fame, also, is passing. Nowadays even the street pianists are ashamed to play *Ah! che la morte*; and the composer of Faust is writing tediously beautiful oratorios, and adding descriptive *melodrame* to the Apocalypse. Still there was Goetz to come, with the greatest comic opera of the century,* except Die Meistersinger; and there was the thirty-year-old novelty Lohengrin. Meanwhile fashionable Italian opera decayed steadily, as those who could sing the music of Rossini and Bellini died and were replaced by others who could only horribly howl and scream the music of Verdi—a race happily unable

---

* Hermann Goetz, Der widerspenstigen Zähmung (The Taming of the Shrew), first performed in 1874. An English translation by the Rev. J. Troutbeck had been performed by the Carl Rosa company at Drury Lane in 1878 and at Her Majesty's in 1880. It is one of the most shamefully neglected operas of the XIX century.

to survive a year of Wagner, whose music is singable, but by no means howlable or screamable.

All this prolific period—from Weber to Bizet; from Beethoven to Wagner; from Rossini to Goetz; from Grisi, Rubini, and Tamburini to Materna, Unger, and Karl Hill—fell within Hullah's experience. How far he kept touch with it may be gathered from his *causeries* in the *Globe*, and from his lectures on the history of music; but certainly not from his biography, which, to tell the truth, deals far too much with events which, like Rogue Riderhood's imprisonment,* "might have happened to any man." This, however, is not wholly the fault of the biographer. Nearly all of Hullah's history that concerns the world, besides what is recorded in the *causeries*, the lectures, and in his official reports as Inspector of Music, might be conveyed in a brief essay.

He was an amiable man, fond of domesticity (he was twice married and had two families), fond of society, of reading, of writing, of talking, of singing, of sketching, of architecture, of music, and of travel. He had quite a mania for holiday trips, and never moved without luggage enough to embitter the autumn migrations of three ordinary men. A convivial trencherman and a late riser, he always lived as far beyond his income as his wife allowed him to; nor was he more provident in accepting work, which he undertook as it was offered, without the least reference to the limits of time and human endurance. His musical aims were wide and humanitarian. He saw that the people spent their leisure hours in dissipation mainly because they had no sufficiently attractive alternative; and he believed that music was such an alternative, and that it could successfully compete with beer and skittles. As to the method of teaching novices to read it, he insisted on the fixed *do*

* In Dickens's Our Mutual Friend.

[452]

and the staff notation with the conviction of a man gifted with the power of recollecting the absolute pitch of musical sounds, and therefore insensible to the difficulties imputed by the tonic-sol-faists to his favorite Wilhem method. He seems to have regarded Curwen, Chevé, and all other inventors of movable *do* systems as quacks;* yet he accepted their results without demur, and declared that teachers would teach best upon the systems in which they happened to believe and to which they were most accustomed. His main point was that the children should be taught to read music by one means or another; and no man did more than Hullah to convince a Philistine nation that it really was a point worth gaining.

In his last years he attempted an autobiography, and produced a few very readable chapters, which bring the narrative of his life past the year 1836, in which he composed music to The Village Coquettes,† by Charles Dickens. The work, which afterwards perished in a fire, was fairly successful. Nevertheless, he speaks of it slightingly, and adds: "With Mr Dickens I remained, till nearly the close of his life, on excellent terms. He had, like the majority of literary Englishmen of that day, no critical knowledge of music; but I fear he never quite forgave me for being mixed up with him in this matter." Nearly a quarter of a century elapsed between the point reached by the autobiography and the

* Guillaume Wilhem (1781–1842), director general of all Paris schools, published many treatises on his method of "mutual instruction." The Rev. John Curwen (1816–80) was the first to advocate the Tonic Sol-fa system (1842) and later founded a college (1875) to exploit the system. Emile Chevé (1804–64), a physician, published pamphlets attacking the method advocated at the Paris Conservatoire.

† Comic opera produced at the St James's Theatre, London, 6 December 1836.

beginning of the period of which his biographer—the second Mrs Hullah—writes from her personal experience. Here, accordingly, the book brightens; and frivolous details are admitted more easily. Pleasant as the writer's touch is, we feel that a little more of Hullah in his intercourse with Mark Pattison, F. D. Maurice,* Dickens, and others, and perhaps a little less of him in his packings and unpackings and Channel crossings, would have given us a deeper insight into the man. But, as Mrs Hullah could not accompany him on his inspecting circuit, she was not present at all the feasts of reason at which he was a guest. A supplement to her account from the hands of Lady Dilke† and others of his hostesses would do much to complete it.

Hullah was a Liberal-Conservative in music, countenancing Schumann, but sticking at Wagner. In politics he was not so much a Conservative as a hater of Radicalism, which is the more noteworthy because his father, it appears, was something of a Jacobin. He inherited his musical talent from his mother. [U]

LISZT

I

The Dramatic Review, 10 April 1886

"The favorite of Fortune" has revisited us at last, and is installed as the Grand Old Man of music. Many persons of literary and artistic tastes are now reading with genuine enthusiasm the newspaper chronicles of his

---

* Pattison, originally a follower of Newman, became a scholarly journalist and author of a highly introspective Memoirs (1883). Maurice, scholar and theologian, was chief founder of Christian Socialism.

† Lady Dilke (Emilia Frances Strong), the widow of Mark Pattison, was a much-published critic of the fine arts.

pilgrimage—in all human probability his last pilgrimage—to the land of Purcell. Sonnets will spring—are springing daily, perhaps—from irrepressible impulses to worship the white-haired hero; the contemporary of Schumann, Berlioz, Chopin, Mendelssohn, and Goetz; who was sped on his career by Beethoven; who was the cherished friend of Wagner; who has all his life conversed with the immortals, and been envied by most of them for his pianoforte playing and his pluck before the public. You cannot read about such a man without emotion. If music be to you only a glorious dream, an unknown language transcending all articulate poesy, a rapture of angelic song, a storm-cloud of sublimity discharging itself into your inmost soul with thrilling harmonious thunder; then for you especially the voice of man's innate godhead will speak in whatever Liszt plays, whether he extemporizes variations on Pop goes the Weasel or faithfully re-utters for you the chromatic *fantasia* of Bach. The great player is to you no mere pianist: he is a host of associations—George Sand, Lamartine, Victor Hugo, Paris in the days of the Romantic movement, and what not and who not? Happy hero-worshiper! No generous infidel will grudge you your ecstasy, or untimely urge that it is intense in inverse ratio to your knowledge of music. Indeed, if one felt disposed to throw cold water on such genial transports, it would be difficult to find any just now to throw, Liszt having the gift that was laid as a curse upon the Scotch laird who made icy water bubble and boil by touching it.*

Yet Liszt's associations do not by themselves entitle him to take precedence of many worthy citizens whose very names are unknown to history. The servant who

* See "Wandering Willie's Tale" in Scott's Redgauntlet (1824).

opened Balzac's door to his visitors, and who must have been no mean connoisseur in creditors, was perhaps more interesting from this point of view than Liszt. As to the gentlemen who turn over the leaves for the pianists at St James's Hall, is there a great *virtuoso* with whom they are not familiar? What exciting tales they could tell of their breathless efforts to follow incredibly swift *prestos*; and what pleasant reminiscences they must enjoy of delicious naps stolen in the midst of dreamy *adagios* with a nice long repeat included within one open folio. For they sleep, these men: I have seen one of them do it at the elbow of a great artist, and have forgotten the music in contemplating the unfathomable satiety of the slumberer, and in speculating on the chances of his waking up in time for the *volte subito*. The eyes did not fail to open punctually; and their expression, unmistakably that of the sleeper awakened, relieved me of the last doubt as to whether he had not been ecstatically drinking in the music with his eyes shut. What are Liszt's experiences compared to those of a man so prodigiously *blasé* that not Madame Schumann herself can fix his attention for the brief space of two pages? Clearly it is by his merit as a player or composer that Liszt's reputation must stand or fade.

There are not many people of anything like a reasonable age in England who have heard Liszt play. This statement may become false by the time it is printed—I hope it will; but at present it is true. That he was once a great player, one who far more than any interpreter of his time could play a sonata as the composer thought it, reading into every quaver the intention with which it was written there, is proved to us, as firmly as any such thing can be proved, by the crowning testimony of Wagner. Having the gift of governing men too, he was a great conductor as well as a great pianist. Whether he is as great as he was is just what we are all at present very curious to ascertain. We cannot expect him to formally undertake a public performance of Beethoven's Opus 106, his playing of which was ranked by Wagner as a creative effort; but there is abundant hope that he may be tempted to touch the keyboard at some concert at which only his presence can be promised. Already he has yielded to the desire of the Academy students; and the public wishes itself, for the nonce, a corps of Academy students and not a mob of mere ticket purchasers, whose applause and lionizing an artist is bound to mistrust if not to despise. Perhaps, under the circumstances, the best policy would be one of exasperation. Treat the master to a few examples of average British pianism; and a desperate longing to take the sound of it out of his ears, tempered by a paternal willingness to shew us what real playing is, may urge him to fulfil our hearts' desire.

Of Liszt's merits as a composer, those who heard his St Elizabeth at St James's Hall last Tuesday have, no doubt, their own opinion. To some of us his devotion to serious composition seems as hopeless a struggle against natural incapacity as was Benjamin Haydon's determination to be a great painter. To others the Dante symphony and the symphonic poems are masterpieces slowly but surely making their way to full recognition. Mr Bache has pressed the latter opinion hard upon us, and has backed it heavily. The present is not the time to insist with any grace on the former view. Fortunately, much of Liszt's music is admired on all hands. Sceptics who think it no more than brilliant, inspiriting, amusing, applaud as loudly as believers who revere it as significant, profound, and destined to endure with the works of Bach and Mozart. So, since we all enjoy it from one point of view or the other, we can very well unite in making as pleasant as possible the sojourn among us of an artist who has come clean-handed out of the press of three generations of frenzied XIX century scramblers for pelf, and of whom even hostile critics say no worse than that he has failed only by aiming too high.

II

The Pall Mall Gazette, 2 August 1886; unsigned

The foreboding that many of us must have felt last spring when Liszt left England with a promise to return has been verified by the news of his death at Bayreuth. Such news always comes too soon; but in this case Time has exacted less than his traditional due: three score and fifteen years were allowed to Liszt to work out what was in him. He had twice as long to utter himself as had Mendelssohn, who was only two and a half years his senior; or Mozart, who might have done things quite unimaginable in their effect on modern music if he had been allowed another thirty years of life. Of Liszt, we at least know that he said his say fully, such as it was. He was a Hungarian, born at Raiding in 1811, with the pianoforte at his fingers' ends. His career as a public player began when he was nine years old; and his success led him to Vienna and then to Paris, where he was excluded by his nationality from the Conservatoire and Cherubini's instruction. Of his plunge into the Romantic movement; his Saint-Simonianism; his Roman Catholicism; his connexion with the Countess d'Agoult (Daniel Stern); his career in his middle age at Weimar, where he did for the opera what Goethe had done before for the theatre; his championship of Wagner, who became his son-in-law, and whose widow is his sole surviving child; his unique position as the idol of all the pianoforte students in the world—all of these we have been lately put in mind by the great overhauling of his history, which took place when he revisited us this year after nearly half a century's absence. He first played here at the Philharmonic Concerts in 1827. Fifteen years later he gave us another trial out of which we did not come with perfect credit. That was, perhaps, why he stayed away fortyfour years before he came again, and as an old man, half priest, half musician, stirred up all the hero worship in our little world of music and all the lionizing in our big world of fashion. That little world will grieve awhile to learn that his third absence must be the longest of all. The big world will probably feel none the worse for having had something to talk about at breakfast this morning. Between it and the dead artist there was little genuine love lost. He cared so little for even dazzling it that he adopted the profession of pianist with repugnance, and abandoned it for that of conductor and composer as soon as he could afford to.

It was as a composer that Liszt wished to stand high in the esteem of his contemporaries, or—failing their appreciation—of posterity. Many musicians of good credit think that he judged himself rightly. Mr Bache, for instance, has given us concert after concert of his favorite master's works with a devotion that has extorted applause from audiences for the most part quite convinced that Liszt and Mr Bache were mistaken. Wagner, who spoke very highly of Liszt as a conductor, declared that his playing of Beethoven's greater sonatas was essentially an act of composition as well as of interpretation; he did not, however, commit himself on the subject of the Dante symphony or Mazeppa. There is a consensus of opinion in favor of Liszt as a player. His songs, too, have affected many musicians deeply; and though they are not generally familiar, their merit has not been at all emphatically questioned. His studies and transcriptions, if not wholly irreproachable in point of taste, shew an exhaustive knowledge of the pianoforte; and, unplayable as they are to people who attack a pianoforte with stiff wrists and clenched teeth, they are not dreaded by good pianists. The brilliancy and impetuous fantasy of his Hungarian Rhapsodies are irresistible, as Herr Richter has proved again and again at St James's Hall. But his oratorios and symphonic poems—especially the latter—have not yet won the place which he claimed for them. A man can hardly be so impressionable as Liszt was and yet be sturdy enough to be original. He could conduct Lohengrin like Wagner's other self, and could play Beethoven as if the sonatas were of his own moulding; but as an original composer he was like a child, delighting in noise, speed, and stirring modulation, and indulging in such irritating excesses and repetitions of them, that decorous concert-goers find his Infernos, his battles, and his Mazeppa rides first amusing, then rather scandalous, and finally quite unbearable. A pleasanter idea of the man can be derived from the many eulogies, some of them mere schoolgirl raptures, others balanced verdicts of great composers and critics, which, whether the symphonic poems live or die, will preserve a niche for him in the history of music as a man who loved his art, despised money, attracted everybody worth knowing in the XIX century, lived through the worst of it, and got away from it at last with his hands unstained.

THE REDEMPTION AT THE CRYSTAL PALACE

The Dramatic Review, 8 May 1886

Why should the Handel Festival occur only once in every three years? Would it pay to make it biennial, annual, half-yearly, quarterly, weekly? Cannot something be made out of our gold-laden visitors from the colonies this year by a festival or two? An experiment in the direction of answering these questions was made last Saturday at the Crystal Palace, when M. Gounod's Redemption was performed at the Crystal Palace by the Handel orchestra, with three thousand singers in the choir, and four hundred players in the orchestra. Additional solemnity was given to the occasion by the prohibition of the sale of intoxicating liquor at the refreshment bars during the performance (so I was assured by a neighbor on his return from a short and unsuccessful absence); and nothing was allowed to distract the attention of the audience from the oratorio except a large signboard with the inscription "OYSTERS," which was conspicuous on the left of the orchestra. The audience behaved much like a church congregation, stolid, unintelligent, and silent, except once, when Madame Albani took her place on the orchestra after the first part, and again when one of her highest notes excited the representatives of that large and influential section of the public which regards a vocalist as an interesting variety of locomotive with a powerful whistle.

M. Gounod is almost as hard to dispraise as the President of the Royal Academy. Both produce works so graceful, so harmonious, so smooth, so delicate, so refined, and so handsomely sentimental, that it is difficult to convey, without appearing ungracious or insensible, the exact measure of disparagement needed to prevent the reader from concluding that M. Gounod is another Handel, or Sir Frederick Leighton another Raphael. And indeed M. Gounod does not express his ideas worse than Handel; but then he has fewer ideas to express. No one has ever been bored by an adequate performance of the Messiah. Even a Good Friday tumble through it at the Albert Hall—ordinarily the worst thing of its kind in the whole cosmos—inspires rage and longing for justice to Handel rather than weariness. But the best conceivable performance of the

Redemption would not hold an audience to the last note if the half-past five train back to town from Sydenham were at stake, much less make them impatient for a repetition of the oratorio, which is, in truth, an extremely tedious work, not because any particular number is dull or repulsive, but because its beauties are repeated *ad nauseam*. We all remember how, at the awakening of Margaret in the prison scene of Faust, we were delighted by the harmonic transitions from phrase to phrase by minor ninths resolving on stirring inversions of the common chord of a new tonic (technically unskilled readers will kindly excuse this jargon), as her voice rose semitone by semitone to the final cadence. It was a charming device; and M. Gounod used it again and again in his other operas. But when he gives us a long oratorio, consisting for the most part of these phrases on successive degrees of the chromatic scale, not only do we get thoroughly tired of them, but the pious among us may well feel scandalized at hearing the central figure in the tragedy of the atonement delivering himself exactly in the lovesick manner of Romeo, Faust, and Cinq Mars. No one expected M. Gounod to succeed in making the Redeemer differ from Romeo as Sarastro, for example, differs from Don Giovanni; but he might at least have made him as impressive as Friar Laurence. Instead, he has limited himself to making the Prince of Peace a gentleman; and one cannot help adding that he could have done no less for the Prince of Darkness.

And such a smooth-spoken gentleman! There is a plague of smoothness over the whole work. The fact that M. Gounod has put too much sugar in it for the palate of a British Protestant might be condoned if the music were not so very horizontal. There is nearly always a pedal flowing along, and the other parts are slipping chromatically down to merge in it. Mr Compton Reade used to be fond of calling Handel the great Dagon of music. But when, at the end of the second part of the trilogy, the celestial choir demands Who is the King of Glory? words cannot express the longing that arises to have done with M. Gounod's sweetly grandiose periods, and to hear great Dagon answer concerning The Lord strong and mighty; the Lord mighty in battle. And again, in the chorus of mockers at the crucifixion, Ah, thou that dost declare, though the composer's dramatic instinct does make a faint struggle against his love of suave harmony, the lamenting listener's memory reverts enviously to the sinister turbulence of great Dagon's sardonic He trusted in God that He would deliver Him. If Mr Compton Reade, or anyone else, still doubts that M. Gounod is to Handel as a Parisian duel is to Armageddon, let him seek greater wisdom at the next Crystal Palace performance of the Redemption or Mors et Vita. Depend upon it, he will be forced either to change his opinion, or to accuse Handel of an extraordinary lack of variety in rhythm and harmonic treatment, and an essentially frivolous sentimental piety in dealing with a subject which, to a genuinely religious Christian composer, must be the most tremendous in universal history.

The execution of the work on Saturday last was as fine as one has any right to expect under mundane conditions. No doubt a choir of angels would sing M. Gounod's ethereal strains better than a massive detachment from the ranks of the British *bourgeoisie*; but no reasonable exception can be taken to the steady middle-class manner and solid middle-class tone of the Festival choristers. The basses seemed to me to be weak; but that may have been due to our relative positions. Some of the orchestral effects were enhanced by the vast space. Thus, at the beginning of the second part, the chords of the violins pulsating above the veiled melody of the horns, answered by the clear and brilliant notes of the trumpets

[463]

in the gallery, transported us all into cloudland. Later, in an orchestral interlude full of mystery, entitled The Apostles in Prayer, the perpetual tonic pedal ceased to be tiresome, and almost excused M. Gounod for being unable to tear himself away from the few devices which he uses so exquisitely. Of Madame Albani, Miss Marriott, Madame Patey, Mr Lloyd, Mr King, and Mr Santley, nothing need be said, except to congratulate them on the easiest Festival engagement that ever fell to the lot of six such vocalists.

MEMOIRS OF A FAMOUS FIDDLER

Unsigned review of Sara C. Bull's Ole Bull. The Pall Mall Gazette, 5 July 1886

We have at last an English memoir of Ole Bull, not before it was urgently needed. For, it being nearly a quarter of a century since the great Norwegian violinist played publicly in the United Kingdom, it had come about that while young America knew Ole Bull as well as we know Joachim and Sarasate, young England very commonly supposed him to be an octogenarian negro. That we failed to attach him to us as a yearly visitor was rather our misfortune than our fault. It is true that he was intrigued against and cheated here; but there was nothing peculiar to us in that. Bull invariably assumed his fellow men to be honest until he found out the contrary; and it is due to the alert commercial spirit of Europe and America to say that, to his cost, he almost invariably did find out the contrary. In whatever quarter of the globe he sojourned he found the general public ready to heap gold upon him, and the particular man of business equally ready to relieve him of it. In America a hasty speculator, who had just made a large haul in this way, was foolish enough to attempt to take off by poison the goose that laid the golden eggs. On another occasion a ruder pioneer of civilization, coveting a diamond which sparkled in the magic fiddle bow, approached the player, knife in hand, with a view to its extraction. But Ole Bull, like Sinfjotli,* instinctively saw death in the cup, and refused to drink, whilst the unfortunate pioneer with the bowie knife took nothing by his enterprise except a rough estimate of how much nerve and muscle go to the making of a Norseman who can play the violin in four-part harmony.

Ole Bull's gain, on the whole, greatly exceeded his loss. Wherever he went he soon found himself the focus of all the hero worship in the place. He knew everybody worth knowing; he never was seasick; and he never grew stout. His strength, courage, and skill did not wane as his popularity grew. Though he ventured to start a colony in America, and was even rash enough to attempt the foundation of a national theatre in his own country, he died a rich man with fair estates. Illnesses, brought on by overwork and misadventures in the course of his traveling, occurred sufficiently often to impress upon him the value of his happier hours. Litigation and the demoralizing worry of being cheated he probably brought upon himself by his unbusinesslike habits; but as these meant nothing more than a natural repugnance to treat men as knaves by tying himself and them down with stamp and signature in the strong bonds of the law (which is the essence of businesslikeness), perhaps he gained as much as he lost even on this point. For, gold magnet as he was, even he found men honest occasionally. On the whole, there is reason to believe that though

* Nordic hero in the Volsung saga, which Shaw had read in the William Morris—E. Magnússon translation (1870).

he suffered, like all great artists, from the hucksterdom of his environment, he yet succeeded in doing it more good than it did him harm. Genius was not in him a disease: he enjoyed robust moral as well as physical health, and, indeed, illustrated in his person the interdependence of the two.

As a violinist, he was of no school, and somewhat of Paganini's sort. His beginnings scandalized the orthodox disciples of Lafont, Rode, and Baillot; and, though he subsequently assimilated the essence of the Italian classical tradition, he became famous, not as an interpreter of the great composers, but as the utterer of a poetic inspiration which he claimed to have had direct from the mountains of Norway. He played his own music; but he had the power of making all genuinely popular music his own. Wherever he went, he found either folk songs, which he immediately regenerated for the people so that they no longer sounded hackneyed; or else, for audiences too highly civilized or sophisticated to be won over in this way, he played his own Norse music, and brought the foreigners under the spell it had laid on himself. His physical aptitude for his instrument enabled him to acquire a prodigious command of it; and in displaying his power in all its phases and in all its exuberance he did not escape the reproach of charlatanism. But he must have been far more than a charlatan to have conquered the world as he did, and to have gained the respect of so many artists who thoroughly knew the value of a player's work. His appreciation of and capacity for music of the highest class is proved by his successful devotion to the music of Mozart, which, whilst it makes extraordinary demands on an artist's sensibility, affords no cover for his shortcomings. Besides his mastery of the manipulative difficulties of violin-playing, Ole Bull knew well the shades of tone and expression of which the alternative resources of the four strings afford such

[466]

rich variety, and which only a born fiddler can exhaustively learn and use.

Mrs Sara Bull's memoir of her gifted husband is for the most part an itinerary, enlivened with anecdotes and favorable newspaper criticisms. As her personal knowledge of him dates only from the year 1868, its advantages hardly counterbalance the partiality entailed by close and affectionate relationship. In truth, the Ole Bull described in her pages is no real man, but an ideal Norse hero—a Berserk or Viking, with a dash of Orpheus and the Pied Piper—a product, not of nature, but of XIX century imaginative literature. A widow's biography of her husband has necessarily something of the defect and excess of an epitaph: it omits faults, and records common instincts as special virtues. But a widow who regards her husband as the embodiment of a poetic ideal which grew up in the course of her reading and daydreaming before she knew him must be even less than ordinarily trustworthy as a critical biographer. That Ole Bull was thus idealized by his second wife is much to his credit; but he must surely have had a failing or two. One would like to hear the devil's advocate before pronouncing a verdict.

The anecdotes concerning Ole Bull are very like the anecdotes about Paganini, Liszt, and the rest of the great *virtuosi*. It is inspiriting to learn that he did not need police protection against canine pets, though his kicking the Princess Damerond's snappish doggie into the chandelier is not so suggestive of tenderness towards animals as the mode of his touching reconciliation with the Danish poet Ohlenschläger, who narrates it as follows:—

When he at one time, on board the steamer, had caused my displeasure by a too severe criticism of the Swedes, and I had taken my seat on a bench, he came leaping towards me on his hands and feet, and barked at me like a dog. This was a no less original than amiable manner of bringing about a reconciliation.

On a Mississippi steamer he astonished a rowdy who was shocked at his unnatural objection to whisky by performing upon him the feat known to British wrestlers as "the flying mare." When the rowdy came to, he offered his bowie knife as a tribute to the strongest fiddler he had ever seen.

Fiddle fanciers will find much to interest them both in the memoir and appendix. Ole Bull was a fancier as well as a player, and, like Paganini, never used a Stradivarius, preferring the purer, if less even, tone of the masterpieces of Amati and Guarnerius. Eventually he used almost exclusively a violin by Gasparo da Salò, whom he believed to be identical with Gaspard Duiffoprugcar, a lute-maker patronized by Francis I. His instrument must therefore have been the oldest of its kind in use. His bow was a heavy one, exceeding the customary length by two inches.

A BOOK FOR ORATORS AND SINGERS

Unsigned review of Morell Mackenzie's Hygiene of the Vocal Organs. The Pall Mall Gazette, 26 July 1886

Though there must by this time be in existence almost as many handbooks for singers and speakers as a fast reader could skip through in a lifetime or so, publishers still find them safe investments. Young people who are born into that fringe of the musical and theatrical professions from which we draw our great stock of deadheads are generally much at a loss when the question of earning a living comes home to them. They find, to their surprise, that they can neither read nor write the various languages in which they have so often chattered to the musical foreigner. Their knowledge of the ways of mummers and minstrels will no more pass with managers and *impresarios* as artistic skill and culture than a sexton's opportunities of helping the beneficed clergy into their surplices would recommend him to a bishop as preacher or theologian: yet they do not recognize their unfitness for an engagement, as a sexton, to do him justice, recognizes his unfitness for ordination. Their ineptly stagey manners and appearance, like their morals, are the impress of an environment of bismuth and rouge, overcoats with Astrakhan collars, moustaches, sham concerts for the benefit of sham singers out of engagement, and an atmosphere which creates an unquenchable craving for admission without payment to all sorts of public entertainments, especially to the Opera. An engagement at £200 a night at Covent Garden usually strikes them as a peculiarly eligible means of subsistence; and their parents, eager to have a *prima donna* in the family to exploit all to themselves, encourage the project while there is a spark of life in it. Unsuspicious of their own futility, they have some distorted ideas of practice, but none of study. They are always in search of a method—especially the old Italian one of Porpora; and they will even pay cash for a handbook of singing, a set of unintelligible photographs of the larynx, or an ammoniaphone from which to suck a readymade compass of three octaves, with the usual fortune attached. They are not damped even by the reflection that if *prima donnas* could be made on these terms the supply among the Western nations would exceed the demand by several millions, and the market value of an Elsa or Valentine sink to eighteen shillings a week exclusive of expenses. Madame Patti can build castles because, besides the wages of a highly skilled workwoman, she enjoys the rent of her monopoly of a highly popular form of ability. If everyone with a musical turn could do as much as she after a course of complimentary tickets and a few whiffs from the ammoniaphone, there would be no more castles for poor Madame Patti: she would at once be reduced to the needy ranks of unskilled labor.

It may seem unjust to Dr Morell Mackenzie to harp in this place on a parasitic class to which his book is not specially addressed. But he has himself created the association by a certain facetiousness and quotativeness that would vanish from his mind in the presence of an audience upon whose scientific and artistic culture he could rely. There is hardly a chapter in which he does not seem to be making allowances, with goodhumored contempt, for the untrained reason of vulgar readers in one sentence, and in the next writing down to their level with a sort of jocoseness permissible at a musical at-home, but decidedly not good enough for a carefully weighed treatise. It is ill to be dull even when correct; excellent to be lively, witty, and vernacular as well as correct; but intolerable to be chatty and trivial in manner merely to reconcile slovenly people to the correctness and authority of your matter. Dr Morell Mackenzie's backsliding in this direction would not be worth insisting on but for the importance of his book, which is the most interesting English record of laryngoscopic investigation since Madame Seiler's.* He recognizes two vocal registers, which he calls long reed and short reed respectively, asserting that in chest voice "the pitch is raised by means of increasing tension and lengthening of the cords," whilst in head voice the same result is brought about "by gradual shortening of the vibrating reed." He does not regard the closure of the

* Emma Seiler's Altes und neues über die Ausbildung des Gesangorganes ... (Leipzig, 1861), was translated as The Voice in Singing (Philadelphia, 1868).

cartilaginous ends of the cords as a change of register, because the reed still lengthens as the pitch rises. It is when "stop closure" of the ligamentous glottis takes place, and the reed begins to shorten with the ascent of the voice, that he admits a change of register. He has discovered eminent singers, tenor and soprano, singing throughout the whole compass in the long reed register, although the quality of tone seemed unmistakably that proper to the short reed, the laryngoscope thus ruthlessly discrediting judgment by ear. His table of fifty voices examined by him is full of curious points; and his remarks on the difficulty of learning to manipulate the laryngoscope and read the image aright, carrying all the authority of his exceptionally extensive practice with the apparatus, are very suggestive as to the contradictory observations of previous investigators. His general hints to singers and speakers are practicable: he does not irritate the reader by prescribing habits, clothes, diet, and hours that would cut an artist off from human society under existing arrangements. There is the inevitable warning against tight lacing, high heels, open mouths, sudden changes of temperature, and excesses of all kinds, which will probably prove just as effectual as previous admonitions to the same effect. With respect to what is called the "breaking" of the voice in adolescence, he points out that only about seventeen per cent. of boys' voices actually crack; and he declares his ignorance of any reason for disusing the voice during the change that would not justify disuse of the limbs during the growth of the long bones of one's skeleton.

Dr Mackenzie is perhaps the great living authority on such matters, and, notwithstanding the defects of style which we have pointed out, this volume deserves to be widely read, as a most authoritative treatise on a subject in which we are all of us interested.

ADVICE ON PIANOFORTE PLAYING

Unsigned review of A. Christiani's Principles of
Expression in Pianoforte Playing. The Pall Mall
Gazette, 31 July 1886

[U] Professor A. Christiani of New York has, in a
copiously illustrated 300 page quarto, formulated what
he has to teach on the subject of pianoforte playing.
When a musician is intelligent enough to feel the need
of arranging his knowledge, he is commonly astonished
at the ease with which he can introduce order into chaos
by adopting a few rough categories. Unsuspected
analogies and logical links come to light at every step of
his work. No one having suggested them to him he is apt
to conclude that they have never occurred to anybody
before. Hence it is rare to meet with a handbook by a
trainer of artists without an exordium in which the
writer's crude stumblings on the metaphysics and
psychology of his subject are announced in good faith as
epoch-making developments of speculation and
research.

Mr Christiani has not quite escaped this pitfall; but
the practical part of his book is none the worse in
consequence. His protest against Schumann's perplex-
ing trick of writing whole movements with the bar
divisions and time signature proper to some quite
different rhythm is likely to raise some controversy
among those who persist in believing—as Schumann
presumably did—that a commonplace theme will sound
odd to the audience because its notation looks odd to the
player. The point can be tested experimentally by
playing from Schumann's notation and Mr Christiani's
alteration of it successively, and challenging the hearer
to distinguish them by the effect on the ear alone. In

dealing with phrasing, accent, pauses, and retardations of speed, Mr Christiani indicates very clearly the artistic treatment which he approves of. Of the merits of his favorite style the reader must judge for himself. *De gustibus non est disputandum.* [U]

A VOLUME ON VOICE TRAINING

Unsigned review of J. P. Sandlands' How to Develop General Vocal Power. The Pall Mall Gazette, 12 November 1886

[U] Of this little "Book for Everybody" the author hopefully says "It will be useful to the general public. It will serve to brighten and sharpen articulation, and render conversation more intelligible." And no doubt it will, if its precepts be discreetly followed; for it is not a bad book of its kind, in spite of such funny sentences as "The word horse calls up into the presence-chamber of the mind a certain animal with four legs and without feathers"; or "The student may think out for himself the color he would like to give to the several phrases in Ex. 6. There is no better practice than applying the color of anger"—a recommendation which suggests that at Brigstock, of which Mr Sandlands is vicar, the parishioners are accustomed to energetic and even comminatory sermons. In the same vein are many misleading exhortations to "tease it out," to "strive after power," and the like. The singers and speakers who "strive after power" are those who never get it. They do, as Talma said, "*ce que font tous les jeunes acteurs.*"* One is afraid to

* François-Joseph Talma (1763–1826) was a celebrated French tragedian of the Théâtre Français. Charles Mathews (who died in 1878), John Hare, George Grossmith, W. S. Penley, George Giddens, and George Barrett, who are mentioned in the following paragraph, were popular English actors.

think of what the Rev. Mr Sandlands would say to Talma's calm estimate of "at least twenty years" as the necessary apprenticeship for a man who would move assemblies.

Another of the vicar's questionable bits of advice is to read at the pitch of "F in the bass," and to persevere at it in spite of difficulty. This is, in another form, the old pet precept of second rate teachers to "get it from the chest." What would Charles Mathews, whose voice never aged, and who gave the widest of berths to F in the bass, have said to it? And what would our curates, with their "clergyman's sore throat," brought on by persisting in what Artemus Ward called "a sollum vois," say to it? "F" Mr Sandlands assures us "is the foundation tone; and the student must get it. It is as necessary for good speaking as a good foundation is for a building that is meant to be permanent." This means simply that Mr Sandlands has a bass voice; that its normal pitch in speaking is F; and that he therefore concludes that all other men have bass voices with the same normal pitch, or, if they have not, that they ought to be made have them. Imagine the effect of a sepulchral course of lessons in the key of F on Mr Hare, Mr Grossmith, Mr Penley, Mr Giddens, Mr George Barrett, or Signor Salvini! These so-called "foundation tones" vary with each individual: Delsarte's* favorite one was B flat, which was at least less likely to be generally mischievous than F. Then, as to speaking with gutta-percha balls in the mouth (a practice not unknown among schoolboys), we are told that Demosthenes used pebbles; so doubtless there is something to be gained by the exercise, though it is hard to see exactly what.

* François Delsarte was the French inventor of a system of vocal and physical calisthenics, designed to develop co-ordination, strength, and grace.

The stress laid by Mr Sandlands upon the importance of seeing in the mind's eye what one speaks about shews that he possesses the faculty which Mr Galton[*] has named "visualization," and that he supposes every one else to possess it too, which is by no means the case. Besides, speakers are not always engaged in describing material objects. So much for Mr Sandlands' errors, which are those of robust innocence and impatience rather than of pretence and quackery—the usual failings of the voice-trainer. As a set-off against them may be taken his ingenious and useful exercises, of which two specimens may be quoted: "The soldiers steer the boat. The soldier's tear fell on the page." Here the point is of course not the sensibility of the literary soldier, but the difficulty of differentiating "soldiers steer" from "soldier's tear." Again, "Violins and violoncellos vigorously vamped with very versatile voices vociferating various strains very vehemently vexes Valentine's violent valet" is good practice. So is "The zealot Zephaniah rode a zebra zigzag up Zeboim." On the other hand, it is nothing short of a duty to protest against the student saying in "full voice"—or, indeed, in any voice whatever:

Not a drum was heard, not a funereal note.

An excellent feature in the book is the condemnation of the rule that, if the consonants are watched, the vowels will take care of themselves. An Englishman who can pronounce *do, re, mi, fa* decently is a *rara avis*.[U]

[*] (Sir) Francis Galton was an English scientist, with whose work Inquiries into Human Faculty ... (1883) Shaw was familiar.

MUSIC IN 1886

Unsigned note in The Pall Mall Gazette, 3 January 1887

[U] In music the market was brisk, but the wares stale. Liszt, after many years' absence, visited us, and, though he would not give a recital in public, was the cause of an epidemic of pianomania, by which Rubinstein greatly profited. This chance of seeing Liszt proved our last: he died between the summer and autumn. Mr Carl Rosa, after a brief season, during which he produced a new opera by Mr A. C. Mackenzie, abandoned the London lyric stage to various unfortunate experimenters on the corpse of fashionable opera, the first of whom did not succeed even in making the ghost walk. The continued success of The Mikado left Sir Arthur Sullivan free to attend to his Golden Legend, which found everybody determined to believe that the popular composer of Patience had only to set himself seriously at it to produce as solid stuff as Beethoven or Handel. The Golden Legend was successful; but Sir Arthur's previous reputation as a composer was confirmed rather than extended by it. A performance of Bach's Mass in B minor, under his direction, by the Leeds choir, with the genuine trumpets and the *oboi d'amore* restored, dwarfed all subsequent festival events, although these included new works by Dvořák, Mr Mackenzie, Mr Villiers Stanford, and others. Besides the usual symphony concerts, a new series has been attempted by Herr Henschel; and there is no doubt that his enterprise, if adequately and judiciously prosecuted, must succeed, as the dearth of opportunities for hearing orchestral music at a reasonable cost in London has been a disgrace to our metropolitan culture. Among the losses which the musical profession sustained in the course of the year, even that of Liszt startled the public less than the sudden death of Joseph Maas, the popular tenor. The obituary contains also the names of two tenors whom many must have believed long since dead—Tichatschek and Templeton.[U]

SOMETHING LIKE A HISTORY
OF MUSIC

Unsigned review of J. F. Rowbotham's A History of Music, Vols. I and II. The Pall Mall Gazette, 11 January 1887

[U] Has the reader ever wiled away a few hours with a popular history of music—one of those innocent compilations which rattle one along from Tubal Cain's time to yesterday, when poetry and music, having coyly approached oneanother in Beethoven's Choral Symphony, at last rapturously embraced in Tristan und Isolde, or, if you prefer a more whistlable instance, Trial by Jury? How learned we used to think the historian when he told us of how Hucbald discovered the delightful art of writing in consecutive fifths, often since independently struck out by amateur composers who never heard of Hucbald! What a capital story that was about Porpora keeping Caffarelli at a single sheet of exercises for six years, and then, when the pupil, as pupils will, ventured to ask for a song, saying to him "Go, young man: you are now the greatest singer in the world"! What desperate hashes of biography, anecdote, and criticism answered for the history of modern music from Bach to Goetz! How the dark ages of the art were stumbled through on outrageous assumptions that there could not possibly have been more music then in the

[477]

world than in the surviving treatises of the pedants! How ignominiously the Greeks were dismissed with the remark that they knew nothing of harmony! and oh, how all the newest composers used to catch it at the end! These books made, and still make, merry times for students who are not too desirous to learn anything important, as well as for the cultured art worshippers who feel extremely musical when reading about the great composers, and extremely sleepy while listening to great compositions.

Mr Rowbotham's history is of a different sort. It will be to English what Ambros's Geschichte der Musik is to German, and Gevaert's Histoire et Théorie de la Musique de l'Antiquité to French readers. Mr Rowbotham goes beyond these authors in claiming that it is possible, "by a certain divine intuition, to penetrate the secrets of ancient nations, which else must have remained unknown to us." Whether his intuitive account of the birth and growth of music is true history will not be easily settled. It is a work of the reconstructive imagination; and all that can be confidently said is that it is plausible, fascinating, and supported with remarkable ingenuity, learning, and research, taking us back into ages which have left no records, and tracing the development of prehistoric music through a drum stage, a pipe stage, and a lyre stage, "which" says Mr Rowbotham "are, it seems to me, to the musician what the Theological, Metaphysical, and Positive stages are to the Comtist, or the Stone, Bronze, and Iron ages to the archeologist." Now, the reconstructive imagination, indispensable as it is to the historian, is apt to get itself out of dark places by the help of pure invention. Hence the extraordinary boldness with which Mr Rowbotham exercises it is anything but reassuring. He gives nearly all his conjectures as authentic history, and offers his descriptions with the confidence of an eye-witness. He criticizes the orchestras of the builders of the Pyramids as confidently as the musical critic of this journal criticizes the last Saturday afternoon performance at the Crystal Palace. He helps us to a knowledge of the Greek theatre by the methods of the descriptive reporter and interviewer, and tells us about Sappho just as Mr William Archer tells us about Mrs Kendal.* Yet it is hard to catch him speaking without warrant. Every detail is an inference, sometimes far fetched, but always conceivably right, from some hieroglyph or old instrument, or traveler's tale, or poem, or passage from ancient literature or extant document of one kind or another.

There is less room for doubt in the analytic part of Mr Rowbotham's work. His discovery of fugue subjects and answers in Pindar may seem supersubtle; but the lines at least can be referred to for confirmation, although unhappily the Greeks had no phonograph to transmit Pindar's delivery to us on a tinfoil cylinder. Nevertheless, Mr Rowbotham is quite satisfied that he knows how Pindar pronounced and scanned. He gives "analytic programs" of the Odes, and restores the lyre accompaniments according to rule. He finds in the strophe, antistrophe, and epode of Stesichorus† the three divisions of the modern sonata movement: the strophe corresponding to the themes, the epode to the free fantasia, and the antistrophe to the repetition of the themes. He attributes the fact that Haydn, whom we fondly call the father of the sonata, put the epode between the strophe and antistrophe instead of after them, to the divorce of music from dancing. His account

* Margaret Kendal, reigning star of the St James's Theatre, of which her husband and John Hare were at this time managers.

† Pindar (522?–443 B.C.) and Stesichorus (632–533 B.C.) were Greek lyric poets, the latter a contemporary of Sappho.

of the evolution of rhythm, and of how poetry was danced into lines and melody into strains, is interesting, and fairly conclusive; and his view of the growth of the scale, though there is a missing link or two in the argument, is likely to serve us until some future writer improves on it. Comic songsters will be glad to learn that mankind has always sung in the key of G; but we are told nothing as to the pitch of this G.

Mr Rowbotham's style is one that challenges special attention. In the second volume, which is entirely devoted to Greek music, he becomes saturated with Hellenism, and not only begins all his sentences with "And," as Edgar Poe did in his more affectedly written tales, but actually ventures on such constructions as "a voluntary omission for the purpose of producing a pleasing effect on the ear, which how it did so we cannot now judge." This sort of English is pardonable in a Greek or in Mrs Gamp,* but not in an historian whose native tongue is English. The effect of the "which" is only laughable; but the superfluous "ands" are more serious: they disturb, irritate, and finally infuriate the reader. On the characteristically rare occasions when an opinion is advanced doubtfully, Mr Rowbotham's form is "the present writer seems to think," or "I seem to imagine." In point of grammar, the following sentence leaves something to be desired: "And how does Pindar play with it, and makes offers at it, as in the second line of the strophe!" The use of "bid" and "forbid" for "bade" and "forbade," is not even good Greek. However, as Mr Rowbotham says, "to mince with exceptions is to miss the joy of generalization"; and it is joyfully and generally true that he writes well, even when he writes not quite soberly. Fine writing indeed he frankly goes in for; and it does not misbecome him as it would a less imaginative

* Character in Dickens's Martin Chuzzlewit.

[480]

author. When he follows music into the domain of morals he begins to deal in epigram, telling us that "credulity is the flower of love, but scepticism is the offspring of hate," and that "imitation is a distrust of oneself, and a desire to be like other people. And it is Hesitation incarnate, and Cowardice transfigured."

The third volume of the history is as yet only promised. When it comes, readers of the first and second are not likely to leave it uncut.[U]

FROM MOZART TO MARIO

Unsigned review of Louis Engel's From Mozart to Mario. The Pall Mall Gazette, 2 February 1887

[U] Readers of The World will pounce avidly on these two volumes, in which their musical guide, philosopher, and friend, the unique "L. E.," gives them his Reminiscences of Half a Century, comprised, with characteristic indifference to ordinary computation, between the years 1756 and 1886. Dr Engel is really an extraordinary man. His rapid surveys of the composer of any age leave an impression that there is not a composer of eminence among his contemporaries who has not confessed his influence; nor a European potentate who has not buttonholed him for half an hour's pleasant chat and wise counsel. Popes and cardinals have conferred with him at the Vatican; and he has been a spiritual father—sometimes "worse than two fathers," as the American humorist puts it*—to all the queens of song in Christendom. The extent of his stock of secondhand

---

* Artemus Ward in London, Part II, in Charles Farrar Browne, Complete Works (1871).

epigrams (all the good ones are secondhand by this time) is only less remarkable than the capriciousness with which he ascribes them to the first historical or unhistorical personage who happens to occur to him as his pen runs on. Appreciating the ways of professional musicians as one who has worked and played with them without catching their illusions or losing touch with the unprofessional and unmusical world, he has learned to temper his partialities with a cynicism which is far more effective in the orbit of Mr Yates's journal* than a comprehensive philosophy could be. For he has partialities, and strong ones.

He is a partisan of Madame Patti against Madame Nilsson; of Meyerbeer against Wagner; and of Rossini against the verdict of posterity: always writing hard at the Opposition save when, in short-lived moments of patriarchal calm, he rises above mundane strife, and, Jacob-like, gives to Tweedledee all that is left after the blessing previously accorded to Tweedledum. In explaining the intentions of a composer, he fortifies himself impregnably by the *ipse dixit* of the Master, just as Dr Furnivall,† by a simple citation of what Mr Browning told him, or what Shelley told his father, dumbfounders all rival commentators on these poets. Popular ignorance of the subject which he treats places the public at his mercy. In a land where the majority of educated ladies and gentlemen will tell you with half-concealed pride that they dont know one note from another—where they are awed by such mystic words as "subdominant" and "diminished seventh," as Whitefield's disciple was awed

* Edmund Yates was founder and editor of the weekly journal The World.

† Frederick J. Furnivall, English philologist and editor, founded the Chaucer, New Shakespere, Browning, and Shelley societies.

by "Mesopotamia,"* a man as accomplished as Dr Engel is more than a critic: he is an oracle.

The book now in hand is introduced in a preface as "a child sent forth with its father's best wishes." Says "L. E." modestly "Maybe its babbling will amuse; it has learned, if that be any recommendation, to speak the truth." Unfortunately for this position, the truth, in criticism, is a matter of opinion; and the child's opinions, like those of other clever children, are old-fashioned. A nurseling that has nothing better to tell us about Wagner at this time of day than that he "wrote music without melody"; wickedly drank his coffee from a golden cup; and shewed the "blackest ingratitude to Meyerbeer," should be sent to bed until it submits to acknowledge its past errors. Yet its little heart is in the right place, for it assures us that "there is no mother who would not willingly give her all for her child, be she high or low born, from the lamented Princess Alice down to the poorest woman." A beautiful doctrine; but one has to be a child indeed to believe it and deliberately set it down nowadays. Very babyish, too, is the long inventory of Madame Patti's jewelry, and the apparent confusion of her wreaths, her rings, her bracelets, her hairpins, her fans, and her combs with her vocal and artistic accomplishments. The innocence of childhood peeps out funnily in the statement that Madame Nilsson "was born a little tow-headed girl." Among ineptitudes of another sort is a translation of *glissando* as a "sliding scale"; but one has to be both pianist and trade-unionist

* George Whitefield (1714–70) was an English religious leader, associated with Wesley, who became famed as an evangelist. W. E. H. Lecky, in his England in the Eighteenth Century (1878–90), notes: "[David] Garrick is reported to have said, with a pardonable exaggeration, that Whitefield could pronounce the word Mesopotamia in such a way as to move an audience to tears."

to catch the full flavor of its exquisite absurdity. A more commonplace blunder is the Englishing of "la propriété" as "possession," of course with reference to poor Proudhon, who no more "went so far as to say that possession is theft" than any Briton goes so far as to speak of his hat or stick as his estate. Even when on its own ground as a musical prodigy, the child makes a slip or two. When it declares that in the Nibelungen Ring the singers "have intervals to sing which it does not matter a bit whether they sing as they are written or not, for false they are at any rate," it is either talking nonsense or playing—not elegantly—upon words. To say that "just as Beethoven created the power of the orchestra in the concert room, so Meyerbeer established it in the theatre," is to ignore Mozart and Weber. Even from the point of view of the mid-century Parisian, which "L. E." has never quite forgotten, it ignores Gluck.

Of Dr Engel's two volumes generally, it need only be said that they have the merits and defects of the weekly articles which have made him known as a writer. Quaintly written, chatty, discursive, first-personal, and occasionally also pointedly third-personal, they are the fruit of native shrewdness, long intercourse with musicians, and desultory reading. Favorites are idolized, foes unsparingly pilloried, friends and heros unconsciously belittled as they appear reflected in the mind of the musical man about town, which is the character frankly adopted by Dr Engel for his purpose. The book is not, on the whole, edifying; but it is amusing, and contains scraps of information which musical biographers will find worth referring to.[U]

FIRST NIGHTS AT SECOND HAND

*Unsigned review of H. Sutherland Edwards's Famous
First Representations. The Pall Mall Gazette, 28
February 1887*

[U] Mr Sutherland Edwards is, better than most men,
in a position to make a considerable contribution to the
history of the stage during as much of the latter half of
the present century as any one is yet in a position to
speak of with confidence. His experience as a "first
nighter" has been great. He was not an absolute novice
when he produced his History of the Opera in 1862; and
since then there have been many "famous first representations." With some of these, notably the popular
successes of Verdi, Gounod, Bizet, and Thomas, he has
already dealt. But there remained the production of the
Niblung's Ring and Parsifal, at Bayreuth; Goetz's
Taming of the Shrew; the commotion about Wagner
when Lohengrin was produced in London, and popularly supposed to be an audacious novelty (it was
twentyeight years old in 1875); the earlier attempt (1870)
with The Flying Dutchman at Drury Lane, when
Madame Ilma di Murska and Mr Santley sang in it, and
its great popular success in English at the Lyceum six
years afterwards; the second night of the Poet Laureate's
Promise of May at the Globe, with the famous oration
of the Marquess of Queensberry;* the production of

* Tennyson's village tragedy The Promise of May has, as its
central character, a gentleman who is a selfish intellectual,
bereft of moral sense or religious conviction. On the second
night, 13 November 1882, the Marquess of Queensberry had
arisen from the audience and, "in the name of Free Thought,"
harangued against "Mr Tennyson's abominable caricature."

The Cup by Mr Irving; the appearance of the Saxe-Meiningen Court Company at Drury Lane; the first night of Signor Salvini's Othello; Messrs Booth and Irving in the same play;* and the birth of Gilbert-Sullivan comic opera on the first night of Trial by Jury.

All or most of these Mr Sutherland Edwards could probably have chronicled with the authority of an eyewitness. Instead, he has given us descriptions of fifteen performances, nearly all of which took place before his own first night in his cradle. The result is a book which had better be avoided by those who are tired of Mr Samuel Pepys's adventures with Nell Gwynne; who have already learned that The Beggar's Opera made Gay rich and Rich gay;† who are satisfied that Handel's Messiah was first performed in Fishamble-street, Dublin; who have read Otto Jahn's Life of Mozart; and who know all about Hernani, Théophile Gautier's red waistcoat, and Mlle Mars's not wholly unreasonable objection to call her stage lover "her lion."‡ Of course there are growing millions who have yet to learn these things, and to such Mr Sutherland Edwards may be recommended for his light and unaffected style, his inexhaustible stock of more or less stale titbits for use as padding when he is gravelled for lack of matter, and his

* Henry Irving played Iago to Edwin Booth's Othello at the Lyceum Theatre on 2 May 1881; on 9 May they reversed the rôles. Ellen Terry was the Desdemona and William Terriss the Cassio in this celebrated production.

† John Rich (1692–1761) made so much money from John Gay's The Beggar's Opera (1728), which he produced at his Lincoln's Inn Fields theatre for a run of two seasons, that he was able to build a new theatre in Covent Garden with the profits.

‡ Mlle Mars [Anne Boutet] (1779–1847) was a renowned French comedienne of the Théâtre Français.

sense of the vanity of all criticism that requires mental effort to follow.

As a musical critic he is conservative in principle, Italian and frivolous in taste. He began well as a faithful admirer of Mozart; but then the composer of Don Giovanni and Die Zauberflöte was a man of great range: you may delight in him for a knack that he shared with Offenbach, or admire him reverently for qualities that class him with Molière and Goethe, Praxiteles and Raphael. Not that Mr Sutherland Edwards is deaf to all the notes in Mozart's compass except those within the Offenbach register. Though we may suspect at times that Il Barbiere is his favorite opera, we cannot suppose that he considers it as great a work as Le Nozze di Figaro, or, to put it generally, that he stops short of perceiving that Mozart's capacity at least exceeded that of Rossini, Donizetti, or Signor Verdi. But this is almost as mild a critical achievement as the discovery that Mr Swinburne is not, on the whole, so great as Shakespear, or that Miss Braddon's novels* are of cheaper quality than Scott's. The two really crucial tests which the musical experts of this century have undergone have been the successive developments of the art by Beethoven and Wagner. Mr Sutherland Edwards escaped the first; for by the time he took up the pen it was obvious to much less keen intellects than his that it was all up with the old estimate of Beethoven as an obstreperous madman who had attempted to conceal lack of melody by excess of discord. But the fashion of abusing Wagner on exactly the same grounds and in practically identical terms had just set in; and Mr Sutherland Edwards's great chance as a critic was that

* Mary Elizabeth Braddon was the author of some eighty novels, the best known of which was Lady Audley's Secret (1862).

of being beforehand with us in appreciating "the music of the future." The question for him and his generation was not of the relation of Il Barbiere to Le Nozze, but of Die Meistersinger to Il Barbiere. It was a severe but not unfair examination test; and Mr Sutherland Edwards was plucked in the good company of Hector Berlioz and others who should have known better. His utmost concession was a relenting towards Meyerbeer, of whose works he has given some appreciative descriptions, which are very different in tone from his earlier allusions to that unaccountably striking composer. Now, to praise Meyerbeer is, in a manner, to affront Wagner, who hated the musical ways of the curiously gifted Jew. Mr Sutherland Edwards would not have Wagner at any price; and the honesty of his opinion is proved by the courage with which he sticks to it now that he no longer has even the largest mob on his side.[U]

MR MAPLESON'S EXPERIMENT

Unsigned note in The Pall Mall Gazette, 14 March 1887

[U] On Saturday, Mr Mapleson began his Covent Garden experiment in Italian opera at ordinary prices. Result: a house packed from floor to ceiling, though the ceiling was probably more remunerative than the floor. The announcements had not been very inviting: the cast [of La Traviata] included only one artist concerning whom any illusions were possible; and she—Mlle Lilian Nordica—was said to have failed elsewhere. Happily it very soon became apparent that if Miss Norton (English for Nordica) ever really did fail anywhere, it was not through incompetence. She is competence itself, with a brisk attack, bright style, good method, and admirable control over the middle of her voice, which is unforced and sound all over except for a trace of *tremolo* in the lowest register. She takes her high notes easily and in tune; her execution is accurate and brilliant in florid passages; and her *cantabile* singing is pure and pleasant. She is not an artist of the very first class; for her manner lacks exceptional distinction and grace; and her acting is the conventional opera house gesticulation which we for some reason tolerate at Covent Garden, though we should certainly think the St James's company stark mad if they indulged in it. But she is far better than any experienced opera-goer had dared to expect; and if her colleagues were equally accomplished, the success of Mr Mapleson's venture would be assured.

Signor Runcio was promised as Alfredo; but he did not appear. His place was taken by Signor Ria, an Italian artist who has been heard at concerts and at some minor operatic performances in London during the years of his residence here. In making some rather disastrous experiments with an unmanageable *mezza voce* in the first act, he incurred the lasting displeasure of the less considerate members of the audience, and so he can hardly be said to have proved equal to the occasion; but by dint of omitting every bar of his own part that was not indispensable to the others, he succeeded in averting a change of program. Curtailment, it may be added, was the order of the night. Signor del Puente played Germont. His voice was as usual, loose, loud, unsteady, monotonous, and incapable of blending with Miss Norton's well formed tone in *Dite alle giovine*. Still, he was heard well throughout the house, bearing himself, like one used to the footlights, with much self-possession and self-satisfaction; and the audience were satisfied with him. Signor Ciampi, as the Baron, comported himself with the extreme gravity of a buffo resolved to do justice to a serious part. Madame Lablache appeared as Flora Bervoix.

The performance was not the scratch one it unfortunately might have been without surprising any one. A good deal was left out; but what was retained had evidently been fairly rehearsed, and went steadily, though Signor Ria was naturally at a loss once or twice. Signor Logheder, the conductor, handled Verdi's music with spirit and sympathy; and his "big guitar," sixty strong, strummed the accompaniments with promptitude and despatch, if without the precision and refinement they had in Costa's time, or the feeling, power, and delicacy that Richter could extort from them. The chorus were in uproarious strength and spirits at their new engagement. The costumes illustrated various periods of history: the ladies clinging to the XIX century; and the gentlemen ranging from Louis Quatorze to the Renascence. The stage arrangements were those to which we have grown accustomed: poor Violetta living and dying in prodigious apartments like the public rooms at the Freemasons' Tavern or Willis's, and entertaining such troops of choral friends as no private income could provide refreshment for.

The old strains were welcome for the sake of old times. *Libiamo; Parigi, o cara; Sempre libera*; and the rest are never quite indifferent to those who are, operatically speaking, old fogies. But, reflecting calmly and sanely on the manifold absurdities of the entertainment in its Covent Garden shape, one cannot help wondering what the beginners think of it.[U]

MAX BRUCH'S CONCERTO

Unsigned note in The Pall Mall Gazette, 21 March 1887

[U] In spite of the biting weather, the concert room at the Crystal Palace was full on Saturday afternoon when Dr Joachim played Max Bruch's Concerto in G minor and the Trillo del Diavolo.* The attraction was in the violinist, certainly not in the program. There was just one great composition: the overture to Don Giovanni, now exactly a hundred years old and still able to make three or four ambitious orchestral works of yesterday seem stale, vulgar, and tedious by comparison. Max Bruch's concerto can hardly ever have sounded more hopelessly third-class, notwithstanding the dignity given to the slow movement by Dr Joachim's very finest tone. C. M. Widor's Symphony in A was performed for the first time in England, and very possibly for the last. Berlioz himself, in his uninspired moments, could not have been more elaborately and intelligently dull, and the dulness is only relieved by the recurrence of phrases beginning with an exasperating octave skip, which reminds the adept musician of innumerable bad *fugatos*, and the initiated of a plague of grasshoppers. Smetana's Lustspiel Overture is ingenious and jolly; Mr Henry Gadsby's Forest of Arden is sentimentally pretty and mechanically bucolic by turns. On the whole, it was a case of Mozart first, Mendelssohn and Tartini second, Smetana fifteenth (say), and the rest nowhere. Miss Adelaide Mullen, who introduced Mendelssohn, was the vocalist. She knows how to produce her voice safely and well; and further cultivation of her somewhat

* Giuseppe Tartini's Sonata in g for Violin.

indifferent skill in pronunciation and phrasing will make a very satisfactory artist of her.[U]

TWO BOOKS FOR MUSICAL PEOPLE

Unsigned review of W. Beatty-Kingston's Music and Manners and C. Hubert H. Parry's Studies of Great Composers. The Pall Mall Gazette, 13 April 1887

[U] Mr Beatty-Kingston, though he lacks that perfection of ignorance which enables many of our novelists to impart unearthly vocal accomplishments to their heros and heroines, is yet not too deep in music to gossip with people who like to sport on the surface. He knows a good deal about executants, composers, and compositions; and he spreads out his information before you without insisting on co-ordinating it into some brain-breaking synthesis of *Tonempfindung*; just as he knows much of men and affairs, but is happily free from theories of human nature or politics. He admires music of all sorts, and instead of rancorously insisting on proving that the composers whose music does not happen to please him are so many incarnate principles of social decay, he saves his temper for judicious expenditure on ill-ventilated opera houses with uncomfortable stalls. His estimate of Gounod's Faust as "the noblest opera of modern times" may be a weakness; but it is an amiable and a popular one; and, after all, he does not make any pretence of being ready to go to the stake for it: perhaps he would say as much another evening for Tristan or Traviata. A writer who describes an ellipse as "an oblong circle" must not be taken *au pied de la lettre.* On the whole, the musical public will find that Mr Beatty-Kingston, as a pleasant gossip, nobly upholds the reputation of the Imperial Order of the Medjidieh, the Royal Orders of the Redeemer, Star of Roumania, Crown of Roumania and Takovia of Servia, the Imperial Order of Francis Joseph, and of the I.R. Austrian Order of Merit of the First Class, &c., with all of which he has, as we gather from the title page, been variegated.

The decorators have not gone to work in this hearty fashion on Mr C. Hubert H. Parry, who is only a doctor of music. He has composed sonatas, string trios, and a setting of Shelley's Prometheus Unbound; and as he is nevertheless evidently not in want of food and leisure, it may safely be inferred that he is a gentleman of independent means; for to the unpropertied musician who would express himself in the classic forms nowadays, society offers its pet incentive to honorable industry— certain ruin. Mr Parry is a thoughtful writer, not pretentious, heavy, nor given to unprovoked metaphysics, but a library friend for all those to whom music is something more than a mere peptic to help away the dulness of after-dinner. Many a Philistine would be surprised, if not disgusted, at the number of perfectly serious people who owe all the happy and wholesome part of their experience to music. To these music does not mean the sum of the public performances they have witnessed. In the concert room and salon there are amateurs; there is the woeful fact that no earthly music is ever perfectly in tune; there is bad ventilation, fatigue, an unmusical neighbor in the throes of boredom, an uninteresting number in the program, and a dozen other flies in the ointment. It is when, tired of work and of the world, the musician gets to his own pianoforte, that he has hours which all the desperate execrations of the people in the next house cannot interrupt or embitter. Less serenely lofty, but perhaps more agreeable to the other citizens, are the musical reveries into which the amateur falls when walking on his business through the town. His music then disturbs no one; and his involuntary gestures are rather attractive than otherwise to observant street boys.

One cannot help liking those modern enthusiasts in whom no doubt has ever arisen that music gained by the turn given to it by Beethoven, the first great composer who deliberately introduced the baser elements of popularity into the symphony. To Mr Parry, at least, it has never occurred that Haydn, shaking his head over Beethoven's early work, may have done so with prescience of the obscene musical orgies which are familiar to us, and which affect even their professed admirers exactly as brandy affects intemperate people. Beethoven was riotous because he liked excitement, and never could see why he should not indulge his humor. The experiment succeeded because the public liked excitement too; and consequently many pages of demoralizing mænad music, fruit of the misdirected ambition and aborted genius of Berlioz, Raff, Liszt, and others of less note, are now figuring at their true level as plagiarisms in the scores of our comic operas. Wagner, who has been blamed for much of this, really rescued music from it. It is true that the Tannhäuser ballet music is a flagrant example of it; but then the Tannhäuser ballet music was an abomination expressly put forth as such—as a thing intolerable for any length of time by any man with a possibility of salvation left in him.

However, Mr Parry was right not to mar his study of Beethoven by cavilling at the faults of his hero's qualities. Of his chapters on Bach and Wagner, it is high praise to say that they are adequate, whilst those on Weber and Mendelssohn are written with fine tact and just appreciation. The Schubert article is one of the best of its kind that has been written. Mr Parry writes kindly and generously, even of Haydn and Mozart—no favorites with his school; and one cannot doubt that he is quite sincere when he writes that Mozart was indifferent to the quality of the librettos he set, mad as that statement appears to any one who has more than a superficial acquaintance with Mozart's operas. There is only one merely conventional remark in the book. It is to the effect that all Berlioz's orchestral effects were sure to sound as he intended. No one can possibly tell whether they did or not; and it is certain that many of them sound very differently at different performances. But this little carelessness is a very small blemish on a very pleasant book.[U]

BEETHOVEN WELL-RUBBED-IN

Unsigned note in The Pall Mall Gazette, 22 April 1887

[U] On one spring day in every year musical people go down to the Crystal Palace to have Beethoven well rubbed into them by Mr August Manns. Thus, this year, the Leonore overture (No. 3), the Choral Fantasia, Adelaide, and the Choral Symphony followed hard upon oneanother between three and five o'clock, for the entertainment of a devoted but only moderately numerous audience. The pianist was Herr Kwast, a sufficiently ambidextrous and self-possessed gentleman, but not as yet a very impressive or deepsighted interpreter of Beethoven. A brief and by no means inspiriting struggle with Adelaide alone separated the Fantasia from the Symphony, which might have been better handled. The *scherzo*, and indeed all the portions of the work which depend on rhythm rather than on melody, were played with faultless precision; but the slow movement was less satisfactory, with the *adagio* too fast, the *andante* too slow, the florid developments of the melody played thoughtlessly as mere accompaniment or embroidery, and the pitch of the wood wind disturbed

throughout by a flat clarinet. Too fast and too slow are
matters of opinion; true intonation, even from a clarinet,
is not.[U]

WAGNER ON ORCHESTRAL
CONDUCTING

*Unsigned review of Richard Wagner's On Conducting,
translated by Edward Dannreuther. The Pall Mall
Gazette, 28 May 1887*

When this little work was published at Leipzig in 1869,
it was not worth any publisher's while to have it
translated into English. To the few who had then heard
of him here, Wagner was known as a pretentious and
quarrelsome person who persisted, on principle, in
writing ugly music in spite of repeated failure, and who
had been dropped by the Philharmonic Society (admittedly the greatest authority on music in the world) after
a couple of trials as conductor. Times have changed now
with a vengeance. No other music than his can be
depended on to draw large audiences to orchestral
concerts; the intensity of Beethoven's popularity is
waning as that of the newer tone-poet's waxes; and
selections and arrangements from his operas take
precedence of symphonies and concertos in programs
that are nothing if not classical. And this concise treatise
of his on orchestral conducting will be sought for today
as a monograph, unique of its kind, by the greatest
composer, conductor, and critic of our own time.

It is perhaps as well to explain that Ueber das
Dirigiren is not an academic textbook of time-beating.
It does not offer diagrams supposed to be traced by a
bâton indicating four in a bar, six in a bar, &c.; nor
advice as to how to manage the three simultaneous

dances in Don Giovanni. Nor does it contain the slightest recognition of that adroitness in driving inefficient orchestras through scratch performances which many professional musicians, and even some critics, regard as the first and last qualification of a conductor. "The whole truth of the matter is" says Wagner "that in a proper performance the conductor's part is to give always the proper *tempo*." His insistence on this may do us some service; for we suffer much from conductors who can do everybody else's business in the orchestra so well—even to counting their rests for them, and shewing them how to finger difficult passages—that no one dares to hint that their own special function of choosing the proper *tempo* is never successfully discharged when really great work is in hand. The illustrations given from the Freischütz overture, the Eroica, C minor, and choral symphonies, and Mozart's symphony in E flat will come home to all loving students of these works. It is as true here as in Germany that "if music depended on our conductors, it would have perished long ago." How well, too, we have reason to groan with Wagner at the habitual opera mutilation which provoked such a passage as "Cut! Cut!—this is the *ultima ratio* of our conductors: the pleasant and never-failing means of accommodating to their own incompetence the artistic tasks which they find impossible." Again—"They have no notion that, with even the most insignificant opera, a comparatively satisfactory effect on educated minds can be secured by correctness and completeness in performance." Does Mr Carl Rosa agree here; and, if so, would it be too much to ask him to give us Lohengrin, if not complete, at least without such butcherly cuts as that sometimes made in the instrumental prelude to the second act? Much that Wagner has said about famous orchestras trading on the departed excellence they were wrought up to by some deceased or seceded conductor, might have been written of the Covent Garden orchestra when, though some of its nightly performances would have disgraced a circus, it was still generally spoken and even written of as the first orchestra in England, merely because it had been so under the direction of Costa, who had then returned to the rival house, and had of course taken the orchestral supremacy with him. To this day there are people who talk of the Covent Garden orchestra as if there were in the neighboring cabbages a musical magic of which nothing could rob a band in Bow-street.

The disappointing impressions which Wagner complains of having received from public performances of classical music in his earliest youth were common and indeed inevitable experiences in London before he brought Her Richter to conduct his festivals at the Albert Hall. The new conductor certainly had his work cut out for him. He had to reveal Wagner; to save Beethoven from vulgarization; and to restore Mozart, whose music was almost extinct. For when Herr Richter first conducted the great Symphony in E flat here, concert-goers had fallen into the habit of expecting nothing from Mozart but a certain vapid liveliness—the English phase of that "Mattigkeit der Mozartschen Kantilene" which so astonished Wagner when he, too, began to suffer from incompetent conductors. That such a difference could have been made by merely changing the man who noiselessly waved the stick has puzzled many people, and reduced them either to incredulity or to irrelevant statements—offered with an explanatory air—as to Herr Richter's extraordinary memory and his practical acquaintance with the art of playing the horn. Those who desire some more intelligent account of what constitutes a good conductor will find it in this book, which will, it is to be hoped, be read or re-read by the expert as well as by the general reader and the student.

Mr August Manns, for example, might take, as to the slow movement of the Ninth Symphony, a hint from Wagner which would come as an impertinence from any ordinary critic. And Sir Arthur Sullivan might find something to interest him in the trenchant passages in which Wagner points out that the modern Mendelssohnian "culture," with all its refinements, its elegance, its reticence, and its "chastity," is far too negative to equip a conductor for a struggle with Bach or Beethoven.

Mr Edward Dannreuther is not responsible for the wording of all the passages quoted above. His version of them, though adequate when taken with the context, happened to be inconvenient for quotation. The variations are therefore by no means offered as improvements. Mr Dannreuther has done his manuscript very conscientiously, and with an evident sense of its being well worth doing for its own sake. The acknowledgment must, however, be strictly limited to the manuscript. "Procrustus" and "ultimo ratio" are only mild examples of the results of careless proof correction, undiscovered even by the compiler of the list of errata, which is itself an inexcusable adjunct to a book of one hundred and twentytwo pages.

HENRY SEIFFERT

Unsigned notes in The Pall Mall Gazette, 1887–8

I

17 June 1887

[U] Violinists will be interested to learn that Wieniawski's diabolically difficult Romances Russes have at last been played to a London audience, and that too by a young and comparatively unknown artist. Mr Seiffert, the gentleman in question, achieved the feat without perceptible effort or anxiety, manipulating a fine Amati violin with remarkable power and mastery. The florid interspersed harmonics which make the piece so perilous seemed to present no special difficulty to him; and though he has neither the passion nor the noble and eloquent style without which no command of the instrument will make a violinist great, these may yet come to Mr Seiffert; and in the meantime it is something to be probably the only fiddler within ordinary ken in Europe, except Musin, who ventures upon the Romances Russes in public. Miss Seiffert also made a favorable impression, partly by her prepossessing manner and distinguished appearance, and partly by her fine voice, the lower register of which, however, she has not yet learned to manage. The concert took place at Messrs Collard's.

II

13 December 1887

The success of the Heckmann quartet is moving the fiddling world to emulation. Mr Van der Straeten, the violoncellist, tried an experiment on Monday evening at Steinway Hall with a quartet led by Mr Henry Seiffert, a young Dutchman who made some sensation last summer at a small concert at Collard's by playing with apparent ease Wieniawski's very difficult Romances Russes. His quartet-playing, however, is unsatisfactory. He played on Monday without effort, but also without sustained attention, dashing at the *finale* to Beethoven's quartet in C minor (Op. 18) with great spirit, but often with no more regard to correct intonation than if his instrument was the tambourine. The impression he made last summer remained unaccounted for until he played Max Bruch's romance for the violin, when the power of his tone and the perfect intonation of his chords in the double stopped passages made a very marked effect. He is undoubtedly a player of exceptional promise. A Miss Ernestine Seiffert, presumably a sister of the violinist—though her appearance agreeably contradicts all British notions as to Dutch types of young womanhood—sang with considerable intelligence and refinement. Mr Walter Wesché's MS. quintet in C minor proved passionately fluent, as quartets in a minor key have generally tried to be since Mozart's time; but it revealed nothing new.

III

22 June 1888

Mr Henry Seiffert, the young Dutch violinist, gave a concert last night at Prince's Hall. He was not very brilliantly supported; he was particularly unfortunate in his accompanist; and he was injudicious enough to begin his first series of solos by an air of Bach's which made leather and prunella of the subsequent pieces, especially as Mr Seiffert played it with all the richness, power, and freedom of tone which first brought him into notice. His other efforts were for the most part luckless struggles between the violin and the pianoforte, in which the violin, save in a victorious moment or two, got the worst of it. On the whole, Mr Seiffert will probably hereafter look back on the concert as one of the injustices of his early career. He needs to be tested by a hearing at St James's Hall with an orchestra at his back.[U]

For Part IV see Vol. 3, Appendix, p. 774.

DEFLATING DRURY LANE

Unsigned note in The Pall Mall Gazette, 21 July 1887

[U] Mr Augustus Harris's operatic experiment has been so handsomely recognized by the press and public that his artists may at any moment wax unmanageable with too much praise. If he should find it necessary to abate their self-satisfaction, perhaps the following remarks apropos of last night's performance of Les Huguenots may be of use. The orchestra, in spite of Signor Mancinelli's talent and enthusiasm, is coarser in the bass strings and in the brass than we like them here except in ballets. Signor [Jean] de Reszke, popular as his fine voice has made him, needs to be told that the late Signor Agnesi accustomed us to a good deal of brain work in operatic acting. We therefore feel the repetition of three gestures and a plunge at the footlights rather a limited treatment of the part of the Count di San Bris. To M. del Puente we would say that we are satisfied with the music written for De Nevers by Meyerbeer, and that corrections by the singer are well meant but unnecessary, and as Sir Michael Costa taught us that Meyerbeer's operas only require intelligent study and strict discipline never to fail of their effect, we would ask why it is that so many famous points fall flat or are missed altogether at Drury Lane. As to the singers, those who know how to sing—notably Mesdames Nordica and Engle—have had sufficient praise. Those who do not are safe from our criticism. It is not English to hit even an Italian opera singer when he (or she) is down. [U]

SOME BOOKS ABOUT MUSIC

Unsigned review of J.F. Rowbotham's A History of Music,
Vol. III; Louis S. Davis's Studies in Musical History;
and George T. Ferris's The Great Composers. The Pall
Mall Gazette, 12 October 1887

[U] The only disappointing feature of the third volume
of Mr Rowbotham's work is the word Finis at the end.
It would be unreasonable to complain of it, since, when
the historian of music has faithfully guided us through
the dark ages, shewing us how the recitations of the
early Christians became Gregorian chants, or picked up
a pagan grace or two and became Ambrosian hymns;
when he has traced the grafting of the peasant's dance
and the vagabond's ballad, and the influence of Arabian
science and subtlety; when he has followed the tedious
evolution of the art of writing music to its final
employment in replacing improvized descants by preconcerted harmony, then only a word or two more is
needed to shew the fugue form in embryo in the popular
forms of the Middle Ages: the rest, as far as Western
Europe is concerned, is plain sailing to all who have a
fair knowledge of living music, from the compositions
of the great Netherlanders and Palestrina to Mr Cowen's
last cantata. Still, his company through the unknown
land was so interesting that the denial of an expected
stroll through familiar fields with him is disappointing.
His vivid descriptive criticisms of Terpander, Sappho,
St Ambrose, and Notker make one long to verify the
soundness of his taste by hearing him on Bach, Haydn,
Mozart, Beethoven, and Wagner, about whom we have
our own opinion to compare with his. Besides, Western
Europe is not the world; and Mr Rowbotham is just the

man to tell us all about the music of those nations whose strains are never heard at the Crystal Palace on Saturdays. So it is to be hoped that he will reconsider his Finis, and go on whilst there is any ground left for him to cover. Meanwhile, one or two points in which the history as it stands is deficient had better be mentioned.

First, there are no dates. The student has to keep his reckoning by repeated references to biographical dictionaries and bald chronologies, just as he has to peep into bakers' shops for the hour when his watch is in pawn. Then there is no sharp line between fable and history, conjecture and record, deduction and guess, so that though Mr Rowbotham's remark that "to controvert the givings out of tradition is but an unamiable thing to do, and of inconsiderable importance in the due conception of history" may be true, it is not reassuring. The historical method is strictly applied throughout; but experience has proved by this time that the historical method is quite as likely to lead to pure romance as the *a priori* method to hypothetic and unreal conclusions; and if Mr Rowbotham can defy us to prove that any of his pages are not history we can no less confidently defy him to prove that some of them are not romance. Further, his free use of the ordinary notation for describing divisions of the scale in various systems, and for writing ancient or foreign melodies and harmonies, is not accompanied by any warning to the modern reader—who is apt to run to his pianoforte or organ to try the effect—that the tuning of our keyed instruments in equal temperament is a new and not altogether happy device, and that the absolute pitches of the Greek modes can only be guessed on the assumption that the cultivation of the voice in Greece had much the same results as among us, which is, to say the least, a discouraging view of Greek art. The next edition of the work will give Mr Rowbotham an opportunity of remedying such of these omissions as he has not made on principle. In the meantime he may congratulate himself on having produced the foremost work of its kind in the contemporary English literature of music.

Mr Louis Davis, an American musician, has nothing new to say, nor does he say the old things with any literary skill; but the great heart of the world (as he is quite capable of calling it in one of his grandioso passages) will surely go out to him for saying "We have all reason to thank the Lord that so few men and women are able to sing; or, whether they can or not, that so few do sing." Equally true, though less profound, is the remark that "without the ear the organ would have never existed; without the continuance of the ear it would immediately cease to exist." "This" adds Mr Davis gravely "is a glimpse into a field into which, at some future day, I hope to enter more fully." Gentlemen who write indignant letters to the papers about church bells will appreciate his statement that "the fact is, the bell is not in sympathy with the age; but with the Church it is different." His sense of the power of music to express ratiocinative processes may be gathered from his exclamation: "Among great thoughts, what is there more similar than a Bach fugue and an essay by Mill?" But when the seeker for biographical information concerning William the Silent is referred to Beethoven's Eroica Symphony in preference to Motley's Dutch Republic, one feels that it is time to dismiss Mr Davis as too rash a guide for the old-world student, however eagerly the new may have received him.

Another American writer upon music, Mr George T. Ferris, has been chosen by Mrs William Sharp to enrich the Camelot Classic series with sketches of the great composers. Whether he is responsible for the orthographic peculiarities of the volume, or whether they have been touched in by editor or printer, is not clear; but such names as Massinet (Massenet), Bonacini (Buononcini), Metastasia (Metastasio), and Les Trojans (Les Troyens) flourish abundantly through the pages. Giving Mr Ferris the benefit of the doubt as to inaccuracies of spelling, pass we on to his inaccuracies of statement. He calls Allegri's Miserere "Allegri's great mass"; he says that the mysterious stranger who ordered Mozart's Requiem was Count Walseck (Walsegg) in person; he repeats the hackneyed and absurd statement that the overture to Don Juan was composed as well as written down in six hours; he ascribes the failure of the "conflagration" in Berlioz's Sardanapalus, caused by a mistake in the orchestra, to the effect of the music; and he describes the score of Donizetti's Lucia as "strongly flavored by Scottish sympathy and minstrelsy." Sometimes he is inaccurate as if accuracy were not worth the trouble: sometimes as if the truth were not romantic enough for his pages. He is a capricious critic, now severely noting "scientific faults" in La Sonnambula and undramatic treatment in Donizetti's Lucrezia, and anon easily declaring Gounod's Faust the greatest of modern operas, or quoting without protest the claim of a French critic for superior "insight into the spiritual significance of Goethe's drama" on the part of Berlioz. With the calmness of one who utters a truism, he begins a sentence with the words "However deficient Wagner's skill in writing for the human voice." Some of his enthusiasms are not unwelcome as echoes of a bygone time, when Semiramide and William Tell seemed the grandest of operas; when Meyerbeer was daring, original, and new; when the hero worship of opera singers was as fashionable in Mayfair as it now is in Maida Vale; when there was no such person as Goetz; and when Wagner was known chiefly as the arranger of the pianoforte score of Donizetti's Favorita. If the Camelot Classics are intended to "strike a chord," as Mr Guppy* said, in the breast of the old fogey, then no doubt Mr Ferris was well chosen for the musical part of the task. Young students desirous of being abreast of their time may confidently be recommended to seek fresher counsel.[U]

THE DON GIOVANNI CENTENARY

The Pall Mall Gazette, 31 October 1887; signed "By our Special Wagnerite"

When I was requested by the Pall Mall Gazette to attend the centenary concert recital of Don Giovanni on Saturday last at the Crystal Palace, I felt strongly disposed to write curtly to the Editor expressing my unworthiness to do justice to the beauties of XVIII century opera. However, I was by no means sure that the Editor would have appreciated the sarcasm (editors, as a class, being shocking examples of neglected musical education); and, besides, I was somewhat curious to hear the performance. For though we are all agreed as to the prettiness of Mozart's melodies, his *naïve* touches of mild fun, and the touch, ingenuity, and grace with which he rang his few stereotyped changes on the old-fashioned forms, yet I have observed that some modern musicians, in the face of a great technical development of harmony and instrumentation, and an enlargement even to world spaciousness of our views of the mission of art, yet persist in claiming for Mozart powers simply impossible to a man who had never read a line of Hegel or a stave of Wagner. I am not now thinking of the maudlin Mozart idolatry of M. Gounod, whom I of course do not consider a great musician; but rather of

* Character in Dickens's Bleak House.

the unaccountable fact that even Richard Wagner seems to have regarded Mozart as in some respects the greatest of his predecessors. To me it is obvious that Mozart was a mere child in comparison with Schumann, Liszt, or Johannes Brahms; and yet I believe that I could not have expressed myself to that effect in the presence of the great master without considerable risk of contemptuous abuse, if not of bodily violence.

So I resolved finally to venture hearing poor old Rossini's pet *dramma giocosa*. Before starting, I took a glance at the score, and found exactly what I expected—commonplace melodies, diatonic harmonies and dominant discords, ridiculous old closes and half-closes at every eighth bar or so, "florid" accompaniments consisting of tum-tum in the bass and scales like pianoforte finger studies in the treble, and a ludicrously thin instrumentation, without trombones or clarinets except in two or three exceptionally pretentious numbers; the string quartet, with a couple of horns and oboes, seeming quite to satisfy the Mozartian notion of instrumentation. These are facts—facts which can be verified at any time by a reference to the score; and they must weigh more with any advanced musician than the hasty opinions which I formed at the concert when in a sort of delirium, induced, I have no doubt, by the heat of the room.

For I am bound to admit that the heat of the room produced a most extraordinary effect upon me. The commonplace melodies quite confounded me by acquiring subtlety, nobility, and dramatic truth of expression; the hackneyed diatonic harmonies reminded me of nothing I had ever heard before; the dominant discords had a poignant expression which I have failed in my own compositions to attain even by forcibly sounding all the twelve notes of the chromatic scale simultaneously; the ridiculous cadences and half-closes came sometimes like answers to unspoken questions of the heart, sometimes like ghostly echoes from another world; and the feeble instrumentation—but that was what warned me that my senses were astray. Otherwise I must have declared that here was a master compared to whom Berlioz was a musical pastrycook. From Beethoven and Wagner I have learned that the orchestra can paint every aspect of nature, and turn impersonal but specific emotion into exquisite sound. But an orchestra that creates men and women as Shakespear and Molière did—that makes emotion not only specific but personal and characteristic (and this, mind, without clarinets, without trombones, without a second pair of horns): such a thing is madness: I must have been dreaming. When the trombones did come in for a while in a supernatural scene at the end, I felt more in my accustomed element; but presently they took an accent so inexpressibly awful, that I, who have sat and smiled through Liszt's Inferno with the keenest relish, felt forgotten superstitions reviving within me. The roots of my hair stirred; and I recoiled as from the actual presence of Hell. But enough of these delusions, which I have effectually dispelled by a dispassionate private performance at my own pianoforte. Of the concert technically, I can only say that it was practically little more than a rehearsal of the orchestral parts.

SPRING WHISTLING AT THE CRYSTAL PALACE

Unsigned note in The Pall Mall Gazette,
13 February 1888

[U] The first of the spring series of Saturday concerts at the Crystal Palace was heralded by the familiar announcement that Mr Sims Reeves would sing, followed by the no less familiar announcement that Mr Sims Reeves would not sing. His place was taken by Mr Charles Banks, who has acquired his method and manner, and is now striving very creditably, with the help of a rich and unspoiled tenor voice, to catch the unrivaled eloquence of his delivery. The orchestra made a splendid beginning with Wagner's Faust overture, but were rather badly beaten by Mozart's great Symphony in E flat, their performance of the first and third movements of which was mechanical and vulgar almost to the extremity of suggesting a couple of suburban schoolgirls playing a pianoforte duet.

Pan Franz Ondricek played Dvořák's Violin Concerto quite as well as it deserved,* and subsequently gave a couple of compositions which were trash, but which enabled him to bring down the house by making his instrument whistle in a manner that recalled Sivori, and set some of us wondering whether that delicate artist can still produce the ethereal harmonics which linger in our memories, somewhat to the disparagement of Pan Franz Ondricek's less exquisitely pure tone. The concert ended with Berlioz's transcription of Weber's Invitation, played stolidly and unimaginatively by the strings, but magnificently by the brass, which brought out the full effect of Berlioz's ingenious and astonishing version of the first of the two sections in C major.[U]

* In a very brief musical note in the "Art Corner," Our Corner, May 1886, Shaw had noted: "At the second Philharmonic concert, Herr Ondricek, a Hungarian violinist, played a concerto by Dvořák. He plays with some breadth of style and strength of tone in slow movements; but he scrambles through rapid passages haphazard, leaving the intonation to take care of itself, which it of course does not do."

ON THE GODLINESS OF DANCING

The Star, 14 April 1888; signed "a correspondent iconoclastic and irreverent"

The late conflict between the Bishop of London and the Rev. Stewart Headlam* as to the godliness of dancing ended practically in the excommunication of the dancers and the inhibition of the popular clergyman, whose version of the Thirtynine Articles includes Land Nationalization, Free Speech, Communion for Stage Players, and a Democratic Constitution for the Church. Mr Headlam's teaching nevertheless seems to have traveled further than the Bishop's, for we hear from Georgia of a troop of factory hands removing the benches from their church on a Friday evening, and having a hearty dance. At a church in North Carolina, a brass band was allowed to perform some stirring rhythmical hymn tunes for the edification of a negro congregation. These pious colored persons, we are told, "began to grow a little nervous and restless about the feet, and in a short time the whole crowd was indulging in a regular old break down." This is shocking, no doubt, to our insular conception of a church as a place where we must on no account enjoy ourselves, and where ladies are trained in the English art of sitting in rows for hours, dumb, expressionless, and with the elbows uncomfortably turned in. But since people must enjoy themselves

* The Rev. Stewart D. Headlam was a Christian Socialist minister and member of the Fabian Society, founder of the Church and Stage Guild (1879), whose activities had led to the controversy over ballet. The Bishop, Frederick Temple, later became archbishop of Canterbury.

sometimes, why not in their own churches as well as in places where drinking bars, gambling tables, and other temptations to enjoy themselves unhealthily and indecently are deliberately put in their way? "Dancing is an art" says Mr Headlam. "All art is praise" says Mr Ruskin. Praise is surely not out of place in a church. We sing there: why should we not dance?

The Puritans, from whom we inherit out prejudice against such a proposal, objected to dancing and singing in all places and at all seasons. Merry England never shared that objection: we admit it in church only because we can afford to dance elsewhere. But how about the people who have no such opportunities: no drawing rooms, no money, no self-control in the presence of temptation and licence? We do not want to see Westminster Abbey turned into a ballroom; but if some enterprising clergyman with a cure of souls in the slums were to hoist a board over his church door with the inscription "Here men and women after working hours may dance without getting drunk on Fridays; hear good music on Saturdays; pray on Sundays; discuss public affairs without molestation from the police on Mondays; have the building for any honest purpose they please—theatricals, if desired—on Tuesdays; bring the children for games, amusing drill, and romps on Wednesdays; and volunteer for a thorough scrubbing down of the place on Thursdays"—well, it would be all very shocking, no doubt; but after all, it would not interfere with the Bishop of London's salary.

THE BACH CHOIR

The Star, 14 May 1888 ; unsigned

The number of empty seats at the performance of Bach's Mass in B minor at St James's Hall on Saturday afternoon did little credit to the artistic culture of which the West End is supposed to be the universal centre. This Mass towers among the masterpieces of musical art like Everest among the mountains; but we still prefer Elijah. The performance suffered from the want of energy and impetus which is one of the hampering traditions of Herr Goldschmidt's conducting, and which Mr Villiers Stanford, as a younger hand, and an Irishman, ought to have proved the very man to correct. But under him, as under Herr Goldschmidt, the wonderful Kyrie dragged tediously along without fire or emphasis, and without a touch of expression in the recurring cadence, which is so moving a point in the score. The later choruses were more effective, though there was a want of power in certain passages which demand a crushing sonority from the mass of voices and instruments. This was notably the case in the Cum Sancto Spiritu. In the Et Resurrexit Mr Stanford made the astonishing mistake of retarding the great passage for the basses, Et iterum venturus. But, in spite of these shortcomings, the stupendous march of Bach's polyphony, and the intense and touching expression of his harmonies produced their inevitable effect. The restored trumpet part, first played for us at the Albert Hall by Herr Kosleck at the bi-centenary performance in 1885, was played on Mr Mahillon's two-valved trumpet by Mr Morrow, who vanquished nearly all the impossibilities until just at the end, when his lip tired, and the notes above the high A became uncertain. At the famous Sanctus Mr Stanford made an attempt, successful unfortunately, to manufacture a tradition similar to that by which English audiences stand during the Hallelujah Chorus in the Messiah. When such an act of homage is the spontaneous impulse of the people it is worthy of jealous conservation. But when a conductor deliberately attempts to produce an imitation of the Hallelujah custom by making his solo singers stand up and then turning to the audience and beckoning them to rise, which they of course do under the impression that it is an established practice, he is really guilty of a sort of forgery. Probably, however, people will not be so easily persuaded to stand up when they come to know how long the Sanctus is.

It should be mentioned that there were plenty of shilling seats: a great improvement on the high prices of the early days of the Bach Choir.

THE SECOND RICHTER CONCERT THIS SEASON

Unsigned note in The Pall Mall Gazette, 15 May 1888

[U] The first matter that excited remark at the second Richter concert last night was the fact that the great conductor had grown visibly stouter in the course of the week. Creditable as this is to British hospitality, it is impossible to contemplate without alarm the probability of the phenomenon continuing progressively through the whole series of nine concerts. The orchestra distinguished itself by a magnificent performance of the prelude and death song from Tristan; but in the Valkyrie Ride the brass was clumsy, and, if the truth must be told, phrased in the style of a second-rate military band. Miss Pauline Cramer heroically attempted the closing scene of the Götterdämmerung, and came off, if not quite victorious, yet with great credit. As for Mr Villiers Stanford's Irish symphony, it is only an additional proof that the symphony, as a musical form, is stone dead. Some such structure as that used by Liszt in his symphonic poems would have admirably suited Mr Stanford's fantasia on Irish airs. The effect of mechanically forcing it into symphony form has been to make it diffuse and pedantic. Since Bach's death, the rule as to fugue has been "First learn to write one, and then dont." It is time, and has been ever since Beethoven's death, to extend the rule to the symphony.[U]

FORGING THE SWORD

The Star, 3 July 1888; unsigned

Herr Richter has added to his Nibelung's Ring selections for concert use the great scene of the forging of the sword in the forest stithy, from the first act of Siegfried. It is one of the most effective he has made, and proves again that Wagner can work on the imagination with voice and orchestra in ways beyond the arts of the actor and stage manager. Mr Edward Lloyd, pretending to forge a sword on the stage, with one eye on the conductor, would be ridiculous; but last night in St James's Hall the leviathan breath of the bellows with its great train of sparks, the roar of the flame, the fierce hiss of the red-hot steel plunged into the water, the ringing of the hammers, the crooning of the old dwarf in the corner, and the exultant shouting of Siegfried at his work, culminating in a yell of excitement from the orchestra as the finished sword smites the anvil in two, made a tremendous effect, and gained an ovation for Mr Lloyd and the conductor.

There was no other novelty except a Bach concerto, one of those incomparable works which tax every quality of a first-rate player, and which, to tell the truth, speedily found out some of the weak places in the wind band. The concert ended with Beethoven's symphony in A, the final movement of which went off with astonishing dash and vigor.

A CURIOUS REVIVAL

The Star, 4 July 1888; unsigned

To old opera-goers a performance of Verdi's Ballo in Maschera brings reminiscences of bygone days and forgotten singers: of Titiens in the trio in the cave scene and Giuglini in the quintet. Fortunately for you, dear reader, it produces no such effect on me; for I never heard the opera on the stage before, and never heard Giuglini, though I knew most of the music in my cradle or thereabouts. As to the young opera-goers, one can really only wonder what they think about it. Its interminable string of *cavatinas*, its absurdly Offenbachian *finale* to the first act, its inexhaustible vein of melodramatic anguish, its entire impossibility from any rational point of view from beginning to end, must all help to puzzle those who were never broken in to that strange survival of Richardson's show, the so-called acting of genuinely Italian opera. These are untimely reflections, perhaps; but they rise unbidden at a performance of Un Ballo. The work, nevertheless, contains one capital scene: that in which Samuel and Tom (who are called Armando and Angri in the bills in these squeamish days) meet Renato innocently escorting his own wife, veiled, from an assignation with his dearest friend, and force her to unveil. Verdi has done nothing better than the combination of the raillery of the two rascals, the humiliation of the woman, and the distress of the husband. But at Covent Garden they do not seem to think that there is much in this. Samuel and Tom were solemn as sextons; and M. Lassalle merely stretched forth his sword to the stalls, as if he were about to perform the familiar feat of cutting an apple in two on Signor Mancinelli's head. He sang the part very well from a French point of view, which the audience, it was most encouraging to observe, flatly declined to accept. Mlle Rolla does not understand the English people. She may sing consistently sharp here with impunity. Though the assembled Britons will not like it, they will pretend to, thinking that she knows best. But to begin a note in tune, and then force it up quarter of a tone is neither popular nor humane. It is better, on the whole, to sing in tune all through, as Mlle Rolla decided to do towards the end of the performance. Her acting consisted of the singular plunge, gasp, and stagger peculiar to the Verdi heroine, whose reason is permanently unsettled by grief. Miss Arnoldson added Oscar to the list of her successes. Jean de Reszke was Riccardo. Some of the tediousness of the opera was due to the senseless conventionality of the representation and to the slow *tempi* adopted by Signor Mancinelli; but Mr Harris will do well to face the fact that, until fortune sends him an extraordinarily sensational dramatic soprano, he will do well to leave such old-fashioned affairs as Un Ballo on the shelf.

DE LUSSAN'S FLORESCENT DÉBUT

The Star, 9 July 1888; unsigned

[U] On Saturday a rather slovenly performance of Carmen brought forward Mlle Zélie de Lussan, who looked the part well and sang it not at all badly, though the comparative weakness of the middle of her voice prevented her from doing her music the fullest justice. As an actress she shewed intelligence and self-possession; but she has hardly sufficient distinction of style to take a leading position in grand opera. She made the castanet song or lilt in the tavern scene quite ineffective by disregarding the *nuances* indicated by the composer. Her greatest success was in the third act. The extremely cool reception given her by the audience at the close of the performance was the result of a ridiculous scene at the end of the first act, when two of the attendants entered the stalls with a cargo of flowers, which were duly handed up and received by the *prima donna* with manifestations of surprise and delight. When the drop-curtain fell for the third time, a porter had to help to carry away the floral trophies. On this occasion Mlle de Lussan drew a rose from one of them and impulsively handed it to Signor Mancinelli, who accepted it with mixed feelings.

A word is needed as to the other performers. The Toreador is a *rôle* which Signor del Puente is supposed to have made peculiarly his own. We appeal to Mr Harris to make it peculiarly somebody else's who will at least take the trouble to sing it accurately and carefully. And we beg to assure Miss Macintyre that a less charming Micaela would have run some risk of being soundly hissed for the graceless interpolation with which she spoiled her part in the *finale* to the third act. Those who advise her to deface a composer's work by interlarding it with commonplaces by her singing-master are no doubt quite ignorant enough to believe that Bizet's music needs improvement. Audiences nowadays know better, and they expect Miss Macintyre to know better too.[U]

AÏDA FILLS THE HOUSE
The Star, 16 July 1888 ; unsigned

Aïda filled the house at Covent Garden on Saturday quite as effectually as Il Trovatore emptied it earlier in the week. Not that Aïda, comparatively fresh and varied in interest as it is, is at bottom at all a more rational entertainment than Il Trovatore, but simply because Aïda is now put on to give the best artists in the company a chance, whereas Il Trovatore is put on only to give them a rest. The performance of the first two acts was unsatisfactory. Madame Nordica, brown enough as to face and arms, was colorless as to voice. Signor Mancinelli conducted the court and temple scenes barbarically, evidently believing that the ancient Egyptians were a tribe of savages, instead of, as far as one can ascertain, considerably more advanced than the society now nightly contemplating in "indispensable evening dress" the back of Signor Mancinelli's head. Not until the scene of the triumphal return of Radames from the war did the gallery begin to pluck up and applaud. Fortunately, an incident which occurred at the beginning of the fourth act confirmed the good humor thus set in. Ramfis, Amneris, and their escort were seen approaching the temple in a state barge. On its tall prow, which rose some five feet out of the water, stood an

Egyptian oarsman, urging the craft along the moonlit bosom of the Nile. Now this was all very well whilst the royal party were on board to balance him: but when they stepped ashore on to the stage, the barge went head over heels; the native went heels over head; and Signor Navarrini's impressive exhortation to *Vieni d'Iside al tempio* was received with shrieks of laughter. Whether the operatic gods were appeased by the sacrifice of the luckless boatman (who never reappeared from beneath the wave), or whether his fate made his surviving colleagues more serious, is a matter for speculation; but the fact is beyond question that the representation greatly improved from that moment. Madame Nordica's voice, no longer colorless, began to ring with awakened feeling. Her admirable method, to which she is, unfortunately, not invariably faithful, was exemplified in the ease, skill, and perfect intonation with which the higher notes were produced. It is an inexpressible relief to the jaded opera-goer to hear notes above the treble stave taken otherwise than with the neck-or-nothing scream of the ordinary *prima donna ma ultima cantatrice.* M. Jean de Reszke also rose to the occasion, and so astonished the house by a magnificent delivery of *Io son disonorato! Per te tradii la patria! . . . Sacerdote, io resto a te,* that the curtain descended to an explosion of applause. It is true that M. de Reszke utterly missed the simple dignity of his part of the duet with Amneris in the first scene of the last act; but that did not obscure his great success: the audience, delighted with him, accepting his version with enthusiasm. Signor d'Andrade, in coffee color and tiger skins, ranted as Amonasro in a manner against which commonsense ought to have guarded him. Why the Ethiopian captive king should be conceived on the Italian stage, not even as an antique Cetewayo, but as a frenzied Hottentot, is hard to understand. Verdi certainly had no such intention, as the character of the music proves. Madame Scalchi played Amneris with passion and a certain tragic grace that might make her an actress, if it were possible for anyone to become an actress in such an atmosphere of incongruity and nonsense as that which an operatic artist is condemned to breathe.

BOÏTO'S MEFISTOFELE
The Star, 18 July 1888 ; unsigned

Boïto's Mefistofele is chiefly interesting as a proof that a really able literary man can turn out a much better opera than the average musician can, just as he can turn out a much more effective play than the average poet. We have by this time accumulated such a huge stock of orchestral effects, rhythms, and modulations, all of which are quite accessible to any person who starts with sufficient musical gift to pick up He's all right when you know him by ear, that the composition of a passable opera or ballet will be as mechanical an achievement before the end of the century as the writing of a passable novel is now. Meanwhile, let us take Mefistofele as seriously as Die Zauberflöte, and suggest to Mr Harris that the effect of the oncoming of night in the first act with the gradual melting of the town ramparts into the gloom of Faust's study, should not be performed with lights turned up, and stage carpenters bustling through the gauze and cheerfully shouting "Pull it back, sir? Yessir. Go on, Tom," and so forth. One would also suppose that such inexpensive articles of *diablerie* as will-o'-the-wisps might be supplied more plentifully in the Brocken scene, if only to give some point to the erratic flights of tootling in the orchestra. However, these are but details, only to be noted at Covent Garden, because so much is there sacrificed to spectacularism on the highest scale.

The singing was—as to the chorus—hurried, jaded, flat, and ineffective in the prologue, where it most needs to be majestic and penetrating; as to the principal persons, various. Signor Ravelli, much used up, spurted bravely at times, but hardly did justice to his part. Signor Edouard de Reszke, as the fiend, used his fine voice with great effect in certain passages, but left extensive room, as usual, for intelligence and variety. The honors of the evening were carried off by Miss Macintyre. She played Margaret like a novice, but her novitiate is full of promise and charm. Of Helen let it suffice to say that she received, amid scanty applause, a vast basket of flowers, which was not generally believed to be a spontaneous tribute from the front of the house. The audience seemed well pleased throughout, and Mefistofele will probably be brought forward oftener next year. The last act, one of the best sections of the opera, made a marked impression in spite of the late hour; and it is a pity that it is not likely to be secured an earlier hearing by the omission of the Brocken business, which is musically and scenically childish. So many scenes have already been cut from the original score that the additional injury to the composer's feelings would hardly be felt by him.

THE INJURY TO MR MALCOLM LAWSON

Unsigned note in The Pall Mall Gazette, 23 July 1888

[U] It is somewhat startling to hear that Mr Malcolm Lawson has been so severely disabled in an unlucky encounter with a cab that the concert for his benefit at the Kensington Town Hall this afternoon must be supplemented by a benefit fund in order to secure him the prolonged rest needed to set his injured shoulder to rights. Society certainly owes Mr Lawson something for good work which must have brought him more thanks than halfpence, and very little of either. He fought hard to make London understand what a great classic they were neglecting in Gluck, and his revival of Alceste at the Tenterden-street rooms, with Mr T. Marzials as Hercules, was a really memorable performance. He also did a service to English music by letting us hear what a grand piece of choral work we have in Henry Purcell's Yorkshire Feast, which was heard as well as the Dido and Eneas, at concerts of the Gluck Society.

That society, of course, did not pay, and when Mr Lawson could hold out no longer he fell back on the St Cecilia Choir, the nucleus of the forces with which he still gives concerts of exceptional historical and artistic value. The democracy also owe him a score. Last November, when the unfortunate Linnell was killed by Sir Charles Warren's cavalry, Mr Lawson set Mr William Morris's dirge to music, and conducted it beside the grave at Bow.* On the whole, Mr Malcolm Lawson has treated his fellow citizens handsomely. An accident has left him helpless for a season, and now it is his fellow citizens' turn. Mr Heseltine Owen, of 3, Milborne

* On 13 November 1887 London's radicals converged on Trafalgar Square in defiance of the Home Secretary's order forbidding its use for a protest demonstration against the Government's Irish policy. The marchers were attacked by police and military, under orders from the Metropolitan Police Commissioner, Sir Charles Warren. A bystander, Alfred Linnell, was badly beaten by the police, dying of his injuries, and thus becoming an unwitting martyr. William Morris, who had participated in the riot, supplied the lyric for a "Death Song" which Lawson composed and performed at the funeral.

Grove, The Boltons, S.W., is treasurer for the concert and benefit fund. [U]

THE MORAL OF THE MAPLESON MEMOIRS

The Star, 20 September 1888; signed
"By a Musical Reformer"

James Henry Mapleson, alias Enrico Mariani, commonly and unaccountably spoken of as Colonel Mapleson, one time professional viola player, later operatic vocalist, and finally for twentyseven years London *impresario* at Drury Lane and Her Majesty's Theatre, has written The Mapleson Memoirs. They are very amusing, especially to readers who, like the Colonel himself, have no suspicion that his record covers a period of hopeless decay. The financial record is depressing enough; but that is nothing new in the history of Italian Opera in England, since all the *impresarios*, from Handel to Laporte and Lumley, lost money, and lived, as far as one can make out, chiefly on the splendor of the scale on which they got into debt. Nevertheless they kept the institution afoot in the good old style, with absurd high-falutin' prospectuses, expensive ballets, rapacious star singers and star dancers, and unscrupulous performances in which the last thing thought of was the fulfilment of the composer's intentions. What was wanted, after Lumley's retirement, was a manager with sufficient artistic sensibility to perceive that these abuses, which Wagner and Berlioz had quite sufficiently exposed, must be done away with if the opera house was to hold its own against the ordinary theatre. Unfortunately, Colonel Mapleson's most indulgent friends can hardly claim for him any such musical

[524]

and dramatic conscience. The period between the disappearance of Mario and the advent of Jean de Reszke is hardly to be recalled without a shudder, in spite of Christine Nilsson, and such fine artists as De Murska, Trebelli, Santley, and Agnesi. Costa maintained rigid discipline in the orchestra; and Titiens's geniality, her grand air, the remains of her great voice, and even her immense corpulence covered for a time her essential obsolescence as an artist; but the prevailing want of life, purpose, sincerity, and concerted artistic effort would have destroyed a circus, much less the Opera; and the enterprise went from bad to worse, until it finally collapsed from utter rottenness.

Colonel Mapleson's negative contributions to this result may have been considerable. His positive contribution was the selection of such a line of tenors, all straight from La Scala, and all guaranteed beforehand to replace and eclipse Mario and Giuglini, as we may fervently hope never to hear again. Colonel Mapleson hopes to take the field again next season; and no one can help wishing that his perseverance may be rewarded with success. But if he proceeds on his old plan, or want of plan, he will only add another failure to his list. If he has learnt at last that the lyric stage cannot lag a century behind the ordinary theatre; that the days of scratch performances are over; that Donizetti is dead; that Wagner is the most popular composer of the day; that the Costa conception of orchestral conducting has been succeeded by the Richter conception; and that people will not pay to see heros and gentlemen impersonated by tenors who are not distinguishable in manners, appearance, voice, or talent from the average vendor of penny ices, then, and not otherwise, he may succeed. It is only fair to add, by the way, that Colonel Mapleson is by no means the only *impresario* who has hitherto failed to take this lesson to heart.

SUCH A THUMPING OF PIANOS

The Star, 10 October 1888; unsigned

The recorded humors of musical enterprise include few
more entertaining freaks than that of Mr Alexander
Alexandroff at the Albert Hall. It will be especially
relished by those who know that London is a city of high
schools for girls, and how on prize distribution day,
every half-year, the British parent attends school to be
entertained by a performance of the overture to
Masaniello, or perhaps, in establishments where taste is
severe, the overture to Egmont, played on innumerable
pianofortes by his daughters, two to each instrument.
M. Alexandroff's idea of engaging fifty young ladies and
twentyfour pianofortes to go through this characteristically British performance, and offering it to London as
Russian national music, has a certain not unattractive
naïveté about it. It may well be, of course, that they do
this sort of thing in Russia, where the education of
women greatly flourishes. But let not M. Alexandroff, or
any other intelligent foreigner, suppose for a moment
that we do not do it in England. It is a product of the
ladies' school, and no nation can boast a monopoly of it.
The effect it produces at Kensington can easily be
imagined. Everybody knows what a Brinsmead pianoforte is like—its bright dry sound at the top, as of a
sonorous brick struck with the edge of a trowel, its
precise touch, and its clear tone in the middle and bass.
Everybody knows also what a dashing young lady pianist
is. Imagine a Brinsmead pianoforte standing to others in
the relation of the Albert Hall to the Court Theatre,
with two proportionately magnified young ladies playing
a duet on it, and you have imagined this speciality

"as performed at St Petersburg and Moscow." The public are taking to it amazingly, and it is worthy the attention of those students of instrumentation who look forward to the realization of Berlioz's dream of an orchestra of 467 players, thirty of them pianists. And it must be admitted, in favor of Berlioz, that there is more room at present for innovation in orchestras by the addition of instruments of the lyre type than in any other direction.

As to the singers, the natural material is Russian, but the manufacture is French. The men sing with the fervor, the *vibrato*, and the ruthless and continual slurring that MM. Faure, Maurel, Lassalle, and others have tried for years to make us like, and which we are no doubt often ashamed to confess that we do not like. That, however, is not Russia's fault; and Mr Michael Winogradow, for instance, deserves to be acknowledged as a very accomplished and effective singer of his school, with a fine voice. But magnanimity has its limits, even towards the French school; and Mlle Veber's *vibrato* oversteps those limits. She is by no means without expression and artistic feeling; but a lady whose notes are a chain of imperfect shakes is out of court in England. Madame Olga Pouskowa's powerful contralto voice makes everyone in the vast auditorium both feel and hear it. She sings a vocal waltz which, for its combination of triviality with Oriental passion, might have been composed in Maida Vale. The tenor, M. Pavel Bogatyrioff, finds the Albert Hall rather large for his voice. Mr Alexander Laroff is another operatic baritone in the French manner. The choir is not bad; and the orchestra is very good, especially in Glinka's Kamarinskaja, which we have all learned by heart at the Richter concerts. The omissions and delays which called forth so many complaints at the first performance were all remedied last night; and Mr Alexandroff may now fairly claim public support for his enterprise, in spite of the somewhat hackneyed character of some of his novelties.

A SATURDAY POP

The Star, 26 November 1888; unsigned

A new quintet by Dvořák brought a large audience to St James's Hall on Saturday afternoon. The success of a popular concert is always a question of luck; for if the leader of the quartet be out of sorts, or the pianist indisposed, the affair is a grief and a disappointment to all except those devotees whose enthusiasm for great compositions and great artists is a manufactured literary product, capable of standing any quantity of wear and tear. Nobody will ever know how much Messrs Chappell owe to their having made St James's Hall a fool's paradise, and how much to genuine musical taste and culture. On Saturday, happily, all went well. By the time the trio of the opening quartet (Mozart's in B flat: the first of the Haydn set) was reached, it was apparent that Madame Neruda was in the vein, and was about to display all her superb qualities: her fire and precision, her perfect artistic relation to her fellow artists, her unerring intonation and unflagging and unforced expression. Her playing was especially admirable in the Mozartian slow movement, which is, as great artists know, one of the most delicate and searching tests a player can undergo. After it the quintet was a trifle; and it goes without saying that she carried Dvořák through brilliantly, making his work seem as delightful as her playing of the first violin part, which it by no means is. With worse executants it would have been found too full of odds and ends from the common stock of musical phrases, with the usual Dvořákian dressing of Bohemian

[528]

rhythms and intervals, which give the analytical programmist an opportunity of writing about "national
traits," and save the composer the trouble of developing
his individual traits. The quintet is chiefly remarkable
for the advance it marks in the composer's constructive
ability, both as regards polyphony and the sonata form.
The first movement is well balanced and shapely; and
in the *andante* Dvořák has successfully contrived a form
of his own. If the quintet were as fresh as it is well put
together it would be a valuable addition to our store of
chamber music. As it is, it will not be so popular without
Madame Neruda's help as it proved on Saturday.

Of Miss Betha Moore's singing it is only necessary to
say that she selected Sullivan's Orpheus, as all ladies do
who can take a high B flat *pianissimo*, and Grieg's setting
of Solveig's song from Ibsen's great poetic drama Peer
Gynt.

Sir Charles Hallé played Beethoven's sonata in D
major, No. 3 of Op. 10. Sir Charles is not a sensational
player; but nobody who has heard him play the *largo* of
this sonata has ever accepted the notion that his playing
is "icy and mechanical." Is there any audience in the
world that would come to hear Rubinstein play a
Beethoven sonata for the twentieth time? Yet Hallé (to
drop the prefix which he shares with the ex-Chief
Commissioner of Police) is always sure of his audience,
no matter how often he has repeated the sonata he
chooses. The secret is that he gives you as little as
possible of Hallé and as much as possible of Beethoven,
of whom people do not easily tire. When Beethoven is
made a mere *cheval de bataille* for a Rubinstein, the
interest is more volatile. The "classical" players have the
best of it in the long run.

See also "Dvořák's 'Nationality'" in Vol. 3, Appendix, p. 773.

A FEARFUL PLAYER

The Star, 3 December 1888; unsigned

Mr Manns might have arranged his program at the Crystal Palace on Saturday afternoon more considerately. Schumann's concerto in A minor is a beautiful work; and the Rhenish symphony is not to be despised. But to play them one after the other, with only one incongruous interruption in the shape of Rossini's *Bel raggio* between, is, to say the least, not a tactful proceeding. Why an inoffensive Saturday audience, all devoted to Mr Manns, should be compelled to wallow for an hour and a half in the noisy monotony and opacity of Schumann's instrumentation is not to be guessed on any benevolent theory of concert administration. However, what is done is done. In the present instance it is not even necessary to describe how it was done, further than to say that the pianist was Madame Essipoff. That lady's terrible precision and unfailing nerve; her cold contempt for difficulties; her miraculous speed, free from any appearance of haste; her grace and finesse, without a touch of anything as weak as tenderness: all these are subjects for awe rather than for criticism. When she played Chopin's waltz in A flat, it did not sound like Chopin: the ear could not follow the lightning play of her right hand. Yet she was not, like Rubinstein at that speed, excited and furious over it: she was cold as ice: one felt like Tartini on the celebrated occasion when he got the suggestion for his Trillo del Diavolo. Additional impressiveness was given to the performance by the fact that Madame Essipoff has no platform mannerisms or affectations. When the applause reached the point at which an *encore* was inevitable, she walked to the pianoforte without wasting a second; shot at the audience, without a note of prelude, an exercise about 40 seconds long, and of satanic difficulty; and vanished as calmly as she had appeared. Truly an astonishing— almost a fearful player. Mlle Badia's songs would have done excellently at a concert in Paris in the year 1850; but after Schumann they were anachronisms.

MADAME ESSIPOFF'S PERFECT DIGNITY

Unsigned note in The Pall Mall Gazette,
4 December 1888

[U] Madame Essipoff's performance of Schumann's concerto at the Crystal Palace on Saturday would have been astonishing if she had betrayed the least consciousness of the difficulty of the work. Probably she does not find it difficult. She played a waltz by Chopin at a speed which might be turned to account by Mr Francis Galton in testing quickness of hearing. Another composition contained a chain of *grupetti* in thirds for the left hand, which seemed to give her no more trouble than if they had been divided between the first and second violins. All this was done with perfect dignity, and with faultless precision and intelligence. It was not touching, but it was impressive; and the applause was of the solidest sort.

As to the program generally, it suffered from too much Schumann. Moszkowski's procession music is a mere operatic triviality. Thomas's overture to Raymond, dashingly played as it was, was hardly worth the trouble. Sterndale Bennett's Paradise and the Peri begins to wear out, as all secondhand music (secondhand Mendelssohn in this case) does sooner or later; and Miss Badin's

Rossinian *fioriture*, coming between the concerto and the Rhenish Symphony, sounded hopelessly out of place. Even in the Rhenish Symphony itself, coming directly after the concerto, the perpetual activity of the wind band became very tiresome after forty minutes or so.[U]

THE WHIRLIGIG OF TIME

Unsigned note in The Pall Mall Gazette,
10 December 1888

[U] The honors of the afternoon concert at the Crystal Palace on Saturday afternoon went to M. Marsick after Mr Manns and the orchestra had taken their usual share. M. Marsick began indifferently; but when he came to himself the intensity and delicacy of his playing produced on the audience an effect that many a violinist with a fuller tone and broader style might have envied. Schubert's setting of the 23rd Psalm, admirably scored by Mr Manns from the original pianoforte version, was sung by the ladies of the choir with that reverent avoidance of fervor, and even of meaning, which Englishwomen display whenever they experience, from any cause, the sensation of being in church.

Berlioz's Francs-Juges overture is like a translation of one of Poe's tales into music. On its performance one would remark that when three trombones and a tuba have, in Mr Patrick Molloy's phrase, a free run for their money, each man should not play—or rather bark—as if the whole volume of sound depended on his individual exertions. The symphony was Mozart's, in G minor. Although it might have been much more delicately handled, it sounded fresher than Beethoven's in C minor does nowadays. The whirligig of time brings its revenges in music as in other things.[U]

CRYSTAL PALACE VARIETY

The Star, 10 December 1888; unsigned

Mr August Manns evidently made up his mind last week that nobody should reproach him again with want of variety in the Saturday program. Mozart, Schubert, Berlioz, Mr Hamish MacCunn, and Sir Arthur Sullivan were represented by some of their most characteristic work. The concert began with the overture to the Yeomen of the Guard, by way of signalizing the replacement in Gilbert-Sullivan opera of *pot-pourri* prelude by orthodox overture. Then the orchestra got to serious business in the G minor symphony. The performance of the first and last movements only shewed that Mozart can utterly baffle a band for which Beethoven, Berlioz, and Wagner have no terrors. It is useless to try to make the G minor symphony "go" by driving a too heavy body of strings through it with all the splendor and impetuosity of an Edinburgh express. That has been tried over and over again in London, with the result that Mozart's reputation positively declined steadily until Hans Richter conducted the E flat symphony here. Wagner has told us how, when he first began to frequent concerts, he was astonished to find that conductors always contrived to make Mozart's music sound vapid. Vapid is hardly the word for any performance conducted by Mr Manns; but on Saturday, except in the slow movement and minuet, his energy was unavailing. It was magnificent; but it was not Mozart. When M. Marsick began Wieniawski's concerto in D minor, it at first seemed that a disappointment was in store. Wieniawski's work, which is much more truly

[533]

violin music than the Beethoven and Mendelssohn concertos, requires above all a violinist who can play with perfect spontaneity, and even with abandonment. M. Marsick was constrained and mechanical, and his instrument, not at all in the vein, whined comfortlessly. Not until the movement was half over did his spirits improve. In the *andante* he completely recovered himself, and the final *allegro* was a triumph for him. A handsome recall at the end put him on the best of terms with the audience, who subsequently applauded him enthusiastically for a very pretty Dans Slavacque, which he played exquisitely. The vocal pieces were sung by Miss Antoinette Trebelli, who imitates, with the facility of a child, what she has heard other people doing around her all her life; but who certainly displays as yet no individuality, style, purpose, or even earnest respect for her work. For the sake of the distinguished artist whose name she bears, Miss Trebelli has been allowed a very favorable start. But she will lose that start if she allows herself to be spoilt by the foolish people who recalled her for an immature trifling with *Non mi dir*, an aria which only very intelligent, refined, and sympathetic singers should attempt. Miss Trebelli not only attempted it without these qualifications, but actually tampered with the concluding bars by way of improvement upon Mozart. Mr Hamish MacCunn's happy thought of setting Lord Ullin's Daughter in the freest and easiest way for chorus and orchestra was as successful as ever. Pearsall would have laughed at the cheapness of the success; but Pearsall would have been wrong; the *naïveté* with which Mr MacCunn has gone to work in the simplest fashion is his great merit. The concert ended with Berlioz's first overture, Les Francs-Juges, one of the most striking examples of his curious gift of brains and brimstone. A few old-fashioned bars of Rossinian tum-tum in it sounded odd beside the poignantly expressive section in C minor, the effect of which will not readily be forgotten by those who heard it for the first time.

WAGNERIANA

The Star, 12 December 1888; unsigned

The Wagner Society has just completed the opening volume of its journal The Meister by the issue of the fourth quarterly part at the modest price of a shilling. At first sight The Meister suggests a quarto edition of the Hobby Horse; but closer inspection reveals a cover from the slapdash drawing of which the Century Guild would recoil, and a printed page which certainly cannot be compared to the "solid set" letterpress which enabled the Hobby Horse, at the Arts and Crafts Exhibition, to hold its own beside the most beautiful of old Italian books. It is the content rather than the form that makes The Meister respectable. Mr Charles Dowdeswell's Schopenhauer articles are admirably done; and the translation of Art and Revolution is one that no Socialist should be without. The editorial tone, however, is not Wagnerian: there is an evident indisposition to provoke hostility. This, with respect be it spoken, was not an indisposition to which the Meister himself was at all subject. There is one editorial footnote in the volume which he would have regarded as recreant. To be quite satisfactory, The Meister wants three things: a title page by Mr Selwyn Image or Mr Walter Crane; a printer who appreciates the Hobby Horse, and is not above taking a hint from it; and a fighting editor.

Messrs Rudolph Ibach and Co. are exhibiting, at 113 Oxford-street, Beckmann's picture of Wagner in the music room at his Bayreuth home, Wahnfried. Cosima is seen in profile, seated on the composer's right; and Liszt sits with his back to the window and the score of Parsifal on his knees. The picture is already known by the photogravure reproduction which has found its way into one or two shop windows. Mr Ibach was a personal friend of Wagner's; and the picture is to be seen free of charge at his pianoforte rooms until its voyage to America, which is close at hand.

PARRY'S JUDITH

The Star, 18 December 1888; signed "By 'The Star's' Own Captious Critic"

London has now had two opportunities of tasting Mr Hubert Parry's Judith, the oratorio which he composed for this year's Birmingham festival. It was performed on the 6th of this month at St James's Hall, and again on Saturday last at the Crystal Palace, with Dr Mackenzie in the seat of Mr Manns (gone to Scotland), and the Palace choir replaced by that of Novello's oratorio concerts. The truth about the oratorio is one of those matters which a critic is sorely tempted to mince. Mr Parry is a gentleman of culture and independent means, pursuing his beloved art with a devotion and disinterestedness which is not possible to musicians who have to live by their profession. He is guiltless of potboilers and catchpennies, and both in his compositions and in his excellent literary essays on music he has proved the constant elevation of his musical ideal. Never was there a musician easier and pleasanter to praise, painfuller and more ungracious to disparage. But—! yes, there is a serious but in the case on the present occasion; and its significance is that when a man takes it upon himself to write an oratorio—perhaps the most gratuitous exploit open to a XIX century Englishman—he must take the consequences.

Judith, then, consists of a sort of musical fabric that any gentleman of Mr Parry's general culture, with a turn for music and the requisite technical training, can turn out to any extent needful for the purposes of a Festival Committee. There is not a rhythm in it, not a progression, not a modulation that brings a breath of freshness with it. The pretentious choruses are made up of phrases mechanically repeated on ascending degrees of the scale, or of hackneyed scraps of *fugato* and pedal point. The unpretentious choruses, smooth and sometimes pretty hymnings about nothing in particular, would pass muster in a mild cantata: in an oratorio they are flavorless. It is impossible to work up any interest in emasculated Handel and watered Mendelssohn, even with all the modern adulterations. The instrumentation is conventional to the sleepiest degree: tromboned solemnities, sentimentalities for solo horn with *tremolo* accompaniment, nervous excitement fiddled *in excelsis*, drum points as invented by Beethoven, and the rest of the worn-out novelties of modern scoring.

Of the music assigned to the principal singers, that of Judith is the hardest to judge, as Miss Anna Williams labored through its difficulties without eloquence or appropriate expression, and hardly ever got quite safely and reassuringly into tune. Madame Patey as Meshullemeth discoursed in lugubrious dramatic recitative about desolate courts and profaned altars. She was repaid for her thankless exertions by one popular number in the form of a ballad which consisted of the first line of The Minstrel Boy, followed by the second line of Tom Bowling, connected by an "augmentation" of a passage from the *finale* of the second act of Lucrezia Borgia, with an ingenious blend of The Girl I Left Behind Me and We be Three Poor Mariners. It will be understood, of course, that the intervals—except in the Lucrezia Borgia case—are altered, and that the source of Mr Parry's unconscious inspiration is betrayed by the accent and measure only. Manasseh, a paltry creature who sings Sunday music for the drawing room whilst his two sons are cremated alive before his eyes, was impersonated by Mr Barton McGuckin, who roused a bored audience by his delivery of a Handelian song, which has the fault of not being by Handel, but is otherwise an agreeable composition, and a great relief to the music which precedes it. Indeed matters generally grow livelier towards the end.

The Israelites become comparatively bright and vigorous when Judith cuts Holofernes' head off. The ballad is gratefully remembered; the enchanting singing of Manasseh's son is dwelt upon; the Handelian song is quoted as a fine thing; and so Judith passes muster for the time.

One of the painful features of oratorio performances in this country is the indifference of most English singers to the artistic treatment of their own language. Hardly any of them shew the results of such training as that by which Italian singers used to be kept at *do, re, mi, fa* until they acquired a certain virtuosity in the sounding of the vowel and the articulation of the consonant. On Saturday afternoon it was not pleasant to hear Mr Barton McGuckin singing line after line as if he were vocalizing for the sake of practice on the very disagreeable vowel *aw*. By a singer who knows this department of his business, such a word, for example, as "command" is a prized opportunity. Mr Barton McGuckin pronounced it "co-monnd" and spoiled it. It is somewhat unlucky that artists who are aware of the full importance of pronunciation, and whose cultivated sense of hearing keeps them acutely conscious of distinctions to which the ordinary singer seems deaf, are also for the most part persons with a strong mannerism, which makes it unsafe to recommend them as models for imitation. Advise a student to pronounce as Mr Irving does, as Mr Sims Reeves does, as Mrs Weldon* does, or as Madame Antoinette Sterling does, and the chances are that that student will simply graft on to his own cockney diphthongs and muddled consonants an absurd bur- lesque of Mr Irving's resonant nose, of Mr Sims Reeves's lackadaisical way of letting the unaccented syllables die away, of Mrs Weldon's inflexible delivery and shut teeth, or of Madame Sterling's peculiar cadence and Scottish-American accent.

The importance of this question of English as she is sung is emphasized just now by the advertisement which announces Mr Leslie's very laudable and farsighted plan of making the new Lyric Theatre an English opera house. English opera suggests at once the Carl Rosa style of entertainment. Now, with all due honor to Mr Carl Rosa's enterprise and perseverance, the performances of his company have never, even at their best, achieved a satisfactory degree of distinction and refinement. But what is peculiar to its representation is the slovenliness in uttering the national language. In an institution which ought to be a school of pure English this is disgraceful, the more so as the defect is, of course, not really the result of social and educational disadvantages, but only of indifference caused by colloquial habit, and by want of artistic sensibility and vigilance.

The Gilbert-Sullivan form of opera caused a remark- able improvement in this respect by making the success of the whole enterprise depend on the pointed and intelligible delivery of the words. It is an encouraging sign, too, that in the success of Dorothy a very important

* Georgina Weldon, English soprano, composer, and mis- tress of Gounod, retired from the concert hall in 1884.

share has been borne by Mr Hayden Coffin, an American, who is a much more accomplished master of his language than many older and more famous baritones of English birth. If Mr Leslie is well advised he will test the artists whom he engages for his new theatre no less carefully as speakers than as singers.

The other day a small but select audience assembled in one of Messrs Broadwood's rooms to hear Miss Florence May play a pianoforte concerto by Brahms. An orchestra being out of the question, Mr Otto Goldschmidt and Mr Kemp played an arrangement of the band parts on two pianofortes. Brahms's music is at bottom only a prodigiously elaborated compound of incoherent reminiscences, and it is quite possible for a young lady with one of those wonderful "techniques," which are freely manufactured at Leipzig and other places, to struggle with his music for an hour at a stretch without giving such an insight to her higher powers as half a dozen bars of a sonata by Mozart. All that can be said confidently of Miss May is that her technique is undeniable. The ensemble of the three Broadwood grands was not so dreadful as might have been expected, and the pretty *finale* pleased everybody.

(The above hasty (not to say silly) description of Brahms's music will, I hope, be a warning to critics who know too much. In every composer's work there are passages that are part of the common stock of music of the time; and when a new genius arises, and his idiom is still unfamiliar and therefore even disagreeable, it is easy for a critic who knows that stock to recognize its contributions to the new work and fail to take in the original complexion put upon it. Beethoven denounced Weber's Euryanthe overture as a string of diminished sevenths. I had not yet got hold of the idiosyncratic Brahms. I apologize. (1936).)

HOW HANDEL IS SUNG

The Star, 3 January 1889 ; unsigned

On New Year's night at the Albert Hall, Messiah is the affair of the shilling gallery, and not of the seven-and-sixpenny stalls. Up there you find every chair occupied, and people standing two or three deep behind the chairs. These sitters and standers are the gallery vanguard, consisting of *prima donna* worshipers who are bent on obtaining a bird's-eye view of Madame Albani for their money. At the back are those who are content to hear Handel's music. They sit on the floor against the wall, with their legs converging straight towards the centre of the dome, and terminating in an inner circumference of boot soles in various stages of wear and tear. Between the circle of boots and the circle of sightseers moves a ceaseless procession of promenaders to whom the performance is as the sounding brass and tinkling cymbals of a military band on a pier. The police take this view, and deal with the gallery as with a thoroughfare included in the Trafalgar Square proclamation, calling out "Pass along, pass along," and even going the length of a decisive shove when the promenade is at all narrowed by too many unreasonable persons stopping to listen to the music. The crowd is a motley one, including many mechanics, who have bought Novello's vocal score of the oratorio and are following it diligently; professional men who cannot afford the luxury and are fain to peep enviously over the mechanics' shoulders; musicians in the Bohemian phase of artistic life; masses of "shilling people" of the ordinary type; the inevitable man with the opera-glass and campstool; and one enthusiast with a blanket on his shoulder, who has apparently been ordered by the police to take up his bed and walk.

To those who heard the Albert Hall Choral Society for the first time on Monday evening, the performance cannot have been a very lively one. The "cuts" (*i.e.* numbers omitted) were many and audacious. They actually included For He shall purify, one of the finest and most popular of Handel's choruses. And with His stripes, Their Sound has gone out, The Trumpet shall sound, and others were also ruthlessly excised. The choruses retained for the occasion were sung in the old prosaic jog-trot. Unto Us a Child is Born was sung correctly, and with admirable purity of tone; but in spirit and feeling it might have been the congratulations offered to a respectable suburban family on the latest addition to the nursery: one whose name could not by any stretch of imagination be called Wonderful! Counselor! The Everlasting Father, the Prince of Peace. Through that fierce and sardonic tumult of mockery, He trusted in God that He would deliver Him, the choir picked its way with a gingerly decorum that suggested a hampering sense of the danger of prosecution for blasphemy. And, later on, in the most famous of all famous choruses, there was not one real, rapturous, transporting Hallelujah. The truth is that Mr Barnby has done with those thousand choristers everything that a conductor can do—except kindle their imagination. That exception places Messiah beyond their reach. Until he can make them rejoice and exult like all the hosts of heaven, and scorn and deride like all the fanatics in Jewry, young London will grow up ignorant of the wonderful qualities which underlie the mere brute amplitude of one of the greatest treasures in their musical heritage. How fast those qualities are being forgotten—how little they are missed, is shewn by the conventional praise which each performance like that of Monday elicits from their appointed assayers in the press.

But if the foregoing must be said in justice to Handel and music, a word must also be said in justice to Mr Barnby. Only those whose memories of the choir go back at least a dozen years can appreciate the wonders he has done with it. In its raw state, its aptitudes for everything except the production of pure vocal tone were manifold and extraordinary. It could hiss, it could growl, it could choke, buzz, gasp, seethe, and whistle until the Albert Hall was like the King's Cross Metropolitan station, with four trains in, all letting off steam, and an artillery wagon coming full gallop up the Gray's Inn Road, whilst somewhere at the heart of the hurly-burly All We like Sheep were being imperfectly kept from going too much astray by Dr Stainer thundering at the organ. Then the orchestra, the indolent, callous, slovenly orchestra, that thought the accompaniments to the old Messiah the cheapest of easy jobs, that was killing Covent Garden by its slovenliness, killing the Philharmonic by its perfunctoriness, under the anxious and estimable Mr Cusins, respecting nobody but Mr August Manns, and fearing nobody but Sir Michael Costa! Mr Weist Hill, too, got some notable work out of them, but he did not shake their conviction that they could not be done without, and in that conviction they hardened themselves until Richter came and beat them easily with what they considered a scratch band of rank outsiders. Those were terrible days for Mr Barnby; but his present achievement gathers lustre from their darkness and confusion. The choir now sings, and abstains from unlovely noises. The tone might be more voluminous considering the multitude of singers; but it could hardly be purer and clearer. And the orchestra, thoroughly reformed, respects itself and its conductor. Mr Smith's

[543]

conquest of the House of Commons* is a joke in comparison. Mr Barnby has made a noble position as an immense, indefatigable worker and a consummate musician. Now is the time for him to consider whether he has not also a poet somewhere in him. If *he* were forthcoming, what a conductor Mr Barnby would be!

There is not much to be said about the four principal singers of Monday. Their work required a very beautiful and eloquent delivery of some of the most touching and impressive passages in our language. It also required complete forgetfulness of the vanities of vocal display. On both points Madame Patey got the better of Madame Albani; but neither lady succeeded in perfectly realizing her true artistic relation to the oratorio. Madame Albani altered the ending of her songs for the worse in the bad old fashion which is now, happily for London, vanishing to the provinces. This time no old gentleman got up to exclaim "Woman, for this be all thy sins forgiven thee" at the end of He shall feed His flock; for the singer of that exquisite strain was too bent on finishing "effectively" to finish well. However, the two voices were grand voices, and so could not wholly miss the mark at any time. Mr C. Banks was the tenor. The English tradition as to the tenor music of the Messiah is distinctly a maudlin tradition, and it is much to Mr Banks's credit that he was not unmanly in his pathos. For the rest, his performance lacked distinction. By the bye, he—or Mr Barnby—took Every Valley so fast that it was spoiled. The audience was much pleased by Mr Watkin Mills's delivery of Why do the Nations, and was a little astonished at his omitting The Trumpet shall Sound.

* William Henry Smith, bookseller and news agent, had succeeded Lord Randolph Churchill as Leader of the Commons.

GOODBYE, PATTI

The Star, 23 January 1889; unsigned

Madame Patti kissed hands last night, in her artless way, to a prodigious audience come to bid her farewell before her trip to South America. The unnecessary unpleasantness of the most useful of Mr Louis Stevenson's novels makes it impossible to say that there is in Madame Patti an Adelina Jekyll and an Adelina Hyde; but there are certainly two very different sides to her public character. There is Patti the great singer: Patti of the beautiful eloquent voice, so perfectly produced and controlled that its most delicate *pianissimo* reaches the remotest listener in the Albert Hall: Patti of the unerring ear, with her magical *roulade* soaring to heavenly altitudes: Patti of the pure, strong tone that made God Save the Queen sound fresh and noble at Covent Garden: Patti of the hushed, tender notes that reconcile rows of club-loving cynics to Home, sweet Home. This was the famous artist who last night sang *Bel raggio* and Comin' thro' the Rye incomparably. With Verdure Clad would also have been perfect but that the intonation of the orchestra got wrong and spoiled it. But there is another Patti: a Patti who cleverly sang and sang again some pretty nonsense from Delibes' Lakmé. Great was the applause, even after it had been repeated; and then the comedy began. Mr Ganz, whilst the house was shouting and clapping uproariously, deliberately took up his *bâton* and started Moszkowski's Serenata in D. The audience took its cue at once, and would not have Moszkowski. After a prolonged struggle, Mr Ganz gave up in despair; and out tripped the *diva*, bowing her acknowledgments in the character of a petted and

[545]

delighted child. When she vanished there was more cheering than ever. Mr Ganz threatened the *serenata* again; but in vain. He appealed to the sentinels of the greenroom; and these shook their heads, amidst roars of protest from the audience, and at last, with elaborate gesture, conveyed in dumb show that they dare not, could not, would not, must not, venture to approach Patti again. Mr Ganz, with well-acted desolation, went on with the *serenata*, not one note of which was heard. Again he appealed to the sentinels; and this time they waved their hands expansively in the direction of South America, to indicate that the *prima donna* was already on her way thither. On this the audience showed such sudden and unexpected signs of giving in that the *diva* tripped out again, bowing, wafting kisses, and successfully courting fresh thunders of applause. Will not some sincere friend of Madame Patti's tell her frankly that she is growing too big a girl for this sort of thing, which imposes on nobody—not even on the infatuated gentlemen who write columns about her fans and jewels. No: the queens of song should leave the coquetry of the footlights to the soubrettes. How much more dignified was Madame Neruda's reception of the magnificent ovation which followed her playing of Bazzini's Ronde des Lutins!

It is unnecessary to say more of the rest of the program than that *E che! fra voi la tema** brought back pleasantly the days when Mr Santley trod the stage, and that Wallace's ridiculous Let me like a Soldier Fall was treated as it deserves, even though it was Mr Edward Lloyd's breast that "expanded to the ball." Miss Gomez made a very favorable impression by her singing of Sir Arthur Sullivan's Sleep, my love, sleep. Madame Patti, it may be added, looks very well and strong, and her voice is as good as ever.

* For note, see Vol. 3, Appendix, p. 783.

DR FRANCIS HUEFFER

The Star, 23 January 1889; unsigned

The unexpected death of Dr Hueffer is a loss to the best interests of music in London. Fortunately, his warfare was accomplished before he fell. The critics who formerly opposed him on the ground that Wagner's music had no form and no melody, that it was noisy and wrong, and never ought to have been written, and could never be popular, came at last to be only too grateful to Hueffer for his willingness to forget their folly. He was a thorough and industrious worker in many departments, and much better equipped for his work both by his capacity and acquirements than many of his colleagues who were by no means so modest.

Personally he was an amiable man, shy and even timid; but he did not look so, and he often produced the most erroneous impressions on those who were only slightly acquainted with him. His long, golden-red beard, shining forehead, and accentuated nostrils made him a remarkable figure at musical performances. Formerly he was careless of his dress and appearance; but of late years he became rather the reverse. His work as a critic was not confined to music: the present writer last met him at the press view of the Arts and Crafts Exhibition at the New Gallery, and at his own request introduced him to Mr Walter Crane, certainly without the slightest presentiment that the meeting was final.

TOO POPULAR

The Star, 23 January 1889; unsigned

The Saturday Popular concerts are almost too popular to be comfortable. Standing room is exhausted before three o'clock. This on the last occasion was not due to Haydn's quartet in C, with the variations on the Austrian hymn. It was not wholly due even to Mr Santley with The Erl King, and To Anthea. It was very largely caused by the announcement of Beethoven's septet.* The way in which people flock to St James's Hall when a few wind instruments are added to the fiddles is only one out of many symptoms of the thirst for orchestral music which remains unsatisfied in London. Private enterprise is a curious thing. When an eminent French engineer suggests an impossible canal through Central America millions are forthcoming instantly. Yet London clamors in vain for a West End concert room capable of accommodating on every Saturday afternoon enough people at a shilling a head to support an orchestra 200 strong. It not only clamors, but gives repeated proofs of the sincerity of its demands and the readiness of its shillings. But no; Panama will be dug through, the Channel Tunnel finished, and the Northwest Passage carpeted before we escape from St James's Hall, where either the orchestra is too small, as with Mr Henschel, or the prices too high, as with Herr Richter. Will not some American millionaire take the matter in hand; build the hall; and give the *bâton* to Mr Theodore Thomas to revenge on the English conductors the wrongs of the American actors?

* Septet in E flat for Strings and Winds, Op. 20.

[548]

Howbeit, this particular concert squeezed itself into St James's Hall until, as has been intimated, St James himself could not have been accommodated with a place. It is unnecessary to say how the quartet was played. Listening to the septet, it was impossible to avoid indulging in some stray speculations as to the age of Mr Lazarus. Fifty or sixty years ago, when the great clarinetist was beginning to rank as a veteran, the subject might have been a delicate one. Today it is difficult to know how to treat him critically; for it would be absurd to encourage him as if he were a promising young player; and yet there is no use in declaring that he "played with his usual ability," because his ability is still, unfortunately for us, as far as ever from being usual. The usual clarinet player is stolid, mechanical, undistinguished, correct at best, vulgar at worst. A phrase played by Mr Lazarus always came, even from the unnoticed ranks of the wood wind at the opera, with a distinction and fine artistic feeling that roused a longing for an orchestra of such players. And his phrases come just that way still. When, in the slow movement of the septet, Mr Lazarus would not have it so fast as Madame Neruda wanted, the question arose whether the difference was one of taste or of age. But when Madame Neruda led off the final *presto* at full speed without sparing a flash of her Hungarian fire, Mr Lazarus answered the question by following her spirited challenge, without slackening one demisemiquaver. For the rest, Mr Paersch managed the horn part with perfect discretion, and Mr Hollander handled his viola admirably; but Signor Piatti was out of sorts, and got quite amazingly out of tune in the trio.

But the highest plane of musical enjoyment during the concert was attained in Beethoven's pianoforte sonata in A flat (Op. 110). Unfortunately, this plane is a select one: it is not everyone who feels at home on it. Among the people who dont may generally be classed

[549]

those who hunt after popular vocalists and never brave the inclemency of classical music except when Mr Sims Reeves or some other famous singer is in the bill. On Saturday, all the chinks and crannies in the audience were stuffed with ballad-convert enthusiasts who had come solely to hear Mr Santley. When Madame Haas began to play Beethoven's Op. 110 they held out for a while in silent misery. Then they began to cough. Now Madame Haas was beginning an exquisite work, most beautifully—most poetically—and was indeed so rapt in it that it is quite impossible that the spell may have been too delicately woven to reach her more distant hearers. It may be, too, that even the regular frequenters of the concerts are accustomed to have Beethoven's later works soundly thumped into them; and Madame Haas is certainly no thumpist. But when every possible excuse is made for the people who coughed, it remains a matter for regret that the attendants did not remove them to Piccadilly, and treat their ailment there by gently passing a warm steamroller over their chests. It is to be hoped that they did not succeed in shaking Madame Haas's faith in her artistic instinct; for it guided her unerringly through the first movement of the sonata. As to the other movements, my impotent exasperation at the idiots on whom such playing seemed lost deprived me of all power of forming a trustworthy judgment. Beethoven in this third manner, and Madame Haas in her smoke-colored silk domino, were got rid of in due course, to be replaced by the idolized baritone.

Mr Santley was a little nervous, and both in The Erl King and To Anthea he forced the pace at the end, and tried to "rush" the effect. It is a pity that he should lack the calm confidence which so many of his rivals derive from their complete innocence of the art of singing. His voice is as fresh and his method as unfailing as ever. He had to repeat To Anthea to console his more obstreperous admirers for their sufferings at the hands of Madame Haas.

Madame Ilma di Murska is dead; and an ungrateful world is describing her obituarily as a person remarkable for a compass that extended to F in alt. Reader, believe it not. What lack has there ever been of F's in alt? Is not that note attainable by Etelka Gerster, Miss van Zandt, our sister's schoolfellow Miss Smith, and many others? Yet they are not di Murskas. It is true that the F's in those famous *fioriture* of the Queen of Night used, when Di Murska sang the part, to chime with a delicate ring and inimitable precision of touch which made *Gli angui d'inferno* her especial property, and gave her a monopoly of the part of Astriffiamante. But she was no less unapproachable as Elvira, in Don Giovanni, a creation to which only a great artist can do justice, and which is usually thrown over to a second-rate "dramatic soprano." The highest note in it is a fifth below the vaunted F, so that "exceptional range" has certainly nothing to do with success in it. Yet who but di Murska was ever rapturously encored for *Mi tradi quell' alma ingrata*, which the general public so often finds "classical," by which it means rather dull and too long? Even Christine Nilsson was nothing to her in this crucial part.

In Italian opera proper she was also unique. Out of a confused memory of dozens of Lucias one remembers only di Murska's. This, remember, was the di Murska of twenty years ago, even then a fabulously old woman and a monstrously made-up woman, the middle of whose voice was not unjustly compared to an old tin kettle. Her makeup had the curious effect of making her seem very young and pretty at close quarters and very artificial and vague in facial outline at a distance. Probably she was by no means the Ninon de l'Enclos that gossip made her out to be. Her eccentric ways of traveling, her menagerie of pets, and such whims as her objection to be watched upon the stage by people in the wings started a vein of small talk about her, which all somehow tended to the exaggeration of her age.

Grove's dictionary gives the date of her birth in Croatia as 1843. A usually well-informed critic suggests 1835 as nearer the truth. The first date is certainly wrong: it is impossible to believe that the consummate artist of 1870 was only twentyseven. It is to be hoped that the story of her daughter's suicide is as untrue as most of the odd stories that attached themselves to her during her lifetime. In her great days here she was a small, slight, fragile woman, with a refinement of manner and delicacy of taste that made itself felt in everything she did on the stage, and that led to all the de Murska legends, beginning with the statement that she was "a lady of position." However that may have been, she was unquestionably a woman of exceptional intelligence and peculiar artistic gifts; and her skill at vocal pyrotechnics was only a small part of the powers which give her a claim to a place among the greatest operatic artists of her day.

MUSICAL MEMS: BY THE STAR'S OWN CAPTIOUS CRITIC*

The Star, 15 February 1889

The other evening, at the London Symphony Concert, I had an idea—an invaluable idea. The first movement of the Eroica symphony was being played; but, as usual,

* This was the first Shaw contribution to bear the signature of "Corno di Bassetto." All subsequent criticisms in The Star, except as noted, were signed either "Corno di Bassetto" or "C. di B."

it was going haphazard. The band had not really studied
it with the conductor; and the conductor was taking his
chance with the band. This was nobody's fault; it was
caused by the customary length of the program, and the
cost of rehearsals relatively to the sum of the payments
for admission to St James's Hall. To the orchestral
player, as to other men, time is money, and money is
livelihood. If he is to devote several days to a thorough
study with Mr Henschel of the Eroica—not to mention
the other half-dozen items in the program—he must be
paid for it. But the hall will not hold money enough. So
what is to be done pending the erection of a new hall,
with a magnificent orchestra endowed by the County
Council, from a poll tax on amateur tenors? Evidently,
either put up with scratch performances or else shorten
the programs. Now, by this time we all know the Eroica
symphony as well as we know Hamlet or Macbeth; and
I, for one, am tired of scratch performances of it.

The best rehearsed dramatic companies (this is not a
digression: the idea is coming) are those itinerant ones
which repeat the same performance half a dozen times
a day before successive audiences. Why should not Mr
Henschel take a hint from them? On Tuesday last he
might have dropped the latter half of his program, and
concentrated his preparation on the Lohengrin prelude,
the song, and the symphony, which are quite as much
as a large crowd (even with improved ventilation and
electric light) can take in at a time. Then, with the prices
reduced to three and ninepence, two shillings, one
shilling, and sixpence, he should have begun at eight
o'clock instead of half-past. At a few minutes past nine
the concert would have been over. Then clear the room,
and begin again before a fresh audience at a quarter to
ten, finishing at eleven. To this plan there are absolutely
no drawbacks. It would not involve the hiring of a single
additional assistant or artist, and the cost of the room

would remain the same. The public would hear a well-rehearsed performance of just the right length, for half what they now pay for a tedious scratch affair. The suburban amateurs would come to the first concert and get away by early trains in excellent time; the late diners and late risers would patronize the second concert. Above all, the sixpenny admission would bring in the enormous class of patient and serious people with a love for art, who cannot afford a shilling for a concert.

Who is this that, after taking it upon himself to tell me how old Mr Lazarus is, adds that wind instruments are injurious to the player's health? I deny that statement flatly. It is so far from being true that the only difficulty is to restrain enthusiasts from prescribing the trombone for all the diseases under the sun. It has been seriously declared that the workmen of the celebrated firm of Courtois of Paris—the name familiar to all *virtuosos* of the cornet—enjoy immunity not only from affections of the lungs, but from cholera and smallpox. They all, it would seem, die of old age, at a hundred and upwards, breathing their last into an ophicleide. I have often wondered myself why the waits do not die of exposure at Christmas. Everybody wishes they would; but they do not seem even to catch cold—at least I never saw a wait with a cold. There must be something in it.

However, there are two sides to this question. The physical effects of artistic activity, especially musical activity, have never been explained. It is quite certain that although the practice of the finest artists is beneficial to them, yet it is possible to sing, act, or play an instrument with demoralizing and even fatal results. Violent and impatient people, who try to overcome difficulties by force, always come to grief. When you begin to sing, or to play a wind instrument, you have to bring into voluntary action muscles of the throat and lips which are weak and involuntary because you have never used them before. However futile and ridiculous your first attempts may be in consequence, you must "suffer it up" in patience and hope. It is from the people who are in too great a hurry that we get the young lady who lost her voice by singing too often (though she never, for the life of her, could venture upon as much vocal exercise in a week as a good artist gets through with pleasure and benefit in a day), as well as the man who lost his teeth and got hemorrhage of the lungs by playing the French horn. Further, it is to be carefully remembered that Art pursued for the sake of excitement would be as mischievous as drinking or gambling, if there were as few obstacles to immoderate indulgence in it.

I am a member of the Wagner Society, and am therefore ready to roll its log at all times, but I do not think I shall contribute to its journal, The Meister. I can stand a reasonable degree of editing, but not even from the all but omniscient editor of The Star would I bear a series of footnotes contradicting every one of my opinions. If the Meisterful method were introduced at Stonecutter-street, my criticisms would appear in this wise:

On Tuesday last a numerous and crowded audience were attracted to St James's Hall by the announcement that Miss Pauline Cramer would sing Isolde's death song, that most moving piece of music ever written. (Note by ED.—Surely our gifted contributor has forgotten Let Erin remember the days of old, in making this sweeping statement.) It is unquestionably the greatest of Wagner's works, and is far superior to the compositions of his earlier period. (We agree, on the whole; but would point out that both in his Tannhäuser March and in his wellknown William Tell overture, Wagner has attained a more engaging rhythmic emphasis, and, at least, equal sweetness of melody.—ED.) Those who heard Miss Cramer's performance must have forgotten for the moment all previous experiences of the kind. (Has our critic ever heard Miss Bellwood's rendering of What cheer, Ria? If so, we can hardly let this statement pass without a protest.—ED.) And so on.

As to the recital of Tristan und Isolde at the Portman Rooms, with pianoforte accompaniment, it was, of course, a terribly shorn and meagre affair in the absence of an orchestra. But such performances are much better than no performances at all. I hear rumors of following up Tristan with the entire Ring. If this comes off, Mr Armbruster must devote all his energy in the first instance to securing the intelligibility of the performance. Unless the audience hear and understand every word, five-sixths of the Ring will be voted a senseless bore. The singers should read their lines together without music, as if they were rehearsing an ordinary drama. If they cannot do this tolerably well, they will never make anything of the music. I do not believe that any person who heard Tristan for the first time at the Portman Rooms without the assistance of a libretto could have passed the most superficial examination as to what the poem was about.

The paragraphs provoked by the revival of L'Etoile du Nord by Mr Carl Rosa in the provinces prove how soon the lapse of years turns a stale opera into a novelty. I have not seen the new performance, but I am certain that it is not a perfect one, for the simple reason that perfect operatic representations are still economically impossible in this country, the result not being worth the trouble. Besides, Meyerbeer's works are so long that they are always mercilessly cut up for performance; and Mr Carl Rosa is one of the old cutting school of managers whom Wagner so righteously denounced. One of the very worst cuts I can remember was the excision from the prelude to the second act of Lohengrin of the burst of music from the palace. This was at a Carl Rosa performance at Drury Lane, conducted by Mr Randegger. If we only had a few thoroughly vindictive critics, who would never let a manager hear the last of an outrage of this sort, we should bring the opera houses to their senses in half a season. The critic is the policeman of the opera. Unfortunately, sheep make bad policemen.

It has been hinted to me that the responsibilities of The Star are already sufficiently heavy without the addition of an anonymous column of criticism which the unique descriptive genius of the sub-editor has led him to label "captious." My colleague Musigena (E. Belfort Bax] also declares that he goes in bodily fear of being mistaken for me. For my own part I am against anonymous criticism, and therefore sign my name and title in full without hestitation. The di Bassettos were known to Mozart, and were of service to him in the production of several of his works. The title was created in 1770. We are a branch of the Reed family, but I have been in Scotland in my life. All complimentary tickets, invitations, and bribes meant specially for me should be addressed to the care of The Star.

Corno di Bassetto.

MUSIC AT BOW

The Star, 21 February 1889

On Monday the editor of The Star summoned me to a private conference. "The fact is, my dear Corno" he said, throwing himself back in his chair and arranging his moustache with the diamond which sparkles at the end of his pen-handle "I dont believe that music in London is confined to St James's Hall, Covent Garden, and the Albert Hall. People must sing and play elsewhere. Whenever I go down to speak at the big Town Halls at Shoreditch, Hackney, Stratford, Holborn, Kensington, Battersea, and deuce knows where, I always see bills at the door announcing oratorios, organ recitals, concerts by local Philharmonic and Orpheus societies, and all sorts of musical games. Why not criticize these instead of saying the same thing over and over again about Henschel and Richter and Norman-Neruda and the rest?" I replied, as best I could, that my experience as a musical critic had left me entirely unacquainted with these outlandish localities and their barbarous minstrelsy; that I regarded London as bounded on the extreme northeast by Stonecutter-street, on the extreme southwest by Kensington Gore, on the south by the Thames, and on the north by the Strand and Regent-street. He assured me that the places he had mentioned actually existed; but that, as I was evidently hurt by the suggestion that I should condescend to visit them, he would hand the ticket he had just received for a Purcell-Handel performance at Bow, to Musigena. "What!" I exclaimed, "Purcell! the greatest of English composers, left to Musigena! to a man whose abnormal gifts in every other direction have blinded him to his utter ignorance of music!" "Well, the fact is" said the editor "Musigena told me only half an hour ago that he was at a loss to imagine how a writer so profound and accomplished as di Bassetto could be in music a mere superficial amateur." I waited to hear no more. Snatching the tickets from the editor's desk, I hastily ran home to get my revolver as a precaution during my hazardous voyage to the East End. Then I dashed away to Broad-street, and asked the booking-clerk whether he knew of a place called Bow. He was evidently a man of extraordinary nerve, for he handed me a ticket without any sign of surprise, as if a voyage to Bow were the most commonplace event possible. A little later the train was rushing through the strangest places: Shoreditch, of which I had read in historical novels; Old Ford, which I had supposed to be a character in one of Shakespear's plays; Homerton, which is somehow associated in my mind with pigeons; and Haggerston, a name perfectly new to me. When I got into the concert room I was perfectly dazzled by the appearance of the orchestra. Nearly all the desks for the second violins were occupied by ladies: beautiful young ladies. Personal beauty is not the strong point of West End orchestras, and I thought the change an immense improvement until the performance began, when the fair fiddlers rambled from bar to bar with a certain sweet indecision that had a charm of its own, but was not exactly what Purcell and Handel meant. When I say that the performance began, I do not imply that it began punctually. The musicians began to drop in at about ten minutes past eight, and the audience were inclined to remonstrate; but an occasional apology from the conductor, Mr F.A.W. Docker, kept them in good humor.

Dido and Eneas is 200 years old, and not a bit the worse for wear. I daresay many of the Bowegians thought that the unintentional quaintnesses of the amateurs in the orchestra were Purcellian antiquities. If so, they were never more mistaken in their lives. Henry Purcell was a great composer: a very great composer indeed; and even this little boarding-school opera is full of his spirit, his freshness, his dramatic expression, and his unapproached art of setting English speech to music. The Handel Society did not do him full justice: the work, in fact, is by no means easy; but the choir made up bravely for the distracting dances of the string quartet. Eneas should not have called Dido Deedo, any more than Juliet should call Romeo Ro-*may*-oh, or Othello call his wife Days-*day*-mona. If Purcell chose to pronounce Dido English fashion, it is not for a Bow-Bromley tenor to presume to correct him. Belinda, too, was careless in the matter of time. She not only arrived after her part had been half finished by volunteers from the choir, but in Oft She Visits she lost her place somewhat conspicuously. An unnamed singer took Come away, fellow sailors, come away: that salt sea air that makes you wonder how anyone has ever had the face to compose another sailor's song after it. I quote the concluding lines, and wish I could quote the incomparably jolly and humorous setting:—

Take a bowsy short leave of your nymphs on the shore;
  And silence their mourning
  With vows of returning,
Though never intending to visit them more.

SAILORS *(greatly tickled)*. Though never—!
OTHER SAILORS *(ready to burst with laughter)*. Though never—!
ALL *(uproariously)*. Inte-en-ding to vi-sit them more.

I am sorry to have to add that the Handel choir, feeling that they were nothing if not solemn, contrived to subdue this rousing strain to the decorum of a Sunday school hymn; and it missed fire accordingly. Of Alexander's Feast I need only say that I enjoyed it thoroughly, even though I was sitting on a cane-bottomed chair (Thackeray overrated this description of furniture)* without adequate room for my knees. The band, reinforced by wind and organ, got through with a healthy roughness that refreshed me; and the choruses were capital. Mr Bantock Pierpoint, the bass, covered himself with merited glory, and Mr John Probert would

* The Cane-Bottom'd Chair, in W. M. Thackeray, Ballads (1855).

have been satisfactory had he been more consistently careful of his intonation. Miss Fresselle acquitted herself fairly; but her singing is like that of the society generally: it lacks point and color. Mr Docker must cure his singers of the notion that choral singing is merely a habit caught in church, and that it is profane and indecorous to sing Handel's music as if it meant anything. That, however, is the worst I have to say of them. I am, on the whole, surprised and delighted with the East End, and shall soon venture there without my revolver. At the end of the concert, a gentleman, to my entire stupefaction, came forward and moved a vote of thanks to the performers. It was passed by acclamation, but without musical honors.

P.S. The Handel Society appeals urgently for tenors, a second bassoon, and horns. Surely every reader of The Star can at least play the second bassoon. Apply to Mr P. L. G. Webb, 3 Chandos-street, Cavendish Square, W.

CONCERTS: WAGNER AND MENDELSSOHN

The Star, 23 February 1889

One of the reflections suggested by the musical events of the last seven days is a comparison of Mr Hamish MacCunn's luck with Wagner's. It is exactly six years since Wagner died at Venice, aged 70. Mr Hamish MacCunn was born yesterday—or thereabouts. Yet whereas Mr MacCunn's Last Minstrel was performed at the Crystal Palace last Saturday, even the overture to Wagner's Die Feen was not heard in London until Tuesday last, when Mr Henschel kindly gave it a turn at the London Symphony Concert. This Die Feen (The Fairies) was written in 1833 for the Würzburg Theatre, where Wagner was chorus master at ten florins a month, which was probably considered a handsome thing for a young man of twenty. It must by no means be supposed that at that age he was a crude amateur. He was certainly a crude Wagner; but if his object had been to turn out a businesslike opera overture, he could evidently have managed as well as Sir Arthur Sullivan or Mr Ebenezer Prout; for the shortcomings of Die Feen are not those of mere illiteracy in music. And there is something of the enchantment of twenty about it. At that age fairyland is not forgotten. The impulse to hear "the horns of elfland" is genuine and spontaneous. At twentysix fairyland is gone: one is stronger, more dexterous, much more bumptious, but not yet much deeper: sometimes not so deep. Accordingly, it was not surprising to find a charm in this *Vorspiel* that is wanting in the empty and violently splendid overture to Rienzi. It is more Wagnerian, for one thing. For another, it has youthful grace and fancy as well as earnestness. At the end, after a little juvenile tearing and raging, it weakens off into an echo of Weber's jubilant mood, and the *coda* is spoilt by the boyish repetition of a piece of energetic commonplace. But the earlier part is well worth the trouble Mr Henschel took with it. The only later work foreshadowed in it is the Faust overture of 1840.

I was astonished, and indeed somewhat hurt, at Mr Henschel's apparent oversight of my proposal that there should be two concerts instead of one. However, he doubtless had my comments in his mind when conducting the Magic Flute overture; for though he did not allow the band to try how fast they could rattle the notes off, as the fashion used to be with Mozart's orchestral works, neither was he able to sound the depths of this great composition, not is he likely to until he can afford to make a thorough study of it, and devote several rehearsals to its preparation. The Haydn symphony (B flat, No. 12), a masterpiece in every sense, went delightfully; and Liszt's Hungarian rhapsody in D, after the usual preliminary bunkum from the horns and bassoons, sparkled, tinkled, warbled, soared, swooped, and raced along so that it was almost impossible to resist the itching to get up and dance. Mr Johann Kruse's performance of Beethoven's violin concerto was not particularly bad except in the opening strokes of the first cadenza, and not particularly good except in a few of the simpler passages. This was the last of the subscription performances. An extra concert, at which we shall have the Leeds choir and the Ninth Symphony, will finish the season next Wednesday afternoon.

Whatever faults the St James's Hall audience may have, susceptibility to panic is not one of them. Although the cooking arrangements connected with the restaurant occasionally scorch the concert room and produce the most terrifying odors of shriveling paint and reddening iron, nobody budges. On Tuesday night I sat trembling, convinced that the whole building was in flames, until a lady gently slipped out and came back with an assurance from the attendants that there was no danger, a smell of fire being one of the wellknown attractions of the hall. Then my past life ceased to run panoramically before my mind's eye; and I settled down to listen to the music. But I respectfully submit that everybody is not gifted with my iron nerve, and that in a very heavy crush the consequences of an inopportune scorch might be disastrous.

The Popular Concert last Saturday afternoon would hardly have provoked me to comment if there had been nothing else to remark than Dr Mackenzie's set of six pieces for the violin, even though three of them were played for the first time by Madame Neruda. They are sentimentally pretty, especially where the programist tells us that in the Benedictus "rapture succeeds to awe"; but there is nothing to prevent Dr Mackenzie carrying out his expressed intention of composing some more. If Madame Neruda would like to contract for such pieces by the dozen, I do not see why the accomplished president of Tenterden-street* should make any difficulty. Neither do I mean to say much about Miss Zimmermann's playing of the Waldstein sonata. Everybody acknowledges that the first movement of the Waldstein is a colossal piece of pianoforte music. I confess I have never been able to see it. It certainly was not colossal as Miss Zimmermann scampered through it, and for the life of me I do not know what else she could have done with a long, scrappy movement which is neither *bravura* nor tone poem, though it asserts itself occasionally in both directions. The *allegretto*, which is the really popular and interesting part of the sonata, was admirably played, the exposition of the theme being particularly happy. Miss Zimmermann got a double recall.

But what I really bring this concert in for is to ask why Mendelssohn's quartet in E flat major is to be thrust into our ears at the point of the analytical program, as one of "the happiest productions of the composer's genius." Also why Mendelssohn is described as "a master yielding to none in the highest qualifications that warrants the name." The man who would say these things nowadays would say anything. Long ago, when the Mendelssohn power was at its height they were excusable; but programs dating from that period are out of date by this time. We now see plainly enough that Mendelssohn, though he expressed himself in music with touching

* Alexander Campbell Mackenzie became principal of the Royal Academy of Music in 1888.

tenderness and refinement, and sometimes with a nobility and pure fire that makes us forget all his kid glove gentility, his conventional sentimentality, and his despicable oratorio mongering, was not in the foremost rank of great composers. He was more intelligent than Schumann, as Tennyson is more intelligent than Browning: he is, indeed, the great composer of the century for all those to whom Tennyson is the great poet of the century. He was more vigorous, more inventive, more inspired than Spohr, and a much abler and better educated man than Schubert. But compare him with Bach, Handel, Haydn, Mozart, Beethoven, or Wagner; and then settle, if you can, what ought to be done to the fanatic who proclaims him "a master yielding to," &c. &c. &c.

These remarks will doubtless have the effect of instantaneously inducing Messrs Chappell to discard their stereotyped program of the E flat quartet. To replace it they should select some person who is not only void of superstition as to Mendelssohn, but also as to the sacredness of sonata form. If the first movement of this quartet was not "a model of construction," it would perhaps be a genuine piece of music instead of the mere dummy that it is. Surely the musical critics ought to leave to their inferiors, the literary reviewers, the folly of supposing that "forms" are anything more than the shells of works of art. Though Bach's natural shell was the fugue, and Beethoven's the sonata, can anybody but an academy professor be infatuated enough to suppose that musical composition consists in the imitation of these shells: a sort of exercise that is as trivial as it is tedious? The fugue form is as dead as the sonata form; and the sonata form is as dead as Beethoven himself. Their deadliness kills Mendelssohn's St Paul and the "regular" movements in his symphonies and chamber music. Fortunately, the people are sound on this question. They are not indifferent to the merits of the first and second subjects in a formal sonata; but to the twaddling "passages" connecting them, to the superfluous repeat, the idiotic "working out," and the tiresome recapitulation they are either deaf or wish they were. I once asked an energetic and liberal-minded young conductor what he thought of Liszt's music. He replied with the inelegant but expressive monosyllable, "Rot." I was much less scandalized than I should have been had he applied that term to Mendelssohn's music; and yet I have no hesitation in saying that we have in Liszt's *Preludes* a far better example of appropriate form than any of the "regularly constructed" works of Mendelssohn.

AN EMBARRASSMENT OF RICHES

The Star, 1 March 1889

There are twentyfour concerts this week. Consequently I give myself a holiday; for if anyone asks me what I thought of this or that performance, I reply "How can I possibly be in twentyfour places at the same time? The particular concert you are curious about is one of those which I was unable to attend." And, indeed, only a few out of the two dozen require any more special notice than an ordinary day's business at a West End shop. Musigena has told you all about Otto Hegner, and has undertaken to look after the two performances of the Ninth Symphony by Mr Henschel on Wednesday and Mr Manns on Saturday. The Hackney choir gave St Paul on Monday; but as they did not invite me to be present—instinctively divining, perhaps, that I detest St Paul, and might pitch into them for its contrapuntrocity—I did not go. As to Mr Grieg, at the Popular Concerts, I tried to get in on Saturday, but found the room filled with young ladies, who, loving his sweet stuff, were eager to see and adore the confectioner. So on Monday I forbore St James's Hall altogether, lest my occupying a seat should be the means of turning away even one enthusiastic worshiper. Mr Isidore de Lara is to be at the Steinway Hall this afternoon, and were I a dark-eyed Oriental beauty from Maida Vale or Sutherland Gardens doubtless I should go; but being what I am, I refrain. Not that Mr de Lara cannot sing very well from my point of view when he likes; but I am always mortally afraid of his beginning to sing well from the dark-eyed point of view, which infuriates me. I have already taken and described my Farewell of Madame Patti at the Albert Hall; and although she is kind enough to repeat the ceremony, I shall not repeat the description. For the other concerts, they are not yet; and sufficient unto the day, &c.

Still, one must go somewhither, after all. That was my feeling, last Tuesday, when, turning over my invitations, I found a card addressed to me, not in my ancestral title of Di Bassetto, but in the assumed name under which I conceal my identity in the vulgar business of life. It invited me to repair to a High School for Girls in a healthy southwestern suburb [Clapham], there to celebrate the annual prizegiving with girlish song and recitation. Here was exactly the thing for a critic. "Now is the time" I exclaimed to my astonished colleagues "to escape from the stale iterations of how Mr Santley sang The Erl King, and Mr Sims Reeves Tom Bowling; of how the same old orchestra played Beethoven in C minor or accompanied Mr Henschel in Pogner's Johannistag song or Wotan's farewell and fire charm.* Our

* Veit Pogner, the goldsmith in Wagner's Die Meistersinger, sings *Das schöne Fest* in Act I. Wotan's farewell is the closing scene of Die Walküre.

business is to look with prophetic eye past these exhausted contemporary subjects into the next generation—to find out how much beauty and artistic feeling is growing up for the time when we shall be obsolete fogies, mumbling anecdotes at the funerals of our favorites." Will it be credited that the sanity of my project and the good taste of my remarks were called in question, and that I was absolutely the only eminent critic who went to the school!

I found the school on the margin of a common, with which I have one ineffaceable association. It is not my custom to confine my critical opinions to the columns of the Press. In my public place I am ever ready to address my fellow citizens orally until the police interfere. Now it happens that once, on a fine Sunday afternoon, I addressed a crowd on this very common for an hour, at the expiry of which a friend took round a hat, and actually collected 16s. 9d. The opulence and liberality of the inhabitants were thus very forcibly impressed on me; and when, last Tuesday, I made my way through a long corridor into the crowded schoolroom, my first thought as I surveyed the row of parents, was whether any of them had been among the contributors to that memorable hatful of coin. My second was whether the principal of the school would have been pleased to see me had she known about the 16s. 9d.

When the sensation caused by my entrance had subsided somewhat, we settled down to a performance which consisted of music and recitation by the rising generation, and speechification by the risen one. The rising generation had the best of it. Whenever the girls did anything, we were all delighted: whenever an adult began, we were bored to the very verge of possible endurance. The deplorable member of Parliament who gave away the prizes may be eloquent in the House of Commons; but before that eager, keen, bright, frank, unbedevilled, unsophisticated audience he quailed, he maundered, he stumbled, wanted to go on and couldnt, wanted to stop and didnt, and finally collapsed in the assuring us emotionally that he felt proud of himself, which struck me as being the most uncalled-for remark I ever heard, even for an M.P. The chairman was self-possessed, not to say hardened. He quoted statistics about Latin, arithmetic, and other sordid absurdities, specially extoling the aptitude of the female mind since 1868 for botany. I incited a little girl near me to call out "Time" and "Question," but she shook her head shyly and said "Miss — would be angry"; so he had his say out. Let him deliver that speech next Sunday on the common, and he will not collect 16s. 9d. He will be stoned.

But the rest of the program was worth a dozen ordinary concerts. It is but a few months since I heard Schubert's setting of The Lord is my Shepherd, sung by the Crystal Palace Choir to Mr Manns' appropriate and beautiful orchestral transcript of the accompaniment; but here a class of girls almost obliterated that memory by singing the opening strain with a purity of tone that was quite angelic. If they could only have kept their attention concentrated long enough, it might have been equally delightful all through. But girlhood is discursive; and those who were not immediately under the awful eye of the lady who conducted, wandering considerably from Schubert's inspiration after a while, although they stuck to his notes most commendably. Yet for all that I can safely say that if there is a little choir like that in every high school the future is guaranteed. We were much entertained by a composition of Jensen's, full of octaves and chords, which was assaulted and vanquished after an energetic bout of fisticuffs by an infant pianist who will not be able to reach the pedals for years to come.

[569]

Then there was the inevitable scene from Athalie, rather anglicized as to the vowels and "t's" and "r's," but intelligently and intelligibly done. Josabeth had the *maintien* of the French stage in a degree that would have enraptured A. B. Walkley.* Joas was so spirited and artless that one forgave Racine the atrocious priggishness of the character; and Athalie did very well indeed. The recitations reached a climax in The Power of Life, a verse dialogue in which the lead was cleverly taken by a sharp and almost bumptious child, who brought out her mother in a wonderful way. I am almost tempted to mention the name of the young lady who spoke the mother's lines, so admirably was it done. It was more in the manner of Miss Beatrice Lamb† than that of any other public performer I can recall. There were many other numbers in the program, but let it suffice to add that when God save the Queen was sung, the substitution of two quavers for the triplet at the beginning of the last line so completely spoiled it that I instantly suspected the headmistress of being a Fenian. She was a slender, elegant lady, who somehow reminded me of Mrs Kendal in Coralie‡; and there was certainly nothing revolutionary in her aspect. But, unless my suspicion is well founded, she had better restore that triplet.

On the whole, as I hurried back by the common, with a fine driving snow dispeling all chance of an impromptu repetition of the sixteen-and-ninepenny experiment, I was able to rejoice in the thought that we may look forward to the persistence of the enormous improvement

* Arthur B. Walkley, drama critic of The Star under the pseudonym "Spectator," later became drama critic of The Times. He was an ardent Francophile.

† A young leading lady in popular comedy and drawing-room drama admired by Shaw.

‡ A play by G.W. Godfrey, which Shaw had seen in 1881.

which has taken place within the last fifteen years in the average taste, general culture, and artistic capacity of our singers, players, and the audiences of appreciative amateurs, upon which everything really depends in the long run. And of you, wise and discriminating reader, I ask whether my account of the high school does not interest you more than the highly scientific account of Dr Mackenzie's Dream of Jubal, which I have left myself no room for, but which may descend on you at any time when I happen to be short of humanly readable copy?

SOME INSTRUMENTS AND HOW TO PLAY THEM

The Star, 8 March 1889

Before I hurry away to St James's Hall to hear the Bach Choir and Joachim, I must snatch a moment to reply to the numerous correspondents who have been struck by my recent remarks as to the salutary effects of wind-instrument playing. It is impossible to answer all their questions in detail, but a few general observations will cover most of the cases.

First, then, as to the constantly recurring question whether the practice of musical instruments is likely to annoy the neighbors. There can be no doubt whatever that it is; and when the man next door sends in to complain there is no use in quarreling over the point. Admit promptly and frankly that the noise is horrible, promise to cease practising after half-past twelve at night, except when you have vistors; and confess that if he in self-defence takes up another instrument you will be bound to suffer in turn for the sake of his health and culture as he is now suffering for yours. This is far more sensible and social than to place the bell of your instrument against the partition wall and blow strident fanfares in defiance of his nerves, as I foolishly did when a complaint of the kind was made to me. But I was little more than a boy at the time, and I have never since thought of it without remorse.

As to my correspondent who inquires whether there is such a thing as "a dumb French horn," analogous to the "dumb piano" used for teaching children to finger the keyboard, I am happy to be able to assure him that no such contrivance is needed, as the ordinary French horn remains dumb in the hands of a beginner for a considerable period. Nor can anyone, when it does begin to speak, precisely foresee what it will say. Even an experienced player can only surmise what will happen when he starts. I have seen an eminent conductor beat his way helplessly through the first page of the Freischütz overture without eliciting anything from the four expert cornists* in the orchestra but inebriated gugglings.

The amateur will find, contrary to all his preconceptions, that the larger the instrument the easier it is to play. It is a mistake to suppose that he has to fill the instrument with expired air: he has only to throw into vibration the column of air already contained in it. In the German bands, which were dispersed by the Franco-Prussian war, mothers of households used to observe with indignation from the windows that these apparently lazy and brutal foreigners always placed the burden of the largest instrument on the smallest boy. As a matter of fact, however, the small boy had the easiest job; and I recommend amateurs to confine themselves to the tuba or bombardon, the chest-encircling helicon, the ophicleide, or at most the euphonium. The euphonium is an

* This was set as "cornets" (see Shaw's comment on 16 March).

extraordinary sentimental instrument, and can impart a tender melancholy to the most ferocious themes. The accents of the Count di Luna, raging to inflict *mille atroci spasimi* on Manrico, in the last act of Trovatore, are bloodcurdling. Transcribed for the euphonium in a military band selection they remind you of The Maiden's Prayer.

Of course, you will not take my advice. You are bent on learning the flute or the cornet. As to the flute I do not greatly care: you will get tired of it long before you can play *Ah! non giunge*, even without variations. But the cornet is a most fearful instrument, and one with which self-satisfaction is attainable on easy terms. The vulgarity of the cornet is incurable. At its best—playing *pianissimo* in heavenly sweet chords scored by Gounod, or making the sword motive heard, in the first act of Die Walküre—it is only pretty. But in trumpet parts it is simply perdurable. Yet there is no getting rid of it.

Two cornet performancers have left an abiding memory with me. One was M. Lévy's variation on Yankee Doodle, taken *prestissimo*, with each note repeated three times by "triple tonguing." This was in the open air, at the inauguration of Buffalo Bill; and it was preceded by a spirited attempt on the part of Madame Nordica to sing The Star Spangled Banner to an entirely independent accompaniment by the band of Grenadier Guards. The other was The Pilgrim of Love, played by an itinerant artist outside a public house in Clipstone-street, Portland Place. The man played with great taste and pathos; but, to my surprise, he had no knowledge of musical etiquette, for when, on his holding his hat to me for a donation, I explained that I was a member of the press, he still seemed to expect me to pay for my entertainment: a shocking instance of popular ignorance.

I dwell on the cornet a little, because in my youth I

was presented by a relative with absolutely the very worst and oldest cornet then in existence. It was of an obsolete rectangular model, and sounded in B flat with the A crook on. Its tone was unique; my master—an excellent player, of London extraction—once described it as "somethink 'ellish"; and he did it no more than justice. I never come across Scott's line, "Oh, for a blast of that dread horn,"* without thinking of it. After devastating the welkin with this remarkable instrument for some months, I was told that it would spoil my voice (perhaps in revenge for having had its own spoiled); and though I had not then, nor ever have had, any voice worth taking care of, I there and then presented the cornet as a curiosity to my instructor, and abandoned it for aye. It turned his brain eventually; for he afterwards spread a report that *I* was mad.

I believe that a taste for brass instruments is hereditary. My father destroyed his domestic peace by immoderate indulgence in the trombone; my uncle played the ophicleide—very nicely, I must admit—for years, and then perished by his own hand. Some day I shall buy a trombone myself. At the Inventions Exhibition Messrs Rudall and Carte displayed a double-slide trombone, which I felt insanely tempted to purchase. Of the merits of this instrument I was, and am, wholly ignorant, except that I inferred that its "shifts" were only half as long as on the ordinary trombone; and I ascertained that its price was 13 guineas. If ever I have so vast a sum at my command I shall probably buy that trombone, and ask Herr Richter to engage me for the next concert at which the Walkürenritt or Les Francs-Juges is in the program.

By the bye, I do not agree with Musigena that Mr Manns keeps his brass too quiet at the Crystal Palace. I

* Marmion (1808), Canto 6, Section XXXIV.

admire two things at Sydenham: the brass and Mr Manns himself. The strings are often snappish and mechanical, the wood wind stolid; but the brass is generally noble. I have never heard the statue music in Don Giovanni more finely played than at Mr Manns' centenary recital of that masterpiece; and this is as much as to say that Mr Manns feels for the trombone like Mozart and myself. But I certainly believe that the time is approaching when it will be admitted that the doubling, trebling, and quadrupling of the strings which has taken place in the modern orchestra requires a proportional multiplication of the wind instruments to balance them. In spite of the splendors of the Boehm flute, it is often lost in passages where the old flute used to tell when violins were less numerous. For ensemble playing there ought to be at least six bassoons instead of two. And though I never want Mr Manns' trombones to play four times as loud—the trombone being a tender plant that must not be forced—I sometimes want twelve trombones instead of three. This would satisfy Musigena, though it would run into money.

But I must not leave my inquiring amateurs without a word for those who most deserve my sympathy. They are people who desire to enjoy music socially: to play together, to explore the riches of concerted chamber music for mere love of it, and without any desire to expand their lungs and display their individual virtuosity. Yet they are too old to learn to fiddle, or, having learnt, cannot do it well enough to produce tolerable concord. Their difficulty is, fortunately, quite easy to solve. The instrument for them is the concertina: not the Teutonic instrument of the midnight Mohock, but the English concertina of Wheatstone. I presume Wheatstone and Co. are still flourishing in Conduit-street, although Mr Richard Blagrove and his quartet party have not been much in evidence lately. You can play any instrument's part on a concertina of suitable compass, the B flat clarinet being most exactly matched by it in point of tone. The intonation does not depend on you any more than that of a pianoforte. A good concertina is everlasting: it can be repaired as often as a violin. It costs from 16 guineas for a treble to 24 for a contrabrass.

BASSETTO'S UNCLE AND PEER GYNT

The Star, 16 March 1889

I am sorry to say that a postcard has been forwarded to me inscribed as follows:—"'My uncle played the ophicleide for years, and then perished by his own hand.'— Corno di Bassetto, in Star.

> "Bassetto, so expert you are
>   With anecdote and wrinkle,
> To keep the readers of The Star
>   For ever on the twinkle;
> Of playing ophicleides, in sooth,
>   You make us feel quite funky;
> But, tell us—*was* it gospel truth,
>   That death of poor old Nunky?
>
> "With this ancestral tale of woe
>   Youve set us all a-sighing,
> Until we deeply crave to know
>   The manner of his dying.
> Did he fall slain by field or lake,
>   By poison, or stiletto,
> Or did his nephew's stories take
>   His breath away, Bassetto?   S.

Nature must be dead in the man who can thus trifle with a family feeling. I regret now that I mentioned the matter. My statement was true; but I decline, for two reasons, to satisfy the morbid curiosity of S.* The reasons are: (1) the evidence at a coroner's inquest does not come under the head of musical memoranda; and (2) the details are so grotesquely extraordinary—so absolutely without precedent in the records of self-destruction—that, often as I have told the story, it has never once been believed.

Another correspondent, writing in vivid prose, describes me as "an ignorant ass" for having spoken of "four cornets" in the overture to Der Freischütz. I own the soft impeachment generally, but demur to the particular instance of it. Sir Isaac Newton confessed himself an ignorant man; and though I know everything that he knew, and a good deal more besides, yet relatively—*relatively*, mind—I am almost as ignorant as he. The term "ass" I take to be a compliment. Modesty, hard work, contentment with plain fare, development of ear, underestimation by the public: all these are the lot of the ass and of the last of the Bassettos. But I think the superior information and sagacity of my censor might have enabled him to detect an obvious misprint. "Four expert cornets" (*vide* last week's column) is nonsense, and would be so even if the instruments referred to—horns, of course—were really cornets. What I wrote was "Four expert cornists." My correspondent is an idiot.

Hitherto I have not been a great admirer of Edvard Grieg. He is a "national" composer; and I am not to be imposed on by that sort of thing. I do not cry out "How Norwegian!" whenever I hear an augmented triad; nor "How Bohemian!" when I hear a tune proceeding by

* Identified by Shaw, in London Music (1937), as Henry S. Salt.

intervals of augmented seconds; nor "How Irish!" when Mr Villiers Stanford plays certain tricks on sub-dominant harmonies; nor "How Scotch!" when somebody goes to the piano and drones away on E flat and B flat with his left hand, meanwhile jigging at random on the other black keys with his right. All good "folk music" is as international as the story of Jack the Giant Killer, or the Ninth Symphony. Grieg is very fond of the augmented triad; but his music does not remind me of Norway, perhaps because I have never been there. And his sweet but very cosmopolitan modulations and his inability to get beyond a very pretty snatch of melody do not go very far with me; for I despise pretty music. Give me a good, solid, long-winded, classical lump of composition, with time to go to sleep and wake up two or three times in each movement, say I.

However, let us be just. The pretty snatches are not only pretty, but both delicately and deeply felt by the composer. And they are, at least, long enough to make exquisite little songs, which Madame Grieg sings in such a way as to bring out everything that is in them. There is a certain quaintness about the pair. Grieg is a small, swift, busy, earnest man, with the eyes of a rhapsode, and in his hair and complexion the indescribable ashen tint that marks a certain type of modern Norseman. For Madame's appearance I cannot answer so fully, as I have had no opportunity of observing her quite closely; but she holds herself oddly and sings with unrestrained expression. The voice, unluckily, does not help her much. I know half a dozen commonplace young ladies with better, fresher, more flexible voices; but they will not take Madame Grieg's place yet awhile. Most of them, too, would regard a habit of musical composition on their husband's part as one of those conceited follies to which men are subject. It is really a stupendous feat, this of making your wife believe in you.

Grieg's Peer Gynt suite, which he conducted at the Philharmonic on Thursday, was written for use in the theatre at the performance of the play. Now Peer Gynt (Pare Yoont is about as near as you can get to it in English) is a great play: a masterpiece of Norwegian literature, as Faust is a masterpiece of German literature. Like Faust, it is a fantastic drama in rhymed verse. Like Faust, again, it is full of scenes that haunt a composer and compel him to give them musical expression. Grieg, however, has not attempted to wrestle with a giant like Ibsen. His Aase's death music, for instance, does not deal with that wonderful imaginary ride to the castle east of the sun and west of the moon with which Peer, having harnessed the cat to his mother's deathbed, beguiles the worn-out old woman painlessly from the world. Grieg deals rather with the earlier part of the scene, where Aase lies deserted, awaiting her last hour. The music, a quiet crooning harmonic motive, is deeply pathetic. On Thursday it moved an audience which knew nothing of Peer Gynt. For the rest, the dawn music is charming, and so is Anitra's dance, which begins like the waltz in Berlioz's Fantastic Symphony. The Dovregubben orgy is a riotous piece of weird fun. All four numbers are simply frank repetitions, in various keys and with different instrumentation, of some short phrase, trivial certainly, but graceful and fancifully expressive. But they pleased the Philharmonic audience more and more as they went on; and finally Grieg, after two recalls, had to repeat the Dovregubben piece.

On next Wednesday afternoon Grieg will have a concert all to himself. He will play his Holberg suite (Holberg was the Molière of the North); Madame will sing five of his songs, besides playing duets with him; and Johannes Wolff will play a violin sonata of his. Mr Wolff is a Dutchman, like Mr Henry Seiffert, who played the other day at the Ice Carnival, which I did not attend, as my skates are out of order. The violin is capricious in its choice of nations. Formerly all fiddlers were Italian. Then the French had a turn, and then the Hungarians, Sarasate being a brilliant exception to all rules. But no one ever dreamt of a modern Dutch musician until the year of the Inventions Exhibition, when a Mr de Lange and his brother, conductor and organist respectively, gave two concerts of the music of the great old Netherlandish school of Sweelinck, Okeghem, Orlandus Lassus, and the rest of them, the execution of which, by eight singers from Amsterdam, made an extraordinary impression on the few musicians who happened to be present. After that, when at a concert at Steinway Hall I heard Mr Seiffert play a couple of pieces by Max Bruch and Wieniawski, with remarkably powerful tone and startling execution, I was not surprised to hear that he was a Dutchman. Subsequently, at the same hall, I heard Mr Wolff, who struck me, before he began to play, as the most goodnatured-looking violinist I ever saw: a man whom no one would have the heart to criticize adversely. I do not remember what he was set down to play: it may have been the Kreutzer Sonata for all I know; but in answer to an *encore*, he gave us the oddest tune I ever heard in a concert room. He must have picked it up from some very old itinerant fiddler in the street. It was only about forty bars, played with immense humor and perfectly appropriate expression. I have not forgotten it yet. Advance, Holland!

THE PERFORMANCE OF GRIEG'S
PEER GYNT IN LONDON

First appeared as "Special Correspondence" in Dagbladet (Oslo), 18 March 1889, signed G. Bernhard Shaw. Re-translated from the Norwegian for the present edition by Harley J. Refsal, Department of Scandinavian Studies, Luther College, Decorah, Iowa

[U] The London appearance of Edvard Grieg and his wife has aroused lively interest in musical circles. Each time Grieg has performed at the so-called "Monday and Saturday Popular Chamber Music Concerts," all available seats, except the most expensive ones, have been filled a half hour before the concert begins. On Thursday, when he conducted his Peer Gynt for the Philharmonic Society's opening concert, the hall was filled to overflowing. The Prince and Princess of Wales were among those in attendance. Following the Dovregubben piece Grieg was twice re-called for a bow, and the applause remained so strong and persistent that he finally had to mount the podium again and repeat the number. You Norwegians cannot accuse us of a lack of appreciation for your composers!

Of course, it can hardly be said that Grieg came here an unknown man. His lyric pieces for piano have been favorites among the cultured London musical set for years. Especially our young women seem to be enchanted by his joyous inventions and well conceived, melodious short compositions with their sweet modulations. When they hear that augmented triad for which he shews such a preference, they sigh "How Norwegian! How fitting for one who hails from the land of the fjords and the midnight sun! What local color!" And then they proceed to sing Solveig's Song for us, in German of course, adhering all the while to Ibsen's original text which, incidentally, they mutilate in a most shocking manner.

Grieg has therefore visited England, parlor by parlor, before he called on us in person. And now he is well-known to an extent which would otherwise have been impossible, even if all his works had been intended for performance in enormous concert halls and opera houses. Madame Grieg is also very popular, and much sought after by the many amateurs who wish to learn the proper method of singing their favorite Grieg songs. The composer's wife can undoubtedly impart more knowledge than others.

Moreover, it must be noted that even the general public is beginning to understand that the Norwegian people are not simply a poor and wretched lot whose land is prized as a refuge for wealthy foreign hunters and fishermen. They are also commencing to be thought of as a people with a vast modern literature and a remarkably interesting political history. Shakespear's supremacy in our own literature has long led us to believe that there is one great dramatist who dominates each national literature. We are used to the idea of one central figure, around whom all the others group themselves. Therefore we are intensely interested in each new word about that "modern Shakespear" looming in Scandinavia—Henrik Ibsen—whose plays, it is said, would amaze and move us if ever translated into our language.

The thought of undertaking such translations has already tantalized literary and artistic minds for years. Mr. H.L. Brækstad, who in a quiet but effective way is a kind of private Consul General for Norway in London, is frequently involved in various official undertakings, and has initiated ties between Norway and Norwegians, being the one who first persuaded Mr Edmund Gosse to write about Ibsen. There appeared a couple of easily forgotten translations of plays from Ibsen's later period. These failed to convince anyone that Ibsen was a great writer, although one clearly perceived him to be a serious, profound social reformer and an experienced drama critic.

But then one of our most able drama critics, William Archer, who is quite familiar with the Norwegian language and literature, delivered a series of lectures at the Royal Institution on dramatic literature, and in one of these discussed Brand and Peer Gynt. The latter work he described with such effectiveness that the listeners were seized by curiosity to become acquainted with the play. A short time after this lecture the excellent translator of Dante, linguist and literary critic, the Reverend Philip Wicksteed delivered a series of lectures on Peer Gynt. Professor Karl Pearson of University College, famous among other things for his refreshing work The Ethic of Free Thought, then published a pamphlet, the motto of which was derived from Peer Gynt. Briefly stated, Peer Gynt was "in the air." So when Grieg presented his work with the same wellknown title he reaped the advantage of an interest which the Ibsen play had inspired beforehand among the educated public.

Grieg has undoubtedly been surprised with the way in which the Philharmonic Society's Orchestra performed his work. I attended the first rehearsal, which took place Wednesday morning, and I can testify that the rehearsal was deplorable. Several members of the orchestra failed to appear for the rehearsal, and the others certainly were not prepared to overexert themselves. But Thursday evening, when they were face to face with the audience, Grieg himself was amazed by the expressive interpretation of his music. The *pianissimo* opening section of Aase's Death made a deep impression even on those who were not familiar with the author. It must be pointed out that those who knew the play felt the music was perhaps a bit trivial. We forgot for the moment that it was written to accompany a dramatic work, and therefore would be governed by certain prescribed circumstances on stage. We are referring to that imaginary ride to the castle "east of the sun and west of the moon." That, as we heard, was rendered with deep expression, and Grieg is more than ever now the public's favorite.

Concerning Madame Grieg I must admit that we have many voices which are better, fresher, and more flexible than hers, but we are enchanted by the incomparable way in which she interprets each and every nuance in Grieg's songs. We are delighted with her precise articulation, and admit that we are most uninformed, but very anxious to gain familiarity with the sound of the Norwegian language. [U]

THE GRIEG CONCERT

The Star, 21 March 1889; unsigned

The Grieg concert yesterday afternoon at St James's Hall is an event which the musical world of London may look back upon with considerable pleasure and satisfaction. The Norwegian composer and his wife will also, no doubt, carry back with them the pleasantest recollections of their enthusiastic reception at the hands of a highly appreciative St James's Hall audience. It is, indeed, a rare occurrence to be present at a concert the program of which not only consists wholly of one composer's works, but which is performed by the composer himself and his wife. The concert opened with his Holberg Suite, or "Suite in old style," as it was called on the program. This suite was composed on the occasion of the Holberg Jubilee in 1884, when the Danes and Norwegians celebrated in great style the 200th anniversary of the birth of Ludvig Holberg, the father of the literature of those countries, and who, by the bye, is a townsman of Mr Grieg. The composer has succeeded in reproducing with much fidelity the spirit of those "good old times," and it is almost unnecessary to say that he rendered his own composition in his elegant and attractive manner. The suite has already been performed at one of the Popular Concerts this season, but it was yesterday again received with hearty applause.

Mrs Grieg sang Ragna and Hope, both characteristic of those "melodies of the heart" which have made her husband famous. The more we hear Mrs Grieg the more we are convinced that no one else can sing these songs so feelingly, and do such justice to them, as she. What would not most composers give for such wives, such better halves, to interpret their songs! Mr and Mrs Grieg next played a piano duet, Norwegian Dances (Op. 35). Here again the wife proved herself a valuable partner, and both she and her husband were enthusiastically applauded. In this composition Mr Grieg shews how ingeniously and artistically he contrives to weave the national melodies of his country into his composition.

The event of the day was, however, no doubt, the performance of his Sonata in C minor (Op. 45) for piano and violin. It was an excellent idea to secure the services of the brilliant violinist, Mr Johannes Wolff, for the violin part in this very spirited composition. It is some time since we heard a violinist who displayed so much fire and power of execution. There were moments when we were forcibly reminded of the style of Grieg's great countryman, the late Ole Bull. No virtuoso on the violin can desire a better accompanist than Mr Grieg. Both Mr Grieg and Mr Wolff were rapturously applauded, and had to appear three times in response to the calls of the delighted audience.

Mrs Grieg sang three more songs, With a Water-lily, Margaret's Cradle Song, and The Rosebud. Forced to sing an *encore* she gave Björnson's well-known song *Dagen er oppe* (Day is breaking) in her most spirited and effective style. In conclusion Mr Grieg played three of his piano pieces, Berceuse, a most original and elegant composition, Humoreske, and the well-known Bridal Procession. The last is, undoubtedly, one of Grieg's most characteristic pieces for the piano, but it is necessary to hear the composition played by the composer himself the better to understand its peculiar character.

RICHARD ORCHESTRATED
The Star, 23 March 1889

A. B. Walkley has had the unspeakable audacity to advise "the frolic Bassetto" to go to Richard III. at the Globe Theatre. This is a gibe at my earnestness, which perhaps makes my column appear heavy to those who are accustomed to the trivialities of dramatic criticism. But I believe I have the support of those who are weary of levity, of egotism, of senseless facetiousness, of self-advertisement, and, I will add, of ignorance and presumption. If, as Walkley implies, I have no sense of humor—and I do not deny it nor regret it—at least my readers are protected against misplaced jests and fleers at men who feel their responsibility and do not trifle with their mission.

As a matter of fact, I did go to the Globe, not because Walkley wished me to hear "Mr Edward German's fine music, with its *leitmotivs* after Wagner's plan" (ha! ha! ha!), but because a musician only has the right to criticize works like Shakespear's earlier histories and tragedies. The two Richards, King John, and the last act of Romeo and Juliet depend wholly on the beauty of their music. There is no deep significance, no great subtlety and variety in their numbers; but for splendor of sound, magic of romantic illusion, majesty of emphasis, ardor, elation, reverberation of haunting echoes, and every poetic quality that can waken the heart-stir and the imaginative fire of early manhood, they stand above all recorded music. These things cannot be spectated (Walkley signs himself Spectator): they must be heard. It is not enough to see Richard III.: you should be able to *whistle* it.

However, to the music! Mr Mansfield's* execution of his opening *scena* was, I must say, deeply disappointing. When I heard his rendering of the mighty line—

> In the deep bosom of the ocean buried,

which almost rivals "the multitudinous seas incarnadine" I perceived that Richard was not going to be a musical success. And when in that deliberate staccato—

> I am determinéd to be a villain,

he actually missed half a bar by saying in modern prose fashion, "I am determin'd to be a villain," I gave him up as earless. Only in such lines as—

> Framed in the prodigality of nature,

which simply cannot be put out of joint, was his delivery admirable. And yet his very worst achievement was—

> Bound with triumphant garlands will I come,
> And lead your daughter to a conqueror's bed.

* Richard Mansfield, American actor-manager, who later introduced Shaw's plays to the United States with his productions of Arms and the Man (1894) and The Devil's Disciple (1897).

Spectator, with reckless frivolity, has left his readers to infer that the magnificent duet with Miss Mary Rorke in which these lines occur, with the famous section beginning.

> Send to her, by the man that slew her brothers,
> A pair of bleeding hearts,

is by Cibber. "*Ecce iterum!* this scene is Cibber again" says Spectator. And this, mind, not that he does not know as well as I do that the lines are Shakespear's, but simply because, as Cibber was a sort of dramatic critic (he was an actor who wrote an apology, by no means uncalled for, for his own existence, though in justice I must add that it is still the best book on the English theatre in existence, just as Boswell's Journey to the Hebrides is still the best guidebook), Spectator wishes to prove him superior to Shakespear!

To return to Mr Mansfield. It is a positive sin for a man with such a voice to give the words without the setting, like a Covent Garden libretto. Several times he made fine music for a moment, only to shew in the next line that he had made it haphazard. His acting version of the play, though it is an enormous improvement on the traditional Cibberesque, notably in the third and fourth acts, yet contains some wanton substitution of Cibber's halting, tinpot, clinking stuff for noble and beautiful lines by Shakespear, which would occupy no longer time in delivery. Why, for instance, is this passage avoided?

RICHARD'S MOTHER: . . . I prithee hear me speak;
> For I shall never speak to thee again.

RICHARD: So.

HIS MOTHER: Either thou wilt die, by God's just
> ordinance,

Ere from this war thou turn a conqueror;
Or I with grief and extreme age shall perish,
And never more behold thy face again.

And so on. Is Mr Mansfield deaf, that he allows the dead hand of Cibber to filch this passage from Miss Leclercq and the audience? Or is a gentleman connected with this paper, who has shewn a suspicious familiarity with the Globe arrangements, the real author of the Mansfield version? If I were playing Richard I would sacrifice anything else in the play sooner than that monosyllable "So"; which tells more of Richard than a dozen stabbings and baby smotherings.

The last act also presents some unaccountable inconsistencies. Mr Mansfield valiantly gives every word of the striking solo following the nightmare scene; and he rejects "Richard's himself again" with the contempt it deserves. But instead of finishing the scene in mystery and terror by stealing off into the gloom to eavesdrop with Ratcliff, he introduces that vulgar Cibberian *coda* in the major key:—

Hark! the shrill trumpet sounds. To Horse! Away!
My soul's in arms and eager for the fray.

Imagine a man at dead midnight, hours before the battle, with cold, fearful drops still on his trembling flesh, suddenly gasconading in this fashion. Shakespear waits until Richard is in the field, and the troops actually in motion. That is the magnetic moment when all the dreadful joy of the fighting man surges up in him, and he exclaims—

A thousand hearts are great within my bosom.

And now, as to Mr Edward German's music, "with its *leitmotivs* after Wagner's plan." Here is the principal theme of the overture:—

[589]

etc.

And whenever Richard enters you hear the bassoons going: Pum-pum-pum, pum, pum, Paw! It is a *leitmotiv* certainly; but this very primitive employment of it is not "after Wagner's plan." Hang it all, gentlemen critics of the drama, have you never been to the opera? Surely you have heard at least Der Freischütz or Robert le Diable, or even Satanella, with their one or two comparatively undeveloped, unaltered, and uncombined *leitmotivs* labeling stage figures rather than representing ideas. Yet you can hardly have supposed that these were "after Wagner's plan."

What Mr Edward German has done is this: having had about twentytwo players at his disposal, he has wisely written for the old Haydn-Mozart symphony orchestra: two flutes, two oboes, two clarinets, two bassoons, two horns, drums, and strings: no trumpets or trombones. He has also necessarily economized in the strings by doing without cellos. For these hardly Wagnerian forces he has written an overture and a series of intermezzos, all pretty and well put together, but none presenting a single point of novelty. The style is the style of—say Max Bruch: that is, everybody's style: Guonod's, Bizet's, Mendelssohn's, Verdi's, all styles *except Wagner's.*

The first *entr'acte* begins with a prolonged bassoon note and a slow triplet, which makes you rub your eyes and ask whether the curtain is not about to rise on the tower scene from Il Trovatore. The prelude to the last act is a reminiscence, and a very vivid one too, of the prelude and gypsy dance at the beginning of the tavern scene in Carmen. In short, Mr German knows his business, and has come off with credit; but his music is not specially dramatic in character, and would suit The

Lady of Lyons just as well as Richard III. By the bye, why has he not taken the pastoral opportunity offered by the scene in which Richmond and his army scent the morning air on Bosworth Field? He should have divided the honors of this most effective bit of scene painting with Mr Telbin*.

I have been asked to say something about Tamberlik; but I imagine he must have flourished a little before my time. At any rate, I only heard him once, about twelve years ago, and then he was not a good singer, nor did he convince me that he was even the remains of one. The opera was Rossini's Otello, which proved worth half a dozen Semiramides. At the end of the duet with Iago, Tamberlik rushed at the footlights and delivered an eldritch squeal, which was all that was left of the famous *ut dièse de poitrine*. I had almost as lief have been played upon by a fire-engine. He had a superb figure, and certain traditional phrasings which the old-fashioned training used to knock into singers, usually knocking the voice out of them at the same time. No doubt when he was young, with a fresh larynx, and able as well as willing to shout, he found no difficulty in carrying off some of the very doubtful honors of middle Victorian Italian opera. But if ever he was a fine artist, then I do not know what a fine artist is—which, as you justly observe, kindly reader, is a perfectly admissible hypothesis.

* William Lewis Telbin, one of the most highly regarded scenic artists in the British theatre.

SATURDAY'S MUSIC: ROKEBY

Unsigned note in The Pall Mall Gazette, 25 March 1889

[U] There was a good bill at the Crystal Palace on Saturday afternoon, for in addition to the music there was the annual show of spring flowers and the very excellent exhibition of the specimens of the photographer's art. The concert program, however, was unusually strong, and included the production of a new overture by Mr Ebenezer Prout, a thorough musician, whose works are not heard very frequently. He has founded his present composition on Sir Walter Scott's Rokeby, and therein recognized the wonderful affinity there is between music and the sister arts of painting and poetry. It is "more an exhibition of feeling than a painting," and in it Mr Prout has given a free rein to his really scholarly musicianship. It is full of sweet melody, and in the opening movement, *andante con moto*, his melodic invention and original method of handling the orchestra are both effective and skilful. The very large audience applauded heartily, and the composer acknowledged their enthusiasm in person.

Not a little interest attached, too, to the appearance of Herr Stavenhagen. He chose for his *début* Liszt's celebrated, eccentric but hardly beautiful, concerto for pianoforte and orchestra in A, No. 2, possibly to display his really wonderful technique. The work is full of technical difficulty, and the last and well-beloved of the Abbé's pupils shewed that he had caught not a little of his master's genius. Other features of the program were an addition to the Crystal Palace *répertoire* of Saint-Saëns' symphonic poem Phaëton, and a splendid rendering of Raff's idyllic, if slightly fantastic, Lenore symphony. A new soprano, Miss Elsa, sang.[U]

"THE CAPTIOUS FROLIC"

The Star, 30 March 1889

I grieve to say that a member of the Globe orchestra has written a long letter to the editor most unbecomingly alluding to me as "the captious frolic," and seeking to prove that I am no musician. As well try to prove the earth flat. With all the gentleman's ingenuity and exceptional opportunities of knowing Mr German's score, he has succeeded in convincing me of only fifteen mistakes in an entire column of The Star: a result which speaks for itself.

On one or two points I have a remark to offer—I trust respectfully, and with good temper. If the music printer of The Star subjects my quavers to a course of Darwinian evolution from which they issue without tails, and so, to quote my critic, "gets the value of four crotchets in a bar of three-four time," is that my fault? Further, when I am told that "the two trumpets and trombone were there right enough," the implication is that I regarded their apparent absence as a culpable omission. So far was this from my thoughts that I am now disposed to reproach Mr German with wasting three players on instruments which made no effect. For they were lost to hearing as completely as to sight, except in a few warlike passages, which I innocently accounted for by concluding that the four stage trumpeters had been for the moment pressed into the orchestra, and of course pressed carefully out of sight, as their costumes would have been anachronic off the stage.

If there were really "about thirty" players instead of twentytwo, where were they? The editor's correspondent, a man of humor as well as of music, suggests that "my eye was off color"; but my eye, during the overture,

[593]

counted twentytwo. This, assuming that "off-color" means temporary incapacity for duty, makes exactly eleven men seen double. But, as a matter of fact, my eye retained its normal ultramarine; and I believe I counted accurately. True, there may have been not only the trumpets and the solitary trombone "right enough" under the stage, but also a bass clarinet in the scene dock, an English horn in the flies, third and fourth horns in the boxoffice, and a harp on the roof. I can answer only for what I saw and heard; and I can assure Mr German that the Bayreuth device of an invisible orchestra is also inaudible on the floor of the Globe, whatever may be the case upstairs. Besides, I confess I do not feel quite easy concerning the estimate of "about thirty," made by one who is in a position to be exact. It suggests more than twentynine and less than thirty: possibly twentynine and a boy.

My critic, who signs himself The Amused One, becomes almost sarcastic over my suggestion that the scene of the dawn on Bosworth Field is a fit opportunity for a pastoral symphony. "Fancy a Pastorale where Bassetto wants it: *i.e.* in the Bosworth Field scene, which is full of mail-clad warriors!" Well, my friend, why not? Does not the mail-clad Ratcliff tell us that the early village cock hath thrice done salutation to the morn? Am I to be told that the early village cock is not pastoral? And again: "Mr German *has* grasped the pastoral opportunity and written a beautiful Pastorale as a prelude to the Road to Chertsey scene: a fitting place for it, I say." Will it be believed that this more fitting place than Bosworth Field is a road full of corpses and mourners? Surely a field is more pastoral than a road!

However, these matters are but trifles, like my amused correspondent's mistaking the prelude to the first act for the Pastorale before the second, and, consequently, correcting me where I was, as usual, perfectly right. The true force of his letter is in the feeling it expresses that I have been unjust to Mr Edward German. No doubt I have: who am I that I should be just? But if I had said that Mr Edward German had written an original and adequate overture and *entr'actes* to Shakespear's Richard III., I should have set his music on a level with Beethoven's Egmont, and himself above Verdi, Gounod, Dvořák, Grieg, and Brahms; for I do not believe that one of these composers could tackle Richard III. successfully. Some of the dramatic critics have lightheartedly gone this length. If I followed that example, Mr Edward German would probably be the first to protest that I was making him ridiculous. So I shall confine myself to suggesting that the overture and one or two of the preludes might very well be subjected to expert criticism at one of our orchestral concerts this season. Many less meritorious compositions by Moszkowski and others have been admitted there.

(Sir Edward German's overture, re-scored for full orchestra, has survived as a concert overture, and is familiar to wireless listeners. It is a much more serious composition than my readers could have gathered from my remarks 47 years ago; but its excellence has nothing to do with Richard III.: it stands by itself as a composition in overture form. 1936.)

At the last Philharmonic Concert, by the bye, I paid a shilling for my program. The editor informs me that, with the law of libel in its present unsatisfactory condition, I must not call this a fraud, a cheat, a swindle, an imposition, an exorbitance, or even an overcharge. Therefore, I have resolved to sulk and call it nothing. Formerly the Philharmonic programs were sixpenny yellow-covered quartos, written by Macfarren. The Crystal Palace Saturday programs are still sixpence. But the Richter programs are a shilling; and shilling books are creeping in at special oratorio performances even at the Crystal Palace.

Doubtless, these prices pay. It is more lucrative to sell 200 programs at a shilling than 2000 at a penny, the maximum of profit coinciding with the minimum of utility. In the same way, it paid Messrs Chappell the other day, at Grieg's recital, to turn away the shilling frequenters of the orchestra—their most faithful patrons—by charging three shillings instead of one; and to allow more than half, not not quite two-thirds, of the seats to remain empty. Though that cannot be helped at present, there is a way of smashing the program fr—— I mean of bringing down the prices of programs, as follows.

Let some publisher employ a competent person— myself, for instance—to write analytical programs of all the standard symphonies, overtures, Wagner selections, and the like, keeping the collection up to date by punctual piracies from German programs; and, in the case of works produced in England, paying the composer a reasonable sum for the necessary particulars. Translations of songs, and opera libretti, combining sane if unsingable English versions, with a few remarks descriptive of the chief points of the opera, might also come into the scheme. Then put these on the market at $\frac{1}{2}$d. apiece, or 2d. the halfdozen. Packets containing the pieces of any concert could be made up from the advertisements. There is no reason to fear that concert givers would at once dish the outside competitor by lowering their prices; for the outside competitor, supplying all audiences, could sell with profit at a price that would not cover the cost of production to separate concert givers, each having only his own particular audience to fl—— that is, to deal with.

Besides, analytical programs are wanted elsewhere than at St James's Hall. Amateurs would buy them for information, for guidance in purchasing music, and for distribution at private performances. Critics would buy them for reference. Literary men would buy them for the charm of their style. Composers would buy them to find out what their compositions meant. Fellow citizens: there is a Golconda in this idea. For the sake of its public utility I dedicate it freely to whoever will advance the capital.

LUCIFER AND RICHTER
The Star, 5 April 1889

If the performance of Benoît's Lucifer had been put off for four days Madame Lemmens-Sherrington would have made her re-entry on the 33rd anniversary of her first appearance in London. On that occasion she was, if I mistake not, twentytwo. Experienced mathematicians will find no difficulty in calculating Madame Sherrington's age from these data. It is an age at which singers usually find themselves incapacitated by what physiologists call "ossification of the larynx." I do not pretend to be a physiologist; but I may mention that I have frequently known cases of "ossification" occur at twentyfour and earlier in the cases of singers who did not know how to sing, wheras the other sort of singers— who are, I admit, a rare species—hold out unimpaired until the public absolutely refuses to believe its ears, and concludes that a singer over eighty *must* retire. And yet it will crowd Bingley Hall to hear Mr Gladstone, who might be Madame Sherrington's father, speak for an hour and fifty minutes at a stretch.

Madame Sherrington's method was always of the safest; and she has the advantage, not common among artists, of being a clever and sensible woman. Within the natural limitations of her talent almost her only fault was a somewhat too ready recognition of the undeniable advantage, from a commercial point of view, of a spice of claptrap. And though she never carried it so far as Madame Patti and others of her contemporaries, still, when that basket of flowers was handed up the other evening, it awakened memories; and it is perhaps as well to say at once that preconcerted ovations of this kind are by this time happily acquiring a *rococo* air which warns artists with an alert sense of modernity to avoid them. Untamed young *prima donnas* from America occasionally insist on them in spite of advice; but the result is now generally disappointing. At Covent Garden last year it was more than once rather worse than disappointing, except to those who, like myself, regard the ovation machinery as an impertinence, a nuisance, and a sham. Madame Sherrington's basket of florist's goods, and the *claque* which the management had judiciously provided for the reception of Lucifer, were fortunately swept into insignificance by a hearty spontaneous reception which she acknowledged with all her old grace. And, save once, when she pulled down the pitch during an unaccompanied chorus, and so made the entry of the organ an appalling catastrophe, there was no falling-off to complain of.

When I say that there was no falling-off discernible in Madame Lemmens-Sherrington, I wish I could say the same for Musigena, who sat next me. He fell off repeatedly; and when I awakened him he yawned as I have never seen even a musical critic yawn before. I am bound to admit that there was nothing whatever in M. Benoît's music to keep him awake; but I think he went too far when, on my venturing a criticism as we left the building, he cut me short with: "How do *you* know? You were asleep all the time."

If criticism is to have any effect on concerts, it must

clearly be published before they come off. On this principle it behoves me at once to say a word about the Richter Concerts, which will take place every Monday, except Whit Monday, from 6 May to 8 July inclusive. First, then, I want to know whether the orchestra is going to be any better than it was last year. Because last year, as Dr Hans Richter knows quite as well as I do, it was not up to the mark. I remember one scramble through the Walkürenritt which would have disgraced a second-rate military band; and the general want of refinement in detail, especially in the wind, was apparent in nearly all the Beethoven symphony performances. Nobody was more delighted than Bassetto by the breadth and force which Richter taught our orchestras after a period of stagnation that cannot be recalled without a shiver. Nobody thrilled with more savage and vengeful glee when the old, heartless, brainless, purposeless, vapid, conceited, jack-in-office, kid-glove, St James's-street, finicking Philharmonic fastidiousness was blown into space by him. But, contemptible and inadequate as this genteel fastidiousness was in the mass, it had its good points in detail; and Sir Arthur Sullivan's delicate taste, individuality, and abhorrence of exaggeration and slovenliness raised it to a point at which, if it still did nothing, it at least did it with exquisite refinement.

The possibility of such refinement being thus demonstrated, and being in no way essentially bound up with the nothingness, why should we tolerate any degeneracy in this respect from the Richter orchestra? For it is degeneracy. Some seasons ago they played Schubert's Unfinished Symphony with unsurpassable delicacy, the wood wind attaining a *piano* which I can only compare to the rustling of leaves in the gentlest of breezes. At that time, too, they could play a Liszt rhapsody with precision, a habit of which they have since broken themselves. There is a book—I forget the author's name, but it is the Posthumous Papers of some club or other—in which a man says to his son, "Vidth and visdom go together, Sammy." I rather doubt the statement; for I have noticed that as Hans Richter grows wider season after season he is more inclined to let things take their chance, and to depend on snatching an occasional magnificent success from the inspiration of the moment.

A word or two about the season's program. I am not sorry to see the Seventh Symphony, which Richter has done to death in past seasons, replaced by the joyous Eighth, in which I hope we shall hear the beautiful trio taken slowly, on Wagner's lines, and not raced to destruction on Mendelssohn's. Talking of Mendelssohn, one of the happiest additions to the list is the poetic Athalie overture. The *maestoso* which closes that work is a masterpiece of harmonic stucture: one of the grandest pages Mendelssohn ever penned. Liszt's Mazeppa is sufficiently novel, though it has been played here more than once. When I first heard it at the Crystal Palace I tried vainly to recollect what the rushing, swishing triplets which represent the galloping of the horse were like. At last a rustic-looking young lady behind me said very audibly, "Oh, *isnt* it like frying rashers?" And so it was, exactly.

Richter's affection for Weber's vulgar Euryanthe overture is one of the things I do not understand. Nor, considering that perhaps his greatest triumph here as a conductor has been his resuscitation of the great symphony in E flat, can I imagine why he is so chary of the works of Mozart. However, he promises the symphony in D. There are lots of Mozart symphonies in D; but this is Köchel No. 504, a mark of identification which—Köchel not being at hand as I write—conveys no impression whatever to my mind, though doubtless it does to yours. A less hackneyed example of Cherubini than the Anacreon overture might have been found without much trouble; and Glinka's Kamarinskaja will be the better for a rest after this season.

("Weber's vulgar Euryanthe overture" rather staggers me nowadays. But in Euryanthe Weber's music is thickening into Wagner's, and losing the unique charm and perfume of Der Freischütz, Oberon, and the Konzertstück for piano and orchestra. Knowing as we do now what Wagnerism was going to mean to music, the loss to Weberism does not affect us as a vulgarization; but then!—well, there the word is; and I really meant it. 1936.)

The Wagner selections are to be increased by the duet with Venus in the first act of Tannhäuser. The vein in which this scene, and much of Tristan und Isolde, is written is restless, passionate, harsh, and intolerable to those who agree with the composer who displayed his tact by saying to Berlioz, "I like music that puts me to sleep." A nobler additon to the repertory is the scene from Die Walküre, in which the Valkyrie warns Siegmund that he is fated presently to die and accompany her to Valhalla, which, on carefully examining her as to how he will be situated there, he flatly declines to do. The music is perfectly simple and indescribably impressive.

The extension of the musical arrangements at the Shakespearean theatres is bearing fruit. I hear remarks on the appearance of the Flying Dutchman overture in the bill at the Lyceum. By the way, I was at the Lyceum on Tuesday, and found Mr Irving playing very finely indeed, and quite irreproachable in my department. He and I are the only two men—not professional phonetic experts—in England who can distinguish a vowel from a diphthong. What a Lady Macbeth Miss Terry is! I would trust my life in her hands. It was a luxury to hear her speak of "the owl, the fatal bellman which gives the stern'st goodnight." I had not heard "goodnight" said in that exact tone since I saw her in the balcony scene in Romeo and Juliet.

THE POPULAR MUSICAL UNION
The Star, 13 April 1889

A gentleman recently condoled with me on the immense number of concerts a critic has to attend. He then asked me somewhat abruptly when I had last been at one. His intention being plainly to suggest that I am in the habit of neglecting my duties, I explained to him that the ear of a critic is a far more delicate organ than the larynx of a singer, and to keep it fresh and sensitive it must be used sparingly. But the fact is that I have so much to say about music that I forget about the concerts. For example, I made a special excursion last month to a concert in a place called Bermondsey, at the invitation of the Popular Musical Union, and then clean forgot to write a word about it.

The Popular Musical Union was formed in 1882 for the musical training and recreation of the "industrial classes." By subscribing a guinea you become an "honorary member" (I always thought that the point in honorary membership was that you paid nothing) and have a concert all to yourself at Grosvenor House once a year. You are patronized by the Lord Mayor, presided over by the Duke of Westminster, and vice-presided over and councilled by nearly five dozen illustrious persons, including Sir Charles Russell, Sir Frederick Leighton, handfuls of earls, a dean, a county councillor, an oculist, an amateur actress, three bishops, half a dozen members of Parliament, *et hoc genus omne*.

The Union opens singing or other musical classes

wherever "a sufficient number of ladies and gentlemen" signify to the hon. sec. (Mrs Ernest Hart) their intention of joining. And here I would dubiously ask whether ladies and gentlemen belong to the industrial classes? Surely the quintessence of gentility is doing nothing, and making the industrial classes keep you. I submit that the Popular Musical Union should resolutely refuse to train and recreate ladies and gentlemen who can presumably very well afford to recreate and train themselves.

The Union has given two imposing concerts lately. At the last one Gounod's Redemption was performed in the People's Palace. I did not go, because I cannot stand listening to a band and chorus practising the chromatic scale in slow time for nearly three hours even when it is harmonized by Gounod. Progression by semitones is too gradual for my ardent nature. I understand that various members of the industrial classes of Mile End pretended to enjoy it, which shews how the hypocrisy of culture, like other cast-off fashions, finds its last asylum among the poor. Now, in my opinion, the East Enders ought to be ashamed to have anything to do with the affectations of their parasites in the West. If the East listens patiently for a while, and never condescends to pretend to like what bores it, it will save itself from much tedium and consequent prejudice against pseudo-sacred music. Roughly, the novices of the East End may take it that the only Scriptural oratorios worth listening to are those of Bach, Handel, and Haydn. After Mozart struck the modern secular humanitarian note in The Magic Flute, and Beethoven took it up in his setting of Schiller's Ode to Joy, oratorio degenerated into mere sentiment and claptrap. With the exception of a few cantatas by Mendelssohn, all the Biblical music of this century might be burnt without leaving the world any the poorer. If the Musical Union is wise, it will train its

[603]

audiences to XIX century vocal music by means of opera recitals.

Here I am, as usual, wasting all my space on the concert I was *not* at. The one at Bermondsey was in the Town Hall of that region. The vocalists announced in small print were Mlle de Lido, Miss Helen Trust, Mr Dyved Lewis, "the Welsh tenor," Mr Albert Reakes, and Mr Bertram Latter. The vocalist announced in colossal letters suitable to a star of the first magnitude was Lady Colin Campbell. This piece of snobbery annoyed me to begin with. Then I was not formally received, as I should have been, by the Mayor and Corporation of Bermondsey. Further, in spite of my card of invitation, I was only admitted to a seat worthy of my dignity on payment of sixpence extra. But I never spare money in the service of the public. Bang went that coin without a murmur from me.

The generosity with which "the industrial classes" applaud you if they think you have "done your bit" heartily, even if you have not done it particularly well, was not abused on this occasion, as it too often is at concerts for the people. The Welsh tenor was excellent, and kept his temper in spite of grievous maltreatment from the accompanist in Deeper and deeper still. That gentleman, when he came to Waft her, angels, discovered that the accompaniment of alternate dotted semiquavers and demisemiquavers would make a rattling galop, which he forthwith led off with such spirit that he got nearly to the end of the page before Mr Dyved Lewis had finished the first bar. However, Handel and the Welsh tenor triumphed in the end, for the aria was encored. To avoid further Terpsichorean difficulties, the successful singer substituted Gounod's setting of Victor Hugo's serenade,* highly bowdlerized

* *Sérénade* (1855).

[604]

in the course of translation so as to spare the blushes of Bermondsey.

Mr Bertram Latter greatly distinguished himself by singing a duet with a baby. His intention was to sing Sullivan's Thou'rt Passing Hence as a solo; but the baby joined in at the end of the first line and continued *sempre crescendo e piu lamentevole* until a little before the end, when it collapsed, leaving Mr Latter, like Orpheus, master of the situation. Great and deserved was the applause elicited by his fortitude and his artistic singing under exceptionally trying circumstances.

Messrs W. Marshall & Co., of 70 Berners-street, have sent me some music for review. Here, for instance, is a volume of airs from Maritana for violin and piano. But of what use is that to me? I cannot play the violin and piano at the same time. Musigena can play violin parts with exquisite virtuosity through a sheet of tissue paper on a comb, his wide-toothed register being remarkable for its fulness and capability of dramatic expression; but he scorns Maritana. And, indeed, I think Messrs Marshall might have sent me the Kreutzer or the Strinasacchi sonata instead of Herr Meissler's waltzes arranged for the flute, The State Ball Album, The Children's Ball, and M. de Faye's arrangements of Braga's Serenata, and the like. My good sirs: do you think that di Bassetto regards this sort of thing as serious music?

BASSETTO THE SHIRK
The Star, 20 April 1889

I regard with immense approval the formation of a Concert Guild by ex-scholars and ex-students of the Royal College of Music. Three of the rules deserve to be quoted. 1. Members of the Guild are not to employ for professional purposes any title or designation of their membership. 2. The services of members taking part in the performances shall be gratuitous. 3. Any surplus arising from the concerts shall go towards the foundation of a benevolent fund for the members. The spirit of these rules is full of promise. They suggest the question whether political economy is included in the curriculum of the Royal College of Music. Highly interesting examination papers could be set by an experienced professor. For instance:—How do you propose to reconcile the artistic interests of society with the individual pecuniary interest of an exceptionally gifted artist? Explain why Madame Patti, instead of assisting at least twice a week all through the year in complete artistic performances of the best operas before large audiences, is at present doing mere jobbing work in South America. Point out, from the point of view of sound national economy, the advantage of a system which makes it the interest of the greatest artists to perform as seldom as possible, and that, too, only before the fewest and richest people. Expatiate on the native vulgarity and insensibility to the refining influences of art evinced by those who insist on the interest which the public has in getting for their collective moneys as many performances out of an artist as may be compatible with his or her health and reasonable happiness. Enumerate the benefits conferred on the French nation by the secession of Madame Bernhardt and M. Coquelin from the Comédie Française on the ground that strolling pays them better. Shew how a progressive income tax would affect art. Is it or is it not a corrupt proceeding for a singer to sing a worthless song for the sake of a royalty on every copy sold? To what extent has the spread of education reduced the percentage of private pupils who are unaware that they can buy their own music for less than half the marked price, or a pianoforte for from 20 to 25 percent less than the figure named in the catalog?

I could extend this list of questions considerably if I had nothing else to do just now. Sometimes it is not the artist, but the manager, who needs a lesson in political economy. The late Patti concerts at the Albert Hall were curious examples of managerial innocence. At them the singer obtained £700 for each concert. The managers of the hall should have demanded £200 extra as the rent of the hall, to be deducted from Madame Patti's fee. She would have objected, of course; but the managers need only have invited her to go elsewhere. As there is no other eligible hall in London capable of seating a sufficiently large audience to cover the ordinary return to the investment and leave £500 for the *prima donna*, Madame Patti could not have gone further without faring worse. The fact is, there were two monopolies concerned: Madame Patti's monopoly of herself, and the Albert Hall's monopoly of its unique size. Both monopolies have their "rents"; and the managers were childlike and bland enough to allow her to add £200 of the rent of their monopoly to that of hers. Had Bassetto been the manager that would not have occurred.

We are to have Italian opera at two houses this season: Verdi's Otello at the Lyceum, after the departure of Shakespear's Macbeth, and the usual series at Covent Garden. I take the opportunity of contrasting the modesty of Mr Augustus Harris with the ambition of actor-managers like Mr Wilson Barrett, Mr Irving, and Mr Mansfield, who produce no plays except those in which they themselves figure prominently. Mr Harris has been so self-denying in this respect that very few people in London know that he is an operatic artist as well as *impresario*. The first time I had the pleasure of seeing him was in Der Freischütz, in which he played Zamiel, the demon huntsman. The part is not a singing part, so I am unable to speak critically of Mr Harris's voice; but his vivid and agile pantomime made a deep impression on me, and I felt strongly that I had witnessed the performance of an enthusiast: so strongly, indeed, that I prophesied that if ever he became bankrupt it would be by trying to revive Italian opera.

I lost sight of him for some time after this until, happening to be present one evening at a performance of Pink Dominoes, I recognized in one of the characters the strange personality of Zamiel. The moment I heard that he had entered upon a career as manager, I foresaw all the glories of the present *régime* at Covent Garden. May I now venture to suggest that Mr Harris should revive Weber's masterpiece, and permit the present generation of Londoners to see him in a character which he has made his own?

If Mr Harris has a fault as an *impresario* it is his too indiscriminate attachment to the traditions of the operatic stage. Instead of making up his mind to a clean sweep of all its barnstorming absurdities, he has cultivated them on the largest scale. He should go to his singers and say gently "Do not saw the air thus. You think yourselves fine fellows when you do it; but the public thinks you idiots. The English nation, among whom I am a councillor, no longer supposes that attitudinizing is acting. Neither would I have you suppose that all amative young men wear dove-colored tights, and have pink cheeks with little moustaches. Nor is it the case that all men with grownup daughters have long white beards reaching to the waist, or that they walk totteringly with staves, raising hands and eyes to heaven whenever thay offer an observation. The daughters of Albion do not, when in distress, leave off wearing bonnets in the open air, assume mourning, keep their hands continually on their hearts, and stagger and flop about like decapitated geese." And so on. Harris's advice to the opera singers would become more celebrated than Hamlet's to the players.

OPERA IN AMSTERDAM
The Star, 27 April 1889

Two new operas were produced last Saturday: Doris at the Lyric Theatre in London, and Brinio at the Park Theatre in Amsterdam. There has been of late a Dutch fashion in art setting in here. We all know that the Netherlands formerly produced such painters as Rembrandt, Jan Steen, and de Hooghe, and such musicians as Sweelinck and Orlandus Lassus. These glories were supposed to have departed until the modern school of Dutch landscape and seascape painters arose and brought Holland again to the front as a rheumatic mother of great painters. And, we naturally asked, if great painters, why not great composers, too? Are there no Dutchmen who do in music what James Maris, his brother Matthew, Mesdag, Weissenbruch, Neuhuys, Bosboom, and others are doing in painting? Somebody suggested Peter Benoît; and it is only a few weeks since Mr Barnby went to the trouble of producing Lucifer at the Albert Hall. The work, as it turned out, had not an original bar in it. However, the announcement of a new opera on a national subject at Amsterdam was not to be neglected. I have been described as "a shirk" in an envious headline by the sub-editor of The Star. But I was at my post in Amsterdam nevertheless; and I think that if the sub-editor had seen me on my way thither, when I had been rocked in the cradle of the deep for an hour, he would have blushed for the first time in his life.

Brinio is a grand opera in four acts by S. van Milligen.

The book is by Flower of the Snow, a memorable name. The characters include William Tell and Ophelia in the relation of brother and sister, our old friend Oroveso the Druid from Norma, Pollio from the same opera, and an unpopular Roman governor, who is addressed through-out by the Ethiopian title of Massa, and who may possibly have been suggested by Pontius Pilate. The action takes place in Batavia during the ascendency of the Romans. Brinio (W. Tell) is a patriotic Batavian with two sisters, one of whom is mad and the other sane, although I am bound to add that there is but little to choose between them except that Rheime overdoes the makeup of her eyes and plays hysterically with straws and poppies. Ada, the uncertified one, is beloved by Aquilius, a Roman officer, and by Massa, both of whom, accordingly, cultivate Brinio's acquaintance. Massa, however, is out of the question, for he not only drinks—he emptied a large goblet seven times in the course of one act without turning a hair—but he seems to have had something to do with Rheime's mental affliction. Consequently Brinio invites Aquilius to dinner, and shuts the door in Massa's face.

In the second act Massa further exhibits his sybarite nature by reclining on a couch whilst a bevy of maidens sing a chorus and strew flowers on him. Then comes an amazing scene in which Vulpes, the confidant of Massa, conducts a sort of conscription among the Batavians, much as Falstaff did at Justice Shallow's house on his way to Coventry. The rest of the act I totally forget, except that Massa ordered the Roman soldiery to arrest Aquilius, which they refused to do on any terms.

The third act takes place at night, in the depths of a primeval forest. Ada and Rheime happen to be strolling there in their ordinary indoor costume. Rheime sings to a tambourine accompaniment, which indicates that she is distraught. Ada sings then without the tambourine;

and finally the two repeat their parts simultaneously in a manner much affected by Sir Arthur Sullivan in his operas. Massa then enters, unobserved, with two villains in cloaks, to whom he laboriously points out Ada—mind! *Ada*, not Rheime, because the villains of course subsequently get hold of the wrong woman. Massa and his hateful hirelings then retire in order to give a chance to Aquilius, who comes in and has a love duet with Ada, Rheime meanwhile sitting on a stump in a dumb paroxysm of flower and straw mania. Aquilius and Ada then elope, leaving Rheime an easy prey to the two villains, who re-enter and approach her by a series of strategic movements from tree to tree, as if she were a regiment of sharpshooters. At last they bear her off, wrapping her head in a veil, lest they should recognize her and spoil the last act. Brinio comes in with Ada and Aquilius: at least, I think it happened this way. Anyhow, Oroveso the Druid comes in with a host of mistletoe worshipers, and, after declaiming unintelligently at insufferable length in a colorless bass voice, appeals to the heavenly powers, who ring a bell, which causes the limelight man to cast a dazzling ray on Brinio, thus unmistakably pointing him out as the savior of his country.

In the last act, Massa is found with his bevy of maidens, drinking like a Roman Coupeau, and inviting everybody to hail his approaching bride. The bride appears with her head wrapped up; but even before she is unveiled, the friskings of the tambourine convince Massa, to his entire disgust, that in spite of his plain directions the two villains have mistaken the sisters. Vulpes now announces the advance of the foe, who come charging cautiously over the battlements, preoccupied with the real danger of breaking their necks rather than with the illusory perils of a stage battle. Massa, after a tremendous draught of Dutch courage, takes his sword, with which, to the utter astonishment of the audience, and in flat defiance of poetic justice, he kills Brinio, whereupon most of the Mistletonians fall down dead. Suddenly, however, Aquilius appears; and the Roman soldiery in turn fall down dead, apparently of heart disease precipitated by excitement. Massa is disarmed and removed in custody; and Ada and Aquilius are happily united. Rheime's reason is perhaps restored by the sight of her brother's mortal pangs, for the tambourine is heard no more; but on this point I cannot, in the present stage of my acquaintance with sung Dutch, speak with certainty.

The opera was received with a considerable show of enthusiasm. At the end of the first act Rheime rushed to the conductor's desk and shook hands impulsively with Heer van Milligen amid cheers. When the forest scene was over the poet and the manager came upon the boards. Vast trophies of laurel and national bunting were handed up and hung upon the arms of the manager, who peered through the greenery like Birnam forest coming to Dunsinane, and made a glowing speech about his heart (just like Mr Wilson Barrett), about the Amsterdam public, about the Netherlands public, about the public of the whole universe, about the triumphant establishment of a great national school of opera, about the inspiration of della Neve, the genius of van Milligen, and heaven knows what not. When he had finished he began again, as public speakers will, and repeated his speech at least twice. Finally, he handed over the trophies to the blushing van Milligen; the applause broke out afresh; the trumpets blared forth victorious fanfares; and the audience dispersed in quest of refreshments.

With all due respect for the manager, I am unable to agree with him in his estimate of Brinio. Had the poem been as rational as even an exceptionally bad Drury

Lane melodrama, it might have passed as an opera libretto with that unfortunately large section of the public which does not consider opera-making a serious or responsible profession. But it was not so rational, nothing like it. The music was vigorous, ambitious, elaborately scored, glib in the sentimental parts and strenuous in the martial, but without a phrase, progression, or rhythmical figure that could by any stretch of international courtesy be described as moderately fresh. As to any attempt at that distinctively dramatic power of suiting the music to the character as well as to the action and emotion, Heer van Milligen seems to have exhausted his endowment of it in devizing the tambourine part to which I have alluded.

On the whole, though Brinio is not without the sort of plausibility that has secured for Lucifer a troublesome and expensive hearing in London, there is no reason why it too should be brought across the North Sea. But the example of the manager who produced it might be imitated by our *impresarios*. Mr Goring Thomas can do Heer van Milligen's work, and do it far better. So can Mr Villiers Stanford, who is sprightly enough when he is not gratifying his fancy for the pedantries of sonata form. Why Mr Augustus Harris does not get a grand opera out of Sir Arthur Sullivan, who is never dull, is one of the unaccountable things in modern management. Perhaps Mr Harris does not understand that he is expected to produce new work. If so, he is mistaken. Far too many nights last season were wasted in rattling the drying bones of Un Ballo and Il Trovatore; whilst works like Goetz's Taming of the Shrew and Wagner's Die Walküre, both of them beautiful and popular works, were left on the shelf. If that happens again, the readers of The Star shall learn my opinion of such senseless proceedings.

CARL ROSA

The Star, 1 May 1889

The importance which was attached yesterday to the news of Mr Carl Rosa's death measures the position he had made for himself in England. His special work was the organization of opera in English, as opposed to the fashionable opera in Italian. In this he was so far successful that he leaves his company firmly established in London and the provinces, not without a certain artistic prestige, though the artistic side was never the strong side of his undertakings. His career as an *impresario* grew out of his marriage with Madame Parepa, whom he met in the United States in 1867, in the course of a concert tour, for which the late Mr Bateman had engaged him as violinist. He was then twentyfour years of age, and had played in this country at the Crystal Palace. With Madame Parepa's talent to support him, he turned conductor and manager, in which capacities he proved so competent that, after some years' experience in America, he directed his attention to England. The death of Madame Rosa in 1874 upset his calculations; but he persevered until his reputation was established in the provinces. In the winter of 1875 he tried a season in London. Mr Santley's performance of the part of the water-carrier in Cherubini's Deux Journées immediately gave the enterprise an artistic position which it certainly could not have gained by its performances of Faust and Il Trovatore in English. Next year, at the Lyceum, the great success of Wagner's Flying Dutchman, with Mr Santley as the Dutchman and Mlle Torriana as Senta, still further raised the status of the company, emboldening Mr Carl

Rosa to produce a real English opera, entitled Pauline, of which, in consideration for the composer and librettist, no further particulars need here be raked up. The next stride was made in 1879, when there was a season of opera in English at Her Majesty's Theatre. Rienzi was produced with the late Mr Joseph Maas in the title part; and Miss Georgina Burns burst on us as the Messenger of Peace. Nothing comparable with this achievement has been since done here in choral and spectacular opera with the exception, perhaps, of the revival of William Tell by Mr Harris last season at Drury Lane. In 1880 Goetz's Taming of the Shrew, with Miss Minnie Hauk as Katherine, was produced at Her Majesty's. This also was an excellent performance; and it was the last really great work introduced to us by Mr Carl Rosa. The operas by Dr Mackenzie, Mr Goring Thomas, and Massenet, which he afterwards undertook, had their merits; but they were far inferior in their artistic importance to the works of Wagner or Goetz.

Mr Carl Rosa was a capable man of business; and as conductor and *impresario* his judgment was to be depended upon to a certain point. But it had its limits. His finest artists—Mr Santley, Miss Minnie Hauk, and Madame Marie Roze, for instance—were not discovered by him; and though he brought forward several singers with bright, strong voices and plenty of hard work in them, yet it is impossible to believe that he enlisted the best talent available in his time in young England, in point of grace, refinement, and intelligence. His recruits, though robust enough, were often rather raw, with Irish, Scotch, Canadian, provincial English or Welsh dialects, and no stage training. With him they found no traditions of the Comédie Française order to improve them. To this day the diction and deportment of the Carl Rosa artists leave everything to be desired; and it is this deficiency which compels the criticism that their spiritual director was not as eminent an artist as he unquestionably was an eminent organizer and man of business. On the purely musical side he had sufficient vigor, individuality, and even enthusiasm; and he certainly knew how to get himself respectably served in the matter of stage management and decoration. As *impresarios* go, all this was no mean endowment; and we could have better spared many worse men whilst we wait for Providence or Bayreuth to train us a manager with the requisite administrative ability—one fully sensible of the pictorial, the poetic, the dramatic, and the musical sides of great operas, and able to co-ordinate them into an ideal representation towards which it shall be the business of an English opera house constantly to work.

The name of Rosa was a phonetic version of the German "Rose." The deceased *impresario's* complete title was Carl August Nicolas Rose, and he was born at Hamburg in 1843.

OPERA: EAST END *VS* WEST END
The Star, 4 May 1889

I have been amusing myself this week by comparing English opera at the West End of the town with English opera at the East. The most important result so far has been the discovery of a magnificent theatre in a place called Shoreditch: a palatial opera house in which you get an orchestra stall for two shillings, or a ruby velvet chair in the front row of the balcony for half-a-crown. More modest arrangements can be made for fourpence; and there are no fees, except a penny for a program. Here have we all been for years paying half-guineas and half-crowns for admission to paltry Strand playhouses, unwitting that there was an East End Covent Garden accessible for fourpence. I had heard of Shoreditch as the home of an industrious population, of persons who never will be slaves earning their modest shilling a day by 16 hours' work; but its celebrity as a theatrical centre was unknown to me.

When Mr Melville, the proprietor and manager of the National Standard Theatre, informed me of his intention to produce Macfarren's Robin Hood on Monday last, I resolved to be there. I do not mind confessing that though, as a professional critic, I know everything, yet there are a few matters that I have not yet got quite at my fingers' ends. Among them are the works of Macfarren, who, like Cherubini, acquired such a reputation as a pedant that it was almost forgotten that he had once been a composer. And just as people with a dread of Cherubini's pedantry are always agreeably surprised by the overture to Anacreon, so was I years ago pleasantly taken aback by the overture to Chevy Chase. Indeed, it was partly on the strength of Chevy Chase that I went to hear Robin Hood.

Robin Hood was written for Her Majesty's Theatre in 1860. In that year English opera sung by Sims Reeves, Santley, and Madame Lemmens-Sherrington, and conducted by Hallé, was given night about with Italian opera conducted by Arditi and sung by Titiens and Giuglini. Such things have been, and may be again. As far as I know, Robin Hood has been shelved ever since; so that the performance on Monday was practically a first one to most of the audience.

Twentynine years after Robin Hood, and one and a half after the death of its composer, we have Mr Alfred Cellier's new English opera Doris produced at the Lyric Theatre, Shaftesbury Avenue, under the disadvantage of the absence from England of Corno di Bassetto. He, however, frequented the first two acts on Tuesday evening last, and proceeded to compare Doris with Robin Hood, with a view to determining how far English opera had advanced in the meantime. He regrets to have to announce quite decisively that it has not advanced at all. Macfarren put forth his musicianship and strained his fancy to trick out a libretto which barely pretended to be serious; and history has repeated itself with some minor variations, as, for instance, that Mr Cellier's songs are gayer, and his *finales* and concerted pieces flimsier, than Macfarren's. Mr Stephenson, too, lightheartedly drops even the pretence of seriousness. Otherwise there is not a pin to choose between the opera of 1860 and the opera of 1889. In one case the trifling is solemn: in the other, it is inane and flippant, that is all.

Doris is the more aggravating of the two at first, because the music seems to interrupt the action until it becomes apparent that there is no action to interrupt. When Martin, catching Carey in the act of kissing Doris's hand, stops to sing her a song before he takes any further steps, you pay no more attention to the story, and feel defrauded of what you have paid already. In Robin Hood the music generally advances matters: you feel that you are getting along, even though you are obviously in a no-thoroughfare. And although after a certain age—say ten—it is not easy to laugh very heartily at the Sumpnour, he is a veritable Falstaff compared with the buffoon at the Lyric, who, in spite of such pleasantries as changing his breeches and getting too drunk to find the keyhole of his door, would be quite intolerable if it were not for a certain natural drollery in Mr Arthur Williams which enables him to pretend to write a letter as Mr Crummles's comic countryman pretended to catch a fly: that is, funnily enough to make a cockney laugh.

Where the East End audience suffered in comparison with the West was not in the quality of the opera, but in

[618]

the manner of its performance. Mr Hawes Craven's Highgate scene at the Lyric is full of the true Bank Holiday feeling for nature, besides being thoroughly carried out in detail so as to make the illusion as easy to the spectator as possible. Further, Mr Ivan Caryll has trained his orchestra to play with such spirit and daintiness that it ranks as quite the best orchestra of its kind in London when the individuality of the conductor is placed to its credit. Then all the artists are good enough for their work: some of them, indeed, much too good. Mr Hayden Coffin's artistic intelligence is so completely wasted on his parts that by the time he has played three or four more of them—he will then be about fifty, judging from the run of Dorothy—his higher faculties will certainly have decayed from disuse. Meanwhile the West End hears its Doris to great advantage.

Not so the East End Robin Hood. With the singers at the Standard I have no serious fault to find, although I may remark that Mr Turner has probably no idea of how unsatisfactory his intonation is when he is not bringing down the house with stentorian high notes. For the chorus I have nothing but praise: the men deserved the thundering *encore* they got for the unaccompanied chorus in the second act. The scenery, though of the old-fashioned sort, was sufficiently plausible. But the orchestra should not have been inflicted on Shoreditch, as it certainly durst never have been inflicted on Shaftesbury Avenue. And here, again, I make magnanimous allowances. The economies in the wood wind I pass over: the sufficiency of the brass I acknowledge. But imagine the effect, in a theatre of the largest size, of a string band consisting of five violins, one tenor, and two cellos, none of the players being, to say the least, Nerudas or Hollmans! When the feeble and mistuned scraping got very bad—and once or twice it could hardly have been worse—doubtless the packed pittites said reverently "This is classical music. This is above our heads, this is." Perhaps they even thought that it was quite the operatic thing for the conductor to wield his *bâton* with one hand and play the harmonium with the other. If so, they were far too kind in their estimate of the management's sense of its artistic duty to them. I hate to see the East End imposed upon; and I felt strongly inclined to rise between the acts and inform the house that more and better strings would have made an enormous difference for the better, and ought to have been provided.

The last time I ventured on a remark about music in the East End, I brought upon myself a letter from a correspondent at Camberwell which exasperated me beyond measure. He accused me of having said that working-men "could not enjoy the high-class oratorios of their superiors"; of running down the Peckham Choir in order to disparage the Tonic Sol-fa; and of wanting to burn "all the cantatas written since Mendelssohn's Ode to Joy." These intolerable aspersions are apparently founded on my opinion that Gounod's Redemption is, as a whole, such a bore that the audience of the People's Palace cannot have been sincere in pretending to enjoy it; on a distinct and unqualified compliment paid by me to the Peckham Tonic Sol-fa Choir; and on my disparagement of all scriptural oratorios written since Mozart's Magic Flute and Beethoven's setting of Schiller's Ode to Joy, *except* certain cantatas by Mendelssohn. It is infuriating to be misunderstood in this way, particularly as it is admitted in literary circles that I write the best English in the world. For the future, I positively decline to answer letters founded on inexcusable misreadings of my column.

Another correspondent—this time a model one—asks whether Miss Grace Pedley really said, as The Star reported, that her compass was four octaves. I cannot answer the question, as it was not I who interviewed Miss Pedley; but a compass of four octaves is not impossible. I believe Mr Corney Grain is gifted to that extent. However, people are apt to make statements of very doubtful value on this subject. For instance, between my lowest growl and my highest squeak there lies a compass of more than three octaves; but if I attempted to range far outside an octave and a fifth in singing, I should be asked to leave off. The service from which my correspondent quotes the bass must have been written either *by* a greenhorn or *for* a Russian choir. I was not aware that the textbooks differed as much on the subject as my correspondent says; but surely no textbooks encourage a student to expect bass chorus singers to be equally ready with C's below the stave and E naturals above it. The average basso cannot be trusted below G or above E flat.

LIONS OF THE SEASON: HAMISH MacCUNN
The Star, 7 May 1889

Mr Hamish MacCunn, at twentyone years of age, is better known than most of the rising young men of fortyfive or so who infuse some of the light and promise of early youth into the productive branches of the fine arts in London. The fame of the more important of his works will have reached every amateur who takes any interest in modern music; and even the main facts of the composer's personal history are already known wherever any curiosity exists concerning them. It is no news that he was born at Greenock in 1868; that his home was an actively musical one; that he was often brought to

London, and spent one season, when he was eight years old, at Sydenham, where he heard Mr Manns' orchestra every day; that he took a scholarship at the Royal College of Music when he was fifteen, and worked under Dr Parry, picking up his orchestral experience as a viola player; that his works, which came out without the slightest flavor of Dr Parry or South Kensington, were first heard in the studio of Mr J. Pettie, R.A., the attraction of whose household for Mr MacCunn will probably be explained in the course of the year; and that the last commission given by the late Mr Carl Rosa was to the composer of The Lay of the Last Minstrel for an opera on the subject of Waverley, to be written by Mr Bennett, the musical critic of the Daily Telegraph. Personally Mr MacCunn is such a very significant-looking young man that he appears taller than he actually is. His hair is dark; he speaks with the accent of a Scottish gentleman; he is by no means unlike the bust of him by Mr D. W. Stevenson at the Royal Academy. There are certain youthful portraits of Mendelssohn, Chopin, and Weber, a composite of which would give some interesting suggestions of Hamish MacCunn. His noble forehead, fine, clear eyes, and particularly pleasant and open expression, partly account for the reminiscence of Mendelssohn. A glance at our portrait will shew that his nose is his own and Scotland's, and that in the length of his head and the development at the base of the skull behind (where these men of war have their powder magazines) his photograph recalls Mr Herkomer's portrait of Wagner.

First, then, as to Mr MacCunn's view of the musical situation in England. He has no doubt that we are entering on a period of genuine musical activity. The necessary conditions for it are: the men, the money, and the public. As to the men, what difficulty should there be about that? We have produced the greatest of men in the fine arts, from Shakespear downwards; and there is no magician's circle drawn about music more than about any other art. Money we have in plenty. As for the public, you want one with enthusiasm, idealism, and—purchasing power. The idealism of the British public is proved, not by the fact that a few of them are fond of Beethoven's symphonies, but by the extent to which they suffer themselves to be aristocracy-ridden. Needless to say, Mr MacCunn, at twentyone, and proud of a newly taken place in the Republic of Art, is no worshiper of aristocracy. But he sees that others worship it, and he finds comfort in the spectacle; for he knows that we do not worship aristocrats wholly because we are a nation of snobs: we idealize them first, and only give our homage to our ideal. Now, says Mr MacCunn, with a salt touch of humor that goes along with the clearest earnestness in him, whilst the British are able to idealize the British aristocracy, nobody can say that they have not a tremendous fund of idealizing capacity ready for the service of Music as soon as she comes to claim it. Questioned as to his favorite composers, Mr MacCunn simply protested: "You might as well ask me which I like best, my arms or my legs." Yet he has tenderness towards certain composers. Weber—the Weber of the Freischütz and Oberon rather than of Euryanthe—is a special favorite of his; and he is strong in praise of M. Gounod, for the beauty and dramatic force of the prelude to whose Faust he has no words to express his admiration. With reference to the old composers, he said more than once, "They carry us very far back; even Gounod takes you very far back"—which means that Mr MacCunn is going to take us as far forward as he can. Mr MacCunn has made no secret of his conviction that the music of the future will be dramatic and descriptive, not "abstract." He has always put programs to his works on the simple ground that, as he always meant something when he wrote them, he may as well tell people what the meaning is. In this there is a touch of Scotch rationalism which cropped up again when, replying to a question as to whether he ever felt impelled to adopt Wagner's practice of writing his own words, he said "I have not the vocabulary. I can find music but not words. Besides, if I write the book, you will be expecting me to paint the scenery too, on the same principle." He added that if a librettist brought inadequate words, the composer could always refuse to set them; but on this score he is evidently void of anxiety and fraternal jealousy. Indeed, he rather insists on the social character of opera production than on the composer's individual share in it. His view about symphonies and abstract music generally is that we have as much of it as we want, and that we cannot advantageously replace the old symphonies with new ones. If he were to write a symphony, he says, Beethoven's in C minor would be better worth listening to; that would be all. As to professors' music generally—"organist's music," as Wagner called it—the professor is always ashamed to do the very thing he is there to do: namely, to make an effect; and so he does nothing.

I at last had the hardihood to ask Mr MacCunn for his notions of press criticism.

"I think" said the composer, fixing his eye on me to indicate that he felt confident of my approval "that criticism, above all things, should not be flippant, because if it is, nobody respects it."

MUSIC OF THE REVOLUTION

The Star, 13 May 1889

This week seems to be devoted to celebrating the French
Revolution of 1789 which produced such an effect on
music that it has never been the same since. I can bring
the connexion down to this very week; for the first
musical product of the Revolution was the Eroica
Symphony, utterly unlike anything that had ever been
heard in the world before. That very symphony, though
nobody feels particularly excited about it now, was
performed at the first Richter concert the other day.
This would be an excellent opportunity to introduce a
criticism of the concert; but unluckily I was not there—
though that, of course, need not prevent me from
writing a notice of it. I had gone down to Surrey to
inspect the newest fashions in spring green; and when
the concert began I was communing perplexedly with
Nature as to the probability of catching the last train but
one from Dorking.

Between ten and eleven, as I sat at Redhill Junction
awaiting the arrival of the ten minutes to ten train, I
meditated on the Revolution music—on its grandiose-
ness, splendioseness, neuroseness, and sensationalose-
ness; on its effort, its hurry, its excitement, its aspiration
without purpose, its forced and invariably disappointing
climaxes, its exhaustion and decay, until in our own day
everything that was most strenuously characteristic of
it seems old-fashioned, platitudinous, puerile, forcible-
feeble, anything but romantic and original. Just think
of the mental condition of the enthusiastic musicians
who believed that the operas of Meyerbeer were a higher
development of those of Mozart, that Berlioz was the

[625]

heir and successor of Beethoven, Schubert an immortal tone poet as yet only half come to light, Rossini such another as Handel, and Wagner a cacophonous idiot! It is not twenty years since this was quite an advanced program.

If, however, we are to have a Revolution, do not let us sing the Marseillaise. The incurable vulgarity of that air is a disgrace to the red flag. It corresponds so exactly in rhythmic structure with the Irish tune called The Red Fox, or, as Moore set it, Let Erin Remember the Days of Old, that the two airs can be harmonized, though not in what Cherubini would have considered strict two-part counterpoint. But compare the mechanical tramp and ignobly self-assertive accent of Rouget de Lisle's composition with the sensitiveness of the Irish melody and the passion that is in all its moods. My own belief is that the men of Marseilles were horribly frightened when they went to the front, as any sensible person would be; and Rouget de Lisle's tune enabled them to face it out, exactly as Ta-ran-ta-ra encouraged the policemen in The Pirates of Penzance.

On Saturday evening, during one of my East End expeditions, I discovered the People's Palace, which consists of a board with an inscription to the effect that if I choose to produce £50,000, the palace will be built for me forthwith.* This rather took me aback; for I had thought that the palace was an accomplished fact. But no: there was a huge concert room, a reading room, and shanties containing a bath, a gymnasium, and a restaurant; also a little clubhouse, but no palace. In the concert room some unfortunate artists were bawling

* The People's Palace in Mile End Road grew out of an imaginary picture in Walter Besant's novel, All Sorts and Conditions of Men (1882), of a great palace of education and recreation in East London for working men and women. Partially completed, it had been functioning since 1887.

ballads in the vain hope of fixing the attention of an immense audience. But the thing was impossible: the place was too big. Hundreds of young people loafed and larked, or stared and wandered in and out, at the end of the room. I thought of the late Edmund Gurney—of his useless big book to prove that Wagner's music was *wrong*, and his invaluable little plea for an orchestra for the East End. One hundred and twenty good players, under an able conductor, could make that concert room useful. They would cost money, too; but why not stick up a board and ask for it?

But there is another way of getting music afoot there. Why not buy first-rate wind instruments; engage a really competent instructor-bandmaster; and then invite the East End to come in and play for itself. There is plenty of musical talent knocking about misused or misdirected among the wage workers. I have often heard a knot of East End amateurs with a few brass instruments helplessly making the most hideous discord, because they had never been taught to tune their slides or warned against the impossibility of making up a band with a fortuitous concourse of deadly weapons tuned to different pitches and only agreeing in the single point of having been purchased at a pawnbroker's. With properly assorted instruments and a little simple instruction, these enthusiasts would have made excellent music. The proletarian bands of the industrial north and of the Salvation Army prove it.

From the People's Palace I went to the Bow and Bromley Institute. There I found a sixpenny and threepenny audience, of discouragingly middleclass aspect, listening to M. Gigout, who was performing on the "kist o' whustles" which is the pride of the Institute. Presently came Madame Belle Cole, a robust lady with an extraordinary voice and an effective adaptation of the style of Madame Antoinette Sterling. She sang

Gounod's Entreat me not to Leave Thee to such purpose that the audience, instead of entreating her to leave them, insisted on her singing again, whereupon she gave Home, sweet Home. The next artist that turned up was Henry Seiffert, the Dutch violinist, whose breadth of tone and command of his instrument completely confirmed the very favorable opinion I formed of him when he first played in London. The audience clamored for an encore; but a gentleman came forward in the midst of the hubbub, and when his evident wish to speak had produced a breathless and expectant silence, said he wanted somebody to give a theme for M. Gigout to improvize upon. This simply struck us dumb. Then he smiled reassuringly, and his eye began to travel slowly along the bench where I sat. Ere it reached my vacant chair I was safe on the roof of an Aldgate tram.

A TYPICAL CONCERT
The Star, 17 May 1889

I do not know anything more annoying at a concert than a man who beats time. He is a sort of modern prophet with a Kentish fire shut up in his bones, so that, like Jeremiah, he is weary with forbearing and cannot stay. He generally does stay, notwithstanding, right through to the very end. It seems unreasonable to hate him so venomously for attempting what the big drum and cymbals may be achieving at the same time with your entire approval; but, reasonably or not, the thumping of his boot distracts and annoys you beyond expression, and you gloat vindictively over his defeat when a syncopated passage throws him out.

Among these death watches of the concert room there are some terribly destructive varieties. I remember a tenor who used to mark time by shooting his ears up and down. If you have ever seen a circus clown twitch his ear you know how it makes your flesh creep. Imagine the sensation of looking at a man with his ears pulsating 116 times per minute in a quick movement from one of Verdi's operas. That man permanently injured my nervous system by rehearsing in my presence (unsuccessfully) the arduous part of Ruiz in Il Trovatore. But he was eclipsed by a rival who marked time with his eyes. You know the fancy clock in which an old man with a pistol looks out of a rustic window, glancing from side to side for burglars as the clock ticks. That was how he did it; and never shall I forget the shrinking of my whole nature from his horrible ocular oscillations. Feeling that I should go mad if I ever saw such a thing again, I left the country (he was not an Englishman), and have never revisited it.

Time, the great healer, eventually effaced his detested image from my memory. But on Wednesday afternoon I happened to be at Mr Henry Phillips's concert at St James's Hall, contemplating Mr Frederic King, who was singing *O du mein holder Abendstern*. To confess the truth, I was not minding the song so much as Mr King's fashionable trousers, made according to the new mode in which the tailor measures you round the chest, in order to get the correct width for the knee. I am rather an outsider in these matters, as it is my practice to make a suit of clothes last me six years. The result is that my clothes acquire individuality, and become characteristic of me. The sleeves and legs cease to be mere tailor-made tubes; they take human shape with knees and elbows recognizably mine. When my friends catch sight of one of my suits hanging on a nail, they pull out their penknives and rush forward, exclaiming "Good Heavens! he has done it at last."

However, the musical critic presently prevailed over

the clothes philosopher; and I lifted my gaze to Mr King's face as the piano began the six-eight rhythm of the Romance. To my intense horror, he instantly beat time horizontally with his eyes for a whole bar. Unbearable memories crowded upon me. I held on to the back of my seat in a silent struggle with homicidal mania. It was a terrible moment; for my place was within a few yards of Mr King's throat. Mercifully, his eyes stopped. Unconscious of the peril through which he had just passed, he began to sing in his best manner; and the effect was like that of David's singing on Saul. Still, I cannot help thinking that it is just as well that I am not in the habit of carrying a javelin. Though now that I think of it, how musical performances would improve if all critics of fine taste carried javelins—and used them!

These afternoon concerts are odd affairs. The tickets are half-a-guinea apiece; and nine-tenths of the audience are obviously deadheads. The artists sing to oblige oneanother: about 70 guineas' worth of them turned up on this particular occasion, and helped Mr Phillips to entertain a few of his friends and a host of strangers who never did and never will contribute a farthing to the gate money upon which Music depends for her living. When I arrived the attendants were strictly carrying out a regulation which I have often insisted on as indispensable to the comfort of artists and audience, but which I now denounce as intolerable. I allude to the practice of closing the doors during each piece. I should not have objected had I been on the right side of the door; but I came late, and so was on the wrong side during the performance of the first movement of Grieg's violin sonata (Op. 13) by Miss Sasse and Henry Seiffert. I was utterly disgusted with the selfishness of the people who, to save themselves a momentary discomfort, kept me on the stairs for nearly three minutes.

When I got in I found Miss Sasse playing Grieg in a hopelessly un-Grieg-like fashion, and Mr Seiffert, who had apparently lost interest in the transaction, absently playing the violin part. Even when he reappeared to give us Wieniawski's Legende, he once or twice took down his instrument and looked perplexedly at it as one communing with himself thus: "What on earth is this thing under my chin? Looks like a fiddle. Gad! this must be a concert; and I expect I've been put up to do something at it. Wonder what she's playing! It sounds like Wieniawski. Yes, by Jove! it's the Legend. I must wake up; here goes!" And in these brief intervals of wakefulness he played very finely, though he seemed to master the polyphonic difficulties as easily asleep as awake. I am always inclined to believe in a violinist who can play Wieniawski. Beethoven and Mendelssohn were great composers of music for the violin; but Wieniawski was a great composer of violin music. There is all the difference in the world between the two.

I have no space to tell of the rest of this typical concert—of how Mr Herbert Sims Reeves, whose determination never to force his voice has been rewarded by a considerable growth in its power and beauty, sang a couple of those Italian songs which are the ultimate perfection of utter brainlessness; of how Madame Patey, with ruthless affectation and exaggeration, used a fine song of Handel's merely to give a thundering display of her voice and power; of how Miss Pauline Cramer astonished everybody by her majestic stature and the brightness and impetuosity which make her genuine German sentiment so acceptable; and of how cleverly and expressively Miss Rosina Filippi recited Henry the Fifth's wooing (Henry V. was an insufferable Jingo snob; but that is not Miss Filippi's fault), besides leaving all the other ladies nowhere in the point of artistic dressing. I say I have no space to tell of these things; nor for Signor di Giambattista's concert in the evening, except that I should recommend the application of vinegar and brown paper to the pianoforte on which he played, especially to the bass.

The Spanish Students* at the Café Monaco seem to have made a poor job of their academic studies, as most of them carry wooden spoons in their hats as trophies of their performances under competitive examination. When I entered I was the fortieth arrival; and about a hundred more came in before I left: chiefly Spaniards, though some English people were there to study the thing from an ethnological point of view. In one of the Henry VI. chronicle plays which Shakespear had a hand in, there is a ghost who abruptly closes a conversation by saying "Have done; for more I hardly can endure." It was with much the same feeling that I withdrew at the end of the first part, leaving the Spanish part of the audience to sit out the second, and astonish the natives by stamping and shouting after the Iberian manner. The guitar and mandolin band, with its tum-tum melodies and simple-minded contrasts of *forte* and *piano*, is pretty; but I had heard the sort of thing before, and a little of it went far with me. Señor Cano played on himself very smartly with a tambourine; Señorita Reyes sang exactly as an Irish fish-wife cries "Dublin Bay Herrings!"; two Andalusians danced as the Carmens of real life dance; the guitarist accompanied very quaintly and skilfully; and—and, in short, I came away.

* A company of Spanish singers, dancers, and instrument-alists, calling themselves Estudiantina Española, were holding forth in the International Hall, a new concert room of the Café Monaco in Piccadilly Circus.

BIZET ITALIANIZED

The Star, 20 May 1889

To lovers of poetry the pearl fisher is known as one who "held his breath, and went all naked to the hungry shark."* To the patrons of the Opera he is now familiar as an expensively got-up Oriental, with an elaborate ritual conducted in temples not unlike Parisian newspaper kiosks, the precincts whereof are laid out, regardless of expense, in the manner of a Brussels tea garden. The chief ceremony is a ballet; and though here, if anywhere, we might expect to find our pearl fisher in the condition mentioned by Keats, such is by no means the case. He—or rather she—is clothed and, within operatic limits, in her right mind. As to holding his breath, he turns that accomplishment to account for the better execution of *roulades* and *fiorituras*. He keeps the hungry shark in order by the prayers of a virgin priestess, who remains veiled and secluded from all human intercourse on a rocky promontory during the oyster season.

Out of these simple and plausible conditions we get a pretty poem. Leila is the priestess. Nadir and Zenith—no: I find on looking at the libretto that the name is Zurga—fall in love with her. Nadir sacrilegiously serenades her on the promontory. She responds; and the two, amid a hideous tempest, are seized and condemned to the stake. Zurga effects a diversion, and enables them to escape by setting Ceylon on fire: an extreme measure; but then, as he doubtless reflects, you cannot have an omelet without breaking eggs. The natives then burn

* John Keats, Isabella (Poems, 1820).

him; and really, under the circumstances, it is hard to blame them. That is all.

Of the choral music, the dance music, the procession music, and the melodramatic music, by all of which the dainty little poem of the two friends in love with the veiled priestess has been stuffed and padded into a big Covent Garden opera, it is needless to speak. It is effective and workmanlike enough; but a dozen composers could have done it to order as well as Bizet. The best of it is the choral unison in the first act—*Colui, che noi vogliam, per duce,* which has something of the swing and frankness of Donizetti's choruses. (These, by the bye, have been discovered by the Salvation Army: I heard one of their bands playing *Per te d'immenso giubilo* capitally one Sunday morning last year down at Merton). The leading motive which runs through the opera is very beautiful, but no more Bizet's than the chorale in Les Huguenots is Meyerbeer's: it is simply that wonderful old Dies Iræ which has fascinated generations of musicians and worshipers. Bizet is only himself—his immature self—in the love music, which has that touch of divine rapture which a young poet's love music should have, and which has the distinction and charm of the Carmen music without the firmness of its style. In the first act, the conventional amorous cavatina for the tenor is replaced by a duet in which the two rivals recall the romantic atmosphere of that evening at the gate of an eastern city when they caught their first glimpse of Leila. The duet, and all those parts of the opera which are in the same vein, are enchanting. He who has no indulgence for their want of solidity is fit for treasons, stratagems, and spoils.

The cast was only four strong. M. Talazac, whose figure offered a terrible temptation to the hungry shark, has a pretty and fairly steady *mezza voce,* besides some sweet head notes; but the *tremolo* with which he uses his chest register will prevent him from attaining popularity here. Signor F. d'Andrade is a useful artist, free from conspicuous faults, and in earnest about his work. Miss Ella Russell is an accomplished singer of the Patti school, with a fine ear, and a voice of enviable quality, range, and flexibility. Her shortcomings are lack of distinction and bad pronunciation. She has not the intense dramatic instinct which has enabled some singers to take a foremost place as by natural right without the acquired culture and habits of thought which are becoming more and more necessary for success on the lyric stage; but a lady of Miss Russell's energy and confidence can do much for herself in this direction if she shuns the seductive illusion that no more remains for her to do. At all events, she should at once take a set of lessons in Italian so as to avoid such achievements as

> Bentosto una barbarar gentay
> Accor minacciantay, furentay.

It may be said that this is one of the consequences of operas performed in a language which is not that of the country, not that of the singer, and not that in which the opera was written.

Signor Mancinelli conducted, as he always does, like a man of character and energy, and the orchestra minded their business accordingly. With such players as there are at Covent Garden, nothing more is needed to secure satisfactory results in such work as the score of the Pearl Fishers.* Tonight, Faust, with Miss Macintyre and M. Montariol. M. Winogradow, the sole success of the ill-fated Russian troupe,† will be the Valentin; and

* The Covent Garden production was retitled Leila.
† Vladimir Lubinoff had brought his Russian National Opera Company to the over-sized Albert Hall, where he disastrously offered as highlights of his opening bill on

Mephistopheles will be played by Signor Castelmary, who used to make the part curiously fantastic and interesting, not by his wolflike singing, but by his peculiar realization of the grotesque aspect of the character.

PERFUNCTORY NOTES ON FAUST
The Star, 21 May 1889

Last night's performance at the Royal Italian Opera, Covent Garden, was rather of the subscription kind: that is, Jean de Reszke was not the Faust, nor Edouard the Mephistopheles. The success of the evening was Winogradow's Valentin. At first the savage fervor and rich tone which made such an effect at the Albert Hall were missing, but they speedily returned. *Dio Possente* aroused a cold and listless house to an *encore*, which was declined. His share of the sword chorale and duel *trio* were given magnificently. The Faust, M. Montariol, did not make a favorable impression at starting. His declamation in the first act was forced and unskilful. Later on it appeared that he was not without his merits. He took his high notes, which are slightly veiled, quietly, and was comparatively guiltless of *tremolo*; so, on the whole, there was much to be thankful for. As Miss

---

8 October 1888 a few operatic selections and orchestral pieces of Glinka, and 48 lady students of the Guildhall School of Music playing works like Willem Coenen's Caprice Concertant on 24 grand pianofortes. He subsequently transferred his company to the Jodrell Theatre, where he produced Rubinstein's opera The Demon on 22 October, in which Michael Winogradow sang one of the leads. The production was a failure, but Winogradow made a great personal success.

Macintyre's Margaret unquestionably delighted the audience it is nobody's business to demur to her performance; but I must add that she perpetrated a shocking Vandalism in ending the final *trio* on the high B natural. Castelmary is less slim and sudden than of yore: he has got an additional chin, too, and has become a Mephistopheles of the Rabelaisian variety, rather short of wind. He retains his old diabolical enjoyment of the part, and annoys the house, as he always did, by his occasional abandonment of all artistic method and self-control. The soldiers' chorus went with thundering vigor. The orchestra left something to be desired in point of delicacy and balance; but they will probably improve as the season goes on, as they did all last year. Excuse these perfunctory notes scrawled between the acts.

THE PHILHARMONIC
The Star, 24 May 1889

There was a rush at St James's Hall last night to hear the famous Belgian violinist who had made such a sensation at the previous concert. The cheapest seats were crammed long before the concert began, although the heat was so great that violin strings soon began to snap in all directions. In the last movement of the Mendelssohn concerto Ysaÿe's *chanterelle* went, and he, like Joachim at a previous performance of the same work at the Philharmonic, had to swap fiddles with one of the first violins, whose instrument was certainly not a Stradivarius.

The concert began with Mozart's Figaro overture. If you want to ascertain whether a musician is hopelessly belated, benighted, out of date, and behind his time, ask him how this overture should be played. If he replies "In three and a half minutes," away with him at once; he is guilty. I am sorry to have to add that Mr Cowen finished inside the three and a half minutes, and, in order to do it, necessarily made all play of artistic feeling impossible. However, the overture, so treated, is undeniably useful to boil eggs by, though I prefer them boiled four minutes myself. After the Figaro came a new symphony by Mr C. Hubert H. Parry. And here I protest against the cruelty of these professional exercises in four mortal movements. I respect Mr Parry; I enjoy his musical essays; I appreciate his liberal views; I know the kindly feelings his pupils at the Royal College have for him. If he would only be content with an overture, I should praise it to the skies sincerely; for I like to hear just one specimen of shipshape professional composition in sonata form occasionally. But I really cannot stand four large doses of it in succession—*Allegro con spirito*, in C; *Andante sostenuto*, in A minor; *Allegro scherzoso (scherzoso* indeed!) in F; and *Moderato*, with variations (two repeats in each)—twelve variations, as I am a living man! I hate to be told that "the figure in the first bar should be observed on account of the prominence to which it is destined in the working out." That is exactly why it should *not* be observed by anybody who can get comfortably to sleep like the man who sat next me, or the man who has a Standard to read, like the lady two bars in front of me—I mean two benches. Mr Joseph Bennett, the programist, says of the symphony:—"It has been described by the composer as a 'little' work; *and amateurs may remember that Beethoven used the German equivalent of the same term in connection with his No. 8.*" I leave the world to contemplate those words in silence: no comment of mine shall disturb its inexpressible thoughts.

Ysaÿe disappointed me. His technical skill is prodigious, his tone strong and steady, his effect on the public unquestionable. But he is an unsympathetic player. In the *cadenza* of the concerto he played every phrase so as to make a point; and the audience whispered "How clever, and how difficult that must be!" But they did not recognize that the phrase was an integral part of the movement—a fragment of the opening theme. Now when Sarasate played the same *cadenza* on Saturday, everybody recognized the reference, and nobody had the feat of execution obtruded on them. It was the same throughout. The spirit of the composition was always missed, and the wonders of the fiddling always insisted on. At last, by dint of having the virtuosity of Ysaÿe thrust down their throats at the point of the bow, the audience burst into exclamations of astonishment at feats for which other violinists neither expect nor receive any special credit. When it came to one of Paganini's studies and Wieniawski's *polonaise*—which were certainly played with consummate dexterity—they were quite enraptured.

For my part I have no hesitation in saying that Ysaÿe's performance was chiefly valuable as a foil to Miss Janotha's playing of Beethoven's G major concerto. Her execution, like his, is exceptionally dexterous; but it is also beautiful, suggestive, poetic. I first heard this young Polish artist at a Philharmonic concert, and she played the G concerto then also. My comment was that here at last was someone who could replace Madame Schumann. The concerto charmed me last night as much as before. Though Miss Janotha occasionally breaks out in waywardnesses and displays of strength, suggestive of possession by a fitful musical demon, yet I know no pianist of her generation whose playing is more sustainedly and nobly beautiful than hers.

Of Herr Karl Meyer I can only say that I should like to hear him sing Tom der Reimer again. Provided you understand German, you will find in his performance the intelligibility and interest of recitation with the charm of song. I noticed that in playing the Jubilee overture the band did not rise when they came to God Save the Queen. They always used to at the Philharmonic. A Home Rule demonstration, I presume.

ABSOLUTE PITCHERS
The Star, 24 May 1889

Now that the season is in full swing, I am afraid I shall have to drag in the subject of music rather often in this column. I know that it is my King Charles's head; and I can assure my readers that I do what I can to avoid it. But when there are several concerts every afternoon, and an opera in the evening, I cannot, in spite of my diligence in not going to them, quite keep them out of my memoranda. Nobody knows better than I do that a musical critic who is always talking about music is quite as odious as an ordinary man who is always talking about himself. I venture to hope that I have never been guilty of the latter vice; and I shall try to steer clear of the former. Therefore, it is with no desire to talk shop that I proceed to confess that I did not go to the Tonic Sol-fa meeting at Exeter Hall on Monday, though The Star was duly represented there.

My chief reason for not going was that one of the items in the program was a collection, a form of musical composition to which I have an incurable repugnance, except when I am myself the performer. A subordinate reason existed in the necessity for my being elsewhere: at Covent Garden, in fact. But I wish carefully to disclaim any hostility whatever to the Tonic Sol-fa. I will go further, and declare my suspicion (my experience is not sufficiently wide to justify me in calling it a conviction) that the Tonic Sol-faists do undoubtedly teach people to read music. That the staff notationists, as a rule, dont, I take as granted on all sides.

An ordinary choir generally contains a few people naturally gifted with the power of recollecting the absolute pitch of notes. If you met them in the middle of the Sahara and said "How do you do? Will you kindly give me A flat?" they would give it to you promptly. John Hullah seems to have supposed that because he could do this all the world could do it. Teach such people the symbols which, in the staff or any other notation, denote the sounds used in music, and they can read whatever you put into their hands. Almost all the champion sight-reading pupils who are brought forward as samples of the efficacy of the staff system, the Chevé system, the Tonic Sol-fa system, or any other system, are persons with this sense of absolute pitch, their proficiency proving nothing except the mere literary legibility of the notation they have before them. They have in their heads not only a fixed "*Doh*," but the other 11 notes in the octave fixed as well, and they use the Tonic Sol-fa as a "fixed *Doh*" system, just as many staff-notation readers use the staff as a movable *Doh* system, and would not be in the least put out if all their parts were written in the key of C, like horn parts in an orchestral score.

The system is undoubtedly the di Bassetto system, as practised by me and by the great majority of sight readers throughout the world. I should explain that I cannot remember the absolute pitch of notes, and that though I can imitate an interval instantaneously, by ear, I cannot calculate it with sufficient presence of mind to carry me through a *presto con fuoco* movement at sight. For instance, if you asked me for A flat in the Sahara, I should borrow a tuning fork and listen to its note. Then, if I saw C stamped on the handle, I should, after some minutes' careful calculation warble the minor sixth above, which would of course be A flat (more or less). But my practical choir method renders reference to a tuning fork unnecessary, and entirely dispenses with mental arithmetic. At the first rehearsal I depend mainly on my natural power of improvizing what is called "a second." By keeping my eyes and ears open, I soon identify the few who are really able to read at sight. These are generally, of course, absolute pitchers. The rest is easy. I simply get beside one of them, and sing what he sings until I have picked up my part. The merits of this method are proved by its almost universal adoption. I have no hesitation in saying that for one person who reads music on the Curwen system or the Hullah system, there are fifty who read it on mine.

In confessing to a deficiency in the sense of absolute pitch: a deficiency which prevents me from detecting a transposition of one of the numbers in an opera, except when (as in the case of *Dio dell'or*, as sung by Castelmary the other night in Faust) the wrong key is attained by a flagrantly burglarious transition without any alteration of the previous modulating cadence, I may as well say that I wish Mr F. Galton would open a critico-metric laboratory to test scientifically the pretensions of those who have perfect faith in the infallibility of their ears. I daresay that you, exacting reader, would not give twopence for a critic who, hearing a note out of tune, could not say whether it was sharp or flat. Well, have you seen, in the New Gallery, Mr Phil Burne-Jones's portrait of Lord Rayleigh in his laboratory, seeking the philosopher's stone with the aid of a retort, a few test tubes, and a secondhand kettledrum?

Lord Rayleigh once lured some eminent musicians into that laboratory, and proceeded with coldblooded physicist's scepticism to test their pretensions. He began by putting pairs of notes just sufficiently out of unison for the eminent ones to recognize that there was a difference in pitch. Then he asked them which was the higher of the two. They answered confidently; and, lo! they were just as often wrong as right. And when he varied the quality of the notes, making the lower one shrill and the higher one dull and veiled, he had them every time. I do not defend Lord Rayleigh's conduct in playing it thus upon men before whom he should have been awestricken, and whose ears were diviner instruments than his soulless mechanical reeds. Still, there is food for reflection in the matter.

I could write quite a treatise on the imaginary powers which musicians have attributed to themselves in perfect good faith, and in the absence of any scientific verification; but it is time to pass on to other matters. I think it must have been on some evening last week that I found myself celebrating the silver wedding of Mr Lansdowne-Cottell, at a recklessly overcrowded concert in St James's Hall. Here I paid sixpence—people seem to think I am made of sixpences—for a program about eight inches by ten, containing a dozen pages of advertisements and two of program. If everybody bought one and got a ticket for nothing, the silver wedding cannot have been wholly in vain. However, the sensation of that part of the evening which I spent there was a performance by Miss Anna Teresa Berger on the cornet. I do not know why a lady should play the cornet: indeed, I do not know why anybody should play it; but her right is as valid as a man's. Miss Berger's double-tonguing verges on the unattainable; and in keenness of blare she rivals Mr Howard Reynolds at his loudest.

Sarasate, whose first concert I missed, played Mendelssohn's concerto last Saturday. But I had as lief hear him play Pop goes the Weasel as any classic masterpiece;

and what is more, I believe he would himself just as soon play one as the other. They say he runs through a new composition once with his pianist, and then has it by heart for ever afterwards; and I can believe it; for he often produces tedious affairs that no artist of his reputation would find it worth while to learn if it cost any trouble. I have never been able to detect any preference on his part for Mendelssohn over Dr Mackenzie, Bernard, Lalo, Max Bruch, or anyone else. He never interprets anything: he plays it beautifully, and that is all. He is always alert, swift, clear, refined, certain, scrupulously attentive and quite unaffected. This last adjective will surprise people who see him as a black-haired romantic young Spaniard, full of fascinating tricks and mannerisms. It will surprise them still more to hear that the person they so idealize produces the whole illusion with his fine eyes alone, being for the rest a man of undistinguished stature, with hair very liberally sprinkled with grey, and a plain square face with more than a fair fortyone years' allowance of marks from Time's graver. There is no trace of affectation about him: the picturesqueness of that pluck of the string and stroke of the bow that never fails to bring down the house is the natural effect of an action performed with perfect accuracy in an extraordinarily short time and strict measure.

SETTING FAUST TO MUSIC
The Star, 29 May 1889

Faust, no matter who writes the music to it, will remain the most popular opera story of the century until some great musician takes Henrik Ibsen's Peer Gynt as a libretto. Boïto's version seems almost as popular as

Gounod's, though Gounod's is a true musical creation, wheras Boïto has only adapted the existing resources of orchestration and harmony very ably to his libretto. In short, Gounod has set music to Faust, and Boïto has set Faust to music.

The house likes Boïto's prologue, in spite of the empty stage and the two ragged holes in a cloth which realize Mr Harris's modest conception of hell and heaven. The great rolling crashes and echoes of brazen sound in the prelude transport us into illimitable space at once; and the tremendous sonority of the instrumentation at the end, with the defiant devil's whistle recklessly mocking each climax of its grandeur, literally makes us all sit up. Perhaps I am reading into the score what the composer never intended: Boïto may have meant no more by the piccolo here than Beethoven meant by it in the last bars of the Egmont overture. If so, that does not invalidate my remark: it only shews how much the critic can add to the work of the composer.

There is a great deal in Mefistofele that is mere impressionism; and like impressionism in painting it is enchanting when it is successful, and nonsensically incoherent when it is the reverse. In the unrestrained colloquialism of private conversation I should not hesitate to describe a good deal of the Brocken scene and some of the rampart scene as ingenious tiddy-fol-lol. The witches' revel, with the spurious *fugato* at the end, is stuff for a pantomime, not for serious opera. But at innumerable points the music is full of suggestive strokes and colors in sound, happiest sometimes when they are mere inchoate instrumentation. The whole work is a curious example of what can be done in opera by an accomplished literary man without original musical gifts, but with ten times the taste and culture of a musician of only ordinary extraordinariness.

There was little novelty in the representation last

night. Miss Macintyre doubled Helen and Margaret for the first time at Covent Garden, and sang the duet in the classical interlude in the most exaggerated vein of romanticism. She did not wholly resist the temptation to force her chest voice up in the prison scene, which is likely to prove a terrible engine of voice destruction among dramatic sopranos in this particular and most fatal way. She relied largely for her acting on the exploitation of what is nothing but a bag of tricks; and it is quite true, as a ruthless critic tells her this week, that she walks badly and twists her mouth to one side. But, with all these drawbacks, her natural talent and refinement, and the charm of her unspoiled young voice, carried her triumphantly through the two parts. Signor Massini cannot act; but his throatiness and his aptitude for singing flat were established beyond question in the first act. He improved greatly afterwards, getting quite into tune in the garden scene, and coming off with some credit in the final act; but he is, on the whole, rather useful than distinguished as a *primo tenore*. Signor Castelmary was announced for Mefisto. He would have been hopelessly out of breath after three bars or so had he appeared; so nobody was disappointed at his replacement by Signor Novara, who played the part with unexpected success, delivering the text with clearness and purpose, and acting without any senseless posturing and point-making. The part exactly suits his voice. Madame Scalchi was good as Martha—not so good as Pantalis.

Signor Mancinelli conducted. He again dragged that irresistible hysterical quartet in the garden scene; and again it missed the effect it never failed to produce when Christine Nilsson was the Margaret. In the prologue, on the contrary, he took the choruses too fast; they were gabbled in a way that suggested anything but the ethereal whisper intended by the composer. The stage

management and scene-shifting were occasionally need-
lessly careless and destructive of stage illusion. An oath
or two from Mr Harris will no doubt improve matters
in this respect.

A BUTCHERED LOHENGRIN

The Star, 31 May 1889

It is a sign of the shallow musical culture of the classes
that they come late for Lohengrin merely because it
begins at eight instead of half-past. A set that will not
sacrifice its cheese and ice pudding to hear the Lohengrin
prelude—the first work of Wagner's that really conquered the world and changed the face of music for us—
may be a smart set for dancing; it is the reverse at music.
When the *élite* of the *beau monde* did come they found
that Mr McGuckin had sprained his ankle badly, and
had refused all proposals to go through his part in a Bath
chair. His place was accordingly taken by Signor A.
d'Andrade, who phrased his narrative in the last act very
nicely. Miss Nordica turned Elsa of Brabant into Elsa of
Bond-street, by appearing in a corset. She produces her
voice so skilfully that its want of color, and her inability
to fill up with expressive action the long periods left by
Wagner for that purpose, were the more to be regretted.
Madame Fürsch-Madi, who has been subject to Italian
opera for many years, got severe attacks of spasms and
staggers at the emotional crises of her part. Her music,
however, was not ill sung. Signor F. d'Andrade rather
distinguished himself as Telramond; but on the whole,
the principal singers lacked the weight, breadth of style,
richness of voice, and sincerity of expression needed for
Lohengrin. Signor Mancinelli's Italian temperament

came repeatedly into conflict with the German temperament of the composer. Where the music should have risen to its noblest and broadest sweep he hurried on in the impetuous, self-assertive, emphatic Southern way that is less compatible than any other manner on earth with the grand calm of the ideal Germany. He perpetrates, too, that abominable butcherly cut in the prelude to the second act, which is an odious inheritance from the bad old times. I confess that I cannot speak amiably of performances at which I am subjected to wanton outrages of this sort. There are reasons for the other cuts: bad reasons, but ones which must be let pass under the circumstances. But this particular cut is without excuse. Under its exasperating influence I proceed to complain that the choristers shouted instead of singing. This is an improvement on the old choristers, who could not even shout; but shouting should not be the goal of even an operatic choir's ambition, and I do not see why, if Mr Mansfield has trumpets on the stage in Richard III., the Royal Italian Opera should be unable to get anything better than four vile cornets. And I wish those ladies of the chorus whom Mr Harris has provided with train-bearers and splendid dresses, would learn to walk in the true *grande dame* manner, and not make the bridal procession ridiculous by their bearing. And I should have liked more precision and delicacy from the orchestra. And, generally speaking, I do not think they can do Lohengrin worth a cent at Covent Garden; and that is the long and short of it. This is the sort of temper you get a critic into when you carry your eternal Cut! Cut! Cut! a bar too far.

ECONOMICS AND MUSIC

The Star, 1 June 1889

Elsewhere you will find a letter on The Music of the
People, by Mr Marshall-Hall, a young composer who
is much spoken of among the young lions of Mr Hamish
MacCunn's generation. At one of Mr Henschel's
concerts Mr Santley sang some portions of an opera, the
poem and music of which were by Mr Marshall-Hall. I
was not at that concert, so I am quite out of it as far as
Mr Marshall-Hall's music is concerned; but I am
delighted to find him, as a representative of young
genius, denouncing the stalls, trusting to the gallery,
waving the democratic flag, and tearing round generally.

Young genius has rather a habit, by the way, of
writing to my editor to denounce me as flippant and
unenlightened, and to demand that I also shall tear
round and proclaim the working man as the true knower
and seer in Art. If I did, the working man would not
think any the better of me; for he knows well enough
that society is not divided into "animated clothes-pegs"
on the one hand and lovers of Beethoven in ligatured
corduroys on the other. For Beethoven purposes society
is divided into people who can afford to keep a piano and
go to operas and concerts, and people who cannot. Mr
Marshall-Hall's idea that the people who cannot are
nevertheless screwed up to concert pitch by honest,
thorough, manly toil, shews that, though he be an expert
in the music question, in the labor question he is a
greenhorn.

Take a laborer's son; let him do his board-schooling
mostly on an empty stomach; bring him up in a rookery
tenement; take him away from school at thirteen; offer

him the alternative of starvation or 12 to 16 hours work a day at jerry building, adulterated manufactures, coupling railway wagons, collecting tramway fares, field labor, or what not, in return for food and lodging which no "animated clothes-peg" would offer to his hunter; bully him; slave-drive him; teach him by every word and look that he is not wanted among respectable people, and that his children are not fit to be spoken to by their children. This is a pretty receipt for making an appreciator of Beethoven.

The truth is, that in the innumerable grades of culture and comfort between the millionaire on the one hand, and the casual laborer on the other, there is a maximum of relish for art somewhere. That somewhere is certainly not among the idle rich, whose appetites for enjoyment are not sharpened by work, nor is it among those who, worn out by heavy muscular toil, fall asleep if they sit quiet and silent for five minutes of an evening. Professional and business men of musical tastes who work hard, and whose brains are of such a quality that a Beethoven symphony is a recreation to them instead of an increased strain on their mental powers, are keen patrons of music, though, in outward seeming, they belong to the animated clothes-peg section. Middle-class young ladies, to whom there is no path to glory except that of the pianist or *prima donna*, frequent St James's Hall with astonishing persistence, and eventually form musical habits which outlast their musical hopes.

The musical public is the shilling public, by which I mean the people who can afford to pay not more than a shilling once a week or so for a concert without going short of more immediately necessary things. Music can be better nourished on shilling, sixpenny, and three-penny seats than on the St James's Hall scale. The laborers are so enormously numerous that the absolute number of their exceptional men—men who will buy books out of 13s. a week in the country and 18s. in a town, and find time to read them while working 12 hours a day—is considerable. The more comfortable members of the artisan class can often afford a shilling much better that the poorer middleclass families; but it has a certain customary and traditional scale of expenditure, in which concerts stand at threepence or sixpence, shillings being reserved for the gallery of a West End theatre, and half-crowns for Sunday trips to Epping Forest and for extra refreshments.

After these come the innumerable "poor devils" of the middle class, always craving in an unaccountable way for music, and crowding the Promenade Concerts on classical nights, the Albert Hall gallery, and wherever else decent music is to be heard cheaply. To these three classes Mr Marshall-Hall must look for the little that is now possible in the way of a musical public. Even when we have supplied all three with as much music as they can stomach, the laborer in ligatured corduroys will still open his eyes to darkness, and the vapid snob grub like a blind puppy in the light. What we want is not music for the people, but bread for the people, rest for the people, immunity from robbery and scorn for the people, hope for them, enjoyment, equal respect and consideration, life and aspiration, instead of drudgery and despair. When we get that I imagine the people will make tolerable music for themselves, even if all Beethoven's scores perish in the interim.

Pending these millennial but perfectly practical measures, I must beg my readers not to blame me if the progress of the race makes it more and more apparent that the middleclass musical critic is the most ridiculous of human institutions. I do not take my function seriously, because it is impossible for an intelligent man to do so; and I am an eminently intelligent man. I often yield to quite romantic impulses. For instance, when Miss Adrienne Verity sent me a ticket for her concert at Collard's the other day, I went because Adrienne Verity struck me as being a pretty name. And I must own that I found her a pleasant-faced, well-grown lass, with refreshingly unceremonious ways and a healthy boisterousness which would make her the life and soul of a haymaking. But a singer! an artist! not yet. The way in which that young lady plunged into *Saper vorreste*, and rampaged through Be wise in time, and fired off Cherry Ripe at us, was bewildering. When ladies and children came forward with trophies of flowers, and did her floral homage as a Queen of Song, my brain reeled. And now I suppose that Miss Verity, having invited me to hear her sing, expects me to give her my opinion. My opinion is that she will either study hard with a competent teacher for a couple of years to come, learning to sing, to speak, to walk, to bow, and to abjure premature concerts and flower offerings, or else she will find a place in Mr D'Oyly Carte's or Mr Leslie's chorus, and there unskilfully scream her voice away in less than six months. And whoever gives her a more flattering opinion will do her a very cruel kindness.

Of the numerous concerts which I unavoidably missed, none caused me any particular regret, except the performance by pupils of the Royal Normal College for the Blind at the Crystal Palace, and a Board School contest at Hampstead, which the headmaster was quite right in bringing under my notice. It was, for example, much more important than Miss McKenzie's concert at Dudley House, which has been much written about, and concerning which I have nothing whatever to say except that it went off very successfully; that Mr Giddens amused me by his recitation; that the Dudley pictures interested me more than the music; and that the Dudley livery of black and yellow continually reminded me of the contrast between the gildings in Park Lane and the gloom of the coal pits wherein that gilding is made.

I need hardly say that my remarks about the Tonic Sol-fa have brought letters upon me insisting on the attractive simplicity of the notation, and even inviting me to learn it myself forthwith. This reminds me of a sage whom I consulted in my youth as to how I might achieve the formation of a perfect character. "Young man" he said "are you a vegetarian?" I promptly said "Yes" which took him aback. (I subsequently discovered that he had a weakness for oysters.) "Young man" he resumed "have you mastered Pitman's shorthand?" I told him I could write it very nearly as fast as longhand, but that I could not read it; and he admitted that this was about the maximum of human attainment in phonography. "Young man" he went on "do you understand phrenology?"

This was a facer, as I knew nothing about it; but I was determined not to be beaten, so I declared that it was my favorite pursuit, and that I had been attracted to him by the noble character of his bumps. "Young man" he continued "you are indeed high on the Mount of Wisdom. There remains but one accomplishment to the perfection of your character. Are you an adept at the Tonic Sol-fa system?" This was too much. I got up in a rage, and said "Oh, dash the Tonic Sol-fa system!" Then we came to high words; and our relations have been more or less strained ever since. I have always resolutely refused to learn the Tonic Sol-fa, as I am determined to prove that it is possible to form a perfect character without it.

THUNDER AND LIGHTNING AT THE PHILHARMONIC

The Star, 7 June 1889; unsigned

Madame Backer-Gröndahl last night played the [Beethoven] E flat concerto again for the Philharmonic Society. She is a famous Norwegian pianist, great in strength and feeling, now urging the pianoforte almost violently to do what a piano cannot do, and anon caressing it to exquisite ripples of sound and streams of keen plaintive melody. I shall not forget her playing of the second subject of the first movement. Her *diminuendo* in the long octave passage near the end of the *allegro* came as an enchanting surprise after the curious rough, sluggish *forte* at which she began it. The point for pianoforte and drum came out as I never heard it come out before; I feel sure that that fine artist, Mr Chaine, must adore Madame Gröndahl for doing him justice in this passage. The circumstances under which the concerto was played were unusually sensational. During the opening movement subdued rumblings, with which Mr Chaine had nothing to do, were heard from time to time. Just as we had all settled down, intent on the hushed melody of the *adagio*, the sky suddenly flashed into view through the windows; the electric light staggered as if from a mortal shock; and the rumbling broke into a crash. Everybody thought of the recent earthquake. A gentleman next me seized his hat and jammed it on his head too tightly for any convulsion of nature to dislodge it, which done, he folded his arms, and glared at Mr Cowen's back. I refrained with difficulty from crawling under the seat. As Madame Gröndahl dashed at the *finale*, a torrent of rain dashed at the windows; the lights, which had partly recovered, again burnt blue; and the pianist had to compete with the elements for our attention, and came out of the competition victorious. Young Mr Frederick Cliffe's symphony in C minor also weathered the storm. It has life and youth in it. A few pardonable displays of scholarship disfigure it here and there; and it is of course not quite free from reminiscences: a drum point from Beethoven, a theme in the trio taken from a beautiful melody in Liszt's Preludes, and so on. But, on the whole, it is fresh, genuine, and interesting. Fräulein Fillunger, who gave us [Weber's] Ocean, thou mighty monster, is not like the gentleman in Shakespear who could sing both high and low.* She can sing high, but not low. The concert began with Cherubini's barren Anacreon overture, and ended with that to Mozart's Zauberflöte, which Mr Cowen darted through as I should not have cared to do with so much lightning about.

THE INTERVAL IS THE ACT
The Star, 7 June 1889

I am indebted to Mr Fisher Unwin for a volume of essays by an American critic, Mr Henry T. Finck, author of Romantic Love and Personal Beauty. I am not sure that I should not have preferred a copy of Romantic Love and Personal Beauty, as these are subjects of enthralling interest to me; but perhaps Mr Unwin has not published that work, and so could only send me Chopin, and other Musical Essays. It is not for me to criticize Mr Finck further than to say that his speciality among musical essayists of the lighter sort arises from his unusual grip of the fact that we, having reached the

* See note p. 280.

eighteen-eighties, are well out of the eighteen-forties. This enables him to tell us a good deal that is interesting about the rise of German opera in New York, and to repeat some very old stories from a fresh point of view. For instance, he has shared the common lot in giving way to the temptation to narrate how Porpora kept Caffarelli singing the same sheet of exercises for five years (it used to be six), and then said "You have no more to learn. You are the greatest singer in the world." But instead of glorifying Porpora therefor, and lamenting that we have no such teachers as he nowadays (the truth being that we hàve far too many of them), he sensibly cites the anecdote as a proof that Porpora was a foolish pedant and Caffarelli a mere vocal acrobat.

However, my object in mentioning Mr Finck's book was to make an excuse for quoting the following sentence from it. "The danger is" writes Mr Finck "that the custom of delaying dinner till eight, which is coming into vogue among the English, who care neither for music nor the theatre, will be followed in New York." Last week I pointed out that Lohengrin, in spite of outrageous cutting down, lasted until midnight, though it began at eight instead of half-past. But the stalls and boxes remained half empty until nearly nine o'clock. Mr Mapleson accordingly has fixed the hour for beginning at a quarter to nine. The people for whose convenience this is done also insist on long waits between the acts, in order to get through rounds of visits to oneanother's boxes, conversations in the crushrooms, promenades round the corridors, and cigarettes on the balcony over the portico. To many of them, in short, the act is the interval, and the interval is the act.

Personally, I am not very grievously affected by these matters. Having attained the dignity of an habitual deadhead at the opera, I am soothed by the comparative comfort and coolness of a stall; and the long intervals enable me to scrawl my notices before I leave the theatre. Fifteen minutes after the curtain falls I am at home; in fifteen more the notice is posted, and I am in bed. But if I had paid half-a-crown to swelter in the gallery; if the long intervals brought no possibilities of movement or change of air; if my last train home were the five minutes to twelve from King's Cross, the twelve from Waterloo, or even the ten past twelve from Liverpool-street, then I think I should execrate the habits of the people downstairs, and take it rather ill of the management to ignore my circumstances in making their arrangements.

Under present circumstances, however, it is not only impossible to please everybody: it is actually impossible to please anybody. Aristocratic audiences and wage-workers are exactly alike in respect of loafing in at a quarter to nine, no matter what the appointed hour may be. But then the wage-worker wants to get to bed at midnight, wheras the aristocrat, who can afford to lie late in the morning, holds that the best of all ways to lengthen his days is to steal a few hours from the night. The suburban middleclass amateur either stays in town on the occasion of his visit to the opera and takes his tea at an aerated bread shop, in which case half-past seven would not be at all too early for him; or else he goes home for his wife and sister-in-law, and cannot get back to Covent Garden much before eight. It is to be borne in mind throughout all these calculations that the patron of the gallery, if he wants a good seat, has to go at least half an hour sooner than the man with the numbered stall. And for this class the opera must finish at twentyfive minutes past eleven at latest. Finally, some of the greatest modern operas require not less than five hours for their complete representation, to which should be added, in common humanity, one interval long enough to admit of the whole audience turning out for a walk or a light meal. The social conditions for stalls and gallery are, therefore, irreconcilable, and both are in conflict with the artistic conditions.

What, then, you ask, can I propose for the better adjustment of these affairs? Well, if I were a manager, I should do as Mr Harris does with the long operas: begin at eight, as being on the whole the best arrangement. But if I were a dictator I should settle the matter by enacting a seven hours' working day, taxing the incomes of the stall and boxholders twenty shillings in the pound, and subsidizing a National Opera out of the proceeds of the tax, using convict labor for the chorus and minor rôles, as well as for the scene-shifting. As to the two unfortunate soldiers who are now placed for shew purposes in the vestibule—and I hold that it is an insult and a dishonor to a soldier to make any such use of him—I should transfer them to the stalls, where they could enjoy the opera and turn their rifles to account by occasionally picking off the people who disturb the performance by talking loudly in their boxes. Even under existing circumstances, it is my firm belief that if something is not done to relieve these unfortunate grenadiers they will use their bayonets some evening out of sheer aggravation.

It will be observed that I have said nothing specifically about the performances at Her Majesty's Theatre. Is any explanation necessary? Suppose Mr John Coleman were to take the Haymarket Theatre, reconstruct it on the Buckstone model, double and treble the ordinary prices, and begin playing a round of Green Bushes, The Wreck Ashore, Black-eyed Susan, and The Duke's Motto,* with a provincial company, helped out by a few old stagers! Would any dramatic critic in London be

* The first two of these dramas (1845 and 1830) were by J.B. Buckstone, the third (1829) was written by Douglas Jerrold, and the fourth (1863), a romance, by John Brougham.

expected to criticize these plays gravely, and describe how they were done? Would he not be deemed generous enough if, for the sake of old times, he gave his tickets away to people able and willing to fill up places that would otherwise be empty, and then write a few lines of commonplace, recording the occurrence which he had not witnessed? Well, frankly, I regard Mr Mapleson's case as exactly parallel; and I shall do nothing to encourage his delusion that Il Barbiere, Lucia, and La Sonnambula can do anything for him now except ruin him.

If I had time to go into the fashionable opera business in competition with Mr Harris, I should try German opera, with Seidl or Hans Richter as conductor. I should then hammer away at the Nibelungen tetralogy until all was blue. If Mr Mapleson had the gumption to go to Mr Armbruster even now, and tell him to put up Siegfried or Tristan, with Miss Pauline Cramer and any cast, amateur or professional, that he could scrape together to support her, the whole Wagner-Richter connexion would go to Her Majesty's, and be followed by hundreds of outsiders from mere curiosity. I should, for one. But wild horses shall not drag me to Lucia.

Tchaikovsky's symphonic poem Romeo and Juliet at Sarasate's concert on Saturday proved impressive enough to keep Mr Cusins's orchestra thoroughly alive and alert. The usual thing is for Mr Cusins, looking every inch a fine old English gentleman, to make astounding faces at the band, of which they are too wellbred to take the slightest notice. He is conscious that they are doing nothing right; and they are conscious that they are doing nothing wrong; and between the two one learns how it was that the Philharmonic so narrowly escaped coming completely to grief in Mr Cusins's time, in spite of the rare degree of skill on both sides. Sarasate's tone was wiry and his pitch sharp when he began; but after a few minutes he left criticism gasping miles behind him.

WOODEN FRIGATES

The Star, 7 June 1889

I have been to *Il Barbiere*, *La Sonnambula*, and *Lucia*; but do not quail, reader: I am not going to inflict on you a single word of criticism concerning these antiquities. I know your opinion; and you know mine. As you say, there are pretty things in the dear old Barber. Perhaps you remember Mario in *Ecco ridente*? No? Of course not; you are too young, I ought to have seen that. You used to sing *Dunque io son*? Well, so used I when my voice was more flexible than it is now. Only think of that! And then, talking of *La Sonnambula*, most conciliatory of operas, is not *D'un pensiero* still acceptable even after Wagner; and can you have a finer test of true vocal expression in a singer than the pathetic *Ah! non credea*, and the rapturous *Ah! non giunge*, one after the other? Lucia, as you very pointedly observe, is a vulgar beast of an opera; and yet what passion and what melody there is in every act of it; and what memories cluster for some of us about those melodies! No, with all my experience I cannot tell you why Edgardo never comes on the stage without throwing his cloak on the floor, much as Mr Pickwick cast his spectacles into the middle of the kitchen at Dingley Dell. Sims Reeves used to do it on his great entrance before *Chi mi frena*, but whether he was the inventor of this choice effect I know not. But enough! these are the reminiscences of old fogies. Suffice it to say that Mr Mapleson is hammering away again at Her Majesty's with Il Barbiere, La Sonnambula, Lucia;

Lucia, La Sonnambula, Il Barbiere; and some of us fogies are going—mostly on complimentary tickets.

For the sake of old times, I will let Mr Mapleson's enterprise alone. I know how it must end; how it ended before; how we must all, in the highest interests of the lyric stage, be content that it shall end again. There is something pathetic in Mr Mapleson's conviction that at all hazards he must be an *impresario*. There is something cruel in the reply of the world, *Je n'en vois pas la nécessité*. Yet there is no reason why Mr Harris should have the field to himself, though Mr Mapleson, in opposing him with his present repertory, is pitting a wooden frigate against a modern Minotaur. What about German opera, conducted by Richter, Seidl, or Levy? What about opera in English? What about even Italian opera at popular prices? Alas! Mr Mapleson will not learn from me what he refuses to learn from experience. I can only shake my head over the good money he is throwing after bad, and wish him better success than I can honestly pretend to expect for him.

ALL ABOUT ROMEO AND JULIET
The Star, 14 June 1889

Let me recur for a moment to certain observations recently let fall by Spectator in these columns. Spectator, it will be remembered, went to the Opera, and saw Madame Albani as La Traviata. Far from being impressed by his visit to the temple in which all the arts meet, he spoke of the whole performance with un-qualified contempt, and positively refused to take our eminent lyric *tragédienne* seriously as an actress. What is more—and I recommend this point to all who are interested in opera—Spectator was right. Whatever may be his failings—however deficient he may be in a natural and becoming awe when he alludes to persons whose age and attainments should command his respect—there is no denying that the sort of thing that Madame Albani and her colleagues do at the Opera is beneath the notice of any intelligent student of dramatic art, and that the critics who gravely write about it in terms which would be rather overstrained if applied to Ristori, Sarah Bernhardt, Ellen Terry, Ada Rehan, Janet Achurch, or Mrs Kendal, richly deserve to be waved aside as foolish amateurs by such competent dramatic critics as Spectator, Mr William Archer, Mr —— well, the list is not so long as I thought, so I had perhaps better not continue it.

On Saturday we are to have at Covent Garden Gounod's setting of Romeo and Juliet. It is solemnly announced in the advertisements that Signor Montariol is in a high state of condescension towards Tybalt, which "he has kindly consented to play, although not a leading part (*sic*) in order to assist in making a perfect ensemble." Really handsome of Signor Montariol, is it not? Let us hope that he *will* make the ensemble perfect, as he so modestly promises.

[U] Romeo and Juliet has always been considered a melancholy opera; and Gounod has undeniably shrunk from the Shakespearean nurse and the Shakespearean Capulet, and so lost the relief they bring to the play. The main difficulty at Covent Garden will be to reconcile the huge scale of the representation with the delicacy and dreaminess of the music. How is Signor Mancinelli to turn that big and somewhat obstreperous orchestra of his into an Eolian harp? How is that noisy stage mob to whisper the mysterious choruses? How is that wilderness of a proscenium to be contracted to a conceivable bedroom for a girl, even making allowance for the difference between a Veronese palace and a

Chenies-street lady's flat? The more I think about it the less I believe that Covent Garden can give us Romeo and Juliet as Gounod intended it to be given.

However, a Covent Garden performance is better than none at all. Those who are counting the hours until eight on Saturday will not find themselves disappointed if Covent Garden does its best. Here is a sketch of the opera for them. The prelude begins *fortissimo* with a broad and splendid exordium, relieved in the middle by a dozen bars of harmless fugue. Then the curtain rises and the prologue is declaimed, without accompaniment, by a chorus which should consist of the very best artists available. The curtain falls again, and the prelude concludes with the strains which afterwards introduce the love scene in the fourth act. Then the band bursts into a waltz; and the curtain goes up in earnest on the scene of the ball at Capulet's. The first important number for a principal artist is the Queen Mab fantasy, at the entry of Mercutio. Then comes Juliet's well-worn vocal waltz, followed by the simple and charming madrigal *Ange adorable* (of course) for Romeo and Juliet. Some snorting at Romeo on Tybalt's part supplies a pretence of movement for a few minutes, and then the act ends with a repetition of Capulet's staves, *Allons! jeunes gens; allons! belles dames*, and general chorusing and waltzing.

The second act is the balcony scene. Being by Gounod, it need not be described except to note that it contains—or once did—a desperate comic episode, in which Capulet's retainers, entering in chase of Romeo's page, chaff the nurse by reproaching her for carrying on an intrigue with Romeo. The third act begins with a fine opportunity for Friar Laurence to shew his ability as a *basso cantante* as he chants a marriage service of his own improvisation over Romeo and Juliet: a beautiful piece of music. In the second scene of this act we get brisk action for the first time, and plenty of it. Romeo's page Stephano, a light soprano in tights, comes to look for his master at Capulet's house, and sings an exquisitely saucy little *chanson* under the windows. Out rush the Capulet retainers in great indignation. After a free flow of repartee, Stephano draws on Gregory; and the rest, in quite an English manner, encourage the little 'un to go it. Mercutio comes in and interrupts the duel, exclaiming "*Attaquer un enfant! Morbleu! c'est une honte digne des Capulets!*" Tybalt, arriving in turn, takes this in bad part; and then, in a scene which follows Shakespear closely, and which will try the declamatory intelligence of Mr Harris's artists severely, Romeo interposes between Tybalt and Mercutio; puts up with Tybalt's insults; gets Mercutio killed by again trying to keep the peace; and finally kills Tybalt and is banished by the Prince. The points in this very exciting scene are the entry of the chorus with fierce shouts of "Montagus!" (or "Capulets!") "*Race immonde!*" &c., and the surge and fury of the orchestra in the final duel, in which Romeo annihilates Tybalt.

The fourth act takes place in the chamber of Juliet, and begins with a most wonderful and passionate love duet, sometimes called "the lark duet" because some unspeakable idiot once listened to it, and heard nothing that he understood except at one place, where a tootling in the wood wind is followed by an exclamation from Romeo of "*Ecoute, Juliette, l'alouette déjà nous annonce le jour.*" When Romeo goes, Capulet comes in to bid Juliet prepare for her wedding with Paris; but instead of the Shakespearean scene of rebellion and scolding, Juliet, checked by a nudge from the nurse and the friar, who have also turned up, submits in silent despair. Capulet, therefore, discourses in sweetly solemn and dignified strains throughout. Juliet, left alone with the friar, appeals to him for help, and he gives her the potion and explains its effect. Here he has his second great chance as a singer, in an *andante*, the beauty of which passes description, the orchestra accompanying *pianissimo* with the haunting prelude to the last act, there called The Sleep of Juliet. The rest of the act is made up of a wedding march, an epithalamium, a dance, and the apparent sudden death of Juliet.

The last act consists simply of that part of the tomb scene in the old acting edition of the play which lies between Romeo and Juliet alone, Juliet of course awakening before the death of Romeo. But it occurs to me that I shall have no space for any other subject if I go any further with my description. I have said enough to save you from wasting one and sixpence on a book; and I am now free to remark that Miss Lucie Johnstone, at whose concert in Steinway Hall on Wednesday I was able to spend 15 minutes, sang with exceptional intelligence and feeling. When experience has strengthened her judgment and given her perfect self-possession, her position as a concert singer will be worth having.

It is an odd thing, by the bye, that almost everybody who gives a concert nowadays is Irish. At least they always say so when they send tickets to The Star. I sometimes wonder whether they turn German when they invite the St James's Gazette, or introduce themselves to the Daily Telegraph as maids of Judah. It is necessary to proclaim, once for all, that The Star is not to be suborned by such arts as these. My name reveals the fact that I am an Italian; but as a critic I only know two nationalities among artists—the Good and the Bad. As for the editor,* his politics may be Irish; but his gallantry is thoroughly cosmopolitan.[U]

* Corno di Bassetto's editor was T.P. O'Connor, Irish journalist and Liberal M.P., who founded The Star in January 1888.

GOOD OLD DON GIOVANNI!

The Star, 14 June 1889

"Good old Don Giovanni!" said some vulgar and disrespectful ruffian in the stalls last night. "Good old Arditi!" he continued, as the conductor took his seat. "Good old Robert Elsmere!" he added presently, as Mrs Humphry Ward wandered into his neighborhood in search of her number. "Good old Lady Colin [Campbell]!" he resumed, as the most divinely tall of the art critics took her place in front of me and extinguished my view of the stage. Standing up, he took out his opera-glass and said "Wheres good old Gus?" He then proceeded to musical criticism. "Theres little Van Zandt: aint she a joy? Who's the tenor? Lestellier! Aint he a terror?" And so on. If this should meet the eye of that man, I ask him, as a personal favor to myself, to commit suicide. Nothing in life can become him like the leaving it.

I cannot say that the performance was an adequate one. A musical critic does not write that often in a lifetime about Don Giovanni—unless, indeed, he is given to writing the thing that is not, as many excellent critics do. Signor F. d'Andrade made a passable libertine; but all libertines are not Don Giovannis, though all Don Giovannis are libertines. And on the whole, I think Signor d'Andrade might as well sing *Viva la libertà!* and *Via, buffone!* and other numbers as they are written. At any rate, Mozart's version is good enough for me. Madame Fürsch-Madi, in *Or sai chi l'onore*, mistook the second section for the first, and during one madly anxious moment, Arditi's fringe of hair stood straight out on end. But she picked up the thread again; a smile mantled the back of Arditi's head; and a minute later I had the pleasure of making a note to the effect that Madame Fürsch-Madi had sung the *scena* very well indeed, and richly deserved her double recall. She omitted *Non mi dir*!!! Miss Van Zandt made a quaint and pretty Zerlina. Madame Valda should bear in mind that the fashion of providing gratuitous B flats in Mozart's operas, though it may be coming in in Australia, is going out here. For the rest, she was not the noble and pious Elvira of Molière and Mozart; and she sang with more spirit and spontaneity than classic grace; but she looked superb. M. Lestellier left out *Dalla sua pace*, and will, I hope, leave out *Il mio tesoro* next time, unless he will take the trouble to learn the song in the interim. Of the Leporello let it suffice to say that it was mainly to his exertions that we owed the turning of the incomparably strange and solemn scene of the invitation to the statue into a profane and ridiculous burlesque which severely taxed the patience of the gallery. Masetto was a failure. The Commendatore distinguished himself at the climax of the supper scene by a wrong note that made our very souls recoil. In short—and here is the truth of the matter—the opera had been insufficiently rehearsed; and the last three scenes can scarcely have been rehearsed at all. Even the stage business went all astray. Let us assume that Romeo and Juliet has absorbed all the energy of the establishment.

JEAN DE RESZKE'S ROMEO
The Star, 17 June 1889

It was instructive to compare the effect of the thoroughly prepared representation of Gounod's Romeo and Juliet on Saturday with that of the scratch performance of

Don Giovanni two nights before. In every sort of merit that an opera can have, Don Giovanni is as superior to Romeo as a sonnet by Shakespear to a sonnet by Adelaide Procter; yet on Thursday the house was bored and distraught, wheras on Saturday it was alert and interested. Everything on the stage had been thought about and practised: everybody there was in earnest and anxious. The result was that an opera with an established reputation for tedium became engrossing where another opera, with an established reputation for inexhaustible variety and vivacity, had just fallen flat. Many persons went about asking why Romeo had never been a success before. The question implied too much; for, after all, the opera has had its measure of success in the past. Further, it is quite true that the work is monotonous* in its mood. One greatly misses the relief which Mephistopheles gives to Faust. No doubt when you first fall under the spell of the heavenly melody, of the exquisite orchestral web of sound colors, of the unfailing dignity and delicacy of accent and rhythm, you certainly do feel inclined to ask whether the people who disparaged the work were deaf. Not until you have had your fill of these, and have realized that there is nothing more coming, do you begin to look at your watch. On Saturday the watch would have come out sooner and oftener but for M. Jean de Reszke. He is an artist who cannot be described in a few words. Though a highly intelligent one at his best, he has moments of *naïveté*—not to say stupidity—which seem to run in his gifted family. Again, though he does everything with a distinction peculiar to himself, there is an exasperatingly conventional side to his posing and playing across the footlights. And though he has the true dramatic instinct, and does

* The typesetter misread the adjective as "monstrous"; see Shaw's criticism of 21 June for his reaction.

really throw himself into his part, yet he is not consistently an actor: for instance, no human being—except perhaps a sexton—ever entered a tomb at midnight in the fashion illustrated by him in the fifth act on Saturday night. I do not believe in ghosts; but if I had occasion to visit a mausoleum, even in the daytime, I should not come bounding into it. Under such circumstances one refrains from gamboling until one's eyes get accustomed to the dim light. The charm of De Reszke lies in the beauty of his voice, his sensitively good pronunciation, and the native grace and refine-ment of his bearing, all of which make his manliness, his energy, and his fire quite irresistible. The charm of the man may be separated from the interest in his perform-ance, which is created almost entirely by his declamation. In the pretty duet, the Madrigal which practically begins Romeo's part, he did not make much effect; but when he exclaimed "O douleur! Capulet est son père; et je l'aime!" the effect was electric. At the end of the balcony scene his half-whispered "Adieu, jusqu'à de-main—jusqu'à demain," will surely be remembered by many a woman in the audience. His acting in the duel scene, uneven as it was, was convincing; and he rose to eloquence in the scene which follows the sentence of exile from the Duke: a scene newly written by Gounod. Madame Melba may thank her stars that she had so good a Romeo to help her out in the last two acts. At one or two points in the balcony scene she sang with genuine feeling; and in the tragic scenes she was at least serious and anxious to do her best. In the first act, however, she was shrill and forward, the waltz *ariette* coming out with great confidence and facility, which I think Madame Melba mistook for art. Her fresh bright voice and generally safe intonation are all in her favor at present. Mlle Jeanne de Vigne phrased *Que fais-tu, blanche tourterelle* nicely, and would have got an *encore*— which she evidently wanted badly—had she been content with the simple run up to C and down again of which Gounod made such a perfect ornament. But she *would* try to improve the final phrase; and as her taste is not quite as fine as Gounod's, the *encore* was nipped in the bud, which I think served her right. Madame Lablache had, of course, no trouble with the part of the nurse. Mr Winogradow, as Mercutio, shewed all the symptoms of a short life and a merry one as a singer. No man can, without wrecking his voice, sing on the plan of delivering every note with the utmost possible intensity and vehemence. Unless Mr Winogradow pulls in at once, and learns to get at least nine out of ten of his effects quietly, Covent Garden will soon know him no more. M. Montariol (Tybalt) was as good as his word, as far as improving the ensemble went, though he should have done this without saying anything about it. He played his second-rate part like a first-rate artist, just as he has occasionally played first-rate parts like a second-rate artist. Also he fenced so perfectly that Romeo was able to go for him quite recklessly; and this, of course, is the explanation of the nonsense about his condescending to play Tybalt. If he had not Brer Jean would now be awaiting his trial for manslaughter. M. Séguin also helped materially by playing Capulet. But the honors among the basses went, of course, to Edouard de Reszke, who had a tremendous time of it as Friar Laurence. The family *naïveté* already hinted at peeped out in such brilliant readings as *Dieu, qui fit l'homme à ton image*, delivered in the stentorian manner of masterbuilders when they seek the ear of a bricklayer on a very high scaffold, and the magic word *femme* marked by sudden subsidence to a tenderly respectful *pianissimo*. But the marriage service and the potion scene delighted the audience; and a special cheer was always received for Frère Edouard when the rest, having passed before the

[670]

curtain, left him—he coming last— for a moment in sole possession of the proscenium.

THE DE RESZKES AND THE BAND TAKE A WALK

The Star, 19 June 1889

After the success of the Romeo and Juliet experiment, the substitution of Scribe's original libretto of Les Huguenots for the Italian version, or rather for the mixture of two Italian versions which now does duty at Covent Garden, is only a matter of a little rehearsal— chiefly for Madame Scalchi. Last night we had Brer Jean as Raoul and Brer Edouard as Marcel, who looked remarkably like Sir John Falstaff reformed and teetotalized. Brer Jean altered the ending of his first song because it was too high; and Brer Edouard presently altered the ending of his Lutheran chorale because it was too low. When Piff Paff was duly disposed of, the twain went off for a walk, and—Brer Jean being presently wanted—kept the stage waiting for some time before they returned. On the whole Brer Jean would have been better if he had not been obviously afraid of his part. For some bars before the C sharp in the duel septet, which he did not attempt to sustain, he suffered from something like stage fright; but when it was over he cheered up considerably, though he remained more or less preoccupied and unhappy all through the evening. Yet he sang delightfully in spite of his mood. Marcel is a part that does not suit Brer Edouard. The music is too low for him; and the character is one for a clever actor. Now Brer Edouard's endowment is mainly vocal: if the De Reszkes had been an English country family, he would certainly have gone into the Church. Madame Toni Schläger, the new *prima donna* from Vienna, began badly by a most discouraging display of *tremolo*, and an even more alarming composure, which did not give way in the least when her lover unexpectedly called her names before the whole cast. The calm way in which she arranged herself on M. Lassalle's arm for a comfortable stage faint as the curtain descended presented a spectacle of matronly decorum before which the house quailed. But if Madame Schläger is matronly, she is also extraordinarily comely. Her long dark hair is wonderful. Her voice, too, unsteady and uncertain as it is, asserts itself every now and then with striking power and penetration. Her acting consists in an exhibition of intense sorrowfulness which is oddly impressive. The house, which rebelled against her at first, ended by accepting her. Her final effect, when, on seeing Raoul spring through the window, she uttered a heartrending cry and fell supine into a wavy river of her own hair, won her a demonstrative curtain call. Madame Scalchi, as Urbain, made an astonishing deal of as much of her part as she could manage, and slipped over the rest very cleverly. Miss Russell achieved so many gratuitous vocal feats to propitiate us for not singing exactly what Meyerbeer wrote that I have no doubt she will achieve that feat too some day. Mr Harris provided her with a beautiful milk-white steed in the third act; but it began to waltz the moment she began to sing; and at last Brer Edouard had to lift her down and leave the animal free to return to its native hippodrome. Signor d'Andrade's intonation in the part of De Nevers became very faulty after the first two acts. M. Lassalle was the San Bris. Signor Mancinelli is at his best in interpreting Meyerbeer; but his generalship last night was seriously at fault: more than once he got excited, and failed to keep his forces together. I fear I shall shortly have a rather bad fit of plain speaking on the subject of the band. There are among the first violins some half a dozen or so gentlemen who play with a flow of undisciplined animal spirits which, gratifying as it is to everyone who likes to see young people enjoying themselves, has the incidental disadvantage of destroying all the delicacy, dignity, and grace of the orchestra. The stage business again shewed want of rehearsal and want of thought. In the Pré-aux-Clercs scene the moon rose most naturally, but it shone brightly enough to make ridiculous all that part of the dialogue which derives its point from Marcel's groping after Valentine's voice in the darkness. During vespers the Catholics kept their hats on; and several of the Protestants took them off. Have these choristers no religious feeling that they cannot grasp so simple a situation? The substitution in the gypsy ballet of a *pas seul* for the old business with the soldiers is not, in my opinion, an improvement.

The performance began about twelve minutes past eight. At the end of the fourth act it only wanted five minutes of twelve. The band accordingly cut the entertainment short by going home. Signor Mancinelli, after a moment's hesitation, followed their example. I left several of the audience waiting for the fifth act. I wonder whether they are there still.

AN ANGRY CRITIC AND A VERY QUIET LADY

The Star, 21 June 1889: abridged and revised in London Music, 1937

[U] A good many people have asked me what on earth I meant on Monday in my notice of Roméo et Juliette by saying that its mood is MONSTROUS. These innocent persons seem to think that whatever appears over my signature in The Star is written by me. This is a mistake. I merely supply a manuscript sketch which the printers fill in according to their own fantasy. I believe I did make some such trite observation as that the mood of the work in question was monotonous. The compositor, feeling that the adjective lacked force and compactness, and having his own opinion about Gounod, altered the word to monstrous. When the proofreader came upon the phrase, he naturally exclaimed "What on earth does this mean? This must be one of Di Bassetto's deep things—one of his originalities—one of those inspired utterances which distinguish him from the vulgar critic. It must be displayed in capitals in a line by itself." And display it he did forthwith.

I was on the roof of an omnibus in Oxford-street when I read it. The next thing I remember is standing at the counter of a postoffice, with a superintendent politely but firmly informing me that they were not allowed to transmit messages couched in the terms I had employed. In vain I pleaded for the right of adequate expression: in vain I offered to pay half-a-crown a letter: in vain I insisted that I had used no word that is not in the authorized version of the Scriptures. He was inexorable, and pointed out to me that it would be much cheaper to take a cab to Stonecutter-street and deliver my message verbally. But I felt that I should go flat, like an opened bottle of soda water, during the drive. I demanded how many of my 42 words he would send. He replied, five: to wit, "Correct—misprint—monstrous—to—monotonous." On my threatening to go straight down to the Courts and apply for an injunction to compel him to go an adjective or two further than this, he reluctantly consented to retain one other word—"idiotic." And with this miserable concession I had to be satisfied. [U]

I hope the Royal Italian Opera will not grow conceited on the strength of my general approval of Romeo and Juliet. Lest it should, I hasten to find fault with one or two points in the performance. The unaccompanied prologue, which was sung as Gounod directs, by the principal singers, ought to have been an invaluable lesson to the chorus in distinctness of enunciation, crispness of attack, beautiful tone formation, pure intonation, and finesse in managing the delicate *nuances*. As a matter of fact, it was unintelligible; it buzzed and dragged; the pitch fell during each line so that the harp made us squirm when it came in; and there was much less gradation than a well educated horse shews in his paces. I imagine that the chorus were vaguely trying to help from the wings. If so, they had much better not have interfered. Here, then, is one opportunity for that constant improvement which Mr Harris's artists doubtless thirst for.

Signor Mancinelli misjudged one or two movements so widely that I strongly suspect him of a conscientious attempt to follow the composer's metronome marks: the surest way, need I add, of violating the composer's intentions. In a theatre of reasonable size a very skilful singer, daintily accompanied, could no doubt point all the vagaries of Queen Mab as rapidly as poor M. Winogradow was haled through them on Monday; but, under the circumstances, the result was that the song missed fire. The great duet in the fourth act was taken so fast that the *molto sostenuto* indicated by Gounod, which is the characteristic effect of the movement, was quite lost. And again, the *allegretto agitato: Il faut partir, hélas!* was overdone in the same way. What with Jean de Reszke's impetuosity, and Signor Mancinelli's tendency to rush strong numbers, one sometimes yearns for the advent of Richter, the unhasting, the unresting.

I cannot understand why some account of the very

interesting Doll's House dinner last Sunday at the Novelty Theatre* has not crept into print. It was distinctly understood that the affair was to be kept quiet, and from that I naturally concluded that the Press would be full of it on Monday. I hasten to remedy the tactless discretion of my fellow guests.

It was an odd affair, because, as every discoverable Norwegian in London had been recklessly invited, the company was a queer mixture of people whom everybody knew and people whom nobody knew. Among the latter was a very quiet lady of forty or thereabouts, with some indescribable sort of refinement about her that made her seem to have lost her way and found herself in a very questionable circle. Nobody was taking any notice of her; so I charitably introduced myself (she pretended to know who I was) and tried to make her feel more at home. You shall hear more of her presently.

Then we had supper and toasts and so forth. William Archer led off the speechmaking by toasting Ibsen, with special insistence on the great dramas in verse which preceded the Doll's House order of play. (How often have I not informed composers that the next great opera will not be a setting of Faust over again, but of Peer Gynt?)

Two famous actresses from Christiania, Fru Gundersen and Fröken Reimers, represented the Norwegian stage. Miss Reimers was asked to recite, but said she could not declaim without statuesque drapery. No garment that could by any stretch of imagination be deemed statuesque could be discovered; and we should have lost the recitation had not somebody produced a

* Charles Charrington and his wife Janet Achurch had presented Ibsen's A Doll's House at the Novelty Theatre, London, on 7 June. Their performances brought them instant acclaim.

couple of yards of common white tape. Miss Reimers at once beamed her gratitude; flung the tape over her shoulder; and shewed us what real stage declamation is like, to the manifest depression of the British actors present, who had all picked up their profession anyhow. Their discomfiture was completed by a young Danish actor, whose *maintien* and delivery were so perfect that we frankly threw in our hands and returned to the savage pursuit of British speechmaking. The whole cast of the Doll's House were present, except Mr Royce Carleton and the three youngest members, who had been put to bed. There was also present a Herr Nansen, who was described to me as the brother of the discoverer of Greenland; but I imagine there is some mistake about this, for I have been familiar with Greenland and its icy mountains since my childhood. Then there was Mr Hermann Vezin, at the head of the board. Herr Barth answered for painting, and Dr. Hagerup answered for everything else. Mr H. L. Brækstad*, who has at last succeeded in planting the Norwegian standard firmly in London, was immensely in evidence. Mr Charrington, in a disconsolate manner, made the best speech of the evening, and sat down obviously convinced that he had made the worst. Miss Achurch made two speeches in a brief and fearless manner, which at once exposed the awkwardness and pusillanimity of the unfortunate persons who were trying to look like the stronger sex. "A woman making a speech" said Dr Johnson "is like a dog standing on its hind legs. It is not well done; but the

* Hermann Vezin was an American-born actor and voice coach, friendly with Shaw. Carl Wilhelm Bøckmann Barth was a Norwegian painter of marine subjects. Georg F. Hagerup was a Norwegian jurist and statesman. Hans Lien Brækstad, a fanatical Ibsenite, was a Norwegian journalist and *littérateur* resident in London.

wonder is that is should be done at all."* Now mark my words. The time is approaching when that story will reverse its genders, and be attributed to some female sage. What is more, *it will not lose its point in the process.* I foresaw this long ago; and, with a manly determination to uphold the superiority of my sex, at once adopted the view that public speaking is a despicable art, only fit for women. I declare, in spite of the editor's teeth, that I enjoyed Miss Achurch's speeches far more than I have ever enjoyed Mr Gladstone's; but let Miss Achurch just try her hand at musical criticism and you will soon acknowledge the unassailable pre-eminence of Creation's masterpiece: Man. I am a man myself, and ought to know.

After dinner we all went down to the stage and finished the evening in the doll's house, where the snow on the windowsill, which I had always supposed to be real (knowing Mr Archer's conscientious devotion to naturalism in art) turned out to be a wretched cottonwool imposture which came off on my clothes. The first thing everybody did was to go straight to the stove, open it, and stare into the interior. Then they tried the famous letterbox, and slammed the famous door. Then Mr Vezin plucked up a postprandial courage and recited all the most bloodcurdling poems he could think of. Miss Reimers, who had very nearly upset even my gravity at dinner by asking me with perfect sincerity why the splendid, the intellectual, the free English people had no national theatre, recited Tennyson's Rizpah and the first speech from Schiller's Maid of Orleans in Norwegian. Miss Achurch, rashly called on for a recitation, and being totally unacquainted with that art, adventured

* A misquotation from Boswell's Life of Dr Johnson (1791), in which Johnson speaks of a woman *preaching* and a dog *walking* on its hind legs.

desperately on Kingsley's Three Fishers, and first conveyed to us that she did not know her business at all, and then, in a curiously original way, and not without a touch of extravagance, left us impressed and astonished.

When our resources were at last exhausted and the entertainment was on the point of petering out, our hosts had to play their last card. Could anybody play the Helmer piano and oblige us with a tune. There was general shaking of heads until it appeared that the quiet lady, neglected and unknown, could play some pieces. As she went to the little piano we prepared ourselves for the worst and stopped talking, more or less. To encourage the poor lady I went to the piano and sat beside her to turn over for her, expecting The Maiden's Prayer or an old-fashioned set of variations on The Carnival of Venice. I felt I was being very good to her.

After the first two bars I sat up. At the end of the piece (one of her own composition) I said "Has anyone ever told you that you are one of the greatest pianists in Europe?" Evidently a good many people had; for without turning a hair she said "It is my profession. But this is a bad instrument. Perhaps you will hear me at the Philharmonic. I am to play Beethoven's E flat concerto there."

Her name is Agathe Ursula Backer-Gröndahl. She played upon Helmer's pianoforte as it was never played upon before, and perhaps never will be again. A great artist—a serious artist—a beautiful, incomparable, unique artist! She morally regenerated us all; and we remained at our highest level until we were dragged down by the shrieks and groans of two Italian waiters who started quarreling among the knives in the saloon. Fraternity having been re-established by Mr Charrington, Mr Archer was requested to improvize a *World* article for the entertainment of the company. He blushingly declined. Later on it was felt that the evening would be incomplete without a song from me; and after some pressing I reluctantly consented. The guests then left precipitately; and the scene, a historic one in the annals of the theatre, closed.

ORCHESTRAS AND BANDS

The Star, 28 June 1889

Every reader of this column is, I presume, a lover of music, aware, as such, that noise is not music, and shrinking from the multiplication of drums and cymbals as from an outrage on all true and delicate art. This cultivated state of mind comes of reading high-toned criticism. I cannot say that I have attained it myself—unless noise is defined as mere empty toneless clatter. But if it means magnitude of sound, then I may as well confess at once that I hardly ever get noise enough to satisfy me. I despise an orchestra if its *fortissimo* does not leave me as if an avalanche had come thundering and roaring upon me, sweeping me away like a feather with its mere wind. Until every man has gone to the bottomless depths of sonority potential in his instrument—until the basses are lifting the ground like an earthquake—until the trebles are whistling like a storm through the giant teeth of the Alps—until the middle parts can drown with their impetuous charge the rush of an express train through a tunnel—until even Philharmonic fogeydom believes and trembles, my craving for immense sound is unsatisfied.

I enjoy the Richter orchestra because its *fortissimo* is unapproached by that of any other band in London. After its gorgeous tone paintings the performances of the Philharmonic seem but pretty water-color sketches.

On Monday nights this season I have been so much occupied with the opera—which requires a good deal of parental looking after—that I have missed the whole Richter series so far with the exception of the Wagner Society concert this week. Now, I am not going to waste time in describing how stupendously they played the Rienzi overture and the Kaisermarsch, or how the orchestra made itself a Cyclopean bellows in the forest smithy of Mime, and wafted the air of the medieval burgher town about the meditations of Hans Sachs. No; my business is perpetually to find fault until the limit of attainable perfection is reached. A moment ago I disparaged the Philharmonic orchestra. Now let me say that, though it could not have played the Rienzi overture so as to give me concussion of the brain (which is the right way), yet it would certainly have accompanied Mr Edward Lloyd in the first part of Lohengrin's farewell speech with much more refinement than the Richterians. The wood wind lacked delicacy of touch; and the Grail music was—of all things—mundane.

Mr Edward Lloyd delivers his words better than many English singers; but he was not half so intelligible as Mr Max Heinrich, an admirable baritone singer, whom I had not heard before (probably he has not been singing here for more than a couple of years). Mr Lloyd does Siegfried very well, just as Mrs Kendal would do Schiller's Joan of Arc very well if she were put at it. Still, his laugh, though a very well-bred laugh, is hardly the exultant shout of a young giant over his anvil. Mr William Nicholl should try to get Mime's music safely on his ear. He sings it as if he were reading it at sight, and felt hopelessly bothered by the harmony. In short, he sings it out of tune. The performance of the wonderful Parsifal music was a little labored and uneasy: its divine atmosphere was much clouded and troubled by its technical unfamiliarity; but on the whole it was meritoriously done. The set of sonorous cylinders seem to give me satisfactory bell effects; but surely the fifth in the peal is atrociously flat. Can it not be replaced next time by a fresh cylinder?

On Tuesday I was again in St James's Hall at the concert of the Chevalier Emil Bach. I applaud the Chevalier for engaging the Philharmonic orchestra and Mr Cusins; I deplore his ambition to compose a pianoforte concerto; I protest against his sending me the most uncomfortable seat in St James's Hall: a seat which drove me away, groaning with artificially induced sciatica and lumbago, at the end of the first part. It was the fault of that seat that I did not hear the Chevalier's songs, nor his playing of the Weber polonaise; and I hereby solemnly warn Mr Vert* and the musical professsion in general that if they ever again send me a ticket numbered AA15 I shall destroy it as I would a mad dog.

Mr Cusins seized the opportunity to let us have that charming Fingal's Cave overture of Mendelssohn's, which it is almost as hard to hear nowadays as it is to avoid hearing Cherubini's Anacreon. Madame Sembrich sang *Giunse al fin*; and never have I writhed as I did when Madame Sembrich altered the exquisite and perfect ending of Mozart's exquisite and perfect song. After that her arts were lost on me. I listened sternly to the *scena* from Lucia, with its two touching melodies, and its ridiculous and old-fashioned florid frippery in which the flute enters into a contest of pure foolishness with the human voice. I could not laugh at it as I usually do. Nor was my eye dimmed with emotion when a huge bouquet was brought up by no less a person than Christine Nilsson, who ought to have known better,

* Nathaniel Vert was a concert agent, who managed several leading artists, including Hans Richter.

and the air was filled with bowing and handshaking and wafting of kisses and all the old undignified humbug that even the Opera has outgrown. Sarasate was looking on. I wonder what he thought of it all!

As to the Chevalier's concerto, I shall be brief and frank. The proper place for the first movement is the fireplace. The other two, with a little trimming, may be allowed to survive as pretty little sketches. The program of the concert, by the bye, must have been printed at The Star office. Such a champion misprint as *Spargi d'amaro puanto** could have been achieved nowhere else. As to Miss Isaacson's concert of chamber music at Prince's Hall the same afternoon, with Mr Carrodus and Mr E. Howell, I can only offer my sincere apologies for being unable to get there. Ordinary critics find it almost impossible to be in two places at the same time. I find considerable difficulty in being in one.

I regret to have to announce that the British Bandsman, an excellent paper devoted to the interests of the brass *banditti*, has had the mad presumption to "strongly suspect that I am deficient in knowledge of wind instruments." This is true; but I am not going to be told so by any British bandsman alive. How am I to make myself respected as a critic if the public for a moment suspects that there is anything I dont know? Besides, the B.B. is really too hard on me. The euphonium is not to me "an instrument unknown." I learnt to be gentle and modest, not at my mother's knee, but by listening to the diffident mooings of British bandsmen trying to play Oh, happy days! on the euphonium, in selections from L'Etoile du Nord. As to the ophicleide being obsolete, I did not say it was not. The "chromatic bullock" was born obsolete; but it is no

---

* The aria is *Spargi d'amoro pianto*, from Lucia di Lammermoor.

more obsolete today than it ever was. It seems only the other day that Mr Hughes was playing, Oh, ruddier than the cherry! on it at Covent Garden.

However, I am not punctilious on the subject of the ophicleide. When its part is played on a tuba in the Midsummer Night's Dream overture, I never dream of objecting to the substitution. But when the British Bandsman goes on to speak of the trumpet in the same strain, then I put down my foot. I am aware that there is a delusion rife among bandsmen that the great composers have written trumpet parts out of mere amateurish ignorance of the cornet. I am also rather disposed to laugh occasionally when Mr Morrow or Mr M'Grath, in a sudden fit of classic reverence, solemnly produce the slide trumpet of commerce—a surpassingly obdurate and disagreeable instrument—and blare away with it through Mendelssohn's violin concerto. These trumpets, if it were worth anyone's while to learn to play them, would doubtless give the peculiar close, ringing, penetrating sound that the cornet so completely misses; but then they would probably fail in the soft cornet effects in which Wagner's and Gounod's scores abound. What we really want is a revival of the old Handel and Bach trumpet, which Kosleck, of Berlin, handled so brilliantly at the Albert Hall a few years ago, and which Mr Morrow (I think it was Mr Morrow) tried last year for the Bach Choir. I do not suggest that it should oust the cornet from the orchestra, but only from those trumpet parts in which the cornet is out of place.

(It was after this that the cornet vanished from our symphony orchestras. I do not know what conductor kicked it out; so I may as well claim the credit for the above protest. The slide trumpet, being now played by trumpeters, and not by cornettists forced to take a very occasional turn at an unfamiliar instrument, is no longer obdurate or disagreeable; though I still deny that it is a true trumpet.

We need a great artist reformer, a musical William Morris, to recover for us the character and variety of our wind instruments. 1936.)

ATHALIE NEITHER HERE NOR THERE
The Star, 2 July 1889

The Handel orchestra at the Crystal Palace is not the right place for work so delicately and finely concentrated as Mendelssohn's Athalie. Nor is it, as many people seem to think, a favorable arena for the display of choral excellence. The more fiddlers you have in your orchestra and the more singers you have in any section of your chorus, the less likelihood is there of any defects being noticed, since at any given moment there will be enough performers right to drown a considerable minority who may be wrong. The proportion of error can only be guessed at by the magnitude of the mere indeterminate noise—the buzz and rattle—that comes along with the definite vocal tone. From this the Tonic Sol-faists on Saturday were commendably free: the tone was clean and the intonation very good indeed: much better, I venture to assert, than is usual in staff-notation choirs, where practice mostly begins by taking the reading powers of the members for granted. In volume and penetration the vocal mass was fully up to the ordinary standard; but then the ordinary standard is absurdly low. Considering what a formidable sound can be produced by a single properly trained man or woman of ordinary physique, the mildness of the result of combining 2500 of them on an orchestra is almost ridiculous. It is not too much to say that nine-tenths of the potential efficiency of our choirs is wasted through the diffidence that comes from conscious want of individual skill. The way in which the tone from the sopranos dwindled at every G and A shewed that a large number of these healthy young Englishwomen were deliberately shirking every note above F. Now a soprano, or even a mezzo-soprano, who is afraid of an occasional A simply does not know how to sing; and I would respectfully put it to these fair Sol-faists whether it is of much public use to know how to read if you cannot sing what you read. If a soprano breaks down over Mendelssohn, what sort of a figure would she cut if she were put at, say, the Choral Symphony?

As an exhibition of choral singing the concert was interesting enough: as a performance of Athalie it was neither here nor there. The work is one of Mendelssohn's finest; and it can only be mastered by a conductor who studies his part as seriously as he might study the part of Hamlet if he were an actor. Mr Venables confined himself to beating time for the choir with steadiness, spirit, and—except in one number—with judgment. That number, unfortunately, was the duet with chorus, Ever blessed child, an inspired composition, standing with I waited for the Lord among the most beautiful and touching utterances of Mendelssohn. But, alas! it is in six-eight time; and whenever an English conductor sees six-eight, he exclaims "Ha! Sir Roger de Coverley!" and scampers off up the middle and down again, reckless whether it is Ever blessed child or O thou that tellest that he is murdering. When Mr Venables had duly dragged the duet through by the hair, he changed his mood just in time to quench the fire of the fiercely impetuous Behold, Zion, behold. Otherwise I have nothing to reproach him with. The orchestral effects, notably those striking *fortissimo* chords in The sinner's joys decay, were feeble and scattered in the vast space. The unpublished fugue, which was performed for the first time at the end, is just like any other fugue by a master of Mendelssohn's calibre. The subject begins with the usual skip, and the parts solemnly trudge along to the pedal, after which climax of insanity the welcome end comes with due gravity of cadence. Then Madame Antoinette Sterling, loudly applauded, came on the platform to give away prizes. A huge ribbon, inscribed "Honorable mention" was held up by two respectable citizens. A third citizen then exhibited a placard bearing the name Bayswater, whereat the audience, fugally demoralized, roared with laughter. Further placarding conveyed the gratifying intelligence that Nottingham had borne off the first prize, which Madame Sterling accordingly handed to Mr J. S. Derbyshire, the Nottingham conductor, amid enthusiasm. I then dashed away to catch a low-level train, which I just saved by the desperate expedient of doing the last third of the journey by toboggan, a fearful method of progression. I owe an apology to Mr T. Newton, who was announced to sing a song "in twelve distinctly different voices" at half-past five. Why are not the musical critics invited to hear this gifted polyphonist?

THE TWO BLACK MEN
The Star, 5 July 1889

I must apologize to the Shah for my failure to appear at Covent Garden on Tuesday. He will cut rather a foolish figure in Persia when he confesses—if he has the moral courage to admit it—that he saw the opera without Corno di Bassetto; but if Mr Harris chooses recklessly to select the night of the Hyndman-George debate★ for

★ The Henry George—H.M. Hyndman debate on Single Tax *vs.* Social Democracy was held in St James's Hall on 2 July. Shaw's report of the debate appeared in the August issue of the International Review.

the reception of Persian majesty, he has himself to thank for my absence. Possibly, however, Mr Harris acted out of consideration for me.

Of the program I can only faintly convey the truth by saying that it was the most extravagantly Bedlamite hotch-potch on record, even in the annals of State concerts. It was evidently the work of a committee on which conflicting views had to be reconciled. Thus, view No. 1 was that the Shah is a gentleman of ordinary and somewhat vulgar European musical taste; therefore let him hear the overture to William Tell. View No. 2: The Shah is an idiot; therefore ply him with the mad scene from Lucia. View No. 3: The Shah's artistic culture is deep, earnest, severe, and German; therefore strike up the great Leonore overture by Beethoven. View No. 4: It does not matter what the Shah is: we are going to let him see what Covent Garden can do; therefore let us put on the fourth act of Faust, which is one of our big things. View No. 5: The Shah is a savage and voluptuary; therefore treat him to the Brocken corobbery from Boïto's Mefistofele, as the most unseemly thing we can very well do under the circumstances. How beautifully the Pall Mall's own visitor summed it up as "a scene of brilliancy, *tempered by ladies*."

In dealing with the performance of Les Huguenots lately, I felt strongly tempted to warn Signor Mancinelli that the band parts in use at Covent Garden are inaccurate at the most striking point in the whole score. In the fourth act, when Raoul, in the transport of discovering that Valentine loves him, forgets the impending massacre and the duty of instantly warning his friends, he is suddenly struck dumb by the distant sound of the bell which is the signal for the carnage. The bell strikes the keynote F, and takes a veiled, sinister color from a dull accompanying chord in the lowest register of the clarinets. Almost immediately a clear,

[688]

terrible C is delivered in unison by the brass; and never, not even in Wagner's Flying Dutchman, has the peculiar character of the fifth of the scale been more dramatically employed. But what happens at Covent Garden? Why, they actually bring out a prosaic F with an effect which is perfectly senseless.

I therefore appeal to Signor Mancinelli to look at the horn, trombone, and bassoon parts in the first dozen bars of the *maestoso* movement following the famous *andante amoroso*, and see whether the C's are right in every second bar. Also to exhort the first trombone and the third and fourth horns to give the necessary prominence to that C, which is above the F of the bell. I further appeal to Mr Harris to incur the trouble and expense of placing a first-rate drum player behind the scenes, and providing him with two clangorous bells, accurately tuned to F and C, so that we may hear the scene as Meyerbeer planned it. However, I fear my appeal will be in vain. If it were a new patent moon, or an extra horse, or half a dozen new dresses, or any other unmusical vanity, there would be a rush to meet my views. But a part in the score that nobody bothers about or misses—what stuff! Fulfilment of the composer's intention is not, like evening dress, indispensable.

[U] Those who intend to patronize Verdi tonight at the Lyceum, and who do not understand Italian, may be glad to know something of Otello, in case their finances should run short of the price of a libretto. It is founded on a play of Shakespear's; and though probably not five per cent. of my readers have ever read a line of that author, yet they will have picked up from allusions and quotations a general notion of what the tragedy in question is about.

Act II. of Shakespear is Act I. of Verdi. There is no overture. The orchestra bursts into a roar, and up flies the curtain almost instantly from the quay at Cyprus, during the tempest. The Cypriotes, with Montano and Cassio, are there, making remarks on the weather and the condition of Othello's ship. Trumpets and cannon announce the quality of the voyagers. Then the storm becomes awful. When Othello lands he announces that the Turks, whom he came to fight, are all drowned, whereupon the chorus, giving way to inveterate operatic habits, shout "*Evviva! Vittoria!*" They then prepare a bonfire, whilst Roderigo (a tenor) discusses affairs as in Shakespear, Act I., Scene 1, with Iago (a baritone). When the bonfire flares up the orchestra and chorus flare up too, and have high jinks, the choral writing being in from five to seven parts—tenors and altos divided. Then Iago, in B minor, tempts Cassio to drink; and Cassio, in D major, does so copiously, encouraged by the chorus. Then comes Cassio's fight with Montano, accompanied by the jangling of "the dreadful bell that frights the isle from its propriety." Othello comes in and cashiers Cassio, as in Shakespear; but when the stage is cleared the two left in possession are not Iago and Cassio, but Othello and Desdemona, who finish the act with love, harps, moonlight, and the rest of the enchanting nonsense proper to the occasion.

Act II. takes place in the castle. Iago persuades Cassio to seek Desdemona's intercession, and then, after a grandiose exordium from the orchestra, announces that he believes in the cruelty of God, who has fashioned him in the Divine image. This runs to several pages of the score, and, excepting a single phrase at the end about "the sepulchral worm," is monotonously written in the tearing Verdi manner, almost entirely within the extreme upper fifth of the singer's compass. The "Ha! I like not that" scene follows, with the omission of Desdemona's plea for Cassio. It is interrupted by a five-part chorus in the garden, accompanied first by bagpipes, then by mandolins and guitars. Iago continues rapidly through the first strain, warning Othello. Desdemona returns with Emilia, followed by a procession of sailors, children, and the Cypriote unwashed generally: the natural result being a brief but pretentious quartet and chorus. When the populace go, there is a quartet without chorus, in which Iago gets the handkerchief from Emilia. The retirement of the ladies leaves Othello free to rage at Iago and to bid "farewell the tranquil mind," in the course of which the amateur will discover that Verdi's Othello is no other than our old friend Renato from Un Ballo over again. When Iago begins his "I lay with Cassio lately," Verdi is so anxious lest the singer should be too loud that he actually writes *ppppppp*. It will be interesting to hear—or rather to see— M. Maurel singing *ppppppp*. The act ends with the row of the two men, "Now by yond' marble heaven," &c.

The third act, in the great hall of the castle, begins with a duet in which Othello asks to see Desdemona's hand, as in Shakespear's fourth scene, and makes reiterated demands for the handkerchief. After this the "Come swear it: damn thyself" dialogue from Scene I of Act V. is dovetailed in. A *trio* follows, Iago pumping Cassio about Bianca; and Othello, concealed, supposing that they are talking of Desdemona. The entry in state of Lodovico with the order for Othello's return and supersession by Cassio, and Othello's violence to his wife whilst reading it, are the occasion of an imposing septet with chorus. This act also ends with only Iago and the Moor on the stage. From without comes a cry of "Glory to the lion of Venice." "There is your lion for you" says Iago ironically as Othello falls in a fit and the act drop descends.

In the last act—the bedchamber scene—Desdemona sings the willow song to Emilia, and an Ave Maria by herself. Forty bars for the orchestra alone, whilst Othello enters and extinguishes the light, are made up of the unison passages for the basses, of which so much was said when the opera was produced. The rest of the scene needs no further comment than that the turbaned Turk is cut out, and that Othello, instead of dying upon a kiss, dies rather mawkishly on three. I shall say nothing more until I have taken the music in through my ears. I dont trust my eyes—or anybody else's. [U]

THE MASTERLY RICHTER
The Star, 9 July 1889

Call no conductor sensitive in the highest degree to musical impressions until you have heard him in Berlioz and Mozart. I never unreservedly took off my hat to Richter until I saw him conduct Mozart's great symphony in E flat. Now, having heard him conduct Berlioz's Faust, I repeat the salutation. I never go to hear that work without fearing that, instead of exquisite threads of melody, wonderful in their tenuity and delicacy, and the surpassingly strange and curious sounds and measures, ghostly in touch and quaint in tread, unearthly, unexpected, unaccountable, and full of pictures and stories, I shall hear a medley of thumps and bumps and whistles and commonplaces: one, two, three, four: one, two, three, four; and for Heaven's sake dont stop to think about what you are doing, gentlemen, or we shall never keep the thing together. Last night there was no such disappointment. The Hungarian March I pass over, though I felt towards the end that if it were to last another minute I must charge out and capture Trafalgar Square singlehanded. But when the scene on the banks of the Elbe began—more slowly than any but a great conductor would have dared to take it—then I knew that I might dream the scene without fear of awakening a disenchanted man. As to the dance of will-o'-the-wisps in the third part, Richter's interpretation of that most supernatural minuet was a masterpiece of conducting. I need say no more. The man who succeeds with these numbers does not make the usual failure with the Easter Hymn or the Ride to Hell.

The four principal singers were, in order of praiseworthiness, Mr Max Heinrich, Mr Bantock Pierpoint, Miss Mary Davies, and Mr Edward Lloyd. I put Mr Lloyd fourth only because, there being but three others, I cannot put him fifth or sixth. I do not mind his shirking the C sharps and even the B natural in the duet with Margaret; but I indignantly demand what he meant by wantonly tampering with the Invocation at its finest point, the burst into C sharp major, on the words My soul thrills with delight. If Mr Lloyd had suspected what my soul thrilled with when he made the most annoyingly vulgar alteration I ever heard an artist of his eminence perpetrate, he would, I hope, have refrained. I also object to his ending the beautiful episode in F, Oh, will ye come again, on the higher octave of the note written by Berlioz. Miss Davies is so hampered by the remains of her Academy method that she never seems quite certain of what her voice will do; but if she does not sing safely and happily, she at least sings with taste and feeling, sometimes very sweetly. Mr Pierpoint is always efficient; and Mr Max Heinrich acquitted himself like a fine artist, though the person who told him to pronounce "linings" as "lennix" is unworthy of his confidence.

The chorus did everything to perfection except sing. Their time, their tone, their enunciation, their observance of light and shade, testified to the pains taken with them by the conductor. But not even he could get any considerable volume of sound out of them. As the roaring drunkards of Auerbach's cellar they were polite and subdued; as bragging soldiers they were decent and restrained; as convivial students chanting *Jam nox stellata*, &c., they did not forget that there might be a sick person in the neighborhood; and as devils in Pandemonium their voices were sweet and low. The decorum of these warblers would have done honor to the choir of the Chapel Royal.

HOW NOT TO TEACH SINGING
The Star, 12 July 1889

In my youth I used to speculate upon the curious but almost invariable failure of public music schools—Royal Academies, Conservatories, and the like—to turn out good singers. The case was even worse than this: the voices were not only undeveloped, they were crippled and sometimes utterly destroyed by the process of training to which they were subjected. The moral seemed to be that private teachers were the safest; but I soon observed that private teachers were fully as destructive as public ones. I wonder whether this state of things prevails to any extent at present.

The odd thing was that when I read the treatises penned by the teachers, or conversed with them, I found that they were eloquent in their denunciation of the very faults which their own pupils most flagrantly exemplified. They would insist that the voice should be produced without the slightest effort or constriction of the throat, and with an expiration so steady, gentle, and perfectly controlled that a candle flame would not flicker before the singer's lips. Then they would proudly produce their champion pupil, who, after setting every muscle of the neck and jaws as if she (it was generally she) wanted to crack a walnut with her glottis, would turn on a blast from her lungs sufficient to whirl a windmill, much less flicker a candle. The result generally was that the family doctor interfered when the damage to the student's health had gone too far; and the medical profession soon adopted the notion that singing is a dangerous exercise, only suitable for persons of exceptionally robust lungs and heart.

I assure you it is not pleasant to live next door to a young lady who, from the very common accident of having a loud voice and an aptitude for picking up tunes, has resolved to become a *prima donna*, and, with that view, has engaged Signor Fizzelli, or Fizzini, or Fizzoni to train her for the ordeal of a first appearance at La Scala, Milan, where he broke his voice some years ago on the occasion of his *début* as Arturo in Lucia di Lammermoor, thanks—as he avers—to the intrigues of the jealous nincompoop who, though unable to sing *Fra poco* in the original key, supplanted him in his rightful part of Edgardo. Fitz's training system is the walnut system, scientifically known as "tension of cords and force of blast."

When Fitz tells his pupil to sing on the vowel *a*, she either rolls her tongue up into a ball at the back of her mouth and brings up an *awr*, or else she bleats out the flattest of *ha-a-a-a-h's*. Fitz rages at her until she finds some intermediate sound that suits his taste. Then, on that sound, and on the walnut system, he makes her sing scales in one unvarying slow, deadly grind that would wear the soul and health out of a millstone. You—next door—hear the process getting more difficult, the effort more exhausting, the voice more inhuman every day, until at last a morning comes when Fitz does not appear, and the doctor's brougham does. In the meantime you are desperately tempted to rush out some day as Fitz comes down the front garden after applying the torture, and remonstrate with him on the chance of his assaulting you, and thereby giving you an excuse for killing him in self-defence.

If you actually did remonstrate, he would not hit you. I never knew a hitting voice trainer except one, who declared quite seriously that the only method to make a man produce the vowel *o* in Nature's way was to get him to hold a full breath for fifteen seconds, and then punch him smartly in the thorax. There can be no doubt of the effectiveness and certainty of this plan; but, except when the teacher can punch hard enough to incapacitate the pupil from hasty reprisals, it should be practised only on women and invalids; and even with them it is apt during future lessons to engender a certain mistrust of the professor's intentions which spoils the harmony essential to the relation between master and pupil. But Fitz is not that sort of man. You will sometimes find him unexpectedly intelligent and even sensible as a talker, though you cannot safely depend on this. What you *can* depend on is that he will defend his method on the ground that it is the true Italian method of Porpora, rediscovered and patented by himself; and that every other teacher in the universe is a notorious humbug and quack, the mainspring of whose activity is a despicable jealousy of the same Fitz.

Let me say, however, that I think Fitz's vogue is waning. His failures have been too flagrant and too fearful to pass unnoticed. The young English girls, with sweet and promising voices, who went to Paris to be "finished" in grim earnest by the final attempt to grind them into savagely dramatic Viardot Garcias have invariably disappointed the hopes formed of them. The wobbling, screaming crew, with three horrible high notes and three Richardson's show gestures, who infested the operatic stage twenty years ago—the ignoble Fernandos and Manricos, Lucias and Leonoras—had to retreat before Wagner, since they could no more sing his music than they could sing Handel's. The increase in the number of people who now keep a pianoforte, and amuse themselves at it with cheap vocal scores of operas, is producing a common knowledge of the defects of our standard performers, which enables the critic to attack the inaccuracies, the vulgarities, the innumerable petty artistic dishonesties of the operatic stage with a sense of having the public at his back, which is a new, powerful and most noteworthy factor in musical criticism. The effect of it on me occasionally moves concert givers and managers (otherwise of sound mind) to demand whether it is not obvious that I must be in the pay of their enemies or else maliciously mad.

Just as cheap literature is restoring Shakespear to the stage and banishing gag, Garrick, and Cibber, so cheap music will banish cuts, interpolations, alterations, and perversions from the opera house. It will not teach the people to sing; but it will teach them to miss the qualities which are never forthcoming with bad singers and to value those which are always forthcoming with good ones.

And now, what on earth did I begin all this about? I must have intended to lead up to something; and now I have hardly any room left for it. Ha! I recollect. The performance of Goetz's Taming of the Shrew, by the students of the Royal College of Music on Wednesday afternoon at the Prince of Wales's Theatre.

It struck me that though the students who sang had not received any specially valuable positive instruction in the art of producing the voice, they had been abundantly warned against Fitz and the walnut system. If a man could become a great tenor by dint of doing nothing that could possibly injure his vocal cords, then Mr Pringle, who played Hortensio, would be the Tamagno of the XX century; and doubtless Mr Herbert Sims Reeves would be the De Reszke. Mr David Evans, as Lucentio, certainly knocked up his voice and lost his way in the delightful gamut solo, from sheer want of skill; but he did not seem to have been deliberately taught to sing badly: he has not been taught to sing well: that is all. The opera is such an excessively troublesome one to commit to memory that only students with unlimited opportunities of rehearsal could have afforded to get it up for the sake of one performance as perfectly as it was got up at the Royal College. The rich *finale* to the wedding scene, a sort of comic version of the great ballroom *finale* in *Don Giovanni*, was not so steady or crisp as it might have been: indeed, at one moment it wavered perilously; but on the whole the slips were very few and far between. The solo singing was of course *jejune*, lacking variety and sincerity of expression; and the acting ran into mock heroics on the serious side, and into tomfoolery on the comic; but if experience had not taught me the desperate risk of praising young amateurs, I should be tempted to compliment Miss Emily Davies on her plucky and intelligent effort to play Katherine, and to slap Mr Sandbrook on the back for his hard work as Petruchio. The orchestra acquitted itself admirably, the violins, played exclusively by students, being distinctly above the professional average. The first oboe, one trombone, two of the horns, and the first cornet were manned by professional players from outside. I am sorry to say that the bad custom of bouquet-throwing was permitted; and need I add that an American *prima donna* was the offender. What do you mean, Madame Nordica, by teaching the young idea how to get bouquets shied?* One consolation is, that if the critics cannot control the stars, they can at least administer the stripes.

* Shaw's phrasing appears to be a deliberate echo of James Thomson's The Seasons: Spring (1728): "Delightful task! . . . To teach the young idea how to shoot."

P.S. I have just paid my first visit to Otello at the Lyceum. The voices can all be beaten at Covent Garden: Tamagno's shrill and nasal, Maurel's woolly and tremulous, Signora Cattaneo's shattered, wavering, stagy, not to be compared to the worst of Mr Harris's *prima donnas*. On the other hand, Maurel acts quite as well as a good provincial tragedian, mouthing and ranting a little, but often producing striking pictorial effects; Tamagno is original and real, shewing you Otello in vivid flashes; and the interpretation of Verdi's score, the artistic homogeneity of performance, the wonderful balance of orchestra, chorus, and principals, stamp Faccio as a masterly conductor. The work of the orchestra and chorus far surpasses anything yet achieved under Signor Mancinelli at Covent Garden. The opera is powerful and interesting: immeasurably superior to Aida: do not miss it on any account. But if you go to the five-shilling pit, as I did, remember that there are four rows of stalls under the balcony, and that the pit therefore consists almost entirely of that square hole in the wall at the back which is one of Mr Irving's most diabolical innovations.

AGATHE BACKER-GRÖNDAHL
The Star, 13 July 1889

"Bassetto" said the editor of The Star "you say that Madame Backer-Gröndahl is a great pianoforte player?" "Commander of the Faithful" I replied "one of the very greatest in Europe." "Then what about an interview" cried my chief. "Commander of the Faithful" I said "this lady is so truly fine and noble an artist that I am afraid and ashamed to intrude on her in the ribald character of a journalist." "Your modesty is well known to me; and your feelings do you credit, O Bassetto" he answered "but if you dont go I will send someone else." So I could not choose but go; and on Tuesday evening my hansom jolted slowly along the Marylebone Road, bound for Madame Gröndahl's apartments in Blandford Square. You remember when I first found out Madame Gröndahl. It was at a Philharmonic concert, in Beethoven's great concerto in E flat. You know the long passage in octaves beginning *fortissimo,* with the *diminuendo* at the end. Well, I never heard anything quite so rough and strange at the beginning of those octaves under Madame Gröndahl's fingers. I did with my ears what I do with my eyes when I stare. What follows was no more a mere *diminuendo* of sound than a beautiful sunset in a mere *diminuendo* of light. It was a series of transfigurations—a letting loose of voices imprisoned in the passage—a wonderful suffusion of its steadily beating heart—a delicate lifting of it gradually out of the region of audible sound. A critic can no more express these things in words than he can describe his sensations when an artist of genius appears suddenly in front of the crowd of performers whose varying skills and tastes it is his ordinary business to sort out, patting one on the back and rapping another over the knuckles, like a schoolmaster. On such occasions his feeling for really great playing, which so seldom gets exercised that he sometimes doubts whether he possesses it, awakes like the Sleeping Beauty; and the critic knows that he is not wholly a vain thing.

But what I wanted to find out from Madame Gröndahl was how London had continued to remain for seventeen years unacquainted with a public player whose position is as exceptional, and whose talent is as rare and exquisite, as that of Madame Schumann. For Madame Gröndahl is, in round numbers, forty; that is, she is in the full maturity of her genius. And here you become curious about her personal appearance: you would like a little description. Well, she is what you would call—observe, what *you* would call—a perfectly plain woman. Her hair is not golden like yours: it is, I think, almost ashen: you would call it grey. Her figure and style are—well, quiet, slender, nothing in particular, nothing superb or Junonian: what can I say? Complexion? Quite Norwegian: no cream or coral, nothing to be afraid of there. Eyes? Well, eyes are a matter of opinion: I should rather like you to see them for yourself: they are *memorable*. A noble brow; but then, as you say, how unbecoming to a woman to have a noble brow! Would anybody look at you if you were in the same room with her? Ah, there you have me. Frankly, they would forget your very existence, even if there were no such thing in the world as a piano. For there is a grace beside which your beauty is vulgar and your youth inadequate; and that grace is the secret of Madame Gröndahl's charm.

At Blandford Square I find the invaluable, the ubiquitous H. L. Brækstad, who explains my errand to our hostess, and at intervals corrects my propensity to neglect my business and talk eloquently about myself. In excellent English Madame Gröndahl tells me how, when she was three or four years old, she used to make music for the stories her father told her; how, later on, Halfdan Kjerulf gave her lessons and taught her what expression in playing meant; how she was struck by hearing the late Edmund Neupert play Beethoven; how she was sent to Berlin and studied under Kullak for three years, working six and sometimes nine hours a day; and how she made her first appearance there seventeen years ago. She composes, she says, in the quiet of the evening, when the day's work is done: chiefly, indeed, in the evenings of December, when the year's work is done.

"What work?" I ask, astounded.

"Oh, all the things one has to do" she replies "the

housekeeping, the children, the playing, the three lessons I give every day to pupils." I rise up in wrath to protest against this house, these children, these pupils swallowing up the ministrations that were meant for mankind; but she adds, with a certain diffidence as to her power of expressing so delicate a point in English, that it is as wife and mother that she gets the experience that makes her an artist. I collapse. Bassetto is silenced. He can only bow to the eternal truth, and think how different his column would be if all artists were like this one. Here, then, is the reason why she never came to England before. She was too busy in her own house!

Presently she begins to speak with earnest admiration of some of her compatriots—of Svendsen, for instance, and "Mr Grieg." Her respect for Grieg infuriated me; for she is a thousand times a finer player than he; and I got quite beside myself at the idea of his presuming to teach her how to play this and that instead of going down on his knees and begging her to deliver him from his occasional vulgarity, and to impart to him some of her Mendelssohnic sense of form in composition. In spite of her perfectly becoming consciousness of her gift and her reverence for it she is aggravatingly modest. If I could play like her there would be simply no standing me. But she seems quite as gratefully surprised at her instantaneous success in London as she was when, on her return to Christiania after it, she was presented with a Steinway Grand, which stands in the same relation to the finances of Norway as half a dozen men-of-war to the finances of Mayfair. The presentation had been brewing for a long time, but her London triumph precipitated it.

As it grows dark in the sitting room in Blandford Square I prepare to withdraw; and we have some parting words about her recital on Saturday afternoon at Prince's Hall, where you can hear whether I have at all exaggerated her gifts. She will play Grieg's violin sonata with Johannes Wolff, who, it will be remembered, played it at St James's Hall with Grieg himself. She will not play a Beethoven sonata—thinks it would be too much to ask the public to listen to two sonatas. *Sancta simplicitas!* too much! However, she will play Chopin, of whom she is a famous exponent, and some of her own compositions, of which I shall have a word to say some other day. Today week she leaves us to rejoin Herr Gröndahl in Paris. He has trained a choir, and brought it to the Exhibition, his genius lying in the conducting direction. I venture to prophesy that she will come back, and eventually become as regular a visitor as Joachim or Madame Schumann.

P.S. I asked her about the octave passage in the concerto. She replied "That is the *heroic* point in the work. Von Bülow once drew my special attention to it."

A DESPERATE UNDERTAKING
The Star, 15 July 1889

The spectacle of Mr Augustus Harris making for righteousness with a whole mob of aristocratic patrons hanging on to his coattails is one which deserves to be hailed with three times three. It is difficult to conceive a more desperate undertaking than an attempt to make Die Meistersinger a success at Covent Garden. As well try to make wild flowers spring from the upholstery by dint of engaging tremendously expensive gardeners. There are many things needed for Die Meistersinger: scenery, dresses, persons with voices of a certain strength and compass, a conductor, a band, &c. &c. &c.; but there is one pre-eminent condition, without which all the others are in vain, and that one is the true Wagner-

Nuremberg atmosphere: the poetic essence of the medieval life wherein man, instead of serenading, dueling, crying "*T'amo, t'amo*," and finally suiciding (mostly in B flat or G), went his mortal round as apprentice, journeyman, and master; and habitually demeaned himself by doing useful work. Of this atmosphere there is hardly a breath at Covent Garden; and that is the first and last word of the higher criticism on Saturday's performance. But the practical criticism has to consider not whether the performance was perfectly satisfying, but whether it was better worth doing than letting alone; and on this point there must be a unanimous verdict in Mr Harris's favor.

The first step taken was to secure a large sale for the two-shilling librettos by substituting a colorless translation of the German poem, not into English, because the audience would understand that, nor into Polish, French, or Russian, because then one or two of the singers could have declaimed it with native familiarity, but into Italian, the least congenial language in Europe for the purpose. How *Johannistag* sounds as *solenne di*, and *Wahn! wahn!* as *Si, si*, may be imagined. In order to make quite sure of the librettos going off well, the usual opera bills were carefully removed from the stalls, probably not by Mr Harris's orders; for it is due to him to say that petty dodges of this stamp, characteristic as they are of fashionable entertainments in general and of opera house tradition in particular, are just those of which he has striven to rid Covent Garden. It is greatly to his credit that, in order to do as much of Die Meistersinger as possible, he dared on this occasion to begin at half-past seven, with the encouraging result that the attendance was more punctual than it usually is at eight, or even half-past eight. Yet, though the curtain did not fall until eighteen minutes past twelve on Sunday morning, chunks—absolutely whole chunks—had to be cut out of the very vitals of the work to get it over in time. The first half of Sachs's *Wahn! wahn!* Walter's denunciation of the master's pedantry in the second act, a section of the trial song, a section of the prize song, Beckmesser's scolding of Sachs in the third act, may be taken as examples of the excisions. This could have been avoided only by some such heroic measure as dispensing with the first act altogether: a fearful expedient; but then a single honest murder is better than half a dozen furtive mutilations.

So much for what was not done: now for what was. The honors of the evening went to Lassalle, whose singing was grand, especially in the third act. If he could only learn the part in German, cultivate a cobbler-like deportment about the elbows, and cure himself of his stage walk and his one perpetual gesture with the right hand, he would have very few dangerous rivals in Europe as Hans Sachs. Jean de Reszke, who wandered about the stage as if he had given Die Meistersinger up as a hopeless conundrum, but was always anxious to oblige as far as a tenor part or a spell of love-making was concerned, sang charmingly in the last two scenes. The ever condescending Montariol, as David (which he played with much spirit and evident relish), again sacrificed his dignity as *primo tenore assoluto* on the altar of devotion to the management. Abramoff gave due weight to the music of Pogner. Madame Albani is always at her sincerest—that is, her best—in playing Wagner. In the first scene of the third act she got so carried into her part that for the moment she quite looked it; and the quintet at the end was one of the happiest passages of the evening. Mlle Bauermeister, the invaluable, whom I have heard oftener than any other living artist (I once saw her as Astrifiammante), was Magdalen.

Signor Mancinelli, who was literally dragged twice across the stage in agonies of dorsaflexion, had evidently taken great pains. With fresh impressions of Richter and Faccio rife in the house, his limitations inevitably made themselves felt, especially in the overture and first act, where the orchestra, being in a continual bustle, requires the smoothest and most sympathetic handling to prevent it getting on one's nerves. And the waltz and procession music in the last scene were much too slow: a grave fault at midnight, with watches popping in and out all over the house and the end still distant. The staging of this last scene, by the way, was excellent. The chorus, if the substitution of women for boys must be accepted without a murmur, acquitted themselves very well; but the riot in the second act would have been better if it had either been sung note for note as written, or, as usual, frankly abandoned as impossible and filled up according to the vociferous fancy of the choristers. A combination of the two plans resulted in a failure, both in accuracy and *laisser-aller*. Such misplaced nocturnal buffooneries as the emptying of vessels from the windows on the crowd, and the subsequent clowning of the nothing-if-not-stolid watchman, should be at once stopped. M. Isnardon as Beckmesser set a bad example in this way; and his chief opportunity of really funny acting—the exhibition of the miseries of acute nervousness before the public in the last scene—was entirely missed.

The audience kept together wonderfully at the end, considering the lateness of the hour; and their conduct in suppressing ill-timed applause and insisting on silence after the fall of the curtain until the very last chord was played, was quite delightful. The proceedings ended with a tremendous ovation to Mr Harris, who fished out of the wing a stout gentleman generally but erroneously supposed to be Wagner. The assembly then broke up in high good humor.

EXPLOITING CHILDREN AND CRITICS

The Star, 19 July 1889

I see that Lord Dunraven has undertaken to move in the House of Lords the rejection of the amendment forbidding children under ten years of age to be used for the purpose of making money for their parents and for the proprietors of theatres. The House of Lords is exactly the place for such a heartless piece of mischief. Those who are on the side of social responsibility and of the children in this matter are undoubtedly reinforced for the moment by the party which would abolish the theatre altogether if it could. But that does not blind me to the fact that even Mr Winterbotham's stuff about the children going from the ballet to the streets is more sincere than the speeches of the Infants' Exploitation deputations. If Mrs John Wood can form no higher conception of the duty of the community towards the children whose parents' poverty makes them practically helpless, than that it should leave her free to buy them at so much a week for her pantomime, and ask no questions so long as she is personally—if not socially—kind in her dealings with them, then, it is to be hoped for the credit of the time that Mrs John Wood is fifty years behind it. As to Mr Beerbohm Tree's naïve complaint that the clause would prevent his producing A Midsummer Night's Dream, that, at any rate, was honest. Indeed, all the straightforward opponents of the clause make it pretty plain that the chance of occasionally seeing Pizarro, East Lynne, The Bohemian Girl, and A Doll's House (which I shall not be suspected of undervaluing) is of sufficient importance to justify us in keeping infants working for money between half-past eight and eleven every night for months at a time.

However, there is a way out of the difficulty. The Bill says nothing about amateur help from the nursery. If, then, children are so educated, elevated, and delighted by their exertions in the bracing atmosphere of the gas battens, the parents who are convinced of this will surely not hesitate to send their own olive branches without money or price, to become healthy, wealthy, and wise by staying up late, and to drive home the moral lessons of Ibsen and Shakespear. Until they are prepared to give that simple proof of their sincerity, the managerial cry of "Suffer little children to come unto me" will be set by all sensible and humane persons to the tune of "Will you walk into my parlor?" The reply in either case will, I hope, be a resolute "No."

I must say that I feel somewhat jealous as I read Mr Harris's magnificent half column of Meistersinger testimonials in the daily papers. An acute and critical letter from Mr Kuhe is given *in extenso*. A dispassionate and grave tribute to the "simple perfection" of the performance at Covent Garden, is signed by the "representatives of Wagner's works in England," meaning the publishers, who will probably gain much more by the popularity of the opera than Mr Harris without having incurred his risk. The Morning Post is unjustifiably severe: it says that "the whole production was worthy of the house and its associations." Considering that Mr Harris has succeeded, and deserved to succeed, just in so far as he has turned his back on the associations of the house, it was magnanimous of him to insert this. Perhaps he only did it as a set-off to the heroic eulogies of The Times critic. But what I want to know is why *my* criticisms and letters are never reproduced as advertisements. I protest against this undeserved neglect, which

I can only ascribe to a gross insensibility to the merits of my style and the extent of my influence.

On Saturday afternoon, at Prince's Hall, Madame Backer-Gröndahl not only bore out all that I have said in her praise, but left me considerably her debtor to boot. I adhere to my opinion that she should have played a Beethoven sonata instead of Grieg's violin sonata in C minor; but if we had no Beethoven we had at least Schumann and Chopin. The day has gone by when it was possible for us to get out of our depth in Schumann's pianoforte music: an artist like Madame Gröndahl gets to the bottom of such a composition as the novelette in F, and leaves us wishing that it, and not she, were deeper. But the Traumeswirren* satisfied us ineffably.

There is, however, a special pianistic form of musical genius which Schumann had not, but which Chopin had, and which Madame Gröndahl has. Thus it was Chopin's nocturne in F, bracketed with the fantasia in F minor at the end of the program, that constituted the chief and final test of the occasion. Madame Gröndahl sustained it triumphantly. She was delicate, splendid, everything that an interpreter of Chopin should be; and she leaves England—surely only until next season—with a London reputation as a great Beethoven player, a great Schumann player, a great Chopin player, and, consequently, a great pianoforte player.

I must not leave this subject without a word concerning Madame Gröndahl's compositions. Those for the pianoforte reminded me strongly of Mendelssohn by their sensitiveness, their clear symmetrical form, and their perfect artistic economy. The peculiar Norwegian feeling comes out most in the songs, some half-dozen of which were sung by Miss Louise Philips with a skill and taste which agreeably surprised me; for, as it happened,

* Fantasiestücke, Op. 12, No. 7.

I had not heard of her before; and I instinctively prepare for the worst at a recital when the singer appears. Johannes Wolff played the Grieg sonata with a finish which shewed even more than his usual address. The genial audacity and technical skill with which he made the audience wax rapturous over a detestable polonaise by Laub (called Lamb in the program) were immense.

I heard the Grieg sonata again on Wednesday at a concert given by Mlle de Hoerschelmann somewhere in the wild west of the Old Brompton Road. I was fascinated beyond measure by a Miss Nellie Levey, a young lady with a guitar, an exquisite ear, a quaint vein of humor, and an irresistible smile, who threw such subtle appeal into the words *Perchè tradirmi? perchè fuggirmi?* that I could hardly refrain from rising and earnestly protesting that nothing was further from my intentions. I should like to hear that young lady again.

Mademoiselle de Hoerschelmann—who is, I understand, a Russian—did not sing nor play. She recited in four languages, none of which she pronounced with any special virtuosity. She is, however, a very graphic reciter; and her idea of reading a canto from the Inferno is the right one in the right place. Recitation, as ordinarily practised, is about as entertaining as royalty-song singing. If I ever go into the business I shall simply read Homer or Dante or the Arabian Nights to the audience for an hour or two at a stretch. Mlle de Hoerschelmann's delivery of the third canto would have been a great success had the audience understood Italian. As for me, I never have any difficulty in understanding a play or poem in a foreign language when I know what it is all about beforehand; and I enjoyed Dante much more than I had enjoyed Ostler Joe earlier in the afternoon, when Mrs Kendal favored us with it at the Opera Comique to the utter stupefaction of an audience which had fallen under the strange spell of Ibsen, a spell of which Mrs Kendal, who had just dropped in for her recitation, was happily unconscious.

Note that the Wagner performances at Bayreuth commence on Sunday next. It is well to see Parsifal twice, with Tristan and the Meistersinger in between. Each performance costs a pound for admission alone. It is eminently possible to spend £20 on the trip without exceptional extravagance. But I never met anyone who complained of not having had value for his money.

THE OPERA SEASON AND ITS LESSONS
The Star, 26 July 1889

The season is over. By the end of next week there will be hardly four millions of persons left in London, mostly riffraff, mere working people, for whom nobody thinks of running an opera house or a series of St James's Hall concerts. And what a season it has been! Take the opera alone, and consider what wonderful things have happened. Tamagno was promised, as he had been repeatedly promised before; but this time, in defiance of all precedent, he has actually come, and his magnificent screaming is henceforth among the *sante memorie* of London amateurs. The Covent Garden management promised, above all things, Die Meistersinger and Romeo and Juliet; and both have been carefully produced. These things take away the breath of the old stager. Once upon a time it seemed a law of Nature that a London *impresario* should begin the season with a column of announcements of singers whom he had not engaged, of new works which he had not the smallest intention of producing, of eminent tenors, the undoubted successors of Mario, who were in fact the refuse of the Italian stage. Only a few years have elapsed since then; and yet even Mr Mapleson, who still believes in the irresistible attractiveness of Donizetti (and may therefore be supposed capable of believing in anything), does not venture to resuscitate the old-fashioned prospectus. As to Mr Harris, he thinks nothing of simply saying what he intends to do, and doing it.

When Mr Mapleson made his annual effort with Lucia, Il Barbiere, and La Sonnambula, &c., I flatly refused to waste my own time and The Star's space on an experiment which was of no public interest, and which was certain to fail. In vain the weeping staff held out stall tickets for Her Majesty's Theatre to me with imploring gestures. I folded my arms and said that if the name of Lucia di Lammermoor were mentioned in my presence again my resignation would follow instant-aneously. This threat never fails to bring Stonecutter-street to its knees; though, lest too frequent repetition should blunt it, I am careful not to employ it more than three times in any one week. It was effectual on this occasion; and I did not once set foot in Her Majesty's during the season.

To Mr Harris I have paid much more attention. He is a man with a future: there is something to be got by pitching into him. To let him alone, or to lavish indiscriminating praise on him whilst London is as ill-provided in the matter of opera as at present, is to trifle with the situation. It must never be forgotten that the Royal Italian Opera, far from paying its way, depends on a subvention as much as any Continental opera house. Unfortunately, this subvention is not yet forcibly levied on excessive West End incomes by the London County Council, and by them entrusted to Mr Harris for the purpose of maintaining a serious and progressive artistic institution for the performance of the best dramatic music. Instead, it has to be extracted by him from excessively rich people for the purpose of maintaining a fashionable postprandial resort for them during the season.

The following are the steps by which these munificent patrons make their plutocratic power felt at Covent Garden. They delay the rise of the curtain until half-past eight, and then come late. They insist on intervals of twenty minutes between the acts for what is to them the real business of the evening: visiting and chatting. They waste invaluable space with their comfortless dens of boxes. The percentage of inconsiderate persons among them is so high that there are always at least three parties disturbing the audience by talking and laughing at full pitch during the performance. The prices which their riches enable them to bid for admission drive ordinary amateurs to swelter among the gods, whilst box after box is thrown away on inveterate deadheads whose mission in life is to pester *impresarios* for free admissions. And they impose on the management impertinent sumptuary regulations by which I, for instance, am compelled to attend the opera in the cheapest, ugliest, and least wholesome suit of clothes I possess: regulations which are supposed to afford me a guarantee of the high personal character and perfect propriety in appearance, manners, and conversation of my neighbors. The guarantee is worth nothing. I shall not pretend that the average opera stallholder is in any of these respects a specially offensive person; but I unhesitatingly affirm that the average pittite is at no disadvantage whatever compared to him and is, on the whole, better company. The enthusiastic young students, male and female, whose last half-crown has been dedicated to Wagner, and who, flushed with triumph after a devoted wait at the doors and a long push, a strong push, and a push all together on the stairs, await the rising of the curtain with delightful eagerness, are,

[713]

of course, hopelessly lost to the stalls, though they are the most amusing and interesting of neighbors. As soon as women are educated to understand, as a minority already does, that it is grossly rude to keep on one's headgear in a theatre, the last rag of excuse for "evening dress indispensable" will vanish.

Yet I would forgive Mr Harris's fashionable patrons their class mumbo jumbo if only they would insist also on having the best of everything on the stage and in the orchestra—if they would rise up against those dreary deadly subscription-night Traviatas and Trovatores—if they would ask why more fuss has been made over the production of one Wagner opera in rich London than about the complete cycle of them which was given between the middle of May and the middle of June in comparatively needy Berlin—if they would ask why they are expected to put up with clever accompanists and bandmasters whilst great conductors like Richter, Levi, and Faccio are extant, and presumably open to sufficient offers—if they would ask why the XVIII century fashions in scenic art should be maintained at Covent Garden any more than at the Lyceum—if—

This is getting insufferably long: let me get back to the point. Before Mr Harris can procure money to perfect his opera house, there must be a pressure and a clamor behind him. Before he can effectually humble and terrify his artists (an operatic artist is by nature the most arrogant worm in existence) he must have more criticisms like mine to read to them in the greenroom. Before he can appear in the official gold chain and cocked hat of Chief Superintendent of Operatic and Dramatic Performances to the County Council of London (as Sir Augustus Harris, with a salary of ever so much a year) the Opera must be brought into much closer relation to the life of the people and the progress of dramatic music. As a beginning for next year, I suggest the production of one quite new opera, by a composer under forty; freshly studied and carefully rehearsed performances of Don Giovanni and Le Nozze di Figaro; and the shelving of the old Bellini-Donizetti-Verdi stopgaps to make room for The Taming of the Shrew, Tannhäuser, Tristan, at least one of the four works from the Nibelungen tetralogy, and an old work of some merit called Fidelio, of which Mr Harris may have heard in his youth, though of late years it seems to have escaped his memory. Faust, Mefistofele, Les Huguenots, and Lohengrin can be exploited as usual; but I confess I should not regret seeing Carmen, Les Pêcheurs de Perles, and even Roméo et Juliette handed over to the smaller theatres. Berlioz's Benvenuto Cellini would also excite great interest now that his Faust has become so popular.

Bless my soul! it is later than I thought: I must be off to Bayreuth at once, or I shall be late for Parsifal on Sunday afternoon. *Auf wiederschreiben!*

BASSETTO AT BAYREUTH
The Star, 1 August 1889

Imagine yourself in a state of high indignation at having paid a pound for admission to a theatre, and finding yourself in a dim freestone-colored auditorium, reminding you strongly of a lecture theatre by the steepness of the bank of seats and the absence of a gallery. But wheras most lecture theatres are fan-shaped or circular, with a rostrum at the pivot or centre, this one is wedge-shaped, with a shabby striped curtain cutting off the thin end of the wedge, the difference being that the parallel benches are straight instead of curved. Partition walls jut out at right angles to the wall of the building at intervals along

[715]

the side, and break off short just in time to avoid getting between the people in the end seats and the stage. These walls, which do not quite reach the ceiling, are surmounted by branches of lamps in round globes, which shed a dun-colored light over the dun-colored house. You come prepared by countless photographs and engravings for the shape of the place; but this prevailing dun tone, and the prevailing absence of cushion, curtain, fringe, gilding, or any gay theatrical garniture, with the steepness of the bank of seats (no pictures give you an adequate idea of this), make you inclined to think that the manager might really have touched up the place a little for you. But you have nothing else to complain of; for your hinged seat, though of uncushioned cane, is comfortably wide and broad, and your view of the striped curtain perfect. The highly esteemed ladies are requested by public notice obligingly their hats to remove, and those who have innocent little bonnets, which would not obstruct a child's view, carefully remove them. The ladies with the Eiffel hats, regarding them as objects of public interest not second to any work of Wagner's, steadfastly disregard the notice; and Germany, with all its martinets, dare not enforce discipline. You open your libretto, your score, your synopsis of *leitmotifs*, or other idiotic device for distracting your attention from the performance; and immediately the lights go out and leave you in what for the moment seems all but total darkness. There is a clatter of cane seats turned down; a great rustle, as of wind through a forest, caused by 1300 skirts and coat tails coming into contact with the cane; followed by an angry hushing and hissing from overstrained Wagner-ians who resent every noise by adding to it with an irritability much more trying to healthy nerves than the occasional inevitable dropping of a stick or opera-glass. Then the prelude is heard; and you at once recognize

[716]

that you are in the most perfect theatre in the world for comfort, effect, and concentration of attention. You inwardly exclaim that you are hearing the prelude played for the first time as it ought to be played. And here, leaving you to enjoy yourself as a member of the analytical public, I strike in with the remark that the perfection is not in the performance, which does not touch the excellence of one which Richter conducted at the Albert Hall, but in the conditions of the performance. And I may say here, once for all, that the undiscriminating praise that is lavished on the Bayreuth representations is due to the effect of these conditions before the curtain and not behind it. The much boasted staging is marred by obsolete contrivances which would astonish us at the Lyceum as much as a return to candle-lighting or half price at nine o'clock. Mr Mansfield playing Richard III. in the dress of Garrick, or Mr Irving Hamlet in that of Kemble, would seem modern and original compared with the unspeakable ballroom costume which Madame Materna dons to fascinate Parsifal in the second act. The magic flower garden would be simply the most horribly vulgar and foolish transformation scene ever allowed to escape from a provincial pantomime, were it not recommended to mercy by a certain enormous *naïveté* and a pleasantly childish love of magnified red blossoms and trailing creepers. As to the canvas set piece and Gower-st. sofa visibly pulled on to the stage with Madame Materna seductively reposing on it, the steam from a copper under the boards which filled the house with a smell of laundry and melted axillary gutta-percha linings, the indescribable impossibility of the wigs and beards, the characterless historical-school draperies of the knights, the obvious wire connexion of the electric light which glowed in the ruby bowl of the Holy Grail, and the senseless violation of Wagner's directions by allowing

[717]

Gurnemanz and Parsifal to walk off the stage whilst the panoramic change of scene was taking place in the first act (obviously the absence of the two men who are supposed to be traversing the landscape reduces the exhibition to the alternative absurdities of the trees taking a walk or the auditorium turning round): all these faults shew the danger of allowing to any theatre, however imposing its associations, the ruinous privilege of exemption from vigilant and implacable criticism. The performance of Parsifal on Sunday last suffered additionally from Herr Grüning executing a hornpipe on the appearance of Klingsor with the sacred spear; but this was introduced not as an act of whimsical defiance, but under pressure of the desperate necessity of disentangling Parsifal's ankle fron the snapped string on which the spear was presently to have flown at him.

Now if you, my Wagnerian friends, wonder how I can scoff thus at so impressive a celebration, I reply that Wagner is dead, and that the evil of deliberately making the Bayreuth Festival Playhouse a temple of dead traditions, instead of an arena for live impulses, has begun already. It is because I, too, am an enthusiastic Wagnerite that the Bayreuth management cannot deceive me by dressing itself in the skin of the dead lion. The life has not quite gone out of the thing yet: there are moments when the spirit of the master inspires the puppets, and the whole scene glows into real life. From the beginning of the Good Friday music in the last act, after the scene where the woman washes Parsifal's feet and dries them with her hair—the moment at which Parsifal's true character of Redeemer becomes unmistakably obvious to the crassest Philistine globetrotter present—the sacred fire descended, and the close of the representation was deeply impressive. Before that, a point had been brought out strongly here and there by individual artists; but nothing more. I shall return to the subject and deal more particularly with the two casts later on, when I see the work again on Thursday. For the present I need only warn readers that my censure of some of the scenic arrangements must not be allowed to obscure the fact that the Grail scene is unsurpassed as a stage picture; that the first scene, though conventional, is finely painted; and that the Spanish landscape, from which the magic garden suddenly withers (this is a capital effect), and the Good Friday landscape in the last act, are fine pieces of stage scenery.

IMPRESSIONS DE VOYAGE

The Star, 2 August 1889

I write under difficulties this week. I am not a good sailor. After being rocked in the cradle of the deep all night, I am at present being rocked in a Dutch railway carriage. I have been in it for five hours, and I assure you that if an express were to come in the opposite direction on the same line of rails and smash the whole affair, Bassetto included, into pulp, I should make no unmanly complaints. After all, there is something grand in being able to look death in the face with a smile of welcome; but I should enjoy it more if I could look life in the face without feeling so poorly.

It is later in the day; and I think life is, perhaps, worth living after all. To drive up the Rhine from Bonn to Coblenz, whilst the hours advance from afternoon to night, is better than a dozen press views of different schools of landscape. Cologne Cathedral, too, has affected me. I am extremely susceptible to stained glass, and the old glass there transports me, whilst the new glass makes me long to transport it—with bricks. Yes, I confess I am enjoying the evening. I wish I were undressed and in bed, with twelve hours' sleep before me; I wish that when that terrific shower caught me in Cologne my mackintosh had not split up the back like a trick coat in a farce, throwing the younger posterity of the Three Kings into derisive convulsions. I wish I knew whether that very genial market woman really gave me, as she implied, an enormous bargain for the sake of my *beaux yeux* (one and elevenpence for half a pound of grapes and six little hard pears), or whether she swindled me; and I wish I could go back by Channel Tunnel. But still, for the moment, I do not regret having been born.

Some hours have elapsed, and I now distinctly *do* regret having been born. Imagine reaching Würzburg at two in the morning, and being told to wait two and a half hours for a train to Bamberg. Imagine a wilderness of a German waiting room—a place like a *café* running to seed for want of a little paint—crowded with people in various grades of wakefulness. The young what's-their-names wearing badges, and carrying military paraphernalia wrapped up in umbrella cases, are very wideawake indeed: they are continually breaking into Lorelei, or some other popular air, only to break out of it in quite British fashion the next moment. The men who are stretched on the two broad forms in the middle of the room, and on rows of chairs in the background, might be supposed asleep if a man could really sleep with the back of his neck pillowed on the handle of a traveling-bag, and his occiput taking an impression of the catch. The seated slumberers, with their arms folded on the table and their faces hidden upon them, are probably less miserable, especially those who are not at marble tables. I tried this plan for a moment myself; but it was a failure: after killing ten minutes by the familiar process of making them appear ten hours, I have taken to writing as the best way I know of making time seem too short (*ars longa, vita brevis*, you understand). The fearfully weary woman with the fretful child has just got up and tried a walk, after addressing to me a remark which I do not understand, but which I accept as a commission to see that nobody steals her luggage during her promenade.

Pshaw! describing a scene like this is like trying to draw one of the faces you see in a cloud. Already the noisy youngsters are gone, and the horizontal figures have transferred themselves, during their vertical intervals, to the trains which an official with a brutal bell and an undistinguished delivery enters to announce from time to time. There are but twelve of us now, including the two waiters, myself, and the child, who has, I am happy to say, left off worrying its mother to stare at the tremendous spectacle of Corno di Bassetto writing his sparkling Star column, and looking more melancholy and jaded over it than any infant's mind could have conceived. But hark! methinks I scent the morning air. The shunter's horn—a silly child's affair with a harmonium reed in it—takes a bustling tone as if it were paid so much a week to call the lark in time. A passing engine shews against the sky no longer as a bright gleaming mass of metal against a dead darkness, but as a black shadow on a dim grey galanty-sheet. And it is beginning to strike cold and raw! Ugh! What an idiot I was not to go on to Nuremberg; and what stupids they were to give me tickets via Bamberg! I feel that I shall slate something presently—Parsifal, probably.

After all, Bamberg has its merits. It was worth coming round to see: that affable young German gentleman at Cook's who sold me my tickets evidently knew a thing or two. How Bamberg manages to have so many rivers and bridges and yet to be on top of a group of hills I do not know: it is only another proof of the worthlessness of the commonplace that water will find its own level. The town has such an odd air of being built by persons with artistic instincts, but with the temperament which usually earns for its possessor the title of rum customer, that the climb up from the vegetable market, strong in marrows and carrots, under the Bridge House, decorated with frescos exactly like the ones I used to produce on whitewashed walls with penny paints when I was a boy, and up to the Cathedral, freshened me more than all the naps I had snatched in the train from Würzburg: more even than the delightfully musical German of the two young ladies *en route* for Kissingen, who were my fellow-travelers to Schweinfurth. Really a perfect ante-Gothic cathedral of the plainest and most reasonable beauty, looking its best in the morning light.

Glancing through Baedeker as I bowl along Bayreuth-wards I perceive that the chief feature of the Wagner district is a great lunatic asylum. At Neumarkt an official railway *colporteur* thrusts into my hand a great red placard inscribed with a WARNUNG! (German spelling is worse than indifferent) against pickpockets at Bayreuth. This is a nice outcome of Parsifal. In the town an enterprizing tradesman offers "the Parsifal slippers" at 2m. 50 the pair as "the height of novelty." It is a desperately stupid little town, this Bayreuth. I was never in Bath but once; and then they were trying to make it exciting by a meeting of the British Association which I addressed for a solid hour in spite of the secretary's urging me to be brief.* Trying to make Bayreuth lively by a Wagner Festspiel is much the same thing.

However, there are hills with fine woods to wander through, and blackberries, raspberries, and other sorts of edible berries, about the names of which no two persons agree, to be had for the picking. On the top of

* Shaw addressed the British Association for the Advancement of Science, on The Transition to Social Democracy, at its annual meeting at Bath, on 7 September 1888.

the hill on which the theatre stands is a tower erected to the brave sons of Bayreuth who fell in 1870–71. Except that the tower is round, and that there is no courtly old lady to take toll and sell ginger beer, you might, by a vigorous contraction of the imagination, fancy yourself on Leith Hill. The town contains a bust of Mr John Cobden Sanderson, with somebody else's name under it; also the most extravagantly and outrageously absurd fountain and equestrian statue in the world (of Margrave Somebody). Jean Paul Richter is much commemorated in the neighborhood. I am surprised to find how few faces I know here. Charles Dowdeswell, William Archer, Antoinette Sterling, Stavenhagen, Richter, Karl Armbruster, Pauline Cramer, Rimbault Dibdin, and Benjamin R. Tucker of Boston, are all I can identify. It is desperately hard work, this daily scrutiny of the details of an elaborate performance from four to past ten. Yet there are people who imagine I am taking a holiday.

TRISTAN AND ISOLDE
The Star, 6 August 1889

Tristan and Isolde comes off better than Parsifal by just so much as the impulse to play it is more genuine and the power to understand it more common. To enjoy Parsifal, either as a listener or an executant, one must be either a fanatic or a philosopher. To enjoy Tristan it is only necessary to have had one serious love affair; and though the number of persons possessing this qualification is popularly exaggerated, yet there are enough to keep the work alive and vigorous. In England it is not yet familiar: we contentedly lap dose after dose of such pap as the garden scene in Gounod's Faust, and think we are draining the cup of stage passion to the dregs.

The truth is that all the merely romantic love scenes ever turned into music are pallid beside the second act of Tristan. It is an ocean of sentiment, immensely German, and yet universal in its appeal to human sympathy. At eight o'clock yesterday (Monday) I wondered that people fresh from such an experience did not rashly declare that all other music is leather and prunella; shrug their shoulders at the triviality of *Là ci darem*; and denounce a proposal to try the effect of the fourth act of Les Huguenots as a direct incitement to crime.

The performance on Monday was an admirable one. After the scratch representations we are accustomed to in London, at which half the attention of the singers is given to the prompter, half to the conductor, and the rest to the character impersonated, the Bayreuth plays seem miracles of perfect preparedness. Nothing is forgotten; nothing is slurred; nothing on the stage contradicts its expression in the orchestra. At Covent Garden, where you cannot get an artist even to open a letter or make a sword thrust within four bars of the chord by which the band expresses his surprise or his rage, a tithe of the thought and trouble taken here would work wonders. The orchestra, too, by certain methods of treating the instruments, produce many effects of which the tradition must be handed down orally; for most of them defy such directions as a composer can write into his score with any prospect of being rightly understood. Everything that can be done by educated men thoroughly in earnest is done: the shortcomings are those which only individual gifts can overcome.

That shortcomings do exist may be inferred from the fact that, except at those supreme moments at which the Wagnerian power sweeps everything before it, it is possible for an ungrateful visitor to feel heavily bored. The reason is that the singers, in spite of their formidable physique, thick powerful voices, and intelligent and energetic declamation, are not all interesting. They lack subtlety, grace, finesse, magnetism, versatility, delicacy of attack, freedom, individuality: in a word, genius. I remember how Karl Hill sang the part of Mark when I first heard that second act: how we were made to understand the simple dignity, the quiet feeling, the noble restraint, the subdued but penetrating reproach of the old king's address to the hero whom he had loved as a son, and in whose arms he surprises his virgin wife. Herr Betz gave us hardly any of this. He turned his head away, and lifted his hands and sang most dolefully: nobody was sorry when he had said his say and was done with it. Only a few months ago, at the Portman Rooms, I heard Mr Grove, who makes no pretension to the eminence of Herr Betz, sing this scene with much truer expression. But when Hill sang the part Wagner was conducting; so perhaps the comparison is hardly fair to Betz. In the third act again Vogl surpassed Charles II. in point of being an unconscionably long time dying. Wagner's heros have so much to say that if they have not several ways of saying it (Vogl has exactly two—a sentimental way and a vehement way) the audience is apt to get into that temper which, at English public meetings, finds vent in cries of "Time!" For the fuller a poem is, the duller is an empty recitation of it.

The honors of the occasion were carried off by the women. The men shewed that they had been heavily drilled and were under orders; but Frau Sucher and Fräulein Staudigl played as if the initiative were their own. Frau Sucher, indeed, is not a good subject for leading-strings. Her Isolde is self-assertive and even explosive from beginning to end: impetuous in love, violent in remorse, strong in despair. Frau Sucher has the singer's instinct in a degree exceptionally keen for Bayreuth: she, like Frau Materna, can fall back sometimes on methods of expression solely musical. Fräulein Staudigl's Brangäne was excellent. If I were asked to point to the page of music in which the most perfect purity of tone would produce the greatest effect I think I should select the warning of Brangäne from the tower top to the lovers in the garden. I cannot say that Fräulein Staudigl quite satisfied me in this indescribable episode; but I can praise her warmly for not having fallen much further short of perfection than she actually did. The orchestra, conducted by Felix Mottl, played with an absolute precision and a touch of austerity which reminded me of Costa, who, obsolete as his tastes were, and quickly as he has been forgotten, deserves this reminiscence for having kept his foot down so long on slovenly and vulgar orchestral work. So much so that I sometimes wish he were alive again; though there was a time when—musically speaking, you understand—I heartily wished him dead. Curious, that Tristan and Isolde in Bayreuth should have set me talking about Costa, of all men that ever were!

DIE MEISTERSINGER

The Star, 6 August 1889

Perhaps the reason why these Bayreuth artists interest me so much less than they ought to, is that they make no mistakes, and I am consequently deprived of an irritant to which I have become accustomed in London. Whatever it is, I sighed more than once for ten minutes of Covent Garden. Not, of course, for the Covent Garden orchestra, or the conductor, or the cuts, or the stalls and boxes, or the late hours, or the superficialities, or the general cloudiness as to the meaning of the stage business, or the pointless Italian verse. But I could have borne a stave or two from Jean de Reszke and Lassalle with a tranquil mind. It is true that Herr Gudehus understands the part of Walther much better than De Reszke; he acts with humor and intelligence, and sings by no means without fervor and power. Moreover, he is venerable; wheras our Polish favorite is a mere sprig of forty or thereabouts. Again, Reichmann gives a more characteristic portrait of the cobbler mastersinger of Nuremberg than Lassalle: one, too, much fuller of suggestive detail. And though his voice is much worse for wear, there is, here and there in his compass, still a rich note or two; and he was able to finish the part bravely, though the last hundred bars or so evidently cost him a severe effort. But in musical charm neither Gudehus nor Reichmann touched De Reszke and Lassalle, though at every other point they far surpassed them. I wish some man of science would provide critics with a psychology capable of explaining how the same man may sing through an opera like a genius and act through it like a country gentleman; or, conversely, why he may interpret the book like a student and philosopher, and sing through the score like an improved foghorn. The first case prevails in London and makes Covent Garden frivolous; the other monopolizes Bayreuth and makes the Festival Plays heavy. The performance was an arduous one, the third act lasting two hours. Richter conducted; and this is as good a place as another to say that he is by far the freest, strongest, and most gifted conductor of the three, though he left Parsifal to Levi (it is an open secret that Wagner at first offered the work to the Gentile conductor), and does not always take the trouble to secure the faultless precision attained by Mottl in Tristan. I have heard nothing played here with such effect as the prelude to the third act; and the judgment, the good husbandry, and—at the right moment—the massive force with which

Richter got the maximum of effect in the scenes of crowd and tumult were great feats of generalship. The stage management was above praise: how much it did to make the situations intelligible could only be adequately felt by those who had seen Die Meistersinger in theatres where nothing but a few of the simpler incidents seem to be thoroughly understood by anybody concerned. The final scene was one of the most imposing I have ever seen on the stage; and here, as in the previous acts, the effect produced was not the result of money freely lavished, but of care conscientiously taken. The waltz was charming because it was a dance and not a ballet (I wish I could persuade Stewart Headlam that ballet is the death of dancing). Anyhow, the scene at Bayreuth was no more like that at Covent Garden than a picture by Teniers is like an *Aquarelle* by Dubufe. Of the principal artists, besides those of whom I have already spoken, the most distinguished was Friedrichs, who played Beckmesser like a finished comedian. Fräulein Staudigl again shewed considerable intelligence as an actress in the part of Magdalena; and Fräulein Dressler's Eva was a good Eva as Evas go, though she crowned Walther at the end with an appallingly flat imitation shake. Hofmüller was comparatively bright as David. The remarkable completeness and depth of the impression produced shewed the wisdom of performing great works without mutilation, at whatever tax on the time and endurance of the audience. The flood of melody throughout the work astonished the few survivors of the sceptics who originated the brilliant theory that Wagner devoted his existence to avoiding anything of a musical nature in his compositions.

The place is by this time full of English. I shall retreat to Nuremberg after Parsifal.

THE SECOND PARSIFAL

The Star, 7 August 1889

This Parsifal is a wonderful experience: not a doubt of
it. The impression it makes is quite independent of
liking the music or understanding the poem. Hardly
anybody has the slightest idea of what it all means;
many people are severely fatigued by it; and there must
be at least some who retain enough of the old habit of
regarding the theatre as an exception to the doctrine of
Omnipresence, to feel some qualms concerning the
propriety of an elaborate make-believe of Holy Communion, culminating in the descent of a stuffed dove
through a flood of electric radiance. Yet Parsifal is the
magnet that draws people to Bayreuth and disturbs their
journey thence with sudden fits of desperate desire to go
back again. When you leave the theatre after your first
Parsifal you may not be conscious of having brought
away more than a phrase or two of *leitmotif* mingled
with your burden of weariness and disappointment. Yet
before long the music begins to stir within you and
haunt you with a growing urgency that in a few days
makes another hearing seem a necessity of life. By that
time, too, you will have been converted to the Church
and Stage Guild's view that the theatre is as holy a place
as the church and the function of the actor no less sacred
than that of the priest.

The second performance given during my stay at
Bayreuth was much better than the first. It is sometimes
difficult for a critic to feel sure that an improvement of
this sort is not in his own temper rather than in what he
is listening to; but as I found Klingsor decidedly worse
than before and was conscious of one or two points at

which Fräulein Malten as Kundry fell short of Frau Materna, the difference must have been objective, since, had it been merely subjective, the apparent changes would all have been, like my mood, from worse to better. Malten has several advantages over Materna in playing Kundry. Not only is she passably slim, but her long thin lips and finely-turned chin, with her wild eyes, give her a certain air of *beauté de diable*. Only an air, it is true, but enough for a willing audience. Her voice, though a little worn, is bright; and her delivery is swift and telling. Altogether, one may say that her individuality, though it would not startle London, is quite magnetic in Bayreuth. Frau Materna, the rival Kundry, is not perceptibly lighter than she was when she sang at the Albert Hall in 1877. She is comely, but matronly. Still, as Kundry is as old as the hills no complaint need be made on this score; indeed, the part is one which a very young woman would play worse than a mature one, unless she were a young woman of extraordinary genius and precocity. At moments Materna's singing is grand, and her acting powerful: at other moments she holds up the corner of an absurd scarf as if it had descended to her from a provincial Mrs Siddons. Fräulein Malten also clings to a scarf rather more than is good for the sobriety of spectators with an untimely sense of fun. But nobody laughs. It is a point of honor not to laugh in the Wagner Theatre, where the chances offered to ribalds are innumerable: take as instances the solemn death and funeral of the stuffed swan; the letting out of Parsifal's tucks when his mailed shirt is taken off and his white robe pulled down; and the vagaries of the sacred spear, which either refuses to fly at Parsifal at all or else wraps its fixings round his ankles like an unnaturally thin boa constrictor. Nevertheless, nobody behaves otherwise than they would in church. The performance is regarded on all hands as a rite. Miss Pauline Cramer, if she had no deeper feeling than a desire to oblige the management, like Montariol at Covent Garden, would hardly have volunteered for the silent part of the youth whose whole duty it is to uncover the Grail. As to Frau Materna, it is impossible to believe that when she goes up nearly the whole depth of the Grail scene on her knees, she is only aiming at a stage effect. As such, it is not worth the physical exertion it costs. Van Dyck, though not so steady a singer as Grüning, has a certain impulsive *naïveté* which, with his engaging physical exuberance, makes him the better Parsifal. The part is a unique one, full of never-to-be-forgotten situations. Impressive as the first Grail scene is, nine-tenths of its effect would be lost without the "innocent fool" gazing dumbly at it in the corner, only to be hustled out as a goose when it is over. His appearance on the rampart of Klingsor's castle, looking down in wonder at the flower maidens in the enchanted garden, is also a memorable point. And that long kiss of Kundry's from which he learns so much is one of those pregnant simplicities which stare the world in the face for centuries and yet are never pointed out except by great men.

DR MACKENZIE AND EDWARD FITZGERALD

The Star, 9 August 1889

I see that Dr Morell Mackenzie has again explained the physiology of song, this time in the Contemporary Review. I notice that he describes abdominal breathing as "pushing down the diaphragm and protruding the stomach." Many people—including myself—have always taken it for granted that abdominal breathing means the trick of retracting and depressing the diaphragm as an alternative to lifting the ribs, as a woman or an opening umbrella does. But after a few experiments I find that I can breathe in a manner answering to Dr Morell Mackenzie's description by pushing what I suppose to be my diaphragm forwards and downwards, instead of pulling it inwards and downwards. I quite agree with the doctor that it is a bad plan; but the other variety does not seem to me to be open to the objections he urges. However, I speak with diffidence on a matter which involves a knowledge of the whereabouts of the stomach, because I entirely forget where that organ is situate. It is a long time since I dipped into Huxley and Foster*; and all that comes back to me of their teaching is that they disabused me of my original impression that my stomach was a sort of hollow kernel, situated exactly in the centre of my body. On consideration I recollect that it is shaped like the bellows of a bagpipe, and is all to one side; but which side, or how high up or how low down, I cannot for the life of me remember. Hence the caution with which I offer my opinion.

Dr Morell Mackenzie returns to his old and apparently reasonable contention that children should be taught to sing early, and that the training of the voice need not be discontinued whilst the voice of the boy is breaking into that of a man. He also righteously protests against the height of the English pitch; but in doing so he makes a slip. "Nearly all singers" he says "are in favor of lowering the pitch. The sole exceptions are, I believe, the contraltos, whom a high pitch does not affect so much as it does others. I know of one justly celebrated contralto who produces an extraordinary effect by her low E. If

* Thomas Henry Huxley's Elementary Lessons in Physiology (1866) and Michael Foster's A Course of Elementary Practical Physiology (1876).

the pitch were altered this vocal feat would no longer be so wonderful; and it is natural, therefore, that this lady should wish the present state of things to continue." Dr Morell Mackenzie, to say the least, has not decomposed much brain tissue over this point. Obviously a lowering of the pitch, which eases the high B's and C's of the sopranos, makes the low E's and F's of the contraltos and bassos more difficult. Astrifiammante can only be relieved at the expense of Sarastro. If Dr Mackenzie had written that the lady objected because the change would render her favorite vocal feat impossible he would have been nearer the mark.

The Musical Times has had the happy idea of extracting from Edward Fitzgerald's letters his notes upon music. On the whole, Fitz was a sound critic; by which you will please understand not that his likings and dislikings in music were the same as yours, but that he knew one sort of music from another, and was incapable of speaking of the overtures to Mozart's Zauberflöte, Beethoven's Leonore, and Rossini's William Tell as if they were merely three pieces cut off the same roll of stuff by three different tailors. His walking out of the house after the first act of Les Huguenots because it was "noisy and ugly" was rash but perfectly consistent with his remark on the C minor symphony "I like Mozart better: Beethoven is gloomy." The two criticisms bring to light the whole secret of the extraordinary sensation made by such men as Byron, Beethoven, and Meyerbeer in the first half of the century. Beethoven was the first to write gloomy music for its own sake. Meyerbeer was the first opera composer who had the courage to write persistently lugubrious music for its own sake. This was quite a different thing from writing a funeral march because Saul was dead, tromboning a terrible invocation to the *divinités du Styx* because a heroine had to descend into the shades, or in any of the old tragic ways of purifying the soul with pity or terror. Mozart's Don Giovanni was the first Byronic hero in music; but the shadows cast by him were so full of strange reflections and beautiful colors that such lovers of beauty as Fitz were not alarmed. But when Beethoven came, the shadows were black and gigantic; the forms were rough and bold; the Mozartian enchantment was gone. Instead of it there came a sense of deep import in the music—of, as Fitzgerald says, "a Holy of Holies far withdrawn; conceived in the depth of a mind, and only to be received into the depth of ours after much attention." The translator of Omar Khayyám did not like the black shadows; and though he recognized that Beethoven had "a depth not to be reached all at once," and was "original, majestic, and profound," yet he liked the no less deep and more luminous Mozart better. As to Meyerbeer, who had the lugubriosity of the new school without its profundity, Fitz simply walked out of the house at the end of the first act, and thereby missed the discovery that the arch trifler could rise magnificently to the occasion when his librettist offered it to him.

His worst shot at the music of later days is his description of Carmen as "an opera on the Wagner plan," a description which shews that his notion of "the Wagner plan" was entirely superficial. But his dismissal of Bizet's opera as containing "excellent instrumentation, but not one new or melodious idea through the whole," though it seems absurdly severe, is the natural deliverance of a man who speaks from that zone of Parnassus in which Handel has his place. Fitz appears to have lived on Handel; and Carmen is the very smallest of small beer to a palate accustomed to even Acis and Galatea, much more Samson, Messiah, Israel in Egypt, or Jephtha. But it would never do for Press critics to contemn in this fashion every farce for not being a tragedy. By the way, Fitz saw Carmen at Her Majesty's in 1880; and of the singers he says that "only one of them could sing at all; and she sang very well indeed: Trebelli her name." This shews that he knew good singing from bad, in spite of his fogeyish habit of comparing every singer with Pasta. From the purely musical point of view, Trebelli was certainly the best of all the Carmens.

Tomorrow the Promenade Concerts at Covent Garden begin. Arditi is to conduct. Glancing at the first program: *Ernani, involami, Il segreto, Un di se ben*, and so on, I feel that Arditi will be in his element. But what about the classical nights, on which the prestige of these concerts always depends? I do not mean to imply that Arditi cannot conduct a symphony: he can conduct anything, and come off without defeat, thanks to his address, his experience, and his musical instinct. But symphony is not his department. He knows the Leonore overture, which he has so often conducted at the opera; and I give him credit for the deepest respect for Mozart's Jupiter symphony, to which he is by this time pretty well accustomed. But Beethoven's symphonies are not his affair. I remember once seeing him conduct the slow movement of the Ninth symphony. He smiled; he beat away genially; he checked the entries of the instruments vigilantly; occasionally he ecstatically rose and sank in his characteristic manner like an animated concertina set on end; but a skilled reader of faces could see that he was profoundly puzzled, and could not for the life of him catch the swing of the movement. This was not to be wondered at, since he had begun the first section by briskly beating four in a bar, wheras eight in a bar, at a moderate pace, would just about have got him right. The second section, in three-four time, a ravishing strain which should go much more ardently than the first section, he conducted with funereal solemnity. Since then his acquaintance with the later works of

Beethoven may have ripened; but I doubt it. His temperament is so Italian, and his training has so confined him in the mid-century operatic habit of mind, that I cannot believe that the classical nights will be the strong points in the forthcoming season. If, however, he will follow up *Un di se ben* by plenty of Italian concerted music, I shall applaud him to the echo. Are we never again to hear *Guai se ti sfugge un moto*, *E rimasto*, *Chi mi frena*, *E scherzo od e follia*, *O sommo Carlo*, and half a dozen other delightful concerted pieces which will occur to Arditi at once in this connexion? The singers, it seems, will have sufficiently frequent engagements together to make it reasonable to ask them to get up these beautiful and simple numbers, and so to relieve us from the perpetual solo, solo, solo, varied only by *encores*.

PROMENADE CONCERTS

The Star, 12 August 1889

When I reached Covent Garden on Saturday at eight I found it crowded to the ceiling. Business had begun at half-past seven; and when I entered the orchestra was employed, absurdly enough, upon the ballet music from Ponchielli's Gioconda. For why, in the name of reason, should the accompaniment to a dance be played in public without the dance itself, any more than the accompaniment to a song? I grant you that there are a few dance tunes that are worth listening to for their own sakes, but they are to be found neither in the Gioconda nor any other grand opera ballet. I gathered from the program that the band had already disported itself with the overture to Zampa, the *allegretto* from the Eighth symphony, and other not too severe orchestral compositions. After Gioconda Mlle Tremelli sang *Il Segreto* in an undisciplined manner, running very short in the matter of breath, but achieving an effective shake which sounded as if it were a double-voiced one in thirds. Miss Nettie Carpenter played Svendsen's Romance for Violin, and played it very well, though her tone is just a little soapy, if I may be permitted to use such an expression. Signor Foli followed with I Fear no Foe; and I had just made a note that his voice was entirely gone, when, in singing The Millwheel for an *encore* (everybody was encored), it came back again and relieved him of the arduous task of interpreting the ballad by facial expression alone. Eloquence of feature is one of Signor Foli's strong points. In the waltz from Die Meistersinger I heard no glockenspiel. However, as I was not just then very favorably situated it is barely possible that it may have been tinkling beyond my hearing.

Nikita—the young lady spurns a prefix—gave us *Ernani involami*, which she sang well. Yet if good teaching were common, and an artistic atmosphere prevalent in British homes, every third girl in England would be able to do nearly as much. Nikita has been well taught: she does not scream her high notes nor make shots at them; and she can imitate feeling sympathetically. She is too young, I hope, for her expression to be more than imitation. I was astonished to hear so sensible an artist as Mr John Radcliffe play a ridiculously old-fashioned set of variations for the flute on Irish airs. Surely he does not seriously believe that any human being nowadays cares for such nonsense as the first variation on The Minstrel Boy. The composer named in the bill was Sauvelet. I wonder is this a flautist named Sauvelet whom I heard more than 20 years ago on a concert tour with Madame Demeric Lablache and a tenor, then comparatively unknown, named Edward Lloyd. The last thing I heard was the quartet from

Rigoletto, the success of which proved the wisdom of my advice the other day to the managers to make a feature of concerted music. I came away as the orchestra, abetted by the Coldstream Guards, began a tremendous assault and battery on Carmen. Arditi was in high feather, and shewed his histrionic ability by the cleverness with which he put on that touch of the ringmaster which has been expected from conductors at promenade concerts since Jullien's time.★ He was expansive, paternal, enthusiastic, and liberal with the most extravagantly superfluous leads to his veterans, most of whom could have done their work equally well in the dark.

BAYREUTH AND BACK

The Hawk, 13 August 1889; signed "By Reuter." The editor considered it necessary to explain the pseudonym in a footnote: "The appreciation of this joke lies in the pronunciation of it"

Oh Bayreuth, Bayreuth, valley of humiliation for the smart ones of the world! To think that this Wagner, once the very safest man in Europe to ridicule, should turn out the prime success of the century! To be reduced to a piteous plea that you always admitted that there were some lovely bits in Lohengrin! To know beyond all shifts of self-deception that, when you got your one great chance of discovering the great man of your age, you went the fools among, and made an utter, unmitigated, irretrievable, unspeakable ass of yourself! To humbly and anxiously ask whether there are any

★ Louis Jullien (1812–60), popular conductor and composer of dance music.

tickets left—to pay a pound apiece for them—to crawl, seasick and weary, hundreds of costly miles to that theatre which you so neatly proved to be the crazy whim of a conceited, cacophonous charlatan, there to listen to Tristan and the Meistersinger with the hideous guilt upon you of having once thought Lucia and La Favorita worth a dozen such. This is the sort of thing that takes the starch out of the most bumptious critic.

Yes, the cranks were right after all. And now—now that it is not merely a question of whether he or Offenbach is the more melodious, but of whether he is to be accepted as the Luther of a new Reformation, the Plato of a new philosophy, the Messiah who is really to redeem the fall and lead us back to the garden of Eden, now that the temple is up and the worshipers assembled, now that we are face to face with pretensions for "The Master" in comparison with which the old simple claim to rank as artist and man of genius was a mere joke, dare we pick up our weapons and resume our fight? No, thank you, the fellow is too dangerous. Better call him a man of extraordinary ability as if we had thought so all along, and then lie low and see whether he will really pull off his philosophic and religious venture as he undoubtedly pulled off his musical one, confound him!

You would not catch me talking in this strain if my own withers were wrung. No, I am not confessing my own mistakes; I am only rubbing in the mistakes of others. The first time I ever heard a note of Wagner's music was in my small boy days, when I stumbled upon a military band playing the Tannhäuser march. I will not pretend that I quite rose to the occasion; in fact, I said just what Hector Berlioz said—that it was a plagiarism from the famous theme in Der Freischütz. But a little after this bad beginning I picked up a score of Lohengrin; and before I had taken in ten bars of the prelude I was a confirmed Wagnerite in the sense the term then bore, which committed me to nothing further than greatly relishing Wagner's music. What it commits a man to now, Omniscience only knows. Vegetarianism, the higher Buddhism, Christianity divested of its allegorical trappings (I suspect this is a heterodox variety), belief in a Fall of Man brought about by some cataclysm which starved him into eating flesh, negation of the Will-to-Live and consequent Redemption through compassion excited by suffering (this is the Wagner-Schopenhauer article of faith); all these are but samples of what Wagnerism involves nowadays. The average enthusiast accepts them all unhesitatingly—bar vegetarianism. Buddhism he can stand; he is not particular as to what variety of Christianity he owns to; Schopenhauer is his favorite philosopher; but get through Parsifal without a beefsteak between the second and third acts he will not. Now, as it happens, I am a vegetarian; and I can presume enormously upon that habit of mine, even among the elect. But for an unlucky sense of humor which is continually exposing me to charges of ribaldry, I should have been elected a vice-president of the Wagner Society long ago.

However, these be matters into which this is not the place for a deep dip. The question of the moment is, what is Bayreuth like? Well, it is a genteel little Franconian country town among the hills and fine woods of Bavaria, within two or three hours' rail from Nuremburg. It is not old enough to be venerable, nor new enough to be quite prosaic; and the inhabitants either live in villas on independent incomes or else by taking in oneanother's washing and selling confectionery, scrapbooks, and photographs. There are plenty of street fountains, a nonsensically old-fashioned monument to a person generally described by vulgar English visitors as "old stick-in-the-mud," a factory chimney, a barrack, a lunatic asylum, a very quaint XVIII century opera house, the Wagner Theatre halfway up the hill, and the inevitable *Sieges Turm*, or tower commemorative of 1870–1, quite at the summit, among the pines. Half the main street is the Maximilianstrasse, and the other the Richard Wagnerstrasse. The Master's house is a substantial villa, undistinguishable from other villas except by the famous inscription:—*Hier wo mein Wähnen Frieden fand, Wahnfried sei dieses Haus von mir benannt,** and by a *sgraffito* cartoon much in the manner and taste of Mr Armitage,† representing Wotan the Wanderer. Behind the Master's house is the Master's grave; for Wagner, as I heard an indignant Englishman exclaim, is "buried in the back garden, sir, like a Newfoundland dog." I shall never be a true Wagnerite after all; for I laughed at this explosion of bourgeois prejudice, wheras any decently susceptible disciple would have recoiled horrorstricken. At certain hours the gate between the Wahnfried domain and the Hofgarten is left open; and the faithful go in to deposit wreaths on the colossal granite slab which covers the Master's last bed, and to steal ivy leaves as souvenirs. The only other sentimental journey available at Bayreuth is to the cemetery at the country end of the Erlangenstrasse, near the old town, where you see a boulder of unhewn stone on Jean Paul Richter's grave, and an inartistic and useless outhouse which is the mausoleum of Liszt.

The imagination rather declines to face the notion of life at Bayreuth without Wagner. Walks on the hills through the scented pine woods are always available; but dwellers in the next county to Surrey do not spend

* Literal translation: "Here where my imagination has found peace, this house shall be called by me the peace of imagination."

† Edward Armitage was a contemporary painter of historical and biblical subjects, who led the movement for the restoration of fresco painting in England.

twenty pounds to walk in Bavaria when a few shillings would land them at Guildford or Dorking. There are a couple of show places—the Fantaisie to the southwest, and the Eremitage to the east, which give some sort of aim for a couple of excursions, each capable of slaying two or three hours. They are something between a Wicklow glen and an Isle of Wight chine; and the Eremitage has a *château* with Temple of the Sun, pseudo-Roman bath, dolphins, tritons, and general rococo. On the whole, Bayreuth has to be put up with for Wagner's sake rather than enjoyed for its own. Business begins at the Wagner Theatre at four; but after two the stream of people up the hill is pretty constant, their immediate destination being the restaurant to the right of the theatre, and their immediate object—grub. At a quarter to four a group of men whom you at once recognize as members of the orchestra, as much by a certain air of Brixton or Kentish Town about them as by the trombones and cornets they carry, troop out of the centre door. These, by fearsome blasts, right and left, proclaim that the entertainment is about to begin. In spite of the vile noise they make, they are audible for a very short distance, partly because they stand under the portico instead of on top of it, partly because brass instruments should be blown quietly and musically if the sound is to travel (always excepting the nothing-if-not-violent bugle). In ten minutes or so it will be time to go into the famous theatre.

You have already bought your playbill in the street for a penny; and you will have to find your own seat among the fifteen hundred in the auditorium. However, this is easy enough, as your ticket directs you to, say, Door No. 2, Left Side. That door delivers you close to the end of the row in which your seat is, and as each corner seat is marked with the highest and lowest number contained in the row, you can, by a little resolute brainwork, find your place for yourself. Once in it, you have a stare round at the theatre. It is republican to begin with; the 1500 seats are separated by no barrier, no difference in price, no advantages except those of greater or less proximity to the stage. The few state cabins at the back, for kings and millionaires, are the worst places in the house. All this is pleasant; for if you are an aristocrat, you say "Good! a man can be no more than a gentleman," and if a democrat, you simply snort and say "Aha!" The wonder is that though this theatre has been known to the public for thirteen years, yet we have during that time run up a little host of playhouses, and never once dreamt of departing from the old cockpit-and-scaffold model. What a capital architectural feature is that series of side wings, each with its pillar and its branch of globes, causing the stage to grow out of the auditorium in the most natural manner! Sh-sh-sh! The lights are lowered. Sit down, everybody. Why do not the ladies take off their hats as requested by placard? Ah, why indeed? Now the lights are almost out; there is a dead silence; and the first strain of the prelude comes mystically from the invisible orchestra. And so on. When the act is over, there is a pause of an hour for late afternoon tea. After the second act comes a similar pause for supper. Thus do these ascetics emulate the Buddha.

It is too late in the day to describe the three lyric plays now being repeated at Bayreuth. Tristan—would you believe it?—is thirty years old. Die Meistersinger will be twentytwo next October. Certainly, Parsifal is quite a novelty—only ten years and a half; but Parsifal is not an affair to be sketched in a few lines. All that I shall say here, then, is that though the accounts of the tremendous effect they produce in the Wagner Theatre are not exaggerated, yet the process of getting tremendously affected is by no means a blissful one. I am a seasoned

Wagnerian; and there is no veil of strangeness between me and the ocean of melody, with all its cross-currents of beautiful and expressive themes, in Die Meistersinger. But at Bayreuth, after the third act, I had just energy enough to go home to my bed, instead of lying down on the hillside and having twelve hours' sleep *al fresco* there and then. That third act, though conducted by Hans Richter, who is no sluggard, lasts two hours; and the strain on the attention, concentrated as it is by the peculiarities of the theatre, is enormous. Consider, too, that the singers are not like De Reszke or Lassalle, refreshing to listen to. They are all veterans—hale and respectable veterans, irreproachably competent, with thick voices and intelligent declamation; but they are terribly dry. You are driven for a reviving draught of beauty of sound to the orchestra. Having heard that before, you are thrown back on the inner interest of the poem, and so forced to renew your grip with a closer application on the very thing you sought a moment's relief from. When it is over you are glad you went through with it, and are even willing to face it again; but you recognize that you have achieved edification by a great feat of endurance, and that your holiday, your enjoyment, your relaxation will come when the work of witnessing the performances is finished, and you are returning home down the Rhine. Parsifal, in spite of its prolonged and solemn ritual, is less fatiguing than the Meistersinger, although to the Philistine it is a greater bore; for the Meistersinger, long as it is, is bustling, whilst the shorter Parsifal is slow and serious. Not that the boredom saves any Philistine from the spell of the work; the merest scoffer is impressed, and would not unsee it, even if he could get his sovereign back at the same time. Tristan neither fatigues nor bores, except for a while at the end of the second act, if King Mark is dull, and during the first half of the third if the tenor is uninteresting. The rest is one transport; deafness and impotence combined could alone resist it; you come away hopelessly spoiled for Roméo et Juliette after it.

As to the peculiar merits of the Bayreuth mode of performance, they are simply the direct results of scrupulous reverence for Wagner, thorough study, and reasonable care. What has been said lately about the inferiority of the staging to that at the Lyceum is quite true. Admirable as the orchestra is, we can beat it in London as certainly as we can build the theatre the moment we are wise enough to see that it is worth our while. And the sooner the better, say I, for the sake of our English millions to whom Bayreuth is as inaccessible as the North Pole.

THE DEAD SEASON

The Star, 16 August 1889

This dead season, at least, enables the unfortunate Londoner to hear orchestral music every night for a shilling, and brings into use two-thirds of our stock of opera houses. We have three of them: Covent Garden, Her Majesty's, and Drury Lane. The space occupied by them is of enormous value; and I presume somebody pays the rent of that space to the ground landlord. Yet the theatrical work done by the three could be done equally well at any one of them. When melodrama is raging at Drury Lane, Covent Garden is idle. When Mr Harris goes to Covent Garden for the opera season, Drury Lane closes. Her Majesty's remains closed all the time, except when somebody is seized with an insane impulse to lose a few thousand pounds by providing the

[745]

deadheads of London with a fortnight or so of bad opera. Will some actuarial or mathematical reader kindly add up the square feet of space occupied by the three big houses, and divide the result by the total number of performances given in them during the year? If the result does not prove that we are far more extravagant in the matter of space than they are at Bayreuth, I will eat the paper or even the slate on which the calculation is made. Be it remembered, too, that the extravagance in space is nothing as compared to the extravagance in value; for the site of Her Majesty's alone must be worth half a dozen streets in Bayreuth. Yet when we complain of the inferiority of our theatres, we are always told that the necessity for economy of space makes a reasonable model impossible.

The calculation might be carried on to include all the prominent places of entertainment in London: the Albert Hall, the Globe, Olympic, Opera Comique, Shaftesbury, Novelty, and St James's theatres would of course be in the list. Here again it would certainly be found that a much smaller number of houses, and consequently of square feet of valuable space, would suffice for the work actually done. This is sheer waste of money produced by competition. Now, every intelligent man of business hates competitive waste. He longs to abolish the superfluous expenditure (carefully keeping up prices lest the public should be pauperized) and put the saving into his own pocket. Why should not this be attempted in the case of the theatres? All that is necessary is to substitute combination for competition, American fashion, by forming a Public Entertainments Trust to buy up all the theatres in London and throw them into a common stock. The superfluous ones could then be demolished, and the sites sold or let on building leases. All the older theatres might be demolished and replaced to the necessary extent by new ones, possibly on more favorable sites. The Trust would then have a monopoly of the London theatres: a monopoly which, astutely managed, might make any fresh attempt at competition unprofitable.

I may as well say beforehand that my position as critic would make it impossible for me to accept the position of chairman of the Trust; and the discouragement created by this difficulty may delay the project for some time. But in the meantime, combination is advancing. Mr Harris, for instance, is no longer competing at Drury Lane against the Alhambra, the Royal Italian Opera, and the Carl Rosa Company. He is interested in all three. This makes him powerful as against the race of artists. Suppose you are a lady of the ballet engaged at the opera, and you feel aggrieved at some act of the manager. Once upon a time you could say "Tyrant, I shake the dust of your theatre off my feet" (a dancer can do this very prettily) or "I go to obtain an engagement at the Drury Lane pantomime, where, perhaps, I shall be columbine." And if they annoyed her at Drury Lane, she could say "I will not stand this, I will go to the Alhambra." Nowadays, the three are practically all one establishment. When, after a few more years of competing syndicates, we have a great "combine" of the Harris, Leslie, D'Oyly Carte, and all the other interests, the spread of artistic culture in the meantime continually making pleasant young singers and actors more plentiful, and consequently cheaper, we shall have an agitation for a Factory Act applicable not merely to children under ten, but to all women over seventeen and men over eighteen.

Talking of the children under ten, I see that my friend Archer, in this week's World, returns to the Protection of Children Act by printing a dialogue which took place at Bayreuth between himself and some inconceivable idiot who defended the Act on the ground that Miss

Mabel Love* was a victim of mental overpressure, and generally served himself up on toast for immediate consumption by the eminent critic, who is unfortunately in favor of infant exploitation. Archer, in fact, has become a sort of theatrical Dr Barnardo,† eager to snatch children from the gutter and raise them to the culture and affluence of tinsel fairyland. The choice, he says, is "between the sty and the stage." The homes of the children are such that the stage pittance "converts misery into comparative comfort." Withdraw it, and "Back and side go bare, go bare: Foot and hand go cold."‡ Archer thinks that the demand for theatre children is so immense, and so small the supply of comparatively respectable children whose parents are quite willing to make a few extra shillings by them, that managers have to undertake the education of "sty children!"

But, even if it were so, what would be the effect on the earnings of the family? Archer is confident that the employer would not cut down the father's wage; and he is right: the employer might, on the contrary, have to raise the proffered wage in order to tempt the father to work at all. If I lived in misery in a sty, with my children naked as to their back, their sides, and their feet—that is, dressed in aprons alone—I should have formed a habit of living on, say, from nothing a week to eight or nine shillings, according to luck. And I should earn those shillings by brutalizing drudgery. Now, if some liberal-

* Young actress and dancer, who had recently gained attention in a Gaiety burlesque, Faust Up to Date. A month earlier, the fourteen-year-old performer had attempted suicide.

† Thomas John Barnardo, Dublin-born philanthropist, founded Dr Barnardo's Homes to assist destitute children.

‡ Drinking song in William Stevenson's play, Gammer Gurton's Needle (1575).

minded householder, overlooking the probability of my partner in the sty being by force of circumstances an uncleanly and dishonest person, were to offer her half-a-crown a week for charing, I would certainly not thereupon offer to accept a lower wage from my employer: rather would I take out the half-crown in six or seven hours' relief from my detested toil. And if by any extraordinary accident I had a pretty or shapely child, and that child put on its apron and called on Mrs John Wood to explain that it was in want of an engagement, and that lady benevolently clothed it, fine-tooth-combed it, introduced it to Miss Morleena Kenwigs* and the rest, and gave it five shillings a week, I should promptly retire from active industry altogether, feeling that I was improving myself by withdrawing from degrading and ruinous toil, and at the same time elevating my child in the manner so eloquently set forth by William Archer.

Archer would of course still be able to say quite logically that this was at least better than the former conditions, in which the child never escaped from the sty. The manager, he would argue, will take care that the child is well and happy. Is he not "directly interested in keeping his little troop physically fit?" Must they not "be bright, alert, and well disposed if they are to do their work properly and please the public?" Just like the child acrobat at the circus, with his well brushed hair, his physically fit muscles, his rosy complexion, and his cultivated mind! Just like the charming barmaid who must be bright, alert, and well disposed for fourteen hours a day, if she wishes to keep her place! How much better than being on the streets! The beauty of this sort

* Mrs John Wood was an old-time actress–manageress, still performing in London. Miss Kenwigs, a child attending dancing classes, is a character in Dickens's Nicholas Nickleby.

of logic is that if the system went on unchecked to the point of making children bear the whole burden of breadwinning in the proletarian community, Archer would always be forced to cry "Go on" and to oppose those who cried "Stop." You first put your children between the devil and the deep sea; and then, on philanthropic grounds, you push them to the devil to save them from drowning.

Briefly put, Archer's argument in favor of infant exploitation is that it is a remedy for poverty. Briefly put, the reply is that it isnt. Slightly amplified, the reply goes on to say that even if it were a remedy it would be a surpassingly dastardly one. Specially applied to the mistaken assumption that the theatre children are "sty" children, the reply is that the income of a sty never rises, because the head of it never works one hour more than absolute necessity compels him to. Specially applied to the correct assumption that the children are of the Kenwigs class, the reply is that the assertion that their board school education and drill and their home life are less healthy for them than theatrical training and night work, is an interested one, the commonsense objections to which have been evaded by the "sty" theory. Comprehensively applied to the contention that the managers' interests are identical with those of the children, the reply casts off its logical form and expresses itself through a symbol formed by applying the thumb to the tip of the nose and throwing the extended fingers into graceful action.

PROMS AT HER MAJESTY'S

The Star, 19 August 1889

I was greatly grieved on Saturday at Her Majesty's to see
that out of the 100 orchestral players announced, only
76—even including 20 Scots Guards—were in their
places. The other 24 are, I fear, seriously ill, or they
would hardly have failed Mr Leslie on so important an
occasion. I trust we shall see the poor fellows back at
their posts before the season is over.

The house looked better than I expected; for, if the
truth must out, I was at the private view on Thursday,
and the reason I said nothing about it here was that the
"Old London" decoration seemed to me to destroy the
gaiety of the house and to turn an imposing interior into
a ghastly, zinc-colored travesty of an open-air scene.
However, on Saturday, with the finishing touches
added, with the floor and the muddy sandbanks under
the orchestra hidden by a crowd of promenaders too
closely packed to promenade, and with powerful lights
everywhere, matters were greatly improved; and I am
now prepared to admit that the decorations serve their
turn well enough. Signor Bevignani looked much
pleased with himself, and got on fairly well until he
attempted the shepherds' dance, the storm, and the
thanksgiving *finale* from the Pastoral Symphony (compendiously described in the program as "scherzo"),
when, I am sorry to say, he covered himself, and the
orchestra, with humiliation. The band, instead of
holding the harmonies, attacked them anyhow, and let
the tone tail off at once; and Signor Bevignani, under
the erroneous impression that this sort of kid-glove
trifling with music still passes for orchestral playing in

London, tried to cover up the thin spots by hurrying on, which, of course, made matters worse. I must say that if Signor Bevignani is so hopelessly out of it as not to have learnt that we do things differently nowadays, the band, at least, know better, and ought, for their own credit, to astonish him with some of the sustained tone that Richter would expect—and would get—from them. Mr Howard Reynolds sets a capital example in this respect: indeed, the Waldteufel waltz, which was his *cheval de bataille*, was the only piece in which I heard twopenn'orth of tone from the strings; but I wish Mr Reynolds would not make a point of forcing at least two notes in each solo to the point of splitting the ears of everyone, groundling or other, within range of his cornet. And if he would delicately hint to his two colleagues that they get half the intervals in the opening phrase of Tchaikovsky's Italian Caprice most detestably out of tune, he will greatly oblige me. M. Vladimir de Pachmann gave his well-known pantomimic perform-ance, with accompaniments by Chopin, a composer whose music I could listen to M. de Pachmann playing for ever if the works were first carefully removed from the pianoforte. During the Doris selection I wandered about the house inattentively; but I was struck by the beauty of tone and accuracy of intonation of a euphoni-um soloist—Mr Guilmartin, I presume—who was not mentioned in the program. Mr Edward Lloyd, wildly encored, gave us When other lips, Come into the garden, Maud, and so forth. Miss Alice Gomez sang *Porgi amor* not so effectively as on other occasions, but still attractively. After Mr Lloyd's second appearance I fled, M. de Pachmann being imminent; and I have only to add that the place has a successful air, and that the ventilation is much better upstairs than down.

MOZART AND WAGNER

The Star, 23 August 1889

One cannot be always chronicling promenade concerts, even in August and September. As there is nothing else to chronicle just now, I am thrown back for matter on the letters of my correspondents, and on the general resources of my intellect. In busy times I often wonder whether the gentlemen who take the trouble to write to me about musical affairs ever have their breath taken away by the calmness with which their information is, without the slightest acknowledgment, appropriated and retailed in this column as an original product of the vast factory in which my brain machinery works up the raw material of my experience. Let me explain to them, however, that when their information arrives, I sometimes know already, and sometimes know better.

One epistolarian who went to the "classical night" at Covent Garden on Wednesday, found that the audience liked Herr Friedheim's pianizing better than Mozart's G minor symphony. Indignant thereat, he waited in the hope that the thunders of The Star would avenge Mozart. But he was disappointed; for I did not go to that concert. Why? Because I foresaw that the symphony would, in the words of my correspondent, be "hardly cheered at all." A Mozart symphony at a promenade concert never is cheered except by a few mistaken devotees, who are jealous for the supremacy of the classical masterpieces. But your even Christian wisely declines to cheer, voting the thing as vapid as flat soda water. Give him, he says, something rousing, something warm and alive, something with substance and entrails in it: a rattling selection from Doris, or a solo by Mr

Howard Reynolds that makes his diaphragm vibrate. And he is quite right. His is honest love of music sincerely seeking a genuine gratification. As such it is far more respectable and hopeful than the "culture" that pretends to relish the insipid classic it thinks it ought to like, and with which it is inwardly utterly disappointed.

So then, cries Culture, the low nature of the creature is confessed at last. Corno di Bassetto is a Philistine: he thinks classical music insipid, and prefers cornet solos! Good Mr Culture, be honest. It is you and such as you with your hypocrisies and affectations that keep sham classical performances in countenance. Do you suppose that when the orchestral parts of a Mozart symphony are placed before a body of players who can fiddle off the notes without hesitating, there is nothing more to be done than to set up somebody to beat one-two-three-four, and then let every player rip ahead? Apparently you do; for you pay for it and pretend to like it. What is more, you turn up your nose at the people whom you take for novices because they will not join in your humbug, and who, for all you know, may be experts, aware that the random shots of the orchestra are flying as wide of Mozart's intention as a schoolgirl's shot at the Pathetic Sonata flies wide of Beethoven. Do you really believe that the verdict of a hundred years on Mozart has come from a packed jury of pretenders to culture? If you do, then nothing can be done except leave you to your chance of some day hearing a Mozart symphony played as Mozart meant it to be played. You will applaud with a will then; and you will find plenty of others to help you. In the meantime, kindly recollect that applauding what you dont like is only one out of a great many ways of telling a lie.

By the way, my correspondent must not take these scathing rebukes to himself unless he deserves them. I have no reason to class him with the race of culture humbugs. But this subject of Mozart circuitously reminds me of a viper who has bitten me in a weekly paper—a Sunday paper too. Last Sabbath morning a relative threw me into a paroxysm of fury by reading aloud a paragraph in which the writer asked would I be surprised to learn something. This is an insult—an intentional insult. No matter what it is that I would be surprised to learn, that way of putting it breathes envy, disparagement, rancor, belittlement, and intolerable assumption of superior knowledge. No, sir: I am not surprised to learn that you are quite satisfied that everything that was done at the Bayreuth Festival playhouse when Wagner was alive was done exactly according to his intentions. That is just what I should have expected from a man capable of so injuriously reflecting on a colleague who never injured him.

I ask—addressing myself to the intelligent and well-disposed *alone*—I ask what mortal reason there is for assuming that Wagner ever succeeded in getting one single detail of Parsifal done at Bayreuth to his entire satisfaction? When a lyric dramatist carefully writes a stage direction which clearly suggests a very happy effect, and the attempt to carry it out on the stage utterly fails to realize that effect, am I to be told that the failure is exactly what the composer meant, because he, too, had to put up with it?

Wagner was in a dilemma at Bayreuth. Early in his career he had been disheartened by the inanity of the conventional performances of Mozart's instrumental works; and he had been hugely delighted with the way in which the orchestra of the Paris Conservatoire executed Beethoven's last and greatest symphony. In Mozart's case nothing had come down concerning the composer's own manner of conducting except a tradition that he was extraordinarily exacting in point of expression, and that the orchestras of his time found it hard to

[755]

play some of his *allegros* fast enough to please him. Furthermore, his scores contain very scanty indications of how they are to be dealt with. In Paris, on the other hand, the Conservatoire orchestra kept alive an exhaustive treatment of the Ninth Symphony, formed, in the first instance, by three seasons' dogged rehearsal under Habeneck. Warned by these striking instances, negative and positive, of the value of tradition, he naturally set great store by the establishment of an exceptionally authoritative one for his own works. He not only filled his scores with marks of expression, but contrived at last to build a special theatre for typical performances of his lyric dramas. At that theatre accordingly the artists are in possession of a mass of authentic tradition, the value of which is considerable in the prevalent scarcity of original interpretative talent. But the difficulty is that the tradition includes all the shortcomings as well as the excellencies of the representations personally superintended by Wagner. Every practical artist knows that such shortcomings are, under existing circumstances, inevitable, even when cash does not run short, as it did at the first Bayreuth Festival in 1876. It is therefore perfectly legitimate to appeal to the directions in Wagner's score as against the Bayreuth traditional practice, and perfectly unreasonable to call my omniscience in question for doing so.

Reverting for a moment to the question of cornet performances, I wish the musical ambition which that instrument undeniably inspires in the breast of amateurs were better guided than at present. I am not now speaking of the drawing-room amateur, who ought promptly to be converted into a lethal chamber amateur, but to the members of the brass bands of the volunteer corps, Salvation Army, the police force, and the musicians who play in the clubs of working men, or accompany them in demonstrations. There is no artistic limit to the ambition of a wind band: it may discourse as fine music as any orchestra, and in as worthy a manner. I do not see why we should not in time have in each of our parks a wind band at least a hundred and twenty strong, playing transcriptions of the works of the greatest masters, and educating the people out of their present meek submission to trashy quicksteps and music-hall tunes.

I imagine that the difficulty of getting good band-masters is a more formidable obstacle to improvement than the costliness of good instruments; for I notice that even in pretentious volunteer bands the men do not seem to have been shewn how to make the most of such instruments as they have. The notes produced by the pistons are often horribly out of tune, because the tuning slides have not been adjusted, the guilty performer not knowing the use of them. In processioning and dem-onstrating bands, execrable villains with brass instru-ments are allowed to "vamp": that is, improvize their parts by feeling for a few of the simplest diatonic harmonies, and grunting them out on the off-chance of their fitting in. During a march in the key of G they play F natural and C in alternate bars, occasionally hastily trying B flat when seized with a momentary misgiving that all is not well. I have not space to enlarge on the subject this week; but I think I shall return to it some of these days; for the brass band is really the music of the masses. I remember once making an impassioned speech from the balustrade of Trafalgar Square with a band playing the Marseillaise in four different keys close behind me. That is the sort of thing that makes a critic thoroughly in earnest about his work.

MORE PROMS

The Star, 24 August 1889

The managers at Her Majesty's kindly sent me a ticket for Thursday night to hear a young lady of nine play the violin. I prefer not to be an accomplice in the exploitation of young ladies of nine, so I did not go until the following night, when classical doings were afoot. Signor Bevignani's orchestra has settled down into the most charming drawing-room orchestra conceivable at a promenade concert. It has no force; but it is polite and delicate, and can put in the touches for wood wind and horns into a Mendelssohn symphony or a Mozart accompaniment with the gentlest of breaths. It was, of course, not within ten tons of the weight of the Zauberflöte overture; but not at Bayreuth itself was the Meistersinger prize song more sweetly accompanied. M. de Pachmann also played very prettily. The whole atmosphere was pre-Wagner, reminding one of Mendelssohn and Spohr and the Prince Consort. Also, perhaps, of Poole* and Lincoln and Bennett. I was glad, for the honor of a once famous name, when Miss Marie Tietjens, whom I had not heard before, sang *Vedrai carino* quite unexceptionally, with a voice still fragile, and hardly quite formed yet in the middle, but of remarkably pure and pleasant tone and perfect intonation. To Mr Holman Black, who attempted the serenade from Don Giovanni, and came off rather nervously, I will just say that he has learnt the song from an edition in which the words are wrongly set, a very easy thing to do; for none of the English

* John Poole, author of theatre comedies and farces early in the century.

[758]

editions, as far as I know, except Novello's, contain the restorations of Mozart's phrasing to be found in Breitkopf and Hartel's great edition. The lines *Tu che il zucchero porte in mezzo core*, are now really out of the question as Mr Black sings them. He will find, too, that the effect of the last bar of the song is not in the B, C, D which he makes so much of, but in the lower D. Fashionable baritones can make nothing of the song, because they sacrifice the middle of their voice to the top. When a composer uses the contrast between the upper and lower D—one of the most effective of vocal contrasts with a completely cultivated bass voice—they are at a loss. However, it is better to fail on the low note written by Mozart than to try for a high F sharp, as the fashion once was. Mr Black afterwards rashly sang a new setting of The Minstrel Boy by somebody bearing the illustrious name of Shelley. The audience took this rather in bad part, not unjustifiably; for the new tune was a commonplace march, much inferior to the old one. On the other hand, they encored Mr Lloyd rapturously in the Preislied from Die Meistersinger and in Alice, where art thou? and behaved handsomely to M. Tivadar Nachéz, who fiddled, and to Mr Howard Reynolds. Among the announcements for this evening is "Mrs Shaw, the American Lady Whistler." I cannot make this out: if she is Mrs Shaw, how can she be Lady Whistler? Señor Albéniz takes the place of Mr de Pachmann as solo pianist.

STILL PROMENADING!

The Star, 30 August 1889

Still promenading! I went to Covent Garden on Wednesday to hear the classical program, and to Her Majesty's on the previous Saturday to hear Mrs Shaw,* who is not, after all, the American Lady Whistler, but an American lady whistler, which is not exactly the same thing. Mrs Shaw is a tall, dark, pleasantly-favored woman, with a good deal of cheek, not too chubby, but just slack enough to allow plenty of play to her lips. After the manner of her countrywomen, she travels with enormous wreaths and baskets of flowers, which are handed to her at the conclusion of her pieces. And no matter how often this happens, she is never a whit the less astonished to see the flowers come up.

They say that the only artist who never gets accustomed to his part is the performing flea who fires a cannon, and who is no less dismayed and confounded by the three-hundredth report than by the first. Now it may be ungallant, coarse, brutal even; but whenever I see a fair American thrown into raptures by her own flower basket, I always think of the flea thrown into convulsions by its own cannon. And so, dear but silly American ladies, be persuaded, and drop it. Nobody except the very greenest of greenhorns is taken in; and the injury you do to your artistic self-respect by condescending to take him in is incalculable. Just consider for a moment how insanely impossible it is that

* Alice J. Shaw, who appears to have been equally at home in the concert hall and on the variety stage, was billed as "La Belle Siffleuse."

a wreath as big as a cart-wheel could be the spontaneous offering of an admiring stranger.

If these persuasions do not avail, sterner methods must be taken. The public can protect themselves by organization. There is—or was—an institution called the Playgoers' Club. Some day I shall get up an affiliated Society of Hissers and Hooters, whose mission it will be to attend "first appearances" in force, and hiss all bogus demonstrations until the sight of a basket of flowers becomes more dreadful to a *débutante* than any fear of a cold reception could possibly be. However, I shall not leave my Society plunged for ever in the barbarism from which hissing and hooting survive. It is a savage thing to assail a possibly nervous artist with fierce sibillations and booings. At a well-conducted public meeting a gentle, but very expressive murmur of "Oh! oh!" is quite sufficient to bring to his senses a speaker who says or does anything unbecoming. My club shall be trained to "Oh! Oh!" like cooing doves at a first offence. Only persistent wrongdoing will be dealt with by hissing, or, in the last extremity, by brickbats.

But to return to Mrs Shaw. I cannot say that her performance astonished me. Indeed, when I had conquered my first impulse to laugh at the oddity of this novel *prima donna* gravely whistling Arditi's *Il Bacio* to the orchestral accompaniment, I began to entertain serious thoughts of going into the business myself. I am by no means an exceptionally gifted whistler; but at the very first trial I found that I could get within a sixteenth of a semitone of B natural, which is apparently Mrs Shaw's highest note. As to *Il Bacio*, with its pretty but easy and trumpery *bravura*, who could not whistle that? Now if Mrs Shaw had whistled the waltz from Gounod's Romeo, or the Shadow Song from Dinorah, there would have been something in the feat. The audience seemed hugely amused and delighted; but unless Mrs Shaw can greatly surpass her performance of Saturday, any demand her success may create for lady whistlers is sure to bring forward a dozen equally brilliant performers.

As far as my knowledge of whistling goes there are two methods open to the virtuoso. One, Mrs Shaw's method and mine, is to whistle with the lips and tongue. This produces the best results as far as purity and flexibility are concerned. The other, which totally baffles me, but which comes naturally to a talented friend of mine, is to open a corner of the mouth, tuck it under the ear, and whistle through the back teeth. The tone produced is penetrating in quality, and will attract the attention of a disengaged cabman at a great distance. Mrs Shaw makes no use of this method even in *forte* passages, perhaps because it is somewhat lacking in facial beauty. On the whole, my verdict upon her is that she lacks sustaining power and volume of tone, and that *Il Bacio* is not a sufficiently arduous test to entitle her to claim a first-class as a florid whistler. As a further test, I should suggest the performance by some competent singer of the final air from L'Etoile du Nord, with the double flute *obbligato* by Mr Barretti* and Mrs Shaw. But in order to make the comparison fair, Mr Barrett must wear a corset sufficiently powerful to deprive him of at least half his natural lung capacity.

I invite the attention of the Covent Garden orchestra to the fact that they are completely beaten at Her Majesty's in point of style and discipline. The spirit of Costa is still abroad there. On this particular whistling Saturday I heard hardly any blunders: a more alert and conscientious band could not have been desired at a promenade concert. Their performance of the Masan-

* Barretti was the Italianized name used professionally by the English flautist William L. Barrett, which had led to much chaffing by his colleagues at the Savage Club.

iello overture was brilliant—so brilliant, in fact, that Signor Bevignani lost his head over it and spoiled the *coda* by first letting it run away with him, and then running away with it. The audience recognized the success at once; for, stupidly as the mere bar loafers at these concerts keep up a foolish and mechanical round of applause and encores for everything, good or bad, you hear the difference at once when the clapping is taken up by the people who only applaud when they know why.

At Covent Garden on Wednesday I heard the Lost Chord with the orchestral accompaniment which Madame Antoinette Sterling eschewed after her first experience of it at the Crystal Palace. The scoring of the last verse wants grandeur of tread: it does not march; and much of the effect is lost in consequence. Madame Belle Cole—well, I hardly like to say why Madame Belle Cole's voice is less free and resonant than it was. But how is the importance of physical training for singers to be duly insisted on if critics shrink from personalities? The training of a champion wrestler, who is nothing if not eighteen stone, is one thing: the training of a vocalist is another; but both have, within certain limits, power to choose their own weight. For instance, no human being need weigh more than fourteen stone at most unless he or she pleases. I remember Tietjens as Fidelio and as Margaret; and I cannot help asking myself whether mischief such as she did to the poetry of the lyric drama by for years associating its heroines with monstrous obesity is never to be rebuked or even noticed by a suffering public. Loth as I am to condemn a lady to drink nothing for two months except six gallons of boiling water *per diem*, yet there are circumstances which justify this extremity. I venture desperately to blurt out to Madame Belle Cole that if she continues to grow as she has grown since the middle of the season, she will, in a few years, be quite fat. And fat spoils artists. Look at Hans Richter, the greatest orchestral conductor we know. When he first came here with Wagner, twelve years or so ago, he was only half as wide as he is now, but he was twice as effective. Everybody whispers that there is a falling off of late years. Alas! there is, on the contrary, a putting on, and that is the secret of the growing impatience and incompleteness of his achievements. Macadam designed a little ring, through which he declared that a stone must be small enough to pass before it was fit for paving. The entrance to our concert platforms should be guarded by a hoop of standard diameter—say six feet to begin with—through which all the artists should be compelled to pass successively before taking part in the performance.

A newcomer at this Wednesday concert was the pianist, Madame Roger-Miclos, who played Beethoven's comparatively youthful C minor concerto*: a curious selection for such an occasion. She is a swift, accurate, steely-fingered player, who can make a scale passage sound as if it were made by a dexterous whipcut along the keyboard. I admire Madame Roger-Miclos much as I admire the clever people who write a hundred and eighty words a minute with a typewriter. Her classic Madame de Stael draperies suited her slim figure, Egyptian profile, and cold style. She was the only artist who came off without a mishap. When Madame Belle Cole repeated the last two verses of the Lost Chord, in response to an *encore*, the wood wind got a bar before her at the start. When Mr Barrington Foote came forth to sing Nazareth, the band, insufficiently instructed as to the transposition required, began simultaneously in two different keys. Mlle Colombati, attempting to sing *Batti, batti* on the most superficial acquaintance with it,

* No. 3, Op. 37.

strayed into the second verse during the first, and caused Signor Arditi to turn with a shiver of agony and rage and prompt her by bursting into song himself. His voice, a counter tenor, has a gooselike quality which is startlingly effective. Mr Foote tried to drown the trombone, but was easily overcrowed by Mr Hadfield.

THE OPERA SEASON
The Scottish Art Review, September 1889

It is grim work watching an opera season in London. In his stall sits the English gentleman in evening dress, taking on trust his guinea's-worth of guaranteed Mozart or Wagner as ignorantly as a ploughman takes Cibber or Garrick on trust as genuine Shakespear. He is walled in with a hotly oppressive crimson pigeonhouse of private boxes, filled with countless women in white, glittering and chattering, shaking diamonds and flapping fans. Over his head is a monstrous chandelier, hanging by a huge chain, which may snap, he thinks, at any moment; and clustered about it, on the roof of the crimson pigeonhouse, swelters a crowd representing the general public, at half-a-crown and five shillings a head. On the stage an opera tumbles along with cuts here and cuts there, the detail of the action sometimes slurred, sometimes omitted, never simultaneous with its indication in the orchestra; the singers' opportunities for display are strung together in no relation more organic than that between the feats in a circus; and the prompter is working desperately to make up for insufficient rehearsal and want of forethought. This is the ordinary "subscription night," upon which the subscriber gets for his money the most perfunctory Traviata or Trovatore that the management can venture upon without loss of prestige or flagrant breach of faith. There is little risk at the hands of the critics; for the standard of excellence is very low; and those who are disposed to screw it up, having once exhausted the possible variations on the same complaint, drop the subject lest they should repeat themselves and seem barren. Besides, a musical critic is too busy during the season to pay much attention to ordinary subscription-night performances, even were his editor able to spare space. Moreover, the short-comings are everybody's fault: that is, nobody's fault. If Mr Augustus Harris were asked why his melodramas at Drury Lane are so much better done than his operas at Covent Garden, he would reply—if his startled *amour-propre* did not hide the right answer from him—that if he had to put on a different melodrama every night, the shortcomings of Covent Garden would immediately appear at Drury Lane.

The truth of this will be disputed by no one who remembers what "stock company" acting was. The operatic artist of today is a "stock company" artist. He calls himself a *primo tenore* or a *basso cantante* instead of a juvenile lead or a first old man; but the difference is only technical. Just as the stock actors could take any part in their line at short notice by learning or recalling the lines, and applying their stage habits to the action; so within one week do the Covent Garden artists contrive to get through Lohengrin, La Traviata, La Sonnambula, Aïda, and Le Nozze di Figaro. And just as the old stock company performances as wholes had absolutely no artistic quality, and never produced even a momentary illusion except on the merest novices; so these operatic representations are ineffective beyond endurance by musicians of independent and original culture. The public, however, is still in its novitiate, and has always resented the protests of such critics as Schumann, Berlioz, and Wagner, much as a schoolboy resents his father's impatience of the farce and reluctance to wait for the harlequinade. Mere protest against inferior work never educates the public. The only way to make them intolerant of bad work is to shew them better. It was the traveling company with its repertory of one thoroughly mastered play that drove the stock companies from our provincial theatres, not because the actors were individually cleverer than the members of the stock companies, but because their collective performance had a completeness and produced an illusion, after one experience of which the scratch performances of the stock companies could no longer be endured. The stock company accordingly vanished before the "tour." The change has been described, by advocates of the old-fashioned training, as a triumph of superior economic over superior artistic organization; but the slightest analysis of the economic position will shew that the case was exactly the reverse, since the stationary companies saved, without set-off, the traveling expenses which were so heavy an item in the cost of production of the tour.

This season a remarkable event sounded an alarm for stock companyism in opera. An Italian company came to London with one opera—Verdi's Otello—and astonished the frequenters of Covent Garden by the force and homogeneity of the impression made by its performance. The grip of the drama on the audience, the identification of the artists with their parts, the precision of execution, the perfect balance of the forces in action, produced an effect which, for the first time, justified the claims of Italian opera to rank as a form of serious drama united to purposeful music. The usual romantic explanations of this success were freely offered—Italian aptitude, great artists, La Scala, Wagnerian methods, and so on; but thorough preparation was the real secret. The belief in Italian aptitude for lyric drama is a superstition from

[767]

the Puritani period. Ever since opera began to assume a really dramatic character the Italian singer has lost his place on the stage, and has even come to be recognized as the least teachable and intelligent member of his profession. In the particular case in question there were three parts requiring special artistic excellence for their due presentation. One of them was played by M. Maurel, a Frenchman, who has repeatedly appeared at Covent Garden in leading parts without ever producing a tithe of the effect made by his Iago at the Lyceum. Another, that of Desdemona, was taken by an Italian, who was the one failure of the representation: her artificial stage business, false pathos, and wavering voice being tolerated for the sake of the whole of which her performance was the least worthy part. In that of Otello himself, there was an Italian, Tamagno, undoubtedly a quite exceptional artist, whose voice seems to have reached the upper part of the theatre with overwhelming power, though to others some of the current descriptions of its volume seemed hyperbolical. His voice, at any rate, had not the pure noble tone, nor the sweetly sensuous, nor even the ordinary thick manly quality of the robust tenor: it was nasal, shrill, vehement, sometimes fierce, sometimes plaintive, always peculiar and original. Imitation of Tamagno has ruined many a tenor, and will probably ruin many more; but the desire to produce such an effect as he did with *Addio sante memorie!* is intelligible to anyone who rightly understands the range of an Italian tenor's ambition. Yet it was certainly not to hear *Addio sante memorie!* that the audiences filled the Lyceum night after night during the dog-days: it was to hear Otello; and there was always a protest against the inevitable *encore* on the ground of interruption to the drama. Faccio, the conductor, understands Verdi's music as Richter understands Wagner's. He accompanies with perfect judgment, as he conducts with perfect

[768]

authority. Like the Bayreuth conductors, and unlike the Covent Garden ones, he had only one opera to think about; and the result was a mastery of it quite as complete as Hermann Levi's of Parsifal or Felix Mottl's of Tristan und Isolde. In amplitude and richness of sonority, beauty of tone, delicacy of execution, and distinction of style, the Milan orchestra might justly have claimed precedence of Bayreuth if the tasks of the two had been at all fairly comparable in point of difficulty.

The Otello enterprise was an enormously expensive one, yet we are told that no loss was suffered by the managers. There is hope, then, that the blow which its artistic success dealt to the subscription-night opera of fashion may prove speedily mortal. It has already raised the standard of operatic acting. Ordinarily, the opera singer is satisfied if he can catch some notion of the incidents which come into his own stage business, and of the situations in which he himself figures; and he is usually inoculated with some tradition as to certain characters, as, for instance, that Mephistopheles is a sardonic smiler and *poseur*, Don Giovanni a swaggering libertine. When these vague notions modify his conventional attitudinizing to the extent of giving it an air of energy and purpose, and even suggesting that he knows the story which the opera tells, and is taking some steps to make it clear to the audience, he shines out as comparatively an actor, and is gravely commended by the newspapers in terms which dramatic critics reserve for Mr Irving and Mr Jefferson, Salvini and Coquelin.*

* Joseph Jefferson was an American actor who had performed frequently in Britain. His most famous *rôles* were Rip Van Winkle and Bob Acres in Sheridan's The Rivals. Benoît Constant Coquelin was one of France's greatest actors, a member of the Comédie Française company, who later created the *rôle* of Cyrano de Bergerac.

Thus, at Covent Garden this season, a Monsieur F. d'Andrade made an indifferent De Nevers and a bad Don Giovanni, but displayed some smartness and intelligent interest in his business, and played with much natural expression and sincerity as Telramond in Lohengrin. He was at first acclaimed as a new histrionic genius. But after Maurel's Iago, nothing more was said of d'Andrade. Maurel played like a man who had read Shakespear and had conceived an Iago with which he was thoroughly preoccupied. Having repeated the impersonation for a long period without interruption or distraction, he was practised in identifying himself with it—had got into the skin of it, as the phrase goes. He had, too, emancipated himself from the prompter, and thus left himself nothing to think about but Iago. The result was that he made a considerable reputation as an actor by the ordinary standard, wheras formerly at Covent Garden, where he was expected to play Peter the Great, Valentine, Telramond, Hoel, and Don Juan within a fortnight, he was only an actor by courtesy, and by contrast with colleagues who were still more superficial than he. Now he is an actor on the same plane as Mr Edwin Booth, and may claim to be one of the notable Iagos of his time. It is a strong exaggeration to speak of him as the best Iago on the stage; for he is demonstrative and pretentious to a degree that would hardly pass without a smile at the Lyceum in winter; and the raillery of the critic who described his Iago as "twopence colored" was not without point. But it was none the less a new departure of the most hopeful kind in operatic acting.

At Covent Garden Mr Harris kept up the reputation of his management by the production of some newly-prepared and carefully-rehearsed works. Bizet's Pearl Fishers was not worth the trouble. The scale of the performance was too large; the staging was stupidly unimaginative; and Talazac, the Opéra Comique tenor, whose former appearance in London at the Gaiety Theatre with Miss Van Zandt seemed to be quite forgotten, did not interest the public. He is now a short, stout man, with an odd air of always being in the way on the stage, and nothing attractive in his singing except the power of sustaining for a long time a sweet but rather wheezy *mezza voce*. Gounod's Roméo et Juliette, which followed after the usual padding of ordinary subscription-night performances, was produced on the ground, artistically quite irrelevant, that Madame Patti, having recently appeared as Juliette in Paris, had given the opera a valuable advertisement. As a "grand opera" it has never been satisfactory. Its delicate music requires an exquisite tenderness of handling which would be lost in Covent Garden; and the great length of the work, which, except the fiery third act, is in the same vein throughout, makes it tedious in spite of the beauty of the music. The Shakespearean original itself seldom passes without an occasional yawn; but if four of the acts had been rewritten by Lamartine we should go fast asleep over it, though the result would have been a perfect literary analogue to Gounod's opera, enjoyable only under conditions more favorable to contemplative serenity than a fashionable opera house affords.

A more important event was the production of Die Meistersinger, or as much of it as there was time for between half-past seven and a quarter-past twelve. In neither of these sufficiently arduous achievements was there any drawback that can justly be laid to the charge of the management. The preparation was elaborate and thorough, the mounting costly even to extravagance. Unfortunately the all-important functions of the conductor, with whom it lies to make much or little of the opportunities provided by managerial expenditure, were not quite adequately discharged. Signor

Mancinelli's industry was most praiseworthy; he has his work at heart—which is a hundred points in his favor; and he is fairly competent for something more than the ordinary work of a conductor of Italian opera. But in dealing with works in which violent musical crises have to be marshaled with vigor and coolness—Les Huguenots, for instance—he loses control; and he has never succeeded in impressing on his players that distinction of style which a band always receives from a fine conductor. In Die Meistersinger the performance of the overture was the worst on record in London, and in the broader and more complex sections throughout the instrumental effect was noisy and confused. The close comparison with Richter at St James's Hall and Faccio at the Lyceum brought all these shortcomings into mercilessly strong relief. A conductor of Richter's calibre would soon win for Covent Garden the artistic rank which its wealth of artistic material renders possible. A strong chief is wanted there all the more because the string band is largely manned by young and very rough players, to whose artistic conscience Signor Mancinelli has not been able to penetrate.

The main strength of the company has been, as usual, vocal, though there has been no attempt to "star" on important occasions. The cleverness of Madame Melba and Miss Russell, remarkable in degree, is commonplace in quality; and Miss Macintyre, though her position is now an assured one, is still too young and amateurish to make it possible to predict whether she will be developed by her internal artistic instinct, or spoiled by her early prima-donnaship. Madame Albani's "heavy lead" was challenged only by Madame Toni Schläger (from Vienna), who, as Valentine, looked like a magnificent woman in deep distress, and sang like a great singer who had for the moment forgotten how to sing. She certainly made her mark; but it is beyond human wit to say whether she failed or succeeded. Though she is a much more tragic person than Madame Marie Roze, she nevertheless resembles her in a curious combination of unusual ability and endowment with a sort of helpless beauty that disarms criticism of her want of skill. The men, on the whole, distinguished themselves more than the women. M. Jean de Reszke's inbred refinement of bearing, the charm of his voice, and his occasionally inspired declamation made him an ideal Romeo. M. Lassalle's Sachs far surpassed all his previous achievements: if Theodor Reichmann could only sing the part with Lassalle's voice, we should have an ideal Mastersinger. As San Bris in the unfortunate performance of Les Huguenots which brought forward Madame Schläger, he made much less effect than Edouard de Reszke, who played it last year, but relinquished it this time to take the part of Marcel, which proved too low for his voice, and considerably overtaxed his histrionic intelligence. The management was at a loss for a heavy basso more than once, the Commendatore in Don Giovanni coming heavily to grief in the hands of Signor de Vaschetti, whose failing is a propensity to sing startling wrong notes. Montariol was not very interesting as a first tenor; but he was most serviceable as David and Tybalt, concerning which some ridicule was tactlessly brought on him by repeated announcements that in condescending to such parts he was sacrificing his dignity "to oblige the management." The performance of Roméo et Juliette in the original French was the most important step in advance made during the season. It pleased everybody, wheras the perversion of Die Meistersinger into Italian pleased nobody, except perhaps the lazier members of the chorus.

Mr Mapleson's attempt at Her Majesty's to interest the public with the old Italian repertory for its own sake—he had no artists of special note—was a decisive failure. The Bayreuth performances pointed the moral of this failure, and drove home the lesson of the Lyceum.

AN OCCIDENTAL MECCA?

The Star, 6 September 1889

I notice that my respected colleagues speak with humble submission, and even with approval, of the intention attributed to Madame Wagner of reserving the right of performing Parsifal for Bayreuth exclusively. In other words, the whole world is to be robbed of one of its most precious heirlooms for the glorification of a stupid little Bavarian town about as large as Notting Hill Gate and its neighborhood. Such a report, if I believed it, would almost reconcile me to the custom of suttee. As it happens, I do not believe it; but I am none the less amazed at the frame of mind which can accept it as tamely as if such a monstrous exercise of the rights of property were perfectly natural and proper. It is bad enough that such rights should, under any circumstances, be vested in an irresponsible private person; but the mere suggestion of enclosing Parsifal for the autumnal sport of a few thousand tourists and journalists ought to elicit a vehement protest from the exponents of musical opinion from one end of Europe to the other. It is not for Madame Wagner to say where or by whom any of Wagner's works shall be performed, except that she may reasonably insist on having, besides her royalties, some guarantee that the performances will be of sufficient merit to maintain the commercial prestige of the copyright. The rest is between us and our artistic consciences.

The whole tendency to make Bayreuth an occidental

Mecca ought to be resisted tooth and nail in England. The English people have little enough part in fashionable opera in London, with its guinea stalls; but Covent Garden is a people's palace compared with Bayreuth, to witness a single performance at which costs a Londoner at least five days' absence and £12 out of pocket. Such luxuries concern the ordinary Englishman about as much as the Criterion five-shilling dinner concerns the docker on strike. Madame Wagner ought to disestablish Bayreuth, and urge all the Wagner societies to get Parsifal performed in their own countries.

I see by a stray paragraph that Blondin* has an orchestrion, or high-class automatic barrel organ, to which he loves to listen whilst it grinds out hundreds of operatic selections. Once upon a time I looked on these machines with a placid contempt which, like that of a Low Church divine for the theatre, excluded even the curiosity necessary to stimulate me to take steps to hear one play. At last I happened to dine with a man who, after dinner, asked me would I like some music. I secretly mistrusted his intentions (the most unlikely sort of men will sometimes pull out a cornet or concertina, or call upon you for the accompaniment to When other lips), but, of course, I politely said Yes, as he expected me to. "Will you have Dinorah, or national airs?" said he. I hastily declared for Dinorah. Then he took what looked like a thick roll of wall paper into the next room. Presently Dinorah started, and he came back with an air of modest elation. The machine really performed very handsomely. It phrased with almost affected elegance, and made pauses and *ritardandos* and *accelerandos* in the most natural manner. The tone was sweet and low: an excellent thing in orchestrions after dinner; but it occasionally asserted itself with strenuous majesty. Since

* A celebrated French tightrope walker.

then I have had much more respect for music machines; and I no longer wonder at Madame Patti delighting in one at her burglarproof castle in Wales.

I wonder why our theatre managers do not get their music done by machinery. Usually the highclass theatre orchestra is like a threadbare garment, full of holes, parts left out, harmonies incomplete, the thread of melody thin and ineffectual, the whole impression paltry and timid. The inferior theatre orchestra is music-hally, blatant, thumping, out of tune. If I were an actor-manager I would announce an "invisible orchestra," as at Bayreuth and the Criterion, and invest in an orchestrion. In melodramas I would start the accompanying slow music myself by a button placed under my foot on the stage, exactly as the captains of penny steamboats have worked the engine-room signals since the abolition of riparian callboys. Of course, if the suggestion were generally adopted some thousands of instrumentalists would have to go down to the docks for a living; but then that is our established way of making progress: always over somebody's body.

An *obbligato* to a song is rather a questionable advantage to a singer. On Monday last I happened to look in at Her Majesty's. Presently out came Mr Howard Reynolds, looking so like the champion of England, and Mr Reginald Groome, looking so like the master of the ceremonies that I half expected an exhibition of gold belts and an invitation to buy one of Mr Reynolds's handkerchiefs for a sovereign. However, what actually ensued was Balfe's ancient, absurd, and charming In this old chair my father sat, with cornet *obbligato*. It was rather a pretty performance: Mr Groome was soft and sentimental, and Mr Reynolds merciful. But it happened that the cornet had the last word in the little *ritornel* which ends the song; and when Mr Reynolds came to the penultimate note he lifted up his cornet and blew two of the most terrific blasts that have been heard on earth since Jericho fell. His pent-up opinion of the human voice and of Balfe thus let loose, he retired with the greatest gravity, followed by the deafened tenor, who kept his countenance admirably, and looked quite pleased and amiable.

Besides Mr Reynolds, no less than three *virtuosi* performed. There was Mrs Shaw, who again gave us Il Bacio, with fuller tone than on the first occasion. Mrs Shaw's main secret is that she whistles in tune. It is true that there are not many public performers who habitually sing and play falsely enough to justify one in saying that they are out of tune; but between that and being in tune lies generally the whole difference between a very ordinary singer and a very successful one. I remember once going to a music hall to see a very clever juggler. Before the juggler came a gentleman who sang a song which made brutal fun of a particularly painful divorce case then proceeding. But he sang in tune, and with a quick sense of the lilt and swing of the refrain. After the juggler came a lady who ridiculed the higher education of women by presenting herself in a chintz sunbonnet and spectacles and singing an inane composition entitled Dr Mary Walker. She, too, could sing in tune in a high ringing voice, with engaging impetuosity of rhythmic movement. Her name, if my memory serves me aright, was Bellwood, and the gentleman was hight Macdermott. They were the only two artists whose songs did not bore my neighbors, by whom, strange to say, the success seemed to be attributed to their vulgarity. This was obviously a mistake: they had no monopoly of vulgarity. They *had* a monopoly of singing musically (comparatively speaking), and that was the true secret of their success.

M. Tivadar Nachéz, the violinist at Her Majesty's, has gained his success in quite the opposite way to Miss

Bellwood. He plays some easy affair like Raff's cavatina with the air of a man who is making a masterly conquest of untold difficulties, the members of the orchestra, who know better, looking on the while with mingled feelings. An *encore* follows, and he thereupon plays a *bravura* piece as fast as he can bow it. He has, of course, very little time to spend in aiming at the exact pitch of the notes; but he seems well satisfied when he gets within half a semitone of the bull's eye. But in my opinion a miss is as good as a mile at work of this sort; and I do not see why M. Nachéz should have come all the way from Spain to do what plenty of our native violinists can, if they try in earnest, do quite as badly. Señor Albéniz, the pianist, though a finer artist, is content to achieve similar feats under the easier conditions of an instrument which takes care of the intonation for him. His playing of harpsichord music is prodigiously swift and dainty; but it gives no gauge of his capacity for serious playing.

THE 789TH PERFORMANCE OF DOROTHY

The Star, 13 September 1889

Last Saturday evening, feeling the worse for want of change and country air, I happened to voyage in the company of Mr William Archer as far as Greenwich. Hardly had we inhaled the refreshing ozone of that place for ninety seconds when, suddenly finding ourselves opposite a palatial theatre, gorgeous with a million gaslights, we felt that it was idiotic to have been to Wagner's Theatre at Bayreuth and yet be utterly ignorant concerning Morton's Theatre at Greenwich. So we rushed into the struggling crowd at the doors, only to be informed that the theatre was full. Stalls full; dress circle full; pit, standing room only. As Archer, in self-defence, habitually sleeps during performances, and is subject to nightmare when he sleeps standing, the pit was out of the question. Was there room anywhere, we asked. Yes, in a private box or in the gallery. Which was the cheaper? The gallery, decidedly. So up we went to the gallery, where we found two precarious perches vacant at the side. It was rather like trying to see Trafalgar Square from the knifeboard of an omnibus halfway up St Martin's Lane; but by hanging on to a stanchion, and occasionally standing with one foot on the seat and the other on the backs of the people in the front row, we succeeded in seeing as much of the entertainment as we could stand.

The first thing we did was to purchase a bill, which informed us that we were in for "the entirely original pastoral comedy-opera in three acts, by B. C. Stephenson and Alfred Cellier, entitled Dorothy, which has been played to crowded houses at the Lyric Theatre, London, 950 and (still playing) in the provinces 788 times." This playbill, I should add, was thoughtfully decorated with a view of the theatre shewing all the exits, for use in the event of the performance proving unbearable. From it we further learnt that we should be regaled by an augmented and powerful orchestra; that the company was "Leslie's No. 1"; that C. J. Francis believes he is now the only HATTER in the county of Kent who exists on the profits arising solely from the sale of HATS and CAPS; and so on. Need I add that Archer and I sat bursting with expectation until the overture began.

I cannot truthfully say that the augmented and powerful orchestra proved quite so augmented or so powerful as the composer could have wished; but let that pass: I disdain the cheap sport of breaking a daddy-long-legs on a wheel (butterfly is out of the question, it was such a dingy band). My object is rather to call attention to the condition to which 788 nights of Dorothying have reduced the unfortunate wanderers known as "Leslie's No. I." I submit to Mr Leslie that in his own interest he should take better care of No. I. Here are several young persons doomed to spend the flower of their years in mechanically repeating the silliest libretto in modern theatrical literature, set to music which, pretty as it is, must pall somewhat on the seven hundred and eighty-eighth performance.

As might have been expected, a settled weariness of life, an utter perfunctoriness, an unfathomable inanity pervaded the very souls of "No. I." The tenor,* originally, I have no doubt, a fine young man, but now cherubically adipose, was evidently counting the days until death should release him from the part of Wilder. He had a pleasant speaking voice; and his affability and forbearance were highly creditable to him under the circumstances; but Nature rebelled in him against the loathed strains of a seven hundred-times repeated *rôle*. He omitted the song in the first act, and sang Though Born a Man of High Degree as if with the last rally of an energy decayed and a willing spirit crushed. The G at the end was a vocal earthquake. And yet methought he was not displeased when the inhabitants of Greenwich, coming fresh to the slaughter, encored him.

The baritone had been affected the other way: he was thin and worn; and his clothes had lost their lustre. He sang Queen of My Heart twice in a hardened manner, as one who was prepared to sing it a thousand times in a thousand quarter hours for a sufficient wager. The comic part, being simply that of a circus clown

* Shaw's brother-in-law, Charles Butterfield, husband of Lucy Carr Shaw, who appeared opposite him as Dorothy. He used the stage name Cecil Burt.

transferred to the lyric stage, is better suited for infinite repetition; and the gentleman who undertook it addressed a comic lady called Priscilla as Sarsaparilla during his interludes between the *haute-école* acts of the *prima donna* and tenor, with a delight in the rare aroma of the joke, and in the roars of laughter it elicited, which will probably never pall. But anything that he himself escaped in the way of tedium was added tenfold to his unlucky colleagues, who sat out his buffooneries with an expression of deadly malignity. I trust the gentleman may die in his bed; but he would be unwise to build too much on doing so. There is a point at which tedium becomes homicidal mania.

The ladies fared best. The female of the human species has not yet developed a conscience: she will apparently spend her life in artistic self-murder by induced Dorothitis without a pang of remorse, provided she be praised and paid regularly. Dorothy herself, a beauteous young lady of distinguished mien, with an immense variety of accents ranging from the finest Tunbridge Wells English (for genteel comedy) to the broadest Irish (for repartee and low comedy), sang without the slightest effort and without the slightest point, and was all the more desperately vapid because she suggested artistic gifts wasting in complacent abeyance. Lydia's voice, a hollow and spectral contralto, alone betrayed the desolating effect of perpetual Dorothy: her figure retains a pleasing plumpness akin to that of the tenor; and her spirits were wonderful, all things considered. The chorus, too, seemed happy; but that was obviously because they did not know any better. The pack of hounds darted in at the end of the second act evidently full of the mad hope of finding something new going on; and their depression, when they discovered it was Dorothy again, was pitiable. The S.P.C.A. should interfere. If there is no law to protect men and women from Dorothy, there is at least one that can be strained to protect dogs.

I did not wait for the third act. My companion had several times all but fallen into the pit from sleep and heaviness of spirit combined; and I felt as if I were playing Geoffrey Wilder for the millionth night. As we moped homeward in the moonlight we brooded over what we had seen. Even now I cannot think with composure of the fact that they are playing Dorothy tonight again—will play it tomorrow—next year—next decade—next century. I do not know what the average lifetime of a member of "No. 1" may be; but I do not think it can exceed five years from the date of joining; so there is no question here of old men and old women playing it with white hair beneath their wigs and deep furrows underlying their makeup. Doubtless they do not die on the stage: they first become mad and are removed to an asylum, where they incessantly sing, One, two three: one, two, three: one, two, three: one, two, be wi-eyes in, ti-I'm oh, Ph-ill is, mine, &c., until the King of Terrors (who ought to marry Dorothy) mercifully seals their tortured ears for ever.

I have always denounced the old-fashioned stock company, and laughed to scorn the theorists who fancy that they saw in them a training school for actors; but I never bargained for such a thing as this 789th performance of Dorothy. No: it is a criminal waste of young lives and young talents; and though it may for a time make more money for Mr Leslie, yet in the end it leaves him with a worn-out opera and a parcel of untrained novices on his hands when he might have a repertory of at least half a dozen works and a company of fairly skilled artists able to play them at a day's notice. We exclaim at the dock directors' disregard of laborers' bodies; but what shall we say of the managers' disregard of artists' souls. Ti, rum ti ty, rum ti ty, rum ti ty, rum m m: tiddy tum

[782]

tiddy tum tiddity, tum! Heavens! what hum I? Be wi-
eyes in—Malediction!

ALL ABOUT THE BRIGANDS

The Star, 20 September 1889

Since Monday, when I saw Offenbach's Brigands at the
Avenue Theatre, I have been trying to make up my
mind whether I run any serious risk of being damned
for preferring the profligacy of Offenbach, Meilhac, and
Halévy to the decorum of Cellier and the dulness of
Stephenson. Perhaps an item more or less in the account
can make not very great difference to me personally;
but I warn others solemnly that Offenbach's music is
wicked. It is abandoned stuff: every accent in it is a snap
of the fingers in the face of moral responsibility: every
ripple and sparkle on its surface twits me for my
teetotalism, and mocks at the early rising of which I
fully intend to make a habit some day.

In Mr Cellier's scores, music is still the chastest of the
Muses. In Offenbach's she is—what shall I say?—I am
ashamed of her. I no longer wonder that the Germans
came to Paris and suppressed her with fire and thunder.
Here in England how respectable she is! Virtuous and
rustically innocent her 6-8 measures are, even when
Dorothy sings "Come, fill up your glass to the brim!" She
learnt her morals from Handel, her ladylike manners
from Mendelssohn, her sentiment from the Bailiff's
Daughter of Islington. But listen to her in Paris, with
Offenbach. Talk of 6-8 time: why, she stumbles at the
second quaver, only to race off again in a wild
Bacchanalian, Saturnalian, petticoat-spurning, irre-
claimable, shocking *can-can*. Nothing but the wit of a

[783]

Frenchman shining through the chinks in the materialism of English comic opera artists could make such music endurable and presentable at the same time.

When Mr Gilbert translated Les Brigands for Messrs Boosey, years ago, he must have said to himself "This Meilhac-Halévy stuff is very funny; but I could do it just as well in English; and so I would too, if only I could find an English Offenbach." In due time he did find his Offenbach in Sir Arthur Sullivan. Accordingly, when Falsacappa the brigand chief exclaims "Marry my daughter to an honest man! NEVER!" we are not surprised to recognize in him a missing link in the ancestry of the Pirate King of Penzance. The relationship of the carbineers to the policemen is too obvious to be worth dwelling on; but there are other ties between the two phases of musical farce. The extremely funny song in the second act, *Nous avons, ce matin, tous deux*, is closely allied to When I First put this Uniform on in Patience; and the opening chorus *Deux par deux ou bien par trois* is first cousin to Carefully on Tiptoe Stealing in H.M.S. Pinafore.

I cannot, however, suppose that Mr Gilbert's objection to the use of his libretto was founded on an idiotic desire to appear "original." The people who regard the function of a writer as "creative" must surely be the most illiterate of dupes. The province of the fictionist is a common which no man has a right to enclose. I cultivate that common myself; and when someone claims to have grown a new plant there, different from all the rest, I smile sardonically, knowing that that selfsame plant grows in all our plots, and grew there before he was born. And when he discovers in my plot a plant which he has raised in his own or seen in his neighbor's, and thereupon cries out "Stop thief! Stop plagiarist! Stop picker of other men's brains!" I only smile the widelier. What are brains for, if not to be picked by me and the rest of the the world? In my business I know *me* and *te*, but not *meum* and *tuum*.

Mr Gilbert's book as played at the Avenue is much nearer in spirit to the original than Henry Leigh's. Leigh's lyrics sometimes flowed more smoothly than Mr Gilbert's; but his libretti were silly and raffish: the fun too often degenerated into tedious tomfoolery: his feeble and fleshy whimsicalities are inferior in grit and sparkle to even the most perfunctory paradoxes of Mr Gilbert. His Royal Horse Marines, commanded by Marshal Murphi, and his brigands Jacksheppardo, Dickturpino, and Clauduvallo, only shew how French wit of no very high order can yet be degraded by translation into English fun. The horse-collar bar-loafing buffoonery is not in the least like the genuine Meilhac and Halévy *opéra bouffe*, in which the characters, primarily persons of engaging culture, reasonableness, amiability, and address, are made irresistibly ridiculous by an exquisite folly, an impossible frivolity of motive, which exhibit them as at once miracles of wit and sensibility and monsters of moral obtuseness. Mr Gilbert has given us the English equivalent of this in his own operas; and a curiously brutalized, embittered, stolidified, middle-classical, mechanical equivalent it is; but the essential wit and incongruity are preserved. In translating Les Brigands, he naturally did not wholly miss these qualities; though, oddly enough, his version makes hardly anything of a couple of points which might have been expected to appeal specially to him: to wit, the family sentiment of Falsacappa, and the conscientious scruples of Fiorella on the subject of robbing handsome young men (just as the Pirates of Penzance drew the line at orphans).

As to the performance at the Avenue, I do not grudge the admission that Messrs Van Biene and Lingard's company is a good one as provincial companies go. But as companies for the performance of Offenbach's operas *ought* to go, in the provinces and elsewhere, its members are as babes and sucklings playing at Meilhac and Halévy in the nursery. The orchestra is not large enough, not dainty enough, not immoral enough to supply that inimitable effervescence which is the great achievement of Offenbach in orchestration. In the second act, the Princess of Grenada, entering with Gloria-Cassis and her suite, should look like the court in Ruy Blas, grave, punctilious, an assembly of etiquette-ridden grandees, with their appearance in the wildest contradiction to the Spanish dance rhythm movement of *Jadis vous n'avez qu'un patrie* (transferred at the Avenue from Gloria-Cassis to the Princess, Miss Marie Luella, who caught the musical intention of the song perfectly and brought down the house with it). The only point attempted was by Mr Maurice de Solla, who made himself up as Gloria-Cassis into an exact likeness of Mr Robert Browning! In the name of Sordello, why?

The third act depends altogether on Antonio, the ancient treasurer of the Duke of Mantua, who has squandered the contents of the treasury on his love affairs. His song, *O mes amours, O mes maîtresses!* with its refrain, *Vl'a-a! Vl'a-a! Vl'a mon caractère*, ending in falsetto on high D, is the most important number in the act. At the Avenue it is omitted, the part being taken by a gentleman who presumably cannot sing, and who seems to have derived his ideas of character acting from the antics of Lurcher in Dorothy. Undaunted by Mr Gilbert, he "gagged" the line about the sundries in his accounts, and gagged it so senselessly that Mr Gilbert would only have pitied him and passed on. Under these circumstances the act was even less worth waiting for than the third act of a farcical performance usually is. Years ago, somewhere or other, I saw Mr Edward Royce, of Gaiety fame, double a brigand's part with that of Antonio very cleverly indeed. I wish he had been at the Avenue on Monday.

Falsacappa was gigantically impersonated by a Mr Hallen Mostyn, who sings so noisily that he cannot hear what key the orchestra is playing in, and so, though his ear is sound enough, occasionally sings in a different one. The whole company did this at one place (where a cut had been newly restored) for about 15 bars in the first act. Serve them right, say I, for scamping their work in the provinces with their cuts! The vocal forces were economized by knocking the parts of Campotasso and the carbineer captain into one; but as a set-off the Princess's part was made worthy of a *prima donna* by the aforesaid transfer of Gloria-Cassis's song to her. Fragoletto was originally a woman's part: such lines as *Nous avons pris ce petit homme : Il est tout petit, mais en somme*, &c., refer to the feminine proportions of the hero. However, the opera is all the better for the substitution of Mr Frank Wensley, who lilts *Falsacappa! voici ma prise* very prettily. Miss Delaporte is, I have no doubt, a capital Fiorella, now that she has had time to recover from the fatigue which a little oppressed her and veiled her voice on the first night. Fiorella, by the way, should not be announced in the bill as the sister of Falsacappa. Young women do not present their portraits to their brothers.

NO ACCOUNTING FOR TASTE
The Star, 27 September 1889

The 16th November will be a dreadful afternoon at the Crystal Palace Saturday concerts. It is to be devoted to Mendelssohn's St Paul. I suppose this would not occur unless there were people capable of enjoying such musical atavisms as XIX century scriptural oratorios. There is no accounting for taste. In the last century people used to like sham Shakespear: tragedies in five acts and in blank verse, in which the hero, usually a compound of Macbeth, Richard III., and Iago, used to die declaiming "Whip me, ye grinning fiends" at the ghosts of his murdered victims. In the same way legions of organists and academy professors have turned out sham Handel for the use of festival committees anxious to vindicate themselves from the charge of neglecting English art. Now I grant that Mendelssohn is better than the organist, the professor, the Mus.Bac., and the Mus.Doc.; just as Tennyson is better than Cumberland or Colman.* But compared with Handel he is what Tennyson is compared with Shakespear. If you are shocked at these sentiments, I challenge you to go to the Crystal Palace on 16th November; to set all that dreary fugue manufacture, with its Sunday-school sentimentalities and its Music-school ornamentalities, against your recollection of the expressive and vigorous choruses of Handel; and to ask yourself on your honor whether there is the slightest difference in kind between "Stone him to death" and "Under the pump, with a kick and a thump," in Dorothy. Then blame me, if you can, for objecting to the Palace people pestering mankind with Mendelssohnic St Pauls and Gounodic Redemptions and Parrysiac Judiths and the like, when one hardly ever hears Jephtha or a Bach cantata. But of what use is it to complain? If my cry were heeded, the Palace directors would simply say "Oh, he likes Handel, does he? How nice! We rather think we can meet his views

* Richard Cumberland (1732–1811) and George Coleman the younger (1762–1836) were dramatic authors. The latter was for more than twenty years manager of the Haymarket theatre.

in that direction." And they would straightway kidnap five or six thousand choristers; put Israel in Egypt into rehearsal; and treat me to a dose of machine thunder on the Handel orchestra. It would be utterly in vain: I should complain worse than ever: the machine thunder is as unimpressive as the noise of the thousand footsteps in Oxford-street.

WAGNER IN BAYREUTH

The English Illustrated Magazine, October 1889. An abridged version, under the title Bayreuth Denying the Master, appeared in The Transatlantic, Boston, 1 November 1889

There are many reasons for going to Bayreuth to see the Wagner Festival plays. Curiosity, for instance, or love of music, or hero worship of Wagner, or adept Wagnerism—a much more complicated business—or a desire to see and be seen in a vortex of culture. But a few of us go to Bayreuth because it is a capital stick to beat a dog with. He who has once been there can crush all admirers of Die Meistersinger at Covent Garden with— "Ah, you should see it at Bayreuth," or, if the occasion be the Parsifal prelude at a Richter concert, "Have you heard Levi conduct it at Bayreuth?" And when the answer comes sorrowfully in the negative, the delinquent is made to feel that in that case he does not know what Parsifal is, and that the Bayreuth tourist does. These little triumphs are indulged in without the slightest remorse on the score of Richter's great superiority to Herr Levi as a Wagnerian conductor, and of the fact that a performance of the Parsifal prelude by a London orchestra under his direction is often much better worth a trip from Bayreuth to London than a performance by a German orchestra under Levi is ever worth a trip from London to Bayreuth. It is not in human nature to be honest in these matters—at least not yet.

Those who have never been in Germany, and cannot afford to go thither, will not be sorry when the inevitable revolt of English Wagnerism against Bayreuth breaks out; and the sooner they are gratified, the better. Ever since the death of Beethoven, the champions of Music have been desperately fighting to obtain a full hearing for her in spite of professorship, pedantry, superstition, literary men's acquiescent reports of concerts, and butcherly stage management—all trading on public ignorance and diffidence. Wagner, the greatest of these champions, did not fight for his own hand alone, but for Mozart, Beethoven, and Weber as well. All authority was opposed to him until he made his own paramount. Mendelssohn was against him at a time when to assert that Mendelssohn's opinion was of less weight than his seemed as monstrous as it would seem today to deny it. People do not discriminate in music as much as they do in other arts. They can see that Lord Tennyson is hardly the man to say the deepest word about Goethe, or Sir Frederick Leighton about Michael Angelo; but Mendelssohn's opinion about Beethoven was accepted as final, since the composer of Elijah must evidently know all about music. In England, since not only Mendelssohn, but Costa, the Philharmonic Society, The Times, and The Athenæum were satisfied when they had dried Mozart into a trivial musical box, when the overture to Le Nozze di Figaro was finished within three and a half minutes, when the beautiful trio of Beethoven's Eighth Symphony was made a mere practical joke on the violoncellists, when the famous theme in the Freischütz was played exactly in the style of the popular second subject in the Masaniello overture, the public could only conclude that these must be the classical ways of conducting, and that dulness was a necessary part of the classicism. Wagner did not succeed in putting dulness out of countenance until he became a classic himself. And now that he is a classic, who is to do for him what he did for his predecessors? For he is not going to escape their fate. The "poor and pretentious pietism" which he complained of as "shutting out every breath of fresh air from the musical atmosphere" is closing round his own music. At Bayreuth, where the Master's widow, it is said, sits in the wing as the jealous guardian of the traditions of his own personal direction, there is already a perceptible numbness—the symptom of paralysis.

The London branch of the Wagner Society, unobservant of this danger signal, seems to have come to the conclusion that the best thing it can do for its cause is to support Bayreuth. It has not yet dawned on it that the traditional way of playing Tristan und Isolde will, in the common course of mortality, inevitably come to what the traditional way of playing Mozart's G minor symphony had come to when Wagner heard Lachner conduct it; or, to take instances which appeal to our own experience, what Don Giovanni came to be under Costa in his later days, or what the C minor symphony is today at a Philharmonic concert. The law of traditional performances is "Do what was done last time": the law of all living and fruitful performance is "Obey the innermost impulse which the music gives, and obey it to the most exhaustive satisfaction." And as that impulse is never, in a fertile artistic nature, the impulse to do what was done last time, the two laws are incompatible, being virtually laws respectively of death and life in art. Bayreuth has chosen the law of death. Its boast is that it alone knows what was done last time, and that therefore it alone has the pure and complete tradition—or, as I prefer to put it, that it alone is in a position to strangle

[791]

Wagner's lyric dramas note by note, bar by bar, *nuance* by *nuance*.

It is in vain for Bayreuth to contend that by faithfully doing what was done last time it arrives at an exact phonograph of what was done the first time, when Wagner was alive, present, and approving. The difference consists just in this, that Wagner is now dead, absent, and indifferent. The powerful, magnetic personality, with all the tension it maintained, is gone; and no manipulation of the dead hand on the keys can ever reproduce the living touch. Even if such reproduction were possible, who, outside Bayreuth, would be imposed on by the shallow assumption that the Bayreuth performances fulfilled Wagner's whole desire? We can well believe that in justice to those who so loyally helped him, he professed himself satisfied when the most that could be had been done—nay, that after the desperate makeshifts with which he had had to put up in his long theatrical experience, he was genuinely delighted to find that so much was possible. But the unwieldy toy dragon, emitting its puff of steam when its mouth opened, about as impressively as a mechanical doll says "Mamma": did that realize the poet's vision of Fafner? And the trees which walk off the stage in Parsifal: can the poorest imagination see nothing better by the light of Wagner's stage direction in the score than that? Is the gaudy ballet and unspeakable flower garden in the second act to be the final interpretation of the visionary bowers of Klingsor? The Philistine cockney laughs at these provincial conceits, and recommends Bayreuth to send for Mr Irving, Mr Hare, Mr Wilson Barrett, or Mr Augustus Harris to set the stage to rights. It is extremely likely that when A Midsummer Night's Dream was first produced, Shakespear complimented the stage manager, tipped the carpenters, patted Puck on the head, shook hands with Oberon, and wondered that the make-believe was no worse; but even if this were an established historical fact, no sane manager would therefore attempt to reproduce the Elizabethan *mise en scène* on the ground that it had fulfilled Shakespear's design. Yet if we had had a Shakespear theatre on foot since the XVII century, conducted on the Bayreuth plan, that is the very absurdity in which tradition would by this time have landed us.*

Tradition in scenery and stage management is, however, plausible in comparison with tradition in acting, singing, and playing. If Wagner had been able to say of any scene "I am satisfied," meaning, not "I am satisfied that nothing better can be done for me; and I am heartily grateful to you—the painter—for having done more than I had hoped for," but "This is what I saw in my mind's eye when I wrote my poem," then successive scene manufacturers might mechanically copy the painting from cloth to cloth with sufficient accuracy to fix at least a good copy of the original scene for posterity to look at with new eyes and altered minds. At any rate the new cloth would not rebel, since it could be woven and cut at will to the pattern of the old picture. But when it is further sought to reproduce the old figures with new persons, then comes to light the absurdity of playing Procrustes with a dramatic representation. I remember once laughing at a provincial Iago who pointed the words "Trifles light as air," by twitching

* The Comédie Française, in performing the plays of Molière, still keeps as closely as possible to the stage arrangements of the author's own time. Even in this instance, where the tradition has the excuse of being the most trustworthy record of the manners of the period represented, the effect on the plays themselves is sufficiently depressing; and its reaction on the French stage at large is a main factor of the immense superiority of English acting, undrilled and inartistic as our novices are, to French. [GBS]

his handkerchief into space much as street hawkers now twitch the toy parachute made fashionable by Mr Baldwin.* An experienced theatrical acquaintance rebuked me, assuring me that the actor was right, because he had been accustomed to rehearse the part for Charles Kean, and therefore had learnt every step, gesture, and inflexion of that eminent tragedian's play. Unfortunately, he was not Charles Kean: consequently Charles Kean's play no more fitted him than Charles Kean's clothes. His Iago was a ridiculous misfit, even from his own shallow view of acting as a mere external affectation. In the old provincial stock companies, most of which have by this time died the death they richly deserved, there was often to be found an old lady who played Lady Macbeth when the star Shakespearean actor came his usual round. She played it exactly as Mrs Siddons played it, with the important difference that, as she was not Mrs Siddons, the way which was the right way for Mrs Siddons was the wrong way for her. Thoroughly sophisticated theatre fanciers carried the fool's logic of tradition to the extremity of admiring these performances. But of those with natural appetites, the young laughed and the old yawned.

Consideration of these cases suggests the question whether we are to be made [to] laugh and yawn at Bayreuth by a line of mock Maternas and sham Maltens? If not, what can Bayreuth do that cannot be done as well elsewhere—that cannot be done much more conveniently for Englishmen in England? If Bayreuth repudiates tradition, there is no mortal reason why we should go so far to hear Wagner's lyric dramas. If it clings to it, then that is the strongest possible reason for avoiding it.

* In 1888 a Mr Baldwin had performed the astonishing feat of leaping from a soaring balloon with a parachute, which opened as he fell and floated him safely to the ground.

Every fresh representation of Parsifal (for example) should be an original artistic creation, and not an imitation of the last one. The proper document to place in the hands of the artists is the complete work. Let the scenepainter paint the scenes he sees in the poem. Let the conductor express with his orchestra what the score expresses to him. Let the tenor do after the nature of that part of himself which he recognizes in Parsifal; and let the *prima donna* similarly realize herself as Kundry. The true Wagner theatre is that in which this shall be done, though it stand on Primrose Hill or in California. And wherever the traditional method is substituted, there Wagner is not. The conclusion that the Bayreuth theatre cannot remain the true Wagner Theatre is obvious. The whole place reeks of tradition—boasts of it—bases its claims to fitness upon it. Frau Cosima Wagner, who has no function to perform except the illegitimate one of chief remembrancer, sits on guard there. When the veterans of 1876 retire, Wagner will be in the condition of Titurel in the third act of Parsifal.

It would be too much to declare that the true Wagner Theatre will arise in England; but it is certain that the true English Wagner Theatre will arise there. The sooner we devote our money and energy to making Wagner's music live in England instead of expensively embalming its corpse in Bavaria, the better for English art in all its branches. Bayreuth is supported at present partly because there is about the journey thither a certain romance of pilgrimage which may be summarily dismissed as the effect of the bad middle-class habit of cheap self-culture by novel reading; partly by a conviction that we could never do the lyric dramas at home as well as they are done at Bayreuth. This, if it were well founded, would be a conclusive reason for continuing to support Bayreuth. But Parsifal can be done not merely as well in London as in Bayreuth, but better. A picked London orchestra could, after half a dozen rehearsals under a competent conductor, put Herr Levi and the Bayreuth band in the second place. Our superiority in the art of stage presentation is not disputed, even by those who omit Mr Herkomer and the Bushey theatre* from the account. There remain the questions of the theatre and the singers.

The difference between the Wagner Theatre at Bayreuth and an ordinary cockpit-and-scaffolding theatre is in the auditorium, and not in the stage, which is what any large stage here would be were space as cheap in London as in the Fichtelgebirge.† The top of the partition between the orchestra and the seats curves over hoodwise towards the footlights, hiding the players and conductor from the audience. The instruments are not stretched in a thin horizontal line with the trombones at the extreme right of the conductor, and the drums at his extreme left: they are grouped as at an orchestral concert: first violins to the left; seconds to the right; basses flanking on both sides; woodwind in the middle, opposite the conductor; brass and percussion behind the woodwind and under the stage. From the orchestra the auditorium widens; and the floor ascends from row to row as in a lecture theatre, the rows being curved, but so slightly that the room seems rectilinear. There are no

* Hubert von Herkomer, Bavarian-born painter, who was Slade Professor of Fine Arts at Oxford (1885–94) founded a school of art at Bushey in 1883. It included a tiny theatre, opened in 1888, in which Herkomer produced and often acted in musical productions written, composed, and designed by himself. The most recent of these, An Idyl, for which he did all but write the lyrics, was performed in June 1889, conducted by Hans Richter.

† The Fichtelgebirge is a mountain range which extends eastward toward Czechoslovakia. Bayreuth lies at its western slope.

balconies or galleries, the whole audience being seated on the cross benches in numbered stalls, with hinged cane seats of comfortable size, in plain strong wooden frames without any upholstery. The most striking architectural feature is the series of short transverse walls with pillars and lamps, apparently suggested by the old-fashioned stage side wing. Each of these wings extends from the side of the room to the edge of the stalls. Between the wings are the doors; and as each ticket is marked with the number not only of the seat, but of the nearest door to it, the holders find their places for themselves without the intervention of attendants. Playbills are bought for a penny in the town, or in the street on the way to the theatre. The wall at the back contains a row of *loggie* for royal personages and others who wish to sit apart. Above these state cabins there is a crow's nest which is the nearest thing to a gallery in the theatre; but the conditions of admission are not stated. The prevailing color of the house is a light dun, as of cream color a little worse for smoke. There are no draperies, no cushions, no showy colors, no florid decoration of any kind. During the performance the room is darkened so that it is impossible to read except by the light from the stage.

The artistic success of this innovation in theatre-building is without a single drawback. The singers and the players are easily and perfectly heard, the merest whisper of a drum roll or a *tremolo* traveling clearly all over the house; and the *fortissimo* of the total vocal and instrumental force comes with admirable balance of tone, without rattle, echo, excessive localization of sound, or harsh preponderance of the shriller instruments. The concentration of attention on the stage is so complete that the after-image of the lyric drama witnessed is deeply engraved in the memory, aural and visual. The ventilation is excellent; and the place is free

[797]

from the peculiar odor inseparable from draped and upholstered theatres. The seats between the last doors and the back do not empty rapidly; but in case of fire the occupants could easily step over into the sections which empty at once, and so get out in time to escape suffocation or burning.

Compare this theatre with our fashionable opera houses. In these there is for persons of average middle-class means a stifling atmosphere, a precarious and remote bird's-eye view of the crowns of the performers' hats, and an appalling risk of suffocation in case of panic. For rich people there is every circumstance that can distract the attention from the opera—blazing chandeliers, diamonds, costumes, private boxes for public chattering, fan waving and posing, fashionably late arrivals and early departures, the conductor gesticulating like an auctioneer in the middle of the footlights, and the band deafening the unfortunate people in the front rows of the stalls. Under such conditions a satisfactory representation even of Il Barbiere is impossible. Thus, though we have orchestras capable, under the right conductor, of playing the prelude to any Wagner lyric drama better than it is played at Bayreuth, yet we can never produce the effect that is produced there until we have a theatre on the Bayreuth model to do it in. Why should we not have such a theatre, accommodating 1500 people, on equal terms at a uniform charge per head. The dramas performed need not always be lyric; for it must not be overlooked that the actual Wagner Theatre is also the ideal Shakespear Theatre.

In considering whether such an enterprise would pay, the practical man should bear in mind that opera at present does not pay in the commercial sense, except in Bayreuth, where the charge for admittance to each performance—£1—is prohibitive as far as the average amateur is concerned. At Covent Garden, Mr Augustus Harris has his subvention, not from the Government, as in Berlin or Paris, but from a committee of private patrons whose aims are at least as much fashionable as artistic. To carry a season through without losing some thousands of pounds is a considerable feat of management. Consequently no demonstration that the money taken at the doors of a Wagner Theatre here would not cover expenses of performance, plus rent, interest, and the ordinary profits of skilled management, is conclusive as against the practicability of London enjoying the artistic benefit of such an institution. The London Wagner Theatre might be an endowed institution of the type suggested by Mr William Archer; or it might be a municipally subventioned theatre. It might be built as an ordinary commercial venture, and let for short periods to tragedians temporarily in want of a Shakespearean theatre, like Mr Mansfield, or to *impresarios* like Mr Harris, Mr Leslie, Mr Mapleson, or the managers of the Carl Rosa company. Its novelty and the celebrity of its original would launch it: its comfort and its enormous artistic superiority to its rivals would probably keep it afloat until the time when its special function as a theatre for lyric drama would be in constant action throughout the year.

In any case we should not waste our Wagner Theatre as the Bayreuth house is wasted, by keeping it closed against all composers save Wagner. Our desire to see a worthy and solemn performance of Parsifal has been gratified; but what of the great prototype of Parsifal, Die Zauberflöte, hitherto known in our opera houses as a vapid, tawdry tomfoolery for shewing off a soprano with a high F and a bass with a low E? Mozart is Wagner's only peer in lyric drama: he also made the orchestra envelop the poem in a magic atmosphere of sound: he also adapted a few favorite rhythms, modu-

[799]

lations, and harmonies, to an apparently infinite variety and subtlety of accent and purport. If we are asked whether Die Meistersinger is greater than this or that lyric comedy, we say yes with contemptuous impetuosity until Le Nozze di Figaro is mentioned; and then, brought up standing, we quote Michael Angelo's "different, but not better." There is no parallel between Tristan und Isolde and Don Giovanni except in respect of both being unique. At Bayreuth we have heard Tristan und Isolde from the first note to the last, faithfully done according to the composer's score, under the best theatrical conditions possible. But whither shall we turn to hear Don Giovanni? At the opera houses they occasionally try to lick the sugar off it—to sound that part of its great compass which is within the range of the shallowest voluptuary—that part within which the hero is at the level of his ancestor Punch. If the Wagnerites do not ardently desire to hear a dignified and complete representation of Don Giovanni, with the second *finale* restored, they are no true disciples of "The Master."

Then there is Fidelio, always grimly irreconcilable with the glitter of the fashionable opera house, and needing, more than any other lyric drama, that concentration of attention which is the cardinal peculiarity of the Wagner Theatre. Verdi, by dint of his burning earnestness about the dramas he has found music for, and of the relevance of every bar of his mature scores to the dramatic situation, has also placed his best operas beyond the reach of Covent Garden. Many persons were astonished at the power of his Otello as performed this year at the Lyceum by the Milan company; but an equally careful and complete performance of his Ernani would have been quite as unexpected a revelation after the intolerable Traviatas and Trovatores of ordinary "subscription nights." Those victims of

Wagneritis (a disease not uncommon among persons who have discovered the merits of Wagner's music by reading about it, and among those disciples who know no other music than his) may feel scandalized by the suggestion of Verdi's operas at a Wagner Theatre; but they must be taught to respect the claims of the no less important people for whom Molière and Mozart are too subtle, Schopenhauer and Wagner too abstract. The simple tragedy of Victor Hugo and Verdi is what these novices have to depend on for the purification of their souls by pity and terror; and they have a right, equally with the deepest of us, to the most careful and earnest representation of any art work which appeals seriously to them. As for the composers who were chiefly musicians, or who were dramatic only by fits and starts, or whose dramatic purpose seldom rose above the production of imposing stage effects—Gounod, Rossini, Meyerbeer, and their imitators—a single Wagner Theatre would always have something better to do than to produce their works, pitiful as it would be to abandon them to the incredible slovenliness and flippancy of the fashionable houses. But perhaps the example of a Wagner Theatre might induce rival *impresarios* to consider the moral of the fact that Wagner himself has recorded the satisfaction he enjoyed from an uncut performance of Il Barbiere in which, for once, Rossini's authority was placed above that of the stage manager. Did he not point, in his practical fashion, to the superior artistic completeness gained in ballets through the necessity of giving the artistic inventor his own way on the stage?

The uses of a London Wagner Theatre would by no means be limited to the presentation of the works of Mozart, Beethoven, Verdi, Wagner, and perhaps Goetz. The spoken drama, in spite of the artistic ambition of our actor-managers, is almost as forlorn in England as the lyric. The people for whose use dramatic literature exists have lost the habit of going to the theatre, because they so seldom find anything there that interests them. Occasionally the more enterprising of them may be seen at some amateurish venture of the Browning or Shelley Society, or at the Lyceum. But there is no theatre in London which is the natural home of the plays they want to see. Shakespear's plays, Schiller's, Goethe's, Ibsen's (Peer Gynt and Brand), Browning's—what chance have we at present of knowing these in the only way in which they can be thoroughly known? for a man who has only read a play no more knows it than a musician knows a symphony when he has turned over the leaves of the score. He knows something about it: that is all. Are we then for ever to offer our children the book of the play to read, instead of bringing them to the theatre? The appetite for serious drama exists: that much has appeared whenever it has been put to the proof by a competent manager with sufficient resources to hold out whilst the lovers of serious drama were overcoming their incredulity as to any theatrical entertainment rising above the level of the commonest variety of novel. This year there was a revival of hope because Mr Pinero, in a play* produced at the Garrick Theatre, walked cautiously up to a social problem, touched it, and ran away. Shortly afterwards a much greater sensation was created by a Norwegian play, Ibsen's Doll's House, in which the dramatist handled this same problem, and shewed, not how it ought to be solved, but how it is about to be solved.

Then came out the deplorable fact that it is possible for men to attend our ordinary theatres as professional critics constantly for years without finding occasion to employ or understand the simplest terms used in

* The Profligate, by Arthur W. Pinero.

metaphysical and psychological discussions of dramatic art. Somebody, for instance, having used the word "will" in the Schopenhauerian sense which has long been familiar to every smatterer in Wagnerism or the philosophy of art, the expression was frankly denounced by one dramatic critic as "sickening balderdash," whilst another adduced it as evidence that the writer could not possibly understand his own words, since they were not intelligible. The truth appears to be that the theatre of today, with its literature, its criticism, and its audiences, though a self-contained, consistent, and useful institution, ignores and is ignored by the class which is only interested in realities, and which enjoys thinking as others enjoy eating. The most cynical estimate of the numbers of this class in London will leave no doubt of the success of any theatre which can once make itself known as a Wagner Theatre in a larger sense than Bayreuth yet comprehends. This theatre need not oust the theatre of today, which will retain its place as long as it retains its use. The two can exist side by side without more friction than perhaps an occasional betrayal of the conviction of each that the literature and criticism of the other is "sickening balderdash."

The doubt as to the possiblity of finding singers for an English Wagner Theatre might be disregarded on the ground that London is accustomed to pick and choose from the world's stock. But this plan has not hitherto answered well enough to justify us in relying upon it in the future. Fortunately, Bayreuth has shewn us how to do without singers of internationally valuable genius. The singers there have not "created" the lyric drama: it is the lyric drama that has created them. Powerful as they are, they do not sing Wagner because they are robust: they are robust because they sing Wagner. His music is like Handel's in bringing into play the full compass of the singer, and in offering the alternative of

[803]

either using the voice properly or else speedily losing it. Such proper use of the voice is a magnificent physical exercise. The outcry against Wagner of the singers who were trained to scream and shout within the highest five notes of their compass until nothing else was left of their voices—and not much of that—has died away. Even that arch quack, the old-fashioned Italian singing master, finds some better excuse for his ignorance of Wagner's music and his inability to play its accompaniments, than the bold assurance that German music is bad for the voice. Plenty of English singers would set to work at the Niblung Ring tomorrow if they could see their way to sufficient opportunities of singing it to repay them for the very arduous task of committing one of the parts to memory. Singers of genius, great Tristans and Parsifals, Kundrys and Isoldes, will not be easily obtained here any more than in Germany; and when they are found, all Europe and America will compete for them.

But Bayreuth does without singers of genius. Frau Materna and Fräulein Malten, with all their admirable earnestness and enthusiasm, are only great Kundrys according to that easy standard by which the late Madame Tietjens passed as a great Semiramis and a great Lucrezia: that is, they have large voices, and have some skill in stage business and deportment; but they do nothing that any intelligent woman with their physical qualifications cannot be educated to do. Perron's Amfortas is an admirable performance; but our next Santley, falling on more serious artistic times, will equal it. Miss Macintyre will have to be very careful and faithful in her career if she wishes to find herself, at Frau Sucher's age, as fine an Isolde; but who can say how many rivals to Miss Macintyre we may have by that time? Theodor Reichmann must have been an excellent Sachs in his time; and he is still worthy of his place at

Bayreuth; but we can produce a Hans Sachs of the same order when we make up our minds that we want him. Friedrichs, a capital comedian, and Van Dyck, who makes his mark as Parsifal by a certain *naïveté* and rosy physical exuberance rather than by any extraordinary endowment as a singer, exhaust the list of artists whose performances at Bayreuth this year were specially memorable. Gudehus as Walther and Vogl as Tristan proved themselves as capable as ever of carrying through two very heavy tenor parts; but though their conscientiousness and intelligence were beyond praise, they are neither young nor youthful (it is possible to be either without being the other), and their voices lack variety and charm.

Can we hope to replace the three great conductors? The chief part of the answer is that there is only one great conductor, and him we have bound to us already. Whoever has heard the Tristan prelude conducted by Richter on one of his fortunate evenings at St James's Hall, or the Parsifal prelude as he conducted it on one memorable occasion at the Albert Hall, knows more than Bayreuth can tell him about these works. Herr Levi shews what invaluable results can be produced by unwearying care and exhaustive study. Herr Felix Mottl's strictness, refinement, and severe taste make the orchestra go with the precision and elegance of a chronometer. Discipline, rehearsal, scrupulous insistence on every *nuance* in a score which is crammed with minute indications of the gradations of tone to be produced by each player: these, and entire devotion to the composer's cause, could do no more. But they are qualities which exist everywhere, if not in everyone. If Wagner's work can call them into action in Germany it can call them into action here. With Richter the case is different. He, as we know, is a conductor of genius. To make an orchestra play the prelude to Parsifal as Herr

Levi makes them play it, is a question of taking as much pains and as much thought as he. To make them play the introduction to the third act of Die Meistersinger as they play it for Richter is a question of the gift of poetic creation in musical execution. The perfection attained by Herr Mottl is the perfection of photography. Richter's triumphs and imperfections are those of the artist's hand.

Before Wagner, the qualities which distinguish the Bayreuth performances were rarer in Germany than they are now in England. His work inspired them there: what is to prevent it doing so here? No more of Bayreuth then: Wagnerism, like charity, begins at home.

A DEFENCE OF BALLET

The Star, 4 October 1889

It is all but thirteen years since I went to the Lyceum Theatre one November evening to hear the Carl Rosa Company perform for the first time an opera by Mr Fred Cowen entitled Pauline (surnamed Deschapelles, of course). I was not then the lenient, almost foolishly goodnatured critic I have since become; and I am afraid I rather dropped into Mr Cowen over his opera. At that time it was the fashion to say that History repeats itself. At present it is the fashion to point out that it does not; but, however that may be, the fact remains that on Tuesday I received an invitation from Major Cockle to attend the dress rehearsal of his new opera The Castle of Como at the Opera Comique the same evening at half-past seven. Happening to have engagements of an unmusical nature for the first night, I eagerly seized the opportunity of escaping it, and so took care to be in the theatre punctually at a quarter to eight.

When I entered, I was much puzzled to find a huge orchestra thinly scraping through a minuet, which the composer was conducting in a state of the wildest excitement, occasionally stopping for a frantic altercation with the stage manager, who declared—as managers will—that it would be "all right tomorrow," an assurance with which the composer-conductor, mindful of the great truth that "tomorrow never comes," altogether declined to be satisfied. Claude Melnotte and Pauline were dancing the minuet conscientiously in a dingy apartment, whilst Monsieur Deschapelles slept on a sofa. Presently, to my utter confusion, Pauline said she was going to marry her father; and Claude reproached her on the ground of a prior attachment, contracted when they were children together. M. Deschapelles then rose, and, declaring that he had overheard every word of their conversation, said, "You are a noble fellow" to Claude, and magnanimously withdrew in his favor and blessed the union of the young people. These transactions, conducted in language of wasting dreariness, drove me to appeal to my neighbor as to whether the opera was over, or whether they were taking the last act first. He told me it had not yet begun; that this was only a curtain-raiser; and that the excited conductor was Mr Milton Wellings. I gazed with inexpressible awe at the illustrious composer of Some Day; for I know as well as M. Dumas *fils* how much merit it takes to make even a small success. And I admire a man who is as desperately anxious about a hopelessly dull little piece to which he has written a dance tune as Wagner was about the 1876 Nibelungen performance at Bayreuth. *Sang-froid* can be acquired: earnestness is the gift of the gods.

Here let me respectfully offer Mr Milton Wellings and the management a piece of advice which they will probably not take. Let them cut out the dialogue and the old man, and turn the curtain-raiser into a masque consisting either of the minuet alone or of a set of dances which Mr Milton Wellings can add. In the Jubilee year a masque was performed at Gray's Inn, with a success from which no manager has yet taken a hint. The dancers were amateurs, but the performance was interesting and pretty: much more so than the pedantries of the modern ballet, which presents the art of dancing at the very deepest depths of degradation. Pious people who are not ashamed to confess that they have never been to a theatre think the ballet indecent. Would it were! Just as a burglar, having some sort of rational human purpose in him, is a more hopeful subject than an idiot; so indecency is better than the blind stupidity which substitutes proficiency in a set of technical forms and feats for the attainment of beauty and significance, which are the true life of all art forms that really are alive. The ballet indecent! Why, it is the most formal, the most punctilious, ceremonious, professor-ridden, pig-headed solemnity that exists. Talk of your fugues, canons, key relationships, single and double counter-point, fifty orthodox resolutions of the chord of the minor ninth and the rest of it! What are they to the *entrechats*, *battements*, *ronds de jambes*, *arabesques*, *élévations*, that are the stock-in-trade of the art of theatrical dancing? The man who said that the British bishop is unique had never met a ballet master or the president of an academy of music. I have often wondered that the essential identity of mental attitude presented by them has not opened Stewart Headlam's eyes to the fact that an ordinary ballet is no more a true dance than an ordinary Church of England service is a true act of worship.

Fortunately, public opinion is sound upon this matter. At one period of my chequered career I made a point of seeing every ballet produced at the Alhambra in order to study one of the most remarkable artistic institutions of the time. The virtuosity of the principal dancers was the result of a training of a severity and duration unknown among singers since Porpora taught Caffarelli. Even the rank and file were skilled to a degree unknown in opera choruses, and by no means common in orchestras. The grouping and coloring were thought out by real artists. A ballet called Yolande, produced about twelve years ago, when Aurelia Pertoldi was dancing her best, reached a standard of technical perfection which would have been received with astonished acclamation in any other art. Yet nobody of any intelligence cared two straws about the Alhambra. The brainless artificiality of the ballets was too much for the public. People went and stared; but the quality of the applause was always poor. I gave it up at last as a hopeless affair; and though it was not I who set fire to the old Alhambra, I stayed in Leicester Square nearly all night watching it burn without a pang of regret.* Then, in 1885, came Excelsior at Her Majesty's, the delightful dance in Mary Anderson's revival of The Winter's Tale [1887], and the Gray's Inn masque, all successful in waking up the public love of dancing. In Excelsior two dances caught the public: one executed by men in heavy boots and spurs; the other a simple piece of shawl waving and handkerchief fluttering (I could have done it myself) by Miss Kate Vaughan, at whose success the unappreciated pirouettists and entrechatists looked on as indignantly as an organist who can write tonal fugues looks on at the success of Mr Milton Well—. Bless my soul! that reminds me: I have forgotten all about The Castle of Como. To business!

* The Alhambra, built in 1856 and operated as a music hall since 1860, was completely demolished on 7 December 1882. Newly rebuilt, it opened on 18 October 1884 as the Alhambra Theatre of Varieties.

Well, as I was saying, Mr Cowen had to make Claude Melnotte a baritone for the accommodation of Mr Santley, who was then Carl Rosa's trump card. The tenor in Pauline was Glavis. Major Cockle makes Glavis a contralto, and so adds another woman-man monstrosity to the Maffio Orsinis, Urbains, Siebels, Oscars, and Adrianos of the past. There are duets, solos, declamatory *recitatives* instead of dialogue, choruses, ballets, wedding processions, visions, bells, orchestral effects, and so on. Have I not often enough declared that these things can be as easily manufactured by an intelligent man with a musical turn as a shilling shocker by an idiot with a literary turn? Major Cockle blazes away most courageously with horse, foot, and artillery: strings, wind and drums, taking his effects where he can get them, in the school of experience (of other people's works) after the eclectic fashion of Max Bruch and M. Massenet. But the plan of listening to twenty operas and then saying "Go to: let us make a twentyfirst," though it may make a beginning for a composer, will never make a reputation for him. And The Castle of Como is such a beginning and nothing more. The orchestration, handled in the coarsest Italian manner under Signor Coronaro, who forgot that the Opera Comique is not quite as large as La Scala, and that his men are very rough performers indeed compared to those of Signor Faccio, is spirited but not very adroit, the woodwind parts especially being piled up in a heap in the most undistinguished fashion. The notion of illustrating Claude's description of the "palace lifting to eternal summer" by an ill-contrived vision of a Mediterranean gambling hell is a folly that will probably not survive the laughter of the first few representations. The principals are fairly competent as far as singing goes, which is as much as one can say at present for the raw levies of English opera.

Leaving The Castle of Como at the end of the second

act, I was able to look in at the Avenue Theatre in time for Mr Solomon's musical version of The Area Belle. I do not know whether they measure and number a policeman like a hat, by adding his length to his breadth and halving the result; but unless they do, Mr Penley is not credible as a member of the police force. However, it is traditionally correct to have a very short policeman and a very tall soldier. Mr Solomon's tunes are neat, fluent, and lively; and when he interpolates a stave of The Girl I left behind me the dramatic critics recognize it and hail it as a high contrapuntal achievement. But when Mr Penley, in the middle of a concerted piece, ridiculously warbled a line to the tune of Come into the garden, Maud, the allusion was, I noticed, too subtle: nobody laughed. I was sorry to see how new methods of education are sweeping old jokes into oblivion. The girl in the piece was called Penelope solely to give the soldier an opportunity of saying "I love Penelope," and so provoking the policeman to retort, in the words of Lindley Murray,* "Penelope is loved by me." Will it be believed that Mr Penley actually says "*She* is loved by me"? I should have demanded my money back on the spot had I not been fascinated by Miss Alma Stanley's perfect intonation, excellent delivery of her words when singing, and the thorough and hearty care she took of her part. The ghost business—always a weak point in this funny old-fashioned farce—is much too long.

I have left myself too little space to speak of my trip to Camberwell on Monday to hear the South London Choral Association songfully illustrating a lecture on Mendelssohn by Mr F. G. Edwardes, organist of the St John's Wood Presbyterian Church. I cannot say that the part-songs had any relevance to the lecture beyond the

* Scottish-American grammarian (1745–1826), noted for his Grammar of the English Language (1795).

fact that Mendelssohn composed them; and I should like to ask Mr Edwardes rather pointedly whether it is not time to leave off that Mendelssohn petting which is as essentially inappreciative as it is childishly uncritical and unintelligent. Surely we have suffered enough of it at the hands of Mr Bennett in the Daily Telegraph and Musical Times without having it perpetuated by younger men. But my main purpose in mentioning the occasion was to proclaim the excellence of Mr Venable's choir. The quality of sound produced was admirable: all tone and no noise; and its volume was so well under control that Mr Venables shewed some disposition to shew it off, like an organist with a new swell shutter. I have no doubt, from the way Mr Gatehouse played the part of the violin concerto, that he is a very capable leader for the Institute orchestra.

VOICES AND REGISTERS
The Star, 11 October 1889

On Thursday evening last week, something drew away my attention from the fact that I am The Star musical critic. I have recollected it only this moment, when it is too late to go anywhere in search of a performance to write about. Therefore there will be no column this week, as I have made up my mind resolutely to check my tendency to discursiveness, and confine myself to a simple direct account of current musical events. It is plain that people do not buy The Star to read about my private affairs and opinions; and since I have missed the Leeds Festival, whither I unquestionably ought to have gone, I had better hold my tongue until I have something to say. I really regret Leeds, not so much on account of

[812]

the music as of the improving influence of all the oratorios and cantatas.

Just a word before I affix my signature. The gentleman who wrote to the Daily News insisting that tenors should sing in the register called falsetto (or "short reed," as Dr Morell Mackenzie calls it) has been promptly assailed by another gentleman, who reminds him that Mario and Jean de Reszke began as baritones. As Mario began without the advantage of my critical super-audition, I cannot say anything about him, except that he certainly ended as a baritone, and a bad one, at an age which left Mr Sims Reeves's voice pure and undiminished. De Reszke's baritone days I remember very well. He was by no means the deep powerful *basso cantante* his brother Edouard now is. Don Giovanni and Valentin in Faust were his best parts (though he was, of course, quite an immature Don): his voice was light, delicate, and of a charming quality; he was slim, and the handsomest young man I ever saw on the stage; and out of a score of Don Juans and Valentins he is the only one I specially remember. Nowadays he is a tenor, robust in person and method, still goodlooking and distinguished, but, except when something wakes him up, comparatively— well, I do not like to say inane. Let us call it disillusioned.

And now, will Mr Palmer or Dr Morell Mackenzie, or some other expert, tell us what has happened, physiologically, to De Reszke's voice? The aerial upper register of the baritone is now the thick middle register of the tenor; and the change has been from less to greater power and vigor, and not the converse, as the change from baritone to tenor seems to have suggested to Mr Palmer's critic. Was the gain of an extra fourth at the top of his compass an incident in his physical growth, like the appearance of an eye tooth? Did the middle of his tenor voice, which was so much lighter and purer when it was the top of his baritone voice, change from a short reed or falsetto register to a long reed or chest one? Finally, can anyone explain how the trick is done? I am a baritone myself; but my disposition is so romantic that I have kept off the lyric stage because nearly all the romantic parts are written for tenors. Still, if De Reszke and Mario raised themselves from baritones to tenors, why should not I?

Though I loathe nothing more than the commonplace that the truth always lies between the two extremes (truth being quite the most extreme thing I know of), I venture to suggest that the balance of advantage lies with singers who can use both registers effectively, and who have intelligent instincts of self-preservation to prevent them from forcing the long reed production above its safe limit. Mr Sims Reeves and his son, and Maas in his later days, are samples of Mr Palmer's system. So, in speaking, was Charles Mathews. They all saved their voices from coarsening, and from wear and tear; but they also sacrificed dramatic vigor to coddle their falsettos, and were insufferably lackadaisical except where the appropriate expression of the music fell within the limits of their method.

I heard Mathews* play Used Up when he was so old that his throat was externally like wrinkled parchment; and I was struck with the perfect lightness and preservation of his voice. But in the last act, where Sir Charles Coldstream lifts up the cellar trap and sees the man whom he has, as he thinks, murdered, a vehement exclamation is required; and this Mathews could not manage, just as Maas, when playing Don Cæsar de Bazan, could not challenge the captain of the guard like a man, but warbled at him like a querulous dove. On the other hand, the plan of using the long reed production

* C.J. Mathews, actor and author of the comedy Used Up (1845), adapted from the French.

all over the voice destroys, first, the quality of the voice, then the power of adjusting the overstrained vocal cords to the right pitch, and finally the voice itself. Tietjens once warned a friend of mine against this in terms which shewed how keenly she felt its danger. Yet within a year or so she took up the contralto part of Leonora in La Favorita, and became such a slave to the practice she had denounced that she speedily became a mere wreck. Not long before her death I heard her in Fidelio. At the end of *Komm Hoffnung, lass den letzten Stern*, she, by a frantic effort, sang the B natural with her chest voice, or, at least—to use the Mackenzie terminology—with as long a reed as she could humanly bring to bear on it. During the rest of the opera she failed to get a single note in tune—and failed consciously. A tragic hearing!

These terms, "long reed" and "short reed," are an improvement on the old "chest voice, head voice, falsetto," &c. Perhaps I should explain what "registers" are. Well, inquiring reader, your windpipe is furnished at the top with a pair of lips; and when you whistle with these lips instead of with your facial ones, the result is: singing. When you are whistling through their whole length and altering the pitch by lengthening or shortening the organ pipe formed by the back of your throat—a process involving only very slight modifications in the tension of these inner lips—you are singing with your chest voice, or *voce di petto*, or long reed register, whichever you please to call it. When you want to get up to notes which could be better produced if the lips were shorter and thinner, you perform a curious operation called changing the register: that is, you shut the lips at one end far enough to leave only the convenient length open, and with the "short reed" so left, you start again on a new plane, adjusting the length of the organ pipe as before. Then you are singing falsetto, or in *voce di gola*, or throat voice, or short reed register. The most striking example of change of register is when a man sings a low note in his natural voice and then another high up in imitation of a woman. This high voice is what used to be called *voce di testa* or head voice, before the names got so appallingly confused as they are at present. A more agreeable and subtle, but still very distinct contrast of registers may be heard whenever Madame Patey sings Beethoven's Creation's Hymn. The laryngoscope has proved that the old tradition of three voices, giving the sensation of coming from the chest, the throat, and the head respectively, had, in the registering mechanism, a foundation of physiological fact; but as to how many registers can be made, how many *should* be made, whether any at all ought to be made, whether the old names should be retained, which was which, and what practical conclusions the singing master should draw: on all these points there exist not only differences of opinion, but feuds—deadly, implacable vendettas—in which each party regards all the others as impostors, quacks, voice smashers, ignoramuses, rascals, and liars.

Somehow, musicians are amazingly ill-conditioned controversialists. They are almost as bad as scientific men: not quite so dogmatic or so insolent perhaps, but still equally void of good humor and sense of social solidarity with their opponents. Just as, in my boyish days, I hardly ever met a schoolmaster who seemed to know that he was as much bound to be polite to me as long as I behaved myself as to my father as long as he paid the bill, I seldom read a musical paper now without wondering whether the writers are as unmannerly in private life as they are in print. It is my schoolmaster over again. He had a notion that his whole duty was to know, or pretend to know, more about Euclid or Virgil than I; and the result was that his obvious limitation, incompleteness, and lack of social charm made me resolve to shun the mathematical and classical influences which had apparently made him what he was. And the musical papers seem to think that *their* whole duty is to know more about music than anybody else. If some unfortunate amateur calls a tuba a bassoon, or a sonata a symphony, they write of and to him as Colonel Newcome* (a pestilential humbug) spoke of and to the Hindoos.

Mr William O'Brien† obeyed a right instinct when he told the people of Dublin to demand "that Irish music shall be heard and honored on Irish soil before the music of Italy or Germany." But the thing is impossible at present. The best modern music is the fruit of a complex culture which no Irishman can enjoy today in his own country. To honor Professor Villiers Stanford more than Wagner, or Balfe more than Mozart, is as impossible as to place Moore above Shelley, or Lever above Ibsen. If Ireland were to set about honoring Irish musicians tomorrow, what would she do? Would she go to the only class that is nationally alive: the peasantry, and give a wreath to the countryside lilter, or whistler, or piper, whose unwritten tunes made the best real music? Not a bit of it: she would go to the educated class—a class nationally dead, and artistically as sterile as Sodom and Gomorrah; pick out some plausible imitator of the hated foreigner; and then desperately pretend to think him a great Irish composer. Why, Mr O'Brien delivered this very speech in support of a concert-giver who made his reputation, not as an Irish singer under his real name of Ledwidge, but as an imitation Italian opera singer calling himself Mr Ludwig. It was not Ireland, but a lucky chance of escaping from Ireland under a foreign *impresario* (Carl Rosa), that made Mr Ludwig. Nations,

* Character in Thackeray's novel The Newcomes (1854–5).
† Young Irish nationalist leader and journalist, who had been an M.P. since 1883.

like individuals, put off opera writing until they have got out of prison. Ireland has not reached the Wagnerian stage yet. I have been there; and I know.

CENSORSHIP FOR MUSIC HALLS?

The Star, 18 October 1889

I notice with alarm that the parties to the great music hall discussion are talking about "the want" of a censor for comic songs, as if that were something to be deplored. This is encouraging, hopeful, helpful, quite delightful. Reader: can you not hear my teeth gnash as I pen these sarcasms? But I will be calm. Listen. We have got a censor of plays at present. We have had him for a considerable time. He will, I hope, excuse me if, in the exercise of my duty as a critic, I describe his function as an unmitigated nuisance. I repeat, an unmitigated nuisance. It prevents serious plays from being acted, and consequently prevents them from being written. And according to the uncontradicted statement made by Mr George Conquest* the other day to the Pall Mall Gazette, it has led him to force East End managers to cook their plays to suit his social prejudices and class interests by inducing them to alter plays in which the villain of the piece is represented as a gentleman by condition.

If he prohibited bad plays as well as good ones, and impartially reduced stage dialogue to the inanity of drawing-room conversation, there might be some excuse made by shortsighted and conventional people for his censorship, on the ground that in depriving the thoughtful of their theatre he also deprived the vicious

* Lessee since 1885 of the Surrey Theatre in Blackfriars Road, co-author of more than a hundred melodramas.

of theirs. But he never objects to a thoroughly immoral play. Mind: I do not say that I should approve of a censorship if it did forbid immoral plays. But since such prohibition is the sole ground on which the advocates of "official licensing" defend it and declare it necessary, I hasten to point out once more what has already been pointed out again and again; *i.e.* that you can perform any number of farcical comedies which from beginning to end turn upon the stage humors of adultery and prostitution; but you cannot perform Shelley's Cenci; and if you were to spend a considerable capital in preparing one of Ibsen's great works, you would do so at the risk of being forbidden to proceed at the last moment by the licenser.

This state of things is not the fault of Mr Pigott*: it is inherent in the institution of censorship. On the whole, if Mr Pigott were not a little better than his function, he would hardly have been tolerated so long. But at best he must either virtually abolish his office (except as to salary) by licensing everything indiscriminately, which would be neither honest nor, considering the moral responsibility improperly put upon him, reasonably possible; or else he must, to the best of his judgment, license the plays which seem to him tolerable and forbid those which he deems objectionable. Certainly, if I were censor, this is what I should do, short of abdicating in favor of someone who would be no less a nuisance than I. And the result would be that whilst I should never dream of objecting to the Cenci or Ibsen, I should prohibit such plays as Still Waters Run Deep, Impulse,† and The Profligate, as being, to my way of

* E. F. S. Pigott was censor of plays for the Lord Chamberlain until his death in 1895.

† Tom Taylor's Still Waters Run Deep (1855) was successfully revived at the Criterion in October 1890. B. C. Stephenson's Impulse was first performed in 1882.

thinking, false in sentiment and therefore essentially depraving to the spectators.

Obviously I should at once be recognized as an insufferable tyrant by Mr Robert Buchanan,* and by that large section of the British middle class which he typifies as far as his view of the morals of dramatic fiction is concerned. But I should not care a snap of my fingers for him. The question of the censorship has not yet reached Parliament; my salary could not be dwelt on for hours in Committee of Supply, like that of the Chief Secretary for Ireland. It would be necessary of course to keep the public in good humor by keeping my hands carefully off the farcical comedies; but, for the rest, my contention would be that since I had been appointed as Pope of the playhouse to decide by my own inner light what was good for the English people and what not, I could do no less than assume my own infallibility, and despotize away to the top of my bent.

I submit, then, that the result of establishing a new censor for the music halls is foreknown by all persons who have watched the institution at work over our theatres. It will not stop the indecency, the frivolity, the inanity; and it will stop all progress upward from them. If we can think of no more effective machine than a censor for making music halls better than the people who go to them, we may as well try *laisser-faire* for a while. Mr McDougall† himself saw the futility of suggesting a censorship of the lines sung; for the indecency, innocent Mr Juggins,# is always between

* Poet, novelist, and prolific playwright, who was a vehement anti-Ibsenite.

† John McDougall, chairman of the London County Council.

Although "juggins" had been employed since the early XVII century as a slang term for a simpleton or gull, it had

[820]

the lines, where nothing but virgin paper would meet the eye of a licenser. He was quite right in concluding that the only way to bring the music halls into accord with his ideas of what they should be, was to force on them the alternative of that or peremptory closure.

As to the general question of the quality of music hall entertainment, I have nothing to say about that: I am not a representative of the true music hall public, which consists partly of people whose powers of imaginative apprehension and attention are too limited to follow even the most incoherent melodrama, and partly of people who like to sit smoking and soaking in lazy contemplation of something that does not really matter. What astonishes a theatregoer at a music hall, or an educated woman when she realizes one of her most cherished dreams by at last persuading either her husband or the man-about-towniest of his friends to take her to the London Pavilion or the Empire, is the indifference of the audience to the performance. Five out of six of the "turns" are of the deadliest dulness: ten minutes of it would seal the fate of any drama; but the people do not mind: they drink and smoke. Under these circumstances the standard of interest, much less of art, is low, the strain on the management or the artists to keep it up being of the slightest. It is rising slowly, in spite of the influence of that detestable product of civilization, the rich man's son, who now represents a distinct class, technically described as "masher," and growing with the accumulation of riches in idle hands produced by our idiotic industrial system. If left to develop freely, our best music halls would in course of

---

recently been popularized by the sobriquet "Jubilee Juggins" bestowed upon a young idler, Ernest Benzon, who squandered a fortune betting on horses in 1887, around the time of Victoria's jubilee.

time present a combination of promenade concert, theatre, and circus (minus the horses): that is, you would have a good band, decent concert singers, acrobats, jugglers, ballets, and dramatic sketches, all in the same evening. And the refreshment department will probably develop also, as 'Arry develops into the noble Juggins, and begins to prefer the aerated bread shop to the public house.

Of course the theatre monopolists fear that this would ruin most of them. But it does not follow; though if it did we should allow them to be ruined just as complacently as we allowed the stage coach proprietors to be ruined by the introduction of railways. The manager whose patrons prefer a variety entertainment can give them what they want by turning music hall manager. The houses whose patrons prefer the drama have simply to stick to the drama, and they will not be ruined. When a theatre has been playing down as nearly as possible to the music hall level, it will lose the tail of its audience when the music halls are set free from their present medieval shackles; but it can, and ought to, recruit its thinned benches by playing up to the level of the thoughtful people who now avoid the theatre because the life and morals of the stage are a century behind those of the educated world. All these results are at present hindered by absurd monopolies, censorships, and protective regulations which are enough to make Adam Smith turn in his grave, so completely do they defeat their professed public ends.

[U] I have been asked whether I would let music hall singers do just what they please. I reply that there is no question of any such anarchy. If a man speaks or behaves indecently in public, he is liable to punishment for the misdemeanor. Music hall singers at present enjoy a special exemption in this respect, because the place is "licensed." I would withdraw that license, and throw the full responsibility for the song upon the singer, who would be liable to prosecution in the ordinary course by any outraged member of the audience—perhaps Mr McDougall and his friends in person, present expressly for that purpose.[U]

Just consider this one fact. A newspaper or book containing lewd matter can do a thousand times more harm than any indecent song or dance. Yet there is no censor of the Press. Nothing but a sense of public responsibility, and the prospect of being called to account before a jury, prevents the proprietors of The Star from turning it into a broadsheet of obscene anecdotes. Yet the editor would never dream of allowing such pleasantries into his columns as the official licenser of plays hallmarks for public use on the stages of the Avenue, the Criterion, the Gaiety, and the Comedy Theatres. I shall not insult the public intelligence by again drawing the moral.

FAUST AT THE ALBERT HALL
The Star, 31 October 1889

A stroll round the gallery of the Albert Hall last night during the first part of Berlioz's Faust brought me past so many wage-working men of a type unknown at oratorio performances that I must at once say something which members of the Church Establishment had better skip lest they be shocked beyond recovery. It is nothing short of this—that a large section of the most alert-minded, forward, and culture-capable of the London artisan class are eager to gratify their curiosity about this wonderful art of music, if only they can get it dissociated from the detested names—dont be shocked, reader, it is quite true—of St Paul, Elijah, Saul, and the other terrors

[823]

of the poor man's Sunday school. It is useless to blink the fact. Just as the workman, long after he wanted to give up bad beer and spirits for coffee and cocoa, yet refused to enter the coffee tavern until he could get what he wanted there without a tract and an inquiry as to whether he was saved, so he will keep out of the concert room until he feels certain that he will not be reminded there of the hated "religious instruction" to the hypocrisy of which his own poverty bears unanswerable testimony. He hates fugues because they remind him of anthems; an oratorio makes him feel as if he were in church, which is the most horrible sensation known to him short of actual bodily pain, because there is no place where he is forced to feel the shabbiness of his clothes and the unsocial contempt in which he is held by church-going respectability, as he is forced to feel it there.

Therefore, I plead for more secular music for the workman—for picturesque dramatic music that will hold him as a novel holds him, whilst his ear is automatically acquiring the training that will eventually make him conscious of purely physical beauty. Faust he evidently likes, and he would perhaps relish it even more if Mr Barnby could be persuaded to conduct a trifle less canonically. Berlioz has told us how the audience rose in a wild tumult of patriotic enthusiasm when he first gave them his version of the Rákóczy March. At the Albert Hall last night the audience, with admirable self-control, kept their seats, and did not even *encore* the march. Mr Barnby is certain to be made a knight some day in the ordinary course; but before it is too late let me suggest that he should be made a bishop instead. At the same time I must again bear testimony to the enormous pains he has taken to drill that huge and stolid choir, and to the success with which he has taught them to produce genuine vocal tone and to do their duty with precision and some delicacy, if not with intelligence. I wonder he was not killed by the struggle with their thousandfold pigheadedness (this is not polite, I know; but, bless you, the Albert Hall choristers never read Radical newspapers). I had to leave at the end of the first part, and so did not hear Margaret. Mr Iver McKay, the Faust of the evening, was not in brilliant voice; he was more often flat than not. Mr Henschel sang the Mephistopheles music, which suits his peculiarities, cleverly—more cleverly, perhaps, than could any of his rivals in the part, except Mr Max Heinrich. Mr Ben Grove was an excellent Brander, again shewing himself to be what I declared him when he sang King Mark's music at Mr Armbruster's recital of Tristan, a capable, trustworthy, self-respecting, and Art-respecting singer.

A PORTFOLIO OF NEW MUSIC

The Star, 1 November 1889

This week, dear reader, we shall have some nice little reviews of recent musical publications. But do not on that account resolve too hastily to skip me: the subject has its lively side, unless you happen to be on the premises whilst the reviewer is trying them over. Publishing enterprise must have recognition and encouragement—when it deserves them. For I must add that one or two eminent firms have seen in the simplicity of my character only something to practise upon with lays that they would not impose on a City Father after a heavy dinner.

Here are a couple of samples of the sort of thing sent to me on the off—the exceedingly off—chance of my having been born recently enough to describe them respectively as "a graceful and effective drawing room song, compass F to G," and "a dashing nautical ballad, with swinging chorus, suitable for a smoking concert, and within the resources of a robust baritone."

Are they all forgotten?
    Moments that are past?
Have they fled for ever?
    Moments that are past.
        A-a-a-a-a-a-a-a-ah!

Only come again
    As you came to me that day
When the sun was on the river
    And the scent was in the hay.
        A-a-a-a-a-a-a-a-a-a-ah!

Only come again
    As you came to me that day
When we sat and talked together
    As true lovers only may.

Here is the other—

Dead! Men! No! secrets tell
    Mer! Cy! But! scant we shew
Young or old we seize their gold
    Then up the plank they go
Jolly good luck to our flag so grim
    Emblem of deeds we do
Millions of wealth, long life and health
    To the Vam-Pire's crew.

The last verse explains that "England, hearing rumors of bloodshed and marauding, dispatched a cruiser ably armed and manned, commanded by a Briton (by danger nothing daunted) to mete out vengeance with relentless hand. They fell in with the schooner and brought her soon to action. The combat raged with fury fierce and long. The pirates, taken captive, were hanged beside their leader, who never more will sing his gruesome

> Dead men no, &c. &c. &c."

My readers will hardly believe that such things have been thrust upon my notice; but they have. I do not think I have deserved it. At any rate I decline to put myself in danger of hell fire by calling the people who admire such trash by their proper name.

Messrs Novello have treated me far more handsomely. And yet there is one thing in their contribution which I must declare inferior to the Vam-Pire's Crew, because there are unquestionably idiots in the world who like the Vampire; but no human being ever liked a Church Cantata written to order for one of our provincial Festivals. Here it is, in the familiar Novello buff and brown cover, price two shillings. The words, I blush to say, are by a brother critic. Listen!

> Rest thee, my Savior, rest Thy head meetly.
> Angels watch over Thee sleeping so sweetly.
>> No dream alarm
>> With thought of harm
> Till night and its shadows have vanished
> completely.

Take it away, Messrs Novello, take it away. Burn the whole edition, lest any choral society should waste its time on rhyme-jingling that never once rises to the level of blasphemy, and on music-mongering that is enough to make every intelligent student in England forswear counterpoint. I suppose the stewards of the —— Musical Festival thought they were encouraging English music by ordering a cantata; and I am bound to assume that my colleague of the largest circulation in the world is honestly and infatuatedly unconscious of how detestable his verses are from a literary point of view, and how their essential triviality must jar on all sincere Christians. But there are limits to the allowances I am prepared to make. In future it will be necessary to square The Star if the truth about these matters is to remain untold any longer. Either I must have my share of the libretto-making or I blow the gaff.

WORKING MEN AND SACRED MUSIC
The Star, 8 November 1889

Here is a gentleman from Somersetshire wishing to know how I can "reconcile the statement that working men care not for oratorios on account of their sacred or religious character to the fact that at the People's Palace Elijah, Messiah, &c., draw enormous audiences." Now I tell the gentleman from Somersetshire once for all that it wont do. I never speak of "working men" as if they were a consignment of regulation boots, all alike except as to assorted sizes.

There are working men who delight in piety—who join the Salvation Army, or drag their unfortunate children evening after evening to dismal chapels, where their poor little imaginations are filled with eternal torment, vengeance, sin and the devil. Others there be who go to secular halls, and revel in demonstrations that Moses thought the earth flat, and that if any of the four evangelists told the truth the other three necessarily told lies. Of the two extremes, that of extracting nothing from Hebrew literature but discrepancies and absurdities is on the whole more religious than extracting nothing but wrath and terror from it. Both practices, regarded as rites, are essentially savage; but the prevalence of one gives a certain humor to the other, and indeed grows inevitably out of it.

The majority of churchgoing workmen, probably, are heathens like the rest of us, going as a matter of habit, just as they wear neckties, because their respectability would be doubted if they omitted the observance. Some abstainers who are lazy or prefer their club approve of churchgoing as an institution, and make their children go. Others, again, go because they like it or are used to it, but dont attach sufficient importance to it to insist on their families coming with them. Hundreds go because they have a vague sense of higher duties owed somewhere, and can find no other means of payment. And the reasons for abstention are quite as various and inconsequent as those for attendance.

Hence, in speaking of the working men who go to hear Berlioz's Faust, but are repelled by Scriptural oratorios, I was careful to speak of them as a section only, though I mentioned certain reasons for regarding them as a section important to cater for: numerous, curious, aspiring, intelligent, and comparatively independent in their judgment. It is not necessary for me to repeat here what I then said; but I desire to impress on my Somersetshire correspondent that oratorio performances at prices within the means of working men are so few relatively to the huge bulk of the working class that if there were twice as many of them, and these twice as crowded, they would be as dust in the balance against the general presumption that the average laborer knows and cares no more about Elijah than he does about the Thirtynine Articles. It is true that wherever human life is there also is music, and a belief in the supernatural; and probably no slum in Europe is without denizens who will sing or dance or send at point of death for a priest. But that does not make every slum contribute to the congregation of St Paul's or the audiences at the

Albert Hall. The unlucky majority still want bread and butter much more than they want Bach and Beethoven.

Another correspondent asks me to decide a wager for him. The question at issue is whether alto parts are not frequently sung in our churches by men as well as by boys. I am hardly the man to settle such a point. In my small boyhood I was a victim of the inhuman and absurd custom of compelling young children to sit out morning service every Sunday. To sit motionless and speechless in your best suit in a dark stuffy church on a morning that is fine outside the building, with your young limbs aching with unnatural quiet, your restless imagination tired of speculating about the same grownup people in the same pews every Sunday, your conscience heavy with the illusion that you are the only reprobate present sufficiently wicked to long for the benediction, and to wish that they would sing something out of an opera instead of Jackson in F, not to mention hating the clergyman as a sanctimonious bore, and dreading the sexton as a man likely to turn bad boys out and possibly to know them at sight by official inspiration: all this is enough to lead any sensitive youth to resolve that when he grows up and can do as he likes, the first use he will make of his liberty will be to stay away from church. Anyhow, I have not attended a service seven times in the last twentyfive years, nor do I propose to stir up gloomy memories and wrathful passions by altering my practice in this respect. Therefore, all I can say on the subject of my correspondent's wager is that adult male alto and countertenor singers, though no longer as common as they once were, are still to be heard in all directions singing the parts specially written for their kind of voice by the composers of the great English school: not the secondhand Handels and Mendelssohns of the past century and a half, but the writers of the glees, madrigals, and motets and services which are the true English musical classics. Nowadays, however, since the opera and the concert platform offer golden opportunities to a tenor or a baritone, wheras an alto or countertenor is confined to the choir or the glee quartet all his life, a promising choir boy gets rid of his treble as soon as Nature permits him. The effect of this in diminishing the number of adult altos must be considerable.

Thackeray students will remember that when Colonel Newcome returned from India, and obliged a convivial circle by singing a ballad in a countertenor voice with florid ornaments in the taste of his own heyday, he was astonished to find everybody laughing at him. But I myself have seen a singer—a young man—appear before an audience of "the classes" in a blue evening coat with brass buttons, and gravely sing a song by Mendelssohn in an alto voice. The effect was by no means disagreeable; but it was so strange and unexpected that the room positively vibrated with suppressed laughter. The same thing would happen at one of Messrs Boosey's ballad concerts if an alto were engaged; though downstairs, at the Christy Minstrels, an alto, black with burnt cork, might at the same moment be piping away as a matter of course to an audience quite familiar with his voice. Thus to some people the man alto is an everyday phenomenon, whilst to others he is either a Thackerayan tradition or an extravagant novelty. Hence wagers!

Before quitting the subject of church music, I may mention that an exciting discussion has been raging in the Musical World on the proper accentuation of the Nicene Creed. Archbishops have joined the fray; and their letters, mostly in Greek, form a pleasing variety to portraits of Madame Patti. This is all to the good: any discussion which brings into relief the inadequacy of mere musical grammar to qualify a Mus.Bac. or Mus. Doc. to raise human speech to the eloquence which

Purcell and Handel gave it will help music. I observe with immense approval that the Musical World now makes room for criticism of all the arts. Nothing more unmusical can be imagined than a musical paper all about music.

The students of the Royal Academy of Music had a concert of chamber music all to themselves at St James's Hall last Monday afternoon. It was a very creditable performance, especially the Mendelssohn pianoforte trio, the first three movements of which were excellently played, in spite of an accompaniment from somebody on the roof with a hammer, who produced exactly the effect of Hans Sachs in Beckmesser's serenade. Pupils' work cannot be criticized from a merely technical point of view, as the performers are carefully doing what they have been taught instead of following their own original impulse. The choir of young ladies, in unnecessarily ugly arrangements of white dress and red sash, sang correctly; and there was less than I had feared of that baneful grinding of the voice which has always been the curse of Academy and Conservatoire teaching. But the diction was bad throughout. As far as I could distinguish the words sung, the articulation was distinct but not pure; and the vowels were often as corrupt as they could be. A professsor of really fine elocution is needed in Tenterden-street.

[U] On Tuesday I fulfilled my threat of going down to Blackheath to hear Mr Burnett's string quartet play a work of Paganini's. They also played Brahms's pianoforte quintet in F minor; and in this they shewed their English qualities—a formidable body of tone (they would have drowned the strings of a moderate German orchestra), precision, contempt for difficulties, vigor, and workmanlike earnestness. On the other hand, they decidedly lacked sensitiveness; there were no half tones in the pictorial sense; their *fortes* and *pianos* (with hardly anything between) were treated rather as opportunities for letting themselves go and necessities for holding themselves in than as variations in mood or gradations in depth of feeling. They were not subtle enough to create the magic atmosphere which is the first condition of the highest success in instrumental music. A considerable share of the failure in this respect was due to the gentleman at the piano, who, though an enviably dexterous and accurate keyboard manipulator, was no pianist: possibly the organ is his instrument. Blackheath, if it knows anything about music—which I regard as improbable—will support Mr Burnett strenuously; for the quartet is one of exceptional capability, and would be encouraged, on principle, in any place which was alive to the importance of artistic culture to its rising generation.[U]

LOVE AND BONNETS
The Star, 11 November 1889

There is no harm in saying now that when Madame Falk-Mehlig was Miss Anna Mehlig she was not my favorite pianist. She was well taught, diligent, and accurate; but she used to leave me in the frostiest and most forlorn condition, because she was still in the schoolgirl phase of being troubled with a conscience. Now you cannot be a great artist until you have outgrown your conscience—until in playing the right way you are doing exactly what you like because you like it. When the news came that Miss Mehlig had married, and retired—in other words, had sacrificed her sonata playing for love—I counted it as the first genuine artistic act in her career. Accordingly, nothing can be more natural than her return to her art after some years in full possession of a ripened talent expressing itself freely and sympathetically with a warmth and charm that were lacking in the old days. She was cordially welcomed at the Crystal Palace on Saturday, when she sat down to the famous Beethoven concerto in E flat; and she played it for the greater part very prettily. I say for the greater part, because the last movement, the peculiar accentuation of which requires the finest rhythmical management, baffled her; only a few bits of graceful passage-playing in it being really worth listening to. Madame Nordica, with her capital method, light vocal touch, and bright tone, all in complete working order, gave us a song of Marschner's—one so German as to be nothing if not sentimental—with a surprising want of feeling. As to the ballad by Gomez, which was her second contribution, it sounded like the very last sweepings of the refuse of the Rossini school. Liszt's Campanella, a piece of rank drawing-room rubbish, sounded serious and original in comparison. I appreciate Madame Nordica, I hope; but there are two things about her that I cannot get over: the transparent superficiality of her artistic feeling; and her bonnets, which may be excellently confected from the bonnettist's point of view, but which give her an air of not being at home in the very place where an artist should feel and look most at home. They make us feel as if we had interrupted her on the point of going out for a walk. The orchestra gave an appetizing taste of its quality in the concerto, the horn parts in particular coming out quite beautifully, though I must add that these instruments met with reverses later on, in the intermezzo to the Goetz symphony. Concerning which noble work by a great composer, I would ask Sir George Grove whether he has become at all conscious of the obvious absurdity of the patronizing tone which he and Macfarren adopted when Goetz's works were first produced here. Sir George

[834]

was not so bad as Macfarren, who could find nothing more sensible to say about the joyous Spring overture than that it contained consecutive sevenths; but he programmed in a pat-the-young-man-on-the-back style which was a very unworthy response to such an inmost confidence; for the symphony is of no less sacred a nature. But, now that I think of it, Sir George patronized everyone in his programming days: even Beethoven. The new rhapsody by Lalo has a second movement which would make a suitable and spirited *entr'acte* for a Norwegian play; but from the dignified standard of the Crystal Palace concerts I must describe it compendiously as tiddy-fol-lol.

St Paul next Saturday. I shall go expressly to abuse it.

THE COPYRIGHT QUESTION
The Star, 15 November 1889

I must apologize to the Musical Guild of ex-scholars and ex-students of the Royal College of Music for having missed their first concert at the Kensington Town Hall on Tuesday. Last season, appreciating the importance of such a society, I was one of the first to call attention to it and to recommend its opening concerts to the public. The Guild shewed its sense of my foresight and magnanimity by not inviting me even once. This time I forgot all about it; and the result is, of course, an invitation to the whole series of concerts. Such is musical life. However, I did not introduce the subject to complain of the slights and ingratitudes to which my zeal in the public service and my too indulgent attitude as a critic expose me, nor even to make it known that the second concert will be given on next Wednesday week, and will include the Kreutzer sonata and Brahms's trio

in E flat for pianoforte, violin, and horn, Op. 40. I simply
wish to explain my absence on Tuesday.

The fact is, I was at Leicester delivering to the
midlanders an impassioned appeal for a remodeling of
their municipal institutions on Bassettoist principles.
Now it happened whilst I was in the greenroom of the
Co-operative Hall, contemplatively enjoying the "Bayreuth hush" which preceded my bodily appearance on
the platform, my eye fell on a writing upon the wall.
Curiosity is one of my finest traits; and I at once began
to read the document. It was a list of the songs which can
only be sung subject to performing rights held by a
certain Mr Harry Wall, who made himself famous in
the eighteen-seventies by the persistence with which he
mulcted in penalties singers of all degreees who had
unsuspectingly warbled his property. The difficulty
always lay in finding out what songs were Mr Wall's and
what were not. The London Figaro, which pursued him
throughout with relentless disapproval, noted the songs
which he had made the subject of legal proceedings, and
published a list for the guidance of singers. The writing
on the wall at Leicester is probably a copy of this list.

The list had no direct interest for me at the moment,
as I did not propose to entertain the audience with
minstrelsy. But it reminded me that there is at present
in the field a formidable and more dignified representative of performing rights in the person of Mr Alfred
Moul, whom bandmasters and arrangers and "selection"
makers of all sorts, accustomed to free communism in
musical compositions, are now vigorously denouncing
as a blackmailer. This means that he has been making
people pay for something which they have hitherto
pirated for nothing. Before I say anything as to the
merits of such a proceeding I may mention that the
denunciations of Mr Moul specially amused me, because
he is an old acquaintance of mine; and I derive the usual

entertainment from seeing people whom I privately know in a vigorous row of any kind.

When I first came across Mr Alfred Moul some twenty years or so ago, I took him to be a young man of about eighteen, unnaturally self-sufficient and finished for his age, and a very clever pianist, though not then a professional one. When I last saw him, at the "private view" of Her Majesty's Theatre as decorated for Mr Leslie's recent promenade concerts, the lapse of two decades had made the gravest alterations, not to say ravages, in my own aspect; but Moul (I lapse for the moment into the familiarity of private intercourse) was still eighteen. The effect of this curious phenomenon was totally to destroy my faith in my original estimate of his years. He may have been threescore all along: he may be the Wandering Gentile, if there is such a person. Certain it is that age cannot wither him; and as to custom staling his infinite variety, I can only say that I have had glimpses of him through the smoke of the battle of life during the twenty years in question, as pianoforte virtuoso, conductor, voice trainer, composer, publisher, artist, professor, and man of business. But he has always been elegant, and always eighteen.

As a composer I never could elude him for long. As he invariably gave up an enterprise the moment he succeeded in it, and so was never the same thing for long; so he never composed under the same name for more than a month. When I got a bundle of music to review, it was sure to contain a song, or a waltz, or a pianoforte piece by Cyril This, or Prosper That, or Stephen the Other (he was particularly fond of Stephen); but the first six bars would reveal the style of Moul; for *le style c'est l'homme*. At first I used to hail these discoveries with pleased surprise. Later on I received them with imprecations, having exhausted every form of words that logrolling amenity could take.

[837]

Then he disappeared for a long time; and I was mourning him as dead or married or otherwise extinguished when a colonial *prima donna* told me of a great pianist named Alfred Moul who had given concerts at the Antipodes. Some time after this I began, from the tops of omnibuses, to catch glimpses in passing hansoms of a figure which I supposed must be that of a son of Moul's, wonderfully like his father. Later on the figure accosted me, and convinced me that he was Alfred Moul himself, looking perhaps six months younger, but, save for a certain added mellowness of manner, otherwise the same. In his latest incarnation he is Agent-General for the British Empire of the French Society of Authors, Composers, and Music Publishers; and his business is to enforce the rights created by copyright legislation as interpreted by the articles of the International Convention held at Berne in 1887. And in my opinion the society is to be congratulated on having got hold of a very capable representative.

If I could gather from current complaints that the new Agent-General had enforced these rights offensively, or made unreasonable and extortionate demands, or aggrieved the complainants in any other way than in making them pay for what they had been accustomed to lay hands on freely, I should have hurried to 40 Old Bond-street, and called upon him to explain or amend his life before I alluded to the subject in print. But there is no case against him. There is a case against the law— against its ambiguity in the abstract—against the difficulty of ascertaining its bearing on any particular emergency—against the uselessness of the Stationers' Hall register—against the impossibility of finding whether the law's bite is as bad as its bark by any other process than the risky one of putting your head into its mouth. But these are not the fault of any Agent-General: they are the fault of our legal machinery. There is also a case—a very strong case—in favor of Communism as against Private Property; but the implied suggestion that Communism should be the rule as to works of art whilst Private Property remains the rule for everything else is unworkable. We cannot reasonably deny to the author or composer those rights (or wrongs) against others which others have against him. Copyrights and patent rights are as a matter of fact the least objectionable forms of private property in permanent sources of wealth and pleasure; because, unlike the analogous property rights in land and capital, they are limited in duration, and their reversion to the entire community is eventually secured. Shorten their duration by all means if expedient—I have always urged that copyrights should be shortened as they extend internationally—but whilst they last they are the means by which the author or composer gets paid for his labor. If Mr Moul is a blackmailer for enforcing them, then so is any agent who enforces the payment of a patentee's royalty; so equally is the concert-giver who enforces payment of a shilling at the turnstile; and so doubly is the agent who enforces payment of a landlord's rent or a shareholder's dividend. I might as well complain of blackmail whenever I pay for admissions to musical entertainments, because, forsooth, I am often invited to attend such entertainments freely as "a gentleman of the Press."

Therefore, I advise conductors who make potpourris and selections from the works of living composers to pay their shot without abusing the collector, except in cases where they admit the audience either for nothing or at a cost barely sufficient to cover the rent of the room and the gas bill, in which case they would, of course, have some ground for an appeal to the generosity and public spirit of the composer. But when they are simply trading in music for profit I am at a loss to see why the composer should allow them to exploit a single semiquaver of his without getting his share of the money it attracts. Moral therefore: Agitate (as a Communist) for the repeal of the Copyright Acts if you will; point out the inconveniences of its operation as much as you please; but in the name of common sense let the innocent and useful Mr Alfred Moul alone.

I have quite a mass of other subjects to deal with this week; but I find that this copyright question has mopped up all the ink I have space for. I must, however, call attention to one real grievance. A remarkable drawing has arrived here representing a young lady who has cast herself despairingly on the floor amid the ruins of what seems to be a voluminous manuscript. Underneath is written "When your heart is rent at sight of this, P.T.O." Turning over as requested, I find that the subject of the picture is my correspondent (resident at Brook Green) after Mr Barnum's steam organ has begun its fourteenth repetition of its repertory of a waltz, a polka, and variations on the National Anthem. "I need not describe the sound" she says "you can hear it at Stonecutter-street if you open the window." I have opened the window and can hear it quite distinctly. I appeal to Mr Barnum's chivalry. Can he not either stop it or play *con sordino?*

ORATORIO FOR THE CLASSES AND THE MASSES

The Star, 18 November 1889

To sit on hard chairs listening to oratorios from three to half-past ten, with a few intervals of train and tramcar, is not the liveliest way of spending a Saturday half-holiday, especially when one of the oratorios is St Paul. But since the other was Judas Maccabæus there were compensations in my lot on Saturday: at any rate, my last state was not worse than my first. St Paul, you will understand, was done on Saturday afternoon at the Crystal Palace concert; and Judas followed in the evening at the People's Palace. Of the first of the two performances, I need not renew my weariness by writing much. After all, Mendelssohn was Mendelssohn, who, even in his emptiest *tours de force* where he had no message to deliver and nothing to feel deeply about, yet felt deeply about nothing, and wrote beautifully, if not pregnantly, because he could not endure to write otherwise. But even beauty does not make subjectless music interesting; and I had as lief talk Sunday-school for two hours and a half to a beautiful woman with no brains as listen to St Paul over again. As to the performance, the orchestra was good; the choir was odious—simply odious; Mr Lloyd was in his best vein; and Mr Brereton, I must charitably hope, in his worst. If Miss Anna Williams's intonation were as pure as her voice, what distance would I not travel to hear her? I do not mean that she habitually sings out of tune, but she has to take conscious aim at the pitch, and some intervals never get quite on the centre of the bull's eye. I see that some critic complains of Miss Marian McKenzie as not up to her usual mark in the contralto music. I thought she sang But the Lord is Mindful of His Own particularly well. You really cannot believe what critics say.

The exchange value of the difference between the Crystal Palace oratorio and that at the People's Palace was exactly six and fivepence, including traveling expenses. It was a great occasion at Bow—their first oratorio—and I looked round expectantly for a great muster of critics. But I looked in vain. If it had been St James's Hall with Joachim playing the Mendelssohn concerto, or Mr Edward Lloyd singing Lend me Your Aid for the hundredth time, they would have been there by dozens. In my solitude I was enjoying a sense of superior virtue, when in walked Mr Fuller Maitland, of the Times. You might have knocked me down with a feather. The performance began with great spirit, the strings, in full harmony, giving delusive promise of excellence. When the fugue broke them into parts, it became evident that though the second violins meant quite as well as their rivals under Mr Manns, yet they were not equally able to give effect to their intentions. However, they got through with an occasional lift from the organ, and one or two pauses for tuning, during which each fiddler scraped his A string, found that it was about an eighth flat; and left it so with apparent satisfaction. The choir got on capitally, putting to utter shame the multitudinous dolts who are the bane of Mr Manns' artistic life. They sang with admirable spirit and earnestness, and there was not a dull moment in the oratorio, which, to be sure, was slightly curtailed. As to the principals, the only one who was not equal to the occasion was the tenor, who was heavily overweighted by his part, and not in the best of voice to attempt it. Miss Margaret Hoare astonished the natives with From Mighty Kings, and a young lady named Miss Hoskins, whose fine contralto voice has the first bloom still on it, brought down the house with Father of Heaven: to Thy Eternal Throne. I do not think Miss Hoskins quite knew that she was singing one of the most beautiful songs ever written, even by Handel; but she would at her present stage have sung it all the worse if she had sung it more consciously. Mr Bertram Latter sang the baritone music without a fault: the comparative ineffectiveness of his songs was the fault of the conductor, who took both of them too slowly. Arm, arm, ye brave, in particular, went at exactly half the proper speed. On the whole, I enjoyed the concert, which is more than I can truthfully say of the Sydenham performance. And the crowd which filled the great hall seemed to be of my opinion.

JUVENILE OPERA

The Star, 19 November 1889

At the Avenue Theatre, at half-past two every day, an "opera" is sung by children. At least, they are all guaranteed under fourteen. But some people are not children at fourteen: they are hobbledehoys; and there is no charm in hobbledehoyhood. A child should have a child's ways, a child's stature, above all a child's voice. The giantess at the Aquarium, for instance, is not, artistically considered, a child. And the young ladies of the ballet in the first act of Belles of the Village are as unchildlike as the ballet itself, which is no less inane and artificial than genuine children's dances are interesting and pretty. The rest is pleasant enough. Nothing could be more naïve than the rustic drama by Hugh Foster, or more innocent than the music by John Fitzgerald. Master Fred Allwood takes himself with commendable seriousness as Will Green, the Jack Tar. His dancing of the sailor's hornpipe is beyond belief: it brought down the house. But Master Allwood sings precociously in the voice, not of the passing boy, but of the coming man; and I am greatly afraid that he will some day find that voice considerably the worse for his present efforts. Master Alfred Bovill, as the beadle, shewed himself a comedian of genius. He is the first operatic vocalist I ever saw leap into popularity by a *couac*, as the French call it. There was one note in his song upon which his voice broke every time with irresistibly comic effect; and the audience encored him again and again for it, going into convulsions at each repetition of the catastrophe. Of what the effect on a sensitive child would have been I shudder to think; but Signor Bovill had no more

[843]

delicacy about making comic capital of his precarious upper notes than Coquelin has in exploiting the curled tip of his nose. Master Frank Mettrop, as the oldest inhabitant, also brought off a small part with some comic talent. Of the girls, only two are really child singers and actresses, namely, Miss Bessie Graves, a little artist ready made by nature, who sings very sweetly, and Miss Lizzie Primmer, who has doubtless had to study rather harder, her fairy godmothers having been stingier than Bessie's. Miss Annie Fieber and Miss Bessie Colman are only spoiling their adult voices by using them prematurely; and Miss Fieber's coquetries will sit better on her when she is older. Miss Lizzie Dungate, a little more grown than the others, is staid, but pleasing. When Master Allwood was resting, flushed with triumph, after his miraculous hornpipe, she said, as if it were one of her lines (which can hardly have been the case) "You will be encored again for that, tomorrow," whereat the house laughed indulgently. On the whole, the grown-up people were decidedly amused; and as people generally bring their children to the plays, and buy them the toys that amuse themselves, I take it that the Belles of the Village is likely enough to serve its turn through the winter.

TWO ANONYMOUS COMMUNICATIONS

The Star, 22 November 1889

Of all the thousands of Star readers who have delighted in Mendelssohn and loved him only one has cared enough to hurl a postcard at me for what I said about St Paul. Here it is.

"AN IGNORANT SELF-CONCEITED ASS is the Star musical critic (!) who scribbles on Mendelssohn and the Oratorio of St Paul at the Crystal Palace on Saturday!!!

"He should be put under a glass case and exhibited at Barnum's menagerie; for SURELY he has the LONGEST PAIR OF EARS IN ALL LONDON.

"The animal!

"Who was his father?—and who his mother? The breed should be perpetuated as a curiosity!!!"

My heart warms to this anonymous correspondent. The postcard is an outburst of genuine feeling about music, somewhat unsocially expressed, perhaps, but still heartfelt. Yet I shall probably often again wound that feeling, because, for the musical critic in England, Mendelssohn is The Enemy. Until we have got far enough to recoil from Elijah flippantly rattling off his atrocious God is angry with the wicked every day, we shall never fathom the depths of truly great music. Mendelssohn, who was shocked at Auber's writing an opera [Fra Diavolo] in which a girl sang *Oui, c'est demain* (meaning "Tomorrow I shall be a bride") at her looking-glass before going to bed, was himself ready to serve up the chopping to pieces of the prophets of the grove with his richest musical spice to suit the compound of sanctimonious cruelty and base materialism which his patrons, the British Pharisees, called their religion. If my correspondent will compare such work as his with Parsifal, and his career with that of the man who produced Parsifal, he (or she; for the handwriting is of uncertain sex) will understand why Wagner once said, speaking of an occasion when Mendelssohn invited him to applaud an orchestral full gallop through the beautiful slow trio of Beethoven's eighth symphony, "I thought I saw before me an abyss of superficiality." The Philharmonic orchestra scampers through its work in the same elegantly superficial manner to this day, thanks to

Mendelssohn. Probably all my correspondent really means is that Mendelssohn composed music of exquisite grace and tenderness. I am no more insensible to that than was Wagner, who used to ask his pianist friends to play Mendelssohn's overtures for him. But when I am asked to spend an afternoon listening to oratorios that must stand or fall, not by the grace or tenderness of their prettiest strains, but by the depth and moral dignity of their conception, then Mendelssohn gets roughly handled; and it serves him abundantly right.

Here is another communication marked "Private," which I shall answer publicly, as there may be others interested in my reply.

"Dear Sir,—As I believe your opinion to be one of the best in London [this is a man of sense], would you, as a great favor, be kind enough to give me information about the following matter:

"I think of taking singing lessons from Professor ——, of ——, and I wish to know if you consider him competent to teach in opera and oratorio—provided that in course of time I found I had sufficient voice and ability to lead me to hope that by hard study and perseverance I had a chance of rising so high.

"I have never had any singing lessons; but my voice has been tried and found to be rather powerful.—Yours faithfully,

X Y Z."

Now observe here how much more vaguely a musical career is conceived than one in any other art. Had X Y Z wished to go on the stage he would hardly have asked whether Mr Hermann Vezin is "competent to teach *drama*." Just as there is no such thing as teaching drama, so there is no such thing as teaching opera or oratorio. Mr Hermann Vezin can, of course, take a novice and coach her in the part of Juliet to the point of enabling her to go through it with verbal accuracy and with a certain propriety of gesture and deportment: even that depending, however, on the extent to which the pupil's natural gifts make her capable of understanding the teacher's instructions. Similarly Professor —— is no doubt competent to coach a pupil in the part of Jephtha or Manoah, Faust or Mephistopheles. But if artists could be turned out in this fashion, Mr Hermann Vezin and Professor —— could at once open shops, and supply Juliets and Gennaros to the managers as Mr Clarkson supplies wigs. The truth is that the artist must be at once his own master and everybody's pupil. If he cannot learn from all that he sees and hears, and then teach himself the practical application of what he has learnt, art is not his affair, and he had better remain an amateur. Mr Joseph Jefferson, as indisputably the most finished comedian among English-speaking actors as M. Coquelin is among French-speaking ones, years ago repudiated the notion that any part of an actor's business could be learnt off the stage. And my own art of literary composition, much the most difficult in the world, was certainly not taught me by a master, nor do I propose to take apprentices.

I can, however, tell X Y Z some of the things he must learn in order to become a fine artist—things which he will never learn by shutting himself up twice a week for an hour with the same man and the same pianoforte in the same drawing room. First, he must learn to sing: that is, to touch or sustain any note within his compass with certainty of pitch and beauty of tone, and withal with an unembarrassed management of it, so that it may be lightly or vigorously touched or sustained, just as he wishes. Second, he must learn to pronounce with purity the syllables *do*, *re*, *mi*, *fa*, so that his more or less genteel variations on the original cockney *dow*, *roy*, *meey*, *fawr* may become utterly repugnant to him, and that he may no longer ignorantly laugh at Mr Irving for saying simply "gold" instead of the customary "gah-oold." He must also learn foreign vowels, so as to be able to sing *re* both as *ré* or *rè*, and sustain them without ever closing, English fashion, into an *ee* at the end. All this must be checked by his own ear, not his master's. There is no use in getting other people to listen to him: he must listen to himself with his whole soul until his ear has grown exquisitely sensitive to minute shades of intonation and pronunciation—until he cannot go wrong without literally hurting himself.

This cultivation of the ear never stops. The fine artist improves until age unmakes more progress in the year than culture can make. But how is X Y Z to set about cultivating his ear? Alas! how indeed? in this British world of ugliness and noise! But he can, according to his means, keep good music sounding in his ears. He can go to concerts—to the Crystal Palace on Saturday afternoons, at least sometimes (always is too dear); to the Saturday and Monday Pops; to the Philharmonic; to the Richter concerts; to the best of the numerous suburban oratorio performances; to the opera occasionally; and to the theatres. Let him make studies of inferior, good, and first-rate artists in point of intonation and pronunciation. Any friend will oblige him with a song in the first capacity. Then let him try how much better in these points he finds Mr Edward Lloyd, Mr Henschel, or Mr Max Heinrich. Finally, let him try Madame Patti in Within a Mile, or Home, Sweet Home.

A fresh course can be gone through on pronunciation. Look through Mr Alexander J. Ellis's little book on Speech in Song (I think Messrs Novello published it some years ago), in order to get some idea of what to watch for; and then call in a friend again—a vulgar friend, if you have one. Study his vowels, and how loud he thinks it necessary to speak. Then go to the theatre and compare with his the speech of a mediocre actor. Then try an actor of the rank of Mr Kendal. Finally, go and hear Mr Irving; and also the masterly Coquelin in Les Précieuses Ridicules if possible; for in that you will hear how beautifully in tune he can sing. Then begin over again with the women, thus—1. Vulgar lady friend. 2. Actress of good position, not specially famous as a speaker: say Miss Amy Roselle. 3. An actress who is famous for clever but not for beautiful speaking: say, Mrs Kendal. 4. An actress who speaks very cleverly and most beautifully—there is only one—Miss Ada Rehan.* 5. An intentionally musical speaker of the highest class: Sarah Bernhardt. A course of violinists culminating in Sarasate would also be useful; but once the habit of studying has been established there is something to be picked up from the whistle of every locomotive and the hail of every bus conductor.

Pray note, however, that although Mr Irving and Miss Rehan speak so admirably, their personal mannerism is so strong that an attempt to imitate them would be the surest way to court overwhelming ridicule. The problem is to speak as beautifully as possible, and not for a moment to speak like this or that person who speaks beautifully. And further, there must always—what! no more space this week. Then it shall be continued in our next. I will have my say out if I fill The Star with it until Christmas.

* Irish-American actress, leading lady in Augustin Daly's New York company from 1879 until his death in 1899, performing more than 200 *rôles*, ranging from farce to Shakespear and Restoration comedy.

THE RED HUSSAR

The Star, 25 November 1889

Until Mr Leslie gets rid of the Dorothy tradition at his theatre, there will be little to record there except the waste of three excellent artists and a tolerable comedian. Mr H. P. Stephens, author of The Red Hussar, is a Molière, a Sheridan, a Congreve, a very Shakespear compared to the author of Dorothy and Doris; but even he has done nothing except put a smart face on the inanities of his forerunner. Miss Tempest is still a masquerading heiress; Mr Ben Davies still a spendthrift in difficulties; Mr Hayden Coffin still one of Mr Davies's acquaintances with a song; and Mr Arthur Williams is not regenerated by the change from a comic sheriff's officer to a comic corporal. There is the usual second young lady (Miss Dysart) to pair off with Mr Coffin; and there is an old lady to attempt to repeat the dreary tomfoolery of the Priscilla scenes in Dorothy. Towards this part of the affair, however, the attitude of the audience on Saturday night was distinctly threatening. Squire Bantam, though transformed to Colonel Sir Marmaduke Mashem, remains essentially an unmitigated bore, Mr Christian, who impersonates him, being unable to make bricks without straw, as Mr Williams can. Some variety is obtained by sending all the characters campaigning for a while; but the military music of the second act, in which this occurs, is the most mechanical trash imaginable, with noisy, tiresome orchestration, in which a crowd of trivial conceits and contrivances jostle oneanother in the most impertinent and irritating fashion. Something of the same fault appears in the stage management: the soldiers are too often doing pointless scraps of business that were better left out. In fact, there are moments when, what with Mr Solomon fidgeting with the instruments, and Mr Charles Harris fidgeting with the supers, it is hard for a nervous spectator to sit still and refrain from objurgation. The first act is by far the most effective of the three: partly because the audience are unwearied: partly because Miss Tempest sings some bright, if not particularly novel, numbers with that care and feeling for the musical part of her work by which she has made her mark from her first appearance on the stage. Mr Davies also has a capital song, A Guinea here, a Guinea there, which he sang with his eyes shut, but otherwise admirably. The first of Miss Tempest's songs, by the way, has tagged on to it a worn-out scrap of conventional ornament, which Mr Solomon might as well cut off and throw on the musical dustheap. Mr Coffin's voice, as anyone might have foreseen, has been displaced and damaged in quality by the unsuitable work it had to do in Doris. In the concerted music of the first act, his tone was hard and aggressive, and would not blend with the others on any terms. His song, My Castle in Spain, in the second act, was not much better. I almost began to suspect him of deliberately sacrificing the beauty of his voice to its power: the surest way of losing both in the long run. But in the third act he sang a song in his old fashion, and was heartily encored, though it was past eleven, and a suburban god very sensibly called out that it was too late for *encores*. The audience throughout received the work very handsomely.

At the Crystal Palace concert in the afternoon Miss Nettie Carpenter played Saint-Saëns' violin concerto and a few solos in the manner of her master Sarasate, who, had he been present, would have had no reasonable fault to find; for she played very well indeed, and will take high rank as a player if her style matures and her tone amplifies by further experience. The rest of the concert was hopelessly dismal. The muggy, muddy weather had got into the very souls of the audience and performers alike. Mr Manns doggedly went through the program like a brave man fighting a broadsword combat against overwhelming odds. The Flying Dutchman overture would not come right; and the seventh symphony was a mockery. Liszt's Festklänge (sounds of rejoicing!) completed our discomfiture; and we trudged off sadly through the rain, feebly hoping for better luck next time. I forgot to mention that Miss Fillunger sang Schubert's *Auflösung* nicely; but Mendelssohn's Infelice requires a voice which is as good all over as in the upper register, outside which Miss Fillunger seems quite lost.

"CONGENIAL" CRITICISM

The Star, 29 November 1889

[U] Some years ago Mr Walter Crane and Mr Theo. Marzials made a delightful oblong book of old English ballads. Mr Marzials arranged the accompaniments; and Mr Crane designed the pages; but the music and words were printed from type. Messrs Macmillan now send me a thin quarto of songs, verses, and pictures, all down to the very lettering, notation, and design of the end papers by Mr Reginald F. Hallward. I hardly like to pick to pieces a composition in which every part is bound to the other in the unity of a deeply felt impulse which has burst irresistibly into artistic expression; and indeed I have no faith in the validity of any criticism which, when confronted with work in which the underlying sentiment can be seen or heard flowing through every line of progression, can see nothing but the deviations from its own habitual standard of plausible execution. Still, nobody would think much of me as a critic if I did not shew my superiority by finding fault; so here goes for Mr Hallward.

But before I come to the faults, a word as to the facts. This Flowers of Paradise is a book for children; but it is not really a book for young children, except insofar as it is well to keep beautiful things under their eyes. The message of the book is expressed in these lines:

> If thy heart be only open
>   To the lovely message given,
> Walls are not yet built dividing
>   Splendors of the earth from heaven.

Before you can understand that message, you must grow up and then become as a little child again.

Now for the congenial work of pointing out a friend's faults. I say a friend's; for it strikes me that this Reginald Hallward must be a man whom I knew in the days when I was a revolutionist, and said so. He was a revolutionist also, and he, too, said so.* I cannot answer for what he is now, except that I perceive he is still an artist: for my own part, I am more a revolutionist than ever; but I never say so—I even rebuke those who do as wild and dangerous vaporers. I am a Progressive, a Radical. In short, my specialities are political hypocrisy and auto-biographical musical criticism. What I am trying to say, if I could only come to it, is that in noting down his songs, Mr Hallward has sacrificed the neatness and legibility of good music type without attaining the freedom and individuality of manuscript, obviously because he has not written music enough to form a musical handwriting. And I must deplore the inadequate

* Hallward, a colleague of William Morris and Emery Walker, was a member of the Hammersmith Socialist Society.

study of the action of the hands of the violinists in the heavenly choir (though I have seen worse from artists of greater pretensions), besides protesting most vehemently against the angel who is hugging a horrible hermaphrodite of an instrument, half guitar, half violoncello, played by scraping the tailboard with a bow.

I have also to acknowledge the concluding part of the second volume of the Wagner Society's shilling quarterly, entitled The Meister, published by the late George Redway (I do not mean that Mr Redway is dead: he is only amalgamated into a joint-stock company). At the first glance I am struck with the execrable waste of the fine opportunity for artistic printing presented by the quarto pages. These, instead of being set up in the largest old-faced type that can be accommodated by "solid" setting, are leaded like the pages of a treatise on political economy. The margins are like the frame of a schoolboy's slate, even all round, instead of being as narrow as possible at the top and down the middle, and as wide as possible on the outside and at the foot. The title page contains nine leading lines in nine different founts of type, like a jobbing printer's advertisement of a lost dog. The design on the cover is roughly effective in its arrangement of black and white; but the drawing is cheap and slovenly beyond description. Need I add that in the two lines of the publisher's imprint at the foot there are three sorts of type dragged in, making five to the whole page of 14 words. Will the editor, or the committee, or whoever is responsible for these anti-Wagnerian atrocities, take the trouble to step into the King's Library at the British Museum, and gather a hint from the beautiful old MSS. there, and the early books—the Mazarin Bible, for instance—which so faithfully preserved their beauty.

For the literary contents of The Meister I have nothing but praise. The completion of Religion and Art, the second of Wagner's great essays, gives to this volume the same high value that Art and Revolution gave to the opening one. He who has not read these two essays has, for modern purposes, read nothing. Mr William C. Ward's commentary on the Niblung tetralogy is the most interesting and luminous monograph on the subject in English. It, as well as Mr Charles Dowdeswell's Schopenhauer articles (which are exactly what were wanted) also comes to an end in the current part, and so helps to make the volume complete in itself. In four parts, at a shilling a part, it forms about the cheapest book of its kind at present before the public.[U]

One more book, The Story of Music, by W. J. Henderson, an American critic. It is concisely and intelligently written; but I can find little criticism in it that goes beyond a repetition of opinions which have been printed over and over again, and which were formed from the point of view common in 1850 and now obsolete. A critic who at this time of day cannot follow Wagner's harmony, and talks of "false relations" in it, is as hopelessly out of date as he himself would consider the professors who, on the ground that "*mi* contra *fa* diabolus est," object to a chord containing B natural following a chord containing F. When he goes on to inform us that Wagner "did not give sufficient attention to the powers of the human voice," it is time to shut the book. And yet he is by no means an anti-Wagnerite, this Mr Henderson; only his modesty—the critic who is modest is lost—is such that he feels bound to accept as gospel all the stale rubbish of the musical book makers who have been preying on popular ignorance of art since Lord Mount-Edgcumbe's* time. He even declares that

* Richard Edgcumbe (1746–1839), second Earl of Mount-Edgcumbe, was the author of Musical Reminiscences of an Old Amateur (n.d., private circulation only); a second edition was published anonymously in 1827.

Donizetti "wrote tunes simply and solely for their own sake, caring nothing for dramatic significance." Far be it from me to stand between Donizetti and his righteous doom; but whenever there was any dramatic significance to care for he cared for it to considerable purpose, although he was not one of those great masters who, refusing to make the best of hopeless old forms, create new ones for themselves. As to Lucia's *scena*, I have ridiculed its absurd flute tootling and *fioriture* often enough; but I never objected to it, as Mr Henderson does, on the ground that it is a waltz. Why should it not be? Handel's famous *Lascia ch'io pianga* is a saraband; but is it any the worse for that? What are all our song forms but evolved dance measures?

Here is a letter elicited by last week's column:

Sir,—With reference to your article of today, may I be allowed to point out that M. Coquelin and Mme Bernhardt both pronounce French as French is spoken by educated Frenchmen, whereas Mr Irving and Miss Terry pronounce English as no Englishman or English-woman has ever, whether educated or not, spoken the language since the world began. Also that the glorious voice of Madame Patti in Home, Sweet Home is but a melancholy study at best of the demand for music in this "musical people," and supply in a potentially great artist.—Yours faithfully,

H. ASHWORTH TAYLOR.

Hereupon I would observe that Mr Taylor, insofar as his statement about educated French people is true, has put the boot on the wrong leg. It is not M. Coquelin who speaks like the educated Frenchman: it is the educated Frenchman who tries to speak like M. Coquelin, because the diction of the Comédie Française is a standard diction in Paris. Here in England we have no standard (though Miss Glyn once assured me that Mr Gladstone

[856]

had taken Charles Kean for his model as a speaker).* In order to arrive at one, which course would Mr Taylor prefer? the adoption of average colloquial pronunciation by Mr Irving, or the adoption of Mr Irving's pronunciation by the average man? Mind, I say his pronunciation, and not his personal peculiarities: his undershot jaw, for instance, or the shape of the oral and nasal cavities which give his voice quite a different timbre from that of Mr Taylor. As to Miss Terry, the dry, husky quality of her voice is not her pronunciation: neither is the staccato articulation which her imitators catch at. To take another example, Mr Thomas Thorne's trick of pumping up every word with a separate sob is not *his* pronunciation. Mr Taylor does not seem to distinguish these differences; therefore I am at a loss to know whether he means anything more than that Miss Terry and Mr Irving have not got exact doubles anywhere among educated English people.

As to Madame Patti, I think she is never better employed than when she is singing her stock ballads. If she were a great dramatic artist, I should say by all means let her devote herself to Donna Anna, Leonora, and Isolde. But she is not, never was, and never will be. There has not yet been witnessed a dramatic situation so tragic that Madame Patti would not get up in the middle of it to bow and smile if somebody accidentally sprung his opera hat. She is simply a marvelous Christy Minstrel; and when you have heard her sing Within a Mile in the Albert Hall so perfectly that not a syllable or a whisper of it is lost, you have heard the best she can do.

* The veteran actress Isabella Glyn, who had died in May of that year, had told this story to Shaw at one of Lady Wilde's at homes. The actor Charles Kean, second son of the great Edmund Kean, never attained the stature in the theatre that his father did.

And this best of hers is not to be despised; nor is the demand for it any discredit to the taste of the people; for between it and the very highest sort of music (which no sane critic ever supposed to be Madame Patti's affair) there is only a chaos of artificiality, a demand for which would be only a sign of that musical curiosity which people acquire from reading about the subject, and which is very different from the true love of music.

MR SMITH READS THE PAPER

The Star, 2 December 1889

Last week, when my colleagues were filling in their stereotyped "magnificent rendering of the Seventh Symphony by Mr Manns' famous orchestra," I was sorrowfully recording my opinion that the famous ones did not on that occasion play worth a cent. On Saturday they had evidently, to a man, made up their minds to let me know whether they could play or not. This is interesting, by the bye, as proving that Mr J. A. Smith, the eminent drum player (I would give anything to play the drum), is not the only orchestral artist who studies the press (he, I may remark, does so with such diligence that when I compose a symphony for the Palace, or for Herr Richter, I shall not write in the old style, "the drums count" but simply "Mr Smith reads the paper"). He does not mean to annoy me, I am sure; but if he only knew how desperately I long for something to read myself during a tedious movement, he would rightly ascribe my feelings to mere envy. However, whether it was the sharp, crisp weather, or my disparagement of the previous concert, certain it is that the band was on the alert, strings keen and impetuous, woodwind and horns full of soft color, brass noble and splendid. The

Euryanthe overture had "a magnificent rendering," if you like; and Brahms's symphony in D delighted me, though I try to turn up my nose at Brahms. Individual, or rather dual, virtuosity was represented by Mr and Mrs Henschel, who, after making a genuinely valuable contribution to the concert by their Euryanthe selections, in every bar of which Wagner casts his shadow before, unexpectedly relapsed into a feeble drawing-room duet entertainment, in which Mrs Henschel sang in tune, and thereby took the part of the pianoforte against her own husband, which was hardly acting up to her vows. I wonder whether Mr Henschel is conscious of his trick of forcing the intonation just the fiftieth part of a comma to the bad. Let him beware: such habits grow; and there is the spoiling of a good singer in him. As to Sir Arthur Sullivan's Macbeth music, I am eagerly in favor of such performances at standard orchestral concerts, as the anticipation of them causes composers to take their theatrical commissions for incidental music in a much more earnest and lofty spirit, with a view to their subsequent enlargement to the full scale of grand orchestra. By making such events customary, we should at least get a good overture occasionally. This music of Sir Arthur's, clever, skilful, brilliantly scored, catchingly runs the round of the most paying modulations; and there are some ha'porths of true Celtic melody and feeling to boot. Mr Hamish MacCunn's Ship o' the Fiend, which, as it happened, I had never heard before, did not supplant Lord Ullin's Daughter in my affections. The ship is certainly a river steamer in a desperate hurry. I have listened to the sea in all weathers for months together; and whenever I heard four in a bar going, that was a steamer, reader, usually a screw-steamer. Neither oar, wave, nor sailing ship ever made that dread Harwich-Rotterdam Dover-Calais rum-tum accompaniment to the only wishes for death that are really

[859]

sincere. The big drum is fine; but methinks I have heard the effect before—in [Berlioz's overture to] Les Francs-Juges, was it not? Not, of course, that it is any the worse for that.

GRETNA GREEN
The Star, 5 December 1889

There must be a stop put to this sort of thing. Sterndale Bennett, when asked to write an opera, is said to have stipulated that there should be no soldiers' chorus in it. On receiving the libretto, the first thing he saw was "Act I: The Pré-aux-Clercs, Soldiers drinking." He promptly rolled it up, returned it, and never wrote an opera. I warn composers that in future, if the curtain goes up on "Act I: Village inn, with sign, benches, and practicable door L; village lasses and lads discovered singing," I shall presently be discovered making my way home.

I have already hinted that I do not consider Dorothy one of the summits of operatic art; and the last dozen imitations I have been invited to witness have left me slightly restive on the subject. Gretna Green is Dorothy complicated by Erminie.* It will be recollected that the appalling dulness of the beginning of Erminie was dispelled by the introduction of our old friends Robert Macaire and Bertrand.† The melancholy of the first act of Gretna Green is in like manner relieved by the

* Erminie, a comic opera with music by Edward Jakobowski, was produced at the Comedy Theatre on 9 November 1885.

† Macaire and his stooge Bertrand first appeared as the villains of a melodrama, L'Auberge des Adrets (1823), by Benjamin Antiers, Saint-Amand, and Paulyanthe.

appearance of Lurcher in the character of the Sleeper Awakened, otherwise Abou Hassan, otherwise Christopher Sly, and on this occasion Robin Bates, a strolling player. But the upshot is that in the second act the inevitable three men arrive at the inevitable Bramble Hall, in the inevitable disguise, and there dance the inevitable minuet, with the inevitable ladies in powder and patches. What happens in the third act is as dark a mystery to me as are the closing incidents of Dorothy and Doris. Men have died, and worms have eaten 'em, but not for love*; and I have gone to theatres and sat out third acts, but not for Dorothy, not for Doris, not for Gretna Green.

There is an important difference between Dorothies at the Lyric and Dorothies at highly experimental *matinées*. At the Lyric they are forced into success by persistently concentrating upon them the efforts of far better and more popular artists than they deserve. At the *matinées* the little merits they may possess are hidden by defective execution. Mr John Storer, the composer of Gretna Green, is a Mus.Doc., and therefore knows his musical grammar, and I imagine arranges his score with a view rather to the resources of St James's Hall and Crystal Palace than of the Comedy Theatre. He rings the changes on the ordinary trade patterns in music with some fluency and spirit; but too many of the numbers come in just where they interrupt the action instead of advancing it; and the *finales* are without force or interest. The representation was so imperfect that I can hardly believe that the preparation had got as far as a single complete rehearsal. A few of the principals knew their parts; but the band was evidently playing at sight; and the general business of the stage was pushed through

* The words are Rosalind's, in Shakespear's As You Like It, Act IV, Scene I.

at random, not without occasional profane remonstrances from the wings. Miss Leonora Braham and Mr Richard Temple played like experienced hands; and Mr L. Cadwalader, late Claude Melnotte in Major Cockle's opera, was much in earnest over the tenor part. But Mr Cadwalader must do what his countryman Mr Barton McGuckin manfully did before him: face the fact that the nose given him by Nature is out of the question for any part except that of Jack Sheppard; and that until he builds up a new one, Phyllis's exclamation when she catches sight of him, "Oh, I hope the Squire [her unknown betrothed] may be like *him!*" will make even the most considerate audience laugh. And even that will avail him nothing until he learns to sing evenly instead of in a squeezed *mezza voce* broken by an irregular series of shouts on all the ascending intervals. Miss Maude Vena is a plump and pleasing person, but no vocalist. As to Miss Velmi, the heroine, I shall defer criticism until she has had a more favorable opportunity than she had yesterday afternoon.

A TALK WITH DR HUEFFER
The Star, 6 December 1889

I remember once coming to loggerheads with the late Dr Francis Hueffer, about fifteen seconds after the opening of our first conversation, on the subject of musical culture in English society. Whenever the subject arose between us, I declared that English society did not care about music—did not know good music from bad. He replied, with great force, that I knew nothing about it; that nobody had ever seen me in really decent society; that I moved amidst cranks, Bohemians, unbelievers, agitators, and—generally speaking—riffraff of all sorts;

and that I was merely theorizing emptily about the people whom I called bloated aristocrats. He described, by way of example, an evening at Lord Derby's house, where he had greatly enjoyed some excellent music; and he asked me whether I knew that such music was, in a quiet way, a constant grace of the best sort of English social life. I suggested that he should give me an opportunity to judge for myself by introducing me to these circles; but this he entirely declined to do, having no confidence whatever in my power of behaving myself in a seemly manner for five consecutive minutes.

On the first occasion it so happened, fortunately for me, that a firm of music publishers, having resolved to venture on the desperate step of publishing six new pianoforte sonatas, had just sent out a circular containing an appeal *ad misericordiam* that at least a few people would, either in public spirit or charity, take the unprecedented step of buying these compositions. I promptly hurled this at Hueffer's head, and asked whether that looked like evidence of a constant and enlightened patronage such as the upper classes accord to racing, millinery, confectionery, and in a minor degree to literature and painting (for, hang it all! even if the sonatas were not as good as Beethoven's, they were at any rate no duller than the average three-volume novel or Academy picture). There the subject dropped, my method of controversy being at that time crudely unscrupulous and extravagant. Hueffer, I fancy, regarded me as an unschooled dangerous character; but once, when I was perched on the gunwale of a wagon in Hyde Park, filling up some ten minutes of a "demonstration" with the insufferable oratorizing which is the only sort feasible on such occasions, I was astonished to see his long golden beard and massive brow well to the front among the millions of "friends and fellow citizens." He never told me what he thought about the contrast between the new musical criticism demonstrating on wagons in the sunlight, and the old, groping in perpetual evening dress from St James's Hall to Covent Garden Opera House and back again.

One point I might have put to him, but didnt, is that when you get up a musical entertainment for the exclusive delectation of the nobs, you must either be content with a very scanty audience, in which case the nobs will not think it good enough to come again, or else pack the room with a contingent of musical deadheads, who are not nobs, nor even respectable Philistine snobs, but rank outsiders—though you would be surprised at the costly entertainments, operatic and otherwise, that are run solely for their sake, and that of the jaded pressmen. Last Friday, happening to have an invitation from the Grosvenor Club to their "ladies' night" at the Grosvenor Gallery, I thought I would go and see whether things were altering at all. For the Grosvenor Club, you must know, is no vulgar free-and-easy; and its concerts, from 9.30 to midnight, are never wholly nobless.

On entering that Bond-street portal which was brought here bodily all the way from Italy, and approaching the stairs which I have so often worn with the weary feet of an art critic, I found on one side a descending stream of sad and hollow people, and on the other an ascending one, flushed and swollen. By this I perceived that the refreshments were downstairs; and I hurried up with all convenient speed. Here I found a nob or two, a deadhead or two, and a vast majority of solid snobs. No celebrities, no literary lot, no journalistic lot, no artistic lot, no Bohemian lot, nothing (to speak of) except plain snobbery, more or less choice. In short, there were—professionally engaged musicians excepted—not above twelve people in the room known to me; and I should have congratulated Mr Prange on such an entirely satisfactory result if I had been quite certain that he would have appreciated the full force of this final proof of the respectability of the gathering, and of the success of his elimination of the great army of "private view" people.

I could not get a program; and when Signor Ducci went to the piano, and Mr Radcliffe took his flute, Mr Mann his horn, and the fiddlers four their fiddles, I wondered what was coming. It proved to be resurrection pie of the dustiest flavor. For a long time I was at a loss. I thought vaguely of Clementi, of Dussek, of Field, of all the Sir Arthur Sullivans that existed before Mendelssohn's time. Not until several elegantly empty movements had worn themselves out did I hit on the right man: on Hummel, the genteel, the talented, the tastefully barren. Here are serenades by Mozart, chamber music with wind parts by Schubert, by Weber, by Schumann, by Mendelssohn, by Brahms, all ready to Signor Ducci's hand; and he goes and digs up Johann Nepomuk Hummel! One unfortunate gentleman said to me: "These things are very nice, of course; but they are very long." Forgetting that I was for once among respectable people, I morosely expressed an opinion that this particular thing was strongly qualified rubbish. "Oh" said he "you are so very critical: I daresay it does not come up to *your* standard. But it was certainly too long for a place like this." Thus does music get into disrepute. If my friend had heard Beethoven's septet, he would have been delighted. Hearing Hummel instead, he concluded that it was in the nature of classical music to be dull; and he will probably think so to his dying day.

However, the choicer spirits sat in the front of the room and faithfully listened. The others sat at the back and talked. How they talked! One young lady, who must, I should think, be the champion chatterbox of the universe, so outdid with her tongue the most rapid flights of Signor Ducci's fingers that I stole round three times through the east gallery merely to see whether she had stopped from exhaustion; but she was as fresh as an aviary each time. Another lady,* who coaches me in the ways of good society, and makes certain prearranged warning signals to me when I eat with my knife or help myself to potatoes with my fingers, was very severe with me because I took sides with the front of the room and listened to the unimpeachable Johann Nepomuk. "You were a failure there" she said next day. "Everybody was noticing your disgraceful behavior. You will never be a gentleman." "What should I have done?" I demanded. "I say nothing" she replied "about your not bringing us down to the refreshment room, and your furtively leaving before you had seen us off in a cab. But you should at least have come and *talked* to us." "But that would have disturbed the music" I pleaded. "Music!" she retorted, with scorn. "The Grosvenor is a private club where some rather crack people go: not a concert room. People go there to talk. Besides, you *scowled*." On reflection, I daresay I did. I would suggest to Mr Prange that in future a curtain should shut off the east gallery from the west, and that the fireman should be employed to keep the musical section and the loquacious section in different rooms.

On Wednesday, I at last got to Kensington to hear the Musical Guild. By the bye, I recently stated here that the Guild had ungratefully omitted to invite me to their concerts last season. The secretary writes to say that this was a lie. I do not mean that he expressed it exactly in that way: he is far too polite; but there can be no doubt

* Mrs Jane Patterson, Shaw's lover. In his shorthand diary for 2 December 1889 he noted: "I found JP in a rage about my having been inattentive to her on Friday at the Grosvenor."

that it actually was a lie. The invitation was sent; but the Stonecutter-street staff, who have an unquenchable thirst for classical music, boned the ticket, and it never reached me. When I got to the Town Hall on Wednesday, I found that Kensington society, which combines the Philistinism of old Bloomsbury with the frivolity of old Brompton, has left this excellent little Guild in the lurch. A ball at the Kensington Town Hall is always full: a chamber music concert, it appears, is empty. I and Mr du Maurier and about a hundred other people had the room to ourselves. Item the first, a string octet by Mr Holmes, a violinist whom I have had the misfortune to have heard hardly at all since he used to lead the quartet at the Popular Concerts some twelve or thirteen years ago, between the engagements of Madame Neruda, Joachim, or sometimes Herr Straus. As Mr Holmes is a professor, the octet was in regulation form, with four movements, first and second subjects, development, recapitulation, and so on. At first we were all on the alert to hear what the eight fiddles playing all together would sound like; but gradually the orthodoxy of the octet numbed us, and we sat mutely reminding oneanother of the eve of the battle of Agincourt.

> The poor condemnèd English,
> Like sacrifices, by their watchful fires
> Sit patiently and inly ruminate ...*

The worst of it was that Mr Holmes was there, and could see us all; so that we had to applaud like mad. And no doubt his music would have been enjoyable enough had he kept his ideas off the rack of the sonata form, and stopped when he had said his say. As it was, the only people who relished it thoroughly were the experts on my left who had a copy of the score, and so could feast

* Chorus, in Shakespear's Henry V., Prologue to Act IV.

their *eyes* on the construction of the work. The execution was highly creditable: the Kensingtonians are fools to neglect these concerts.

After a Schumann duet on two pianofortes by Miss Annie Fry and Miss Maggie Moore (I do not know which was which) I walked in the teeth of the east wind all the way to the Institute over Prince's Hall, in Piccadilly, where the members of the Wagner Society were having their *conversazione*. There I got for the first time close enough to Miss Fillunger to perceive that the reason her voice is all top and no middle is that her method may be summed up in two words: sheer violence. It is a pity; for she sings certain songs with much taste and feeling. Isolde's Liebestod was a failure; but the fault was partly that of the accompanist. Mr Max Heinrich sang *Anrede*, also to a rather trying accompaniment, very well; Mr Shakespeare warbled in his prettiest toy tenor fashion; and Señor Albéniz, after playing Brassin's transcriptions of the rainbow scene from Das Rheingold and the fire charm from Die Walküre, had a final tremendous wrestle with the Walkürenritt. The dead silence produced by his playing, particularly during the second piece, was the highest compliment he could have desired.

To Herr Rudolph Liebich, who gave a concert at Barnsbury Hall on Wednesday, I could only say "Had I three ears, I'd hear thee."* But I have only two, and these cannot be in different postal districts on the same evening. In short, my apologies: I really could not come. In reply to an inquiry why I said nothing about the concert given by the Hallé Manchester orchestra at St James's Hall some time ago, I can only say that I never heard a word of it until it was over; and then I was not surprised to hear that a concert so carefully concealed

* Shakespear's Macbeth, Act IV, Scene 1.

from me had also apparently been concealed from the general public. At least, this seems the likeliest reason for the thin attendance complained of. I presume that Sir Charles Hallé's concert agent has not yet heard of The Star, and is carefully sending two stalls for every concert to all the crop of sixpenny weeklies which came out in the seventies and died at the half-dozenth number. (You would not credit the stupidities of this sort that go on.) Now, I dont want your tickets, gentlemen agents; but do, in the name of commonsense, send me your prospectuses. If not, you will have your own behind-the-timeness to thank for "a rather thin attendance."

CONFESSIONS OF A NON-SAVOYARD

The Star, 13 December 1889

The past week has, I believe, been a busy one for the musical critics. It has certainly been a busy one for me, but not musically: I have not even been to the Savoy opera. The first night I have to spare, I shall—but stop! I have not seen The Dead Heart yet, nor La Tosca, nor A Man's Shadow.* So let us fix the fourth night I have to spare for The Gondoliers. It will probably come about Easter, or if not then, towards the end of August.

Do not be disappointed at this, eager reader. A new Savoy opera is an event of no greater artistic significance than—to take the most flattering comparison—a new oratorio by Gounod. We know the exact limits of Mr

* The Dead Heart (1859), an historical drama by Watts Phillips, had been revived at the Lyceum on 28 September; La Tosca, from the French of Sardou, opened on 28 November at the Garrick; A Man's Shadow by Robert Buchanan had been holding forth at the Haymarket since 12 September.

Gilbert's and Sir Arthur Sullivan's talents by this time, as well as we know the width of the Thames at Waterloo Bridge; and I am just as likely to find Somerset House under water next Easter or autumn, as to find The Gondoliers one hair's-breadth better than The Mikado, or Gounod's promised Mass a step in advance of Mors et Vita. The Savoy has a certain artistic position, like the German Reed entertainment*; but it is not a movable position. The Red Hussar might have been a new departure at the Lyric; Gretna Green might have been anything; but I am already as absolutely certain of what The Gondoliers is as I shall be when I have witnessed the performance.

One result of this is that I have no real curiosity on the subject. Indeed, I may as well confess that I have no real conviction that I shall ever fulfil my promise to go. Would you be surprised to learn that I have never seen The Sorcerer, Iolanthe, Princess Ida, and Ruddigore at all, nor even Patience, except from behind the scenes at an amateur performance. I have a sorrowfully minute acquaintance with the music of them all; but it has been imposed upon me by circumstances over which I have no control. And as I have seen Trial by Jury only as an afterpiece by a provincial company when it first appeared ever so many years ago; as I saw The Pirates at the Opera Comique, and H.M.S. Pinafore by the secessionists at the Imperial, I begin to realize the fact that I have been only once inside the Savoy Theatre. On that occasion I was haled thither forcibly by a friend

* Mr and Mrs German Reed's Entertainment, established in 1855, catered to middle-class Victorians who spurned the vulgarities of the theatre and music hall. The company was later managed by a son, Alfred German Reed, in partnership with Richard Corney Grain, at St George's Hall, until the untimely deaths of both partners in 1895 brought an end to the popular musical and dramatic enterprise.

who had a spare stall for a Mikado *matinée*. The conclusion is irresistible that the attraction of Gilbert-Sullivan opera is not sufficient to overcome my inertia.

The reason is not far to seek. Mr Gilbert's paradoxical wit, astonishing to the ordinary Englishman, is nothing to me. Nature has cursed me with a facility for the same trick; and I could paradox Mr Gilbert's head off were I not convinced that such trifling is morally unjustifiable. As to Sir Arthur's scores, they form an easy introduction to dramatic music and picturesque or topical orchestration for perfect novices; but as I had learned it all from Meyerbeer (not to profane the great name of Mozart in such a connexion), and was pretty well tired of Offenbach before Trial by Jury was born, there was no musical novelty in the affair for me. Besides, Sir Arthur's school is an exploded one. Neatly and cleverly as he exploits it, he cannot get a progression or a melody out of it that is not the worse for wear. It smells mustily of Dr Day and his sham science of harmony, beloved of the Royal Academy of Music. Give me unaffected melodies consisting chiefly of augmented intervals, a natural harmony progressing by consecutive fifths and sevenths, plenty of healthy unprepared tonic discords and major ninths, elevenths, and thirteenths, without any pedantic dread of "false relations"; and then I will listen with some interest. But no more of Dr Day for me.

By the way, the question of learning harmony reminds me that I never finished the reply I began some weeks ago to the gentleman who asked my advice as to how he should proceed in the matter of taking singing lessons. But I do not know that I have anything to add, except that if he succeeds in finding in one and the same person a master able to teach him to produce his voice and pronounce well, besides helping him with really valuable artistic advice and criticism, I shall be glad to learn that gifted one's address.

Here are a few samples of the teachers who are quite willing to undertake the entire instruction of a public singer, from his first scale to his first ovation at La Scala, Milan, or at the Handel Festival. 1. Competent teacher of voice production. Can speak English with an Irish accent, and pronounce Italian with the same. Pretends to know French and German, but doesnt. Considers Rossini the most famous and popular of contemporary composers; but confesses to have been much struck with the modern innovations in Les Huguenots, Il Trovatore, and Gounod's Faust. Has rediscovered Porpora's method, as taught for six years from a single sheet of exercises to Caffarelli.

2. Frenchman. Great master of pronunciation, style, deportment, and dramatic expression, all, except the pronunciation, of the most artificial, unnatural, and impossible order. Sublimely egotistical, overbearing, but timid if resolutely bullied. Has originated all he knows himself. Considers all other teachers quacks. Relates all the anecdotes of Delsarte as having happened to himself. Has smashed his own voice, and is at present busy smashing everybody's else. Intends to come out at the Grand Opera in Paris some day, and bring the world to his feet, like Farinelli, by singing one note—just one—which will be the revelation of a new era. Shews you how Talma (whom he never saw) declaimed. Also gives imitations of Rachel. Regards the French nation as the most degraded on the face of the earth. Is under the impression (erroneous) that he has composed a great Mass. Teaches Gluck's *Divinités du Styx* to lady pupils, and Schubert's *Erlkönig* to gentlemen.

3. Englishman. Organist, Mus.Bac. Unaffectedly colloquial delivery. Suburban accent. Thinks he ought to know something about singing, considering the number of choirboys he has trained. Was a choirboy himself. Member of the Church of England, except for

the eighteen months when he was an Irvingite, having taken an organ of that persuasion. Was at the opera once, but is not much of a theatregoer. Understands fugue and canon, and wrote a *nunc dimittis* in five real parts for his degree. Successfully "analyzed" the last movement of Mozart's Jupiter symphony on the same occasion. Favorite classics, Handel and Mendelssohn. Favorite moderns, Jackson and Goss. Dislikes foreigners. Can teach the staff notation, and does not see what more a man can do with a pupil who only wants to sing.

4. Alsatian. Native tongue a patois, which he has forgotten. Cannot speak any language, but communicates with his fellow creatures in bad French. Composes fantasias, berceuses, serenades, &c., with great facility. Can play the guitar, roll twentyfour cigarets in a minute, and do Badeali's trick of singing a note and swallowing a glass of wine at the same time. Capital critic of cookery. Can shew you exactly how Malibran sang La Sonnambula, Schröder-Devrient Fidelio, and Cabel Dinorah. Has known every musician and celebrity of the century, and can tell you discreditable things about most of them. Heard Rossini say that the overture to Tannhäuser would sound just as well played backwards, and, with all due deference to you, prefers Rossini's opinion to yours. Considers that Wagner shewed his evil disposition by drinking coffee out of a golden cup, wearing velvet dressing-gowns, and being ungrateful to Meyerbeer. Knows good singing and music from bad in all the old-fashioned styles, and can work introductions, engagements, and press notices for you.

5. German. Enthusiast. Thorough musician. Well read, well educated, fully up to the modern standard of musical culture. Despises the ignorant dolts and dastards who drag music through the mud in England. Tells them so whenever he meets them. Finds that everybody quarrels with him, and asks whether it is not obvious

that this conspiracy against an eminently reasonable and well-disposed man is the work of the Jews, who are the curse of modern civilization. Will unmask them some day; and in the meantime will let them know what he thinks of them whilst he has breath in his body. Has no sense of humor; cannot see from anybody's point of view but his own; cannot understand that any other person should, except from corrupt motives or mental incapacity, have any other point of view; and would infallibly ruin himself by mere incompatibility but for the indispensability of his professional skill, knowledge, and devotion.

[U] I could multiply these types; but enough is as good as a feast, especially with the law of libel in its present uncertain condition. Now, it is evident that my correspondent would be very ill advised were he to apprentice himself to any one of these gentlemen. But they could all do something for him. If he is musically illiterate and does not know B flat from a bull's foot on paper, a few lessons from No. 3 will remedy that in the cheapest way. Then No. 1 could come in until safe habits of using the voice were discovered, when No. 2 could be resorted to, partly for amusement, partly for pronunciation. No. 5 could coach you in modern music and rub off the rococo acquired from the rest; and No. 4, for a due consideration, could give you a tip or two and get you an engagement.[U]

ST JOHN'S EVE
The Star, 20 December 1889

When I went down to the Crystal Palace last Saturday I knew that I was not going to have a treat. Mr Manns was over the hills and far away; and Mr Cowen was installed instead with a cantata. Still, it might have been worse. It might have been an oratorio. So, though straitened, I was not utterly cast down; and I should have reached the Palace in a fairly serene temper had not the train which brought me from Charing Cross to Victoria stuck in the tunnel and lost me the quarter past two express. The next time it happens I will have the law of them, if there is law in England.

Just as a considerate dentist warms his forceps in hot water, and hides it behind his back as he approaches you, so Mr Cowen disguised his cantata as "an old English idyll." But he could not conceal the ominous fact that the libretto is by Mr Joseph Bennett, who also supplies an "analysis" of the music, said analysis being about as difficult as an experienced chemist would find that of a cup of tea. If Mr Cowen had only written an analysis of Mr Bennett's poem, the two authors would have been even with oneanother. As it is, Mr Cowen has all the praise; and Mr Bennett has to be content with a slice of the pudding.

Here are some extracts from the "analysis." Easy rhythmic flow and natural harmonies—effective change of key and tempo—light and sparkling accompaniment—thoroughly appropriate simplicity—the composer reflects the spirit of old English music in almost every phrase—simple suggestiveness of the hushed accompaniment—animated and vigorously written number—frank and straightforward music—very effective return of the first part of the chorus—unaffected beauty of the song—unadorned eloquence of which Mr Cowen's music now presents so many examples—strong and earnest feeling, &c. &c. &c. Here is a final gem: "As for the vocal melody, it is simple and simply melodious, bespeaking, moreover, a manly and healthy sentiment entirely appropriate to the circumstances under which it is introduced."

[875]

The reflections suggested to me by Mr Cowen's simple and simply melodious melodies ran upon the irony of the arrangements of that musical Providence which ordains that blunt English professors shall be set to write about Judith and Jael and Deborah, whilst subtle descendants of the race of these heroines are imitating old English ballad music. St John's Eve is just as like The Vicar of Bray or Down Among the Dead Men as Mr Goschen is like Lord Brassey★ or Mr W. H. Smith. It is the drawing-room music of Maida Vale in an "old English" fancy costume. Mr Bennett has played up to the fancy costume, hardily but vainly, by flavoring his verse with such Augustan spices as "gentle Zephyr," and describing his heroine as "the fair." Which only reminded my irreverence of Mrs Simkins in the ballad of The Resurrection Man.

Then came the Resurrection Man, the corpse resolved
        to raise:
He broke the coffin with his axe, and at the fair did gaze.
Up started Mrs Simkins. Says she, "My gracious Me!
What are you with that axe about?" "Why, axe about,"
        says he,
        With my fol the diddle, ol the diddle, hi fiddle
        dee.

What a capital subject and title for a cantata, by the way, The Resurrection Man would make!

I do not propose to add an analysis of my own to Mr Bennett's. I doubt if I was as attentive to the music as I ought to have been. The opening St John theme set me thinking about a stave of David's in Die Meistersinger.

★ George J. Goschen (later 1st Viscount Goschen) and Thomas Brassey (created first Earl Brassey in 1886) were liberals, both of whom had served as M.P.'s and as lords of the Admiralty.

Then Mr Geard began to play it as a solo on the second trombone; and it immediately struck me as a pity that Mr Manns never gets Mr Geard, with Mr Hadfield and Mr Phasey, to play one of those quaint medieval pieces for organ and three or four trombones, which are so much more pleasant to listen to once in a way than Cherubini's overture to Anacreon played for the fiftieth time.

Happening, as I mused thus, to look down at my program, in a sudden wave of speculation as to why its price should have been doubled in honor of Mr Bennett's verses, my eye caught the heading

ARABELLA GODDARD

"Arabella Goddard stands in need of help. Her health, failing for some time past, is now so impaired that she can no longer follow her profession as a teacher; and this appeal is issued by her friends and admirers in the confident expectation that it will not be vainly put forth." Address, Chappell and Co., 50 New Bond-street, W.

The writer of the appeal is wrong in his dates as far as Madame Goddard's retirement is concerned. She may not have played at the Popular Concerts after 1873; but she did not retire then: I heard her play Beethoven's E flat concerto, and one by Sterndale Bennett at the Crystal Palace as lately as 1876, if not 1877; and at about the same period she was playing some of her old Thalberg pieces at Messrs Boosey's ballad concerts. She was an extraordinary pianist: nothing seemed to give her any trouble. There was something almost heartless in the indifference with which she played whatever the occasion required: medleys, fantasias, and *pot-pourris* for "popular" audiences, sonatas for Monday Popular ones, concertos for classical ones; as if the execution of the most difficult of them were too easy and certain to greatly interest her. I have a notion—which may be

[877]

pure fancy—that she wore wide hanging sleeves long after everybody else had given them up, and that they gave a certain winged grace to the traveling to and fro of her elbows; for she always held her forearm at right angles to the keyboard, never perceptibly turning it out. She was more like the Lady of Shalott working away at her loom than a musician at a pianoforte. I can see her now as she played; but I confess I cannot hear her, though I can vouch for the fact of her wonderful manipulative skill. Professional jealousy ascribed her success to the influence of her husband, who was musical critic to The Times; but no influence could have kept her in the front rank for nearly a quarter of a century without great ability on her part. I hope her old admirers will be generous. She must either have spent a fortune or lost it. I hope she has spent it and enjoyed it; and if she had spent ten, her position as the most famous of English pianists entitles her to ask for the means of enjoying dignity and comfort in her retirement.

I do not know what young women are coming to nowadays. You should see the artful letters with which they practise on the weakest side of my nature when they want to get me to a concert. I very nearly succumbed to the wiles of two concert givers on Wednesday; but I hardened my heart for three reasons. 1. They called me a "musical *critique*," a term which lacerated my literary sensibilities. 2. They sent me a half-crown ticket, though their program mentioned high places at half a guinea and five shillings. They little know how smallminded "critiques" are, if they habitually wound their dignity in this greedy fashion. 3. I was performing myself at Westminster, and could not have come anyhow.

CHRISTMAS IN BROADSTAIRS

The Star, 27 December 1889

The only music I have heard this week is waits. To sit up working until two or three in the morning, and then, just as I am losing myself in my first sleep, to hear *Venite adoremus*, more generally known as Ow, cam let Huz adore Im, welling forth from a cornet (English pitch), a saxhorn (Society of Arts pitch, or thereabouts), and a trombone (French pitch), is the sort of thing that breaks my peace and destroys my good will towards men. Coming on top of a very arduous month, it reduced me last Saturday to a condition of such complete addledness, that it became evident that my overwrought brain would work itself soft in another fortnight unless an interval of complete mental vacuity could be induced.

Obviously the thing to do was to escape from the magnetic atmosphere of London, and slow down in some empty-headed place where I should be thoroughly bored. Somebody suggested Broadstairs. I had always supposed Broadstairs to be a show place at Wapping; but I found that it was halfway between Margate and Ramsgate, in neither of which famous watering-places had I ever set foot. So on Christmas Eve I made my way to Holborn Viaduct, where I found a crowd which I cannot honestly describe as a nice crowd. A blackguard crowd, in fact: a betting, loafing, rowdy crowd, with a large infusion of fighting men in it. The fighting men were much the most respectable of the company. They had quite an air of honest industry about them, being men without illusions, who will calculate your weight and earn your money by the sweat of their brow if the opportunity looks good enough—who are not courageous but fitfully hopeful, not fearful but anxious, fighting being to them not a romantic exploit but a trade venture. The question was, however, what were they doing at Holborn Viaduct?

Well, I suppose they were waiting to hail the return of the heros from Bruges: of the prudent Smith, who is a fairly competent but by no means first-rate artist, and of the heroic Slavin, who is, it appears, a pianist, the Orpheus of the ring.* Also, perhaps, of the referee, whose decision proves that he is versed in the history of the ring, and knows what has happened to referees in the past when they have incautiously declared a winner without considering that by doing so they also declared a loser, and thereby took money out of the pockets of men with wives and families. As I came along in the train I read some indignant articles on the unfairness of the Bruges prizefight, evidently written by men who do not know that the proceedings which caused Mr Slavin to demand with noble indignation whether the occupants of Mr Smith's corner were Englishmen, are in every respect typical of the prize ring, and were as familiar in every detail to our grandfathers as Handel's Messiah is to me. Of course the cornermen were English; and I am bound to say that they seem to have earned their money faithfully, which is more than can be said for the mere betting men—real gentlemen, bent on getting money anyhow except by working for it.

I have no illusions about pugilism or its professors. I advocate the placing of the laborer in such a position that a position in the ring will not be worth his acceptance, instead of, as it now is, a glorious and

* Jem Smith and Frank Slavin fought a draw at Bruges on 23 December 1889, in a bare-fist contest which Trevor C. Wignall, in The Story of Boxing (1924), called "a foul blot on pugilism." It was the last bout under the rules of the London Prize-ring, being succeeded by the Marquess of Queensberry's rules.

lucrative alternative (for a while) to drudgery and contempt. I have not the smallest respect for the people who call the prizefighter a brute, without daring to treat him like one, but who will treat him much worse than one (than their hunter, for instance) if he remains a laborer for wages. I object to gamblers of all sorts, whether they gamble with horses, fighters, greyhounds, stocks and shares, or anything else. I hate foxhunting, shooting, fishing, coursing (a most dastardly pursuit); and I would, if I had the power, make horse traction in the streets, with all its horrors, as illegal as dog traction is. Furthermore, I do not eat slaughtered animals; and I regard a man who is imposed on by the vulgar utilitarian arguments in favor of vivisection as a subject for police surveillance. No doubt, all the other journalists who disapprove of prizefighting are equally consistent.

However, this has nothing to do with Broadstairs. Let no man henceforth ever trifle with Fate so far as actually to seek boredom. Before I was ten minutes here, I was bored beyond description. The air of the place is infernal. In it I hurry about like a mouse suffocating in oxygen. The people here call it "ozone" and consider it splendid; but there is a visible crust over them, a sort of dull terracotta surface which they pretend to regard as a sign of robust health. As I consume in the ozone, this terrible lime-kiln crust is forming on me too; and they congratulate me already on "looking quite different." As a matter of fact I can do nothing but eat: my brain refuses its accustomed work. The place smells as if someone had spilt a bottle of iodine over it. The sea is absolutely dirtier than the Thames under Blackfriars Bridge; and the cold is hideous. I have not come across a graveyard yet; and I have no doubt that sepulture is unnecessary, as the houses are perfect refrigerating chambers, capable of preserving a corpse to the remotest posterity.

I am staying in Nuckell's Place; and they tell me that

[881]

Miss Nuckell was the original of Betsey Trotwood in David Copperfield,★ and that the strip of green outside is that from which she used to chase the donkeys. A house down to the left is called Bleak House; and I can only say that if it is any bleaker than my bedroom, it must be a nonpareil freezer. But all this Dickensmania is only hallucination induced by the ozone. This morning a resident said to me "Do you see that weatherbeaten old salt coming along?" "Yes" I replied "and if you will excuse my anticipating your reply, I may say that I have no doubt that he is the original of Captain Cuttle.† But, my dear madam, I myself am Corno di Bassetto; and in future Broadstairs anecdotage will begin to revolve round Me." Then, impelled to restless activity by the abominable ozone, I rushed off to the left; sped along the cliffs; passed a lighthouse, which looked as if it had been turned into a pillar of salt by the sea air; fell presently among stony ground; passed on into muddy ground; and finally reached Margate, a most dismal hole, where the iodine and ozone were flavored with lodgings.

I made at once for the railway station, and demanded the next train. "Where to?" said the official. "Anywhere" I replied "provided it be far inland." "Train to Ramsgit at two-fifteen" he said: "nothing else till six." I could not conceive Ramsgit as being so depressing, even on Christmas Day, as Margit; so I got into that train; and, lo, the second station we came to was Broadstairs. This was the finger of Fate; for the ozone had made me so

★ Shaw was misinformed. The original of Aunt Betsey in Nuckell's Place, according to a well-informed Dickensian, Leslie C. Staples, was Mary Pearson Strong, who may, however, have been related to the Nuckell family as she shared a tombstone with them in the local cemetery. Her house and the patch of green from which she shooed the donkeys is adjacent to the Albion Hotel.

† Character in Dickens's Dombey and Son.

ragingly hungry that I burst from the train and ran all the way to Nuckell's Place, where, to my unspeakable horror and loathing, they triumphantly brought me up a turkey with sausages. "Surely, sir" they said, as if remonstrating with me for some exhibition of depravity "*surely* you eat meat on *Christmas* Day." "I tell you" I screamed "that I never eat meat." "Not even a little gravy, sir? I think it would do you good." I put a fearful constraint on myself, and politely refused. Yet they came up again, as fresh as paint, with a discolored mess of suet scorched in flaming brandy; and when I conveyed to them, as considerately as I could, that I thought the distinction between suet and meat, burnt brandy and spirits, too fine to be worth insisting on, they evidently regarded me as hardly reasonable. There can be no doubt that the people here are mentally enfeebled. The keen air causes such rapid waste of tissue that they dare not add to it by thinking. They are always recuperating—that is to say eating—mostly cows.

Nevertheless it was with some emotion that I trod sea sand for the first time for many years. When I was a boy I learnt to appreciate the sight and sound of the sea in a beautiful bay on the Irish coast. But they have no confounded ozone in Ireland, only ordinary wholesome sea air. You never see an Irishman swaggering and sniffing about with his chest expanded, mad with excessive oxygen, and assuring everybody that he feels—poor devil!—like a new man.

By the way, I did not escape the Waits by coming down here. I had not walked fifty yards from the railway station when I found them in full cry in a front garden. However, I am bound to confess that the seaside vocal Wait is enormously superior to the metropolitan instrumental one. They sang very well: were quite Waits off my mind, in fact. (This is my first pun: let who can beat it.) A couple of boys and the basso were conspicuous in the harmony. I suspect they were the church choir turning an honest penny.

CANTERBURY KINFREEDERL AND A LIGHTHOUSE

The Star, 3 January 1890; reprinted in abridged form in London Music, 1937. The full text is restored here

The other day, mad for want of something to do, I stood on the edge of the cliff and took a last look at sea and sky before plunging head-foremost to the rocks below. The preceding week had been a deadly one. I had been to Canterbury to see what the boy in Edwin Drood called the Kinfreederl; and my attempt to look right down the building from end to end had been baffled by a modern choir screen compared to which Costa's additional accompaniments to Mozart seemed pardonable and even meritorious. Why cant they let the unfortunate Kinfreederl alone? I rushed off angrily into the wilderness, and after wandering for eighteen miles or so found myself back here at Broadstairs again. I had also gone to Ramsgate to see a melodrama; but I had to leave the theatre at the eleventh murder, feeling that my moral sense was being blunted by familiarity with crime. As a last resource, I had been to the North Foreland Lighthouse to seek employment there; but the resident illuminating artist, whose intelligent and social conversation was an inexpressible relief to me, told me that the Trinity House catches its lighthousists young, as no man with an adequate knowledge of life would voluntarily embrace so monotonous a career. "I have come to such a state of mind in a rock house" he said "that I believed at last that we two in it were the only people in the world."

One thing that struck me about the lighthouse was that it had a certain character and a certain beauty about it, just like the old Cathedral, except in so far as it was not like it at all. The constructors, I have no doubt, did their very best to make a good lighthouse, because they understood the want of such a thing. Now when we start to put up a choir screen—a thing we should never dream of doing on our own spontaneous initiative—we dont understand the want of it. We dont want it, in short. Consequently, when the restorative architect sketches a miserable sham medieval obstruction, we hand the sketch over to the builder as being probably the right thing. The shape is much the same; and, after all, the fellow is an architect, and ought to know. The guide who shewed me the Cathedral told me, as well as I can recollect, that the building was designed by one Thomas Ibbekket, who was killed by the Black Prince. So they made him a saint, and put his shrine near the tomb of the Prince, upon whom the pious pilgrims did poetic justice by stealing the diamonds out of his helmet. Well, if Ibbekket's ghost were set to repair the North Foreland Lighthouse, how would he regard the job? He would say "By'r Lady, here be a bell tower, and eftsoons a gramercifully ill-favored one. The wight that wrought here did but foolishly to seek beauty in curiously fashioned wedges of glass, the whiles forgat he it wholly in the shape of his window; wheras every churl knoweth that the beauty of glass is but in its hue, and eke the majesty of a window in the stone arch that surroundeth it. Fain would I build these fools a new tower; but since they will neither have me do that nor disuse their silly custom of firing a beacon in the loft, I must e'en do what I faithfully can to hide their folly, and shield them from the scoffing of the passing shipman." With such notions, Thomas, it is safe to say, would make a hash of the lighthouse, but by no means such a hash as we have made of the choir screen. To touch that for bungling, Thomas would have to set to at manufacturing dioptric lenses as a sham XIX century optician.

However, I am digressing. When I had exhausted the Kinfreederl and the Lighthouse and the melodrama, suicide, as I have related, seemed the only thing left. But I was loth to cast myself off the cliff; for I had just read Mr Walter Besant's sequel to Ibsen's Doll's House in the English Illustrated Magazine, and I felt that my suicide would be at once held up as the natural end of a reprobate who greatly prefers Ibsenism to Walter Besantism. Besides, it seemed to be rather Walter's place than mine to commit suicide after such a performance. Still, I felt so deadly dull that I should hardly have survived to tell the tale had not a desperate expedient to wile away the time occurred to me. Why not telegraph to London, I thought, *for some music to review?* Reviewing has one advantage over suicide. In suicide you take it out of yourself: in reviewing you take it out of other people. In my seaside temper that decided me. I sent to London at once; and the music came duly by parcels post.

I have tried all the songs over carefully, and am under notice to leave when my week is up. First, then, from John Heywood, of Manchester, I have a song described on the title page as The Peasant's Wooing, by Langford Grey. But surely the right title is Dermot Asthore, and the true author Crouch, of Kathleen Mavourneen fame. There is much curtailment and some alteration; but Mr Langford Grey cannot on the strength of these claim the melody as his own. Mr William Spark, Mus. Doc., and organist of the Leeds Town Hall, has, it appears, written an oratorio called Immanuel. I decline to encourage such proceedings by praising the three extracts sent me. Suffice it to say that the Hosanna is simply a rattling Italian opera march in the style of

Donizetti; and that This is the day which the Lord hath made, makes a good anthem, as anthems go. Mr Mills— not Mr Mills of Bond-street, to whom so many Englishmen owe bills for sheet music, but Mr Mills of 60, Moorgate-street—appeals to The Star's political sympathies with songs about Tullamore Gaol, by Dr A.H. Walker, and about Trafalgar Square, by Russell Lewis. As to Trafalgar Square it is bad enough to have been frightened almost out of my senses there without having doggrel sung about my sufferings afterwards. Tullamore Gaol has more fun in it, Mr T.D. Sullivan being a much better hand at verse than Mr F.G. Halliwell, the singer of the Square.

Messrs Reynolds, of 13, Berners-street, send me songs meant to be comic. But few and far between are the successes in this *genre*. Either an epigram of universal relevance or a tune of irresistible seductiveness is indispensable. Neither is forthcoming in these compositions. Messrs Reid Bros., 436, Oxford-street, submit some songs of the ordinary drawing-room worthlessness. A nautical specimen, with the refrain Sailing away, Sailing afar, Darling, my heart is true, True as the compass to the star, True to Old England and you, should be placed in the drawer set apart for songs not to be sent to Corno di Bassetto. As to Mr G. Percy Haddock's Liebeslied for violin or cello and pianoforte, the melody is very stale and not particularly suited to the violin, though I admit that it is not particularly unsuited to the violoncello. It was, however, an economical idea to dedicate the cello version to Signor Piatti, and the violin version (note for note the same melody an octave higher) to Mr Haddock's brother Edgar. Absurd as this is, it is at least pecuniarily disinterested. The point of this remark lies in the fact that dedicating a song is usually only a polite way of begging, as the dedicatee, if a private person and not a relative, is expected to buy five pounds' worth of copies in return. I take the opportunity of mentioning this custom in the hope that the innocent people who gush dedications all over their title pages may be made aware of the construction which older hands place on such follies. If people do meaningless things, they must not complain at having meanings supplied by other hands.

In coming to the more successful efforts contained in my bundle, I feel far from sure that my standard has not been unduly lowered by trying over the failures. I know a pianoforte dealer who has an artful way of selling indifferent pianos, even to experts. When you go into his showrooms to choose an instrument, he leads you straight to a dashing, rattling, fireirony, "brilliant" atrocity, upon which he half murders your ear before you can stop him. Then, professing to understand by your protests exactly what you really want, he opens just such another, only ten per cent. worse all round. By the time he has assaulted you in this manner some five or six times, you are ready, by force of contrast, to accept a very middling piano as a quite exquisite instrument. This old acquaintance of mine has more establishments in Europe and America than I care to mention.

The book of seven songs by Fred. Whishaw perhaps sounded better after the other ditties sent by Messrs Reid than they would after a course of Schubert and Gounod. Six out of the seven are in three-four time, which is rather too much of a good thing. And there is all the difference in the world between Shelley's

> A widow bird sat mourning for her love
> Upon a wintry bough.

and Mr Whishaw's

> A widow bird sat mourning for her love
> Up on a wintry bough.

[888]

Little Parlez-vous, a children's operetta by Effie Magee and W.H. Jude, turns out to be an insidious attempt to introduce French lessons in the guise of nursery theatricals. But as there is nothing in the work that children cannot pick up without effort; and as the instincts of the authors are obviously more artistic than philological, I think the children will make the French an excuse for the theatricals, quite as much as the parents will make the theatricals an excuse for the French.

Messrs Hopkinson, of 95, New Bond-street, treat me like a reasonable being. These two duets, At Daybreak (soprano and tenor) and Song of the Mill (soprano and contralto), by Mary Carmichael, do not mark a new departure in music; but they are written with fine natural feeling and cultivated taste, and are miles above the illiterate rubbish which some publishers think good enough for the public. Mr Arthur Somervell's songs are also competently written; but Thine am I, my faithful fair, contains a rather too strong reminiscence of an old English ballad—I have the name on the tip of my tongue, if I could only remember it. Where roses blow, by A.H. Behrend, is of the drawing-room drawing-roomy. Gounod's new Ave Maria on Bach's second C minor prelude is an exact repetition of the treatment applied by him years ago to the first prelude in C major. I cannot honestly say that the last is likely ever to be the first in this instance. The old tendency to save himself the trouble of composing by simply setting everything to the ascending chromatic scale overtook Gounod again when he was halfway through this new "meditation" of his. The heavenly felicities of these progressions are by this time palling on me. Have I not sat out The Redemption?

Instrumental music does not prevail to any striking extent in my bundle. Marshalls (Limited), of Berners-street, send me Vol. IV of The Abbey, containing ten voluntaries for harmonium or American organ by Alfred Rawlings. They are very easy and unpretentious; but the harmonic treatment, simple as it is, shews the born musician. Messrs Rudall and Carte tempt me with several numbers of the Clarinet Player's Journal. Of these I prefer the one containing a romance by Mr Edward German, as both the melody and accompaniment belong by right of birth, as it were, to the instruments for which they are written, wheras Mr Hamilton Clarke's melodies, though undeniably graceful, lack special character, and have accompaniments which suggest transcriptions from a score instead of pianoforte music proper. Signor Riccardo Gallico's Mesto pensiero must have been conceived as the utterance of a stagey Italian singer rather than of an instrument. Signor Gallico has, by the bye, very sensibly written the pianist's copy of the clarinet part without transposition. I recommend this course to the attention of Mr German and Mr Hamilton Clarke. Why on earth should I, playing an accompaniment in the key of F to a clarinetist playing in the same key, have his part put before me in the key of G? Of course, he must have his sheet written in G because, as his instrument is pitched a tone lower than the pianoforte, he must finger for G in order to get F. But if I finger for G on the piano, I get G—at least I often get it, and I always intend to get it. I therefore applaud Signor Gallico for relieving me of the useless trouble of transposing.

Ha! the postman. What is this? My ticket for the Press view at the Old Masters on Friday! Hooray! Goodbye, Broadstairs.

A MIDSUMMER NIGHT'S YAWN

The Star, 10 January 1890

Pretty lot of fellows, these dramatic critics. Do you remember Cousin Feenix, in Dombey and Son, who spoke of Shakespear as "man not for an age but for all time, with whom your great grandfather was probably acquainted"? That is much the manner in which the dramatic critics have treated the performance of A Midsummer Night's Dream at the Globe. They have sat it out; yawned; put in a good word for Mr Benson as an Archbishop's nephew and for old William; and then set to work in earnest over their beloved penny dreadful equestrian lions and half-crown dreadful Toscas, and forty thousandth night of Sweet Simpering Lavender,* and stale dramatic dog biscuit generally. However, it is an ill wind that blows nobody any good. When I entered the pit at the Globe on Monday evening, just as the overture was getting under way, I found only four rows occupied, and so had practically a choice of positions and an easy view for my hard-earned two shillings. But the stalls were full; and I noticed that several of the occupants had brought sacred-looking books, and that the men were unusually particular about removing their hats when they came in.

Now, I am loth to spoil such excellent business; but I am bound to avow that I found myself next a gentleman who is an old acquaintance of the manager's, and he assured me (and I have since verified his assurance) that

* Arthur Pinero's enormously successful comedy Sweet Lavender had been running since March 1888. It achieved a total of 683 performances.

the archiepiscopal connexion is a pure invention of the Press, and that Mr F. R. Benson is neither an archbishop, nor an archbishop's son, nor an archbishop's nephew, nor even, so far as can be ascertained, his remotest cousin-german. My first impulse on hearing this was, I own, to demand my money back. But just then Miss Kate Rorke's draperies floated through the arcades; and when she said

> O happy fair!
> Your eyes are lodestars, and your tongue's sweet air
> More tunable than lark to shepherd's ear

Lambeth Palace might have been dynamited across into Millbank for all I cared. Reader: do you remember Shield's three-part song; and have you ever yourself lent a hand with

> O——h! hap-pee hap-pee hap-pee hap-pee fai-air
> Your eyes, are lodestars and your tongue, sweet, air.

Which, I frankly admit, spoils the sense of the verse, but not its music. This generation, I sometimes think, has no sense of word music. They will go to the Arts and Crafts Exhibition, and admire tissues of cottons, wools, and silks; but give them a beautiful tissue of words, and they have no more sense of the art of it than if it was the Post Office Directory. For instance, William Morris has been weaving words into an article on the art and industry of the XIV century in Time. Now watch the reviews, and see whether one of them will draw the slightest distinction between the beauty of this article's verbal fabric and the literary kamptulicon of Mr Blank of the Sterile Club, situate in the region between Dan and Beersheba. But if William Morris had woven a carpet instead, how everybody would have pretended to admire it!

The confounded thing about it is that actors, whose business it is to be experts in word music, are nearly as deaf to it as other people. At the Globe they walk in thick darkness through Shakespear's measures. They do not seem to know that Puck may have the vivacity of a street Arab, but not his voice: his bite, but never his bark; that Theseus should know all Gluck's operas by heart, and in their spirit deliver his noble lines; that Oberon must have no Piccadilly taint in his dialect to betray him into such utterances as

> Be it ahnce, aw cat, aw bea-ah
> Pahd, aw boa-ah with b'istled hai-ah
> In thy eye that shall appea-ah
> When thou wak'st, it is thy dea-ah.

By this time I should be converted to the device of joining consecutive vowels with r's, if conversion were possible. I know that it is easy to say Mariar Ann, and cruelly hard to say Maria Ann. But the thing is possible with courage and devotion. When Mr Benson schools himself to say

> Not Hermia but Helena I love

instead of

> Not Hermia but Helenar I love

I shall be spared a pang when next thereafter I hear him play Lysander. Helenar sounds too like cockney for Eleanor.

On the whole, I fear I must declare sweepingly that Miss Kate Rorke is the only member of the company who is guiltless of verse murder. She is by no means the gentle Helena of Shakespear. The soul of that damsel was weak; but none of Miss Kate Rorke's organs, I take it, is stronger than her soul. Yet by this very strength she forces herself on the part; and I accept her with joy and gratitude. Artist in one thing, artist in all things. The sense of beauty that guides Miss Rorke through the verse, guides her movements, her draperies, her eyes, and everything about her. She has charms in her fingers and charms in her toes; and she shall have music (by Mendelssohn) wherever she goes.

Miss Maud Milton, who played Hermia, took the part at such short notice that she evidently had to learn it during the intervals; for in the first act she left out all about the simplicity of Venus' doves, and a good deal more beside. Later in the evening she was comparatively letter-perfect; and she played with intelligence and force. But she was melodramatic: the indispensable classic grace was wanting: she looked persecuted, and seemed to be struggling through the toils of some forger villain towards a reconciliation with a long lost husband in the fifth act. As to Bully Bottom, I have no doubt he was more Athenian than Shakespear made him; but his stupidity lacked the true unction, and his voice had not caught the Stratford-on-Avon diapason. The rest of the company must excuse me. I never trespass on the province of a colleague. The criticism of acting is Arthur Walkley's business.

About the music, however, I may venture on a word. Mendelssohn's score, even when eked out by Cooke's Over hill, over dale, and Horn's I Know a Bank, falls short of Mr Benson's requirements. Accordingly, not only are two "songs without words," the Spring Song and the so-called Bee's Wedding, pressed into the service, but the Fingal's Cave overture has been cheerfully annexed for the last *entr'acte*. I fully expected a selection from Elijah to crop up in the course of the fifth act. But how different this music is from the oratorio music! how original, how exquisitely happy, how radiant with pure light, absolutely without shadow! XIX century civilization had a job after its own pocket in knocking all that out of Mendelssohn, and setting him to work on Stone Him to Death and the like.

I am glad to be able to say that the XIX century has not utterly defeated the execution of the music at the Globe. True, the orchestra is a little shorthanded, and now and then rather rough; but it greatly enhances the pleasure of seeing the play; and, under the circumstances, I ask no more except that the wedding march should be pulled together and smartened up. At present it is slovenly. The audience behaved stupidly, talking too much during the *entr'actes*, and encoring "I know a bank," a charming piece, but one which does not require to be heard twice over, as its melodic ideas are repeated and elaborated as much as they will bear. The singing was very fair, though here again imperfect training in diction told on the effect. For instance, Miss Townsend's voice was pretty when she was singing old-fashioned florid passages without words; but when she came to tell us about hills and dales, the excessive acuteness of her vowels made the effect grotesque. I must use a French *é* to represent the effect of the first line she sang—

Oveh heels, oveh *déllz*, &c. &c.

But if I harp too much on diction, some idiot will begin to clamor for the introduction of the French system, by which all the actors, instead of cultivating and developing each his own diction, acquire a secondhand article which is much more hateful than the honest incompetence of our British buskineers. (This phrase is at the service of any dramatic critic who would like to write The British Buskineers to the tune of British Grenadiers. For example:

On parle de Mounet Sully: on parle de Coquelin,
De Febvre, Got et Maubant, du sociétaire enfin.

And so on, ending with the dow, roy, meeh, fawr, saorl, lar, see, of the British buskineer.)

The death of Gayarré places it beyond my power to make amends for the injustice—if it really was an injustice—which I did him the first and last time I heard him sing. The occasion was his *début* at Covent Garden in 1877 in the character of Raoul de Nangis. I was not then accustomed to the now happily obsolescent vocal method called goatbleat; and I thought he had a horrible voice and a horrible way of using it, whilst his bearing and acting aggravated rather than redeemed his vocal disadvantages. Not only thought so, reader, but said so; for in those days Italian opera was in the valley of the shadow; and the performances at Covent Garden were one long exasperation from the first note to the last. Mr Harris had not taken matters in hand then: he was, I rather think, playing in Pink Dominoes at the Criterion. Howbeit, I protested vehemently against Gayarré; but although I stand to my opinion of the solitary performance I witnessed, I cannot doubt that in concert rooms, in private, and in theatres too small to frighten him into forcing his voice beyond all reason, he must have been an artist of considerable charm, as his position was not one of those that are to be had for nothing. Cases are by no means uncommon of practised singers and speakers losing all confidence in their old methods in new and alarming conditions as to space. When that happens, they begin to bleat frantically, with the effect that Gayarré produced on me. Actors and singers who have small voices should remember that the problem for them is to make themselves *heard*, and by no means to make themselves *loud*. Loudness is the worst defect of quality that any voice, large or small, can have.

CORNO AT A PANTOMIME

The Star, 17 January 1890

The other day, passing Her Majesty's Theatre, I saw by the placards that a Christmas pantomime [Cinderella] was going on inside. I had not been to a pantomime for fourteen years at least. So I went in; and now I do not think I shall go to one for fourteen years more. It was terribly stupid. The investment it represented may have been anything between ten and twenty thousand pounds. Every thousand of it produces about a farthings-worth of enjoyment, net. I say net, because a balance has to be struck between positive and negative results. In estimating that the entertainment exceeds the annoyance and tedium by a tenth of a farthing per cent., I am making a generous allowance for the inferior tastes of my fellow creatures. As far as I am personally concerned, the balance is on the other side; for I am sorry I went; and wild horses could not drag me thither again.

What struck me most was the extraordinary profusion of artistic talent wasted through mere poverty of purpose. One fiftieth part of it placed at the disposal of a man with the right sort of head on his shoulders would have sufficed for a quite satisfactory pantomime. The scenepainters, costumiers, property makers, armorers, and musicians are for the most part capable artists; a few of the players are actors; and the dancers do not all walk like irresolute ostriches. But they might almost as well have been walking up and down the Strand with their hands in their pockets—or in Mr Leslie's pockets—for all the use that is made of their ability in the Haymarket. In the Strand they would bore nobody but themselves: in the Haymarket they bored Me—Me, that never injured them.

[897]

The whole affair had been, according to the playbill, "invented and arranged by Charles Harris." I have no animosity towards that gentleman; but I must say I wish he would invent a little more and arrange a little less. Take the procession of beetles, for instance. When I was a small boy there was in the house a book on entomology, with colored plates. The beetles depicted in them were so gorgeous and fantastic that it was delightful to turn over ten plates or so. After that they palled, rapid and easy as the turning over of a bookleaf is; for the mind thirsted for a new idea. Now it was a capital notion of Mr Harris's, that of having a processional ballet of beetles. But he has worn the notion to death—or, to put it tropically, he turns over too many plates. The first five minutes are interesting, the second tedious, the third wearisome, the fourth exasperating, and the fifth sickening. As of old, I craved for a fresh idea, and was given a stale beetle. The character of the color scheme never varied, the drill never varied, the music never varied; so that at last I felt as if Mr Harris were brushing my hair by machinery for half an hour on the strength of my having enjoyed it for the first half minute. The fairy tale procession and the Shakespearean procession were far more successful; for here was a world of ideas annexed as cheaply as a slice of Africa by the British Empire.

Perhaps I may seem a little rough on the pantomime, in view of all the praise the papers have lavished on it. But you must remember the fourteen years which have elapsed since my last experience in this line. I have not been let down gently from Christmas to Christmas by a ladder of fourteen steps: I have come down the whole distance with a crash. I used to regret that the performers were merely ordinary actors and not pantomimists as well. Imagine my feelings on finding that they are now not ordinary actors, but "variety artists" without any dramatic training whatever. The reduction of the harlequinade to three or four scenes lasting only an hour or so seemed inevitable owing to the curious scarcity of the sort of talent required to make it really funny. I have never seen a good clown (this is without prejudice to Mr Payne, to whose clowning I am a stranger); and I have my doubts as to whether the character was not as purely idiosyncratic with Grimaldi* as Dundreary was with Sothern.† I remember one brilliant harlequin—Mr Edward Royce—who donned the spangles one evening in an emergency. Also one solitary pantaloon, a member of the Lauri troupe,‡ an imposing old gentleman, punctiliously mannered and beautifully dressed, whose indignant surprise at the reverses which overtook him was irresistibly ludicrous.

But even in its decay, with stupid and vulgar clowning, and harlequins and columbines who had never seen Dresden China or Watteau pictures, the harlequinade still consisted of a string of definite incidents, involving distinct parts for an old woman, a masher (then known as a swell), a policeman, and a nurserymaid. The policeman still plotted, the clown counterplotted, the pantaloon muddled everything he attempted, and the harlequin at least danced. At Her Majesty's I found to my astonishment that all this has dwindled to a single scene, lasting about twenty minutes,

* Joseph Grimaldi (1779–1837) was a celebrated panto-mimist and clown at Drury Lane and Covent Garden.

† E. A. Sothern created on both sides of the Atlantic the *rôle* of the brainless peer Lord Dundreary in Tom Taylor's comedy Our American Cousin (New York, 1858; London, 1861). It was a caricature which earned him lasting fame.

‡ A family of variety and pantomime artists. The pantaloon whom Shaw recalls probably was Charles Lauri Sr., who died in 1889.

during which two clowns, two pantaloons, two police-men, and a crowd, without distinct functions, improvize random horseplay in the feeblest and most confusing way simultaneously in opposite corners of the stage.

This idea of doubling the clown and pantaloon is about as sensible as if Mr Irving were to invite Edwin Booth to come back to the Lyceum and revive Othello with two Othellos and two Iagos.

The question now is, shall we leave it there, and shall I never see a pantomime again? Such a solution is impossible. When Mr Harris and Mr Leslie have gone on for a few years more egging each other on to greater expenditure behind the curtain for the sake of greater weariness before it; when even the grownup people who have learnt to be thankful for small mercies begin to echo the sneers of the cynical little children for whose sake the entertainment is professedly got up; when the essential squalor of the whole affair becomes so obvious that even the dramatic critics will grow tired of writing strings of goodnatured lies about it, then some manager will suddenly strike his forehead and say "Suppose I try a real pantomime! Suppose I get rid of my foulmouthed, illiterate, ignorant stage manager, who, though he dips thousands deep into my treasury, cannot with all his swearing get two supers to walk across the stage in step, much less tread the boards like self-respecting men! Suppose I take the matter in hand myself as an artist and a man of culture!"

Well, suppose he does, how could he set to work? I had better give explicit directions, since it appears that nobody else will. First, then, Mr Manager, get rid of your "literary adviser," if you have such a thing. The theatres which harbor such persons at once become conspicuous by their illiteracy. This done, think over the whole profession as far as you know it, with a view to selecting dancers, acrobats, and comedians who are good pantomimists. At Her Majesty's, for instance, there is a ballet of young ladies who are supposed to represent rabbits. You can pick out at a glance the girls who ever saw a rabbit and who have the faculty of suggesting the peculiar movement of the creature's head and paws. These are the girls to select for the new departure in pantomime. Leading artists are to be found everywhere. At a circus in Amsterdam I saw a troupe which made music out of kitchen utensils. Their leader was a capital pantomimist: his imitation of an orchestral conductor was immense; and his posturing as the ringmaster on a sham horse outdid nature itself. In *Le Voyage en Suisse* there was a Frenchman, Agoust by name if I mistake not, who was a most artistic pantomimist. When Offenbach's *Voyage dans la Lune* was produced at the old Alhambra, Madame Rose Bell, a lively French lady, distinguished herself therein, not more by the qualities which endeared her to the Alhambra audience than by the vivacity and expressiveness of her pantomime. Such examples shew how a company of pantomimists could be selected by a good judge. It must finally contain a pair of young and beautiful dramatic dancers for lover and sweetheart (harlequin and columbine), a good comedian for the intriguing valet (clown), a good old man for the tyrannical father, the rich old suitor (pantaloon), or anything except the detestable Ally Sloper* of today. Finally, you must get a dramatic poet who is a born storyteller and who knows the Arabian Nights better than Two Lovely Black Eyes. The poet will tell you the rest.

* Comic-strip character created in 1867 by Charles Henry Ross, which became a fixture in the comic weekly, Judy.

CHILDREN IN THEATRES

The Star, 24 January 1890

When I laid down my pen last week I thought I had done with pantomimes and Cinderella for ever. But who shall foreknow the ways of Destiny? On Saturday I went to Bristol to fulfil a Sunday starring engagement of an unmusical nature. In the evening, having nothing better to do, I naturally went to the theatre, where I found a packed audience listening to the strains of a comic boy in buttons, who was in sole possession of the stage. I gathered from his song some more or less valuable observations on human conduct in general; but I did not find out what the main business in hand was until the entire family came in, when a glance at the two ugly sisters and the one pretty one shewed me that I had wantonly exposed myself to another Cinderella pantomime. However, I do not complain. The Bristolians, an exacting people, declared that it was not as good as last year's; but I had not seen last year's, and so could only weigh it against the pantomime at Her Majesty's, compared to which it was an entertainment for artists and philosophers.

For instance, there was a musical director, Mr G. R. Chapman, who knew his business, and subdued his orchestra to the merest whisper during the harlequinade and the clog dancing (clog dancing is pretty when the dancer does not wear clogs). At Her Majesty's, Mr Solomon keeps his band scraping and blowing its loudest throughout, until it induces distraction and madness, like the steam organ of a merry-go-round. The variety items are managed so as not to confuse or unduly interrupt the story, which was never quite lost sight of by the actors. These, as actors will in pantomimes, occasionally substituted playing the fool for comic acting, with depressing results; for nothing on earth leads more to gloomy meditation than the spectacle of a grown man playing the fool. Far be it from me to deny, too, that the fun occasionally drooped into stale and vapid vulgarity. But there was nothing like the weariness and dreariness of the London pantomime. If I were forced to choose which of the two I should sit out again on pain of death, I should choose death; but if that alternative were cut off I should unhesitatingly choose Bristol, although I cannot understand why any conceivable railway journey should at this time of day take three mortal hours to accomplish.

But I have not resumed the subject of pantomime merely to heave another brick at the costly follies of our big metropolitan playhouses. Nor would I have done so solely in order to urge most vehemently upon the Jee family, who made a delightful clangor with The Last Rose of Summer on horseshoes and The Harmonious Blacksmith on anvils, that the horseshoe which sounds the keynote is flat, a defect curable in five minutes by any harmonious blacksmith armed with a file. Even the suicidal determination of all the singing ladies to get chest notes or nothing, disastrous as its results must prove to them, would not by itself have moved me to remonstrance, hardened as I am to it by this time. As to the very pretty dance between Mr Edmund Payne and Miss Nellie Murray in the fourth scene, did not the audience sufficiently justify it by an *encore*, as they did also a clog dance (clogless, as aforesaid) by a Miss Lyndale, whose rosy and shapely limbs were unembarrassed to an extent that would have considerably embarrassed my grandmother? Mr John Watson, the scenic artist who designed the admirable effects of light and color in the fairy coach scene and the *Incroyable* ballet, can probably do without any congratulations; and the proprietor-manager with the historic name, Mr John Macready Chute, would, if he is anything like a London manager, consider all the praise I might lavish on him cancelled by the diabolical hatred and personal malice betrayed by my reflection on that single horseshoe that was out of tune. Therefore, I lay no stress on any of these matters, but proceed to the one point that seriously requires publicity.

It was towards the end of last century that this nation, having devoted itself body and soul to the making of money and of everything that would, under pressure, sweat gold, took to making money out of children. I do not propose to make my readers sick by recapitulating the horrible villainies on parish apprentice children which led to the ineffectual Morals and Health Act of 1802, and which were continued on all sorts of poor children without much alleviation almost up to the middle of this wickedest of all the centuries. Every attempt to put these villainies down was met with by declarations that the children liked them, and were benefited by them, and that their little earnings helped to brighten and beautify the dwellings of their affectionate parents. By slow and painful steps Humanity beat back Rascality, Greed, and Hypocrisy until, last year, a point was reached at which the law forbad the employment of children under ten. Unhappily an exception was made in the case of children employed in theatres, who were still left liable by means of a magistrate's special license. This breach was made in the Act solely through the ignorance and prejudice of its supporters with respect to theatres, one gentleman declaring, in effect, that children on the stage were corrupted by association with loose women there, and so forth. The gentleman apologized afterwards; but by that time the mischief was done. The Puritan assumption that every woman on the stage is necessarily a coarse and brazen voluptuary is as offensive as the counter assumption that she is necessarily a fireside angel, supporting a deserving family out of her modest earnings, and never going out without a chaperone. The moment the opposition to the exception in favor of theatre proprietors became identified with the Puritan crusade against beauty and happiness, it was damned, and the children were sacrificed.

But even those who sacrificed them by accepting the fatal amendment never intended that magistrates should do more than, after a strict inquiry, cautiously license here and there the appearance of some indispensable child character in dramas so great that they cannot, without public loss, be banished from the stage. I invite these innocent compliers to take a turn through the theatres and see for themselves how magistrates and petty sessions have been wantonly issuing their licenses wholesale. In this Bristol pantomime, in which the employment of a child under ten was no more indispensable than the appearance of a performing lion, there were at least twenty children under ten on the stage. They were all the better for the Act, which had secured for them a separate room with a fire in it, a restriction of their time at the theatre to two hours, and the vigilance of people of my way of thinking before the curtain, backed by the chance of a visit from the factory inspector behind it. Consequently they romped through and piped out Mr Farmer's Singing Quadrilles much more happily and freely than they would have done in the bad old times. Further, there were only twenty of them as against thirty before the passing of the Act. But the fact remains that they should not have been there at all.

There is some consolation in the reflection that the Bill for the further extension of the Factory Acts—a measure to which the Liberal party is pledged—will contain a clause raising the age under which children may not be employed from ten to twelve, as in Germany and Hungary. No doubt an attempt will be made to renew the present special license clause. But the way in which it is being abused to drive a coach and six through the Act of 1889 will come up in judgment and secure for the children the protection of total and unconditional prohibition. If the comfortable middleclass people are so ready to be persuaded that work on the stage is a harmless pleasure for children, let them send their own young ones gratuitously to enjoy and improve themselves there. The Acts prohibit only employment for hire. In the meantime, I hope that some member of Parliament will seize the earliest opportunity to get from the Secretary of State a return of all the cases in which licenses have been granted. Such a return will open the eyes of the verdant dupes who thought that the licensing clause was passed solely in order to provide Richard III. with a little Duke of York, or A Doll's House with three little Helmers.

ORCHESTRAL CONCERTS
The Star, 31 January 1890

Just listen to this:

"Star Building, Stonecutter Street, E.C.,
"27th January 1890.

"Dear Signor di Bassetto,
"May I respectfully and deferentially invite your attention to the fact that it is about six weeks since we had anything about music in your column, and that the Popular Concerts have been running for the last fortnight in the vain hope of securing a fraction of the

time that can be spared from the enlightenment of humanity at Bristol and elsewhere."

These people seem to think that I have nothing else to do than go to concerts for them. Observe, too, how severe, how classic, their taste. No vulgar pantomime music for them. Monday Popular Concerts or nothing: that is their ultimatum.

It is evident that if I am to maintain my independence as a critic, this spirit of insubordination at headquarters must be checked. But how check it? A vulgar critic would refuse ever again to enter St James's Hall—would perhaps threaten to resign. Not thus do I enforce my authority. I am no despot: when the editorial staff, madly fancying that it knows better than I, revolts against me, I immediately let it have its own way, knowing that before three columns have elapsed it will implore me to resume my sceptre and rescue The Star from the consequences of its presumptuous ignorance. The moment I got that letter I went straight off to a Monday Pop. The following notice of it will, I trust, be found to conform in all respects to the best regulation pattern.

On Monday, the 27th inst., at St James's Hall, Piccadilly, a large audience assembled to enjoy the eleven hundred and fifth of Messrs Chappell's Popular Concerts, an excellent institution, now in its thirty-second season, which has contributed, more than any other cause, perhaps, to the spread and enlightenment of musical taste and culture in England. Lady Hallé, better known to our readers as Madame Norman-Neruda, occupied, not for the first time, the responsible post of first violin; and the violoncello was in the capable hands of the veteran Piatti. It is hardly necessary to say that such artists as these, assisted by Herr L. Ries (second violin) and Herr Straus (viola), gave a perfectly satisfactory rendering of Schumann's quartet in A minor, which, curiously enough, is written in the key of F major, and which, as all know, is the first of the set of three dedicated by Schumann to his friend Mendelssohn. Nor did the share of the program allotted to the once contemned Zwickau composer end here. It is true that Schumann's Papillons can hardly be viewed as an adequate example of his maturest powers; but it furnished Herr Stavenhagen with ample opportunities for displaying the combined delicacy and strength of his execution, which was duly appreciated, and secured for him a merited, but—considering the character of these concerts—inappropriate *encore*. However, it is vain to expect artists to resist these flattering compliments: the initiative in reform must come from the public. The concert concluded with the ever fresh and perennially welcome septet of Beethoven, played—we need not say how well—by Madame Neruda and MM. Ries, Lazarus, Wotton, Paersch, Reynolds, and Piatti, who, if we except Mr Paersch, a comparatively new comer in the place formerly occupied by Mr Harper, have for so many decades charmed us with their unapproachable rendition of this delightful work, of which the composer in his old age pretended to be ashamed. But such are ever the waywardnesses of great geniuses. The vocalist was that promising young singer, Miss Marguerite Hall, who was heard to advantage in songs by Schubert and Brahms, besides seizing the occasion to introduce an unpretentious but thoroughly musicianly setting of O My Love is like a Red Red Rose, by Herr Henschel.

There! How do you like it, O men of Stonecutter Street, and silly friends all who are wont to say of this column that it is "amusing, of course, but not musical criticism"? Now that bitter experience has taught you that no want of capacity, but only sheer mercy for you, restrains me from earning my income cheaply by what

[908]

you in your abysmal gullibility call "musical criticism," perhaps some sense of shame may penetrate your ungrateful hearts. Idiots! I could teach a parrot to twaddle like that if I could catch a sufficiently empty-headed one. To speak more gently, it is mere beginner's work; and no critic should pretend to undertake a *feuilleton* until he has far outgrown it. However, I shall relapse into it some day. When I shall have got on terms of private intimacy with all the artists and *impresarios* in London—when my obligations to them in the way of tickets and scraps of information shall have made it impossible for me to say anything that would make the morrow's meeting disagreeable—when I begin to do a little business in the libretto and analytical program line—when, in short, I am thoroughly nobbled and gagged, then I, too, shall relapse into the beginner's style; and you, if you are wise, will stop reading my column.

Meanwhile, let me say, since I have had the trouble of going to that concert, that the Schumann quartet, though an excellent piece of chamber music, cuts but a feeble figure in a large concert hall; and that I cannot understand why the septet was played with all the old-fashioned repeats. The septet is just fresh enough to make it delightful without the repeats, and just old and hackneyed enough to make it wearisome with them, especially after half-past ten at night. Madame Neruda, by the way, led off the *allegro* about half a mile sharp, and set my ears and Mr Lazarus's on edge to such an extent that when the clarinet took up the theme, neither he nor I could tell whether it was in tune or not. As to Herr Henschel's futile little setting of My Love is like, &c., I can only hope that its very cool reception will help to bring him to his senses when next he gets an attack of providing paltry new tunes for good old words. Brahms's *Guten Abend, mein Schatz*, I had never heard before. It is a quaintly pleasant little duologue in song; and Miss Marguerite Hall hit it off very nicely.

At the Hallé orchestral concert this day week I was inhumanly tormented by a quadrille band which the proprietors of St James's Hall (who really ought to be examined by two doctors) had stationed within earshot of the concert hall. The heavy tum-tum of the basses throbbed obscurely against the rhythms of Spohr and Berlioz all the evening, like a toothache through a troubled dream; and occasionally, during a *pianissimo*, or in one of Lady Hallé's eloquent pauses, the cornet would burst into vulgar melody in a remote key, and set us all flinching, squirming, shuddering, and grimacing hideously. Under these circumstances I became morose, and could see nothing but faults. The Euryanthe overture was hurried, and so missed by a hair's breadth the full grandeur of its march and passion of its flight. When shall we be delivered from this Mendelssohnic curse of speed for speed's sake? The Spohr concerto, in spite of its shapely plausibility, is lifeless and artificial; and if Lady Hallé made the best of the solo part, the orchestra certainly made the worst of the dull empty accompaniments. The intermezzo by Svendsen turned out to be an inferior imitation of Glinka's Kamarinskaja; and there was no sense in encoring Grieg's pretty Spring melody, admirably as it shewed off the qualities of the string band. The interest rose considerably when Berlioz's Romeo and Juliet music, without the vocal numbers, came on. The orgy at Capulet's was very well played: the balance of tone between the dance measure and the broad jubilant chant of the brass was struck to perfection. In several passages the ringing brightness of the tone from the wind came with exactly the effect Berlioz, one feels, must have aimed at. The mass of violins, all executing a prolonged shake in harmonics, fluttered the audience as usual in the Queen Mab scherzo; but I cannot say that I see much beneath the *bizarrerie* of that celebrated movement except a distorted echo of Beethoven's much more beautiful Eroica scherzo.

P.S. I have just been to La Tosca; and the public will undoubtedly expect to know whether I felt like M. Lemaître,* who wanted to get up and say "*Pas cela: c'est lâche*"; or like Mr William Archer, who took it as a pessimist's tonic and felt braced by it. I felt nothing but unmitigated disgust. The French well-made play was never respectable even in its prime; but now, in its dotage and *delirium tremens*, it is a disgrace to the theatre. Such an old-fashioned, shiftless, clumsily constructed, emptyheaded turnip ghost of a cheap shocker as this Tosca should never have been let pass the stage door of the Garrick. I do not know which are the more pitiable, the vapid two acts of obsolete comedy of intrigue, or the three acts of sham torture, rape, murder, gallows, and military execution, set to dialogue that might have been improvized by strolling players in a booth. Oh, if it had but been an opera! It is fortunate for John Hare† that he has only the dramatic critics to deal with.

* Jules Lemaître, dramatic reviewer for the Journal des Débats and the Revue des Deux Mondes, had a reputation as one of the finest literary and dramatic critics of the century.

† Popular actor-manager of the recently-built Garrick Theatre, at which Sardou's La Tosca was playing.

THE MUSIC GUILD'S STUDIO CONCERT

Hampstead and Highgate Express, 1 February 1890;
unsigned

[U] On Thursday evening a concert of chamber music took place in the studio of Mr Henry Holiday at Oak Tree House, Branch Hill, Hampstead Heath. The performers were members of the society called the Musical Guild, set on foot last year by certain ex-scholars and ex-students of the Royal College of Music. Mr Holiday's interest in it is explained by the fact that one of its cleverest violinists is Miss Winifred Holiday, who on Thursday led Beethoven's trio in D, Op. 70, a work which was substituted for the much earlier trio in G in consequence of the illness of the pianist, Miss Annie Fry. The concert did not suffer, however, as Miss Maggie Moore was at hand to take her place; and probably no one present was so unsophisticated as to regret the change from Beethoven's Op. 1 to his Op. 70. Schumann's pianoforte quartet in E flat, Op. 44, and Schubert's quartet in D minor, with a couple of songs from Miss Anna Russell and Mr Daniel Price, completed the program. The performance was carried through without a hitch by the young *artistes*, who played with spirit and precision, their intonation being remarkably just throughout.

Although it must be said that a thoroughly adequate rendering of Beethoven and Schumann was beyond their means, the shortcoming was not due to any lack of skill or devotion in the performers, but rather to that perfectly innocent thoughtlessness which is in itself a charm. If their grip of the graver and more deeply felt movements was weak and uncertain, the gaiety and energy with which they attacked the light and vigorous ones made some amends. Immaturity is a quality as well as a fault in an artist. Beside Miss Holiday, the violins included Messrs Jasper and Wallace Sutcliffe and Mr Arthur Bent. Mr D. H. Squire played the violoncello, except in the Beethoven trio, when Mr J. T. Field took his place. Mr Hobday held the viola throughout. The enjoyment of the evening was considerably enhanced by the surroundings, as Mr Holiday likes to work with the masterpieces of Phidias and Praxiteles under his eye, and has furnished his studio* liberally with casts from them. The audience sat attentively to the end, which is more than can be said of most concerts of chamber music, even when the artists are of European reputation.[U]

EDUCATING ONE'S EAR
The Star, 7 February 1890

One day when I was expatiating to a friend on the importance of teaching people to speak well, he asked me dubiously whether I did not find that most men became humbugs when they learnt elocution. I could not deny it. The elocutionary man is the most insufferable of human beings. But I do not want anybody to become elocutionary. If your face is not clean, wash it: dont cut your head off. If your diction is slipshod and impure, correct and purify it: dont throw it away and make shift for the rest of your life with a hideous affectation of platformy accent, false emphases, un-

* Holiday was an artist and stained-glass designer, whose work graces Salisbury Cathedral.

meaning pauses, aggravating slowness, ill-conditioned gravity, and perverse resolution to "get it from the chest" and make it sound as if you got it from the cellar. Of course, if you are a professional humbug—a bishop or a judge, for instance—then the case is different; for the salary makes it seem worth your while to dehumanize yourself and pretend to belong to a different species. But under ordinary circumstances you had better simply educate your ear until you are fairly skilful at phonetics, and leave the rest to your good sense.

The above remarks express indirectly but unmistakably that I have just been to a students' concert at the Guildhall School of Music. I claim the right to measure the Guildhall School by a high standard. Your "Royal" Academies and Colleges do not appeal to me: I am a Republican, and cannot understand how any person with an adequate sense of humor can consent to have a crown stuck on his head at this time of day. But the Guildhall School is our civic school; and the time is coming when that term will have some real significance in London. Already the young savages and Philistines of the commercial classes crowd thither, and leave the private teacher lamenting and penniless. Now, the first thing that the savages and Philistines need to be taught is the art of speech. A finely skilled professor of diction would be cheap at a thousand a year at the Guildhall School. Fancy my feelings when I found that there is no such functionary in the place.

Doubtless this will strike the teaching staff as unfair. But I did not fail to perceive that the unfortunate pupils had been drilled and drummed into articulating their consonants clearly. When they came to an Italian T or D, in forming which the tongue makes an airtight junction with the teeth until the consonant explodes, they conscientiously tucked up their tongues against their palates in true British fashion and brought out their native T or D much as a Sheffield hydraulic piston would, with plenty of hissing. Such a sound as this, followed by a racy Brixton or Bradford diphthong, produces an effect in an Italian song of the old school that would make a vivisector's mouth water. Imagine a young lady sent out by her master to sing Handel's *Lascia ch'io pianga* without a word to warn her that the reiterated "e che sospire" is not pronounced "Ayee Kayee Soaspearayee." I forbear further illustration. The subject is too painful. Suffice it to say, that if Mr Tito Pagliardini were to hear an air by Stradella or Pergolesi uttered by a Guildhall pupil, he would rush from the building across the Embankment, and bury the horrid memory in the Lethean Thames.

Yet diction is not one of the lost arts. Coquelin does not speak in the Guildhall manner; nor Salvini, nor Joseph Jefferson, nor Henry Irving, nor Ada Rehan, nor Antoinette Sterling, nor Mrs Weldon, nor dozens of other speakers and singers. And remember that, though the public is not an expert, and cannot place its finger on the exact details in which the Guildhall novices differ from these finished artists, yet it hears a difference, though it mercilessly ascribes it to native vulgarity on the one hand and native distinction on the other. But it is absurd to brand young singers as vulgar because they, having spent their lives between the City and Holloway, know no other mode of speech than that which is vernacular in those regions. Half a dozen early lessons in phonetics from someone who knew at least a little about them—not necessarily a Mus. Bac. or Mus. Doc.—would set them in the right way.

Such teachers are to be found, if the Guildhall authorities care to find them. On Saturday last I received an invitation to the Albert Hall from a Mr P. J. Kirwan, who is doubtless a wellknown reciter, but of whom I had never heard until that day. I found him to be an artistic speaker with a cultivated voice and a tact in comedy that enabled him to pass off all his humorous selections at about six times their literary value. His delivery of Drayton's Agincourt* was most musical, though here and there the legitimate mark of the school of Mr Irving intensified into illegitimate Irvingism. One of Mr Irving's objectionable peculiarities is a trick of spoiling a vowel occurring between m and n, by continuing the humming sound of these letters through it instead of letting it flash out clearly between them. Thus his "man" or "men" becomes a monstrosity, which Mr Kirwan has picked up. Again, Mr Irving's "oo" varies from French "eu" to English "aw"; and Mr Kirwan, in pronouncing "fury" as "fieurie" or "fyawry" clearly slips into a mere imitation. Nor is he wholly guiltless of unmeaning pauses. "Along that wild and weather-beaten coast" cannot reasonably be read as "Along that wild and weatherbeaten. Coast." Similarly, the difference between "And did the deed for ever to be sung" and "And did the deed for ever to be. Sung" is the difference between sense and nonsense.

Whilst I am in the way of faultfinding, I may as well say that I protest altogether against the Reciter's theory that verse should be disguised as prose in its oral delivery. All poets read their verses singsong, which is the right way: else why the deuce should they be at the trouble of writing in verse at all? Mr Kirwan recognizes this to some extent; indeed he treated Agincourt quite fairly, and Hood's Equestrian Courtship exquisitely, in this respect; but when he came to Tennyson and Morris the waves of verse were flattened into ripples, and at a few points into dry flat tablecloth prose. I hardly blamed him in Enoch Arden, the desperate commonplace of

* Michael Drayton's Ballad of Agincourt, in Poemes Lyrick and Pastorall (c. 1605).

which would flatten out anybody or anything; but Atalanta's Race* is quite another sort of poetic commodity; and it rather got the better of Mr Kirwan. Since it was much the most difficult piece in the program, he should have placed it earlier in the afternoon. As it was, its difficulties seemed to flurry him a little; and his attempt to make the description of the race sensational by hurrying it was the one error of taste he committed—by which, of course, I mean the one point at which his taste clashed with mine. Anyhow, I heartily wish that Mr Weist Hill would appoint him professor of English diction at the Guildhall School.

Harking back for a moment to that concert, I may say that the terrible old voice-grinding which used to constitute the staple teaching at academies and conservatoires seems much mitigated in these days. The only young vocalist about whom I felt any particular anxiety was a lady who sang Gounod's Worker with the too familiar Academy pressure kept steadily on the middle of the voice. The last note but one was the conventional high note to finish with. She made an unskilful shot at it, and, being young, just saved it. I cannot pretend to think that that young lady is in the right path; but I speak with no better warrant than that of a mere critic. Doubtless her master differs from me with authority.

Mr Richard Shipman, like Mr Kirwan, recites; and as he does his best in a very goodhumored way, I have no objection to offer, although I, somehow, did not sit out his recital as I sat out Mr Kirwan's. I should not mention the matter except to tell Miss Marjorie Field Fisher that many young ladies have done very well in the world as singers with less talent and charm than she possesses. But here again I must point out that the

* Poem by William Morris, in The Earthly Paradise (1868–1870).

excessive acuteness of her enunciation of vowels turns "rage" into "reeje" and "wave" into "weeve": also that "Mizzahreery Dommynee" is not a fair equivalent for "Miserere Domine." This concert, by the way, began by a young gentleman trying a musical joke on the audience. He first played Home, Sweet Home. Then, in a series of insane variations, he mixed it up with the Tannhäuser march, Gounod's marionette march, The Harmonious Blacksmith, and the prayer from Moses in Egypt. Not a soul laughed; and a man near me voiced the impression of the audience by hoarsely whispering "He aint got it off right." Britons are gey ill to joke with on a pianoforte.

Madame Sara Palma, from La Scala, Milan, is, as one would naturally suppose, a young English lady. I did not hear her in Signor Mattei's Prima Donna; and even at her concert yesterday week I did not hear her attempt anything that she could sing. Believe me, oh aspiring and comely young songstresses all: I am not hard to please or chary of praise; but what is the use of trying *Caro nome* on me when you cant phrase, and cant shake, and dont know when or how to breathe, and have no inner impulse to express yourself in that sort of music at all? For the concert was a very creditable one of its kind. On the same evening I went to Mr Henry Holiday's studio at Hampstead, to hear the Musical Guild at work; and capitally they played a Beethoven trio and a Schumann quintet, brilliantly, spiritedly, and yet with an outrageous thoughtlessness proper to their youth and innocence. There was a concert at Prince's Hall on Tuesday night; but I would not go because somebody sent me a visiting card instead of a ticket; and I positively decline to negotiate *billets-doux* or private documents of any description at concert-room doors. [U] It always leads to a discovery of my identity, and a disturbance of the concert by such remarks as "Do you see that short very stout man, with long black hair down his back, and

[918]

the spectacles, next the girl in blue—putting a pencil in his mouth—there! he's just pulled out an orange handkerchief with black stripes? That's Corno di Bassetto."[U]

AN ÉMEUTE AT ST JAMES'S HALL
The Star, 8 February 1890

What shall I do to make Sir Charles Hallé take steps to abate the scandalous nuisance which I vainly pressed upon his notice in the ordinary course last Friday week? This time I took special care to get out of earshot of the quadrille band which plays in the St James's Restaurant, and which can be heard at one end of the concert room over an area quite as large as that occupied by the orchestra at the other. By looking at the agonized faces of the unfortunate people in the half-crown seats I could see what they were suffering; but I could not hear it—at first. But the quadrille band was not to be baffled in that way. It bided its time until we came to those eloquent pauses between the last broken strains of the funeral march in the Eroica symphony—pauses during which you can usually hear a pin drop. But last night it would have been necessary to let Cleopatra's Needle drop to overpower the wild strain of brazen minstrelsy that rushed through the room and doubled me up in my place of fancied safety. It was too much. When, after the march, the applause from the front of the room subsided, a voice was heard raised at the back in impassioned oratory. The stir and sensation which ensued prevented me from catching his speech in full; but the concluding sentence was "We all pledge ourselves to complain, either in writing or by word of mouth." The half-crowners energetically cried "Hear, hear"; and the ladies stood up to see this gentleman who ventured for the common weal to assume the *rôle* of Masaniello or William Tell at a moment's notice, and whom I take this opportunity of publicly thanking for his spirited and proper protest. Then Sir Charles, who betrayed no consciousness of these strange proceedings, started the scherzo; and the insurrection quieted down into dumb discontent, which found vent afterwards in wild suggestions that it was done on purpose out of jealousy of the Manchester band; that a rival conductor was at the bottom of it; that the police ought to put a stop to it; that the papers ought to take it up, &c. &c. But the papers—save one—do not seem to care much what happens to the people who pay a shilling and half-a-crown, so long as those who pay either half-a-guinea or nothing (especially nothing) go undisturbed.

[U] I postpone criticism of the concert to the usual day and place [the Friday "Musical Mems" column], merely warning the public of what they have to expect at orchestral concerts in St James's Hall pending some assurance from the proprietors that steps will be taken to put a stop to the nuisance.[U]

LISZT'S VARIATIONS

The Star, 14 February 1890

I devoted myself to the encouragement of English music at the first Crystal Palace concert of the year on Saturday afternoon by patiently listening to a concert overture "to the memory of a hero."* The particular hero was not named; but there was some doubt about the consecu-

* Concert-Overture: "To the memory of a hero," composed by C.H. Couldery.

tiveness of his memory; for I took him to be a musical amateur in whose head the *finale* of Brahms's violin concerto had got mixed with the overture to William Tell, and whose reminiscences of Mendelssohn were adulterated with incongruous scraps of La Favorita. Sir George Grove declares that the overture is "apparently written on a program, though a program which does not obtrude itself." My opinion of it is also written on a program, which I, too, refrain from obtruding. Such overtures should be contracted for at so much the dozen.

I do not quite know why some of the audience raged so frantically at Liszt's variations on Dies Iræ. The old hymn makes a tremendous theme; and most of the variations are either pretty or fantastic enough to make an occasional performance interesting, though I can by no means endorse Mr Barry's assurance that "Liszt has treated his subject in a thoroughly earnest, serious, and elevating manner." I grant the earnestness: Liszt was always earnest; but I question the seriousness and the elevation. A composer may treat a subject about which he is desperately in earnest in a manner which is neither serious nor elevating, whilst another will set some piece of imposing humbug to most majestic music. It is only your first-rate composer who is both earnest and elevating (seriousness is only a small man's affectation of bigness). Nothing was too artificial for Meyerbeer, or too conventional for Rossini, who nevertheless gave their music exactly the sort of passion and grandeur which Liszt strove so desperately and expensively to force out of an expensive accumulation of the mere materials of music. Like Berlioz, he was rich in every quality of a great composer except musical fertility; and when for a moment some stray breath of inspiration relieved him of this poverty, he was triumphantly successful. But men who had hardly any quality of a great composer except this one that he lacked may

[921]

dispute precedence with him with almost as much public support as the giants, from Bach to Wagner, whose superiority goes without saying. You may respect Liszt, vainly struggling with Dante's Divine Comedy, more than Offenbach featly vanquishing Meilhac and Halévy's Grand Duchess; but you can hardly deny that the Dante symphony is a failure, and The Grand Duchess a success. It does not follow that you would always rather hear the success than the failure. The success is simply enjoyable for the moment: the failure is interesting, suggestive, instructive, stimulating. Sometimes, when listening to Berlioz's cleverest work, its very cleverness forces us to compare its proud poverty with the unassuming affluence of La Sonnambula; but we never doubt for a moment that the world could have spared Bellini much better than Berlioz, or that Offenbach's life, compared to Liszt's, was a wasted one. Hence such Lisztian hero-worshipers as Herr Stavenhagen and the late Walter Bache are to be encouraged and supported: it is good for the public and the players and the conductor to do some hard brain work over a symphonic poem instead of accompanying Madame Patti in *Ah, non giunge*, or fathoming the Sunday School profundities of the pilgrims' march from Mendelssohn's Italian symphony.

This, by the way, does not apply to the Crystal Palace band, which sticks to serious work. They took the Dance of Death in dudgeon, methought; and I tell them to Mr Manns' face that their playing of the intensely fresh and energetic syncopated passages in the first movement of the Fourth Symphony was not worth listening to. And though the slow movement finished admirably, yet that trochaic measure in the drum figure which pervades it began with the customary slovenliness which marks it as the most difficult of all measures to get rightly with an orchestra. It seems as simple as skipping; but somehow when it comes to the point you have the Euryanthe overture sounding vulgar, and the slow movement of Mozart's E flat symphony (a pure dialogue, like the introduction to Weber's Invitation, though wonderfully more elaborate), made the despair of fine conductors. For the rest, the symphony went well; and so did the prelude to Iphigenia in Aulis as edited by Wagner,* which Mr Manns read with admirable dignity.

The Hallé concert this day week brought out Sir Charles's deficiencies as a conductor in a striking way. It began with Cherubini's overture to Anacreon, an absolutely meaningless piece of pure music. I never heard it better played: I doubt if it could be better played; and I do not greatly care whether it could or not. From that we went on to Grieg's *entr'actes* and dance music for Ibsen's great play Peer Gynt. Grieg has done nothing more pathetic and natural than the little prelude to the scene in which Peer's mother, lonely on her deathbed, lies waiting and longing and listening to the silence before Peer steals down from the mountain and beguiles her into believing that the bitter end of her earthly journey is a glorious ride through the air to the castle east of the sun and west of the moon (at the gate of which God Himself orders St Peter to entertain her with coffee and biscuits, which is to her a high and heavenly honor). The way in which Sir Charles Hallé contrived to make us feel before the end of the first bar that all this was a blank to him was quite wonderful. The prelude is nothing if not a tone poem; and nothing it was, accordingly—or less than nothing. I was amazed at

* Wagner had revised Gluck's Iphigénie en Aulide in 1846, altering the orchestrations, rewriting a number of the recitatives, and even introducing an additional character in the third act.

the completeness of the failure. The Eroica symphony is something besides a tone poem: much of it is excellent abstract music from the Cherubini-Anacreon point of view; and so it went along to the strains of its own funeral march, a very handsome corpse. The truth is that no man can conduct a Beethoven symphony unless his instincts are not only musical, but poetic and dramatic as well. Consequently, as Sir Charles is only a musician, the Manchester orchestra has yet to experience the delight of really learning a Beethoven symphony. Bach's concerto in D minor for two violins was refreshing; but Lady Hallé's refinements sort ill with Bach's grand style; and I thought Mr Willy Hess had much the better of it.

I have in my hands the report of the London branch of the Wagner Society, which I peruse with mingled feelings. It is satisfactory that the 52 members of 1884 are now 309; but the balance sheet is enough to drive any sensible Englishman mad. In German-speaking cities at present Wagner's operas are paying enormously. In Dresden, for instance, the announcement of an opera by any other composer empties the house. Even the Bayreuth performances were a financial success last year. In this miserable country a man who has seen Die Walküre on the stage is a much greater curiosity than one who has explored the Congo. Clearly, then, the business of an International Wagner Society is to transfer money from the prosperous Wagnerism of Germany to the languishing Wagnerism of Britain. Yet the London Wagner Society actually sent £46 : 12 : 6 to Berlin (of which city, London, it appears, is a suburb) out of its income of £271 : 19s. In return they got sixtyfour free tickets for the Bayreuth performances, which were balloted for by gentlemen in a position to spend £20 on a fortnight's holiday, to the unspeakable edification and Wagnerian enlightenment of the English nation at large. Having accomplished this masterly consignment of coals to Newcastle, the London branch proceeded to waste £60 odd, under pretext of an orchestral concert, by simply handing that sum over to Mr Vert, in return for which a scratch performance of a bit of Parsifal was thrust into an ordinary Wagner program at an ordinary Richter concert, for which the members received "free" tickets (at four and sixpence a head). The climax of folly was a *conversazione*, or evening party, which had as much to do with "The Meister's" cause as any evening party in Mayfair has, and which cost £43 : 11 : 4. Total money wasted, £150 : 13 : 4. As against this, there was £51 : 16s. well spent on the quarterly journal called The Meister, and some £17 on a recital of Tristan, which was, on the whole, well worth the money. But if I, instead of subscribing my guinea, had paid a shilling apiece for the four Meisters across the counter, and half-a-crown for the Richter concert as one of the public, I should have turned the odd fourteen and sixpence to much better account than the branch has turned it for me. On Wednesday last I went to one of the branch's meetings for the first time, and found, as might have been expected, that nobody present seemed to have the least idea of how such meetings should be conducted. There was no chairman, no discussion, no orderly procedure, no opportunity whatever of raising any question connected with the subject of the evening or with the society. Mr Ellis, the secretary, simply came out; fed us with lecture as if we were a row of animals in the Zoo; and walked off and left us there. The more I think of it, the more I am convinced that now that this German Wagner Society can take care of itself, we want an independent English one. Who shares that opinion?

KNIGHTHOOD AND DANCING

The Star, 21 February 1890

I see that somebody in the Pall Mall Gazette wants to have Mr August Manns knighted. The suggestion will be taken up by the comic journals for the sake of saying that "a Manns a man for a' that." As for me, who am no punster, I ask why Mr Manns should be bothered about it. He knows how we manage these things here. We keep a couple of musical knights (in addition to clerical organist chivalry) in order to make knighthood a little respectable, just as we keep a couple of mounted sentries at Whitehall so as to give the War Office a military air. There is no question of selecting the man who has done most for music: Costa, who had no respect for the past, no help for the present, and no aspiration towards the future—who was equally ready to murder anything old with "additional accompaniments" and cuts, or to strangle anything new by refusing to have anything to do with it—who allowed the opera to die in his grasp whilst it was renewing its youth and strength all over Germany: Costa was made Sir Michael. The gentleman selected by Mr W. S. Gilbert to set his burlesques of grand opera to music is Sir Arthur Sullivan, though music in England would not be one inch further behindhand than she is if he had never existed. Charles Hallé, who endowed England with a second orchestra (Rule, Britannia!), and who is therefore the only man whose services are for a moment comparable to those of Mr Manns, was given a knighthood when he was seventy. No doubt Mr Manns' position is such that he can, if he chooses, confer (at sixtyfive) on a worthless order an honor that it cannot confer on him. But if he receives any such offer, I hope he will politely pass it over to Mr Barnby or Mr Cusins, and go on quietly with his work. I respect him so much that I am always half ashamed to call him Mister. If he became Sir August I should blush every time I penned that cherished distinction of successful brewers and oratorio mongers.

This reminds me that I have a word to say about the last Crystal Palace concert. Mr Manns was immensely in the vein; and the Egmont overture, which at first could only be *seen* in the movement of his *bâton*, at last got into the heads of the band, who finished it as keenly and powerfully as they had begun it sleepily and irrelevantly. There was quite an ovation to the conductor after the Scotch symphony, a work which would be great if it were not so confoundedly genteel. Miss Fanny Davies was full of speed, lilt, life, and energy. She scampered through a fugue of Bach's with a cleverness and jollity that forced us to condone her utter irreverence. The concerto by Rosenhain turned out to be a pleasant and ingenious piece of "absolute music" in the mid-century manner. I had never heard of Rosenhain; and I am surprised at the disingenuousness of other critics in the same predicament, who have hastily read him up, and are pretending that they knew him from boyhood's hour.

Upon Miss Amelia Sinico's first appearance I wish to offer a few general and impersonal observations. If ever you get behind the scenes at the opera, or into musical Bohemia, you will here and there come across some darkeyed little imp of eight or ten, who can sing every opera from cover to cover without missing a note or a word; who can improvize *cadenzas* much more readily than you could invent an alias at a police station; who knows Il Trovatore from Don Giovanni without in the least knowing Verdi from Mozart; who speaks all Western languages and knows none; who is equally used to smacks and kisses, indoor errands and comfits; and whose mother is a *prima donna*. However expensively you educate your daughter for the operatic stage; however many gold medals she may take at the Royal College of Music; when she reaches the opera house (if she ever does) she will be as rank a greenhorn in the eyes of the darkeyed imp as a senior wrangler who takes to the city is in the eyes of a sharp office boy. But just as the office boy finds that the wrangler has a mysterious qualification for important duties which juvenile sharpness aspires to in vain, so the imp, when at eighteen she finds that she is only fit to be a *prima donna*, sometimes finds at thirty that she was not fit even for that. The Miss Macintyres and Madame Melbas, whom she remembers as perfect Jugginses, leave her behind almost without an effort.

I do not wish to discourage the daughters of artists who have, in their time, given me a good deal of pleasure; but when I hear Miss Sinico giving her clever imitation of a *prima donna* singing *Ombra leggiera*, and Miss Antoinette Trebelli doing the same with *Non mi dir*, I cannot accept either feat as evidence that these young ladies have as yet ever begun the serious study of their profession. At the risk of being impertinent, I venture to warn them that only the most exceptional natural capacity can nowadays enable an aspirant to dispense with the general culture and education which nobody expected from an opera singer in London twenty years ago. The capacity for sustained attention, the air of purpose and self-respect that such education gives, makes the person who has received it so much more dignified and interesting that the public are getting more and more intolerant of Bohemianism in art. Now I have no right to say that Miss Sinico's education has been unsystematic; for I know no more about her than any other member of the public. What I have a right to say is that though her Italian is piquant, like her mother's, it is also a little vulgar, *un*like her mother's; and that when she next sings *Batti batti* (which will not be for some years to come, if she is wise) she must understand that, at the Crystal Palace at least, the day has passed for such vulgarisms as ending an octave above the note written by Mozart. I would also whisper to her that she should not naïvely let the public see how fond she is of applause. She obviously must be a *prima donna* or nothing; but it will cost her many years' work and experience before she can expect Mr Manns' Saturday audiences to receive her with any feeling except one of almost paternal indulgence.

Since I do not confine this column exclusively to concerts and operas, all sorts of people suggest that I should go to all sorts of places and give my opinion thereon. Last week, however, one of these suggestions had a binding effect on my conscience. Among my valued friends is a clergyman—I shall not mention his name because, having been afflicted all my life with a constitutional impiety which has led the clerical profession to adopt a general attitude of expecting me to be stricken dead, I am afraid of compromising him. Let us call him the Rev. St*w**t H**dl*m, M.L.S.B. for Bethnal Green; or perhaps it will be shorter and less likely to lead to his identification if I call him simply H. Well, H. enthusiastically admires the art of dancing; and he will have it that I undervalue it—an assumption as baseless as it is injurious, for I was interested in it before he was born. However, when he wrote to me to demand why I never went to a ballet, I could not deny that I had of late years neglected the Alhambra and the Empire. So on Monday, having ascertained that Spectator was indulging his mania for musical criticism at Marjorie or Les Cloches, or some opera or another, I made straight for the Alhambra; saw Asmodeus there at nine; waited for M. Bruet and Madame Rivière; and got to the Empire afterwards in time to see A Dream of Wealth.

I care not a jot about the technology of the art of dancing. I do not know, and, what is more, I positively refuse to know, which particular *temps* is a *battement* and which a *ronde de jambe*. If I were equally ignorant of the technical differences between a tonal fugue and a quadrille, I should be a better musical critic than I am; for I should not so often be led astray from the essential purpose of art by mere curiosity as to the mechanical difficulties created by certain forms of it. All that concerns me is how beautifully or how expressively a dancer can dance, and how best I can stop the silly practice of ending every solo with a teetotum twirl like the old concert ending to the overture to Iphigenia in Aulis. But if you want a rule of thumb to guide you in determining the merits of two dancers comparatively, then simply see *how much of each* dances, and award the palm to the larger quantity. Let me explain. Dancing begins at the feet and progresses upwards. In some people it stops at the ankles: they shine only in clog dancing, hornpipes, and the like. In others it reaches as far as to the hips: these can aspire to kicking through a Gaiety *pas de quatre*, or spurious *can-can*. When the magic fluid reaches the shoulders and invades the arms as far as the elbows, then the dancer pretends to leading business. Many a *première danseuse* holds her position in spite of a neck and wrists which are, dancingly considered, dead as doornails. But the dancer who dances to the tips of her fingers and the top of her head: that is the perfect dancer; for dancing being a sort of pulsation of grace in the limbs which dance, the perfect dancer is all grace; and if she has, to boot, a touch of tragic passion in her, it will find instant and vivid expression in her dancing. To such a nonpareil you would unhesitatingly give, if she asked for it, the head of Adelina Patti or Sarasate in a charger. So perhaps it is just as well that she is the rarest of rare birds.

At the Alhambra the best dancer is a man, Vincenti, an intelligent and cultivated artist and an admirable pantomimist. I leave H. to chronicle the perfection of his *pirouettes* and *entrechats*, and the public to *encore* his amazing revolution about the centre of the stage combined with rotation on his own longitudinal axis, like an animated orrery. I should prefer to illustrate his excellence in pure dancing by an instantaneous photograph taken at the height of his bound into the air, with the crutch in his hands, at the beginning of his first solo. Nothing could be more graceful. Yet Vincenti's figure is by no means heroic; and he has a prodigious head. Signor Albertieri, at the Empire, is a prettier man; but he is comparatively no dancer at all, but only an acrobat and wrestler, who throws Madame Palladino half over his hips and holds her there in an attitude (any pugilist will shew you the trick), as if that were dancing. The opulent Bessone, *première danseuse assoluta* in Asmodeus, is complete from toe to top, a superb, passionate dancer, strong, skilful, and abounding in sensuous charm. Whether she is as great a Serafina as Fanny Elsler was in The Devil on Two Sticks I know not, since I never saw Fanny; but with two such artists as she and Vincenti, and a happily arranged ballet by Casati, on an ever popular legend, the Alhambra now offers between nine and ten every evening an entertainment of high artistic rank, to which everybody should go and bring their daughters, in spite of the abominable atmosphere of tobacco smoke.

I wanted to hear M. Bruet because I remembered his name from a remote occasion when I somewhere heard him give an amazingly exact imitation of a violoncellist. He and Madame Rivière seem none the worse for wear;

and I only wish that all our would-be serious artists had half the musical talent of these two arch mockers. For the rest I cannot deny that the Empire ballet fell flat after Asmodeus, neither Signor Albertieri nor Madame Palladino being able to sustain the formidable and inevitable comparison with their rivals across the square. The jewel casket scene was tawdry: it suffered specially from the vast space of naked floor which makes ballet scenery so hard to manage. Signorina Cavallazzi, however, did excellently as the miser; and some of the pantomime was good. Possibly had I taken the two theatres in reversed order, and seen The Paris Exhibition at the Empire, and Our Army and Navy at the Alhambra, my impression of the respective merits of the houses might have been reversed also. But, as it was, I should like to see Asmodeus again; wheras I have had quite enough of A Dream of Wealth.

When I arrived at my door after these dissipations I found Fitzroy Square, in which I live, deserted. It was a clear, dry cold night; and the carriage way round the circular railing presented such a magnificent hippodrome that I could not resist trying to go just once round in Vincenti's fashion. It proved frightfully difficult. After my fourteenth fall I was picked up by a policeman. "What are you doing here?" he said, keeping fast hold of me. "I'bin watching you for the last five minutes." I explained, eloquently and enthusiastically. He hesitated a moment, and then said "Would you mind holding my helmet while I have a try. It dont look so hard." Next moment his nose was buried in the macadam and his right knee was out through its torn garment. He got up bruised and bleeding, but resolute. "I never was beaten yet" he said "and I wont be beaten now. It was my coat that tripped me." We both hung our coats on the railings, and went at it again. If each round of the square had been a round in a prize fight, we should have been less damaged and disfigured; but we persevered, and by four o'clock the policeman had just succeeded in getting round twice without a rest or a fall, when an inspector arrived and asked him bitterly whether that was his notion of fixed point duty. "I allow it aint fixed point" said the constable, emboldened by his new accomplishment; "but I'll lay a half sovereign *you* cant do it." The inspector could not resist the temptation to try (I was whirling round before his eyes in the most fascinating manner); and he made rapid progress after half an hour or so. We were subsequently joined by an early postman and by a milkman, who unfortunately broke his leg and had to be carried to hospital by the other three. By that time I was quite exhausted, and could barely crawl into bed. It was perhaps a foolish scene; but nobody who has witnessed Vincenti's performance will feel surprised at it.

ON THE SUBJECT OF FIDDLING

The Star, 28 February 1890

I was lucky in looking in to hear Joachim at the Popular Concert last Monday. I must first mention, however, that Joachim was never to me an Orpheus. Like all the pupils of Mendelssohn he has seldom done anything with an *allegro* except try to make speed do duty for meaning. Now that he is on the verge of sixty he keeps up the speed at the cost of quality of tone and accuracy of pitch; and the results are sometimes, to say the least, incongruous. For instance, he played Bach's sonata in C at the Bach Choir Concert at St James's Hall on Tuesday. The second movement of that work is a fugue some three or four hundred bars long. Of course you cannot really play a fugue in three continuous parts on the violin; but by dint of double stopping and dodging from one part to another, you can evoke a hideous ghost of a fugue that will pass current if guaranteed by Bach and Joachim. That was what happened on Tuesday. Joachim scraped away frantically, making a sound after which an attempt to grate a nutmeg effectively on a boot sole would have been as the strain of an Eolian harp. The notes which were musical enough to have any discernible pitch at all were mostly out of tune. It was horrible— damnable! Had he been an unknown player, introducing an unknown composer, he would not have escaped with his life. Yet we all—I no less than the others—were interested and enthusiastic. We applauded like anything; and he bowed to us with unimpaired gravity. The dignified artistic career of Joachim and the grandeur of Bach's reputation had so hypnotized us that we took an abominable noise for the music of the spheres.

My luck at the Monday Popular Concert lay in the fact that Joachim there played very finely, especially in the Brahms sonata. Whilst I am on the subject of fiddling I may as well mention how Madame Neruda rose to the occasion at the Crystal Palace on Saturday before going off to Australia to pick up gold and silver. Madame Neruda is younger than Joachim; but only by about nine years: she is fifty, though you would hardly guess it from her bearing on the platform. But for some years past her style has been contracting a little. Her tone is less distinguished; and her old fire and eloquence are abated. In spite of the care with which she studies her playing, I find that the amateurs of yesterday are disposed to be irreverent when I fully express the admiration which survives in me from the time when her great talent was at the height of its splendor. They will admit that she is an accomplished player, but not an inspired one. That is what I should have said myself had I heard her for the first time when she played Spohr's

Dramatic Concerto at the last Crystal Palace concert or the recent Hallé concert. But I heard her play it so magnificently twelve years or so ago that I will not do her reputation the injustice of pretending that it was no better then than now. Perhaps it was to shew us that it was Spohr rather than Norman-Neruda who has become the worse for wear that she chose a sonata by Handel the Imperishable for her second piece. At any rate it certainly woke up the qualities which made her famous, and earned her an ovation in which the rawest recruits joined heartily.

Though each generation produces its quota of great artists, yet as the favorites of my youth succumb to inexorable Time, I never feel quite sure of their replacement until I actually see and hear their successors. Years ago I went to an afternoon concert at which no less than three eminent pianists appeared. I remember two things about it. One is, that as I entered, a gentleman turned to me trembling with anxiety and asked with the deepest earnestness "Has Cambridge won?" The other, that I heard Madame Schumann for the first time, and recognized, before she had finished the first phrase of Schubert's impromptu in C, what a nobly beautiful and poetic player she was. An artist of that sort is the Holy Grail of the critic's quest. Now, I never had the slightest fear that we should ever be at a loss for successors to Rubinstein and Von Bülow. I was once by no means so sure about Madame Schumann. Concerning one of the most gifted of her pupils, Nathalie Janotha, I reserve my opinion for a few years more, or at least until I happen to hit on a concert at which she plays: a matter in which I have been too remiss, except when I have been irresistibly attracted by an announcement that she is to play Beethoven's concerto in G. But Madame Schumann's true successor at present is Madame Backer-Gröndahl, in whose perfectly original and independent style none of her predecessor's finest qualities are lacking. It will be remembered that when I first heard Madame Gröndahl last June I hailed her as a player of the highest rank. After sleeping over that judgment for a year, I am as confident as ever that events will sustain it; and I shall go to the Crystal Palace tomorrow with an uncriticlike eagerness to hear her play Grieg's concerto and to say "I told you so" to those who last year thought it safer to wait another quarter century or so before they committed themselves to an opinion.

I have rather wandered away from the Bach Choir concert, at which *Wachet auf!** was sung for the second time in public in England. This is the sort of fact that almost disables me from writing another line. What on earth is the use of toiling over a musical column for a nation that has waited 150 years to hear a love poem which had no peer until Tristan und Isolde was written. However, let me not be unjust. England has not been idle. She has produced Costa's Eli and Macfarren's Potiphar's Wife, Dr Parry's Judith, and Dorothy, not to mention some forty thousand performances of Elijah. *Wachet auf!* is a setting of an old love story narrated by Herodotus, which, by a misapprehension which is perhaps the most extraordinary in literary history, came into the Bible under the name of The Song of Solomon, and so happily got set to music by Bach on a plane of idealization to which Herodotus would certainly not have raised him.

Some day, when the County Councils begin to do for music in England what the petty courts of Germany used to do for it, after a fashion, in Germany, I shall try to persuade the nation that a million a year spent on Bach choirs would be a remunerative investment. At present there is no use in telling the people what a great

* Cantata No. 140.

man Bach was, since they cannot help themselves. So I will only say that Mr Villiers Stanford is too thorough an Irishman to be an ideal Bach conductor. He is alert, clever, enthusiastic, facile; but he lacks the oceanic depth of German sentiment that underlies the intense expression of Bach's music.

Still, a clever Irishman is better than the usual alternative: a mediocre Englishman. Let me just suggest to him, in passing, that whether Joachim is playing or not (he played that D minor concerto which Madame Neruda played the other day with Mr Willy Hess), a conductor should always conduct. Mr Stanford modestly effaced himself whilst Joachim and Mr Gompertz were playing the *largo*; and the result was that the basses in the orchestra lagged and got out of step with the soloists. The accompaniment I liked best that evening was the no-accompaniment of the motet; but if you must have an organ muddling matters with its tempered scales, then by all means serve it up to me with trombones in Bach's manner; for I admit that nothing in art can be compared to it except the best medieval building.

Then there is that Crystal Palace concert. I do not return to it to compliment Mr Manns on a capital performance of Schumann's symphony in C; for I simply do not care about Schumann's symphonies: that is the long and short of it. Nor am I going to praise the clear and confident lady who dragged in two fragments, Hear ye, Israel, and the waltz from Gounod's Roméo, into a program consisting otherwise of complete artistic wholes. But I have a word to say about Mr German's overture to Richard III., now that I have heard it under the conditions which were, of course, imperfectly fulfilled at the Globe Theatre. I advise Mr German either to rewrite the work, or else drop Richard III. and simply present it as Overture in G, that is to say, as a piece of "absolute music" in overture form. For if it is to be taken as dramatic I do not see why the Richard motive should be fitted with an "answer" as if it were a "subject," there being nothing in the dramatic idea at all corresponding to such answer. Again, the *fugato* is flat nonsense unless Mr German wished to suggest a troop of little Richards springing up through traps and chasing one another round the stage. I hope Mr German will, on reflection, agree with me that the man who can write a dramatic overture is the man who can invent dramatic motives and develop them dramatically in music. The oftener he breaks down in this arduous task and falls back on the forms of absolute music, the worse his work will be. For instance, the most entirely foolish thing in music is an overture by a Mus. Doc. in orthodox form, written solely with a view to that form, and then sent up for concert use with the general title of Portia and Shylock, and The Caskets, written in blue ink above the first and second subjects respectively. I venture to accuse Mr German of a certain degree of the confusion between "absolute" and dramatic music, of which the above is an imaginary case. Mind, I admit that he has proved his ability as a musician up to the hilt. What remains comparatively questionable is his interest in Shakespear.

The night before last I repaired to the London Institution to see The Shakespear Reading Society recite Much Ado. I have musical associations of all sorts with these recitals. Wagner once pointed out that music would never have survived the omissions and misunderstandings of conductors and concert givers had it not been kept alive in the homes of people whose spare cash went in buying pianoforte scores and the like for private consumption. In the same way, people would know very little about Shakespear if they had no more of him than they get at the Lyceum Theatre. Therefore, as a

Wagnerian, I no sooner saw that Mr William Poel* was devoting himself to making ordinary people get up readings of Shakespear than I at once made a note that he was a much more important art propagandist than Mr Irving. Another musical association was formed by my seeing Mr Poel once play Beethoven to Miss Mary Rorke's Adelaide in a surpassingly unhistoric little drama. I forget when and where it was; but I have mixed Mr Poel up ever since with Beethoven as he appears in a certain sketch which represents him as wearing a Poellian collar. I have no doubt that the first-nighters who imagine that the way to be in everything in London is to keep outside everything will not condescend to encourage Mr Poel's achievement, since the human material with which he works is necessarily rather green. The more reason for an ordinary person like myself to avow that from these simple recitals, without cuts, waits or scenery, and therefore without those departures from the conditions contemplated by the poet which are inevitable in a modern theatre, I learn a good deal about the plays which I could learn in no other way. What is more, I enjoy myself, which is not invariably my experience in the more commercial atmosphere of the West End theatre.

* Actor, manager, and scholar, founder of the Elizabethan Stage Society, who sought a return to the simpler staging of the past and rediscovery of lost works of the theatre.

CONCERTS

The Star, 3 March 1890

On Friday evening last I went to the Wind Instrument
Society's concert at the Royal Academy of Music in
Tenterden-street. Having only just heard of the affair
from an acquaintance, I had no ticket. The concert, as
usual, had been kept dark from me: Bassetto the
Incorruptible knows too much to be welcome to any but
the greatest artists. I therefore presented myself at the
doors for admission on payment as a casual amateur.
Apparently the wildest imaginings of the Wind Instrument Society had not reached to such a contingency as
a Londoner offering money at the doors to hear classical
chamber music played upon bassoons, clarinets, and
horns; for I was told that it was impossible to entertain
my application, as the building had no license. I
suggested sending out for a license; but this, for some
technical reason, could not be done. I offered to dispense
with the license; but that, they said, would expose them
to penal servitude. Perceiving by this that it was a mere
question of breaking the law, I insisted on the secretary
accompanying me to the residence of a distinguished
Q.C. in the neighborhood, and ascertaining from him
how to do it. The Q.C. said that if I handed the secretary
five shillings at the door in consideration of being
admitted to the concert, that would be illegal. But if I
bought a ticket from him in the street, that would be
legal. Or if I presented him with five shillings in
remembrance of his last birthday, and he gave me a free
admission in celebration of my silver wedding, that
would be legal. Or if we broke the law without witnesses
and were prepared to perjure ourselves if questioned

afterwards (which seemed to me the most natural way), then nothing could happen to us.

I cannot without breach of faith explain which course we adopted: suffice it that I was present at the concert. The first item, a septet in E flat, which is, for Beethoven, a tea gardens sort of composition, was not made the best of. Mr Clinton led the first movement, which should be brisk and crisp, slowly and laboriously. The bassoons were rough and ready; the horns rough and not always ready. On the whole, with such artists the performance ought to have been several shades finer. The Spohr septet, a shining river of commonplaces, plagiarisms, and reminiscences, went more smoothly; but then the fiddle, cello, and piano had a hand in that. The piano, by the bye, was played by Mr Septimus Webbe, who, though in his earliest manhood, has, if I mistake not, been a notable player for at least fourteen years past. What a fortune he would have made had the Hofmann-Hegner boom happened when he was in his prime at eight! One movement of an octet by the late, highly respectable Franz Lachner was enough for me. I am much afraid that Wagner's pithy description of him in Ueber das Dirigiren will survive all the obituary notices that were so complimentary to him.

Madame Backer-Gröndahl seems to have brought from Norway a witch-like power of letting loose the elements on her audiences. Last year she played Beethoven's E flat concerto amid storm and thunder, the lightning scaring the veterans of the Philharmonic Society into vain remorse for their misspent musical lives. On Saturday she came to the Crystal Palace in clouds of boreal snow. I should not have minded her bringing the snow if she had left Grieg's concerto at home. I hinted last year, and I now explicitly repeat, that Madame Gröndahl's powers of interpretation are wasted upon scrappy work like Grieg's. If it had been

Señor Albéniz, or Mr Vladimir de Pachmann, or Miss Essipoff, or the composer himself, I should have been content with Grieg. But when you are longing for Mozart in D minor or Beethoven in G, or the E flat over again, then Grieg is an impertinence. The program, as far as the pianoforte was concerned, would have infuriated a saint. Madame Gröndahl put Grieg where she should have put Beethoven, and Chopin where she should have put Grieg. The audience gave repeated proofs of a quite exceptional imbecility. A splendid performance of Mozart's Idomeneo overture, a noble and seldom-heard composition, was hardly noticed; whilst a sentimental show piece for the strings by Dvořák was received with rapture. Sir George Grove's "analysis" of Beethoven's second symphony was such a shameless piece of special pleading that I hasten to remark emphatically that nothing can extenuate the insufferable kitchen clock tum-tum which pervades the first two movements of that overrated work. The *scherzo* and the *finale* are fine if you like; and the band surpassed itself in playing them. The *scherzo* in particular was a triumph of orchestral execution. Mr Braxton Smith's singing pleased the audience, though he does not, as skilful bowlers do, vary his delivery: his organ has but one stop. The two pieces by Saint-Saëns were clever trash.

On our way back to Victoria, a signal stopped our train in the snow, and when it fell the engine gasped and refused to budge. At last another train overtook us, and butted us into Clapham, where, in a paroxysm of ill-temper, I resolved to say nothing more about Madame Gröndahl until after her recital at Steinway Hall on Wednesday afternoon.

MR HENRY SEIFFERT'S CONCERT

The Star, 7 March 1890

Yesterday evening Mr Henry Seiffert gave something between a violin recital and a concert at Steinway Hall. Miss Fillunger sang, very sympathetically and earnestly; and Mlle de Llana played. Indeed Mlle de Llana had to contribute out of all conscience to the work of the evening; for, besides her solos, she had to follow Mr Seiffert vigilantly through a troublesome transcription of the orchestral score of Wieniawski's second concerto, and to play the heavy and difficult pianoforte part in Rubinstein's violin sonata in A minor. Her chief solo, Chopin's Ballade in A flat, got shifted to the end of the concert. The result of this inconsiderate departure from the program was that at one complicated passage her memory and her fingers failed her for a moment; and she had to pause for breath. Unlike M. de Pachmann, who passes off mishaps of this sort so effectively that he has been suspected by evil-minded persons of bringing them about on purpose, Mlle de Llana looked very angry with herself, perhaps because she is too young to know how often the same thing has happened to players of the first rank, from Liszt down to Miss Marie Krebs. In fact it happens to them all at one time or another, genius being but mortal. Mr Seiffert's playing was remarkable, as usual, for breadth of tone, for a strength of style in *cantabile* passages which promises to mature into grandeur and passion, and for extraordinary freedom and intrepidity of execution. He is still apt to slur over the very details which, because they are uninteresting in themselves, depend for their interest on the finesse of the player; in themes like the first subject of the *finale à la zingara* of the Wieniawski concerto one misses in his impetuous attack the smooth, perfectly equal touch and the precision of intonation which Sarasate has associated with passages of that character; and his *pizzicato* is curiously ineffective. But all these imperfections may be expected to disappear long before Mr Seiffert is as old as Sarasate. His talent, striking as it is, is not yet by any means fully developed; and I shall wait for a few years yet before stereotyping my opinion of him.

BASSETTO'S DESTRUCTIVE FORCE

The Star, 7 March 1890

Let me hasten to reassure those who have been terrified by certain striking examples of the destructive force of this column, and who are aghast at such power being wielded by one man. Their fears are vain: I am no more able to make or mar artistic enterprises at will than the executioner has the power of life and death. It is true that to all appearance a fourteen thousand pound pantomime, which the critics declared the best in London, collapsed at a touch of my pen. And the imagination of the public has undoubtedly been strongly seized by the spectacle of the much-written-up Tosca at the height of its prosperity, withering, like Klingsor's garden, at three lines in a postscript to my weekly article. But there is no magic in the matter. Though the east wind seems to kill the consumptive patient, he dies, not of the wind, but of phthisis. On the strong-lunged man it blows in vain. La Tosca died of disease, and not of criticism, which, indeed, did its best to keep it alive.

For my part, I have struck too many blows at the well-made play without immediate effect to suppose that it is my strength and not its own weakness that has enabled me to double it up this time. When the critics were full of the "construction" of plays, I steadfastly maintained that a work of art is a growth, and not a construction. When the Scribes and Sardous* turned out neat and showy cradles, the critics said "How exquisitely constructed!" I said "Where's the baby?" Of course, there never was any baby; and when the cradles began to go out of fashion even the critics began to find them as dowdy as last year's bonnets. A *fantoccini* theatre, in which puppets play the parts of men and women, is amusing; but the French theatre, in which men and woman play the parts of puppets, is unendurable. Yet there was a time when some persons wrote as if Adrienne Lecouvreur was a superior sort of tragedy, and Dora (alias Diplomacy) a masterpiece of comedy. Even now their artificiality passes for ingenuity. Just as a barrister in England gets an immense reputation as a criminals' advocate when a dozen of his clients have been hanged (the hanging being at once a proof and an advertisement of the importance of the cases), so when a dramatist has written five or six plays in which two hours of intrigues and telegrams are wasted in bringing about some situation which the audience would have accepted at once without any contrivance at all, he receives his diploma as a master of play construction!

I promised last Monday to return to the subject of Madame Backer-Gröndahl after her recital, the Crystal Palace concert having left me in a carping temper. But if the concert left me discontented, the recital threw me into a perfect frenzy of exasperation. Do you know that noble fantasia in C minor, in which Mozart shewed

* Augustin Scribe and Victorien Sardou were French playwrights catering to popular taste. Between them they turned out hundreds of "well-made" plays, many of which were adapted for the British stage or converted into operas.

what Beethoven was to do with the pianoforte sonata, just as in *Das Veilchen* he shewed what Schubert was to do with the song? Imagine my feelings when Madame Backer-Gröndahl, instead of playing this fantasia (which she would have done beautifully), set Madame Haas to play it, and then sat down beside her and struck up "an original part for a second piano," in which every interpolation was an impertinence and every addition a blemish. Shocked and pained as every one who knew and loved the fantasia must have been, there was a certain grim ironic interest in the fact that the man who has had the unspeakable presumption to offer us his improvements on Mozart is the infinitesimal Grieg. The world reproaches Mozart for his inspired variation on Handel's The people that walked in darkness. I do not know what the world will now say to Grieg; but if ever he plays that "original second part" himself to an audience equipped with adequate musical culture, I sincerely advise him to ascertain beforehand that no brickbats or other loose and suitably heavy articles have been left carelessly about the room.

My complaints are not at an end yet. I ask Madame Gröndahl why she has so little faith in our appetite for the classics of the pianoforte. Let her consult any of our favorite pianists (Hallé, for instance) as to whether, with all our faults, we ever swerve in our fidelity to an artist who relies on our unquenchable appetite for Bach, Handel, Beethoven, Schubert, and Schumann. What was it that at once secured for Madame Gröndahl a leading position here last year? It was the discovery that she was a great Beethoven player and a great Chopin player. Further, it was the discovery that she could bring to the execution of these composers' works a true pianist's technique, and not the sham orchestral method that breaks down when tested with two bars of an *andante* from a Mozart sonata. The audience that crowded Steinway Hall on Wednesday, and flowed over on to the platform, was deeply disappointed to find, beside the Grieg outrage and the Chopin nocturne (C minor) and ballade (A flat), nothing in the program but drawing-room music. In Norway it may be necessary to extenuate the crime of playing serious music by Neupert's studies, Lassen's crescendos, Ole Olsen's and Grieg's dance tunes and *Bluettes en forme de Valse*, by one Ed. Schütt; but here some of us know a little better than that; and the more exquisite the virtuosity shewn in the execution of these things the more we feel the absence from the program of worthier subjects for its display. And not another word will I say about Madame Gröndahl until I hear her play a Beethoven sonata in public.

It has suddenly struck me that Grieg's appendage to Mozart's fantasia must be Norway's revenge for Mr Walter Besant's appendage to Ibsen's Doll's House.

In my recent notice of the London branch of the Wagner Society, the urgent necessity for pitching into that body and waking up its committee prevented me from saying a word about the paper read by Mr Ashton Ellis on Wagner's letters to Uhlig, Fischer and Heine, published in 1888 at Leipzig by Breitkopf und Härtel (price 9 marks, or in paper cover 7m. 50). First I have to remark that the letters contain passages as to the interpretation of modern music which make the prin-ciples Wagner fought for against Mendelssohn almost plain enough to cure Sir George Grove of speaking of the distinction between "absolute" music and tone poetry as mere critics' slang. I defy any critic to attempt an intelligent classification of modern music without finding this distinction forced on him; and I further defy him to account for the difference between a Beethoven symphony as played by the Hallé and Richter orchestras without seeing exactly how Wagner found in

Mendelssohn the arch enemy of progress in the orchestra. The Heine of the letters, by the bye, was not Heinrich Heine, but a costume designer and ex-comedian of the Dresden Court Theatre. An instalment of Mr Ellis's paper appears in the new number of The Meister, which also contains the first part of a really readable translation of the famous Pilgrimage to Beethoven, and a study of Die Meistersinger, in which I note only one slip: *i.e.*, the description of Hans Sachs as "the lowly shoemaker." A master shoemaker in medieval Nuremberg was, I should imagine, anything but a lowly person.

Whilst on the subject of Wagner, let me point out to those who do not see Messrs Novello's monthly paper, the Musical Times, that Mr Bennett's papers on the life and works of "the Meister" began in the January number, and are still running. They are valuable because they are so perfectly free from Wagnerian hero worship. Mr Bennett is one of those unhappy ones who, having shied all the bricks they could pick up at Wagner whilst he lived, have now reluctantly to build their missiles into a monument for him. In reading them I cannot refrain from chuckling at the conflict between Mr Bennett's old habits and his new and rueful conviction that the game is up. But he is a quite honest Philistine, still convinced that David is an overrated humbug, in spite of his having undeniably overthrown Goliath. The articles are rather more than less interesting for this; and the paper contains other matter that musicians will find readable.

More than a month ago Mr Macready Chute, of the Prince's Theatre, Bristol, wrote to me: "We have 15 children under 10 years of age out of 32 on the stage. They are principally the same children as were engaged last year, when they had a separate room with a fire in it, a matron, &c., exactly as the magistrates required this year, the only restriction being the hour at which they had to leave the theatre. In fact, I have no hesitation in saying that children in the Prince's Theatre, Bristol, are always treated with the same consideration as they now receive under Act of Parliament." The moral of which is that the Act causes absolutely no hardship whatever to humane managers like Mr Macready Chute, whilst it braces all the sordid or indifferent ones up to his level. I hope, however, that next year Mr Chute will go a step further and try to do without those fifteen children. Meanwhile, I congratulate our good old Mrs Grudden* on her new dignity of Parliamentary Matron.

TWO WELL-ATTENDED CONCERTS
The Star, 11 March 1890

The large audience of the Crystal Palace on Saturday may be claimed for Mr Hamish MacCunn or for Wagner, according to bias. My own opinion is that the attraction was Mr Edward Lloyd. Bonny Kilmeny is a juvenile work of Mr MacCunn's; and although a fairy story set to music could have no better quality than juvenility, yet Mr Manns' platform is hardly the right platform for it. We are accustomed there to pregnant, concentrated, purposeful works, and Mr MacCunn's diffuse strains, full of simple feeling and fancy as they are, did once or twice suggest to me that the Sydenham orchestra might be better employed than in accompanying Hogg's verses and tootling the sentimental interludes for the woodwind which occur between every line. The baritone music, exceptionally well sung by Mr

* Character in Dickens's Nicholas Nickleby.

Norman Salmond, alone held its ground in spite of the associations of the place. When I first heard this gentleman at a Popular Concert a week or so ago, I was so much struck by the artistic sense with which he used his voice that I thought I would wait and hear him again before committing myself to a favorable verdict that must necessarily seem improbable in a nation which is apt to model itself, when it sings bass, upon Mr Santley and Signor Foli. However, my impression is confirmed: Mr Salmond is undoubtedly a considerable acquisition for our concert *entrepreneurs*.

Schubert's symphony in B minor shewed off the orchestra to perfection; but the sudden transition to the Homeric bustle and breadth of the Pegnitz scene from Die Meistersinger knocked it to pieces for some dozens of bars at the beginning. When the band had pulled themselves together, Mr Albert Fairbairn (vice Mr Andrew Black, *hors de combat* with influenza) began his impossible task of singing the part of Sachs at sight, with dismal results. Except for Mr Lloyd's prize song, and for the interesting way in which some of the orchestral points came out under concert conditions, the performance can hardly be regarded as a successful one. Mr MacCunn's Land of the Mountain and the Flood, a charming Scotch overture that carries you over the hills and far away, was much applauded. I object, by the bye, to the "working out" section, which Mr MacCunn would never have written if his tutors had not put it into his head. I know a lady who keeps a typewriting establishment. Under my advice she is completing arrangements for supplying middle sections and recapitulations for overtures and symphonies at twopence a bar, on being supplied with the first section and coda.

I was considerably disappointed to find such a crowd at the orchestral concert given in Prince's Hall by the students of the Royal College of Music. Doubtless the students were glad to see the gallery full; but the effect on me was to force me to buy a stall, and to sit among the nobility and gentry instead of in a modest shilling seat. Some of the orchestral students were already familiar to me. For instance, that promising lad, Master W. B. Wotton, is progressing satisfactorily with his bassoon; and the way in which G. Case, C. Geard, and J. Matt handled the trombones would have done credit to any College. W. L. Barrett plays the flute, and H. G. Lebon the oboe quite in a professional manner. (The foregoing is an elaborate and side-splitting joke, the gentlemen named being skilled professors and no students at all.) All the violins were in the hands of students: fourteen lasses and ten lads; and they played capitally: the influence of King Cole at South Kensington appears to have developed fiddling at the college in an extraordinary degree.

Miss Polyxena Fletcher, a young lady with a rich oriental tone in her complexion, gained great and deserved applause by playing Brahms's second pianoforte concerto courageously and even aggressively; for she occasionally, in the abounding strength of her young blood, thumped the keyboard as if it were Brahms's head. And she was quite right: why should she forbear at that age, with an orchestra thundering emulously in her ears? The madrigals and part songs had been well prepared and went with praiseworthy precision; but there was one unsubduable treble voice which pierced through the others like a steam siren, and spoiled the homogeneity of the upper part in the harmony. Mr Pringle's scene from an Italian opera (MS.), with the startling title of Messalina—what on earth do these young spirits know about our friend Messalina?—was sung by Miss Maggie Davies, a very clever young lady whom I heard as Bianca in the students' performance of Goetz's Taming of the Shrew last year, and by Mr E.

Branscombe. Miss Davies's Italian vowels have been looked after; but Mr Branscombe remains an Englishman, and considers that a British "two" is equal to an Italian "tu" any day. I must affirm that the performance was highly creditable to the Royal College, and to the conductor, Mr Villiers Stanford.

BEETHOVEN, BRAHMS, AND BANJO
The Star, 14 March 1890

I used to think myself rather an advanced musician; but Time is overtaking me at last. In five years I shall be an old fogey. A few weeks ago, when Sir Charles Hallé played Beethoven's E flat concerto in Edinburgh, the critics of that town voted it poor stuff, and called it arid, diffuse, and all manner of disparaging epithets. Whereupon Sir Charles up and told them that no person with any musical knowledge could have talked such nonsense. And the Musical World accused them of "an ape-like passion for wanton and destructive mischief"; lamented that it could visit them with nothing worse than "execration"; and called them "venomous fools" and "witlings who, unable to lift their feeble intellects to the level of works to which the world pays grateful homage, endeavor to bring such works down to the lower plane on which they grovel." People call me severe; but I wonder what they would say if I went on in that style.

I submit two points in defence of the Edinburgh critics. 1. If they thought the concerts overrated, arid, and diffuse, they were right to say so. 2. Perhaps the performance *was* arid. Hamlet is a very fine play; but with Charles Mathews in the leading part, it would seem a trifle long and dry. Are you quite sure, Mr Musical

World, that if you were unfamiliar with the Emperor concerto, and heard it for the first time from Hallé in his seventieth year, you would rise fully to the occasion? Besides, listen to what they are beginning to say in London. Last Tuesday a leading evening paper, criticizing the Royal College concert at Prince's Hall, said calmly: "Brahms's E flat concerto is full of inspiration; and the day will come when the most famous pianoforte concerto in this key will be that, not of Beethoven, but of Brahms." That is the sort of statement that sets one looking for grey hairs and thin places on one's crown.

The significance of such criticism lies in its being probably the first sign of a reaction in favor of abstract or "absolute" music against the great Wagnerian cult of tone poetry and music-drama. An eclipse of reputation always becomes visible at Greenwich soon after its possessor's canonization. To take minor cases, Macaulay is only just emerging from the shadow, and George Eliot is in the very black of it. To take major ones, the Restoration conception of Shakespear as vapid and old-fashioned corresponds exactly to the Victorian conception of Mozart, a conception against which the Mozart idolatry of such writers as Oulibicheff availed nothing.* Neither, I suppose, will the many books of Wolzogen avail Wagner when his turn comes. When it does come we shall have two consolations. First, these eclipses are made by critical fashion rather than by popular feeling. Second, when the Wagnerian criticism becomes the mode, it will soon be so vulgarized that we shall be glad to shelve it until its professors are all dead.

I did not go to the Goddard [benefit] concert on

* Alexandre D. Oulibicheff [Ulibishev] (1794–1858), Russian diplomat, was the author of a biography of Mozart. Hans von Wolzogen was the editor of Wagner's *Baireuther Blätter* and author of numerous books on Wagner.

Tuesday, as it was one of those occasions on which a critic's room is worth a guinea more than his company. Besides, the Norwegian colony in London had bidden me to a *soirée* at which they said they were going to entertain Madame Backer-Gröndahl. Needless to say, when I arrived, I found Madame Gröndahl entertaining them. Presently the floor was taken by a violinist who was no stranger to me: to wit, Alexander Bull, son of the famous Ole of that ilk.

Now, nothing will persuade me that Bull knows how to play the fiddle any more than I do. He always reminds me of the too celebrated amateur who, being asked could he play the violin, replied that he had no doubt he could if he tried. Bull grabs the instrument cautiously by the shoulder, and considers how he can best tackle it. Finally deciding that he had better proceed like a man cutting a wedding cake exactly in two, he very carefully draws the bow across it in that manner, keeping a wary eye on the instrument in case it should, in some unlooked for way, resent such treatment. In his inspired moments he stands it on his shoulder and plays in mid air. Each performance has the same odd appearance of being his first attempt; and though he makes less faults than most professional violinists, yet there is something strange about them, because they are not the usual faults. He solves the ordinary player's difficulties by natural magic, and then falls into difficulties of his own which an ordinary player would settle offhand. But his tone is so fine and nervous, and so full of subtle and unexpected inflexions; and his playing is so unflaggingly imaginative that I receive a much more vivid musical and poetic impression from him than I do from Joachim, for instance, or from Ysaÿe, who, they say, can play unbroken chords on four strings with an ordinary bow and bridge, and who is declared by experts the most dexterous of living fiddlers. I can answer for it that he is the most bumptious; but I do not rank bumptiousness high as an artistic quality: perhaps because I am myself singularly free from it. Now Bull is not in the least bumptious: he is chronically apologetic for not being able to play as well as his father. It must be a terrible thing to have such a father if you want to be an artist; for of course he will not teach you, and nobody else will venture to interfere. But the result in Bull's case goes to shew that if you miss a good deal under such circumstances, you also escape something. I never heard his father; but his own playing seems to me unique of its kind.

Madame Backer-Gröndahl will at last appear in her right place at the Popular Concerts tomorrow and on Monday. If the Philharmonic Society will only give us an opportunity of hearing her play Schumann's concerto, we shall have nothing left to complain of.

The other evening I made one of those appalling sacrifices of my own comfort which are the price of a comprehensive knowledge of contemporary music. It takes all sorts to make a world; and each sort must have its music. There is the stupid sort, for instance: the people who cannot follow the thread of any connected entertainment; whose attention cannot stand a ten minutes' strain; who are so credulous that they will sit openmouthed and, in a wellmeaning, joyless, wondering way, applaud anything that goes on in a room which they are not allowed to enter for less than a shilling. No competent musical critic could possibly enjoy an entertainment suited to these worthy people; but since they are eminently gullible, it is his duty occasionally to suffer for an evening in order to see that no inordinate advantage is taken of their artistic imbecility. It was with a vague notion of doing some good in this direction that I lately visited "the unique and incomparable Bohee Operatic Minstrels" at the International Hall over the

Café Monaco. I took the title as a guarantee that the audience would be tolerably simple folk.

They were. But I do not think that the Brothers Bohee presumed unduly on their simplicity. If the singers— especially the comic singers—suppose that the audience can distinguish a single word of their songs without carefully reading the printed copy in the program, most of them deceive themselves enormously; and I must say I am not convinced that if, in choosing subjects, an occasional relief from the deathbeds of darling angel mothers were ventured upon, it would not be rather welcome than otherwise. I will even go the length of suggesting that rhymed balderdash must be quite as troublesome to a dull intelligence as rhymed reason. Still, the verses were inoffensive, the tunes innocuous as bread pills, the tambourines full of spirit, and the choruses deeply affecting when repeated, as they always were, *pianissimo*. The musical conventions of the minstrel style are curious; but I shall reserve a full description of them for my treatise on modern music, which I hope to get through the Press shortly before 1950.*

The Bohee Brothers themselves are banjoists, and would have me believe that the Tsar of Russia affects that weapon. Had I known this last Sunday, I should have made a much more vigorous speech in Hyde Park at the demonstration on behalf of the Siberian exiles. If it be true that the Prince of Wales banjoizes, then I protest against his succession to the throne. The further suggestion that Mr Gladstone "favors the instrument" is enough to bring that statesman down to the International Hall with his axe. The banjo may be as fashionable as the chimney-pot hat; but the Brothers Bohee could no more reconcile me to the one than Messrs Lincoln

* The actual year of his death!

[956]

and Bennett to the other. The more featly they twanged the more evident they made it that no skill of handling could extenuate the enormities of the Ethiopian lute.

EVERYBODY PLAYED WELL
The Star, 17 March 1890

Providence did itself credit at the Pop on Saturday. Everybody played well: Madame Neruda and Madame Backer-Gröndahl played very well. Not that those who only knew Madame Gröndahl from her playing here this season yet know all that she is capable of unless they have caught the full significance of one or two movements in the Grieg concerto at the Crystal Palace, or in the last movement of the violin sonata on Saturday. The fact is, Madame Gröndahl has been rather reserved with us this time. Last year she played so as to let us into all her secrets. This time, having no doubt found out how unworthy a horde of Philistines we are, she has kept us at a certain distance, giving us a great deal, but not all. Personally, I feel snubbed. If that state of mind were more generally intelligible in this town, we should gain that confidence from great artists which alone can win them to make us their favorite confidants. Madame Backer-Gröndahl's technique can be bought; and well worth its price it is; but if you want her to play to you as to a friend whom she glories in pleasing, then you have got to convince her that you are artistically capable of that intimate relationship. On Saturday she played Schumann's Novelette in F, which was, of course, mere child's play, though it would, I admit, take an uncommonly forward infant to manage the modulations of the trio as delicately as Madame Gröndahl did. Chopin's prelude in D flat began the serious business of the

[957]

concert. She played it with a wonderful concentration, holding the thread of it with a grip that never relaxed or lost its sensitiveness, though the web of accompaniment that wraps it up like an atmosphere was all the time floating as if her fingers had nothing else to do but to weave it, and her attention was perfectly free. This indelible impressing on me of a theme; this exhaustion of its uttermost content without abandonment, without passion, without joyousness, with unfailing self-containment and unflagging sense of beauty, put me completely out of countenance when it had been continued throughout Mendelssohn's study in B flat minor, which we could not help encoring, though she had been so terribly severe with us. I was particularly curious to hear how she would get on with Madame Neruda in the Grieg sonata; for I had a vivid recollection of how she ruled Johannes Wolff with a rod of iron when he played it at Prince's Hall with her last year; and I knew that Madame Neruda has a will of her own. But there was no gainsaying Madame Gröndahl's way; and at the end the two artists got into such perfect accord that the performance must stand as so far incomparably the finest yet heard of that sonata in London. I neither expect nor desire to hear a better one. Madame Gröndahl unbent a little, too, in the *finale*; and I was consoled as by a human caress after an angelic discourse. I really have more sympathy now with a gentleman who said to me ruefully after the Crystal Palace concert "She doesnt even play any wrong notes."

Mrs Henschel sang very prettily; and there was something else; but it escapes my memory for the moment.